Modeling Random Systems

Modeling Random Systems

J. R. Cogdell

Department of Electrical and Computer Engineering
The University of Texas at Austin

Upper Saddle River, New Jersey 07458

Library of Congress Cataloging-in-Publication Data

Cogdell, J. R.
    Modeling random systems / John R. Cogdell.
        p. cm.
    Includes index.
    ISBN 0-13-141437-2
    1. Stochastic systems–Mathematical models. I. Title.

QA402.C5355 2004
003'.76–dc22

2003069090

Vice President and Editorial Director, ECS: *Marcia J. Horton*
Vice President and Director of Production and Manufacturing, ESM: *David W. Riccardi*
Executive Managing Editor: *Vince O'Brien*
Production Editor: *Kevin Bradley*
Director of Creative Services: *Paul Belfanti*
Art Director: *Jayne Conte*
Cover Designer: *Bruce Kenselaar*
Art Editor: *Greg Dulles*
Manufacturing Manager: *Trudy Pisciotti*
Manufacturing Buyer: *Lynda Castillo*
Marketing Manager: *Holly Stark*

© 2004 by Pearson Education, Inc.
Pearson Prentice Hall
Pearson Education, Inc.
Upper Saddle River, NJ 07458

Pearson Prentice Hall® is a trademark of Pearson Education, Inc.

Mathematica and the Mathematica logo are registered trademarks of Wolfram Research, Inc., 100 Trade Center Drive, Champaign, IL 61820-7237.

The author and publisher of this book have used their best efforts in preparing this book. These efforts include the development, research, and testing of the theories and programs to determine their effectiveness. The author and publisher make no warranty of any kind, expressed or implied, with regard to these programs or the documentation contained in this book. The author and publisher shall not be liable in any event for incidental or consequential damages in connection with, or arising out of, the furnishing, performance, or use of these programs.

Printed in the United States of America
10 9 8 7 6 5 4 3 2 1

ISBN 0-13-141437-2

Pearson Education Ltd., *London*
Pearson Education Australia Pty. Ltd., *Sydney*
Pearson Education Singapore, Pte. Ltd.
Pearson Education North Asia Ltd., *Hong Kong*
Pearson Education Canada, Inc., *Toronto*
Pearson Educación de Mexico, S.A. de C.V.
Pearson Education—Japan, *Tokyo*
Pearson Education Malaysia, Pte. Ltd.
Pearson Education, Inc., *Upper Saddle River, New Jersey*

Contents

Preface

Why I Wrote This Book

If you are looking for a book that presents all the mathematical tools you need to prepare your best students for your first graduate course in communication theory, you have plenty of excellent choices, but this book is not one of them. If you are looking for an introductory book that can help you teach the typical undergraduate the basic concepts of randomness and how to use these to model random systems, then this book should interest you.

Please take a minute and read why I wrote this book. Of course, it was the usual reason, that I couldn't find another book that was suitable for my course, but there is more to the story than that.

When I resumed teaching a probability course in the early 1990s, I used several books, and I found that they all had one or more of the following weaknesses:

1. They were math books, not engineering books, as indicated by the following:

   - Chapters were named for mathematical topics like "Random Variables," not engineering topics.
   - The style was that of a math book, with theorems and proofs, concise notation, terse discussions, and few graphics.
   - Probability was defined by a set of axioms.
   - The various probability distributions were introduced with scant discussion of the physical contexts in which these might be useful.
   - The problems were mainly mathematical exercises.

2. The audience for the book was electrical engineers only, principally those studying communication systems. Many of the examples presumed the reader had knowledge of and interest in this field of application.

3. The importance of modeling real-life situations and problems was largely neglected.

4. The books were too advanced for the average undergraduate. Often, in the introduction they stated something like "written at the level of an undergraduate elective or introductory graduate course." To me that meant that the book was written at a graduate level. They covered too much and explained too little for the typical undergraduate.

5. There was little or no review of difficult topics that were prerequisite to the probability materials. Students were given little or no help with integrating a function over a region of a plane, performing a convolution, or analyzing a linear system in the frequency domain. My experience is that students need help with these topics, even if they saw them earlier in the curriculum. Indeed, repetition is a fundamental aspect of learning and is not a waste of ink or class time.

The Subject and Intended Audience for This Book

Modeling Random Systems attempts to remedy these flaws. I have taken the usual material on probability, statistics, and random processes and presented it in the broader context of developing useful models for systems involving randomness. My intended audience is the typical undergraduate engineering student at the typical engineering college who is not thinking of graduate school at the time, but rather of getting an engineering job and paying his or her debt to society, and perhaps to a bank. Although I am an electrical engineering educator, this material was developed without undue focus on electrical engineering and should be suitable for anyone seeking to learn the art of modeling systems with random aspects.

To choose an appropriate conceptual and mathematical model for an engineering problem, one must match physical context with mathematical assumptions. In *Modeling Random Systems*, we have attempted to instruct students in the arts of recognizing that a model is possible in a real-life situation, crafting an appropriate model, doing the math, and interpreting the results in practical realities. The following, which is one of the problems at the end of Chapter 3, illustrates the process.

> You borrow your roommate's car and he warns you, "The gas gauge shows empty, but there are somewhere between three and four gallons left." Because you must drive 40 miles and return, you ask, "What kind of mileage does your car get?" "Twenty to twenty-five miles per gallon," is the reply. Find the probability of getting back without running out of gas, assuming you put no gas in the car and the information given by your roommate is valid. Assume independence and, for lack of better information, uniform distributions for the gas and mileage.

Our aim is to teach students to solve such a problem as if to take a calculated risk in making the trip. It is often quoted that "the battle of Waterloo was won on the playing fields of Eton." This surely means, among other things, that the future English military leaders were developing character while enjoying the challenge of schoolboy sports. Our hope is that students will similarly find these problems to be fun and engaging and thus will build their problem-solving skills in the effort to solve them.

A Big Book?

My goal in writing this book was to explain patiently and clearly the basic ideas involved in modeling random systems. I was astonished to see that the book ended up with almost 700 pages, until I did some arithmetic. The end-of-chapter problems take up 226 pages, and the figures another 120 pages, more or less. That leaves about 350 pages for the text itself, which isn't such a big book after all.

I cover this entire book in my classes at The University of Texas of Austin. If you choose a more leisurely pace or choose to include some different topics, you can skip the application materials in Chapter 5 on reliability and queuing theory, and of course you can leave out as much of Chapter 6 on random processes as you wish. Some may wish to skip all or parts of Chapter 4 on statistics, which would have slight effect on coverage in the remaining materials.

An Engineering Book

An engineering outlook is integrated into the entire book, but an engineering point of view is especially evident in the materials listed below. I am not aware that many of these topics are covered in other books.

1. Inclusion and use of units are strong. See pages 462ff and 615ff, plus the index.
2. Errror analysis in systems using random variables is explained. See page 251ff.
3. Readers are given a step-by-step tutorial on how to perform a convolution, with an emphasis on sketching the waveforms. See Appendix B, page 678.
4. Readers are given review sections on power concepts in signal analysis, page 574f, time and frequency domain concepts, pages 588–601, and are shown how to set up integrals in two-dimensional spaces, page 215 and many places.
5. Readers are shown how to estimate the power in broadband noise by measuring the peak-to-peak value. See page 624ff.
6. Readers are shown how to perform non-routine statistical calculations using the Σ key on their calculators. See endnote 6 on page 445 and endnote 14 on page 448.
7. Broadband noise models are motivated and illustrated from a physics and circuit-theory treatment of thermal noise. See page 608ff.
8. Finally, many problems are drawn from real-life situations with which readers are familiar. If there is any hallmark of an engineering point of view, it is this application of engineering knowledge to all of life. See below for a fuller discussion of the problems in the book.

End-of-Chapter Problems

An important feature of any engineering book is the number and nature of the problems that appear at the end of each chapter. Here are some remarks on this aspect of *Modeling Random Systems*.

1. Answers are given to all problems because having the answer enhances learning. Without answers, students will work the problem as best they can and then quit, right or wrong. With answers, students will work until they get the right answer or become convinced that they have a better answer or else come for help, all of which are educational. My view is that homework problems are for learning and not for evaluation of learning.

    If you do not want students to have the answers, then change a number or two in the problem. Students will then work the problem in its original form until they get the right answer and will then rework the problem with your numbers. They will learn much through this process, and you can be sure they are working the problems.

2. The problems are classified by topic and by type. Specifically, problems are either mathematical exercises or else modeling problems described in a scenario. The modeling problems are mostly low-tech, drawn from experiences in life common to everyone (traffic lights, getting busy signals on the phone). High-tech problems (cell phone networks, cryptographic schemes) frustrate students (and faculty like me) who have little knowledge of these areas.

3. Almost all the problems are original to me, which creates advantages and disadvantages. Advantages are that (1) most problems are new to you and your students, so problem-solving skills are developed; (2) the problems fit well the material in the book and foster skills in modeling random systems; and (3) the problems have been class tested on exams and homework assignments. Disadvantages are that (1) certain themes are inevitable, since all problems come from the same source; and (2) there is a shortage of problems in areas that have been added recently to my course, such as hypothesis testing, queues, and discrete-time random processes.

Occasionally, the problems require numerical integration or solving of nonlinear equations. I use Mathematica in such situations, but I have found students to be very resourceful in using a variety of tools to get the answers, including hand calculators.

Problems within each section are classified as "Exercises" or "Modeling Problems." With an exercise, you generally know what to do and you need to apply the techniques illustrated in the text and do the math. With a modeling problem, you first need to decide what to do and then apply the techniques required. Within each classification, I sorted the problems crudely for increasing difficulty. In this case *crudely* means a three-level sort: easier than average, average, and harder than average; and even these classifications are very subjective.

The solutions manual is available to instructors who have adopted the text for classroom use in academic institutions. It is not available to students. Solutions are made available to assist instructors in teaching their courses. They should not be made available to students except as limited extracts within the classroom setting. In consideration of your colleagues who do not want their students to have access to these materials, please respect these restrictions.

On the Use of Mathematica and the e-Book Version

Besides the standard text format, an e-book version of this material is available for purchase from the publisher. For more information visit the Pearson/Prentice Hall probability/random processes (electrical engineering) catalog page at http://vig.prenhall.com/catalog/academic/product?ISBN= 0131414372. With the free MathReader, available at www.wolfram.com, readers can print the text or read the text on their computer display, using the hyperlinks to full advantage. With the student version of Mathematica, the reader can, in addition, perform interactive exercises, use the computational power of Mathematica in solving problems, and use the Mathematica code embedded in the text to explore graphics and simulations. Instructors interested in obtaining an examination copy should contact the electrical engineering publisher at Pearson/Prentice Hall.

Acknowledgments

I am pleased to acknowledge the assistance of the following: Richard H. Williams, for his respect and encouragement; Robert M. Adams, for several critical suggestions and encouragement to write the section on hypothesis testing; Ed Powers, Gary Wise, and J. Wesley Barnes, who welcomed me as an auditor in their classes; Gustavo de Veciana, for several helpful discussions; David Brydon, my son-in-law, who got me started in Mathematica; Thomas H. Phipps, who encouraged me to look into Mathematica as an authoring system and gave me his style sheet to begin with; my anonymous reviewers, who made some wise suggestions; and hundreds of students who worked with me through the many versions of these materials.

I also thank the Fluor Daniel, Inc., for an educational grant supporting this work, and Wolfram Research for assistance in a variety of ways.

I thank my wife, who knows how many hours go into writing a book. Finally, I thank my Creator and Redeemer God for the joy of living and working with my mind and hands.

J. R. COGDELL
Department of Electrical and Computer Engineering
The University of Texas at Austin

1

The Probability Paradigm

1.1 INTRODUCTION TO RANDOM SYSTEMS

1.1.1 The Need for Models for Random Systems

Four experiments

Imagine that the professor arrives on the first day of class with a cardboard box containing four 100-Ω resistors, four 1.5-V batteries, and four digital voltmeters (DVMs). She then performs a series of demonstrations.

First experiment. The first experiment is to interpret the color code of a resistor to indicate a 100-Ω resistor and to read the label on the battery to indicate 1.5 V. From this information, she draws a simple circuit on the board, as shown in Fig. 1.1.1.

She then proceeds to calculate the current in the circuit from Ohm's law:

$$i = \frac{v}{R} = \frac{1.5 \text{ V}}{100 \ \Omega} = 15 \text{ mA} \tag{1.1.1}$$

This type of theoretical model is typical of a beginning course in circuit analysis.

Second experiment. In the second experiment, the professor measures the resistance of one resistor and the voltage of one battery with one of the DVMs. The resistance proves to be 98.1 Ω, and the voltage is 1.563 V, which produces a current of

$$i = \frac{v}{R} = \frac{1.563 \text{ V}}{98.1 \ \Omega} = 15.9 \text{ mA} \tag{1.1.2}$$

1

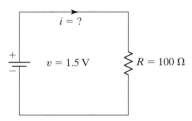

Figure 1.1.1   An ideal circuit model based on the nominal values of the battery voltage and the resistance of the resistor.

This is the sort of empirical model we use in the laboratory. We recognize that this model improves on the circuit-theory model described by Eq. (1.1.1) because it is based on better information.

Third experiment.   The professor then measures with one DVM the four batteries and four resistors and obtains the following results: 1.563, 1.582, 1.460, and 1.498 V for the batteries, and 98.1, 103.7, 98.9, and 96.0 Ω for the resistors. We now can calculate a current for each of the combinations. The results are shown in Table 1.1.1.

Table 1.1.1   The 16 currents from the four resistors and four batteries

Resistance/Voltage	1.563 V	1.582 V	1.460 V	1.498 V
98.1 Ω	15.9 mA	16.1 mA	14.9 mA	15.3 mA
103.7 Ω	15.1 mA	15.3 mA	14.1 mA	14.4 mA
98.9 Ω	15.8 mA	16.0 mA	14.8 mA	15.1 mA
96.0 Ω	16.3 mA	16.5 mA	15.2 mA	15.6 mA

This also is an empirical model, but we are taking another step toward realism because we are acknowledging the unpredictability of any real-world system. In the assembly process, parts are selected more or less at random, so the actual values in the circuit have a random component as well as a nominal value.

Fourth experiment.   The professor then pulls all four DVMs out of the box, and we realize that each of these will likely give slightly different measurements for the batteries and resistors. The 16 measured values each for the voltage and the resistance produce 256 calculated currents. Since this is something of a thought experiment from your point of view, we will assume the following errors for the voltmeter measurements[1]: 0%, +0.78%, −0.51%, and −1.1% on the voltage measurements, and 0%, −0.96%, +0.21%, and +0.44% on the resistance measurements. For convenience we have assumed no errors in the first DVM so that we can retain the preceding calculations.

We will now calculate the resulting currents using Mathematica. If you have not used Mathematica before, we have a short tutorial for you. Our goal in this book is not to teach you to use Mathematica, but you need to know just a little bit to proceed. Click the hyperlink for the tutorial in Appendix A on the CD or refer to Appendix A in this book.

We now calculate all the currents for the measured values of resistance and voltage. The calculations are performed by Mathematica code that is hidden. If you want to look at the code, select the tiny cell bracket above the numbers, go to the "Cell" menu, down to "Cell Properties," and select "Cell Open." If you merely want to execute the code, select the tiny cell bracket and "evaluate" the cell. To evaluate, click anywhere in the cell and hit the Enter key if your keyboard has this key, or Shift-Return if it does not. When you evaluate the cell, it will ask you if you want to automatically initialize all the initialization cells in the notebook. Your answer is always "Yes."

```
{15.9327,16.1264,14.8828,15.2701,16.057,16.2522,
 14.9989,15.3892,15.8515,16.0442,14.8069,
 15.1923,15.7575,15.949,14.7191,15.1022,
 15.0723,15.2555,14.0791,14.4455,15.1899,
 15.3745,14.1889,14.5582,14.9955,15.1777,
 14.0073,14.3718,14.9065,15.0877,13.9242,
 14.2866,15.8038,15.996,14.7624,15.1466,
 15.9271,16.1207,14.8775,15.2648,15.7232,
 15.9144,14.6871,15.0694,15.63,15.82,14.6,
 14.98,16.2812,16.4792,15.2083,15.6042,16.4082,
 16.6077,15.327,15.7259,16.1982,16.3951,15.1308,
 15.5246,16.1022,16.2979,15.041,15.4325,16.0872,
 16.2827,15.027,15.4181,16.2126,16.4097,15.1442,
 15.5384,16.0051,16.1997,14.9504,15.3395,
 15.9102,16.1036,14.8617,15.2485,15.2184,
 15.4034,14.2155,14.5855,15.3371,15.5236,
 14.3264,14.6993,15.1408,15.3249,14.143,14.5112,
 15.051,15.234,14.0592,14.4251,15.957,16.151,
 14.9055,15.2934,16.0815,16.277,15.0217,15.4127,
 15.8756,16.0686,14.8295,15.2154,15.7815,
 15.9733,14.7415,15.1252,16.4391,16.6389,
 15.3557,15.7554,16.5673,16.7687,15.4755,
 15.8783,16.3552,16.554,15.2774,15.6751,16.2582,
 16.4559,15.1868,15.5821,15.8993,16.0926,
 14.8516,15.2381,16.0233,16.2181,14.9674,15.357,
 15.8182,16.0105,14.7758,15.1604,15.7244,
 15.9156,14.6882,15.0705,15.0407,15.2236,
 14.0496,14.4152,15.1581,15.3423,14.1592,
 14.5277,14.964,15.1459,13.9779,14.3417,14.8753,
 15.0561,13.895,14.2567,15.7707,15.9624,14.7315,
 15.1149,15.8937,16.0869,14.8464,15.2328,
 15.6903,15.881,14.6563,15.0378,15.5972,15.7868,
 14.5694,14.9486,16.2471,16.4446,15.1765,
 15.5715,16.3739,16.5729,15.2948,15.6929,
 16.1643,16.3608,15.0991,15.4921,16.0684,
 16.2637,15.0095,15.4002,15.8629,16.0558,
 14.8176,15.2032,15.9867,16.181,14.9332,15.3218,
```

```
15.782,15.9739,14.742,15.1257,15.6884,15.8791,
14.6546,15.036,15.0063,15.1887,14.0174,14.3822,
15.1233,15.3072,14.1267,14.4944,14.9298,
15.1113,13.9459,14.3089,14.8412,15.0216,
13.8632,14.224,15.7346,15.9259,14.6977,15.0803,
15.8573,16.0501,14.8124,15.1979,15.6544,
15.8447,14.6228,15.0034,15.5615,15.7507,14.536,
14.9144,16.2099,16.407,15.1417,15.5358,16.3364,
16.535,15.2598,15.657,16.1273,16.3233,15.0645,
15.4566,16.0316,16.2265,14.9752,15.3649}
```

The output is the 256 currents, which we have converted to milliamps. (Normally we would suppress output like this, but we wanted you to look at the numbers in this case.) Let us plot these in a histogram to show their distribution. To get the histogram, we have to load the package that plots histograms and then ask for the histogram.

```
Needs["Graphics`Graphics`"]
Histogram[AllIs, AxesLabel →
    {"Current, mA","Frequency"}, ImageSize → 400];
```

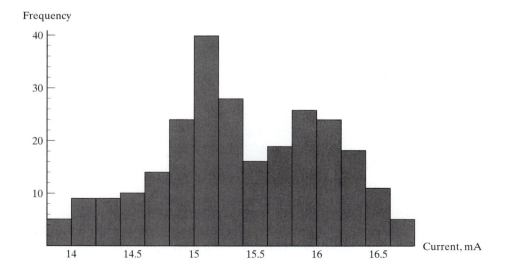

"So what?" you say. The point is that we need a new *kind* of model to describe this sort of system. When we consider that there are hundreds, even thousands or more, of components in the simplest system, and there is uncertainty in the properties of most if not all of them, we conclude that our analysis models need to account for this random factor.

Randomness.   Randomness arises in real systems from many causes: variations in material and manufacturing conditions, age, and the random choice of components in assembling a specific system. Randomness can arise in the sheer complexity of a system, as in the dynamics of gases, or in social systems such as traffic patterns or economic activity. Randomness appears to be inherent in the dynamics of matter and energy at the atomic and subatomic levels, as described by quantum mechanics, and occasionally randomness must be assumed to model our ignorance of true conditions in a system.

1.1.2 Models and Real Systems

Models.   The goal of science is to generate conceptual and mathematical models that allow us to understand and predict phenomena in nature. Early scientists such as Newton and Boyle believed that they were discovering the way things really are, but modern thinkers accept that nature is infinitely complex and ultimately mysterious, and we must be content with successful models of nature. Electromagnetic theory and quantum mechanics are examples of such models.

The goal of engineering is to design and produce safe, reliable, and affordable systems: automobiles, computers, flight control networks, and the like. Scientific, mathematical, and empirical models are vital to the engineering enterprise, and much of engineering education consists in mastering models that have been found useful.

Deterministic and random systems.   A *deterministic system* has predictable output from known inputs. An example would be the response of a linear system to a sinusoidal input of known amplitude, phase, and frequency. Having successful models to analyze and design deterministic systems is vital to engineering; indeed, introductory courses in all engineering disciplines focus on deterministic systems.

Advanced analysis and design usually involve random considerations. All information systems, such as computer and communication systems, process random signals. Environmental factors such as the thermal environment usually exhibit randomness. Social systems such as traffic and elevator operation also have random aspects.

Engineers therefore must have models to analyze and design random systems. In this book we explain the concepts, definitions, vocabulary, and most common models used to describe random systems. Some broad categories to be presented are probability theory, statistics, and random processes.

Probability theory.   Probability theory is a mathematical model used to describe random, or "chance," experiments. We distinguish the probability paradigm, or macromodel, which provides the appropriate framework for describing all random systems, from specific micromodels such as the binomial and Gaussian distributions, which arise from specific additional assumptions about the random experiment. Chapters 1–3 introduce probability theory.

Statistics.   The art of displaying, extracting, and interpreting information from numerical data is called *statistics.* Routine presentations and calculations are known as *descriptive statistics,* but sophisticated statistical studies are based on probability models. Chapter 4 presents some topics in descriptive statistics, the estimation of unknowns, such as the average value of a data source with random components, and hypothesis testing.

Random processes.   The model for a random function is called a *random process.*[2] Information-bearing signals, such as communication signals, instrumentation signals, and computer data, are modeled by random processes. Chapters 5 and 6 present models of simple discrete and continuous random processes that are useful in modeling random events in time and information-bearing signals.

1.1.3 Examples of Random Systems

We give three extended examples to illustrate typical random systems. These will illustrate probability theory, statistics, and random processes, respectively.

Probability applied to manufacturing

Consider a manufacturing facility where large numbers of components, say, semiconductor devices, are produced. One day's production is in the tens of thousands, and these are all tested before being shipped to customers.

Some definitions.   We consider four possible situations, which we call *events,* related to the testing of these devices. Let $G =$ the event that a device is good; $B =$ the event that a device is bad; $V =$ the event that the test gives a valid result; and $W =$ the event that the test gives a wrong result. Figure 1.1.2 suggests the day's production, except you must imagine that there are thousands of points in the large rectangle, one for each manufactured device. The points representing the good devices are on the left and those representing the bad devices are on the right, with a vertical line between them. Points representing valid tests are at the top, and points representing wrong results are at the bottom, with a horizontal line between them.

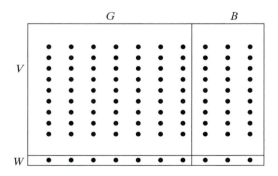

Figure 1.1.2   The day's production of devices is represented by points in the large rectangle. Those in the upper left are good devices that test good (a valid test). Those in the upper right are bad devices that test bad (valid test). Those in the lower left are good devices that test bad (wrong test results). Those in the lower right represent bad devices that test good (wrong test result).

Combinations.   There are four situations, or composite events, that can occur. For example: $G \cap V$ means a good device and a valid test, so the device should be shipped; $B \cap V$ means a bad chip and a valid test, so don't ship; $G \cap W$ means a good chip, but the test indicates bad, so don't ship; and $B \cap W$ means a bad chip that tests good. This bad chip will be shipped, thus creating a warranty problem. The upside-down U symbol is the intersection symbol from set theory, meaning devices that have both attributes.

Success rates.   The experience of the manufacturer is that on a typical day 75% of the devices are good, and the test is valid 99% of the time, and these results are independent. In this context *independent* means that the result of the test is likely to be incorrect (1% of the time) for both good and bad devices. These ratios are approximate, being averages over a large number of days. Actual ratios on a given day would vary from these averages.

These ratios allow us to estimate how many of the devices fall into each of the four categories. We expect that good devices will test good, $G \cap V$, approximately $\frac{3}{4} \times \frac{99}{100}$ of the time. Thus a day's production of n devices will result in approximately $n \times \frac{3}{4} \times \frac{99}{100}$ good devices that test good. These devices are put into the bin to be shipped to customers. The number of bad devices that test bad, $B \cap V$, will be $n \times \frac{1}{4} \times \frac{99}{100}$; these devices are thrown into the recycling bin. The number of good devices that test bad, $G \cap W$, will be approximately $n \times \frac{3}{4} \times \frac{1}{100}$; these also go into the recycling bin. The number of bad devices that test good, $B \cap W$, will be $n \times \frac{1}{4} \times \frac{1}{100}$; unfortunately, these devices are put into the bin to be shipped to customers.

Profit/loss.   Now come profit/loss considerations. It costs $10 to manufacture each device, which sells for $100; however, warranty costs are $10,000 for each bad unit shipped, considering cost of replacement, damage to company reputation, and loss of future business. Thus every device manufactured and tested has a number associated with it. The manufacturer makes a profit of $90 for every good device that is shipped, loses $10 for every device thrown into the recycling bin, and loses $9910 for every bad device shipped to a customer. We map this coupling of the events to profits in Fig. 1.1.3.

Profit calculation.   We can now estimate the profit for a day's production:

$$\text{Profit} = n \times \left[90 \times \frac{3 \times 99}{4 \times 100} + (-10) \times \frac{1 \times 99}{4 \times 100} + (-10) \times \frac{3 \times 1}{4 \times 100} + (-9910) \times \frac{1 \times 1}{4 \times 100} \right]$$

$$= n \times [66.83 - 2.48 - 0.075 - 24.78] = \$39.50 \times n \qquad (1.1.3)$$

Thus the manufacturer expects, on average, to make a profit of about $40 on each device.

We thus see one reason why manufacturers work to improve the quality of their manufacturing and testing operations. Many employees deal with process yield, test, and warranty problems. The high cost of shipping faulty products drives quality programs in every aspect of design, manufacturing, and testing. Thus probabilities have an influence on the bottom line in manufacturing operations.

Summary.   The manufacturing example illustrates probabilistic analysis. The ratios we introduced function like probabilities. We are dealing with repeatable experiments such as selecting a device, testing it, and estimating the profit associated with this unit. In probability theory we model these types of situations with events, sample spaces, random variables, and expectation. These concepts will be defined and explored in Chapters 1 and 2.

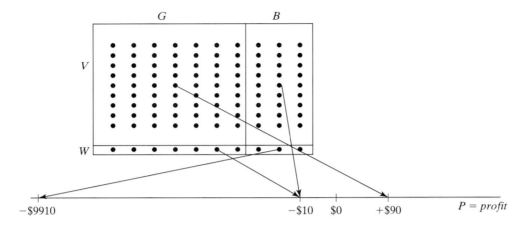

Figure 1.1.3 Each device either makes or loses money for the company. The arrows show the profit for each device manufactured. All the dots (devices) in each category map to the same point on the profit line.

Table 1.1.2 Some data
from student-fee bills

SCH	Fees ($)
9	1011
9	1183
12	1167
12	1262
13	1446
15	1442

A regression analysis of student fees

Fee-bill data. At the University of Texas at Austin, students pay a tuition charge that is scaled to their semester-hour credit load, course-specific fees that have some connection with the resources utilized, fees that are uniform for every student such as the cost of the student shuttle-bus system, and optional fees for admission to athletic events, the yearbook, and the like. On the first day of class one semester, we surveyed six students selected at random about their semester credit hours (SCHs) and their total fees and obtained the results shown in Table 1.1.2.

We then entered these data into a calculator and calculated the best-fit regression line. The calculator program matches a straight line to the data in an optimum manner. The best-fit line was

$$\text{Fee} = 529 + 62.0 \times SCH \tag{1.1.4}$$

The following cell gives the same calculation done with Mathematica. You do not need to evaluate the cell, whose output is shown.

```
FeeData = {{9, 1011},
          {9, 1183},
          {12, 1167},
          {12, 1262},
          {13, 1446},
          {15, 1442}}
Fit[FeeData, {1, x}, x]
```

```
{{9, 1011}, {9, 1183}, {12, 1167},
 {12, 1262}, {13, 1446}, {15, 1442}}
```

```
528.927 + 61.9634 x
```

The output of "Fit" is the best-fit line, which agrees with the result we obtained with the calculator. The data and the best-fit line are plotted in Fig. 1.1.4.

The interpretation of Eq. (1.1.4) is that the estimated fixed fee for the average student is \$529, since that is what he or she would pay in the limit of zero SCHs. The slope, \$62/SCH, was the actual cost of instruction considering tuition and course fees. (We might add that student cost at UT Austin has risen since this experiment was performed.)

A statistical analysis.   The fee-bill analysis illustrates statistical analysis. We recognize that if we selected six other students, or every student in the class, we would get different data,

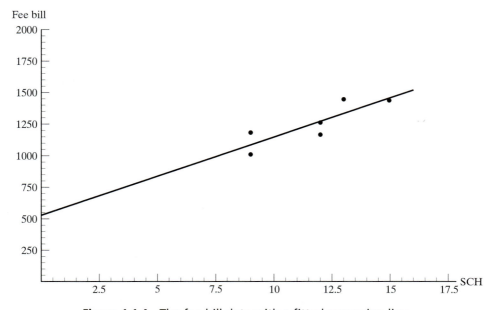

Figure 1.1.4   The fee-bill data with a fitted regression line.

leading to different values for the intercept and slope of the best-fit line. Thus this is a random system.

From another point of view, we have developed a model for predicting fee bills given SCH, but the model is not perfect. The data have some scatter relative to the straight line, with a root-mean-square (rms) error of about $88. The correlation coefficient, another measure of the goodness of the fit between the data and the model, is 0.854. A correlation coefficient of 1 would indicate that every point lies on the line, and a correlation coefficient of zero would indicate that the data are totally random, so the model would be worthless in that event. All these concepts relate to statistical analysis, and we will explore these and other methods of statistical analysis in Chapter 4.

A random-process example: Measuring the speed of light using Venus

The background for the experiment.   At the height of the Cold War in the 1950s, some powerful radar systems were developed to detect hostile aircraft and missiles. One of these systems was an experimental radar designed at MIT Lincoln Laboratory, located at Millstone Hill, northwest of Boston, Massachusetts.[3] This system made the first radar contact with Venus, and the round-trip time for the radar pulses gave a measurement of the speed of light that was approximately ten times more accurate than other measurements prior to that time. The distance between Earth and Venus at the time of the measurement was approximately 28 million miles, meaning the pulses had to travel 56 million miles to make the round trip. Although the receiving equipment was state of the art for the time, the received pulses were so weak that a sophisticated detection technique had to be used. This detection process involved two random processes.

System characteristics.   The radar operated at a frequency of 440 MHz with a peak power of about 300 kW. The antenna gain was 37.5 dB, and the receiver system temperature was 170 K. Venus was assumed to be a good reflector, so a single-pulse signal-to-noise ratio of a 2-ms pulse was calculated to be -10 dB, which means that the return pulses were buried in the noise.

System operation.   The round-trip time to Venus was about 4.5 minutes. The transmitter was operated for 4.5 minutes, sending out 30 pulses per second (except half the pulses were eliminated, as explained below), filling up the space between Earth and Venus with pulses going both ways, and then the transmitter was turned off and the received signals, plus noise, were recorded on magnetic tape. Had a uniform stream of pulses been transmitted, 8191 pulses would have been transmitted, but approximately half the pulses were eliminated on a random basis. The pattern of transmitted pulses was recorded for processing of the received signal, which would be the same pattern, with the return pulses buried in noise.

Detection by cross-correlation.   The received signal was multiplied by the transmitted signal to yield one number indicating detection level. Because the time position of the received pulses was to be determined by the experiment, the received and transmitted signals were lined up at many times to see which position gave the maximum detected signal. In the absence of noise, the expected result should have looked as in Fig. 1.1.5.

The analyzed data received from two-days' operations are shown in Fig. 1.1.6. Here we are dealing with two random processes. The signal is a random process in that it consists of a series of radar pulses with roughly half the pulses eliminated at random, so that the

Figure 1.1.5 The large central triangle appears when all the return pulses line up with the pattern of transmitted pulses. The smaller pulses on either side, of which we have shown but a few, occur because of the basic periodicity of the pulses, but these are half the size of the central pulse because half the transmitted pulses are randomly eliminated.

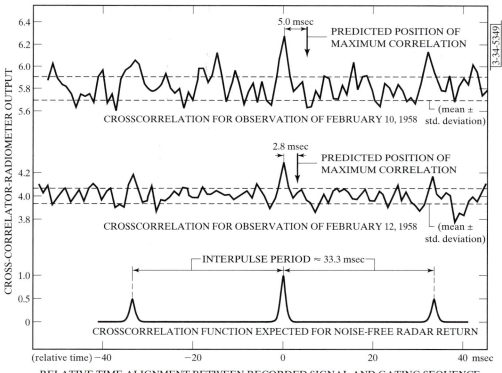

Figure 1.1.6 Radar returns from Venus on the Millstone Hill Radar for February 10, 1958 (top), and February 12, 1958 (bottom). The bottom scan is what the returns would look like in the absence of noise. The signal was detected by cross-correlation between the returns and the transmitted train of random pulses. Taken from the MIT Lincoln Laboratory preprint of *The Venus Radar Experiment*,[4] Robert Price, presented at the 9th General Assembly of the Advisory Group of Aeronautical Research and Development of the Organisation du Traité de L'Atlantique Norde (NATO) at Aachen, Germany, 21 September 1959.

correlation will be highest when the received and transmitted signals are aligned. The noise is also a random process. Theoretical analysis of the expected return signal uses techniques that we will examine in Chapter 6.

Summary.   In this section we showed the need for models that describe random systems. We then gave examples of random systems involving probability, statistics, and random processes. In the remainder of Chapter 1 we develop the basic framework required for the analysis of random systems, which we call *the probability paradigm*. We begin by describing the mathematical language best suited to the needs of this subject.

1.2 THE LANGUAGE OF SET THEORY

In Sec. 1.1 we dealt with three situations that can be modeled by chance experiments. The first involved manufacturing, testing, and shipping parts. In this case we introduced the events G (good part), B (bad part), V (valid test), and W (wrong test result), as well as combinations of those events. In the second situation, data were taken from a class, and a model was fit to the data. In the third situation, random signals were used to measure the speed of light by bouncing a radar signal off Venus. All involved random aspects and could be modeled as chance experiments.

The probability paradigm that we are introducing in this chapter provides a framework for investigating such situations that are modeled by chance experiments. Our immediate need is for a mathematical notation or language in which to express the chance experiment, events, and their combinations. Set theory satisfies this need. After the following brief review of set theory, we define probability and derive useful rules for probabilities in Sec. 1.3.

1.2.1 Set Theory Definitions and Vocabulary

In this section we review the definitions and vocabulary of sets and set operations. If you are familiar with set definitions, with the union and intersection of sets, and with the concept of a partition, you may want to skip ahead to where we discuss how set theory is used in probability theory (Sec. 1.2.3).

Sets.   A set is defined as an unordered collection of distinct (no repeated) elements, for example,

$N = \{1, 2, 3, 4, 5, 6\}$
$C = \{$red, blue, yellow$\}$
$D = \{$spaniel, St. Bernard, mutt, wolf$\}$

Notice that the elements of a set are listed within brackets: {list of elements with no repeated elements}.

Elements.   An element is a member of a set. Examples include $2 \in N$, yellow $\in C$, crow $\notin D$, where the funny e means "is a member of the set," and a line through the symbol means "is not a member of the set."

Subsets.   The set B is a subset of A if every element of B is also an element of A. The relationship is written $B \subset A$, where the sideways u means "is a subset of."

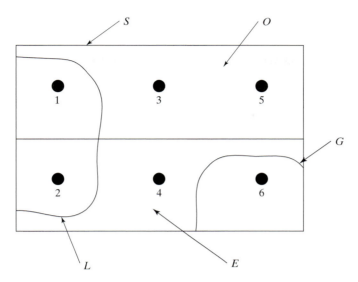

Figure 1.2.1   The rectangle represents the space, the dots represent elements, and the other regions contain subsets.

The space or universal set.   A space S contains all elements and subsets under considera-tion in a given situation or problem. Throughout the remainder of this section we will use for our examples $S = N = \{1, 2, 3, 4, 5, 6\}$. In general, $S = \{s_1, s_2, \ldots\} = \{s_i\}$. This means that the set N is now our space, or universal set; our examples will use only S, its elements, and its subsets.

Equality.   Two sets are equal, $S = N$, if S and N contain the same elements.

Venn diagrams.   Set relationships may be displayed in a Venn diagram. In Fig. 1.2.1 the rectangle represents the space, the dots represent elements, and the areas represent subsets. In Fig. 1.2.1 we show the subsets $E = \{\text{even}\} = \{2, 4, 6\}$, $O = \{\text{odd}\} = \{1, 3, 5\}$, $L = \{s_i < 3\} = \{1, 2\}$, and $G = \{s_i \geq 6\} = \{6\}$, where s_i means all elements having the stated property.

The null, or empty, set.   The null set has no elements and is symbolized by $\emptyset$. The null set is also called the *empty set*. An example is $F = \{s_i > 50\} = \emptyset$.

1.2.2 Combinations of Sets

Union.   The *union* of two sets, written $A \cup B$, contains those elements contained in A or in B or in both. An example in our space and its defined subsets from Fig. 1.2.1 is

$$E \cup L = \{2, 4, 6\} \cup \{1, 2\} = \{1, 2, 4, 6\} \tag{1.2.1}$$

If B is a subset of A, then $A \cup B = A$, since no points in B are outside of A. The union of A and B is shown by the shaded area in Fig. 1.2.2.

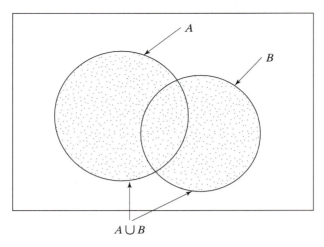

Figure 1.2.2 All elements within the shaded area are in the union of *A* and *B*.

You do it. For Eq. (1.2.2), enter your answer in **myanswer** in the cell box, within the brackets, separated by commas. Once you have entered your answer, click Evaluate for a response.

$$O \cup L = \{1, 3, 5\} \cup \{1, 2\} = ? \tag{1.2.2}$$

```
myanswer = "{?}";
```

```
Evaluate
```

For the answer, see endnote 5.

See Sec. 1.2.2 for a review of the union.

Intersection. The *intersection* of *A* and *B*, written $A \cap B$, contains those elements contained in both *A* and *B*. The crosshatched area in Fig. 1.2.3 shows the intersection of *A* and *B*.

An example of an intersection from our space in Fig. 1.2.1 is

$$E \cap G = \{2, 4, 6\} \cap \{6\} = \{6\} \tag{1.2.3}$$

You do it. For Eq. (1.2.4), enter your answer in **myanswer** in the cell box, within the brackets, separated by commas. Enter "null" for a null response. Once you have entered your answer, click Evaluate for a response.

$$O \cap L = \{1, 3, 5\} \cap \{1, 2\} = \ldots \tag{1.2.4}$$

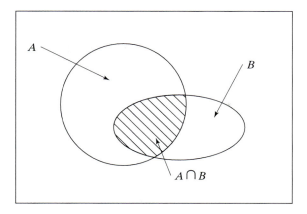

Figure 1.2.3   The crosshatched area is the intersection of A and B.

```
myanswer  =  "{?}";
```

```
Evaluate
```

For the answer, see endnote 6.

Disjoint sets.   The sets A and B are *disjoint* if their intersection is the empty set: $A \cap B = \emptyset$. This means that no element is in both sets. Disjoint sets are pictured in the Venn diagram in Fig. 1.2.4.

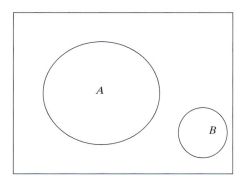

Figure 1.2.4   The disjoint sets A and B have no elements in common.

You do it.   For the sets defined in Fig. 1.2.1, give at least one pair of sets that are disjoint (this entry is case sensitive), then click Evaluate for a response.

```
myanswer = "? and ? are disjoint";
```

```
Evaluate
```

For the answer, see endnote 7.

Complements.   The sets A and B are *complements* if $A \cap B = \emptyset$, and $A \cup B = S$. In words, the two sets are complements if they are disjoint and their union contains every element in the space. Thus every element in the space is in either A or B, but not in both. Complementary sets are indicated by the notation $B = \overline{A}$. If B is the complement of A, then A is the complement of B, $A = \overline{B} = \overline{\overline{A}}$. Figure 1.2.5 shows the space divided into two complementary subsets.

From our space, we note that E and O are complements:

$$E = \{2, 4, 6\} = \overline{\{1, 3, 5\}} = \overline{O} \tag{1.2.5}$$

However, disjoint sets L and G are not complements because their union is missing some elements in S.

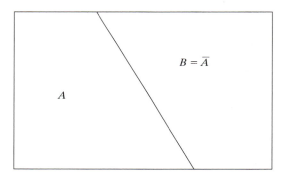

Figure 1.2.5   The subsets A and B are complements if B contains all the elements that are not in A and only those elements that are not in A.

Partitions.   A *partition* is a collection of disjoint sets that together include every point in the space. Figure 1.2.6 shows disjoint sets A, B, C, D, and E, which partition the space.

A way to express a partition within set notation is $S = A \cup B \cup C \cup D \cup E$, and $A \cap B = \emptyset$, $A \cap C = \emptyset$, $B \cap C = \emptyset$, $A \cap D = \emptyset$, and so on, for all pairs. Note that A and $\overline{A}$ are a partition. Another partition is composed of the elementary subsets, $S_i = \{s_i\}$, each of which contains only one element.

Set algebra.   A set algebra can be developed that resembles Boolean algebra. The union corresponds to the (inclusive) OR, and the intersection corresponds to the AND. The results of Boolean algebra carry over into set algebra. For example, deMorgan's theorems are valid for sets:

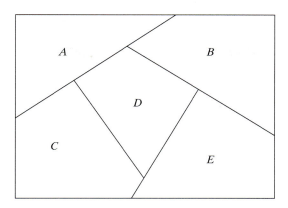

Figure 1.2.6   The sets *A, B, C, D,* and *E* partition the space. Any element in the space must lie in one and only one of these sets.

$\overline{A \cup B} = \overline{A} \cap \overline{B}$, and similarly for absorption rules, distribution rules, and the like. We will not derive these relationships because they are familiar to engineering students.

1.2.3 The Application of Set Theory to Probability

Chance experiments.   Having reviewed the definitions and vocabulary of set theory, we are now able to show how set theory is used to describe chance experiments. Consider a chance experiment, in principle repeatable, with its outcomes. We represent the outcomes as the universal set, *S,* which is called the *sample space* or *probability space.* Thus the elements of $S = \{$sample space or probability space$\}$ are the outcomes of the experiment: $S = \{$outcomes of experiment$\} = \{s_i\}$. Events are then subsets of *S*: $A \subset S$, $B \subset S$, and so forth. When the experiment is performed, one outcome occurs. If that outcome is an element of the set *A*, then event *A* occurred for that performance of the experiment, and vice versa.

The space, *S*, in the probability context is also called the *certain event*, since on every performance of the experiment the event *S* is certain to occur. In the probability context, the null set, Ø, is called the *impossible event,* since it contains no outcomes and thus cannot occur. The elements of the space, s_i, which represent the outcomes of the chance experiment are associated with the elementary events, $S_i = \{s_i\}$. The elementary events are a partition of the space. Every performance of the chance experiment yields one and only one event of any partition.

Example 1.2.1:   Elevator stops —————————————————————————————

The chance experiment.   Consider that five persons get on an elevator at the first floor, and there are four floors in all. All the persons push the button for the floor on which they wish to get off. The outcomes of the experiment are the patterns of the floors at which the elevator stops before all the passengers are discharged, without regard for how many passengers get off. This is a chance experiment with well-defined outcomes.

The space.   The space with its outcomes is

$$S = \{\text{all possible patterns of elevator stops}\}$$
$$= \{\underbrace{2, 3, 4,}_{1 \text{ stop}} \underbrace{2 - 3, 3 - 4, 2 - 4,}_{2 \text{ stops}} \underbrace{2 - 3 - 4}_{3 \text{ stops}}\} \tag{1.2.6}$$

We note there are three ways to have one stop (when all get out on the same floor), three ways to have two stops, and one way to have three stops, making seven elements in the space.

Events.   Events defined in this experiment might be $A = \{\text{exactly three stops}\}$ (one outcome), $B = \{\text{stops on even floors only}\}$ (three outcomes), and $C = \{\text{stops on third floor}\}$ (four outcomes). Upon every performance of the chance experiment, one outcome occurs, and each of these events either does or does not occur.

A probability model?   If we were to continue to develop a model for this situation, we would need to make additional assumptions, or go out and take some data. At this time we are merely introducing an everyday situation that can be modeled in set notation. Section 1.4 introduces probability models.

Here we give, without elaboration, two further examples of chance experiments that show the suitability of the language of set theory for encompassing a wide variety of situations.

Example 1.2.2:   Telephone calls ————————————————————————————
The chance experiment is to call the telephone of your local post office four times at 30-minute intervals: $S = \{\text{call post office four times at 30-minute intervals}\}$. We can represent the result of each call with $0 = \text{busy}$ and $1 = \text{get through}$. Thus the outcomes can be enumerated as 4-bit words: $S = \{0000, 0001, 0010, \ldots, 1111\}$. These words constitute counting from 0 through 15 in base 2, and thus 16 outcomes constitute the sample space. Events might be $O_3 = \{\text{get through on third call}\}$ (eight outcomes in this event), and $O_{1,2,3,4} = \{\text{get through on all calls}\}$ (one outcome in this event).

Example 1.2.3:   Coins ————————————————————————————————
The chance experiment is to flip a coin until you get heads. Here the space is $S = \{H, TH, TTH, TTTH, \text{etc.}\}$. In this experiment we have an infinite number of possible outcomes. Events might be $F = \{\text{get } H \text{ on first flip}\}$ or $E = \{\text{series terminates after an even number of flips}\}$.

Summary.   We introduced set theory as a mathematical language suitable for describing random systems and defined relations between sets. We related set theory to chance experiments in general and several specific situations.

Exercises on set theory

1. Consider the universal set $S = \{0, 1, 2, 3, 4, 5, 6, 7, 8, 9, 10, 11, 12\}$.
   Let $L = \{s_i < 10\}$, $G = \{s_i \geq 4\}$, $E = \{s_i \text{ even}\}$, and $F = \{6\}$.
   a. Find $L \cap G$.

   b. Find $\overline{L} \cup G$.
   c. Find $\overline{E \cup \overline{G}}$.
   d. Find $\overline{E} \cup F \cap G$.

For the answers, see endnote 8.

2. Let $S = \{$all integer values in x and y in a square of 5 on a side having corners $(0, 0)$, $(5, 0)$, $(5, 5)$, and $(0, 5)$. Counting the points on the boundary, this should include 36 elements. Indicate the elements in the space in the following events:
   a. $\{x + y \le 3\}$
   b. $x^2 + y^2 \le 16$. For the answers, see endnote 9.

1.3 THE DEFINITION AND RULES OF PROBABILITY

1.3.1 Random Systems

The chance experiment and its outcomes.   Sections 1.1 and 1.2 presented the probability paradigm with which we model random systems. To reiterate, we require a repeatable experiment with well-defined outcomes. These are the sample space and the outcomes of the experiment, respectively. Events are defined on those outcomes, such that each time the chance experiment is performed, producing an outcome, we can report if the event of interest occurred. In principle we can repeat the experiment a number of times and determine the relative frequency of the event of interest.

We also showed that we have two mathematical needs. We need a mathematical language flexible enough to describe the random system with its outcomes and events. Set theory, presented in the previous section, satisfies this first need. The second need is for a mathematical model for relative frequencies of events. Probability theory, presented in this section, satisfies this second need.

The importance of relative frequencies.   The relative frequency of event A is defined as

$$\frac{\text{number of times } A \text{ occurs}}{\text{number of times the experiment is performed}}$$

In the development of probability theory there is a tendency to regard probabilities as real things and relative frequencies as contrived applications. To the engineer these priorities are backward: relative frequencies are real, and probabilities are a mathematical model. Assume, for example, that you buy a new car. The national average on automobile accidents reveals that the probability of your having an accident in the first year of ownership is 0.2. This means that you would expect one accident in 5 years, on the average. Suppose, however, that you have two serious accidents during your first 2 months of ownership, which you have repaired, but then you total the car in the twelfth month. What matters to you: the theoretical probability of 0.2 or the actual relative frequency of three accidents/year? Clearly, the latter.

For the insurance company the probabilities are accurate models for the relative frequencies of accident rates because insurance companies deal with large numbers of automobiles. But for them, too, the actual number of accidents, not the probabilities, determines the bottom line of loss or profit. As we develop the probability model for relative frequencies, we must keep in mind what is "real" and what is a model.

Statistical stability.   Experience shows that in many chance experiments that are repeated a large number of times, the relative frequencies of events seem to approach a limit. This property reflects statistical stability and is part of what we mean by "*repeatable* experiment." For example, if we flip a normal coin a large number of times, we expect the relative frequency of heads to be close to 0.5. Although the limit of the relative frequency can never be known exactly, it may be determined to a prescribed accuracy provided the experiment is repeated enough times. Thus, as we plot a relative frequency against the number of repetitions, the results should look like Fig. 1.3.1, where the dashed line represents the unknown limit. (You may rerun the experiment by selecting and evaluating the small cell above the plot. To change the number of trials from 100, you must open the cell and change n.)

If the relative frequency does not obey this pattern of statistical stability, then the system is not properly "random" in the sense that we mean when we speak of random systems. In all applications, this assumption of statistical stability should never be forgotten. The ultimate justification of this assumption is the pragmatic test, Does the theory adequately predict relative frequencies of events when we apply it to the real world?

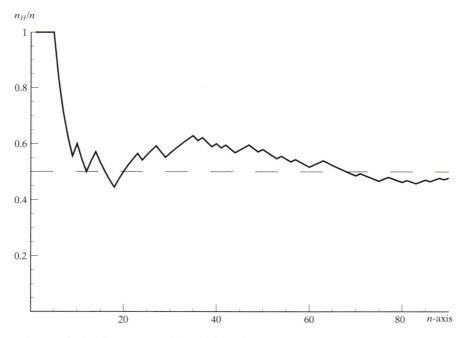

Figure 1.3.1   Relative frequency of heads for a fair coin plotted against the number of flips.

1.3.2 The Rules of Probability

Context.   Consider an experiment described by a sample space, S, of outcomes, and events A and B defined on those outcomes, as shown in Fig. 1.3.2.

We repeat the experiment n times and record the occurrence of A, B, $A \cap B$, and $A|B$ on each repetition. The results appear in Table 1.3.1. At the bottom of the table we total the number of times that A, B, $A \cap B$, and $A|B$ (A given B) occurred.

Measured relative frequencies.   The relative frequencies of events A, B, and $A \cap B$ are defined to be $\frac{n_A}{n}$, $\frac{n_B}{n}$, and $\frac{n_{A \cap B}}{n}$, respectively. The event $A|B$ is called a *conditional event* and answers the question, If B occurred, did A occur also? We put X in the $A|B$ column when B does not occur, since we don't care if A occurred for those times. Thus for a yes in $A|B$, both A and B must occur; hence, the count will be the same for $A|B$ and $A \cap B$, that is, $n_{A|B} = n_{A \cap B}$. The difference comes in the relative frequency of $A|B$, which is defined as $n_{A|B}/n_B$. In words, the relative frequency of the conditional event $A|B$ is the number of times A and B occur together relative to the number of times B occurs. We regard these relative frequencies as "data."

The pattern.   The "probability" of an event will be our mathematical model for the relative frequency of occurrence for the event. The following development of the rules of probability is

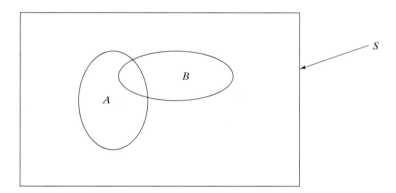

Figure 1.3.2   A space with two events defined.

Table 1.3.1   Experimental results

Repetition	A occurs?	B occurs?	$A \cap B$ occurs?	$A|B$ occurs?
1	yes	yes	yes	yes
2	no	yes	no	no
3	yes	no	no	X
4	no	no	no	X
5	yes	yes	yes	yes
. . .	. . .	. . .	. . .	. . .
n	yes	no	no	X
	n_A	n_B	$n_{A \cap B}$	$n_{A|B}$

based on the concept of a repeatable experiment with definable outcomes, S, and events A, B, and so on, defined on those outcomes. We perform the experiment n times and tabulate the results. The number of times we perform the experiment, n, may be large or small. The general pattern for developing a rule is that we describe a situation, we state its implications for relative frequencies (the data), and we define probability to have the same property as the relative frequency.

Probability rule 1: Definition of probability

Situation: Event A occurs.

Data.   The number of occurrences of A is $0 \leq n_A \leq n$. To convert to a relative frequency, we divide by n. The relative frequency of A must be a positive number lying between 0 and 1, inclusive:

$$0 \leq \frac{n_A}{n} \leq 1 \tag{1.3.1}$$

Probability definition.   The probability of event A, $P[A]$, is therefore defined to be a positive number lying between 0 and 1, inclusive:

$$0 \leq P[A] \leq 1 \tag{1.3.2}$$

The relationship between Eqs. (1.3.1) and (1.3.2) expresses the heart of what we are doing in this section. A model is supposed to act like that which it models in important regards. Here and throughout this section we define the properties of the probability of an event to mimic the corresponding properties of the relative frequency.

Probability rule 2: The certain event

Situation: The certain event, S, occurs.

Data.   In this case the event occurs on every repetition of the experiment, and $n_S = n$. The relative frequency of the certain event is 1:

$$\frac{n_S}{n} = 1 \tag{1.3.3}$$

Probability definition.   The probability of the certain event is therefore defined to be 1:

$$P[S] = 1 \tag{1.3.4}$$

Probability rule 3: The impossible event

Situation: The impossible event "occurs."

Data.   Because no outcomes favor the impossible event, $n_\emptyset = 0$. The relative frequency of the impossible event is

$$\frac{n_\emptyset}{n} = 0 \tag{1.3.5}$$

Probability definition.   The probability of the impossible event is therefore defined to be 0:

$$P[\emptyset] = 0 \qquad\qquad (1.3.6)$$

The meaning of probability.   Reviewing probability rules 1, 2, and 3, we see that probability is a number between 0 and 1, inclusive. At the lowest value lies the impossible event, and at the maximum value stands the certain event. This gives us cause to reflect on the meaning of probability.

Probability and relative frequencies.   Because probability models the relative frequency, we now consider the equation that considers them more or less the same:

$$\frac{n_A}{n} \approx P[A], \text{ or } n_A \approx P[A] \times n \qquad\qquad (1.3.7)$$

Equation (1.3.7) is not exactly true, but if n is large enough, then Eq. (1.3.7) becomes an accurate approximation—how accurate depends on the details. Here we assert, however, that probability not only models relative frequencies but can be approximately equal to the relative frequency. This is an important meaning of probability in the context of an experiment that is repeated a large number of times. Thus, if we know the probability of an event, we know approximately how many times the event will occur in a large number of repetitions of the experiment, as stated in Eqn. (1.3.7).

Subjective probability.   Probability also has a meaning relating to one performance of an experiment. Let us suppose that the experiment has not yet been performed, but we know the probability of event A. From rules 1, 2, and 3, we see that probability is a number between 0 and 1, where 0 represents impossibility and 1 represents certainty. If we know $P[A]$ to be very small, near zero, then we are a bit surprised if A occurs when the experiment is performed, but if $P[A]$ is nearly 1, then we are not surprised.

This subjective meaning of probability describes our anticipations before, and reactions after, an experiment. The subjective meaning of probability is extremely important to the way we organize our professional and private lives and thus should not be thought irrelevant to this subject. When the risk of a business decision is assessed on the basis of a probability model, the decision and ensuing action constitute the only possible performance of the experiment. We risk personal and professional resources on the basis of our expectations before the experiment, and we gain or lose as a result of what happens. Probability calculations, in this context, help us make decisions in the context of uncertainty.

Probability as a mathematical system.   Mathematicians define probability as an axiomatic mathematical system. For them, probability is a measure placed on a mathematical system. A bit later in this section we contrast probability as a mathematical system and as a model for relative frequencies.

Notation.   We state probabilities as $P[\text{event}]$. Brackets are used to distinguish a probability, which operates on an event (a set of outcomes), from a function, $f(x)$, which takes a number or algebraic symbol as an independent variable.

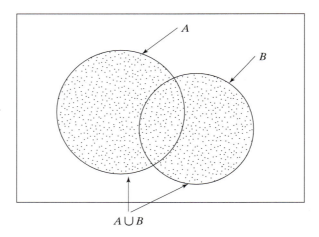

Figure 1.3.3   The shaded area represents the union of A and B.

Probability rule 4: The union of two events

Situation: Event A or B or both, $A \cup B$, occurs. This composite event is the union of A and B, as shown in Fig. 1.3.3.

The number of times the union of A and B occurs is the number of times A occurs, plus the number of times B occurs, minus the number of times A and B occur together, $A \cap B$. We must subtract the number of times the intersection occurs because otherwise the intersection would be counted twice.

Data.   The number of times that A union B occurs is thus $n_{A \cup B} = n_A + n_B - n_{A \cap B}$. The relative frequency of $A \cup B$ is therefore

$$\frac{n_{A \cup B}}{n} = \frac{n_A}{n} + \frac{n_B}{n} - \frac{n_{A \cap B}}{n} \tag{1.3.8}$$

Probability definition.   Hence, we define the probability of the union of A and B to be

$$P[A \cup B] = P[A] + P[B] - P[A \cap B] \tag{1.3.9}$$

Special case: When A and B are disjoint.   Note that if A and B are disjoint, then $P[A \cap B] = P[\emptyset] = 0$, and the probability of the union reduces to

$$P[A \cup B] = P[A] + P[B], \text{ if } A \text{ and } B \text{ are disjoint} \tag{1.3.10}$$

Figure 1.3.4 pictures A and B when disjoint.

Example 1.3.1:   Calculating the probability of the union of two events _____

Consider an experiment in which the outcomes are $S = \{0, 1, 2, 3, 4, 5, 6, 7, 8, 9\}$. Two events are $E = \{0, 2, 4, 6, 8\}$ and $B = \{0, 5, 7, 8\}$. Assume that the probability of an event is proportional

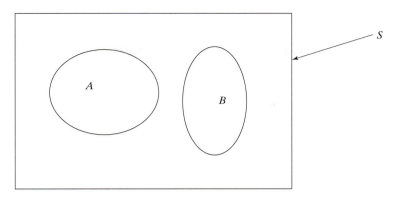

Figure 1.3.4   Events *A* and *B* are disjoint, having no outcomes in common

to the number of outcomes in the event.[10] Thus $P[S] = \frac{10}{10}$, $P[E] = \frac{5}{10}$, and $P[B] = \frac{4}{10}$. Find $P[E \cup B]$.

Solution   From Eq. (1.3.9), $P[A \cup B] = P[A] + P[B] - P[A \cap B]$. Since $P[E \cap B] = P[\{0, 8\}] = \frac{2}{10}$, we have the result $P[E \cup B] = \frac{5}{10} + \frac{4}{10} - \frac{2}{10} = \frac{7}{10}$.

You do it.   For the same space, let $A = \{0, 1, 2, 3, 5\}$ and $C = \{2, 3, 4, 6, 7\}$ and determine $P[A \cup C]$ using Eq. (1.3.9). Enter your answer in **myanswer** in the cell box, and click Evaluate, for a response.

```
myanswer =;
```

```
Evaluate
```

For the answer, see endnote 11.

Probability rule 5: The union of three or more events

Situation: The union of *A*, *B*, and *C*, $A \cup B \cup C$, occurs. Consider the union of three events, $A \cup B \cup C$, as shown in Fig. 1.3.5.

Data.   Here we recognize that in adding the number of times *A* occurs, the number of times *B* occurs, and the number of times *C* occurs, we add the intersections twice, so we subtract the number of times these intersections occur. But the joint occurrence of all three events, $A \cap B \cap C$, is added in three times and then removed three times, so we need to add these in again. The number of times that the union occurs is thus

$$n_{A \cup B \cup C} = n_A + n_B + n_C - n_{A \cap B} - n_{A \cap C} - n_{B \cap C} + n_{A \cap B \cap C} \qquad (1.3.11)$$

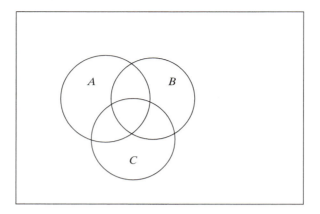

Figure 1.3.5   The most general case, in which all three events overlap; that is, no two are disjoint.

We divide Eq. (1.3.11) by n to obtain an expression for the relative frequency of $A \cup B \cup C$:

$$\frac{n_{A \cup B \cup C}}{n} = \frac{n_A}{n} + \frac{n_B}{n} + \frac{n_C}{n} - \frac{n_{A \cap B}}{n} - \frac{n_{A \cap C}}{n} - \frac{n_{B \cap C}}{n} + \frac{n_{A \cap B \cap C}}{n} \tag{1.3.12}$$

Probability definition.   We define a rule for probabilities to give

$$P[A \cup B \cup C] = P[A] + P[B] + P[C] - P[A \cap B] - P[A \cap C] - P[B \cap C] + P[A \cap B \cap C] \tag{1.3.13}$$

and so forth, for the union of four or more events.

Probability rule 6: The complement of an event

Situation: Event A does not occur, which is the same as saying that the complement of A, $\overline{A}$, occurs.

Data.   Because the number of times that A occurs plus the number of times the complement occurs must add to n, it follows that $n_{\overline{A}} = n - n_A$. The relative frequency of not A, $\overline{A}$, must be

$$\frac{n_{\overline{A}}}{n} = \frac{n - n_A}{n} = 1 - \frac{n_A}{n} \tag{1.3.14}$$

Probability definition.   Thus, the probability that an event does not occur is defined as

$$P[\overline{A}] = 1 - P[A] \tag{1.3.15}$$

You do it.   For the experiment in the previous example and the same assumptions, let $D = E \cap B$. Calculate the probability of $\overline{D}$. Enter your answer as **myanswer** in the cell box, and click Evaluate for a response.

```
myanswer = ? ;
```

```
Evaluate
```

For the answer, see endnote 12.

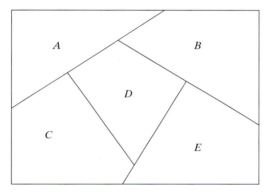

Figure 1.3.6   For the partition, one and only one of the events *A, B, C, D,* and *E* can occur when the experiment is performed.

Probability rule 7: A partition of events

Situation: One of a partition occurs. Consider that a set of events, $A, B, C, \ldots,$ are a partition, as shown in Fig. 1.3.6.

Data.   Because one and only one event of the partition occurs for each repetition of the experiment, it follows that $n_A + n_B + n_C + n_D + n_E = n$. For a partition the relative frequencies must satisfy

$$\frac{n_A}{n} + \frac{n_B}{n} + \frac{n_C}{n} + \frac{n_D}{n} + \frac{n_E}{n} = 1 \tag{1.3.16}$$

Probability definition.   We therefore define the probabilities of the events constituting a partition:

$$P[A] + P[B] + P[C] + P[D] + P[E] = 1 \tag{1.3.17}$$

Thus the probabilities of partitioning events must add to 1.

Examples of partitions.   We give two examples: (1) The events A and $\overline{A}$ are a partition; hence $P[A] + P[\overline{A}] = 1$. This has already been derived as probability rule 6. (2) Consider the sample space $S = \{s_1, s_2, s_3, \ldots, s_N\}$, where N is the number of outcomes in the space. The elementary events are defined as $S_1 = \{s_1\}$, $S_2 = \{s_2\}, \ldots, S_i = \{s_i\}$, and so on. These events consist of one outcome each and hence constitute a partition. Since these events are a partition, it follows that

$$P[S_1] + P[S_2] + \cdots = \sum_{i=1}^{i=N} P[S_i] = 1 \qquad (1.3.18)$$

Thus the probabilities of the outcomes of an experiment must sum to 1. This normalization requirement is useful in deriving and confirming probability models.

Probability rule 8: Conditioned events

Situation: The conditioned event $A|B$ occurs.

Data.   We explained earlier that $n_{A|B}$ is the number of times that A occurs, given that B occurs, which is simply the number of times that A and B jointly occur: $n_{A|B} = n_{A \cap B}$; however, to obtain the relative frequency of the conditioned event, we divide by n_B, not n:

$$\frac{n_{A|B}}{n_B} = \frac{n_{A \cap B}}{n_B} \qquad (1.3.19)$$

The relative frequency of the conditioned event can be expressed in terms of the original experiment as follows:

$$\frac{n_{A|B}}{n_B} = \frac{n_{A \cap B}/n}{n_B/n} \qquad (1.3.20)$$

where we have merely divided numerator and denominator by n, the total number of times the experiment is performed. Of course, these ratios can be calculated only if event B actually occurs, such that $n_B \neq 0$.

Probability definition.   From Eq. (1.3.20) we define the probability of A, conditioned on B, to be

$$P[A|B] = \frac{P[A \cap B]}{P[B]}, \; P[B] \neq 0 \qquad (1.3.21)$$

Another way to write Eq. (1.3.21) is

$$P[A \cap B] = P[B] \times P[A|B] \qquad (1.3.22)$$

which is valid even if $P[B]$ is zero.

Interpretations of conditional probabilities.   We may interpret Eq. (1.3.21) as a renormalization of probabilities, given that B has occurred. Event B has become, in effect, the "certain event" and outcomes outside of B are impossible. Probabilities inside of B, such as $P[A \cap B]$, are scaled up by dividing by $P[B]$.

We may also interpret Eq. (1.3.22) to give the probability of a sequence of actions. Thus the probability that A and B will occur jointly equals the probability that B will occur multiplied by the probability that A will occur, given that B has occurred. This merely models a sequence whereby we first check if B occurred and, if it did, check to see if A occurred also.

Example 1.3.2:   Calculating a conditional probability _____

Consider a space $S = \{1, 2, 3, 4, 5, 6\}$, and $T = \{1, 2, 4\}$, a power of 2. The probability that the outcome is odd, given that it is a power of 2 is

$$P[O|T] = \frac{P[O \cap T]}{P[T]} = \frac{P[\{1, 3, 5\} \cap \{1, 2, 4\}]}{P[\{1, 2, 4\}]} = \frac{P[\{1\}]}{P[\{1, 2, 4\}]} \qquad (1.3.23)$$

If we assume $P[\{1\}] = \frac{1}{6}$ and $P[\{1, 2, 4\}] = \frac{3}{6}$, then

$$P[O|T] = \frac{1/6}{3/6} = \frac{1}{3} \qquad (1.3.24)$$

You do it.   Let $S = \{0, 1, 2, 3, 4, 5, 6, 7, 8, 9\}$, $A = \{0, 1, 3, 5, 7, 9\}$, and $B = \{0, 2, 4, 6, 9\}$. Determine $P[A|B]$, assuming all outcomes are equally likely, and enter your answer as **myanswer** in the cell box. Use Eq. (1.3.21) for your calculation.

```
myanswer = ;
```

```
Evaluate
```

For the answer, see endnote 13.

Absolute and conditional probabilities.   The absolute probability of event A, $P[A]$, can be very different from the conditional probability of event A, given event B, $P[A|B]$.

If A and B are disjoint, as in Fig. 1.3.7, then $P[A|B] = 0$, because A is impossible if B occurs.

At the other extreme, if B is a subset of A, as in Fig. 1.3.8, then $P[A|B] = 1$, since A becomes certain if B occurs. In both cases B gives information about A; there must be some cause–effect relationship or pattern linking the two events,

$$P[A|B] \neq P[A] \qquad (1.3.25)$$

$\uparrow B$ gives information about A

The opposite must also be true: If the conditional probability is the same as the absolute probability, then B _is unrelated to A_.

$$P[A|B] = P[A] \qquad (1.3.26)$$

$\uparrow B$ gives no information about A

This unrelatedness of A and B, called (statistical) _independence,_ leads to our final rule.

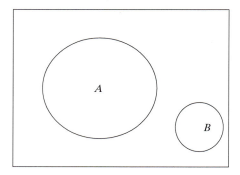

Figure 1.3.7   Here *A* and *B* are disjoint. If *B* occurs, *A* is impossible, and $P[A|B] = 0$.

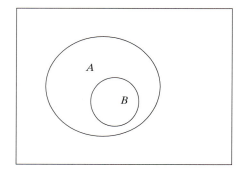

Figure 1.3.8   Event *B* is a subset of Event *A*. If *B* occurs, *A* is certain to occur, and $P[A|B] = 1$.

Probability rule 9: Statistically independent events

Experience tells us that certain events have no connection with one another. Consider the experiment of picking a name at random from the Chicago telephone directory. The event {number of letters in name} and the event {last digit of phone number} must be independent. These events have no cause–effect relationship; they are causally unrelated. This concept of (statistical) independence is important and will be discussed in detail in Sec. 1.5. Here we include it as a new concept leading to a new probability rule.

Situation: *A* and *B* are statistically independent. We assume we have a repeatable experiment with events *A* and *B* defined. We assume *A* and *B* are independent. The picture looks like Fig. 1.3.9, where the crosshatched area corresponds to $A \cap B$.

Data.   We repeat the experiment *n* times, and we are interested in n_A, n_B, and $n_{A \cap B}$. The relative frequencies relevant to this situation are $\frac{n_A}{n}$, $\frac{n_B}{n}$, and $\frac{n_{A \cap B}}{n}$; however, we defer discussion of these relative frequencies until after we have introduced a probability definition.

Probability definition.   If *A* and *B* are independent, the occurrence of one of them, say, *B*, gives no information about the probability of occurrence of the other; thus the absolute and

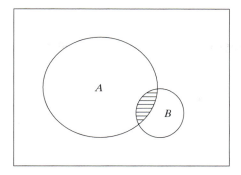

Figure 1.3.9   With *B* neither wholly outside *A* nor wholly inside *A*, *A* and *B* can be independent.

conditional probabilities of *A* are equal. Using conditional probability, we anticipate that if *A* and *B* are independent,

$$P[A|B] = P[A] \qquad (1.3.27)$$

This intuitive concept of independence can be restated using Eq. (1.3.22):

$$P[A \cap B] = P[A|B] \times P[B] \text{ (always)} \qquad (1.3.28)$$
$$= P[A] \times P[B] \text{ (if } A \text{ and } B \text{ are independent)}$$

The first line of (1.3.29) is generally valid, but the second line applies only if *A* and *B* are independent. The definition of independence in Eq. (1.3.27) is based on our intuitive understanding of what probability means and what independence (having no causal connection or pattern) means.

   Data?   How do the data behave? Returning to the relative frequencies, we would translate Eq. (1.3.29) into

$$\frac{n_{A \cap B}}{n} \overset{?}{=} \frac{n_A}{n} \times \frac{n_B}{n} \qquad (1.3.29)$$

We include the question mark in Eq. (1.3.29) because we must ask: Is Eq. (1.3.29) true? In a strict sense, the answer must be no, for in the *n*-fold repetition of an experiment in which *A* and *B* are defined, the relative frequencies will not satisfy Eq. (1.3.29) exactly, at least not most of the time. But if *n* is large, Eq. (1.3.29) will be a good approximation. Equation (1.3.29) is not true automatically or arithmetically but is true "statistically," that is, on the average. We will elaborate in Chapter 2.

   Real and model.   We have now made sufficient progress toward our goal of modeling random systems that we may summarize in Table 1.3.2.

Table 1.3.2   Progress in modeling random systems

Real	Model
a random system	chance experiment
relative frequency	probability
$\frac{n_A}{n}$	$P[A]$
arithmetic of relative frequency	rules of probability
knowledge of causality	statistical independence

1.3.3 Comparing our Rules of Probability with the Axioms of Probability

The style of mathematics.   One goal of mathematics is to develop self-consistent, logical structures based on the minimum number of fundamental assumptions, called *axioms*. At the college level and beyond, this goal takes on a certain style of presentation, both in oral and written form. Mathematicians seek the most general results from the minimum number of assumptions, using the rules of logic. The primary emphasis is on rigorous proof and concise orderly development. Math books typically have few graphics and usually use a carefully defined notation that carries a lot of meaning. The style of mathematics tends to be concise, abstract, and elegant.

The style of engineering.   The goal of engineering is to develop useful machines and processes. In engineering education we use mathematical models to describe and make predictions in physical systems that actually or potentially exist. The style of engineering education should be lucid, concrete, and robust. Important matters are presented from several points of view and explained thoroughly, with the hope that everyone will understand. Many applications are usually presented, and important concepts are generally repeated several times in a variety of contexts. Engineering textbooks generally have many graphical figures, and notation is chosen to be lucid.

Engineering mathematics.   The genre of this text is engineering mathematics, which draws strengths from both traditions and can enrich both. Most works on probability favor the mathematical style, with axioms, theorems, formal definitions, and such. This text, as you have seen, favors an engineering style of presentation. Our concern is to model real-world phenomena, and we have defined probability accordingly.

Comparing our approach with mathematical approaches to probability

Events.   We defined an event as a subset of the sample space, $A \subset S$. Apparently there are situations in which a more exacting definition is required. Thus mathematicians define the concept of a *sigma field*, which refers to all the events that behave properly.

The rules of probability.   We have nine rules, all but one derived from the properties of relative frequencies. The exception is the rule for independence, which is based on intuition. Mathematicians enjoy trimming the list to the bare minimum, which is four rules or axioms, and then proving the rest from those four. The four usually given are as follows:

1. $0 \leq P[A] \leq 1$
2. $P[S] = 1$

3. $P[A \cup B] = P[A] + P[B]$ if $A \cap B = \emptyset$
4. The same as axiom 3 but extended to a countably infinite number of events.

Independence is not an axiom but rather a definition.

Integration.   Integrals represent summations. The standard method for performing integrals in engineering mathematics is the Riemannian integral, which uses the antiderivative. More advanced definitions of integrals exist and must be invoked in special cases that can arise in mathematical probability theory; however, in performing integration on familiar functions, that is, calculating numerical or symbolic integrals, the Riemannian integral is used.

We can be glad that mathematicians are concerned with the logical structure of probability theory. Their diligence assures us that the theory we use is robust and logically consistent, even in the details. Engineering rests on the work of mathematicians, and we repay them with the fruits of engineering.

Probability a paradigm?   We titled this chapter "The Probability Paradigm" because we believe the probabilistic way of thinking and modeling systems is radical and, to some degree, unintuitive. The dictionary definition of *paradigm* is "a pattern, example, or model." The current usage, as in *paradigm shift,* was coined by philosopher of science Thomas Kuhn to describe a broadly accepted way of viewing a large class of phenomena. Standard examples of paradigm shifts are (1) the change from the geocentric solar system of Ptolemy to the heliocentric solar system of Copernicus; (2) the shift from Newtonian mechanics, in which all phenomena are continuous and deterministic, to quantum mechanics, in which changes are discrete and nondeterministic; and (3) the shift from analog to digital representation and processing of information. Such shifts have profound effects on those who experience them.

The repeatable chance experiment, with its outcomes, events, and probabilities defined on those events, requires equally profound changes in one's way of thinking. Behind every probability calculation must lie such a chance experiment, conceivable if not actual. This framework we will call our *macromodel*. As we develop the subject of probability and explore its applications we will derive *micromodels*, such as the binomial or Gaussian distributions, based on this macromodel plus additional assumptions. The next section explores the first of these micromodels.

Exercises on the rules of probability

1. In a given experiment, we have the following information:

$$P[C] = 0.4, \, P[B \cap C] = 0.2, \, P[A \cap C] = 0.1$$
$$P[B \cup C] = 0.7, \, P[A \cup C] = 0.7$$

   a. Find $P[A]$ and $P[B]$.
   b. Are B and C independent?

2. Consider that the sample space, S, is partitioned by a sequence of events, $A_1, A_2, \ldots,$ to infinity. These events are of decreasing probability, of the form $P[A_{i+1}] = P[A_i]/2$.
   a. Find $P[A_1]$.
   b. Let $E = A_2 \cup A_4 \cup \ldots$ to infinity. Find $P[E]$.

c. Let $N = A_1 \cup A_2 \cup \ldots \cup A_N$. Find $P[N]$.

Hint: You must be able to sum a geometric series.[14] For the answers, see endnote 15.

1.4 THE EQUALLY LIKELY OUTCOMES MODEL

1.4.1 Introduction to the Counting Approach to Probability

What we have done so far.   We have shown the need for models of random systems; we have stressed the importance of relative frequencies of events (data); we have introduced the language of set theory; and we have defined the rules of probability, which model the arithmetic properties of relative frequencies and reflect our intuitive sense of independence.

Assumptions.   For any properly random system, we assume statistical stability. This is what we mean by "repeatable experiment." Statistical stability means that the relative frequencies of events behave in such a manner that as more trials are done the relative frequencies approach (unknown) limits. We can determine these limits as closely as we desire by performing the experiment enough times. In many instances we will assume statistical independence as well. As for any model, only real-world applications can ultimately justify our assumptions.

What we have not done.   So far we have not shown how to determine any probabilities. We have developed our macromodel, our framework for all probability analysis. We now will begin exploring *micromodels,* by which we mean specific models that are useful in computing probabilities under specific assumptions. Our first micromodel assumes equally likely outcomes. From this assumption of equally likely elementary events, the probabilities of all other events may be derived. Early workers thought it self-evident that the outcomes of an experiment had to be "equally likely." This is understandable, since this approach works well in games of chance, which were historically important in stimulating the development of probability theory.

Classical definition of probability.   The assumption of equally likely outcomes leads to the classical definition of probability. We will call it *probability by counting,* since the assumption of equally likely outcomes reduces the analysis to the counting of outcomes in the sample space and the counting of outcomes in the events of interest. In this section we investigate this model and present basic techniques for counting.

1.4.2 The Equally Likely Outcomes Model for Probabilities

The equally likely assumption.   We assume a finite number of outcomes, as shown in the sample space in Fig. 1.4.1. All outcomes in $S = \{s_1, s_2, s_3, \ldots, s_N\}$, where N is the number of outcomes in the space, are assumed to be equally likely, that is, to have the same probability. In this section we will use this model to derive probabilities of events.

It is useful to assume the equally likely outcomes model in the following situations.

A random choice.   An integer is chosen at random between 0 and 9, inclusive. This means that one of 0, 1, 2, 3, 4, 5, 6, 7, 8, or 9 is chosen, with no number more likely than any other. Note that here "at random" means equally likely outcomes.

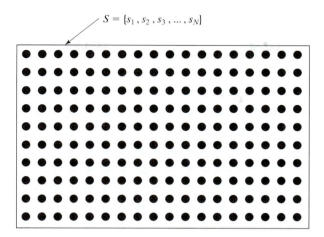

$$S = \{s_1, s_2, s_3, \ldots, s_N\}$$

Figure 1.4.1 The dots represent the *N* outcomes in the sample space. All outcomes have the same probability.

A fair coin. A fair coin is flipped. Here *H* and *T* are the possible outcomes, and being "fair" means that these outcomes are equally likely. Dealing poker hands from a "well-shuffled" deck of cards and throwing "fair" dice fall into this category.

A random telephone number. A telephone number is picked at random out of the Chicago white pages. Although it is moderately challenging to devise a practical scheme for selecting a number to satisfy the "equally likely" criterion, this still is a conceivable experiment.

Normalization of the space. The elementary events of the sample space are $S_i = \{s_i\}, i = 1, 2, \ldots, N$. The elementary events contain all outcomes in the space, $S = \cup_1^N S_i$, and the elementary events are disjoint, $S_i \cap S_j = \emptyset, i \neq j$. In other words, the elementary events are a partition of the sample space. Thus their probabilities must by Eq. (1.3.18) sum to 1:

$$\sum_{i=1}^{N} P[S_i] = 1 \qquad (1.4.1)$$

The equally likely assumption. By assumption, all elementary events (= outcomes) have the same probability; call it *p*. The summation in Eq. (1.4.1) adds *p* to itself *N* times; hence,

$$\underbrace{p + p + \cdots}_{N \text{ times}} = Np = 1 \Rightarrow p = \frac{1}{N} \qquad (1.4.2)$$

where *N* is the number of outcomes in the sample space. Normalization requires that each of the equally likely outcomes have a probability equal to the reciprocal of the number of outcomes in the sample space. Thus we merely count the number of outcomes in the space to determine the probability of each outcome.

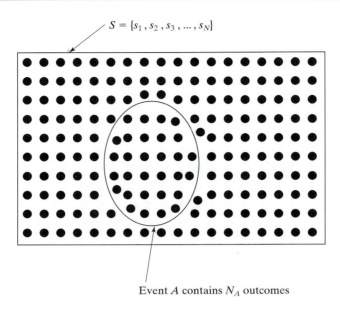

$$S = \{s_1, s_2, s_3, \dots, s_N\}$$

Event A contains N_A outcomes

Figure 1.4.2   The space has N outcomes, and event A is favored by N_A outcomes.

Probabilities of events

Let us find the probability of event A. Assume event A has N_A outcomes favoring it, as indicated in Fig. 1.4.2. The elementary events associated with these outcomes are a partition of event A, and by the same reasoning used in the normalization procedure, we find the probability of event A to be

$$P[A] = \sum_{\text{in } A} P[S_i] = \sum_{\text{in } A} p = N_A \times p = \frac{N_A}{N} \tag{1.4.3}$$

Thus with all outcomes equally likely, the probability of event A is the number of outcomes favoring A divided by the number of outcomes in the space. This is the classical definition of probability. Note that Eq. (1.4.3) is similar to Eq. (1.3.7) but has a totally different meaning. The lowercase n in Eq. (1.3.7) represents the number of times the experiment is performed, whereas the uppercase N in Eq. (1.4.3) represents the number of equally likely outcomes in the sample space. Similarly N_A represents the number of outcomes favoring event A, not the number of times A occurs in n repetitions of the experiment.

Probability by counting.   It follows from (1.4.3) that probabilities may be determined by counting. We must count the outcomes in the sample space, N, and we must count the outcomes in the event, N_A. This is conceptually simple but often a challenge in practice. After discussing some simple examples in which the counting is relatively easy, we will introduce general counting techniques.

Example 1.4.1: Picking a number at random _____
Pick a number at random between 0 and 9, inclusive. Find the probability that the number so chosen is a prime number.

Solution   There are 10 outcomes in the sample space, $S = \{0, 1, 2, 3, 4, 5, 6, 7, 8, 9\}$; thus $N = 10$. We interpret "at random" to mean that all outcomes are equally likely to be chosen. The prime numbers in the space are $A = \{2, 3, 5, 7\}$; thus $N_A = 4$. The probability of picking a prime number is therefore $\frac{4}{10} = 0.4$.

Example 1.4.2: Picking a person at random at a party _____
A party is attended by 47 guests, 20 women and 27 men. What is the probability that the door prize is won by a woman?

Solution   We assume that all guests have an equal chance of winning the door prize. Thus the probability that a woman wins is the number of outcomes in event $W = \{\text{woman}\}$, which is 20, divided by the number of outcomes in the sample space $S = \{\text{guest}\}$, which is 47. Thus $P[W] = \frac{20}{47}$.

Example 1.4.3: Picking a person at random in the United States _____
Find the probability that the last name of a person, picked at random from the population of the United States, begins with A, B, or C.

Solution   Here we have a large number of outcomes that we have no way of enumerating exactly; however, we may approximate the desired probability by assuming some large city has a typical distribution of names and use the white pages of the phone book to estimate the number of entries that begin with A, B, or C. For Austin, Texas, in 1995, the A's began on page 1, the C's ended on page 142.7, and the Z's ended on page 721.5. Thus the requested probability is approximately $P[A, B, \text{ or } C] \approx \frac{142.7}{721.5} = 0.198$.

You do it.   A person buys something in a store, offers a quarter (25¢), and receives some change. In the absence of further information, we will assume all possible outcomes, from 1¢ to 24¢, are equally likely. What is the probability that the change consists of four or more coins, assuming the minimum number of coins of change are given? Enter your answer as **myanswer** in the cell box as a fraction or a decimal number, and click Evaluate for a response.

```
myanswer = ;
```

```
Evaluate
```

For the answer, see endnote 16.

1.4.3 Counting Techniques

Combinatorials

This section on counting techniques introduces the branch of mathematics called *combinatorials,* a standard topic in mathematical texts on probability and discrete mathematics.[17] Many counting operations can be reduced to taking a sample of k objects from a group of n objects or, alternatively, by placing k balls into n bins.

For example, how many pairs ($k = 2$) of letters can be made from the letters A, B, and C ($n = 3$)? The answer depends on the rules for selecting the letters. Two questions must first be answered: (1) Are we allowed to repeat letters? and (2) Does order matter?

Thus there are four possible answers:

- If order matters and we are allowed to repeat letters, there are nine pairs: AA, BB, CC, AB, BA, AC, CA, BC, and CB.
- If order matters and we are not allowed to repeat letters, there are six pairs: AB, BA, AC, CA, BC, and CB.
- If order does not matter and we are not allowed to repeat letters, there are three pairs: AB, AC, and BC.
- Finally, if order does not matter and we are allowed to repeat letters, there are six pairs: AA, BB, CC, AB, AC, and BC.

Selections in which order matters are called *permutations*. Selections in which order does not matter are called *combinations*. Selections that allow repetition are often called *sampling with replacement,* as if something is selected from a general population and then returned to the population before the next object is selected. Selections that do not allow repetition are often called *sampling without replacement.*

Permutations

Consider selecting k distinguishable objects from a population of n objects, with the order of selection noted. These will be permutations, because order matters; for example, AB is different from BA.

Sampling with replacement. We consider first permutations and sampling with replacement. This means that repetition is permitted; all k selections are made from an identical population of n objects. For $k = 1$, we have n choices. For $k = 2$, we have n choices for the first and we have n choices for the second, making n^2 selections possible. In general, there are n^k permutations of a selection of k objects from a population of n when sampling with replacement.

Example 1.4.4: Pairs of letters ——————————————————————
Find the number of ordered samples with replacement of $k = 2$ letters from a population of $n = 3$ letters (A, B, C).

Solution   We may have $n^k = 3^2 = 9$ such samples, which were given previously (AA, BB, CC, AB, BA, AC, CA, BC, and CB).

Example 1.4.5:   Computer passwords ————————————————————————————
How many computer passwords can be made of four, five, or six characters if the first character must be a letter and the remainder may be letters or numerals? Assume letter case, upper- or lowercase, does not matter.

Solution   For four characters, we have 26 choices for the first character and $(26 + 10)^3$ characters for the remaining three characters. Considering four-, five-, and six-character passwords we have $26 \times (36^3 + 36^4 + 36^5) = 1,617,003,648$ such passwords.

You do it.   What if letters and numbers must alternate? Do the calculation, type your answer between the quotes in **myanswer,** and click Evaluate for a response.

```
myanswer = "?" ;
```

```
Evaluate
```

For the answer, see endnote 18.

Sampling without replacement.   We will select k distinguishable objects from a population of n objects, with no repetition of objects permitted. The population is changed by each selection, since repetition is not permitted. As before, there are n choices for the first selection, but now there are $n - 1$ choices for the second, since we cannot repeat the first. Thus for $k = 2$, we have $n(n - 1)$ selections. For $k = 3$ there are $n(n - 1)(n - 2)$. In general, for a sample of size k there are $n(n - 1)(n - 2) \ldots (n - k + 1)$ permutations when sampling without replacement. This result may be written using factorials as

$$\frac{n(n - 1)(n - 2) \ldots (2)(1)}{(n - k)(n - k - 1) \ldots (2)(1)} = \frac{n!}{(n - k)!} \tag{1.4.4}$$

Example 1.4.6:   Forming letter combinations ————————————————————————
When $k = 2$ letters are selected without replacement from $n = 3$ letters (A, B, C) without repetition, there are $3!/(3 - 2)! = 6$, as given previously $(AB, BA, AC, CA, BC,$ and $CB)$.

You do it.   How many four-, five-, or six-character passwords can be formed beginning with a letter followed by letters or numerals if no repetition is permitted. Type your answer in the cell box and click Evaluate for a response.

```
myanswer =  "?" ;
```

```
Evaluate
```

For the answer, see endnote 19.

Example 1.4.7:   Birthdays _____

There are 40 students in a class. What is the probability that no two students have the same birthday?

Solution   We assume 365 equally likely birthdays. There are then 365^{40} possible combinations of birthdays, all of which are assumed to be equally likely (sampling with replacement). Of these

$$365 \times 364 \times \cdots \times 326 = \frac{365!}{(365 - 40)!} \tag{1.4.5}$$

all have different birthdays (sampling without replacement). The required probability is therefore

$$P[\text{no repeated birthdays}] = \frac{365!}{(365 - 40)!\,365^{40}} = 0.108768 \tag{1.4.6}$$

Combinations

We select k indistinguishable objects from a population of n objects. These are combinations, because order does not matter, the objects being "indistinguishable." As before, we have two cases: sampling with and without replacement.

Sampling without replacement.   We seek the number of ways a sample of k objects can be selected, without regard for order, from a population of n objects, without replacement. We can determine the number of such combinations by first considering that the k objects are numbered (distinguishable). We have shown that this condition gives $\frac{n!}{(n-k)!}$ permutations.

Let us designate $\binom{n}{k}$ to be the number of combinations of size k that may be generated from these permutations.[20] If the objects in the combination were numbered, we could rearrange them to create the permutations. Because the k objects can be rearranged $k!$ ways, it follows that

$$\binom{n}{k} \times k! = \frac{n!}{(n - k)!} \Rightarrow \binom{n}{k} = \frac{n!}{k!(n - k)!} \tag{1.4.7}$$

The binomial coefficients.   The numbers $\binom{n}{k}$ defined in Eq. (1.4.7) are commonly called the *binomial coefficients*. The expansion of the binomial expression

$$(a + b)^n = \sum_{k=0}^{n} \binom{n}{k} a^k b^{n-k} \tag{1.4.8}$$

reveals the origin of the name.[21]

Example 1.4.8:   Pairs of letters _____

The number of selections of $k = 2$ letters that may be drawn without replacement from $n = 3$ letters (A, B, C) without repetition and without regard to order are $\binom{3}{2} = \frac{3!}{2!(3 - 2)!} = 3$, as given previously AB, AC, and BC).

You do it.   What if you were interested in triplets of letters drawn from the entire alphabet, without regard to order? Enter your answer in the cell box and click Evaluate for a response.

```
myanswer = "?" ;
```

```
Evaluate
```

For the answer, see endnote 22.

Some calculators have under the "PROB" (probability) menu the functions COMB for combinations and PERM for permutations. In both cases, ENTER n, key k, and then execute the function to determine either the permutations or combinations. In both cases these are "without replacement."

Example 1.4.9:   Team choices _____

A class has 30 men and 10 women. A team of 4 students is chosen at random to participate in a special assignment. What is the probability that the team contains 2 men and 2 women?

Solution   Here we have indistinguishable students except for gender. There are $\binom{40}{4}$ possible teams, all equally likely. For 2 men, we have $\binom{30}{2}$ choices, and for 2 women we have $\binom{10}{2}$ choices. The required probability is

$$P[2M, 2W] = \frac{\binom{30}{2}\binom{10}{2}}{\binom{40}{4}} = 0.2142$$

_____

You do it.   What is the probability of an all-male team? Enter your answer in the cell box to at least four decimal places and click Evaluate for a response.

```
myanswer =        ;
```

```
Evaluate
```

For the answer, see endnote 23.

Sampling with replacement.   The number of combinations for sampling with replacement will not be derived. The answer is $\binom{n+k-1}{k}$. Thus the number of $k = 2$ letters that may be drawn with replacement from $n = 3$ letters (A, B, C) are $\binom{3+2-1}{2} = \frac{4!}{2!(4-2)!} = 6$, as given previously $(AA, BB, CC, AB, AC, \text{ and } BC)$.

Summary.   Probability by counting is conceptually easy but can be challenging in practice. We have very few models, but it takes experience to recognize how to apply these in specific situations. Although this skill is central to traditional probability theory, we will use it only occasionally. The next chapter explores the binomial model, which is used more often. The next section gives fuller consideration of conditional probability, particularly in a special form called Bayes' rule, and the concept of statistical independence.

Exercises on probability by counting

1. A faculty member is seen getting on the elevator on the first floor on a Sunday afternoon and presumably is going to his or her office. An alert probability student knows the number of faculty offices on each floor, as given by the following table

Floor	Offices
1	3
2	3
3	10
4	19
5	17
6	11

Let F = event that faculty member pushes 4, $\overline{T}$ = event that faculty member does not push 2, and G = the event that the faculty member does not push 2 or 3.
a. Describe the sample space.
b. Give the probability of the elementary events.
c. Find $P[F \cap (\overline{T} \cup G)]$.

For the answers, see endnote 24.

1.5 CONDITIONAL PROBABILITY, BAYES' RULE, AND INDEPENDENCE

1.5.1 Definition and Properties of Conditional Probability

Definition of conditional probability.   In Sec. 1.3 we defined the probability of event A conditioned by event B, $P[A|B]$, as

$$P[A|B] = \frac{P[A \cap B]}{P[B]}, \quad P[B] \neq 0 \tag{1.5.1}$$

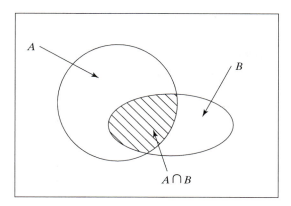

Figure 1.5.1   The determination of the probability of $A \cap B$ by using conditional probability.

Equation (1.5.1) can be put into the form

$$P[A \cap B] = P[A|B] \times P[B] = P[B|A] \times P[A] \tag{1.5.2}$$

which says that the probability that A and B occur together is the product of the probability that B occurs times the probability that A occurs, *given* that B occurs, or vice versa. Note that since the left side of Eq. (1.5.2) is unchanged if A and B are exchanged, the right side must have the same property. This definition is illustrated in Fig. 1.5.1.

   The rules of probability.   Conditional probabilities satisfy all the rules of probabilities with one exception, which we deal with later in this section. For example, a conditional probability must be between 0 and 1, $0 \leq P[A|B] \leq 1$. For other examples, the conditional probability of the union of two events is

$$P[A \cup B|C] = P[A|C] + P[B|C] - P[A \cap B|C]$$

and

$$P[\overline{A}|B] = 1 - P[A|B], \ldots, \text{ for all the rules.} \tag{1.5.3}$$

Rules for conditional probabilities must be the same rules as for ordinary probabilities because, in one sense, the conditioning event merely changes the sample space: B becomes the certain event.

Example 1.5.1:   Picking a number at random ⎯⎯⎯⎯⎯⎯⎯⎯⎯⎯⎯⎯⎯⎯⎯⎯⎯⎯⎯⎯

Let the experiment be picking a number at random from $S = \{0, 1, 2, 3, 4, 5, 6, 7, 8, 9\}$. Recall that "at random" implies equally likely outcomes. Consider the events $A =$ prime number $= \{2, 3, 5, 7\}$ and $E =$ even number $= \{0, 2, 4, 6, 8\}$. Find $P[A|E]$.

$$P[A|E] = \frac{P[A \cap E]}{P[E]} = \frac{P[\{2, 3, 5, 7\} \cap \{0, 2, 4, 6, 8\}]}{P[\{0, 2, 4, 6, 8\}]} = \frac{P[\{2\}]}{P[\{0, 2, 4, 6, 8\}]} = \frac{1/10}{5/10} = 0.2$$

$$\tag{1.5.4}$$

You do it. What if, instead, you wanted $P[E|A]$? Type your answer as **myanswer** in the cell box, and click Evaluate for a response.

```
myanswer = ;
```

```
Evaluate
```

For the answer, see endnote 25.

Example 1.5.2:   Elevator stops
Assume two passengers get on an elevator and each pushes a button for floor 2, 3, 4, 5, 6, or 7. Consider their choices independent and equally likely. Describe the sample space and find the conditional probability that the elevator stops on 2, given that it stops only on even floors. Using Eq. (1.5.1), we find

$$P[T|E] = \frac{P[T \cap E]}{P[E]} \tag{1.5.5}$$

where T = the event that the elevator stops on 2, and E = the event that the elevator stops only on even floors.

Solution   We show the outcomes in Fig. 1.5.2, with circles around the outcomes that favor event E. For example, the point 2,2 means that both passengers push 2, and so the elevator stops on 2 only. This is the sample space. There are nine ways that event E can be satisfied, all equally likely, so $P[E] = \frac{9}{36}$. Only five of the outcomes favor the joint occurrence of T (stops

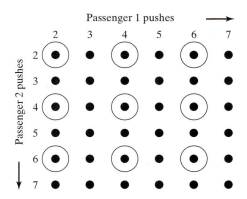

Figure 1.5.2 The sample space for the elevator problem has 36 outcomes, all equally likely. These are conveniently represented in a square array. Each dot in the array represents the buttons pushed. The outcomes in the conditioning event, E, are circled.

on 2) and E (even); hence, $P[T \cap E] = \frac{5}{36}$. Hence, the conditional probability of T given E is
$P[T|E] = \frac{P[T \cap E]}{P[E]} = \frac{5/36}{9/36} = \frac{5}{9}$

You do it.   Let the conditioning event be $L =$ the sum of the elevator floors pushed by the two passengers is less than 8. Find $P[T|L]$. Give your answer to three decimal place accuracy as **myanswer**, and click Evaluate for a response.

```
myanswer = ;
```

```
Evaluate
```

For the answer, see endnote 26.

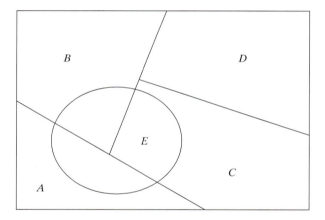

Figure 1.5.3   Events *A*, *B*, *C*, and *D* form a partition; *E* is another event.

Partitions and conditional probability.   Recall that a partition (Fig. 1.2.6) divides the sample space into disjoint events. In Fig. 1.5.3, events A through D are a partition, and E is another event. The probabilities of a set of partitioning events must add to 1:

$$P[A] + P[B] + P[C] + P[D] = 1 \qquad (1.5.6)$$

We can determine the probability of event E by adding the probabilities of the outcomes E has in common with A, B, C, and D:

$$P[E] = P[E \cap A] + P[E \cap B] + P[E \cap C] + P[E \cap D] \qquad (1.5.7)$$
$$= P[E|A] \times P[A] + P[E|B] \times P[B] + P[E|C] \times P[C] + P[E|D] \times P[D]$$

Expressing a probability through the use of a partition and conditional probabilities is sometimes called the *law of total probability*. Equation (1.5.7) is valid because if A and B are disjoint, then $E \cap A$ and $E \cap B$ are disjoint, and so on. In Eq. (1.5.7), the term involving event D is zero because E and D have no outcomes in common. We need, therefore, to include only the events that intersect event E and may ignore events disjoint from E.

Example 1.5.3:   A basketball recruiting scenario _____

A basketball coach is recruiting two basketball players, a forward and a guard. Let $F =$ {the forward accepts} and $G =$ {the guard accepts}. The forward knows that if the guard accepts, he will be more successful, and so he waits until he knows what the guard has decided. The coach makes the following estimates: $P[F|G] = 0.8$; $P[F|\overline{G}] = 0.4$; and $P[G] = 0.7$. This says that the probability that the forward will accept, given that the guard accepts, is 0.8 but is 0.4 if the guard declines. The coach estimates the probability of the guard's acceptance to be 0.7. What is the probability that the forward will accept?

Solution   The sample space in this case is $S = \{F \cap G, F \cap \overline{G}, \overline{F} \cap G, \overline{F} \cap \overline{G}\}$. Outcomes are not equally likely. We calculate the probability of event F by using the partition G and $\overline{G}$. Recall that $P[G] = 0.7$, so $P[\overline{G}] = 1 - 0.7 = 0.3$. Thus

$$P[F] = P[F|G] \times P[G] + P[F|\overline{G}] \times P[\overline{G}] = 0.8 \times 0.7 + 0.4 \times 0.3 = 0.68 \qquad (1.5.8)$$

Comments on the previous example.   Let us note that in this example, the chance experiment is weakly defined. We cannot repeat this experiment again and again to derive a frequency of occurrence. Rather, the probabilities are estimates on the part of the coach, based on his experience, knowledge of human nature, information from informants, and the like. In this case, "probability" is not a model for a numerical frequency of occurrence but rather a model for "likelihood" as estimated by an experienced observer. The rules of probability furnish a means for exploring the implications of such estimates.

Recognizing when a conditional probability is required.   Our experience is that students often have trouble interpreting situations like the basketball scenario just presented. The problem is confusion between conditional probabilities and probabilities of the intersection of two events. In our probability notation, students often confuse $P[A \cap B]$ and $P[A|B]$. The first asks when two events happen on the same performance of the experiment, for example, the forward accepts but the guard does not. The second either states or assumes that some event has happened and, given that knowledge or assumption, asks about another event. For example the question, What is the probability that the forward will accept, given that the guard chooses to go to Notre Dame? is conditional. Or the question, Assuming that the guard joins the Army, what are the chances that the forward will accept? is again conditional. Skill in modeling random systems grows with practice, both in interpreting textbook scenarios and in real life. What may be hard and confusing for you today will become easy and clear with practice.

Sequences of events.   The rule for conditional probability, Eq. (1.5.2), can be extended to more than two events. As an example, consider that a student is selected at random, and we want the probability that the student is a woman majoring in civil engineering. Consider the following events: $E = \{$engineering major$\}$, $C = \{$civil engineering major$\}$, and $W = \{$woman$\}$. The probability we seek is $P[W \cap C \cap E]$. Using conditional probability, we can expand

$$P[W \cap C \cap E] = P[W|C \cap E] \times P[C \cap E]$$
$$= P[W|C \cap E] \times P[C|E] \times P[E] \qquad (1.5.9)$$

This expansion is useful if we know that 10% of the students on campus are engineers (the third term), that 32% of the engineering students are civil engineers (the second term), and 30% of the civil engineers are women (the first term). Using these numbers we obtain the answer

$$P[\text{woman in civil engineering}] = 0.3 \times 0.32 \times 0.1 = 0.0096 \qquad (1.5.10)$$

Equation (1.5.10) demonstrates the way conditional probabilities can be used to break a complicated situation into a number of components.

1.5.2 Bayes' Rule

The context of Bayes' rule. Bayes' rule is a conditional probability that explores causal or logical connections between events, after an event has occurred. We might envision an event D that might be caused, or influenced, by several potential "causes," say, A, B, or C. For example, an airplane might go down (event D) owing to adverse weather (event A), bad equipment (event B), or because the pilot lacks competence (event C). We might diagram this situation as shown in Fig. 1.5.4.

We can describe a situation like this through conditional probabilities; for example, $P[D|A]$ would indicate the strength of the effect of A on D. Such a conditional probability is called a *transition probability*. If this transition probability is small, A will have little likelihood of causing D, or will be somewhat unlikely to cause D to occur, but if the transition probability is near 1, A will almost certainly lead to the occurrence of D.

A partition. We assume that A, B, and C are the only possible causes of D. Thus we rule out all other causes as unimportant. We exclude, for example, a terrorist attack or running out of fuel as potential causes of the plane's going down. We also rule out the joint occurrence of two

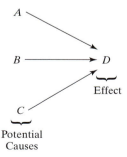

Figure 1.5.4 We assume that either A, B, or C cause D to occur. In other words, we assume that A, B, and C are a partition.

causes, such as an equipment failure during adverse weather. In the language of set theory, we assume our causes to be a partition of the space. These assumptions reveal a weakness of this approach in many applications, because one cannot be sure that all causes are under consideration or that multiple causes cannot occur.

A priori probability.   The term *a priori* means "before the experiment occurs." In this example, this would be before the plane crash. To use Bayes' rule we must know or estimate the probabilities of the various causal factors, $P[A]$, $P[B]$, and $P[C]$, independent of any news about a plane crash. Such estimates come from prior experience.

A posteriori probability.   The term *a posteriori* means "after the experiment has occurred," after the plane has crashed in this example. At this time we know the effect that has occurred, and we want to estimate the probability of the various causes; that is, we want to know $P[A|D]$, the probability that the crash occurred due to adverse weather, and likewise for $P[B|D]$ and $P[C|D]$. This is a situation in which Bayes' rule can be used.

Bayes' rule derived.   We assume that D has occurred, and we want to determine the probability that D occurred due to A. We simply apply the definition of conditional probability:

$$\underbrace{P[A|D]}_{a\ posteriori\ \text{probability}} = \frac{P[A \cap D]}{P[D]} = \frac{\overbrace{P[D|A]}^{\text{transition probability}} \times \overbrace{P[A]}^{a\ priori\ \text{probability}}}{P[D|A] \times P[A] + P[D|B] \times P[B] + P[D|C] \times P[C]}$$

$$(1.5.11)$$

Thus we see that we can calculate the *a posteriori* probability, the probability that A caused D, by knowing the transition probabilities and the *a priori* probabilities.

Example 1.5.4:   Dead squirrels _____

Zoological research reveals that Austin has three types of squirrels. Type S_B turn and go back if a car comes when a squirrel is crossing a street; type S_R run to the other side if a car comes; and type S_F "freeze" if a car comes when the squirrel is crossing a street. Let $K =$ the event that a squirrel is killed. Statistical studies have revealed the following transition probabilities:

$$P[K|S_B] = 0.05,\ P[K|S_R] = 0.08,\ P[K|S_F] = 0.17 \qquad (1.5.12)$$

Equation (1.5.12) says that about 1 in 20 is killed if it turns back, 1 in 12 if it runs to the other side, and 1 in 6 if it freezes. Population genetic studies reveal the following *a priori* probabilities:

$$P[S_B] = 0.6,\ P[S_R] = 0.3,\ P[S_F] = 0.1 \qquad (1.5.13)$$

From this information, calculate the probability that a dead squirrel is an S_F-type squirrel.

Solution   This example is a direct application of Bayes' rule with the *a priori* probabilities and transition probabilities as given. We seek the *a posteriori* probability that the squirrel is S_F-type, given that it has been killed, namely,

$$P[S_F|K] = \frac{P[S_F \cap K]}{P[K]}$$

$$= P[K|S_F] \times P[S_F]/(P[S_B] \times P[K|S_B] + P[S_F] \times P[K|S_F]$$

$$+ P[S_R] \times P[K|S_R]) \qquad (1.5.14)$$

$$= \frac{0.1 \times 0.17}{0.6 \times 0.05 + 0.3 \times 0.08 + 0.1 \times 0.17} = \frac{0.017}{0.071} = 0.239$$

The interpretation of this result is that although one in 10 squirrels is S_F-type, about one in four *dead* squirrels is S_F-type, because S_F-type squirrels are more likely to become roadkill.

You do it. More recent research results show that exactly 25% of the dead squirrels are type S_F. Apparently, the transition probability, $P[K|S_F]$, is in error. On the basis of these latest results recalculate the transition probability, assuming the same *a priori* probabilities. Calculate your answer to three places and enter it as **myanswer** in the cell box, then click Evaluate for a response.

```
myanswer =              ;
```

```
Evaluate
```

For the solution, see endnote 27.

Example 1.5.5: Basketball shooting percentages

In a basketball game, a team can score a goal (event G) in three ways: $F = \{$free throw for 1 point$\}$, $N = \{$normal two-point shot$\}$, and $T = \{$three-point shot$\}$. For a certain team, we have the following shooting percentages: $P[G|F] = 0.7$, $P[G|N] = 0.4$, and $P[G|T] = 0.2$. During a typical game, the number of shots taken is $20F$, $60N$, and $20T$.

    a. Estimate the number of points made by this team on three-point shots in a typical game.
    b. If the ball is shot, what is the probability that a goal is made?
    c. If a goal is made, what is the probability it was made on a normal shot?
    d. If a goal is missed, what is the probability it was either a free throw or a three-point shot?

Solution   First, let's note that the notation is chosen for us, but in a helpful way. G, F, N, and T remind us of goal, free throw, normal, and three-point shot. Defining supportive notation gets us off to a good start in solving a problem.

    Second, we note that there are 100 shots in this "typical" game. This represents 100 repetitions of the "chance experiment," which is to take a shot. The conditional probabilities given in the problem statement all refer to a single shot. The information about the number of shots in the typical game invites us to translate the relative frequencies of occurrence into probabilities. Thus, we assume $P[F] = \frac{20}{100}$, $P[N] = \frac{60}{100}$, and $P[T] = \frac{20}{100}$.

a. The event of interest here is $G \cap T$, that is, a goal is made and a three-point shot was attempted. The probability of this event can be calculated from the conditional probability: $P[G \cap T] = P[G|T]P[T] = 0.2 \times 0.2 = 0.04$. The number of points made would be $3 \times n_{G \cap T} \approx 3 \times 0.04 \times 100 = 12$ points. In this calculation we used a relative frequency to estimate the number of times an event happens with 100 trials.

Students frequently confuse the events $G \cap T$ and $G|T$. The probability $P[G \cap T] = 0.04$ is the probability that if a shot is made (which is the chance experiment), 4% of the time the shot is made and is a three-point shot. The probability $P[G|T] = 0.2$ is the statement that if a three-point shot is attempted, it is good 20% of the time. But this latter probability makes no accounting of the number of times that a three-point shot is attempted.

b. This calls for $P[G]$, the probability that a goal is made on a single shot. The events F, N, and T constitute a partition of the probability space. That is, every shot is one and only one of these three. We can calculate the required probability of a goal by the law of total probability (1.5.7) as follows: $P[G] = P[G|F]P[F] + P[G|N]P[N] + P[G|T]P[T]$. Substituting the numbers we calculate $P[G] = 0.7 \times 0.2 + 0.4 \times 0.6 + 0.2 \times 0.2 = 0.420$.

c. This question is Bayesian in form: given this effect (a goal was made) what is the probability that the cause was a normal shot? We could go through the formal analysis, as we did in the squirrel problem, but the answer is apparent if we look at the expansion for $P[G]$ in part b. The middle term represents the contribution of normal shots. Thus the probability that the goal was made through a normal shot is the ratio of the middle term to the sum: $P[N|G] = \frac{0.4 \times 0.6}{0.7 \times 0.2 + 0.4 \times 0.6 + 0.2 \times 0.2} = 0.5714$.

d. Another Bayesian calculation but just a bit more complicated: $P[F \cup T|\overline{G}]$. First we note that F and T are disjoint, and we note that conditional probabilities obey all the rules (except one, discussed below). Thus we can change $\cup \to +$ and calculate $P[F \cup T|\overline{G}] = P[F|\overline{G}] + P[T|\overline{G}]$. We will work through only the first of these two, since they are similar calculations. This is Bayes' rule again, so we apply the usual form: $P[F|\overline{G}] = \frac{P[\overline{G}|F]P[F]}{P[\overline{G}]}$. But this is $\frac{(1 - P[G|F])P[F]}{1 - P[G]} = \frac{(1 - 0.7)0.2}{1 - 0.42} = 0.1034$. When we add the other term, we get the answer 0.3793.

Bayes' rule discussed.   Bayes' rule requires no new techniques. Rather, it requires the recognition of a situation that investigates the analysis of causes of past events. We also introduced new vocabulary: the terms *a priori*, *a posteriori*, and *transition probabilities*.

1.5.3 Independence

Review of the definition of independence.   The concept of (statistical) independence (probability rule 9) was introduced in Sec. 1.3 as a basic rule of probability. Here we explore this concept in more depth. We say that A and B are independent when knowing that B has occurred has no influence on the probability that A has occurred, and vice versa. In probability notation, this statement translates to

$$P[A|B] = P[A]$$

$$\uparrow B \text{ makes no difference} \tag{1.5.15}$$

From the definition of conditional probability, this implies

$$P[A \cap B] = P[A|B] \times P[B] \text{ (always)}$$
$$= P[A] \times P[B] \text{ (if } A \text{ and } B \text{ are independent)} \qquad (1.5.16)$$

which in words says that the probability of the joint occurrence of A and B is the product of the absolute probabilities of A and B, if A and B are independent.

About the definition of independence. The definition of independence and the associated probability rule are based on intuition and experience. What we mean by statistical independence is: "The two events have no connection, no influence on each other, are not coupled." Both daily experience and carefully controlled experiments justify that events can be independent, that is, that their probabilities obey this definition. Thus this definition, one of the foundations of probability theory, models our intuitive sense of events that are unrelated.

Conditions for independence. Under what conditions might we assume independence? A trivial case is that illustrated in Example 1.5.6, in which independence can be proven mathematically. In advanced statistical analysis such demonstrations are nontrivial. The most common basis for assuming independence, however, is an understanding of the physical causal structure of the events in question.

Example. Consider a radar system that receives a return signal from an aircraft. The return will contain random components and will combine with the noise generated in the receiver, which also has random components. Here we assume independence between signal and noise because these random effects arise from unrelated physical causes. Thus we assume signal and noise are independent because we understand the physical causes of their randomness.

But to assert independence we must also assume that the receiver is operating in its linear region. If either component is large enough to drive the receiver into nonlinear operation, then the outputs due to the two sources will not be independent. Thus deciding independence requires consideration of and experience with the details of the random system.

The following two examples involve independence.

Example 1.5.6: Four-bit register
Consider a binary-coded decimal (BCD) register that is stopped while counting, with any number, 0–9, being equally likely. The 10 equally likely states of the register are shown in Fig. 1.5.5.

We identify the 4 bits with events B_8, B_4, B_2, and B_1 with the occurrence of the event identified with a 1 and the complement of the event associated with a 0. For example, the state 0101 corresponds to the event $\overline{B}_8 \cap B_4 \cap \overline{B}_2 \cap B_1$ and corresponds to $0101_2 = 5_{10}$. We now ask if B_4 is independent of B_1.

Solution To prove independence, we see if the probabilities satisfy Eq. (1.5.16). There are four outcomes associated with the occurrence of B_4, so the probability of this event is $\frac{4}{10}$. Similarly, there are five outcomes associated with event B_1, so this event has a probability of $\frac{5}{10}$. There are two outcomes favoring the simultaneous occurrence of these two events, 0101 and 0111, so the

B_8	B_4	B_2	B_1
0	0	0	0
0	0	0	1
0	0	1	0
0	0	1	1
0	1	0	0
0	1	0	1
0	1	1	0
0	1	1	1
1	0	0	0
1	0	0	1

Figure 1.5.5 The 10 equally likely outcomes of the experiment of stopping a binary-coded decimal (BCD) counter at a random time.

probability of $B_4 \cap B_1$ is $\frac{2}{10}$. To see if B_4 and B_1 are independent, we use Eq. (1.5.16).

$$P[B_4 \cap B_1] \stackrel{?}{=} P[B_4] \times P[B_1]$$

$$\frac{2}{10} = \frac{4}{10} \times \frac{5}{10} = \frac{2}{10} \tag{1.5.17}$$

We conclude that B_4 and B_1 are independent.

You do it. See if B_8 and B_2 are independent. Do your investigation and enter your result (yes or no) as **myanswer** in the cell box, and click Evaluate for a response.

```
myanswer = "yes or no?";
```

```
Evaluate
```

For the answer, see endnote 28.

Example 1.5.7: System reliability

A reliability problem. A system consists of three subsystems such that A must operate and either B or C must operate for the entire system to be functional. Thus, B and C operate in redundancy for increased reliability.

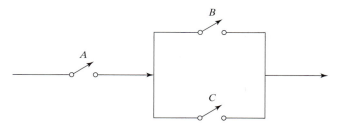

Figure 1.5.6 The switches indicate the system configuration. An open switch indicates a failed subsystem.

The reliability of the subsystems. Let event A indicate that subsystem A is operating (has not failed), with $P[A] = 0.99$, and similarly with B and C with $P[B] = 0.8$ and $P[C] = 0.8$. In words, subsystem A is 99% reliable, and subsystems B and C are 80% reliable. Assume that failures of all subsystems are independent events.

A switch model. The system configuration can be shown in a diagram of switches. An open switch indicates a failed subsystem, and a closed switch indicates an operating subsystem. Continuity between the input and output indicates operation of the system. Clearly A and either B or C must be closed for continuity, as shown in Fig. 1.5.6.

System reliability. What is the overall reliability of the system, given the reliability of the component subsystems and the conditions for system operation?

Solution Event $D = \{\text{system operating}\}$ is expressed by the equation $D = A \cap (B \cup C)$. We know the probabilities of events A, B, and C, and we know all events are independent. The probability of event D is therefore

$$P[D] = P[A \cap (B \cup C)] = P[A] \times P[B \cup C]$$
$$= P[A] \times (P[B] + P[C] - P[B \cap C]) \tag{1.5.18}$$
$$= P[A] \times (P[B] + P[C] - P[B] \times P[C]) = 0.99$$
$$\times (0.8 + 0.8 - 0.8 \times 0.8) = 0.9504$$

You do it. What if B and C are not independent but $P[B|C] = 0.82$ while $P[A]$, $P[B]$, and $P[C]$ remain 0.99 and 0.8, respectively. Calculate the reliability and enter your answer to at least three-place accuracy in **myanswer,** and click Evaluate.

```
myanswer =            ;
```

```
Evaluate
```

For the answer, see endnote 29.

What's the experiment?   One way to place the previous example within our macromodel of probability theory is to assume that many systems containing subsystems A, B, and C are placed into service. The experiment then consists of selecting one of these systems and observing if it is operating. Another model envisions one system in operation, and the experiment is to choose a time and observe if the system is operating. In Chapter 5 we discuss the relationship between these two models for reliability studies.

General independence.   We stated previously that conditional probabilities obey all the rules of probability except one. We now explore that exception. If all the rules of probability apply to conditional probability, then it should be true that

$$\underbrace{P[A \cap B|C] \stackrel{?}{=} P[A|C] \times P[B|C]}_{A \text{ and } B \text{ are independent}} \tag{1.5.19}$$

where A and B are independent, and C is any event. To see if Eq. (1.5.19) is valid, we use the definition of conditional probability:

$$P[A \cap B|C] = \frac{P[A \cap B \cap C]}{P[C]} \stackrel{?}{=} \frac{P[A \cap C]}{P[C]} \times \frac{P[B \cap C]}{P[C]} \tag{1.5.20}$$

For (1.5.19) to be generally true, it must be true that

$$P[A \cap C] = P[A] \times P[C]$$
$$P[B \cap C] = P[B] \times P[C] \tag{1.5.21}$$
$$P[A \cap B \cap C] = P[A] \times P[B] \times P[C]$$

In words, for Eq. (1.5.19) to be valid, A and B must, in addition to being independent of each other, be independent of C. Furthermore, independence among three events entails not only independence of all pairs but also of all three together, as shown in the last line of Eq. (1.5.22).

Generalization.   These results can be generalized to n independent events. To be independent, all events must be independent in all combinations: pairs, triplets, ..., up to all n at once.

Analysis methods

To *analyze* means to take apart for purposes of understanding or solution. Calculus is referred to as "analysis" because it represents large changes by many incremental changes. We have three methods of analysis available by the rules of probability: (1) analysis using conditional probability, (2) analysis using a partition, and (3) analysis using independence.

1. **Conditional probability.** Equation (1.5.2) states that the probability of a complex event $A \cap B$ can be calculated as the product of the probabilities of two simpler events, $A|B$ and

B. Equation (1.5.9) extends this type of analysis to a sequence of events. This technique is useful if the conditional probabilities are accessible.

2. **Partitions.** We showed, in Eq. (1.3.10), that $\cup \rightarrow +$ for the probability of the union of disjoint events. The law of total probability, Eq. (1.5.7), uses this result to expand a probability through a partition (first line of the equation) and then further expands these terms through conditional probability (second line of the equation). Thus a complex event is analyzed in a sum-of-products form.

3. **Independence.** The probability of a complex event $A \cap B$ can be analyzed in terms of the probabilities of A and B if A and B are independent, as shown in Eq. (1.5.22). In this case $\cap \rightarrow \times$.

In computing a probability, one looks for analysis tools. Important questions to ask are, Are conditional probabilities involved?, What is a useful partition?, and Can I use independence?

Exercises on conditional probability, Bayes' rule, and independence

1. An experiment is partitioned by three equally likely events, A, B, and C. A fourth event, D, is related to the partition by the following conditional probabilities: $P[D|A] = 0.9$, $P[D|B] = 0.1$, and $P[D|C] = 0.8$.
   a. Find $P[D]$.
   b. Find $P[B|D]$.
   c. Show that $P[A|D]$, $P[B|D]$, and $P[C|D]$ add to 1.

2. Choose a number at random between 1 and 6, inclusive. We will deal with three events: $E = $ {even number}, $L = $ {less than or equal to 5}, and $T = $ {a member of the sequence 1, 2, 4}
   a. Find the probability that the number is even and less than or equal to 5.
   b. Given that the number is a member of the sequence 1, 2, 4, what is the probability that it is also even and less than or equal to 5?
   c. Given that the number is a member of the sequence 1, 2, 4, what is the probability that it is not even and less than or equal to 5?
   d. Given that the number is not a member of the sequence 1, 2, 4, what is the probability that it is even and less than or equal to 5?
   e. Given that the number is not member of the sequence 1, 2, 4, what is the probability that it is not even and less than or equal to 5?
   f. Given that the number is even and less than or equal to 5, what is the probability that it is a member of the sequence 1, 2, 4?

3. A number is chosen at random between 1 and 12, inclusive. Let $E = $ {even} and $T = $ {exact multiple of 3}.
   a. Are E and T independent?
   b. Is T independent of $O = $ {odd}?

4. Generally, is it true that if B is independent of A, B is also independent of $\overline{A}$?

For the answers, see endnote 30.

1.6 PROBLEMS

1.6.1 Set Notation

Exercises on sets

P1.2.1   Consider a universal set consisting of the digits $S = \{0, 1, 2, 3, 4, 5, 6, 7, 8, 9\}$. Let the subset P be the first five digits in π, E be the first five digits in e (the base of Napierian logarithms), and C be the first five digits in 3^3. *Note:* Take the first five digits, without rounding, and list those that are distinct. Find the elements in the following:
a. $P \cup E$
b. $E \cap \overline{C}$
c. $(P \cap C) \cup \overline{E}$
d. $\overline{P \cup E \cup C}$
A1.2.1 (a) $\{1, 2, 3, 4, 5, 7, 8\}$; **(b)** $\{1, 8\}$; **(c)** $\{0, 3, 4, 5, 6, 9\}$; **(d)** $\{6, 9\}$

P1.2.2   Consider the universal space $S = \{0, 1, 2, 3, 4, 5, 6, 7, 8, 9, 10\}$ and the following subsets: $E = \{\text{even number}\}$, $O = \{\text{odd number}\}$, $B = \{\text{all numbers} > 5\}$, $T = \{\text{multiple of 3}\}$, $M = \{\text{all numbers} \leq 2\}$, $N = \{2, 7\}$, $R = \{3, 4, 5\}$. Give the members of the following subsets:
a. $T \cup O$
b. $(E \cup B) \cap (M \cup N)$
c. $\overline{O \cap T}$
A1.2.2 $S = \{0, 1, 2, 3, 4, 5, 6, 7, 8, 9, 10\}$, $E = \{\text{even}\} = \{0, 2, 4, 6, 8, 10\}$, $O = \{\text{odd}\}$ $= \{1, 3, 5, 7, 9\}$, $B = \{>5\} = \{6, 7, 8, 9, 10\}$, $T = \{\text{multiple of 3}\} = \{3, 6, 9\}$, $M = \{\leq 2\} = \{0, 1, 2\}$, $N = \{2, 7\}$, $R = \{3, 4, 5\}$ **(a)** $\{1, 3, 5, 6, 7, 9\}$; **(b)** $\{0, 2, 7\}$; **(c)** $\{0, 1, 2, 4, 5, 6, 7, 8, 10\}$

P1.2.3   From the sets defined in the previous problem
a. Which are complements?
b. Which are a partition?
c. Which are a subset of another set?
A1.2.3 (a) O and E are complements; **(b)** O and E are a partition, as are M, B, and R; **(c)** no subsets

P1.2.4   Consider the space of all lowercase letters with subsets $E = \{\text{letters in "electrical and computer engineering"}\}$ and $C = \{\text{letters in "computer science"}\}$.
a. Find $E \cap C$.
b. Find $E \cup C$.
c. Find $\overline{E} \cup \overline{C}$.
A1.2.4 (a) $\{c, o, m, p, u, t, e, r, i, n\} = \{c, e, i, m, n, o, p, r, t, u\}$; **(b)** $\{a, c, e, d, g, i, l, m, n, o, p, r, s, t, u\}$; **(c)** $\{a, b, d, f, g, h, j, k, l, q, s, v, w, x, y, z\}$

P1.2.5   A random experiment consists of picking at random an integer between 1 and 30, inclusive. Let $E = \{\text{even}\}$, $O = \{\text{odd}\}$, $T = \{\text{divisible by 3}\}$, $F = \{\text{divisible by 4}\}$, and $P = \{\text{prime}\} = \{2, 3, 5, 7, 11, 13, 17, 19, 23, 29\}$.

a. Which sets are subsets of other sets?
b. Find the set given by $E \cup (T \cap F)$.
c. Find the set given by $T \cap F \cap O$.
d. Find the set given by $\overline{P} \cup O$.

A1.2.5 (a) $F \subset E$; (b) $\{2, 4, 6, \ldots, 28, 30\}$; (c) $\emptyset$; (d) $\{1, 3, 4, 5, 6, \ldots, 29, 30\}$

P1.2.6   Consider sets in which the following is true: A and B are a partition, and C is a subset of A. Give answers if possible, or simplify the following:
a. $C \cup (A \cup B) =$
b. $C \cap B =$
c. $A \cup C =$
d. $\overline{B} \cap C =$
e. $\overline{C} \cap B =$

A1.2.6 (a) S, the universal set; (b) $\emptyset$, the null set; (c) A; (d) C; (e) B

Modeling problems on sets

P1.2.7   Consider the universal set

$S = \{$Atlanta (a), Chicago (c), Paris (p), Johannesburg (j)$\}$ and its subsets
$A = \{$in the Americas$\}$
$N = \{$in Northern Hemisphere$\}$
$E = \{$in Europe$\}$

Find the following:
a. $A \cup N$
b. $\overline{A} \cap \overline{E}$
c. $\overline{A \cup N \cup E} = \overline{A} \cap \overline{N} \cap \overline{E}$

Use the lowercase letters to avoid writing all the names, for example, $A = \{a, c\}$

A1.2.7 (a) $\{a, c, p\}$; (b) $\{j\}$; (c) $\{j\}$

P1.2.8   A card is drawn at random from an ordinary deck of 52 playing cards. Describe the sample space in set notation if suits are taken into account. Let K be the event {king is drawn} or simply {king} and C the event {club}. Describe the following events:
a. $K \cup C$
b. $K \cap C$
c. $K \cup \overline{C}$
d. $\overline{K} \cup \overline{C}$
e. $(K \cap C) \cup (K \cap \overline{C})$

A1.2.8 (a) all kings and all clubs; (b) king of clubs; (c) all kings and all the spades, hearts, and diamonds; (d) all cards but the king of clubs; (e) all kings

P1.2.9   Assume that soft drinks come in bottles (B) or cans, are either carbonated (C) or not, and are either diet (D) or regular. Describe in words the following:

a. $\overline{B \cap D}$

b. $\overline{C \cup D} \cap B$ (You may use deMorgan's theorem.)

c. $C \cup D$

A1.2.9 **(a)** canned diet drinks; **(b)** carbonated regular in a bottle drinks; **(c)** all carbonated and all diet drinks, including carbonated diet drinks

P1.2.10   An airline flies from New York to Los Angeles with two stops along the way. The first stop is Chicago, St. Louis, or Dallas. From any of these locations, the second stop can be Phoenix or Salt Lake City. We can set up a probability problem in which we select at random a flight of this airline from New York to Los Angeles. The outcomes would be the various routes that this flight might take.

a. Determine the outcomes and notate a sample space.

b. On the sample space, mark the following events:

　1. $A = \{\text{pass through Dallas}\}$

　2. $B = \{\text{pass through Salt Lake City}\}$

c. Using your own notation, give the outcomes and interpret in words the following:

　1. $A \cap B$

　2. $\overline{A \cup B}$

A1.2.10   The answer appears here in graphical form.

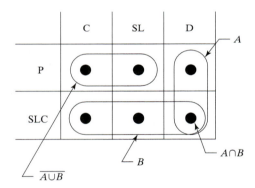

1.6.2 The Definition and Rules of Probability

Exercises on rules of probability

P1.3.1   For an experiment, $P[A \cap B] = 0.15$, $P[A \cup B] = 0.65$, and $P[A|B] = 0.5$. Find $P[B|A]$.

A1.3.1 0.3

P1.3.2   Consider an experiment in which $P[A] = 0.58$, $P[B] = 0.65$, and $P[A \cup B] = 1.0$.
a. Find $P[A|B]$.
b. Find $P[A|\overline{B}]$.

    c. Find $P[\overline{A} \cap \overline{B}]$.
    d. Find $P[\overline{A} \cup \overline{B}]$.

A1.3.2 (a) 0.354; **(b)** 1; **(c)** 0; **(d)** 0.77

P1.3.3   In a restaurant 20% of the customers order appetizers, 30% order dessert, and 40% order an appetizer or a dessert or both. Treat the percentages as relative frequencies.
    a. What fraction orders both appetizer and dessert?
    b. What fraction orders only dessert, no appetizer?
    c. What fraction orders neither appetizer nor dessert?

A1.3.3 (a) 0.1; **(b)** 0.2; **(c)** 0.6

P1.3.4   Consider an elevator in a building with five stories, 1–5, with 1 being the ground floor. Four people enter the elevator on floor 1 and push buttons for their destination floors. Let the outcomes be the possible stopping patterns for all passengers to leave the elevator on the way up. For example, 2-4-5 means the elevator stops on floors 2, 4, and 5.
    a. Find the sample space, S, with its elements (outcomes).
    b. Consider all outcomes equally likely. What is the probability of each outcome?
    c. Let $E = \{$stops only on even floors$\}$. Find $P[E]$.
    d. Let $T = \{$stops only twice$\}$. Find $P[T]$.
    e. Find $P[E \cap T]$.
    f. Find $P[E \cup T]$.

A1.3.4 (a) one stop (four outcomes) $= \{2, 3, 4, 5\}$,
              two stops (six outcomes) $= \{2\text{-}3, 2\text{-}4, 2\text{-}5, 3\text{-}4, 3\text{-}5, 4\text{-}5\}$,
              three stops (four outcomes) $= \{2\text{-}3\text{-}4, 2\text{-}3\text{-}5, 2\text{-}4\text{-}5, 3\text{-}4\text{-}5\}$,
              four stops (one outcome) $= \{2\text{-}3\text{-}4\text{-}5\}$;
              (b) $\frac{1}{15}$; **(c)** $\frac{3}{15}$; **(d)** $\frac{6}{15}$; **(e)** $\frac{1}{15}$; **(f)** $\frac{8}{15}$

P1.3.5   A random experiment has four defined events, A, B, C, and D. Events A and B are complements; C and D are not complements but are independent. Event C is a subset of event A. The known probabilities of the events are $P[A] = 0.1$, $P[C] = 0.05$, and $P[D] = 0.8$. If possible, determine the probabilities of the following events:
    a. $P[A \cup B \cup C \cup D]$
    b. $P[A \cup C]$
    c. $P[A \cap C]$
    d. $P[D \cup C]$
    e. $P[B \cap C]$

A1.3.5 (a) 1; **(b)** 0.1; **(c)** 0.05; **(d)** 0.81; **(e)** 0

P1.3.6   A probability space consists of the integers $S = \{1, 2, 3, 4, 5, 6, 7\}$. Probabilities are assigned to the outcomes such that $P[s_i] = \alpha s_i^2$, $i = 1, 2, 3, 4, 5, 6, 7$, and α is a constant. Let $E = \{2, 4, 6\}$ and $L = \{1, 2, 3, 4\}$.
    a. Find α.
    b. Find $P\left[E \cap \overline{L}\right]$.

c. Show that $P[E \cup L] = P[E] + P[L] - P[E \cap L]$ by direct calculation.

d. Find $P[\overline{E}|L]$.

A1.3.6 **(a)** $\frac{1}{140}$; **(b)** 0.2571; **(c)** $P[E] = 0.400$, $P[L] = 0.2143$, $P[E \cap L] = 0.1429$, and $P[E \cup L] = 0.4714$; **(d)** 10/30

P1.3.7   A random experiment consists in choosing an integer between 1 and 4, inclusive. The probability of choosing a number is inversely proportional to the number. For example, the probability of choosing 4 is half the probability of choosing 2.

a. Using the rules of probability, determine the probabilities of the elementary events.

b. Find the probability that the chosen number is odd.

c. Find the probability that the chosen number is even, given that it is less than 4.

A1.3.7 **(a)** 0.48, 0.24, 0.16, 0.12; **(b)** 0.64; **(c)** 0.273

P1.3.8   A random experiment consists in choosing an integer between 1 and 4, inclusive. The probability of choosing a number is inversely proportional to the square root of the number. For example, the probability of choosing 4 is half the probability of choosing 1.

a. Using the rules of probability, determine the probabilities of the elementary events.

b. Find the probability that the chosen number is odd.

c. Find the probability that the chosen number is even, given that it is less than 4.

A1.3.8 **(a)** $P[S_1] = 0.359$, $P[S_2] = 0.254$, $P[S_3] = 0.207$, $P[S_4] = 0.18$; **(b)** 0.566; **(c)** 0.310

P1.3.9   Consider a chance experiment with events A and B defined, with $P[A] = 0.4$ and $P[B] = 0.3$.

a. Give the minimum and maximum values possible for $P[A \cup B]$.

b. Give the minimum and maximum values possible for $P[A \cap B]$.

c. Assume that $P[A \cup B]$ is the arithmetic average between its max and min values. Find $P[A|B]$.

d. Instead, let $A \cap B = \emptyset$, and let C be another event, such that A, B, and C are a partition. Find $P[C]$ and $P[(A \cup B)|C]$.

A1.3.9 **(a)** min $= 0.4$, max $= 0.7$; **(b)** min $= 0$, max $= 0.3$; **(c)** 0.5; **(d)** 0.3, 0

P1.3.10   A random experiment consists in choosing an integer between 1 and 4, inclusive. The probability of choosing a number is proportional to the square root of the number. For example, the probability of choosing 4 is twice the probability of choosing 1.

a. Using the rules of probability, determine the probabilities of the elementary events.

b. Find the probability that the chosen number is odd.

c. Find the probability that the chosen number is even, given that it is less than 4.

A1.3.10 **(a)** $P[S_1] = 0.163$, $P[S_2] = 0.23$, $P[S_3] = 0.282$, $P[S_4] = 0.325$; **(b)** 0.445; **(c)** 0.341

P1.3.11   Consider an experiment in which the outcomes are the integers $S = \{1, 2, 3, 4, 5\}$. Assume that the probability of selecting an outcome is proportional to the square of the magnitude of the integer. For example, $P[3] = 9P[1]$.

    a. Find the probability of the elementary events.

    b. Find the probability that an even integer is selected.

    c. If an even integer is selected, what is the probability that the integer is 2?

    d. Are the events {even} and {less than 4} independent? Demonstrate.

    e. If the experiment is performed 100 times, approximately how many times will {5} occur?

A1.3.11 (a) $i^2/55$, where $i = $ the number; (b) 0.3636;
(c) 0.2; (d) $0.07273 \neq 0.09256$, not independent; (e) about 45 times

P1.3.12 Consider a probability space with four events defined, A, B, C, and D. We know that A and B form a partition and also that C and D form a partition. Furthermore, we know that $P[A \cap C] = 0.42$ and $P[D \cap B] = 0.12$.

    a. Use combinations of A, B, C, and D to form a partition of the entire space.

    b. Find $P[A \cup C]$.

    c. Assuming $P[D] = 0.3$, find $P[A]$.

    d. Find the probabilities of the partitioning events in part a, assuming $P[D] = 0.3$.

A1.3.12 (a) $A \cap C$, $A \cap D$, $C \cap B$, and $B \cap D$, and there are many other combinations as well; (b) 0.88; (c) 0.6; (d) 0.42, 0.18, 0.28, 0.12

P1.3.13 The outcomes of an experiment are integers between 10 and 20, inclusive; thus $S = \{10, 11, 12, 13, 14, 15, 16, 17, 18, 19, 20\}$. The probability of any outcome is inversely proportional to the number, such that 10 is the most likely outcome, twice as likely as 20. We define some events: $E = \{$even number$\}$, $P = \{$prime number$\} = \{11, 13, 17, 19\}$, and $T = \{$exactly divisible by 3$\}$.

    a. Find $P[T \cup P]$.

    b. Find $P\left[\overline{T \cup \overline{E}}\right]$.

    c. Find $P\left[(E \cap T)|\overline{P}\right]$.

A1.3.13 (a) 0.631; (b) 0.819; (c) 0.284

P1.3.14 Consider a random experiment with 500 outcomes, $S = \{s_1, s_2, \ldots, s_{500}\}$. The probabilities are assigned to the elementary events according to the rule $P[s_{i+1}] = 0.99 \times P[s_i]$.

    a. Find $P[S_1]$.

    b. Let G4 $= \{s_5, s_6, \ldots, s_{500}\}$, that is the event {greater than 4}. Find $P[G4]$.

    c. Let $O = \{i$ is odd$\}$. Find $P\left[O \cap \overline{G4}\right]$.

    d. Find $P[O \cup G4]$.

Hint: This problem involves summing of geometric series.

A1.3.14 (a) 0.01007; (b) 0.96034; (c) 0.019932; (d) 0.98027

P1.3.15 Consider a sample space, $S = \{s_1, s_2, \ldots, s_i, \ldots\}$, where i is all the positive integers from 1 to infinity. Let probabilities be assigned to this space according to the rule $P[S_i] = \dfrac{a}{2^i}$, where a is a constant, and $S_i = \{s_i\}$, the elementary events.

    a. Find a to properly normalize the probability space.

    b. Let $L4$ be the event $\{s_1, s_2, s_3\}$; that is, i less than 4. Find $P[L4]$.

c. Let O = the event associated with $i = 1, 3, 5, \ldots,$ that is, an odd number. Find $P[O]$.

Hint: This problem involves summing of the geometric series.

A1.3.15 **(a)** 1; **(b)** 7/8; **(c)** 2/3

P1.3.16   Consider a sample space $S = \{s_1, s_2, \ldots, s_i, \ldots\}$, where i is all the positive integers from 1 to infinity. Let probabilities be assigned to this space according to the rule $P[S_i] = \frac{a}{i^\pi}$, where a is a constant, and $S_i = \{s_i\}$, the elementary events.
a. Find a to properly normalize the probability space. Four-place accuracy is sufficient in this problem.
b. Let $L4$ be the event $\{s_1, s_2, s_3\}$; that is, i is less than 4. Find $P[L4]$.
c. Let O = the event associated with $i = 1, 3, 5, \ldots,$ that is, an odd number. Find $P[O]$.

A1.3.16 **(a)** 0.8502; **(b)** 0.9735; **(c)** 0.8867

Modeling problems on the rules of probability

P1.3.17   A communication system uses three frequencies because weather can cause loss of signal. There is a 10% chance of losing exactly one channel, a 1% chance of losing exactly two, and a 0.5% chance of losing all three. In normal mode at least two channels must be operating, and in emergency mode at least one is necessary. Let OK = the event that the system is operating.
a. Find $P[$OK in normal mode$]$.
b. Find $P[$OK in emergency mode$]$.

A1.3.17 **(a)** 0.985; **(b)** 0.995

P1.3.18   Identify a chance experiment and take some numerical frequency data. The experiment should not be something you do, like flipping a coin, but something you observe, like people getting on an elevator, the number of cars stopped at a light, and so forth.
a. Describe the space, that is, the possible outcomes.
b. Identify two events, A and B.
c. Take numerical data on a sizable number of repetitions of the experiment for A and B, $\overline{A}$, $A \cap B$, $A \cup B$, $A|B$.
d. Calculate the relative frequency of these events. In the last case, you want the conditional relative frequency.

A1.3.18   no common answer

P1.3.19   A tourist is given instructions to get to a museum. The instructions are poor, so at any intersection of the road there is a 0.7 chance of taking the correct road. The instructions involve five such intersections. Find the probability that the tourist gets lost, assuming that the path is unique. Assume his choices are independent.

A1.3.19   0.8319

P1.3.20 Consider turning on the light in a room. The probability that the power is off in the building due to the power company is 10^{-4}. The probability that the lightbulb is burned out is 10^{-3}. The probability that there is a problem with the switch or wiring in the building is 10^{-5}. Consider that these problems are independent. What is the probability that the light will not light up? Five-place accuracy is required. Consider these independent events.

A1.3.20 1.1099×10^{-3}

P1.3.21 A man carries a key to his house, of course, but also has a spare key hidden under a bush in the yard. There is a probability of 0.05 that he will leave his key at work. There is a probability of 0.6 that his wife will not be home to let him in when he gets home from work. There is a 0.4 probability that one of his teenagers will borrow the key under the bush, since they are always losing their own keys. Find the probability that the man will get locked out of his house and have to sit on the front steps until one of his family returns. State assumptions.

A1.3.21 0.012, assuming independent events

P1.3.22 When you are approached by a waitperson in a restaurant, there are three events that can be determined: whether his or her age is greater than 30; whether the person's birthday month has an even number of letters in it; and whether the person is carrying a driver's license at the time. Let p_A, p_B, and p_C represent the probabilities of these three events. Find the following:
a. $P[A$ or B but not both occur].
b. $P[$none of the three occurs].
c. $P[$all three occur].
d. $P[$exactly two of the three occur].

A1.3.22 **(a)** $p_A + p_B - 2p_A p_B$;
(b) $1 - (p_A + p_B + p_C) + (p_A p_B + p_A p_C + p_B p_C) - p_A p_B p_C$;
(c) $p_A p_B p_C$; **(d)** $p_A p_B + p_A p_C + p_B p_C - 3 p_A p_B p_C$

P1.3.23 A digital chip contains 100 transistors and 400 connections. The probability of a faulty transistor is 10^{-3}, and the probability of a faulty connection is 10^{-4}. What is the probability that a given chip taken at random is defective, assuming all defects are independent?

A1.3.23 0.1307

P1.3.24 When it snows in Austin, there are three things that can happen at the University of Texas: (1) the university remains open and classes continue; (2) the university closes and classes are canceled for the day; and (3) the university opens at noon, and afternoon classes are held. Under the three conditions and for an afternoon class, the average engineering student will attend an afternoon class with probabilities of 0.9, 0.1 (didn't hear about it), and 0.7, respectively. On a snowy day and at an afternoon class, we know two probabilities: (1) there is a 60% chance that a student is in class; and (2) if the student is in class, there is a 50% probability that classes began at noon. For the sake of communication, let us agree on the following notation: C = classes canceled, O = university open, H = half day, and S = student in class.

a. Find the probability that if a student is not in class, classes began at noon.

b. Find the probability that the university closes.

A1.3.24 **(a)** 0.3214; **(b)** 0.2679

1.6.3 Probability by Counting

Exercises on probability by counting

P1.4.1   Consider an experiment with 12 outcomes, all equally likely, as shown in the figure. Two events, A and B, are defined on the experiment and indicated in the figure.

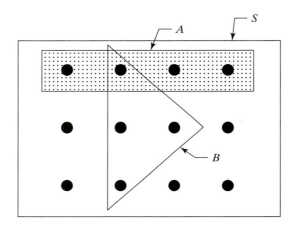

Give the following probabilities:

a. $P[A]$

b. $P[\overline{B}]$

c. $P[A \cap B]$

d. $P[\overline{A} \cap B]$

A1.4.1 **(a)** 4/12; **(b)** 8/12; **(c)** 1/12; **(d)** 9/12

P1.4.2   Use the counting method of permutations to "count" the number of ways that five people can get off an elevator in a five-story building, getting on the elevator on floor 1. How many ways can they get off on even floors? Find $P[\text{even only}]$ using the equally likely model.

A1.4.2 4^5 ways; 2^5 ways; $P[\text{even}] = \frac{1}{32}$

P1.4.3   Find the largest n for which your calculator will calculate $n!$ and give the value of $n!$.

A1.4.3 For my calculator $253! = 5.17 \times 10^{499}$, but $254!$ is off scale.

P1.4.4   For $k = 50$, find the largest value of n for which your calculator will calculate $\binom{n}{k}$ and give the value you get.

     A1.4.4 For my calculator $\binom{2 \times 10^{11}}{50} = 3.29 \times 10^{495}$ is about the largest I can get.

P1.4.5   A computer security system requires an eight-character password, which may contain alphabetical characters or numerals, except for the first character, which must be a letter. The system distinguishes between upper- and lowercase letters.
a. How many possible passwords can be created?
b. How many can be created if the password can be five to eight characters, starting with a letter?

     A1.4.5 (a) 1.831×10^{14}; **(b)** 1.861×10^{14}

P1.4.6   If seven students in a class were picked at random and they wrote down the day of the week for their birthday (assume all days equally likely), what is the probability that all seven days of the week would be covered?

     A1.4.6 0.00612

P1.4.7   Pick a person at random from the local telephone directory white pages. Let

$$A = \{\text{name is Acton}\}$$
$$Q = \{\text{name starts with } Q\}$$
$$T = \{\text{more than two letters in name}\}$$
$$U = \{\text{second letter in name is } u\}$$

Estimate the following:
a. $P[A]$
b. $P[A \cup Q]$
c. $P[A \cap Q]$
d. $P[U|Q]$
e. $P[\overline{U}|Q]$

     A1.4.7 The answers depend on the city. For Austin, Texas, there are about 109 names per column, four columns/page, and 721.5 white pages. The result is approximately $109 \times 4 \times 721.5 = 314,574$ entries, all equally likely. There are seven Actons and about 665 names beginning with Q, of which 13 have something other than u for the second letter, mostly Chinese names like Qi. From this information, we estimate **(a)** $\frac{7}{314,574}$; **(b)** $\frac{672}{314,574}$; **(c)** 0; **(d)** $\frac{652}{665}$; **(e)** $\frac{13}{665}$

P1.4.8   A Mexican restaurant has one item on the menu, enchiladas, but two equally likely sauces, red and green. A party of four comes in and orders.
a. Find the probability that two people order red and two green.
b. If the first person orders green, what is the conditional probability that the final total is $2G$ and $2R$?

     A1.4.8 (a) 0.375 **(b)** 0.375

P1.4.9   If a state in the United States is chosen at random, what is the probability that there will be fewer than seven letters in the name of the state?

      A1.4.9 11/50

P1.4.10 If a person is chosen at random in the current phone book of your city, what is the probability that the first digit of his or her phone number is a 2? (Only an estimate is possible.)

      A1.4.10 about 0.21

P1.4.11 If everyone has one family name and one or two given names, how many different sets of initials exist?

      A1.4.11 18,252

P1.4.12 Use the equally likely model in the following three parts of this problem.
    a. In the college mainframe computer there are 10^6 student IDs (nine-digit numbers) of potential students, former students, and current students. If I type a nine-digit random number into the system, what is the probability that it corresponds to a valid number in the system?
    b. Three students get on the elevator in the engineering building and punch buttons for floors 2, 3, 4, 5, or 6 independently. What is the probability that the elevator does not stop on 4?
    c. A number is chosen at random between 0 and 100, inclusive. (1) Find the probability that the number is less than 50. (2) Find the probability that the number is even. (3) Given that the number is even, what is the probability that the number is less than 50? (4) Given that the number is less than 50, what is the probability that the number is even? Consider zero an even number.

      A1.4.12 **(a)** 0.001; **(b)** 0.512; **(c)** $\frac{50}{101}, \frac{51}{101}, \frac{25}{51}, \frac{25}{50}$

P1.4.13 a. A cube whose faces are painted is cut into 27 cubes of equal size. Find the probability that a cube selected at random from the resulting cubes has at least one painted side.
    b. If the cube is cut into n^3 identical cubes, what then is the probability that a randomly selected cube has at least one painted side?

      A1.4.13 **(a)** $\frac{26}{27}$; **(b)** $\frac{6n^2-12n+8}{n^3}$

P1.4.14 Ten books are arranged at random on a shelf. Three of the books are by Shakespeare. Find the probability that the three books by Shakespeare are next to one another.

      A1.4.14 0.0667

P1.4.15 Four red and six green balls are distributed at random into 10 bins, one ball to each bin.
    a. What is the number of ways the balls can be arranged in the bins? Treat the balls as distinguishable.
    b. What is the number of ways the balls can be arranged in the bins if the balls are indistinguishable?
    c. What is the probability that the four red balls are next to one another?

A1.4.15 **(a)** 3,628,800; **(b)** 210; **(c)** 0.0333

P1.4.16   Assume 365 days in a year and ignore leap day. Assume birthdays are equally distributed during the year. What is the probability that 35 people, chosen at random, all have different birthdays; that is, no 2 have the same birthday?

A1.4.16 0.1856

P1.4.17   Consider a chance experiment in which the numbers 1, 2, 3, 4, and 5 are written on pieces of paper, and three pieces are drawn without replacement.
a. How many ways can the pieces be drawn if order is not considered?
b. If the numbers are made to form a three-digit number between 123 and 543, inclusive (not all numbers are possible, of course), what is the probability that the number so formed will be greater than 420 and divisible by 2? The number is formed by placing the drawn numbers together in the order drawn, which is random.

A1.4.17 **(a)** 10; **(b)** $\frac{8}{60}$

P1.4.18   Consider that there are 10 balls numbered 0 through 9.
a. If there are 10 bins with each one holding one ball, how many ways can the balls be put into the bins with order mattering?
b. If there are 20 bins with each one holding one ball, how many ways can the balls be put into the bins with order not mattering?

A1.4.18 **(a)** 3,628,800; **(b)** 184,756

Modeling problems on probability by counting

P1.4.19   A combination lock dial is numbered 0 to 39. If the dial is spun several times at random, what is the probability that it will end up within ±1 of 26?

A1.4.19 3/40

P1.4.20   A professor puts his pocket change in a jar each night and so starts each day with only folding money. One day he makes one purchase of an item costing between $0.01 and $20.00, with all values equally likely, and pays with a $20 bill. Assume change is made with a minimum number of coins and no 50¢ pieces are used. Consider the change in his pocket at the end of that day.
a. Describe the sample space.
b. Find the probability that he has less than four pennies.
c. Find the probability that he has exactly two quarters, in addition to (possibly) other coins.
d. Find the probability that he has two or fewer coins.

A1.4.20 **(a)** There are 100 outcomes; **(b)** $\frac{80}{100}$; **(c)** $\frac{25}{100}$; **(d)** $\frac{14}{100}$

P1.4.21   Two students get on the elevator in a six-story building on floor 1, and each pushes a button for floors between 2 and 6, inclusive. Consider their choices random and independent. Let L = event that the sum of the floors picked is less than 8, and O = the event that only odd-numbered floors are picked.

a. Describe the sample space.
b. Find $P[L]$.
c. Find $P[O|\bar{L}]$.

A1.4.21 **(a)** 25 outcomes, can be pictured in a square 5×5 array; **(b)** $\frac{10}{25}$; **(c)** $\frac{1}{5}$

P1.4.22 The Coolsville Police Department has 30 police cars, 10 police motorcycles, and 5 police horses. Further, they have 200 policemen and 50 policewomen. You are at a party in Coolsville and a neighbor calls the police (which means the party is a success, right?). Assume a police officer and a means of transportation are selected independently and at random.
a. How many equally likely outcomes are there for the experiment?
b. What is the probability that a policeman arrives on a motorcycle?

A1.4.22 **(a)** 11,250; **(b)** 0.178

P1.4.23 An old-fashioned string of Christmas tree lights has thirty-two 4-V bulbs in series. If a bulb burns out, all the lights go out and one has to search for the bad light. (This is not a good design and is not used anymore, but it was done this way for years.) Assume that all lights are equally likely to be bad, but that only one is actually bad. Consider two search strategies: (a) start at one end and test the lights one at a time with an ohmmeter; or (b) perform a binary search by measuring half the string with an ohmmeter to narrow down the search for the bad bulb, then test half the half, and so on. Find the probability that strategy A will require fewer measurements than strategy B.

A1.4.23 4/32

P1.4.24 A circuit consists of two 50-Ω resistors in parallel in series with two 100-Ω resistors in parallel. If all resistors are functional, the resistance is 75 Ω. Consider that there is a probability of 0.2 that any resistor will be an open circuit, all independent. Find the probability that the total resistance will be greater than 110 Ω.

A1.4.24 0.3856

P1.4.25 In a classroom there are eight seats in the front row. Three students choose to sit in the front row, choosing seats independently and at random.
a. What is the probability that they sit with no empty seats between them?
b. What is the probability that two will sit next to each other but the third will be separated by at least one seat from the pair?
c. What is the probability that no two sit next to each other?

A1.4.25 **(a)** 0.107; **(b)** 0.536; **(c)** 0.357

P1.4.26 A calculator has a bad "5" key that fails to operate one time out of 10. A series of k numbers in the range from 1 to 99 inclusive are added. Consider all numbers in this range equally likely. What is the maximum number of numbers (find k) that can be added before there is a probability of 0.5 or greater of an incorrect answer due to the bad key?

A1.4.26 34

P1.4.27 In a class there are 4 women and 31 men. If four students are picked at random to stand up front, what is the probability that three or more of the students up front will be women?

A1.4.27 2.39×10^{-3}

P1.4.28 Three strangers meet. What is the probability that two or more have birthdays in the same month?

A1.4.28 0.236

P1.4.29 There are 50 people in a class. What is the probability that all have separate birthdays? Ignore leap days.

A1.4.29 0.029626

P1.4.30 Your first assignment as a beginning engineer for MafiaTech, Inc., is to design a system to open combination locks. Your device turns the dial clockwise three times and stops at random. It then turns one turn counterclockwise and then stops at random. Finally, it picks a number at random in the clockwise direction. The dial has 40 numerals, and the dial has to fall within ± 1 of the correct location to work.
a. What is the probability that your system will open the lock on the first try?
b. What is the minimum number of tries before the system has a probability of 0.9 or more of opening the lock?

A1.4.30 (a) $\left(\frac{3}{40}\right)^3$; (b) 5457

P1.4.31 a. In a town laid out on a perfect square grid of streets, Joe's best friend lives two blocks north and two blocks east of Joe's house. What is the minimum distance between the two houses along the streets, and how many routes have that distance?
b. What if Joe's friend lives m blocks north and n blocks east? What is the minimum distance, and how many routes have that distance?

A1.4.31 (a) 4, 6; (b) $m + n$, $\dbinom{m+n}{n}$

P1.4.32 An 8-bit register is used in a digital system. Assume that all possible states of the register are equally likely. The experiment is to pick a state at random (or to observe the state of the register at a random time.)
a. How many outcomes are there?
b. What is the probability that exactly 3 bits in the register are 1?
c. What is the probability that 3 or fewer bits in the register are 1?
d. Rework the problem for a 32-bit register.

A1.4.32 (a) 256; (b) 0.2188; (c) 0.3633; (d) 2^{32}, 1.15×10^{-6}, 1.28×10^{-6}

1.6.4 Conditional Probability, Bayes' Rule, and Independence

Exercises on conditional probabilities, Bayes' rule, and independence

P1.5.1   Numbers are selected at random from a table of random digits, 0 to 9. What is the minimum number of numbers to be selected before the probability of having no even numbers is smaller than 10^{-3}?

A1.5.1 10

P1.5.2   An electric circuit consists of a 100-Ω resistor in series with two 50-Ω resistors in parallel. If there is a 0.1 probability that each resistor is an open circuit and a 0.9 probability that each has its correct value, find the probability that the resistance of the combination is less than 200 Ω. Assume that all resistors fail independently.

A1.5.2 0.891

P1.5.3   a. Under what condition can it be true than $P[A|B] = P[A|\overline{B}]$?
b. Under what condition can it be true that $P[A|B] = P[\overline{A}|B]$?

A1.5.3 **(a)** A and B must be independent; **(b)** $P[A|B] = 0.5$

P1.5.4   A chance experiment has two defined events, with probabilities $P[A] = 0.4$ and $P[B] = 0.6$. For each of the following give the answer requested. It is useful to draw a Venn diagram portraying the situation.
a. Find the maximum value of $P[A \cup B]$.
b. Find the minimum value of $P[A \cup B]$.
c. Find the maximum value of $P[A \cap B]$.
d. Find the minimum value of $P[A \cap B]$.
e. Can A and B be independent? Explain.
f. Can A and B be a partition? Explain.

A1.5.4 **(a)** 1; **(b)** 0.6; **(c)** 0.4; **(d)** 0; **(e)** yes, since it is possible that $P[A \cap B]$ can be 0.24; **(f)** yes, since in parts a and d we have $P[A \cup B] = 1$ and $P[A \cap B] = 0$

P1.5.5   Consider a random experiment with five outcomes, $S = \{s_1, s_2, s_3, s_4, s_5\}$, with corresponding elementary events, S_i. The probabilities of the elementary events follow the pattern $P[S_i] = a^i$, where a is a constant.
a. Find a.
b. Find $P[S_1 \cup S_2 \cup S_3 | S_1 \cup S_2]$.
c. Find $P[S_1 \cup S_2 | S_1 \cup S_2 \cup S_3]$.

A1.5.5 **(a)** 0.5087; **(b)** 1; **(c)** 0.8536

P1.5.6   A fair coin is flipped three times. If two or three heads occur consecutively, a number between 1 and 5 inclusive is chosen at random. If two or three heads do not occur consecutively, a number between 2 and 5 inclusive is chosen at random. Find the probability that an even number results from this procedure.

A1.5.6 0.4625

P1.5.7 For a random experiment with events A, B, and C defined, we know the following:

$$P[A \cup C] = 0.82$$
$$P[B \cup C] = 0.38$$
$$P[A \cup B] = 1.0$$

a. Find the probability of C if A and B are disjoint.
b. What is the largest that $P[A \cap B]$ can be if A, B, and C are independent?

A1.5.7 **(a)** 0.2; **(b)** This leads to a contradiction, so A, B, and C cannot be independent.

P1.5.8 A person has three quarters and seven dimes in his pocket. Two coins are pulled out at random.
a. What is the probability that both are quarters?
b. What is the probability that the first one is a quarter if it is revealed that the second one was a quarter?

A1.5.8 **(a)** $\frac{1}{15}$; **(b)** $\frac{2}{9}$

P1.5.9 A decade counter counts at a high speed and is stopped at random times. For the lowest two digits on the counter, let $A_1 =$ the event that the unit's digit $= 1$, and $A_2 =$ the event that the ten's digit $= 1$.
a. Describe the experiment and its outcomes.
b. Find $P[A_1]$.
c. Find $P[A_2]$.
d. Find $P[A_1 \cap A_2]$.
e. Find $P[A_1 \cup A_2]$.
f. Are A_1 and A_2 independent? Explain how you know.

A1.5.9 **(a)** $\{00, 01, 02, \ldots, 98, 99\}$, 100 outcomes; **(b)** 10/100; **(c)** 10/100; **(d)** 1/100; **(e)** 19/100; **(f)** Yes, $P[A_1 \cap A_2] = \frac{1}{100} = P[A_1]P[A_2]$

P1.5.10 The switches in the following network all have a probability of 0.4 of being open and 0.6 of being closed.

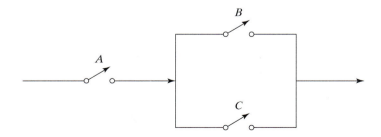

a. Let $A =$ the event that A is closed, $B =$ the event that B is closed, and $C =$ the event that C is closed. What is the sample space of this experiment?

b. Let G = the event that there is continuity between input and output. Express G in terms of A, B, and C.

c. Find $P[G]$. All switch positions are independent.

A1.5.10 (a) $\{A \cap B \cap C, A \cap B \cap \overline{C}, A \cap \overline{B} \cap \overline{C}, \ldots, \overline{A} \cap \overline{B} \cap \overline{C}\}$, eight outcomes; **(b)** $A \cap (B \cup C)$; **(c)** 0.504

P1.5.11   Events A, B, and C partition an experiment. Event D is independent of A and B. The probabilities are $P[A] = 0.2$, $P[B] = 0.5$, $P[C] = 0.3$, and $P[D] = 0.45$.

a. Is D independent of C? Give a proof based on the rules of probability, or else give a clear, plausible argument.

b. Find $P[B \cap D]$.

c. Find $P[A|C]$.

d. Find $P[A \cap \overline{D}]$.

e. Find $P[(A \cup (B \cap D))|D]$.

A1.5.11 (a) Yes, expand $P[D]$ using the partition, use independence on the terms involving A and B, and solve for $P[C \cap D]$; **(b)** 0.225; **(c)** 0; **(d)** 0.11; **(e)** 0.7

P1.5.12   You are at Kerbey Lane Cafe, and you would like to have pancakes and a cup of coffee. The waitress would like to know if you like your coffee light (L) or dark (D) and if you like it sweetened (S) or unsweetened (U). The probability of dark coffee is 0.4 and the probability of sweetened coffee is 0.5. The probability of dark and sweetened coffee ($D \cap S$) is 0.1. Determine the following:

a. $P[L \cap S]$

b. $P[D|U]$

c. $P[U|D]$

d. $P[\overline{S} \cap U]$

e. $P[(U \cap D) \cup S]$

A1.5.12 (a) 0.4; **(b)** 0.6; **(c)** 0.75; **(d)** 0.5; **(e)** 0.8

P1.5.13   Consider a 4-bit register that stores a BCD number, with all numbers from 0 to 9 equally likely. The BCD code is shown in the following table. The power supply current is $i = 0.1 + 0.05k$ μA, where k is the number of 1's in the register.

No.	B_8	B_4	B_2	B_1
0	0	0	0	0
1	0	0	0	1
2	0	0	1	0
3	0	0	1	1
4	0	1	0	0
5	0	1	0	1
6	0	1	1	0
7	0	1	1	1
8	1	0	0	0
9	1	0	0	1

a. Which pairs of bits, if any, are independent?

b. Find $P[B_4 = 1 | B_1 = 1]$.

c. Find the probability that the power supply current is in the range $0.20 \leq i \leq 0.30 \ \mu A$.

A1.5.13 **(a)** B_1 is independent of B_2, B_4, and B_8. No other pairs are independent; **(b)** $\frac{2}{5}$; **(c)** 0.5

P1.5.14   A system consists of four components: A, B, C, and D. The operation of the system can be represented by four switches, with A and B in series, and D and C in parallel with the series combination of A and B, as shown in the diagram. Continuity between input and output means the system is in operation.

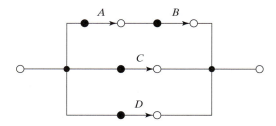

Assume that C and D are 95% reliable, but A and B are 99% reliable, with all failures independent. Represent the event $O = \{$entire system operating$\}$ in terms of the events $A = \{A$ operating$\}$, and so on. Find the overall reliability of the system.

A1.5.14 $O = (A \cap B) \cup C \cup D$, 0.99995

P1.5.15   A decade counter counts at a high speed and is stopped a random time. Considering the BCD form of the 1's digit, let $A_1 =$ the event that the 1's bit $= 1$, and $A_2 =$ the event that the 2's bit $= 1$, etc.

a. Repeat parts a through f in Problem 1.5.9.

b. What about A_8? Is it independent of the A_1 bit? The 2's bit? Explain how you know.

A1.5.15 **(a)** {00, 01, 10, 11}, with probabilities {0.3, 0.3, 0.2, 0.2}; **(b)** 5/10; **(c)** 4/10; **(d)** 2/10; **(e)** 7/10; **(f)** 2/10; **(g)** A_8 is independent of A_1 but not A_2

Modeling problems on conditional probabilities, Bayes' rule, and independence

P1.5.16   A basketball team wins 60% of its home games, but only 45% of its away games. Assume that 55% of the games are played at home, such that for a game picked at random $P[H] = 0.55$.

a. For any game picked at random, what is the probability that the team will win the game?

b. If the team wins a game, what is the probability that it was played at home?

A1.5.16 **(a)** 0.5325; **(b)** 0.620

P1.5.17   A man rushes to the airport to catch a plane. As he gets into his car, he estimates that if traffic is bad, his chances of catching the plane are 0.1. If traffic is not bad, his chances are 0.6. Traffic is bad about one-third of the time.
a. Find the probability that he misses the plane.
b. If the man does miss his plane, what is the probability that the traffic is to blame?

A1.5.17 **(a)** 0.5667; **(b)** 0.5876

P1.5.18   I use my spelling checker to catch typos and misspelled words. If a word is correct, there is a 0.001 probability that the speller will not pass it owing to its limited database, in which case I look the word up in the dictionary and override the checker. If a word is incorrect (not the word I intended), there is a 0.01 probability that the speller will pass it because the result is an English word in its database. I am a poor typist and an even poorer speller: about 5% of the words I type are wrong. Find the probability that a given word in my writing is something other than what I intended.

A1.5.18 5×10^{-4}

P1.5.19   An engineer drives to work by a route that has two traffic lights. The first is green twice as long as it is red from the point of view of the engineer. He has noted that if he makes the first light, he has to stop at the second light about 60% of the time, but if he has to stop at the first light, he makes the second light about 80% of the time. He goes to work along that road five times a week, 50 weeks a year, but returns by another way.
a. Describe the sample space.
b. Estimate the times per year that he will have to stop for the first light.
c. Estimate the times per year that he will have to stop for the second light.

A1.5.19 **(a)** $\left\{ G_1 \cap G_2, \overline{G_1} \cap G_2, G_1 \cap \overline{G_2}, \overline{G_1} \cap \overline{G_2} \right\}$; **(b)** 83; **(c)** 117

P1.5.20   Three marksmen, Able, Billy, and Cary, can hit a target at 500 yards with probabilities of 0.9, 0.8, and 0.7, respectively. One of the marksmen is selected at random and shoots at the target.
a. What is the probability that the target is hit?
b. If the target is hit, what is the probability that either Billy or Cary was the selected marksman?

A1.5.20 **(a)** 0.800; **(b)** 0.625

P1.5.21   Company A makes widgets with a defect rate of 1 in 1000, Company B's widgets have a defect rate of 1 in 1200, and Company C has a defect rate of 1 in 1500. A company buys two-thirds of its widgets from A, one-fourth from B, and the remainder from C.
a. If you select at random a widget from the stockroom, what is the probability that it is defective?
b. If you select a widget at random from the stockroom and it turns out to be bad, what is the probability that it was not made by Company A?

A1.5.21 **(a)** 0.000931; **(b)** 0.284

P1.5.22   Consider a smoke detector. Let $A =$ the event that the detector gives an alarm, $F =$ the event that there is a fire, $B =$ the event of a weak battery, and $M =$ the event of alarm malfunction. We assume $P[A|F] = 0.95$, $P[A|B] = 0.9$, and $P[A|M] = 0.1$. Assume that on the average there is one fire every 20 years, a battery lifetime of 2 years, and an alarm malfunction every 4 years. Find the probability that when the alarm goes off there is a fire.

A1.5.22 0.0909

P1.5.23 A student has an old car with three serious problems: bad tires, bad hoses, and a failing water pump. She sets out for Houston estimating the probability that a tire will fail is 0.1, the probability that a water hose will burst is 0.15, and probability that the water pump will fail is 0.05. When the student is late, her mother, an engineer who knows probability theory, calculates the probability that the water pump failed. What result did she obtain?

A1.5.23 0.167

P1.5.24 The emergency medical service dispatcher knows that on a response there will be an injury in the faster car 50% of the time, an injury in the slower car 40% of the time, and injuries in both cars 20% of the time. Let $N = \{$no injury$\}$, $F = \{$injury in faster car$\}$, and $S = \{$injury in slower car$\}$.
a. What is the probability of an injury on a given response?
b. What is the probability of an injury in the faster car, given that there is an injury at the scene?
c. Which events are disjoint? Explain.
d. Which events are independent? Explain.

A1.5.24 **(a)** 0.700; **(b)** 0.714; **(c)** none; **(d)** F and S

P1.5.25 A company uses CDs from two manufacturers. Although all CDs test good at first, some exhibit an early failure. When the company bought 40% from manufacturer A and 60% from manufacturer B, the combined early failure rate was 3%. When they bought 60% from A and 40% from B, it was 4%.
a. Find the failure rate of disks for manufacturer B.
b. Find the probability that a CD that failed was manufactured by A in the case in which 60% of the CDs were bought from A.

A1.5.25 **(a)** 0.01; **(b)** 0.900

P1.5.26 An engineer drives to work by one of two routes each day. She takes the quicker route about 70% of the time and takes the scenic route the remainder. If she takes the quicker route, there is a 5% chance that she will be late, but if she takes the scenic route there is a 25% chance that she will be late. The experiment is picking a day at random and observing whether she is late.
a. What is the sample space and how many outcomes are there?
b. What is the probability that she is late on any given day?
c. Given that she arrived on time or early, what is the probability that she took the scenic route that day?

A1.5.26 **(a)** $\{Q \cap L, \overline{Q} \cap L, Q \cap \overline{L}, \overline{Q} \cap \overline{L}\}$; **(b)** 0.110; **(c)** 0.2528

P1.5.27   There is said to be a "home court advantage" in sports like basketball. Let us assume that this is true and that the magnitude of the advantage is that the probability of winning at home is greater by 20% than the probability of winning away from home. Use the following notation: W = win the game, and H = play at home. Assume the team plays half its games on the road and half at home. Further assume that the team wins 60% of the time.
   a. Express the home court advantage in the notation given.
   b. Find the probability of winning, assuming that the team plays at home.
   c. If the team wins, what is the probability that it played at home?

   A1.5.27 **(a)** $P[W|H] = 1.2 \times P[W|\overline{H}]$; **(b)** 0.6545; **(c)** 0.5455

P1.5.28   Airline X loses one bag out of 10,000. Airline Y loses one bag out of 8000. Your friend arrives from Dallas on a Thursday and his bag is lost. What is the probability that he flew Airline Y, assuming both airlines are equally likely? (You could get the number of daily flights off the web if these were real airlines. Here assume both airlines have the same number of flights.)

   A1.5.28 $\frac{5}{9}$

P1.5.29   A computer company buys cables from three sources, call them X, Y, and Z, in the ratio 40%, 40%, and 20%, respectively. The cables from X and Z are 99.9% reliable, but the cables from Y are only 99% reliable.
   a. If a bad cable turns up, what is the probability that it came from Y?
   b. Show that the three *a posteriori* probabilities add to 1.

   A1.5.29 (a) 0.8696; (b) $P[X|\overline{R}] = 0.087$ and $P[Z|\overline{R}] = 0.0435$, so they add to 1.0

P1.5.30   A system has three subsystems, A, B, and C. If any of the subsystems is functional, the system operates. Only if all three fail does the system fail. All three are 98% reliable, and C is independent of A and B, but A and B are not independent of each other. Specifically, the probability that A and B continue to operate at the same time is 97%.
   a. Calculate the reliability of the system.
   b. If the system is operating, what is the probability that it is operating with only one of the three subsystems in operation?

   A1.5.30 **(a)** 0.9998; **(b)** 0.0102

P1.5.31   A system operates if subsystems A and B operate or subsystem C operates, or all three operate. The reliability of A is 99%, independent of B and C. Subsystem B is 98% reliable generally but is influenced by C such that if C fails, the reliability of B drops to 96%. The reliability of C generally is 0.95.
   a. Show that the reliability of C must also be influenced by B by finding $P[C|B]$.
   b. Determine the reliability of the overall system by writing an expression for R = reliability of the system and then evaluating $P[R]$.

   A1.5.31 **(a)** 0.9510; **(b)** $R = (A \cap B) \cup C$, 0.9975

P1.5.32 Currently 30% of Americans shop over the web, 20% shop by mail order, and 50% shop in person in a store. Of the people who shop over the web, 90% pay by credit card, and the rest pay by check. Of the people who shop by mail order, 70% pay by credit card, and the rest pay by personal check or mail order. Of the people who shop in person, 40% pay by credit card, and the rest pay by personal check or cash.

   a. What percentage of purchases are paid for by some means other than by credit card?

   b. If a person pays by credit card, what is the probability that he or she did not buy in a local shop?

   A1.5.32 (a) 0.390; **(b)** 0.672

P1.5.33 A manufacturer is concerned about the quality of his product. Experience has shown that on the average, one unit out of 10^4 does not meet specifications. This is not good enough, so tests are performed to catch the bad units. If the unit is OK, the test is 99.9% effective in certifying the unit as OK. But if a unit is defective, the tests are only 80% reliable, meaning that 20% of the bad units test OK. An order of 10^5 units is shipped. How many bad units are expected to be shipped?

   A1.5.33 2

P1.5.34 In Pecos County, 95% of the people always tell the truth, but 5% never tell the truth. A lost traveler spotted two men and asked them, "Is this the way to Belding?" The first man said "Yes," but the second man said, "He's lying."

   a. Describe the sample space, and give the outcomes.

   b. What is the probability that the traveler got to Belding by continuing down the road?

   A1.5.34 (a) $T_1 =$ first man telling the truth, $T_2 =$ second man telling the truth, $S = \{T_1 \cap \overline{T}_2, \overline{T}_1 \cap T_2\}$; **(b)** 0.5

P1.5.35 Abe and Barney go fishing. From past experience we know that Barney catches a fish 80% of the time, that both catch a fish 60% of the time, and at least one of them catches a fish 90% of the time. Treat these percentages as probabilities and use the rules of probability.

   a. Find the absolute probability that Abe catches a fish

   b. Find the conditional probability that Barney catches a fish, given that Abe catches a fish.

   c. Are the events "Abe catches a fish" and "Barney catches a fish" independent? Explain.

   A1.5.35 (a) 0.7; **(b)** 0.857; **(c)** not independent, since $P[A \cap B] \neq P[A] \times P[B]$

P1.5.36 Archie and Bill invest in separate mutual funds. From experience we know that Bill's fund goes up 40% of the time, and at least one of their funds goes up 70% of the time. Furthermore, when Bill's fund goes up, Archie's fund goes up 50% of the time. Treat these percentages as probabilities and use the rules of probability.

   a. Find the absolute probability that Archie's fund will go up.

   b. Find the conditional probability that Archie's fund will go up, given that Bill's fund goes up.

c. Are the events "Archie's fund goes up" and "Bill's fund goes up" independent? Explain.

A1.5.36 (a) 0.5; (b) 0.5; (c) yes, $P[A \cap B] = P[A] \times P[B]$

P1.5.37   Arnold and Billy go shopping. From past experience we know that Billy buys something 20% of the time and that at least one of them buys something 25% of the time. Furthermore, we know that if Billy buys something, then Arnold buys something 50% of the time. Treat these percentages as probabilities and use the rules of probability.
a. Find the absolute probability that Arnold buys something.
b. Find the conditional probability that Billy buys something, given that Arnold has bought something.
c. Are the events "Arnold buys something" and "Billy buys something" independent? Explain.

A1.5.37 (a) 0.150; (b) 0.667; (c) no, $P[A \cap B] \neq P[A] \times P[B]$

P1.5.38   A carnival man hides a pea under one of three nut shells. By a series of complicated movements, he attempts to confuse the bystander so that the bystander no longer knows which of the shells hides the pea. If the bystander follows the sleight of hand, he will be correct. If he cannot detect the proper shell throughout the series of movements, he will pick a shell at random. There is a probability of 0.1 that he will know the correct shell. The game is played, and the bystander points to the correct shell. What is the probability that he knew the correct shell and didn't merely luck out in a guess?

A1.5.38 0.250

P1.5.39   Parts are manufactured and tested with the following results. 5% are defective to the point that they do not work (A); of the remaining parts, 75% meet the specs (B), and 25% work but do not meet specs (C). A part is selected at random and we are interested in its properties.
a. What is the probability that it meets specs? Base your answer on the rules of probability.
b. If a part is tested and found to work, what is the probability that it meets specs?

A1.5.39 (a) 0.713; (b) 0.75

P1.5.40   A student who has taken a data structures course has an 80% chance of landing a job at NetTech Corporation, but a student who has not had such a course has only a 50% chance. If NetTech has one opening and has 5 applicants, estimate the probability that the student hired had data structures. Of a typical group of 23 interviewees, approximately 9 students have had data structures.

A1.5.40 0.507

P1.5.41   A company manufactures coaxial bandpass filters. The manufacturing tolerances are such that one in 10 filters is defective, so the filters are tested before shipping. If the filter is bad, the test is 99% effective, but if the filter is good, the testing is only 80% effective; that is, one in five good filters tests bad.

    a. Out of every 1000 filters that are manufactured, how many good filters are shipped on the average?

    b. Out of every 1000 filters that are manufactured, how many bad filters are shipped on the average?

    c. If a filter is shipped, what is the probability that it is a good filter?

    d. If a filter is shipped, what is the probability that it is a bad filter?

A1.5.41 (a) 720; (b) 1; (c) 0.9986; (d) 1.387×10^{-3}

P1.5.42 An IC consists of 300 transistors, 40 resistors, and 1000 connecting paths. The probability that any transistor is defective is 10^{-6}, the probability that any resistor is bad is 10^{-5}, and the probability that a connection is bad is 2×10^{-6}. Assume all components must function for proper operation of the IC, and all component failures are independent events.

    a. Find $P[\text{IC bad}]$.

    b. Find $P[\text{IC bad due to bad resistor only}|\text{IC bad}]$.

A1.5.42 (a) 2.6964×10^{-3}; (b) 0.148

P1.5.43 In one household with which I am familiar, the wife, who does the cooking, messes up the kitchen stove 80% of the time. The husband, who cleans up, remembers to look at the stove to see if it needs cleaning 70% of the time. If he notices that it needs cleaning, he cleans it 90% of the time, but 10% of the time he does not have time to clean it.

    a. What is the probability that the stove gets cleaned on any night picked at random?

    b. If the stove needs cleaning but does not get cleaned, what is the probability that it was noticed but the husband did not have time to clean it?

A1.5.43 (a) 0.504; (b) 0.189

P1.5.44 A student sets his alarm in time to make his 8 o'clock class. When the alarm sounds, there is a probability of 0.3 that he will get up, a probability of 0.6 that he will hit the snooze button and go back to sleep, and a probability of 0.1 that he will turn off the alarm and sleep for at least 2 more hours. If he hits the snooze button, the alarm will sound again in 10 minutes, and these same probabilities apply the second time, and so on.

    a. What is the probability that the student will get up within 15 minutes of the first alarm?

    b. If the student gets up within the first 25 minutes, what is the probability that the alarm sounded only once?

A1.5.44 (a) 0.480; (b) 0.5102

P1.5.45 An athlete has three tries to jump over a bar. His chances on the first try are 0.7. If he fails on the first jump, he takes the second jump, and if he fails on the second, he gets a third attempt. On the second jump his chances are 0.5 because he tires out, and on the third attempt his chances are 0.3. If he clears the bar on one of the three jumps, find the probability that he was successful on the second jump.

A1.5.45 0.1676

P1.5.46 Furniture dealers know that when a man walks in alone, they make a sale 5% of the time; when a woman walks in alone, they make a sale 15% of the time, but when a man and a woman walk in together, they make a sale 30% of the time. When the front door opens, 90% of the time a woman enters, either alone or with a man, and 40% of the time a man enters, either alone or with a woman. Let $S = \{$sale$\}$, $M = \{$man walks in$\}$, and $W = \{$woman walks in$\}$

a. What is the probability that a man and woman enter together?

b. Each time the door opens, find $P[S]$.

c. If a sale is made, find the probability that the sale was made to a man who entered alone.

d. Are {man walks in} and {woman walks in} independent?

A1.5.46 **(a)** 0.300; **(b)** 0.185; **(c)** 0.02703; **(d)** no

P1.5.47 A repair technician knows from experience that units that come in for repair have power supply troubles 60% of the time, motherboard problems 70% of the time, and connector/keyboard problems 18% of the time; however, sometimes the power supply takes the motherboard with it when it fails, but mechanical problems such as connector/keyboard problems are never found in computers brought in with electronic problems. Consider that these are the only problems. Let $S = \{$computers brought in for repair with one or more of these problems$\}$, $W = \{$power supply fails$\}$, $M = \{$motherboard fails$\}$, and $C = \{$connector/keyboard fails$\}$.

a. Find $P[W \cap M]$, the probability that both the power supply and the motherboard need repair.

b. Find the probability that the motherboard fails, given that the power supply has failed.

A1.5.47 **(a)** 0.48; **(b)** 0.8

P1.5.48 In a certain course there are two sections. Section A is taught by Prof. Cool at a very desirable hour and Section B by Prof. Poor at 8 A.M. Let $A =$ event student gets in Section A, $B =$ event student gets into Section B, and $C =$ event that student does not get into the course at all. Let $E =$ the event that a student registers early. Let $P[A|E] = 0.7$ be the probability that a student gets Prof. Cool and similarly that $P[A|\overline{E}] = 0.4$, $P[B|E] = 0.2$, and $P[B|\overline{E}] = 0.4$.

a. Find $P[C|E]$ and $P[C|\overline{E}]$.

b. The fraction of students who register early is 90%. Find $P[A]$.

c. If a student is selected at random in Prof. Poor's class, what is the probability that this student registered early?

A1.5.48 **(a)** 0.100 and 0.200; **(b)** 0.670; **(c)** 0.818

P1.5.49 A man has 10 unlabeled bottles of wine, and he is seeking to identify one wine by smell. He has a probability of identifying the correct wine of 0.6 after smelling all 10. His wife, who has a better nose for these things, also smells the wines and, without knowing her husband's choice, also identifies the same bottle as he has chosen. If her probability of success is 0.8, what is the probability that the bottle identified by both is correct? Assume all wines except the best wine are equally likely to be chosen by either.

A1.5.49 0.982

P1.5.50 Precision resistors sometimes give problems. In a study it was found that 15% of them have a tolerance of 2% or more. Call this event R, for resistance problem. Another problem encountered was that 10% of them had a 50 parts per million or more temperature coefficient. Call this event T, for temperature problem. It was also found that 10% of the defective resistors had both problems.
a. What is the probability that a precision resistor has both problems?
b. What is the probability that a precision resistor has a temperature problem, given that it has a resistance problem?
c. Are the two problems occurring independently, or is there some causal connection between them? Explain how you know.

A1.5.50 **(a)** 0.02273; **(b)** 0.1515; **(c)** Not independent since $P[R] \times P[T] \neq 0.02273$

P1.5.51 A panel of 2 judges is to choose the best between two wines. Assume that there actually is a "best" wine and that the probability of either judge identifying it is 0.6, with independent judgments.
a. Find the probability that the judges pick the same wine.
b. Find the probability that if the judges pick the same wine, it actually is the better wine.
c. Rework part a if there are four judges and 10 wines, only one of which is "best." Assume that all others are equally likely to be chosen if the judge makes a mistake.

A1.5.51 **(a)** 0.52; **(b)** 0.6923; **(c)** 0.1296 and 0.9997

P1.5.52 A certain rodent can carry two parasites, A and B. Tests have shown that 56% of the rodents are parasite free, 27% carry parasite A, and 6% carry both parasites A and B.
a. What fraction carry parasite B?
b. Does the rodent become more or less likely to have parasite B if it carries parasite A? Explain your answer.

A1.5.52 **(a)** 0.230; **(b)** $P[B|A] = 0.222 < P[B]$, so A makes the rodent less susceptible to parasite B.

ENDNOTES

1. **Independence of calibration errors.** In practice the calibration errors in voltage and resistance measurements on the same meter may not be independent.
2. **Random processes** are sometimes called *stochastic processes,* from a Greek word implying randomness.

3. **The Millstone Hill Radar.** In July 1959, your author, as a beginning graduate student at MIT and a summer employee of MIT Lincoln Laboratory, visited the Millstone Hill Radar during an all-night test of its ability to distinguish aircraft from *chaff*, reflective targets dropped from aircraft to deceive radar operators.

4. **Postscript on the Venus detection.** Sadly, the determination of the velocity of light based on the Venus-bounce experiment was incorrect. The author learned of this recently but has been unable to determine in what way the experiment failed. Certainly our eyes assure us that the detection process was successful, whatever else went amiss.

5. **Answer to you do it on p. 14.** The union of $\{1, 3, 5\}$ with $\{1, 2\}$ is $\{1, 2, 3, 5\}$.

6. **Answer to you do it on p. 15.** $O \cap L = \{1, 3, 5\} \cap \{1, 2\} = \{1\}$.

7. **Answer to you do it on p. 16.** There are three pairs of disjoint sets: E and O, O and G, and L and G.

8. **Answers to exercises on set theory. 1. (a)** $\{4, 5, 6, 7, 8, 9\}$; **(b)** $\{4, 5, 6, 7, 8, 9, 10, 11, 12\}$; **(c)** $(0, 1, 2, 3, 5, 7, 9, 11\}$; **(d)** $\{4, 8, 10, 12\}$.

9. **Answers to exercises on set theory. 2. (a)** $(0, 0)$, $(0, 1)$, $(0, 2)$, $(0, 3)$, $(1, 0)$, $(1, 1)$, $(1, 2)$, $(2, 0)$, $(2, 1)$, $(3, 0)$; **(b)** $(0, 0)$, $(0, 1)$, $(0, 2)$, $(0, 3)$, $(0, 4)$, $(1, 0)$, $(1, 1)$, $(1, 2)$, $(1, 3)$, $(2, 0)$, $(2, 1)$, $(2, 2)$, $(2, 3)$, $(3, 0)$, $(3, 1)$, $(3, 2)$, $(4, 0)$.

10. **Probability assignment.** This is the "equally likely model," which we will introduce fully in Sec. 1.4.

11. **Answer to you do it on p. 25.** In this case, $P[A] = \frac{5}{10}$, and $P[C] = \frac{5}{10}$. The intersection of A and C has two outcomes, $\{2, 3\}$, so $P[A \cap C] = \frac{2}{10}$. Thus $P[A \cup C] = \frac{5}{10} + \frac{5}{10} - \frac{2}{10} = \frac{8}{10}$.

12. **Answer to you do it on p. 29.** Since $D = E \cap B = \{0, 8\}$, it follows from the assumption about probabilities that $P[D] = 0.2$. Thus by Eq. (1.3.15), $P[\overline{D}] = 1 - 0.2 = 0.8$.

13. **Answer to you do it on p. 29.** Since $P[A|B] = \frac{P[A \cap B]}{P[B]} = \frac{P[0,9]}{P[0,2,4,6,9]} = \frac{2/10}{5/10} = 0.40$.

14. **Geometric series.** We give, without proof, the sums of the finite and the infinite geometric series. The finite geometric series is

$$S_n = 1 + a + a^2 + \cdots + a^n = \frac{1 - a^{n+1}}{1 - a} \quad \text{for all } a.$$

For $n \to \infty$ and $a^2 < 1$, the series converges to

$$S = 1 + a + a^2 + \cdots = \frac{1}{1 - a}$$

Note that $a^k + a^{k+1} + a^{k+2} + \cdots = a^k(1 + a + a^2 + \cdots) = \frac{a^k}{1-a}$.

Series related to the geometric series. We also will need the following:

$$\sum_0^\infty k a^k = (a + 2 a^2 + 3 a^3 + \cdots) = a \frac{d}{da}(1 + a + a^2 + a^3 + \cdots)$$

$$= a \frac{d}{da}\left(\frac{1}{1-a}\right) = \frac{a}{(1-a)^2}$$

as well as the following, which extends the same trick:

$$\sum_0^\infty k^2 \, a^k = (1^2 \, a + 2^2 \, a^2 + 3^2 \, a^3 + \cdots) = a \, \frac{d}{da} \left(a \, \frac{d}{da} \left(\frac{1}{1-a} \right) \right)$$

$$= \frac{a(1+a)}{(1-a)^3}.$$

Notice that in the previous two summations, the lower limit can be either $k = 0$ or $k = 1$.

15. **Answers to exercises on the rules of probability 1. (a)** $P[A] = 0.4$, $P[B] = 0.5$, **(b)** Yes, independent; **2. (a)** 0.5, **(b)** $\frac{1}{3}$, **(c)** $1 - (0.5)^N$.

16. **Answer to you do it on p. 37.** From a table listing minimum change for all the outcomes, the results are one coin, 3 times; two, three, or four coins, 5 times each; five coins, 4 times; and six coins, 2 times. That makes four or more coins 11 times. Thus the probability sought is $\frac{11}{24}$.

17. **Combinatorials.** An excellent reference that treats the subject in more depth is Feller, *An Introduction to Probability Theory and Its Applications*, Vol. 1, Chapter 2.

18. **Answer to first you do it on p. 39.** Using the same form as in the example, the number of four-, five-, or six-symbol passwords starting with a letter and alternating letters with numerals would be $26 \times (10^2 \times 26 + 10^2 \times 26^2 + 10^3 \times 26^2) = 19,401,200$.

19. **Answer to second you do it on p. 39.** Using the same format as before, the answer would be $26 \times (35 \times 34 \times 33 + 35 \times 34 \times 33 \times 32 + 35 \times 34 \times 33 \times 32 \times 31) = 1,046,545,500$.

20. **Permutations** deal with distinguishable objects, such that order can be discerned, for example numbered balls. Combinations deal with indistinguishable objects, for example, red balls.

21. **Binomial coefficients.** Another phrase to describe these combinations is "n draw k." $\binom{n}{k}$ is also called the binomial coefficient, for reasons explained in the section. We have written the binomial expansion "backward" from the usual form, starting with the b^n instead of a^n because that's the way the binomial distribution is written. We will study the binomial distribution in the next chapter.

22. **Answer to first you do it on p. 41.** Here $n = 26$ and $k = 3$, so $\binom{26}{3} = 2600$.

23. **Answer to second you do it on p. 41.** There would be $\binom{30}{4}$ ways to choose the team of all men, so the probability would be $P[\text{all men}] = \dfrac{\binom{30}{4}}{\binom{40}{4}} = 0.2999$.

24. **Answers to exercises on probability by counting. 1. (a)** There are 63 equally likely outcomes: for all faculty not officed on the first floor, **(b)** $\frac{1}{63}$, **(c)** $\frac{19}{63}$.

25. **Answer to you do it on p. 44.**

$$P(E|A) = \frac{P(A \cap E)}{P(A)} = \frac{P(\{2,3,5,7\} \cap \{0,2,4,6,8\})}{P(\{2,3,5,7\})} = \frac{P(\{2\})}{P(\{2,3,5,7\})} = 0.25.$$

26. **Answer to you do it on p. 45.** The event L maps into the upper left hand corner of the space, as shown in the following figure.

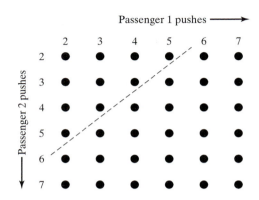

As you can see, there are 10 outcomes in L and of these 7 in $T =$ stopping on two. This leads to the answer $P[T|L] = \frac{7/36}{10/36} = 0.7$

27. **Answer to you do it on p. 49.** When we put in all the numbers except $P[K|S_F]$ and set it equal to 0.25, we have $P[S_F|K] = \frac{P[S_F \cap K]}{P[K]} = \frac{P[K|S_F] \times 0.1}{0.60 \times 0.05 + 0.30 \times 0.08 + 0.1 \times P[K|S_F]} = 0.25.$ This equation yields $P[K|S_F] = 0.18.$

28. **Answer to you do it on p. 52.** Two outcomes favor B_8, and four favor B_2. None favor $B_8 \cap B_2$. Thus they cannot be independent. A glance at Figure 1.5.5 shows that if $B_8 = 1$, then $B_2 = 0$, and clearly there is information in B_8 about B_2, so the correct answer is no.

29. **Answer to you do it on p. 53.** The only difference is that $P[B \cap C]$ changes from 0.8×0.8 to 0.82×0.8. I get 0.9346 for an answer.

30. **Answers to exercises on conditional probability, Bayes' rule, and independence**
    1. (a) 0.6; (b) 0.0556; (c) $\frac{1}{2} + \frac{1}{18} + \frac{8}{18} = 1$
    2. (a) $\frac{2}{6}$; (b) $\frac{2}{3}$; (c) $\frac{1}{3}$; (d) 0; (e) 1; (f) 1
    3. (a) $E =$ even and $T =$ a multiple of three, $P(E) = \frac{6}{12}$, $P(T) = \frac{4}{12}, = \frac{2}{12}$: yes, they are independent; (b) yes
    4. Yes, and easily proved using the rules of probability.

2

The Binomial Model and Random Variables

2.1 BERNOULLI TRIALS AND THE BINOMIAL MODEL

Summary of progress toward our goal of modeling random systems

Our goal in this book is to develop mathematical models for random systems and to develop skills in choosing and applying the right model as needed. Our macromodel is probability theory with its concepts of a repeatable chance experiment with well-defined outcomes, events defined on those outcomes, and probabilities assigned to the events as part of the modeling process.

The probabilities we have used hitherto were simply postulated, such as in the example about recruiting basketball players, or were derived from the "equally likely" model, as in the example about birthdays. In the latter case, computing probabilities reduces to counting, so we introduced basic counting techniques.

In this chapter we explore models arising in experiments that have repeated trials. The resulting models are useful in many practical situations.

2.1.1 Bernoulli Trials

Combined experiments

Flipping a dime and a nickel.   Consider one experiment in which we flip a dime and another in which we flip a nickel. The probabilities are defined as

$$P[H_d] = p_d,\ P[T_d] = 1 - p_d = q_d$$

and

$$P[H_n] = p_n,\ P[T_n] = 1 - p_n = q_n \tag{2.1.1}$$

where H and T represent heads and tails, and d and n represent dime and nickel, respectively. If we assume that the results are independent, the probability of a heads on both would be

$$P[H_d \cap H_n] = P[H_d] \times P[H_n] = p_d p_n \tag{2.1.2}$$

Think again.   Let's think carefully about Eq. (2.1.2). The results that we just described are perfectly reasonable and essentially correct, however, the results are improper, since we are dealing with two separate chance experiments, as we have described the situation. Because probabilities must, strictly speaking, be defined on one experiment, the results are illegitimate in a formal sense because we have multiplied probabilities from two different experiments.

Quick fix.   The remedy is trivial: we combine the two experiments into a single experiment. The sample space for this combined experiment is

$$S = \{H_d H_n,\ H_d T_n,\ T_d H_n,\ T_d T_n\} \tag{2.1.3}$$

The probabilities assigned to each of the outcomes are

$$P[H_d H_n] = p_d p_n,\ P[H_d T_n] = p_d q_n,\ P[T_d H_n] = q_d p_n,\ P[T_d T_n] = q_d q_n \tag{2.1.4}$$

We stress that these probabilities are defined, not derived from some more basic knowledge, apart from the reasoning given in the two-experiment version. We thus make our one-experiment model behave as we anticipate from our two-experiment model, based on intuition and, if necessary, experimentation.

Lest you accuse us of belaboring the obvious, we insist on the importance of having a legitimate macromodel in place to formulate a probability problem. Thankfully, the macromodel framework is sufficiently general to encompass most situations, as here.

Flipping the same coin twice.   If we take the same coin and flip it twice, we can use the same concept of a combined experiment. Using the same coin allows us to drop the d and n subscripts. The space for flipping the same coin twice, with probabilities based on independent trials, is

$$S = \{\underbrace{HH}_{p^2},\ \underbrace{HT}_{pq},\ \underbrace{TH}_{qp},\ \underbrace{TT}_{q^2}\} \tag{2.1.5}$$

Flipping the same coin n times.   With n flips the sample space looks like

$$S = \{\underbrace{HHH \cdots H}_{n \text{ times}},\ THH \cdots H,\ \ldots\} \tag{2.1.6}$$

Note that there are 2^n outcomes to this sample space, since these are permutations with replacement permitted. We assign a probability $p^k q^{n-k}$ to outcomes having k heads and $n - k$ tails. This sample space does not contain equally likely outcomes except in the special case $p = q = \frac{1}{2}$.

Bernoulli and binomial trials.   Consider an experiment that is the n-fold repetition of the same action, called a *trial,* such as flipping a coin or dialing a telephone. Further, consider that we are interested in some event, A, that may or may not occur on each trial, such as {heads on the coin} or {wrong number in dialing the phone}. It is common to call the occurrence of event A a *success.* Such repeated trials with the observation of such an event are called *Bernoulli trials.* In some situations involving Bernoulli trials, the probability of success on successive trials may increase, such as with a *learning curve;* for others the probability of success decreases with increasing trials. Such probabilities may or may not be independent of successes in previous trials. All these are possibilities for a series of Bernoulli trials.

An important special case is that in which the probability of success is the same for each trial and results are independent of all other trials. Such is the case, for example, in the flipping of coins. This special case we will call *binomial trials.* We caution you that commonly this distinction between the special case and the more general case of Bernoulli trials is not made; the special case in which the trials are independent, and the probability of success is the same on each trial, is routinely called Bernoulli trials.

Binomial trials are important for several reasons. Many random systems are well modeled as a binomial trial sequence: saving a file n times, manufacturing n computers, making n independent measurements, polling n subjects, and so on. Binomial trials lead to the binomial, geometric, and Pascal distributions.

Summary of the conditions for Bernoulli and binomial trials

Bernoulli trials require repeated trials with a binary result, that is, something either happens or does not. Binomial trials require that the probability of success on any given trial be the same for all trials, independent of other trials. Binomial trials lead to some important probability distributions: the binomial distribution, the geometric distribution, and the Pascal distribution (or the negative binomial distribution, which is very similar). Here are the additional assumptions that must be made to derive these distributions:

- For the *binomial distribution,* we perform n binomial trials and observe k successes. If we are interested only in the number of successes and not the order, then the result is the binomial distribution: $P[k$ successes in n trials].
- For the *geometric distribution,* we are interested in the trial number for the first success: $P[$first success on nth trial].
- For the *Pascal distribution,* we are interested in the trial number for the kth success. This is a generalization of the geometric distribution: $P[k$th success on nth trial].
- For the *negative binomial distribution,* we are interested in the number of failures before the kth success is observed: $P[j$ failures before the kth success].

These distributions are significant additions to our resources for modeling random systems that we will derive in this section.

Modeling chance experiments.   The concept of binomial trials also gives us closure on our definition of probability. We defined probability as a mathematical model of a relative frequency of occurrence. With binomial trials, we can model the n-fold repetition of an experiment and see if our model behaves correctly. This second application of binomial trials relates to the binomial distribution, to which we now turn.

2.1.2 The Binomial Distribution

Unordered results. Let us consider n binomial trials and an event, A, defined on the results of each trial. For example, we test a part to see if it is good or defective: $A = \{$good part$\}$. If A occurs, we describe this as a *success*. We are interested in determining the probability of k successes in n trials, which is known as the binomial distribution. This corresponds to k good parts out of n parts tested.

Derivation of the binomial distribution. We have already done most of the work. We envision an experiment that is the n-fold repetition of a trial of some sort. We observe if event A occurs on each repetition. The sample space for this experiment is

$$S = \{\underbrace{AAA \cdots A}_{n \text{ times}}, \bar{A}AA \cdots A, \dots, \underbrace{\bar{A}\bar{A}\bar{A} \cdots \bar{A}}_{n \text{ times}}\} \tag{2.1.7}$$

An outcome with k successes and $n - k$ failures would look like

$$\underbrace{AAA \cdots A}_{k \text{ successes}} \quad \underbrace{\bar{A}\bar{A} \cdots \bar{A}}_{n - k \text{ failures}} \tag{2.1.8}$$

except that the successes and failures could occur in any order.

A convenient way to express a binary result is with a 1 and a 0. Let us identify 1 with success and 0 with failure. In that case the space is $S = \{11111, 11110, \dots, 00001, 00000\}$. Reversed in order, these outcome correspond to counting from 0 to 31_{10} in base 2. In general, there are 2^n outcomes in such a sample space, which can be identified with counting from 0 to $2^n - 1$.

If we let the event $K = \{k$ successes in n trials$\}$, the picture looks like Fig. 2.1.1.

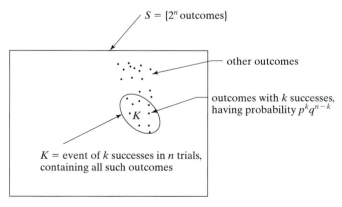

Figure 2.1.1 Event K groups together all outcomes with k successes and $n - k$ failures, all of which have the same probability.

Figure 2.1.1 groups together into event K all outcomes that contain k successes. Each of these outcomes has a probability of $p^k q^{n-k}$, and we merely need to know the number of outcomes in K to determine $P[K]$. Thus we need to count the number of ways that we can have k success in n trials, without regard to order. The number of such combinations is $\binom{n}{k}$, the binomial coefficient.

The binomial distribution. Thus the probability of k successes in n trials, with $P[\text{success}] = p$ and $P[\text{failure}] = q = 1 - p$ on an individual, independent trial is

$$P[k \text{ successes in } n \text{ trials}] = B_n(k, p) = \binom{n}{k} p^k q^{n-k} = \frac{n!}{(n-k)!k!} p^k (1 - p)^{n-k}, 0 \le k \le n$$

$$(2.1.9)$$

We have introduced the symbol $B_n(k, p)$ to represent this discrete distribution, which is called the binomial distribution. We call this a *distribution* because when we fix n and consider the probabilities of all values of k, the probability of the certain event "distributes" among the partitioning events $\{k = 0\}, \{k = 1\}, \{k = 2\}, \ldots, \{k = n\}$.

Normalization of the distribution. Because $\{k = 0\}, \{k = 1\}, \{k = 2\}, \ldots, \{k = n\}$ is a partition of the space, we require that

$$P[k = 0] + P[k = 1] + \cdots + P[k = n] = 1 \qquad (2.1.10)$$

That Eq. (2.1.10) is valid follows from the binomial theorem, since $p + q = 1$:

$$1^n = (q + p)^n = \sum_{k=0}^{k=n} \binom{n}{k} q^{n-k} p^k = \sum_{k=0}^{k=n} B_n(k, p) \qquad (2.1.11)$$

To illustrate this distribution, we show in Fig. 2.1.2 the binomial distributions for $n = 10$ trials, $p = 0.2$.

Most likely value of k. The most likely number of successes of a series of binomial trials is the value of k that gives the maximum value to $B_n(k, p)$. We may determine this value of k by examining the ratio between the kth and $(k-1)$st terms:

$$\frac{B_n(k, p)}{B_n(k - 1, p)} = \frac{(n - k + 1)p}{k(1 - p)} \overset{?}{\underset{<}{>}} 1 \qquad (2.1.12)$$

If the ratio is greater than 1, the probability continues to increase as k increases; if the ratio is less than 1, the probability continues to decrease; and if the ratio is equal to 1, the kth and $(k - 1)$st terms are equal. Equation (2.1.12) can be reduced to the following rule: If $k = (n + 1)p$ is an integer, then this k and the next smaller k are equally likely. If $(n + 1)p$ is not an integer, then the integer part of $(n + 1)p$ is the most likely value of k; however, it should be noted that if n is large, then the most likely value of k yields a small probability. For example, if $n = 400$ and $p = 0.5$, the most likely outcome is the integer part of $401 \times 0.5 \rightarrow 200$. But the probability that exactly $K = 200$ will occur is small: $B_{400}(200, 0.5) = 0.0399$.

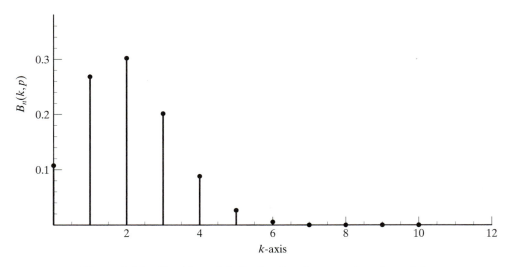

Figure 2.1.2 The binomial distribution for $n = 10$ and $p = 0.2$.

Example 2.1.1:   Telephone registration

Assume that each time you call the telephone registration system to sign up for a course you have a probability of 0.8 of getting through. Find the probability that you get through three times in five calls.

Solution   We assume that the conditions of binomial trials are met. This means that two conditions must be met: (1) It must be true that your success on each of the five calls is independent of your success on the other calls. This implies that you wait a while between calls. (2) The probability of success on every call must the same. This implies that the load on the telephone registration system is constant during the period in which you make the calls. With these conditions met, the answer is

$$P[3 \text{ successes in 5 trials}] = B_5(3, 0.8) = \binom{5}{3} 0.8^3 0.2^{5-3} = 0.205 \qquad (2.1.13)$$

You do it.   What if you want the probability of three or four successes? Do the required calculation, enter your result as **myanswer** in the cell box, and click Evaluate for a response.

```
myanswer =        ;
```

```
Evaluate
```

For the answer, see endnote 1.

Example 2.1.2:   System reliability ——————————————————————————————————
Here is another example in which components in a system are regarded as independent trials. We have a system with 100 components. The probability that a component will fail during a prescribed period of time is 0.005. What is the probability that the system is operating at the end of the period, which requires that no component fail?

Solution   We assume the conditions of binomial trials are met. This means that component failures are independent and that all components are equally likely to fail. In real systems both these assumptions are questionable. Here we have the option to let a failure of a component be a success or to let the nonfailure of a component be a success. We will do the example both ways. Letting a failed component be a success, $p = 0.005$ and $k = 0$ corresponds to no failures. This is the probability:

$$B_{100}(0, 0.005) = \binom{100}{0} 0.005^0 0.995^{100-0} = 0.606 \qquad (2.1.14)$$

For the other viewpoint, counting a nonfailure as a success, $p = 0.995$ and $k = 100$ corresponds to a working system. The probability is $B_{100}(100, 0.995)$, which is the same calculation as Eq. (2.1.14).

——

You do it.   What is the probability that two or more components will fail? Calculate your answer to at least three places, and enter it in the cell box, and click Evaluate for a response.

```
myanswer =            ;
```

```
Evaluate
```

For the answer, see endnote 2.

Note that in the "You do it" exercise, the phrase "or more" suggests working with the complement of the event of interest. This may be generally put into the form

$$P[k \text{ or more}] = 1 - P[\text{less than } k] \qquad (2.1.15)$$

which is generally valid, since the events are complements.

Example 2.1.3:   How large? ——
The ECE Department student population is 14% women. How large does a class have to be before there is at least a 50% chance of containing two or more women?

Solution   We assume the conditions of binomial trials are met. This means that women do not tend to cluster in the same sections but choose randomly from all possibilities; also, that a student picked at random has a 14% probability of being a woman.

Normally, n is known and the probability is calculated as a function of k. Here k and the minimum probability are known and n must be calculated. A good approach is to proceed by trial and error. Because for a class of n students the most likely number of women is $0.14(n + 1)$, a good start would be

$$0.14(n + 1) = 2 \Rightarrow n = \frac{2}{0.14} - 1 = 13.3$$

students. Since we are asked for two or more, we round down and begin with $n = 13$. As previously stated, the sensible way to calculate the probability of two or more is $1 - B_{13}(0, 0.14) - B_{13}(1, 0.14) = 1 - 0.141 - 0.298 = 0.561$. Because this is higher than 0.5, let us try $n = 12$. This leads to $1 - B_{12}(0, 0.14) - B_{12}(1, 0.14) = 1 - 0.164 - 0.32 = 0.517$. This is close to 0.5, and it is easily confirmed that $n = 11$ gives 0.469. We conclude that for a class of 12 students, there is at least a 50% chance of having two or more women in it, subject to the assumptions of binomial trials.

You do it.   What if we want one or more women in the class? Enter your answer as an integer in the cell box, and click Evaluate for a reply.

```
myanswer =              ;
```

```
Evaluate
```

For the answer, see endnote 3.

2.1.3 The Geometric Distribution

The geometric distribution.   In this section we consider a distribution closely related to the binomial. We assume a Bernoulli trial sequence with independent trials and constant probability of success on each trial, i.e., binomial trials. The geometric distribution arises out of the following question: What is the probability in a series of binomial trials with $P[A] = p$ on every trial that the first success occurs on the nth trial?

The sample space.   The sample space for this experiment consists of a series of outcomes in which the first $n - 1$ trials result in failure, and the nth is a success, $S = \{A, \bar{A}A, \bar{A}\bar{A}A, \ldots\}$, a sample space that has an infinite number of outcomes. We will call the desired probability $P_1(n, p)$. We can work out these probabilities using the assumptions of binomial trials.

$P_1(1, p)$ would terminate the series on the first trial:

$$P_1(1, p) = P[A] = p \tag{2.1.16}$$

For $P_1(2, p)$, we must have one failure followed by a success. This probability is

$$P_1(2, p) = P[\bar{A}A] = qp \tag{2.1.17}$$

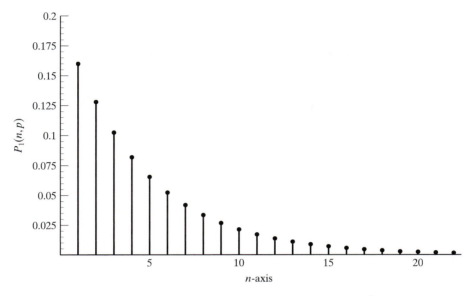

Figure 2.1.3   The geometric distribution for $p = \frac{1}{6}$.

where independence of trials is used. In general, $P_1(n, p)$ will have $n - 1$ failures followed by success, so the general distribution is

$$P_1(n, p) = q^{n-1} p \qquad (2.1.18)$$

The distribution described in Eq. (2.1.18) is called the *geometric distribution* because each term is smaller than the previous by a multiplicative factor, $q = 1 - p$. The most probable trial for success is therefore always the first trial. In the graph we show the geometric distribution for $p = \frac{1}{6}$ (Figure 2.1.3).

Success on or before n.   To find the probability that A occurs on or before trial n, we sum a geometric series:[4]

$$P_1(\text{on or before trial } n, p) = p \times \left(1 + q + q^2 + \cdots + q^{n-1}\right) = p \times \frac{1 - q^n}{1 - q} = 1 - q^n \qquad (2.1.19)$$

where $1 - q = p$. Equation (2.1.19) is readily interpreted as $1 - P[\text{no successes in first } n \text{ trials}]$.

Normalization of the distribution.   Equation (2.1.19) shows that the geometric distribution is properly normalized:

$$\sum_{n=1}^{n=\infty} P_1(n, p) = 1 - q^\infty = 1, \text{ since } 0 < q < 1. \qquad (2.1.20)$$

Note that we exclude $q = 1$, since in that case no success would ever occur and the series of trials would never end. In that case we would not have a legitimate probability distribution function.

Example 2.1.4:   Traffic light _____

A man encounters 10 traffic lights on his way to work. These are on a major highway, so the lights are green twice as long as they are red, from his point of view. Find the probability that he makes all the lights but the last one. We assume conditions for binomial trials, which means the lights are independent, and his probability of making a light is the same for all lights.

Solution   Because the light is green (G) twice as long as it is red (R), we assume $P[G] = 2P[R]$. Since $P[G] + P[R] = 1$ (ignore yellow lights), it follows that $P[R] = \frac{1}{3}$. Thus the probability that he makes all but the last light is $P_1\left(10, \frac{1}{3}\right) = \left(\frac{2}{3}\right)^9 \frac{1}{3} = 0.00867$.

You do it.   What is the probability that his first stop is somewhere between the fifth and tenth lights, inclusive? Calculate your answer to at least three-place accuracy, enter it in the cell box, and click Evaluate for a response.

```
myanswer =            ;
```

```
Evaluate
```

For the answer, see endnote 5.

No memory.   One property of the geometric distribution is that it has no memory, and thus "starts over" with each trial. This property is not surprising in view of the assumptions, but it is interesting to see how it is reflected in the mathematics. Let us say that we have no success in five trials, and we want to calculate the probabilities of success on future trials given that condition. We require a conditional probability $P[\text{first on } n|\text{none in } 5]$. Using the definition of a conditional probability, we have

$$P[\text{first on } n|\text{none in } 5] = \frac{P[\text{first on } n|\text{none in } 5]}{P[\text{none in } 5]} = \frac{q^{n-1}p}{q^5}, n = 6, 7, \ldots \qquad (2.1.21)$$

Note that the effect of the condition in the numerator is to change the values of n that are allowed. When we substitute $n = 6$ into Eq. (2.1.21), the result is $P[\text{first on } 6|\text{none in } 5] = p$, and the result for $n = 7$ is qp, and so on. Thus past failures do not affect the probabilities of future successes.

2.1.4 The Pascal Distribution

The geometric and Pascal distributions.   The Pascal distribution generalizes the geometric distribution by addressing the following question: In a series of independent Bernoulli trials with probability p of success on a given trial, what is the probability that the kth success occurs on the nth trial? The notation we will use is $P_k(n, p)$. Clearly, $P_1(n, p)$ represents the geometric distribution, where $k = 1$, the first success.

Nice try, but. . . .   Here's the *wrong* way to derive the Pascal distribution. We can form the event {kth success on nth trial} as the intersection of two events: {k successes in n trials} ∩ {success on last trial}. This is correct but leads nowhere because the two events are not independent; however, the equivalent {$k - 1$ successes in $n - 1$ trials} ∩ {success on last trial} is the intersection of independent events, by the assumption of independent trials. Hence, the Pascal distribution is

$$P_k(n, p) = P[\{k - 1 \text{ successes in } n - 1 \text{ trials}\} \cap \{\text{success on last trial}\}]$$

$$= P[k - 1 \text{ successes in } n - 1 \text{ trials}] \times P[\text{success on last trial}] \tag{2.1.22}$$

$$= B_{n-1}(k - 1, p) \times p = \binom{n - 1}{k - 1} p^k q^{n-k}, \quad k \le n < \infty$$

Note that the minimum value for the trial number, n, is k, because k successes cannot occur until k trials have taken place. The derivation is based on the binomial distribution, and the answer is almost identical with the binomial distribution.

Example 2.1.5:   Selecting potatoes
A shopper in a grocery store needs two potatoes to bake for dinner. He examines potatoes to make sure they are suitable for baking. Assume that the probability of finding an acceptable potato on a random choice is 0.45. What is the probability that he will have to examine more than three potatoes to buy two? Assume that the conditions of binomial trials are met.

Solution   Because this question asks for "more than three" we will work with the complement, three or less. Thus the problem requires the probability that he will find $k =$ two potatoes on either the $n = 2$ or $n = 3$ trials. In the notation of the Pascal distribution, the solution calls for

$$P_2(2, 0.45) + P_2(3, 0.45) = \binom{2 - 1}{2 - 1} 0.45^2 \times 0.55^{2-2} + \binom{3 - 1}{2 - 1} 0.45^2 \times 0.55^{3-2} \tag{2.1.23}$$

$$= 0.203 + 0.223 = 0.425.$$

The probability that he will have to examine more than three potatoes is therefore

$$P[\text{more than three}] = 1 - 0.425 = 0.575$$

You do it.   What is the probability of picking the second good potato on the fifth trial? Do the calculation, enter your answer in the cell box, and click Evaluate for a response.

```
myanswer =          ;
```

```
Evaluate
```

For the answer, see endnote 6.

Example 2.1.6:   Free throws
A basketball player who is a 70% free-throw shooter misses all five of his free throws in a game. The coach makes him shoot free throws during practice the next day until he hits a cumulative total of 100 free throws. What is the most probable number of free throws that he will have to shoot to hit 100?

Solution   This situation calls for the Pascal distribution for $k = 100$ and $p = 0.7$

$$P_{100}(n, 0.7) = \binom{n-1}{100-1} 0.7^{100} 0.3^{n-100} \text{ for } n \geq 100 \tag{2.1.24}$$

which is plotted in Fig. 2.1.4.

We asked the question, What is the most probable number of throws that he will have to shoot to hit 100? By taking the ratio of $P_k(n, p)$ to $P_k(n-1, p)$, as we did for the binomial distribution, we find that the integral part of $n = \frac{k-q}{p}$ is the most probable value of n for ending the sequence of trials. If $n = \frac{k-q}{p}$ is an integer, it and the next lower integer are equally probable. For our case, the sequence is most likely to end on $n = \frac{100-0.3}{0.7} = 142.4 \rightarrow 142$ trials.

Example 2.1.7:   Recruiting software engineers
A recruiter goes to a university to hire five software engineers. She hires as many EEs as she can and then fills up her quota with CS majors. She interviews only three EEs (they are in

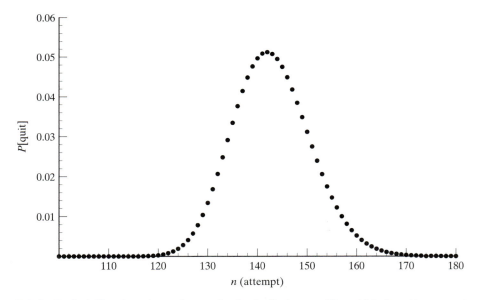

Figure 2.1.4   Probability that the unhappy basketball player will end his free-throw ordeal on the nth attempt. We begin with $n = 100$ because he cannot make 100 unless he shoots at least 100 times.

great demand so only three signed up for an interview) and a large number of CS majors. The probability that she can hire any EE major is 0.4, and the probability that a CS major will accept her offer is 0.7. She offers jobs to all the EEs, and after hearing from the EEs, offers jobs to CS majors until she fills her quota.

a. Find the probability that she hires two EEs and three CS majors.
b. Find the probability that she will have to make offers to more than four CS majors to hire three, as required in part a.
c. What is the probability that she will have to make offers to more than four CS majors generally?

Solution   The EE-hiring process is binomial, and the CS-hiring process is Pascal. The key to the problem is to realize that EEs $= 0, 1, 2$, and 3 partition the experiment. This is the binomial part. Furthermore, the required conditional probabilities are accessible. This is the Pascal part.

a. The probability of hiring two EEs and three CS majors reduces to the probability of hiring two EEs, since there is an unlimited pool of CS candidates to take the remaining three jobs. Thus we require $B_3(2, 0.4) = 0.2880$.
b. This is conditional, with the condition that she has hired two EEs. Thus we require the probability that she will have to make more than four offers to hire three CS majors, which is a Pascal probability. The probability of more than four is calculated as one minus the probability of four or less, which is four or three in this case. Thus the required probability is $1 - P_3(3, 0.7) - P_3(4, 0.7) = 1 - 0.343 - 0.3087 = 0.3483$.
c. The probability that more than four offers are required for CS majors we can work out using the law of total probability, with the partition identified earlier. In general,

$$P[> 4 \text{ CS interviews}] = P[> 4 \text{ CS interviews}|EE = 0] \times P[EE = 0]$$

$$+ P[> 4 \text{ CS interviews}|EE = 1] \times P[EE = 1]$$

$$+ P[> 4 \text{ CS interviews}|EE = 2] \times P[EE = 2]$$

$$+ P[> 4 \text{ CS interviews}|EE = 3] \times P[EE = 3]$$

Parts b and a give us the two components of the third term in the expansion. The first term corresponds to $B_3(0, 0.4)$, since the conditional probability is 1. The second and fourth are similar to the third. The second term is $(1 - P_4(4, 0.7)) \times B_3(1, 0.4)$, and the last term is $(1 - P_2(2, 0.7) - P_2(3, 0.7) - P_2(4, 0.7)) \times B_3(3, 0.4)$. The end result is $0.216 + 0.3283 + 0.1002 + 0.005357 = 0.6498$ when we sum the four terms.

Comparing the binomial and Pascal distributions.

The binomial and Pascal, including the geometric, distributions are based on the same experimental situation—independent Bernoulli trials with constant probability of success—and employ similar notation. We compare and contrast them in Table 2.1.1.

Table 2.1.1   Comparisons between binomial and Pascal distributions

Binomial	Pascal and geometric ($k = 1$)
binomial trials	binomial trials
2^n outcomes in sample space	an infinite number of outcomes in sample space
n fixed and k varies	k is fixed and n varies
order does not matter, only the total number of successes is considered	order does matter because a success must occur on the last trial
$0 \leq k \leq n$	$k \leq n \leq \infty$

The negative binomial distribution

The negative binomial distribution is closely related to the Pascal distribution. In fact, they are the same, except that for the negative binomial distribution the independent variable is the number of failures before the kth success. We may derive the negative binomial distribution from the Pascal distribution. If we let j be the number of failures before k successes, then the total number of trials will be $n = k + j$. Thus we may convert the Pascal distribution to the negative binomial distribution by replacing n by $k + j$, letting j be the independent variable. Thus the negative binomial distribution is

$$P[j \text{ failures before } k \text{ successes}] = \binom{k + j - 1}{k - 1} p^k q^j, \quad 0 \leq j \leq \infty \qquad (2.1.25)$$

Be warned that many authors consider the "negative binomial distribution" to mean the same as the Pascal distribution, although this is incorrect. When someone refers to this distribution, it pays to ask a few questions to make sure you know what they are talking about.

Example 2.1.8:   A learning-curve problem

In this example Bernoulli trials are not independent, and the probability changes between trials. By *learning curve* we mean decreasing the probability of failure and increasing the probability of success with each trial. The trials may or may not end with success. Let's say the probability of failure is 0.6 on the first trial but drops to half the previous value with each trial ($0.3, 0.15$, etc.) and that the trials end on the first success. Thus, $P[\text{success on second trial}|\text{failure on first trial}] = 0.7$, and so on. How many trials do we have to perform to have a 99% probability of success?

Solution   Let S_i indicate success on the ith trial. The probabilities given in the problem statement are conditional in the sense that the ith trial must take place, which entails failure on all previous trials. In this notation, the problem gives us $P[\overline{S}_1] = 0.6$, $P[\overline{S}_2|\overline{S}_1] = 0.3$, $P[\overline{S}_3|\overline{S}_1 \cap \overline{S}_2] = 0.15$, and so on. We now can compute the probability of success. On the first trial, this is 0.4. On the second it is $P[S_2] = (1 - 0.4) \times (1 - 0.3) = 0.42$, which is the probability of failure on the first trial times the probability of success on the second, given failure on the first. Thus success on the first or second trial is $0.4 + 0.42 = 0.82$. Subsequent trials follow the same pattern. On the third, we have a probability of success of $P[S_3] = (1 - 0.82)(1 - 0.15) = 0.153$. Adding that result to the first two trials, we have $0.4 + 0.42 + 0.153 = 0.973$. On the fourth trial the probability of success is $(1 - 0.973)(1 - 0.075) = 0.024975$, and the probability of succeeding on or before the fourth trial is 0.997975. So the answer to the question asked is, four trials.

Comment on this example.   Our observation is that many students think all problems have neat mathematical solutions, such that a step-by-step analysis is unnecessary. It may be true in the present case that some grand equation involving n, the number of trials, can be formed and solved. After approaching the problem by such means for a few minutes we went to the approach given. Trial-and-error analysis is in fact powerful and in many instances the only reasonable approach. Once a pattern is developed, the calculations proceed nicely.

Where we are in our study.   Currently we have derived several distributions: the uniform distribution, the binomial distribution, and the geometric and Pascal distributions. Each has its own unique assumptions and, to some degree, its own notation. The next section unifies these and other distributions through the concept of a random variable.

2.2 RANDOM VARIABLES

2.2.1 The Concept and Definition of a Random Variable

Review of the definition of a function

Ways to describe functions.   The function $x(s)$ means "You tell me s and I'll tell you x." An example is $x(s) = s^2$, $-\infty < s < +\infty$. We may express this function with a table relating s and x, or perhaps with a graph, as shown in Fig. 2.2.1.

```
Plot[s^2, {s, -2, +2}, AxesLabel → {"s-axis", "x-axis"}];
```

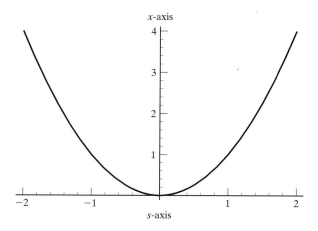

Figure 2.2.1   A graph is one way to express a function.

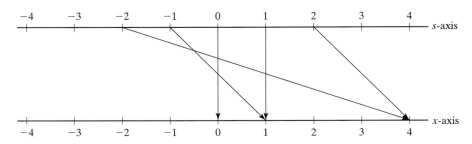

Figure 2.2.2   A function as a mapping of one set of points into another set of points.

Mapping.   A function can also be defined as a rule that maps one variable, s, into another, x. This function can be symbolized as $s \to x$, and pictured as in Fig. 2.2.2, where only a few integer values of s are mapped.

Domain and range.   The *domain* of a function is defined as the set of all values of s for which the function $x(s)$ is defined, in this case, $-\infty < s < +\infty$. The *range* of the function is the resulting set of values of x, in this case $0 \leq x < +\infty$. In the case of the parabola, the domain and range are both real numbers.

Random variables

Definition of a random variable.   When numbers are associated with the outcomes of a chance experiment, the result is said to be a *random variable*. Thus a random variable is a function with the sample space $S = \{s_1, s_2, \ldots, s_N\}$ as the domain, and a set of real numbers $X = \{X(s_1), X(s_2), \ldots, X(s_N)\}$ as the range. This mapping process is shown in Fig. 2.2.3.

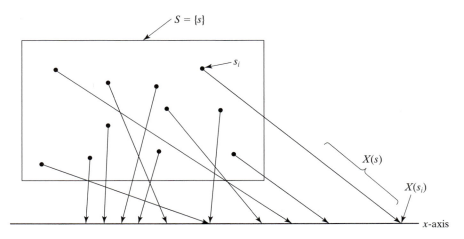

Figure 2.2.3   The random variable is a function that maps the sample space into numbers on the real axis.

Examples of random variables based on binomial trials. Let us say that we perform five binomial trials. Let the event A be associated with a success. The sample space looks like $S = \{AAAAA, \bar{A}AAAA, \ldots, \bar{A}\bar{A}\bar{A}\bar{A}\bar{A}\}$, 32 outcomes in all. Some possible random variables we might define are the following:

1. **The number of successes.** The random variable $X =$ number of successes is the quantity k described by the binomial distribution, $B_5(k, p)$. In deriving the binomial distribution we defined an event K containing all the outcomes with k successes, which is a way to express the same information without recourse to random variables. The range of X is $S_X = \{0, 1, 2, 3, 4, 5\}$.

2. **The trial on which the kth success occurs.** The random variable $X =$ trial for the kth success is the quantity n described by the Pascal distribution, $P_k(n, p)$, except that we must assign a value to X in the event that no kth success occurs. For example, we might define $X = 0$ for no kth success in the five trials. The range of X is $S_X = \{0, 1, 2, 3, 4, 5\}$.

3. **The number of failures subtracted from the number of successes.** This distribution we have not investigated, but it is easily treated. The range of X is $S_X = \{-5, -3, -1, +1, +3, +5\}$.

4. **Binary numbers.** Another possible random variable is $X =$ numerical value of the outcome considering A as 1 and $\bar{A}$ as 0 and interpreting the number in base 2. For example $AAAAA \to 11111_2 \to 31_{10}$. The range of X is $S_X = \{0, 1, 2, \ldots, 31\}$.

Examples of random variables based on picking a number at random. Pick a number at random between and including 0 and 5. Here the sample space is $S = \{0, 1, 2, 3, 4, 5\}$, six equally likely outcomes. Possible random variables might be the following:

1. The number of the outcome, $X(s) = s$. Here the range is $\{0, 1, 2, 3, 4, 5\}$, which is identical with the domain.

2. The function $X(s) = (s - 4)^2$. Here the range is $\{0, 1, 4, 9, 16\}$.

3. We can assign $X = +1$ for even outcomes and $X = -1$ for odd outcomes. Here the range is $\{-1, +1\}$.

Events in terms of random variables. We can define events in terms of a random variable, and these events are equivalent to events defined directly in S; hence, we can associate probability with random variables. Some examples follow of how events can be defined with random variables.

Example 2.2.1: Bernoulli trials

Considering the random variable $X =$ successes in five binomial trials, we note that $\{X = 3\}$ is the event in which three successes occur in the five trials, regardless of order. The probability of the event $\{X = 3\}$ is the value of $B_5(3, p)$, where p is the probability of success on a given trial. We note that $\{X = x\}$ is also an event, where x is an independent variable. This event is the impossible event except for $x = 0, 1, 2, 3, 4, 5$. For $x = 3$, $P[X = x] = B_5(3, p)$.

X **and** *x***?**   We must distinguish between $X(s)$, the random variable, and x, an independent, continuous mathematical variable ranging over the real line. For example, we set $x = 0$ and proceed as follows. We perform the experiment of 5 binomial trials. An outcome occurs. That outcome has 0, 1, 2, 3, 4, or 5 successes. The corresponding value of $X(s)$ is the number of successes, a random variable. If $X(s) = 0$, then the event $\{X(s) = x\}$ occurred since x was set to 0. If 1, 2, 3, 4, or 5 successes occurred, then the event $X(s) = x$ did not occur. For $x = 1.3$, the event $\{X = x\}$ never occurs.

Intervals   In similar fashion we can define events like $\{X(s) \le x\}$ and $\{x_1 < X(s) \le x_2\}$. On any given performance of the experiment (1) a value of s results, s_i; (2) there is a number $X(s_i)$ associated with s_i; (3) we can, for any prescribed value of x, determine if the event $\{X(s) \le x\}$ occurred; and (4) we can determine the probability of this event. Similarly, for specified values of x_1 and x_2 we can record if the event $\{x_1 < X(s) \le x_2\}$ occurred, and we can determine the probability of this event.

Although it appears that we are belaboring this distinction between X and x, our experience is that many students have trouble with this concept and notation. Once more, x is an independent variable that ranges from $-\infty$ to $+\infty$, and X is a number associated with the outcomes of a chance experiment. When we compare X with values or ranges of x, we have an event that has probability.

Benefits of introducing random variables.   Random variables offer many advantages in modeling random systems.

1. Numbers come up naturally in most practical and many theoretical problems. Usually we're interested in some sort of numerical information.
2. Random variables make all experiments alike. The concept introduces a common basis for describing random experiments.
3. Random variables allow us some distance from the chance experiment. In many situations the random variable can be easily identified and measured, whereas the chance experiment may be quite abstract and difficult to define.

2.2.2   Describing the Properties of Random Variables with Probability Mass Functions

Probability mass functions, PMFs

The definition of the PMF.   The *probability mass function,* PMF, is defined as

$$P_X(x) = P[X = x], \quad -\infty < x < +\infty \tag{2.2.1}$$

In words, the probability mass function is the probability that on a given performance of the chance experiment, the resulting random variable, $X(s)$, will be equal to an independent variable x, where all values of x are possible. The PMF, being a probability, is a pure number between 0 and 1, inclusive, having no units.

Notation.   The notation we will use for a PMF is

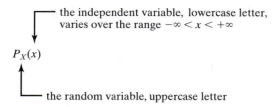

This notation is close enough to the notation we use for probabilities that we need to be clear about the differences. In Eq. (2.2.1) we note three differences. First, in the PMF, the P has a subscript, which is an uppercase letter identifying the random variable. In probabilities there are no subscripts. Second, the PMF has parentheses, like any mathematical function, whereas a probability has brackets, [ ]. Finally, the argument of a PMF is a mathematical variable like x, whereas the argument of a probability expression is an event like $X = x$; however, this last difference is not definitive, since we sometimes shorten the arguments of probabilities.

Probability distributions.   The PMF is a *distribution* in the sense that it tells how the probability distributes over the real numbers when the outcomes are mapped by $X(s)$. An example based on the binomial distribution is shown in Fig. 2.2.4. The random variable is $X(s) = k$, the number of successes in 10 trials with $p = 0.2$ on any trial.

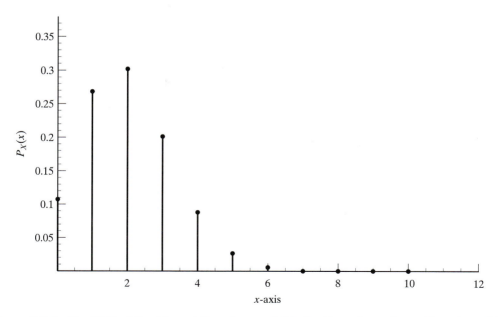

Figure 2.2.4   The PMF of the binomial random variable for the values of $n = 10$ and $p = 0.2$.

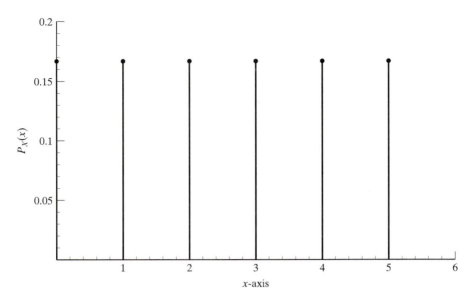

Figure 2.2.5   PMF for six equally likely integers.

Example 2.2.2:   Equally likely outcome _____

Choose an integer at random out of the set of integers, $S = \{0, 1, 2, 3, 4, 5\}$. These integers are the outcomes of the experiment. The random variable associated with them is the same value, $X(s) = s$. Plot the PMF.

Solution   The $N = 6$ equally likely outcomes have a probability of $\frac{1}{N} = \frac{1}{6}$ each. Thus $P_X(x) = \frac{1}{6}$, $x = 0, 1, 2, 3, 4, 5$, (zow[7]) (zero otherwise). The corresponding PMF is shown in Fig. 2.2.5.

The Bernoulli random variable

One simple but very useful random variable is the *Bernoulli random variable*. This is the random variable describing the results of one trial with probability p for success when we assign $X = 1$ for success and $X = 0$ for failure. Thus the PMF is $P_X(x) = q$ for $x = 0$ and $P_X(x) = p$ for $x = 1$, zero otherwise (zow). The PMF of the Bernoulli random variable is shown in Fig. 2.2.6.

2.2.3 Properties of PMFs

The PMF is a probability.   Because a PMF is a probability, it must lie between 0 and 1, inclusive: $0 \le P_X(x) \le 1$ for all x.

PMFs can express probabilities of complex events.   The events in the sample space associated with all values of x are disjoint, because every outcome maps uniquely to some value of x. Thus a partition of the space results, and we may add probabilities. The probability of

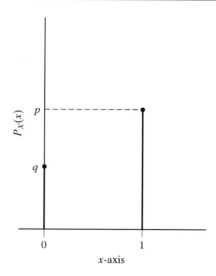

Figure 2.2.6   The Bernoulli random variable is either 0 or 1, with probabilities q or p, respectively.

any event containing certain values of $X(s)$ is therefore given by the sum of the PMF over the independent variable, x, associated with those values. For the example in which an integer is picked at random between 0 and 5, inclusive, the probability of the event $\{1.5 < X(s) < 4.6\}$ includes the outcomes associated with $X(s) = 2$, $X(s) = 3$, and $X(s) = 4$. Therefore, the probability of the event $\{1.5 < X(s) < 4.6\}$ is

$$P[1.5 < X(s) < 4.6] = P_X(2) + P_X(3) + P_X(4) = \frac{3}{6} \tag{2.2.2}$$

Normalization.   Because the event $-\infty < X(s) < +\infty$ is the certain event, it follows that the PMF must sum to 1:

$$\sum_{\text{all } x_i} P_X(x) = 1 \tag{2.2.3}$$

This is clearly true for the uniformly distributed random variable, and we know that the binomial random variable is likewise normalized:

$$\sum_{\text{all } x_i} P_X(x) = \sum_{x=0}^{x=n} B_n(x, p) = 1 \tag{2.2.4}$$

2.2.4 Transforming Random Variables

Functions of random variables.   Assume we have an experiment with a random variable $X(s)$ defined on the outcomes. We know how the probabilities distribute to the outcomes and so

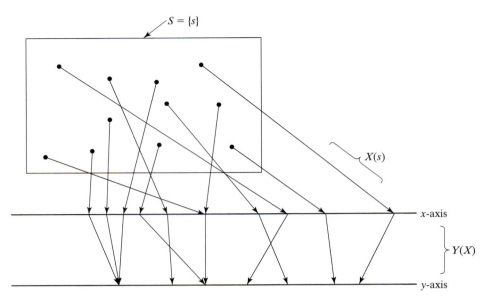

Figure 2.2.7   Mapping from the sample space to one random variable, *X*, and then from the first to a second random variable, *Y*.

we can determine how the probabilities distribute to the various values of the random variable. This information is given by the probability mass function, $P_X(x)$. If we define a second random variable in terms of the first, $Y(X)$, we can determine how the probabilities distribute to the second random variable also. Such a double mapping is shown in Fig. 2.2.7.

Finding the PMF of Y.   How the probabilities distribute to the random variable Y is given by its PMF, $P_Y(y)$. Because the two random variables are related through a mathematical function, the probabilities of X can be mapped into the range of Y, as illustrated in the following example.

Example 2.2.3:   Picking a resistor at random
The basic experiment is to select a resistor from a large bin containing resistors having the values $S = \{50\ \Omega, 60\ \Omega, 70\ \Omega, 80\ \Omega, 90\ \Omega, 100\ \Omega\}$, all equally likely except for the 50-Ω resistors, which are twice as likely as any others because there are twice as many 50-Ω resistors in the bin as each of the others. The resistor selected is connected to a 10-V battery. Find the PMF of the power to the resistor.

Solution   The first random variable is $R(s)$, the value of the resistance. The second random variable is the power, W, where

$$W(R) = \frac{10^2}{R} \qquad\qquad (2.2.5)$$

which is a function of the first random variable.

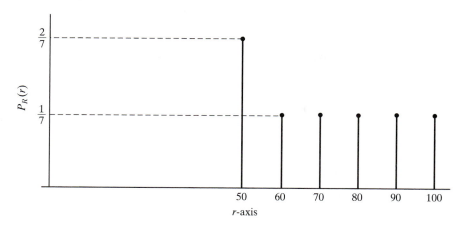

Figure 2.2.8 The PMF of the resistors.

The PMF of R. First, we must determine the PMF of the random variable R. The result is shown in Fig. 2.2.8. We have made the probability of 50 Ω twice the others and normalized to a total probability of 1. This experiment is closely related to the equally likely model. All resistors are equally likely to be chosen, but all values of resistance are not equally likely because there are twice as many 50-Ω resistors as there are resistors of all the other values.

The PMF of W. Because there are six possible values of R, there will be six corresponding values of $W(R) = \frac{10^2}{R}$. The mapping of the R values into the $W(R)$ values is shown in Fig. 2.2.9.

The range of the random variable representing the power is $S_W = \{1.00, 1.11, 1.25, 1.43, 1.67, 2.00\}$. Because $P_R(50) = \frac{2}{7}$, it follows that $P_W(2.00) = \frac{2}{7}$, and similarly for the other pairs. The PMF of the power must therefore be that shown in Fig. 2.2.10.

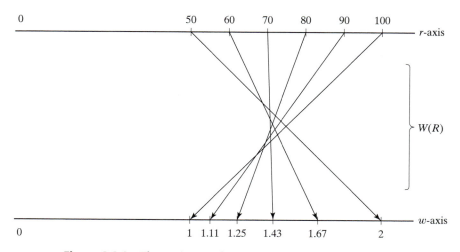

Figure 2.2.9 The resistor values map into the power values.

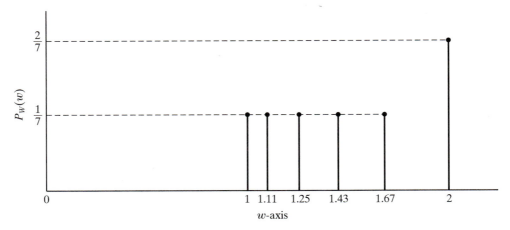

Figure 2.2.10 The PMF of the power in the resistor.

You do it. What if all the resistance values were equally likely? What would be $P_W(1.43)$ in that case? Give your answer to at least three decimal places (or a fraction), and click Evaluate for a response.

```
myanswer =            ;
```

```
Evaluate
```

For the answer, see endnote 8.

Using the PMF of W. From the PMF of W we can find the probability that the power falls in certain regions by summing the PMF over the region of interest, as illustrated in the next example.

Example 2.2.4: Power less than 1.5 Watts _____

Find the probability that the power in the resistor is less than 1.5 watts.

Solution   We may find the probability of the event $W(R) < 1.5$ in two ways:

1. In terms of the PMF of W, it is

$$P[W < 1.5] = \sum_{w_i < 1.5} P_W(w) = P_W(1.00) + P_W(1.11) + P_W(1.25) + P_W(1.43) = \frac{4}{7}$$

(2.2.6)

2. We can also express the event of interest in terms of R, for the event $\{W(R) < 1.5 \text{ W}\}$ maps into the event $\{100/1.5 < R\}$, as shown in Fig. 2.2.11.

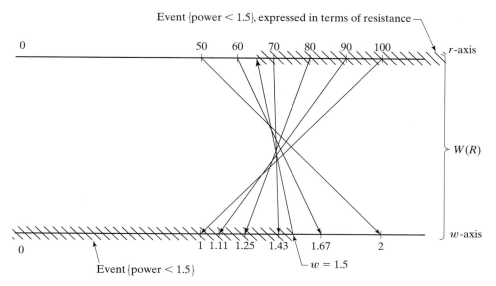

Figure 2.2.11 An event in *W*-space maps into an event in *R*-space.

In terms of R, we can find the probability that the power is less than 1.5 watts by summing

$$P[W < 1.5] = \sum_{\frac{100}{r_i} < 1.5} P_R(r) = P_R(70) + P_R(80) + P_R(90) + P_R(100) = \frac{4}{7} \qquad (2.2.7)$$

You do it.   Consider that the probability of the resistance is proportional to the resistance value. Find the probability that the power is greater than 1.6 watts. Calculate your answer to four places, enter it in the cell box and click Evaluate for a response.

```
myanswer =            ;
```

```
Evaluate
```

For the answer, see endnote 9.

2.2.5 Conditional PMFs

Conditional probabilities are an important analysis tool. Because the definition of a conditional PMF is related to the definition of conditional probabilities generally, we begin with a review of this definition.

Review of conditional probabilities. We recall that the probability of A conditioned on B is defined as

$$P[A|B] = \frac{P[A \cap B]}{P[B]}, \; P[B] \neq 0 \tag{2.2.8}$$

which leads directly to

$$P[A \cap B] = P[A|B] \times P[B] \tag{2.2.9}$$

Conditional probability is a useful analysis tool because it often allows one to analyze a complicated situation in terms of simpler situations.

Definition of a conditional PMF. The conditional PMF of a random variable conditional on event B is

$$P_{X|B}(x) = P[X = x|B] = \frac{P[X = x \cap B]}{P[B]} \tag{2.2.10}$$

For random variables. In the context of random variables, the concept of conditional probability leads to a conditional probability mass function. We can have two types of conditioning events, those defined on the original experiment and those defined in terms of the random variable. As an example of a condition defined on the original experiment, consider the following example.

Example 2.2.5: Conditional PMF for odd outcomes
Pick a number at random between 0 and 5 inclusive. Define a random variable as $X(s) = (s - 4)^2$. Find the conditional PMF $P_{X|O}(x)$, where O is the event $\{s = \text{odd}\}$.

Solution The sample space is $S = \{0, 1, 2, 3, 4, 5\}$, six outcomes, all equally likely. The range of the random variable is $S_X = \{0, 1, 4, 9, 16\}$. The PMF for this random variable is not equally likely because two of the equally likely outcomes, 3 and 5, lead to $X(s) = 1$. The unconditioned PMF is given in Fig. 2.2.12.

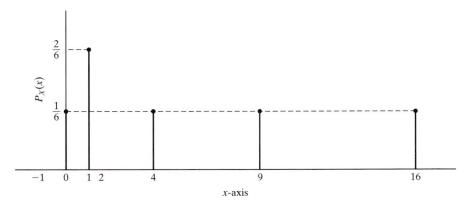

Figure 2.2.12 The unconditioned PMF of X.

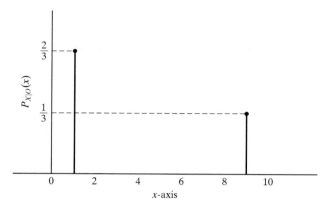

Figure 2.2.13   Conditional PMF for odd outcomes.

We now consider the conditioning event $O = \{s = \text{odd}\}$. The conditional PMF is defined as

$$P_{X|O}(x) = P[(X = x)|(s = \text{odd})] = \frac{P[(X = x) \cap (s = \text{odd})]}{P[s = \text{odd}]} = \frac{P[(X = x) \cap (s = \text{odd})]}{1/2}$$

(2.2.11)

since half the outcomes are odd. The numerator in Eq. (2.2.11) will have a nonzero value only for those values of the random variable related to odd outcomes. For $s = 1$, $X(s) = 9$; for $s = 3$, $X(s) = 1$; and for $s = 5$, $X(s) = 1$ again, so $x = 1$ and 9 are the only values for which $P_{X|O}(x)$ is nonzero. The unconditioned probability that $X(s) = 1$ will be $\frac{2}{6}$, because two of the six equally likely outcomes yield this value; hence, $P_{X|O}(1) = \frac{2/6}{1/2} = \frac{2}{3}$. Similarly, $P_{X|O}(9) = \frac{1/6}{1/2} = \frac{1}{3}$. The conditional PMF is shown in Fig. 2.2.13.

You do it.   Find $P_{X|E}(0)$, where E is the event of an even outcome. Enter your answer to at least four places in the cell box, and click Evaluate for a response.

myanswer =   ;

Evaluate

For the answer, see endnote 10.

Condition in X.   Often the condition in a conditional PMF is expressed in terms of the random variable, not the original experiment, as shown in the following example.

Example 2.2.6:   Condition in X
Find the conditional PMF with the condition $X \leq 5$, $P_{X|X \leq 5}(x)$, where X is the random variable in Example 2.2.5.

Solution   By definition

$$P_{X|X\leq 5}(x) = P[X = x | X \leq 5] = \frac{P[X = x \cap X \leq 5]}{P[X \leq 5]} \tag{2.2.12}$$

Examination of the unconditioned PMF shows that the numerator will be nonzero at $x = 0, 1$, and 4. The denominator in Eq. (2.2.12) is

$$P_X(0) + P_X(1) + P_X(4) = \frac{1}{6} + \frac{2}{6} + \frac{1}{6} = \frac{2}{3} \tag{2.2.13}$$

Consider $x = 0$. For this value of x we have

$$P_{X|X\leq 5}(0) = \frac{P[X = 0 \cap X \leq 5]}{2/3} = \frac{1/6}{2/3} = \frac{1}{4} \tag{2.2.14}$$

Note that the probability value in the numerator comes solely from the $X = x$ part. The $X \leq 5$ part in the numerator merely defines the values for which the conditional PMF has nonzero values. We can handle $x = 1$ and $x = 4$ similarly. The resulting conditional PMF is shown in Fig. 2.2.14

   You do it.   Determine the conditional PMF value $P_{X|X\geq 5}(9)$, enter your answer in the cell box, and click Evaluate for a response.

```
myanswer = ?               ;
```

```
Evaluate
```

For the answer, see endnote 11.

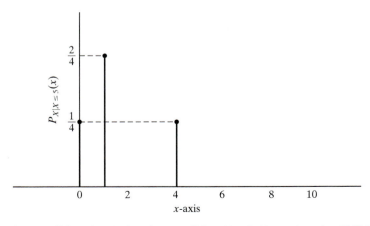

Figure 2.2.14   The conditional PMF for the condition $X \leq 5$. Note that the PMF is properly normalized.

Use of conditional PMFs.   Conditional PMFs arise naturally in many situations. As with conditional probability generally, conditional PMFs allow one to analyze a complicated situation in terms of several simpler situations, as in the following example.

Example 2.2.7:   Defects in manufacture _____

Consider two suppliers of parts, the Excello Corporation and its competitor Mediocre and Sons. Excello has a probability of a bad part of $p_E = 0.01$, and Mediocre has $p_M = 0.02$. There are 100 parts in a box. Find the conditional PMFs $P_{X|E}(x)$ and $P_{X|M}(x)$, where X is a random variable representing the number of bad parts in a box, $E = \{\text{manufactured by Excello}\}$, and $M = \{\text{manufactured by Mediocre and Sons}\}$.

Solution   The experiment is to select a box of parts and to determine the conditional PMF of the number of bad parts in the box for each company. The random variable of interest is the number of bad parts in a box. Conditioning events are M and E. To get the conditional PMF, we select a box and examine it only if the parts were manufactured by the required company. We assume binomial trials (see p. 87) for the number of bad parts. This means that all boxes from each manufacturer are statistically alike, and the probability of getting a bad part is fixed, independent of the other parts in the box.

The PMF, conditioned on E, is $P_{X|E}(x) = B_{100}(x, 0.01)$, and similarly $P_{X|M}(x) = B_{100}(x, 0.02)$, where $x = 0, 1, 2, \ldots, 100$, zow. The function $B_n(x, p)$ is the binomial distribution for x successes (bad parts) in n trials, with a probability of p for a bad part on any trial. Having determined the conditional PMFs, we now use them in the following example.

Example 2.2.8:   Picking a box at random _____

We buy 60% of our parts from Excello and 40% from Mediocre. What is the unconditional PMF for $X =$ the number of bad parts in a box chosen at random?

Solution   Because we buy all our parts from either Excello or Mediocre, these events partition the sample space. The conditional PMFs are simply probabilities, so we can use the usual rules for conditional probability, including the law of total probability, Eq. (1.5.7).

$$P_X(x) = P_{X|E}(x) \times P[E] + P_{X|M}(x) \times P[M] = B_{100}(x, 0.01) \times 0.6 + B_{100}(x, 0.02) \times 0.4$$
$$(2.2.15)$$

For example, the value of $P_X(0)$, which is the probability of selecting at random a box with no bad parts, is $P_X(0) = \binom{100}{0}0.01^0 0.99^{100} \times 0.6 + \binom{100}{0}0.02^0 0.98^{100} \times 0.4 = 0.273$

You do it.   Say you pick a box at random, test a part, and find it good. Using Bayes' rule, calculate the probability that it came from Mediocre? Calculate your answer to at least three place accuracy, enter it in the cell box, and click Evaluate for a response.

```
myanswer =          ;
```

```
Evaluate
```

For the answer, see endnote 12.

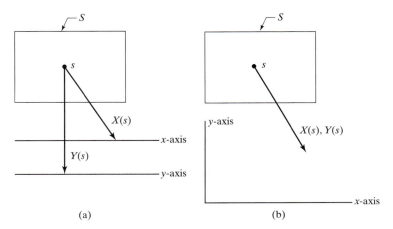

(a)   (b)

Figure 2.2.15   Two ways to view bivariate random variables. (a) Shows a logical extension of the picture for one random variable. (b) Shows mapping into the Cartesian plane, which is generally more useful.

2.2.6 Bivariate and Multivariate Random Variables

Two random variables.   *Multivariate* means having more than one random variable associated with each outcome in an experiment. *Bivariate* means having two random variables. In this section we investigate the bivariate case in detail and point toward a generalization to a larger number of random variables. One way to view the bivariate case, where $X(s)$ and $Y(s)$ are the random variables, is shown in Fig. 2.2.15(a). Here we present the two random variables as parallel real axes. A more common way to view the bivariate case is to consider that the sample space, S, is mapped into the x,y plane, as shown in Fig. 2.2.15(b).

Examples.   The following are three examples of experiments with bivariate random variables defined:

1. Pick a number at random between 0 and 5, inclusive. Let $X(s) = s$, the number picked. Let $Y(s) = (s - 4)^2$. We will consider this situation in Example 2.2.9.
2. Do n binomial trials. $S = \{2^n \text{ outcomes}\}$. Let $X =$ the trial number of the first success, with $X = 0$ for no success in n trials, and $Y =$ the total number of successes.
3. Pick at random an integer in the range $\{1, 2, 3, 4, 5, 6\}$. Call the integer N. Then flip a fair coin N times, with K the number of successes. We will examine this situation in "you do it" following Example 2.2.10.

PMFs for bivariate random variables

We may describe how the probabilities of the experiment map into the x,y plane by the *bivariate PMF*, which is defined as follows:

$$P_{XY}(x, y) = P[(X = x) \cap (Y = y)]$$ (2.2.16)

Properties of the PMF.   The bivariate PMF, also called the *joint PMF,* has the following properties.

1. $P_{XY}(x, y)$ is a pure number with no units because it is a probability.
2. $0 \leq P_{XY}(x, y) \leq 1$, like all probabilities.
3. $\sum\limits_{\text{all } x,y} P_{XY}(x, y) = 1$ because this represents the certain event. The only values of x and y used in the summation are those discrete values where the joint PMF is nonzero.
4. Events correspond to areas in the x,y plane. The probability that event A occurs on a performance of the chance experiment is given by the sum of the bivariate PMF over all values that fall in that area. This probability can be represented by the equation

$$P[A] = \sum_{x_i, y_j \in A} P_{XY}(x, y) \tag{2.2.17}$$

5. If X and Y are considered single random variables, and the relationship between them is not under consideration, their independent distributions are called their *marginal* distributions in the bivariate context. These marginal distributions, $P_X(x)$ and $P_Y(y)$, can be derived from the bivariate PMF. Because, for example, $-\infty < Y < +\infty$ is the certain event, it follows that

$$P[(X = x) \cap (-\infty < Y < +\infty)] = P_X(x) = \sum_{\text{all } y_j} P_{XY}(x, y) \tag{2.2.18}$$

and similarly to find the marginal distribution of Y, $P_Y(y)$.
6. For independent random variables, the bivariate PMF factors into the product of the marginal PMFs, as seen from the definition

$$P_{XY}(x, y) = P[(X = x) \cap (Y = y)] = P[X = x] \times P[Y = y] = P_X(x) \times P_Y(y) \tag{2.2.19}$$

7. Conditional bivariate PMFs can also be defined. For example, the conditional PMF of $X|Y$ would be defined as

$$P_{X|Y}(x, y) = P[X = x|Y = y] = \frac{P[(X = x) \cap (Y = y)]}{P[Y = y]} = \frac{P_{XY}(x, y)}{P_Y(y)} \tag{2.2.20}$$

We now illustrate these definitions and their use in a series of examples.

Example 2.2.9:   Picking a number _____
Pick a number at random between 0 and 5, inclusive. Let $X(s) = s$, the number picked, and $Y(s) = (s - 4)^2$. The range in X is $S_X = \{0, 1, 2, 3, 4, 5\}$, and the range in Y is $S_Y = \{0, 1, 4, 9, 16\}$. The joint PMF is defined as $P_{XY}(x, y) = P[X = x \cap Y = y]$ and is nonzero only at those values of x and y given in the ranges, and then nonzero for only certain combinations of the numbers in the ranges. For example, for $x = 0$, the only value of y for nonzero probability is $y = 16$, and here the PMF is

$$P_{XY}(0, 16) = \frac{1}{6} \tag{2.2.21}$$

since the values $X = 0$ and $Y = 16$ are associated with $s_i = 0$, which has a probability of $\frac{1}{6}$.

A tabular representation. Because there is a unique relationship between X and Y, we can represent the PMF with Table 2.2.1.

In Table 2.2.1, we can see, in a crude way, the shape of the parabola relating X and Y. We can see the parabola even better in the three-dimensional graphical representation of the PMF in Fig. 2.2.16.

Table 2.2.1 A bivariate PMF

$y\backslash x$	0	1	2	3	4	5
0	0	0	0	0	$\frac{1}{6}$	0
1	0	0	0	$\frac{1}{6}$	0	$\frac{1}{6}$
4	0	0	$\frac{1}{6}$	0	0	0
9	0	$\frac{1}{6}$	0	0	0	0
16	$\frac{1}{6}$	0	0	0	0	0

Marginal PMFs. We can also see the marginal distributions on X and Y by summing the rows or columns in Table 2.2.1. If we sum the columns, we get $\frac{1}{6}$ for each, indicating that X has equal probability for values $X = \{0, 1, 2, 3, 4, 5\}$. When we sum the rows, we get $\frac{1}{6}$

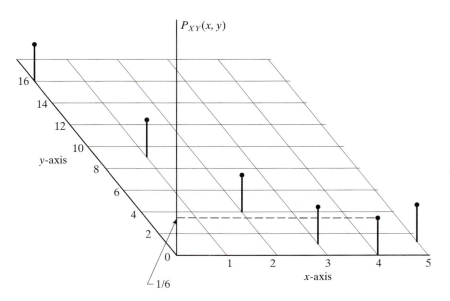

Figure 2.2.16 Joint PMF described by Table 2.2.1. Here the parabolic relationship between the X and Y random variables is evident.

at every point in the range of y except for $y = 1$, where we get $\frac{2}{6}$. This is the distribution shown in Fig. 2.2.12, which we derived earlier in this section, except that we referred to Y as X earlier.

Conditional PMFs.   We may determine conditional PMFs from Eq. (2.2.20). For example,

$$P_{Y|X=0}(y = 16) = \frac{P_{xy}(0, 16)}{P_X(0)} = \frac{1/6}{1/6} = 1 \tag{2.2.22}$$

which means that if X is 0, then Y must be 16.

Example 2.2.10:   Joint PMF based on binomial trials $\rule{5cm}{0.4pt}$
We perform n binomial trials. The sample space contains $S = \{2^n \text{ outcomes}\}$, such as $AAAA\bar{A}$ for $n = 5$. Let $X = $ the trial number of the first success, with $X = 0$ if no success occurs and $Y = $ the total number of successes. We will find the bivariate PMF. The range is between 0 and n in both X and Y. We may derive the PMF by using conditional probability:

$$P_{XY}(x, y) = P[(X = x) \cap (Y = y)] = P[Y = y|X = x] \times P_X(x) \tag{2.2.23}$$

The last, unconditional probability in Eq. (2.2.23) is merely the Pascal distribution (Sec. 2.1.4) for the first occurrence, which is also called the geometric distribution (Sec. 2.1.3), except we have a special case for $x = 0$. The conditional probability in Eq. (2.2.23) is the number of successes, given that the first success occurs on the xth trial. This means that we know that the first $x - 1$ trials were failures, and the xth was a success. Because we are assuming binomial trials (see p. 87), we know the distribution of the number of successes on the last $n - x$ trials to be binomial. Thus the required conditional probability is $B_{n-x}(y - 1, p)$, since there are $n - x$ remaining trials and $y - 1$ remaining successes. It follows that the required PMF is

$$P_{XY}(x, y) = B_{n-x}(y - 1, p) \times P_1(x, p)$$

$$= \binom{n - x}{y - 1} p^y q^{n-y}, \ 1 < x < n, \ 1 < y < n - x + 1, \ \text{zow} \tag{2.2.24}$$

A special case is that no success ever occurs. Here the value would be

$$P_{XY}(0, 0) = q^{-n}, \ P_{XY}(0, y) = 0, \ y = 1, 2, \ldots, n \tag{2.2.25}$$

since this is the probability of no successes. As always, $q = 1 - p$.

You do it.   The following is a nontrivial example for you to work out. (a) We pick at random a number, N, in the range $\{1, 2, 3, 4, 5, 6\}$. Then we flip a fair coin N times, with K the number of successes. Thus we have two random variables, N and K. The first question is, How many points in n, k space have probability associated with them? *Hint:* Draw a picture. Test your answer in the cell box.

```
myanswer =           ;
```

```
Evaluate
```

For the answer, see endnote 13.

(b) The next step is to work out the joint PMF, $P_{NK}(n, k)$. Start with the conditional probability $P[K = k|N = n]$. This will be (pick one) (a) binomial, (b) geometric, (c) Pascal. Enter a, b, or c in the cell box, and click Evaluate for a response.

```
myanswer = "?"      ;
```

```
Evaluate
```

For the answer, see endnote 14.

The condition $N = n$ fixes n, and we are looking for the number of successes. Does that sound familiar? Considering now the PMF of N, derive your formula for $P_{NK}(n, k)$, then compare your values with the bivariate PMF listed in Table 2.2.2, or see endnote 15.

Table 2.2.2   PMF for the $N-K$ bivariate random variables. The values of n run left to right from 1 to 6, and the values of k run top to bottom from 0 to 6

$\frac{1}{12}$	$\frac{1}{24}$	$\frac{1}{48}$	$\frac{1}{96}$	$\frac{1}{192}$	$\frac{1}{384}$
$\frac{1}{12}$	$\frac{1}{12}$	$\frac{1}{16}$	$\frac{1}{24}$	$\frac{5}{192}$	$\frac{1}{64}$
0	$\frac{1}{24}$	$\frac{1}{16}$	$\frac{1}{16}$	$\frac{5}{96}$	$\frac{5}{128}$
0	0	$\frac{1}{48}$	$\frac{1}{24}$	$\frac{5}{96}$	$\frac{5}{96}$
0	0	0	$\frac{1}{96}$	$\frac{5}{192}$	$\frac{5}{128}$
0	0	0	0	$\frac{1}{192}$	$\frac{1}{64}$
0	0	0	0	0	$\frac{1}{384}$

Marginal PMFs.   If we sum vertically to get the marginal PMF for N, we get $\frac{1}{6}$ in each column. Finding the marginal PMF in K requires that we sum in n with k constant. We show the output here and a plot in Fig. 2.2.17.

```
{{0, 0.164063}, {1, 0.3125},
  {2, 0.257813}, {3, 0.166667}, {4, 0.0755208},
  {5, 0.0208333}, {6, 0.00260417}}
```

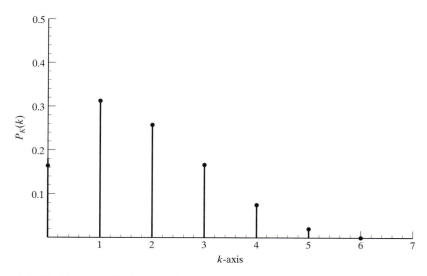

Figure 2.2.17   The marginal PMF of K, obtained by summing the rows in Table 2.2.2.

The multivariate case.   Adding additional random variables makes visualization more difficult but adds no new mathematical concepts. With three or more random variables, we simply have higher-dimensional spaces in which to express the probabilities. In the next section, we give an example of multivariate random variables.

Summary.   In this section on bivariate discrete random variables we defined the joint PMF and presented some of its properties, including marginal and conditional PMFs. Several examples illustrated the definitions.

2.3 THE MEANING AND ALGEBRA OF EXPECTATION

Real and model.   Let us review our progress in modeling random systems, adding the contribution from the last section (data and random variables) and anticipating the contribution of this section (averages and expectation).

Table 2.3.1   Progress in modeling random systems

Real	Model
a random system	chance experiment
relative frequency, $\frac{n_A}{n}$	probability, $P[A]$
math of relative frequencies	rules of probability
knowledge of causality	rule on independence
data	random variables
averages of data	expectation

2.3.1 Averages of Random Variables

What is an average?

Simple averages. In this section we consider simple averages of random variables result-ing from repeated performance of a random experiment. Everyone knows how to take a simple average; for example, the average of 5, 2, 8, and 8 is

$$\text{average} = \frac{5 + 2 + 8 + 8}{4} = 5.75 \tag{2.3.1}$$

In general,

$$x_{\text{average}} = \frac{1}{n} \sum_{1}^{n} x_i \tag{2.3.2}$$

where $n =$ the number of data values and $x_i = i$th data value.

Averages of random variables. Consider a chance experiment with a random variable, X, defined on its outcomes. Let us repeat the experiment n times and call $x(1)$ the value of X resulting from the first performance, $x(2)$ the value resulting from the second, and so forth. The simple average of these numbers is

$$x_{\text{average}} = \frac{1}{n}[x(1) + x(2) + \cdots + x(n)] \tag{2.3.3}$$

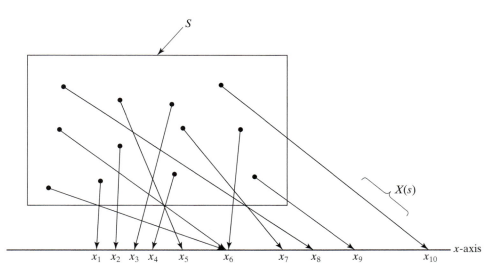

Figure 2.3.1   We number the possible values of the random variable in rank order. Here N is 10.

Rearranging the numbers. Consider that we number the possible values in the range of the random variable in increasing numerical order as $x_1, x_2, \cdots, x_N$, where there are N possible values for the random variable. Note that n is the number of data points we have, whereas N is the number of discrete values the random variable X can take, which is a totally different concept. For example, if X were a Bernoulli random variable (Fig. 2.2.6), its possible values would be 0 and 1, so $N = 2$ (see Sec. 2.2.2 and Fig. 2.2.6). But we might take $n = 1000$ values of the random variable by repeating the experiment 1000 times. The value of N might correspond to each of the outcomes of the experiment, but if more than one outcome mapped into the same value of the random variable, N would be less than the number of outcomes. Figure 2.3.1 shows this numbering scheme.

Distinguishing x_i from $x(i)$.   In Eq. (2.3.3) the values of $x(i), i = 1, 2, \ldots, n$ are arranged in sequence of occurrence. In Fig. 2.3.1 we have shown, in order of increasing numerical value, all the possible values, $x_i, i = 1, 2, \ldots, N$ that can occur in the formula for the average. An alternative approach for computing the average is to tally how many times each value of the random variable comes up in the data. Such a tally would look like the data in Table 2.3.2.

Table 2.3.2 A tally of the values of the random variable resulting from repeated experiments.

Result	Times occurring
x_1	n_1
x_2	n_2
x_3	n_3
$\vdots$	

We can thus rearrange the sequential listing of random variables in Eq. (2.3.3) as

$$
\begin{aligned}
x_{\text{average}} &= \frac{1}{n}(x_1 \times n_1 + x_2 \times n_2 + x_3 \times n_3 + \cdots + x_N \times n_N) \\
&= x_1 \times \frac{n_1}{n} + x_2 \times \frac{n_2}{n} + x_3 \times \frac{n_3}{n} + \cdots + x_N \times \frac{n_N}{n} = \sum x_i \times \left(\frac{n_i}{n}\right)
\end{aligned}
\tag{2.3.4}
$$

where n_1 is the number of times that x_1 comes up in the process, and so forth. Thus we see in Eq. (2.3.4) that we can express the average in terms of the possible values of the random variable times the *relative frequencies* of occurrence of each value. This leads naturally to a model for averaging in terms of probability.

2.3.2 The Definition of the Expectation, $E[X]$

A probability model for a simple average.   Because our model for a relative frequency is probability, we may model Eq. (2.3.4) using probability as

$$
E[X] = \sum_{\text{all } x_i} x P[X = x] = \sum_{\text{all } x_i} x P_X(x)
\tag{2.3.5}
$$

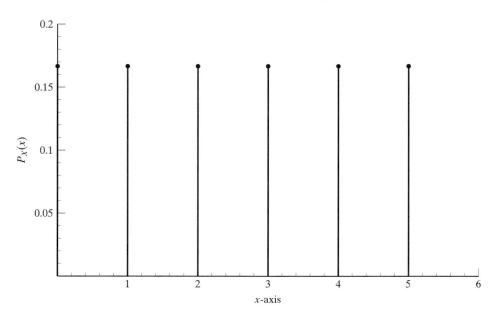

Figure 2.3.2   The PMF of a uniformly distributed random variable of the integers between 0 and 5, inclusive.

where $E[X]$ is called *the expectation of the random variable X* and is a mathematical model for the simple average. Another name for the expectation of X is *the mean of X*. We see that the expectation is the weighted sum of all values of the random variable that can occur, and the weighting factor is the probability that value will occur.

Example 2.3.1:   Uniform PMF
Pick a number at random between 0 and 5, inclusive. Let a random variable be the value of the random number. Find the expectation of the random variable.

Solution   The space is $S = \{0, 1, 2, 3, 4, 5\}$. The random variable is $X(s) = s$, the numerical value of the outcome. The PMF of X is shown in Fig. 2.3.2.

The expectation of X is calculated using Eq. (2.3.5):

$$E[X] = \sum_{\text{all } x_i} x P_X(x) = 0 \times \frac{1}{6} + 1 \times \frac{1}{6} + 2 \times \frac{1}{6} + 3 \times \frac{1}{6} + 4 \times \frac{1}{6} + 5 \times \frac{1}{6} = 2.5 \qquad (2.3.6)$$

We note that Eq. (2.3.6) gives the center of the values of the random variable in Fig. 2.3.2 and is a reasonable result for a model of the average. Another name for the expectation is the *first moment* or even the *center of mass*, considering the probabilities as "mass," as in probability mass function, PMF.

You do it. Find the expectation of the Bernoulli random variable (Fig. 2.2.6). Enter your answer in the cell box, and click Evaluate for a response.

```
myanswer = "?";
```

```
Evaluate
```

For the answer, see endnote 16.

The expectation of the binomial distribution. As a more challenging example, we will determine the expectation of the binomial random variable. Consider a sequence of binomial trials with $p =$ probability of success, and define a random variable $K =$ the number of successes in n trials. Thus K is the binomial random variable, and the PMF for K will be $P_K(k) = B_n(k, p)$. We now determine $E[K]$, the expectation of the binomial random variable K.

The expectation is defined in Eq. (2.3.5) and is applied in Eq. (2.3.7):

$$E[K] = \sum_{k=0}^{k=n} k B_n(k, p) = \sum_{k=0}^{k=n} k \times \frac{n!}{(n-k)!k!} p^k q^{n-k} \tag{2.3.7}$$

where $q = 1 - p$. Because the $k = 0$ term is zero, we can change the lower limit of the sum to $k = 1$. Canceling the k in numerator and denominator and factoring an np out of the sum, we have

$$E[K] = np \sum_{k=1}^{k=n} \frac{n-1!}{(n-k)!(k-1)!} p^{k-1} q^{n-k} \tag{2.3.8}$$

But $n - k = (n-1) - (k-1)$, and also, we can change summation variables from k to $k' = k - 1$. With this change Eq. (2.3.8) becomes

$$E[K] = np \sum_{k'=0}^{k'=n-1} \frac{n-1!}{(n-1-k')!(k')!} p^{k'} q^{n-1-k'} = np \sum_{k'=0}^{k'=n-1} B_{n-1}(k', p) \tag{2.3.9}$$

but the sum now is simply the sum of the binomial distribution for k' successes out of $n - 1$ trials, which must sum to unity. Thus we have proved that

$$E[K] = np \tag{2.3.10}$$

Discussion of Eq. (2.3.10). For $n = 100$ trials and $p = 0.3$, the expectation of the number of successes is $E[K] = np = 100 \times 0.3 = 30$. Recalling that expectation is a model for averaging, we interpret this result as follows: We have an event with probability 0.3. That means it happens about 30% of the time when the chance experiment is performed. We then perform the experiment of 100 trials and note the number of times the event occurs. We expect the number of successes to be about 30, but it could be any number between 0 and 100. This is one "performance" of the binomial-trials experiment. We then repeat the 100-trial experiment again and again and get lots of data for the occurrence of the event. The average of all these data should be near 30, according to the preceding calculated result. If we could perform the experiment an infinite number of times, the average of all the successes obtained on each trial would be exactly 30, according to Eq. (2.3.10).

2.3.3 Expectation of Functions of a Random Variable

The defining situation revisited. Consider again that we have a repeatable experiment with a random variable defined on that experiment. The experiment is repeated n times, as before, but this time we average some function of X, say, $G(X)$. Later in this section, for example, we will consider $G(X) = X^2$.

Here we perform the experiment n times, observe X as before, but instead of averaging the values of X, we average the values of $G(X)$. The average of $G(X)$ resulting from n repetitions of the experiment will be

$$g(x)_{\text{average}} = \frac{1}{n}[g(x(1)) + g(x(2)) + g(x(3)) + \cdots + g(x(n))] \qquad (2.3.11)$$

where, as before, the integers index the sequence of values of the random variable resulting from the first, second, $\ldots$, nth repetition of the experiment. Again, we have only discrete values of X that can occur. Call these as before $x_1, x_2, x_3, \cdots, x_N$. Thus we can again rearrange Eq. (2.3.11):

$$g(x)_{\text{average}} = g(x_1) \times \frac{n_1}{n} + g(x_2) \times \frac{n_2}{n} + g(x_3) \times \frac{n_3}{n} + \cdots + g(x_N) \times \frac{n_N}{n} = \sum g(x_i) \times \frac{n_i}{n} \qquad (2.3.12)$$

This is what we would do with the data, and it leads naturally to the definition in probability theory of the expectation of a function of a random variable as follows:

$$E[G(X)] = \sum_{\text{all } x_i} g(x)P[X = x] = \sum_{\text{all } x_i} g(x)P_X(x) \qquad (2.3.13)$$

Example 2.3.2:   **The mean square value of a uniform PMF** _____
Let $G(X) = X^2$, where $X = \{0, 1, 2, 3, 4, 5\}$, all equally likely. Find $E[G(X)] = E[X^2]$.

$$E[X^2] = \sum_{x=0,1,2,3,4,5} x^2 P_X(x) = (0^2 + 1^2 + \cdots + 5^2) \times \frac{1}{6} = 9.167 \qquad (2.3.14)$$

The expectation of the square of the random variable is called the *mean square value,* or the *second moment,* of the distribution.

Mean square value for the binomial random variable. We now determine the mean square value of the binomial random variable. Let $K =$ number of successes in n binomial trials, with $p =$ probability of success on an individual trial, and $q = 1 - p$. Then $P_K(k) = B_n(k, p)$, which is the binomial distribution. To find the expectation of the square of K, we apply the definition, Eq. (2.3.13)

$$E[K^2] = \sum_{k=0}^{k=n} k^2 B_n(k, p) = \sum_{k=0}^{k=n} k^2 \times \frac{n!}{(n-k)!k!} p^k q^{n-k} \tag{2.3.15}$$

Here we use a trick. Note that $k^2 = k(k-1) + k$. Making that substitution in Eq. (2.3.15) and separating the two terms, we have

$$E[K^2] = \sum_{k=0}^{k=n} k(k-1) \times \frac{n!}{(n-k)!k!} p^k q^{n-k} + \sum_{k=0}^{k=n} k \times \frac{n!}{(n-k)!k!} p^k q^{n-k} \tag{2.3.16}$$

The first summation can be transformed in the same manner as Eq. (2.3.7) to be $n(n-1)p^2$ for the first summation, and the second summation is given by Eq. (2.3.10) as np. Thus Eq. (2.3.16) becomes

$$E[K^2] = n(n-1)p^2 + np = (np)^2 + np(1-p) \tag{2.3.17}$$

This result will be used in the next section.

2.3.4 Special Expectations

Expectation is a general procedure for modeling an average of some result related to a random experiment. Certain expectations have special names, significance, and interpretation. Here we speak of the mean, the variance, and the standard deviation.

Mean and its importance.   The *mean* is defined as the expectation of the random variable:

$$\text{the mean of the random variable } X = E[X] = \mu_X = \sum_{\text{all } x_i} x P_X(x) \tag{2.3.18}$$

Equation (2.3.18) gives the name and two symbols for the mean. The mean models the simple average presented earlier. The mean may be interpreted as the center of mass of the PMF, and sometimes is called the *first moment* in analogy with mechanics. Thus the mean is the balance point of the probabilities, treated as masses.

Variance and its interpretation.   Another special expectation is the *variance*, which is defined as

$$\sigma_X^2 = Var[X] = E[(X - \mu_X)^2] = \sum_{\text{all } x_i} (x - \mu_X)^2 P_X(x) \tag{2.3.19}$$

Equation (2.3.19) gives the definition and two symbols commonly used for the variance of a random variable. The variance is the *second moment* about the mean. It is analogous to the central moment of inertia in mechanics and gives a measure of how spread out the distribution is.

The standard deviation.   The standard deviation is defined as the square root of the variance:

$$\sigma_X = \sqrt{Var[X]} = \sqrt{\sigma_X^2} = \sqrt{E[(X - \mu_X)^2]} \tag{2.3.20}$$

The standard deviation also indicates the width of the PMF, corresponding to the *scatter* of the data values, in the same units as the mean.

An alternative form for computing the variance.   Expanding the definition for variance, Eq. (2.3.19), we find

$$E[(X - \mu_X)^2] = \sum_{\text{all } x_i}(x - \mu_X)^2 P_X(x) = \sum_{\text{all } x_i}(x^2 - 2\mu_X x + \mu_X^2) P_X(x)$$

$$= \sum_{\text{all } x_i} x^2 P_X(x) - \sum_{\text{all } x_i} 2\mu_X x P_X(x) + \sum_{\text{all } x_i} \mu_X^2 P_X(x) \tag{2.3.21}$$

$$= E[X^2] - 2\mu_X E[X] + \mu_X^2 = E[X^2] - \mu_X^2$$

In developing Eq. (2.3.21), we merely treated the mean as a constant, took constants outside the sums, and used the definitions. To obtain the final form, we substituted $E[X] = \mu_X$ and simplified. The term $E[X^2]$ is the mean square value of X. This final form in Eq. (2.3.21) is usually easier for calculating the variance than the definition in Eq. (2.3.19).

Meaning of the variance.   The variance is a measure of the width of the distribution about the mean. A PMF in which all values are clustered close to the mean will have a small variance. A PMF in which all values are scattered far from the mean will have a large variance. These two cases are illustrated in Fig. 2.3.3.

Example 2.3.3:   Variance of the uniform PMF _____
For the random variable uniformly distributed between $X = 0, 1, 2, 3, 4$, and 5, we have determined the mean [Eq. (2.3.6)] to be 2.5 and the expectation of the square [Eq. (2.3.14)], the mean square value, to be $E[X^2] = 9.167$. Find the variance.

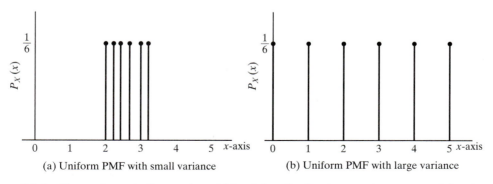

(a) Uniform PMF with small variance   (b) Uniform PMF with large variance

Figure 2.3.3   The variance indicates the width of the distribution, or the scatter of the data as the chance experiment is repeated and values of the resulting random variable are listed.

Solution   From Eq. (2.3.21), the variance is

$$Var[X] = E[X^2] - \mu_X^2 = 9.167 - (2.5)^2 = 2.917 \qquad (2.3.22)$$

and the standard deviation is $\sqrt{2.917} = 1.708$. Note that the standard deviation is about one-third the width of the distribution. This is typical of a symmetric distribution.

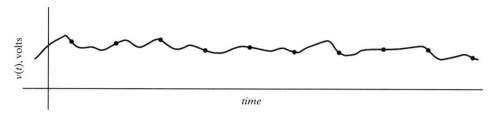

Figure 2.3.4   The graph represents a voltage that varies randomly in time. The black dots represent samples taken at intervals. The mean of the random variables representing these samples would approximate the average value of the voltage. The standard deviation would represent the amount of the variation in the voltage, which would be the noise in the measurement.

The meaning of the standard deviation.   The standard deviation, like the variance, is a measure of the width of the PMF, or the scatter of the data, in units that are the same as those of the data and of the mean. For example, let X be a random variable representing samples of a time-varying voltage, indicated by the dots in Fig. 2.3.4.

Then the mean would have units of volts and would be related to the dc, or time-average, value of the voltage. The mean square, $E[X^2]$, would have units of volts squared and would be related to the total power in the signal. The variance would have units of volts squared and would be related to the power in the fluctuations of the signal. The standard deviation would have units of volts and would be related to the rms value of the time-varying component of the signal.

Variance of the binomial distribution.   The variance of the binomial distribution can be found from Eq. (2.3.21). We think you are up to it, especially since we've already calculated the mean [Eq. (2.3.10)] and mean squared [Eq. (2.3.17)] values for the binomial distribution. Enter your answer between the quotes in the cell box and click Evaluate for a response.

```
myanswer = "";
```

```
Evaluate
```

For the answer, see endnote 17.

Example 2.3.4:   The mean and variance of the geometric random variable _____

Calculate the mean and variance of the geometric random variable, where $P[\text{success}] = p$. The geometric random variable has the PMF that gives the probability of the first success on the nth trial.

Solution   The PMF of the geometric random variable is

$$P_N(n) = pq^{n-1} \tag{2.3.23}$$

where $q = 1 - p$, and n is 1, 2, ... The expectation, given in Eq. (2.3.5) and applied to this random variable, is

$$\mu_N = E[N] = \sum_1^\infty n P_1(n) = p(1 + 2q + 3q^2 + \cdots) = p\frac{d}{dq}(1 + q + q^2 + q^3 + \cdots)$$

$$= p\frac{d}{dq}\left(\frac{1}{1-q}\right) = \frac{p}{(1-q)^2} = \frac{1}{p} \tag{2.3.24}$$

where we used the properties of the geometric series (see endnote 4). The mean square value can be calculated with a similar trick:

$$E[N^2] = \sum_1^\infty n^2 P_1(n) = p(1 + 2^2 q + 3^2 q^2 + \cdots) = p\frac{d}{dq}\left(q\frac{d}{dq}\left(\frac{1}{1-q}\right)\right)$$

$$= \frac{1+q}{p^2} \tag{2.3.25}$$

and therefore the variance [Eq. (2.3.21)] is

$$Var[N] = E[N^2] - \mu_N^2 = \frac{1+q}{p^2} - \left(\frac{1}{p}\right)^2 = \frac{q}{p^2} \tag{2.3.26}$$

Thus if the probability of success is 0.1, it will take on average 10 tries for the first success, which seems reasonable, and the standard deviation of the number of trials will be

$$\sigma_X = \sqrt{\frac{q}{p^2}} = \sqrt{\frac{0.9}{0.1^2}} = 9.487 \tag{2.3.27}$$

This value is rather large and indicates that the number of trials until the first success, though it averages 10, could well vary widely. One rule of thumb that works well for symmetrical distributions is that about two-thirds of the outcomes fall within plus or minus one standard deviation of the mean. In this rather unsymmetrical distribution this rule of thumb does not work well at all, since only 12.2% of the probability falls outside the range $1 \le k \le 19$. To see how the 12.2% was calculated, see endnote 18.

Example 2.3.5:   The mean and variance of the uniform distribution _____

Consider the PMF

$$P_X(x) = \frac{1}{b - a + 1}, x = a, a + 1, a + 2, \ldots, b - 1, b, \text{zow} \qquad (2.3.28)$$

This is the PMF of a uniformly distributed random variable starting on a and ending on b. The number of values in this range is $b - a + 1$. The mean and variance of this random variable are worked out in the following cells:

```
μ = Sum [i, {i, a, b}] / (b - a + 1);
Simplify[%]
```

```
a + b
─────
  2
```

```
Var[X] = Sum [(i - (a + b) / 2)², {i, a, b}] / (b - a + 1);
Simplify [%]
```

```
 1
──── (-2 + a - b) (a - b)
 12
```

Because we require $b > a$, the second expression is more naturally expressed with the signs of the two parentheses changed to $Var[X] = (b - a)(b - a + 2)/12$.

_____

You do it.   Find the variance of the Bernoulli random variable with $p = 0.4$. Enter your answer in the cell box, and click Evaluate for a response.

```
myanswer = ;
```

```
Evaluate
```

For the answer, see endnote 19.

2.3.5 Conditional Expectation

Just as conditional probabilities allow us to break down a larger problem into several smaller problems, so conditional expectations allow us to calculate expectations under prescribed conditions. In this section we define and illustrate the use of conditional expectations.

Definition of conditional expectation.   If A is some event, the definition of the conditional expectation of the X with condition A is

$$\mu_{X|A} = E[X|A] = \sum_{\text{all } x_i \in A} x P_{X|A}(x) \tag{2.3.29}$$

where $P_{X|A}(x)$ is the conditional PMF of X given condition A. Consider the following example.

Example 2.3.6:   Student weights _____

Let $W = $ a random variable describing the weight of a student chosen at random in a group of students. Let $M = \{\text{man}\}$ and $F = \{\text{woman}\}$. Then M and F constitute a partition of the space. Develop a formula for the expected weight of a student chosen at random.

Solution   The problem calls for the PMF of the weights of all students, but this is naturally expressed in terms of the conditional PMFs based on gender. Thus we have

$$P_W(w) = P_{W|M}(w) \times P[M] + P_{W|F}(w) \times P[F] \tag{2.3.30}$$

The expected weight of a student chosen at random would be

$$E[W] = \sum_{\text{all } w_i} w P_W(w) = \sum_{\text{all } w_i \in M} w P_{W|M}(w) \times P[M]$$

$$+ \sum_{\text{all } w_i \in F} w P_{W|F}(w) \times P[F] \tag{2.3.31}$$

In Eq. (2.3.31), the probabilities $P[M]$ and $P[F]$ are constants and come outside the summations, which are conditional expectations, as defined by Eq. (2.3.29). Equation (2.3.31) becomes

$$E[W] = E[W|M] \times P[M] + E[W|F] \times P[F] \tag{2.3.32}$$

Thus if, on average, the men weigh 150 pounds and the women 110 pounds, and 80% of the class are men, the expected weight would be

$$E[W] = 150 \times 0.8 + 110 \times 0.2 = 142 \tag{2.3.33}$$

The previous example has a condition defined on the basic experiment. Often, the condition is expressed in terms of the random variable, as in the next example.

Example 2.3.7:   Uniform PMF _____

Pick a number randomly in $S = \{0, 1, 2, 3, 4, 5, 6, 7, 8, 9\}$. Let the random variable X be the selected number. Find $E[\sqrt{X}|X^2 < 50]$.

Solution   The condition that the square of X be less than 50 eliminates 8 and 9, but the remaining values are equally probable. Thus the conditional PMF is

$$P_{X|X^2<50}(x) = \frac{1}{8}, \quad x = 0, 1, 2, 3, 4, 5, 6, 7, \text{zow} \tag{2.3.34}$$

The required conditional expectation therefore is

$$E[\sqrt{X}|X^2 < 50] = \sum_{\text{all } x_i \in x^2 < 50} \sqrt{x}\, P_{X|X^2<50}(x)$$

$$= (\sqrt{0} + \sqrt{1} + \sqrt{2} + \sqrt{3} + \sqrt{4} \qquad (2.3.35)$$

$$+ \sqrt{5} + \sqrt{6} + \sqrt{7}) \times \tfrac{1}{8} = 1.685$$

You do it.   For the same random variable, calculate $E[X^2|\sqrt{X} > 2.4]$. Enter your answer in the cell box to at least three-place accuracy, and click Evaluate for a response.

```
myanswer =              ;
```

```
Evaluate
```

For the answer, see endnote 20.

The vocabulary and interpretation of expectation.   The word *expectation* is used with a number of related meanings, depending on context.

1. The expectation is the probability model for a numerical average of the results of repeated experiments. This is the meaning we have used to justify the definition, Eq. (2.3.5).
2. The expectation of a random variable is the mean [Eq. (2.3.5)], or center of mass. Here expectation is a constant characterizing the PMF.
3. The expectation is an operator. It operates on functions of random variables as $E[\text{function of } X] = \sum_{\text{all } x_i}$ same function of $x \times P_X(x)$. Clearly, the expectation is a linear operator, since $E[a \times F(X) + bG(X)] = a \times E[F(X)] + b \times E[G(X)]$. We will explore this and other properties of the expectation operator in the next section.
4. Expectation is a weighted average. The weighting function is the PMF, which is the probability of the occurrence of the allowed values of X.

2.3.6 The Algebra of Expectation

The importance of expectation

Bridge to the real world.   Expectation is a very important concept in dealing with random systems because, in one sense, all we have are averages when we deal with real random systems. Therefore, the probability model for averages, the expectation, provides the bridge between real systems and our models.

Significant parameters in many distributions.   Many of the properties of the most successful models are derived from, or expressed in terms of, expectations such as the mean and variance. In other words, the expectations are important footprints of the various distributions that are useful in modeling random systems.

The algebra.   We now present an algebra of expectation that affords us many quick results in analyzing random systems. Although we develop this algebra in the context of discrete sample spaces, all our results will be valid in the continuous and mixed (part discrete, part continuous) sample spaces introduced in Chapter 3.

The algebra of expectation as it relates to a single random variable

In this section we assume a random variable, X, described by the PMF $P_X(x)$.

The definition.   The definition [Eq. (2.3.5)] and conventional notation for expectation is

$$E[X] = \sum_{\text{all } x_i} x P[X = x_i] = \sum_{\text{all } x_i} x P_X(x) \tag{2.3.36}$$

The definition in Eq. (2.3.36) is used in the following section to show various properties of the expectation operator.

Expectation of a function of a random variable.   The expectation of a function, $G(X)$, of a random variable, X, is:

$$E[G(X)] = \sum_{\text{all } x_i} g(x) P_X(x) \tag{2.3.37}$$

where $g(x)$ and $G(X)$ are the same function. This operation was illustrated in the previous section in calculating the mean square [Eq. (2.3.14)] and the variance [Eq. (2.3.19)] of a random variable.

Expectation of a constant.   The expectation of a constant is simply that constant. This result follows from the normalization for a PMF:

$$E[a] = \sum_{\text{all } x_i} a P_X(x) = a \sum_{\text{all } x_i} P_X(x) = a \times 1 = a \tag{2.3.38}$$

Because the constant appears in every term of the sum, it can be factored out of the summation.

Expectation is a linear operator.   The expectation of the sum is the sum of the expectations:

$$E[aG(X) + bH(X)] = \sum_{\text{all } x_i} \big(ag(x) + bh(x)\big) P_X(x)$$

$$= a \times \sum_{\text{all } x_i} g(x) P_X(x) + b \times \sum_{\text{all } x_i} h(x) P_X(x) \tag{2.3.39}$$

$$= a E[G(X)] + b E[H(X)]$$

where $g(x)$ and $h(x)$ are arbitrary functions.

Example 2.3.8: Expectation of a random variable minus its mean ———————

Find the expectation of $X - \mu_X$.

Solution Applying linearity and Eq. (2.3.38), we have

$$E[X - \mu_X] = E[X] - E[\mu_X] = \mu_X - \mu_X = 0 \qquad (2.3.40)$$

by definition of the mean [Eq. (2.3.18)].

You do it. Say we have a random variable X that is equally likely to be 0, 1, or 2. Find the expectation of $e^X - 2X$. Calculate a numerical value to three places and enter it in the cell box, then click Evaluate for a response.

myanswer =   ;

Evaluate

For the answer, see endnote 21.

Variance. The two equivalent forms for the variance also follow from the linear property:

$$\begin{aligned}
\sigma_X^2 &= E[(X - \mu_X)^2] = E[X^2 - 2\mu_X X + \mu_X^2] \\
&= E[X^2] - 2\mu_X E[X] + \mu_X^2 = E[X^2] - 2\mu_X^2 + \mu_X^2 \qquad (2.3.41) \\
&= E[X^2] - \mu_X^2
\end{aligned}$$

A shift in origin. Shifting the origin of X shifts the mean by the same amount:

$$E[X - a] = E[X] - a = \mu_X - a \qquad (2.3.42)$$

however, a shift in origin for the random variable does not affect the variance. This result follows from the definition of variance, Eqs. (2.3.19) and (2.3.42):

$$Var[X - a] = E[((X - a) - (\mu_X - a))^2] = E[(X - \mu_X)^2] = Var[X] \qquad (2.3.43)$$

This is reasonable, because the variance is a measure of the width of a distribution.

Change of scale. If the scale of the random variable is changed by a factor a, the scale of the variance changes by the square of a. This result follows from the definition of variance:

$$Var[aX] = E[(aX - a\mu_X)^2] = a^2 E[(X - \mu_X)^2] = a^2 Var[X] \qquad (2.3.44)$$

This property reflects that variance is a square-law operator. Of course, the standard deviation would be scaled linearly.

Conditional expectations.   All the preceding properties apply to conditional expectations; simply use the conditional PMF. We illustrated some properties in earlier examples in Sec. 2.3.5.

Two or more random variables

Joint PMF.   We now consider the bivariate case, two random variables, X and Y, with a joint PMF of $P_{XY}(x, y)$. The corresponding results are readily generalized to more than two random variables.

The expectation of a function of two random variables.   We may, in general, define the expectation of a function of the two random variables as

$$E[G(X, Y)] = \sum_{\text{all } x_i} \sum_{\text{all } y_i} g(x, y) P_{XY}(x, y) \qquad (2.3.45)$$

Linearity.   This expectation is linear in several ways. An interesting case is

$$
\begin{aligned}
E[aG(X) + bH(Y)] &= \sum_{\text{all } x_i} \sum_{\text{all } y_j} \big(ag(x) + bh(y)\big) P_{XY}(x, y) \\
&= \sum_{\text{all } x_i} ag(x) \sum_{\text{all } y_j} P_{XY}(x, y) + \sum_{\text{all } y_j} bh(y) \sum_{\text{all } x_i} P_{XY}(x, y) \\
&= a \sum_{\text{all } x_i} g(x) P_X(x) + b \sum_{\text{all } y_j} h(y) P_Y(y) \\
&= aE[G(X)] + bE[H(Y)]
\end{aligned}
\qquad (2.3.46)
$$

The latter expression drops out because if, say, y is only in the PMF, it sums out, leaving the marginal PMF on X, which leads to the expectation in X only.

Use of conditional expectations.   We may calculate the bivariate expectation of a function of two random variables using conditional expectation as follows. Using Eq. (2.2.20), we may express the expectation of $G(X, Y)$ as

$$E[G(X, Y)] = \sum_{\text{all } x_i} \sum_{\text{all } y_j} g(x, y) P_{Y|X}(x, y) P_X(x) = \sum_{\text{all } x_i} \left[\sum_{\text{all } y_j} g(x, y) P_{Y|X}(x, y) \right] P_X(x)$$

$$(2.3.47)$$

The term in the brackets of Eq. (2.3.47) is by definition the conditional expectation of $G(X, Y)$, given X; hence we have

$$E[G(X, Y)] = \sum_{\text{all } x_i} E[G(X, Y)|X] P_X(x) = E[E[G(X, Y)|X]] \qquad (2.3.48)$$

Thus the expectation of $G(X, Y)$ can be calculated as the expectation of the conditional expectation.

For the inner expectation, X is held constant and the expectation is performed with respect to Y, resulting in a function of X only. The outer expectation then is performed with respect to X.

Example 2.3.9:   Expectation of the N-K random variable

We earlier described a two-step bivariate experiment in which an integer, N, was chosen at random from $\{1, 2, 3, 4, 5, 6\}$, and then a fair coin was flipped N times and the number, K, of heads was noted. We derived the bivariate PMF, $P_{NK}(n, k)$. We ask now for the expectation of K, using Eq. (2.3.48).

Solution   We require $E[K]$. The conditional expectation $E[K|N]$ is the expectation of a binomial random variable with $p = \frac{1}{2} : E[K|N] = Np = \frac{N}{2}$. Note that the conditional expectation is a random variable. Finally, we take the expectation of this conditional expectation with respect to N. Since N is uniformly distributed between 1 and 6, inclusive, we have

$$E\left[\frac{N}{2}\right] = \tfrac{1}{2} \times \tfrac{1}{6} + \tfrac{2}{2} \times \tfrac{1}{6} + \tfrac{3}{2} \times \tfrac{1}{6} + \tfrac{4}{2} \times \tfrac{1}{6} + \tfrac{5}{2} \times \tfrac{1}{6} + \tfrac{6}{2} \times \tfrac{1}{6} = \tfrac{7}{4} \qquad (2.3.49)$$

Independence.   When X and Y are independent, the joint PMF can be factored as shown in Eq. (2.2.19)

$$P_{XY}(x, y) = P_X(x)P_Y(y) \qquad (2.3.50)$$

It follows then that the expectation of any product function of X and Y can be factored into the expectations in X and Y separately:

$$
\begin{aligned}
E[G(X)H(Y)] &= \sum_{\text{all } x_i} \sum_{\text{all } y_j} g(x)h(y)P_{XY}(x, y) \\
&= \sum_{\text{all } x_i} \sum_{\text{all } y_j} g(x)h(y)P_X(x)P_Y(y) \\
&= \sum_{\text{all } x_i} g(x)P_X(x) \sum_{\text{all } y_j} h(y)P_Y(y) \\
&= E[G(X)]E[H(Y)]
\end{aligned}
\qquad (2.3.51)
$$

Thus when X and Y are independent, the expectation can be distributed to $G(X)$ and $H(Y)$.

Sums of independent random variables.   Equation (2.3.39) is valid for all random variables, including independent random variables. One simple and useful consequence is that the mean of the sum of two or more random variables is the sum of the means of the random variables:

$$E[X + Y] = E[X] + E[Y] = \mu_X + \mu_Y \qquad (2.3.52)$$

It is important to show that for the sum of two or more independent random variables the variance of the sum is equal to the sum of the variances. Here we consider two random variables, but this result can be extended to more random variables by induction. Equation (2.3.53) calculates the variance of the sum of two independent random variables:

$$Var[X + Y] = E[(X + Y - \mu_X - \mu_Y)^2] = E[(X - \mu_X + Y - \mu_Y)^2]$$

$$= E[(X - \mu_X)^2] + 2E[(X - \mu_X)(Y - \mu_Y)] + E[(Y - \mu_Y)^2] \qquad (2.3.53)$$

$$= Var[X] + 0 + Var[Y]$$

In Eq. (2.3.53) the middle term vanishes according to Eqs. (2.3.51) and (2.3.40).

$$E[(X - \mu_X)(Y - \mu_Y)] = E[(X - \mu_X)] \times E[(Y - \mu_Y)] = 0 \times 0 = 0 \qquad (2.3.54)$$

Thus for independent random variables, the variance of the sum is the sum of the variances. Equations (2.3.52) and (2.3.53) will now be used to determine the mean and variance of the binomial random variable.

2.3.7 The Bernoulli, Binomial, and Pascal Distributions

This section revisits the distributions based on binomial trials and uses the algebra of expectation to derive results already derived by more laborious methods. The key idea is to represent the results of each trial as a Bernoulli random variable and to use the independence of the trials (and thus the independent Bernoulli random variables representing the results of the trials) to get a quick result.

The Bernoulli random variable

Review of the Bernoulli random variable. We introduced the Bernoulli random variable (Fig. 2.2.6) in Sec. 2.2 and had you calculate its mean earlier in this section. The Bernoulli random variable has values of 0 and 1 with probabilities $P[X = 0] = q$ and $P[X = 1] = p$, where $p + q = 1$. The mean of the Bernoulli random variable is

$$E[X] = \mu_X = 0 \times q + 1 \times p = p \qquad (2.3.55)$$

The mean square value is

$$E[X^2] = 0^2 \times q + 1^2 \times p = p \qquad (2.3.56)$$

These results give the variance of the Bernoulli random variable to be

$$Var[X] = E[X^2] - \mu_X^2 = p - p^2 = p(1 - p) = pq \qquad (2.3.57)$$

These expectations plus the independence of the trials yield a direct analysis of the mean and variance of the binomial distribution.

The binomial distribution analyzed with the Bernoulli random variable

In this section we rederive the mean and variance of the binomial distribution. We were able to derive these earlier by applying the definitions of mean [Eq. (2.3.10)] and variance (see endnote 17), changing variables, and manipulating the results into a familiar form. We found that the mean is np, and the variance is npq. We now rederive these results using the Bernoulli random variable and the algebra of expectation.

Using the Bernoulli random variable as a binary indicator. Consider a series of n binomial trials, each with a probability of success of p. We know the sample space has $S = \{2^n \text{ outcomes}\}$ of the form $AA\bar{A}A\bar{A}$ for $n = 5$. We define n random variables on this experiment. The first random variable, X_1, is 1 if the *first trial* is a success and is 0 if the first trial is a failure. The second random variable indicates success on the second trial, and so forth until X_n, which indicates success on the last trial. In this way we map each outcome in the sample space into a point in n-dimensional space. For example, the outcome given above maps into $X_1 = 1$, $X_2 = 1$, $X_3 = 0$, $X_4 = 1$, and $X_5 = 0$. The random variables X_1 through X_n are Bernoulli random variables, which we analyzed in the previous section, and they are independent because we are assuming independent trials.

The count of successes. We now define a random variable K as the sum of all the Xs:

$$K = X_1 + X_2 + \cdots + X_n \qquad (2.3.58)$$

Clearly, K is the number of successes: $K = 3$ for $AA\bar{A}A\bar{A}$. Using the algebra of expectation we can find the expectation of K:

$$
\begin{aligned}
E[K] = \mu_K &= E[X_1 + X_2 + \cdots + X_n] \\
&= E[X_1] + E[X_2] + \cdots + E[X_n] \\
&= p + p + \cdots + p = np
\end{aligned}
\qquad (2.3.59)
$$

This is the result we derived in Eq. (2.3.10) by summing an infinite series involving the binomial distribution.

The variance. Because the Bernoulli random variables are independent, the algebra of expectation shows in Eq. (2.3.53) that the variance of the sum is the sum of the variances,

$$
\begin{aligned}
Var[K] &= Var[X_1 + X_2 + \cdots + X_n] \\
&= Var[X_1] + Var[X_2] + \cdots + Var[X_n] \\
&= pq + pq + \cdots + pq = npq
\end{aligned}
\qquad (2.3.60)
$$

This is the result that we derived earlier through a direct application of the PMF (see endnote 17). Equations (2.3.59) and (2.3.60) use the properties of the Bernoulli random variable plus the algebra of expectation to derive the mean and variance of the binomial random variable with far less mathematical effort than was expended earlier to get the same results.

The Pascal distribution analyzed using the geometric random variable and the algebra of expectation

We can calculate the mean and variance of the Pascal distribution similarly. Consider a series of independent Bernoulli trials, with a probability p of success on a given trial. The Pascal distribution, $P_k(n, p)$, gives the probability that the kth success will occur on the nth trial. The Pascal distribution is derived in Sec. 2.1.4, and its mean and variance can be derived from the mean and variance [see Eq. (2.3.24) and (2.3.26)] of the geometric distribution, which is derived in Sec. 2.3.4. Here we show how to determine the mean and variance of the Pascal random variable using the algebra of expectation.

The geometric random variable.   Earlier in this section we determined the mean and variance for $k = 1$, the first success. If we let X be the geometric random variable describing the number of trials to the first success, we find

$$E[X] = \tfrac{1}{p} \text{ and } Var[X] = \tfrac{q}{p^2} \tag{2.3.61}$$

The Pascal random variable.   We can calculate the number of trials to the kth success by adding the number of trials for the first success, X_1, to the number of trials between the first and the second success, X_2, and so on. The number of trials until the kth success is the sum of the X's:

$$N = X_1 + X_2 + \cdots + X_k \tag{2.3.62}$$

By the assumption of independent trials, the random variables X_1 through X_k are independent geometric random variables. In Eq. (2.3.62) N is the random variable describing the number of trials to the kth success, and the expected value of N is

$$\begin{aligned}
E[N] = \mu_N &= E[X_1 + X_2 + \cdots + X_k] \\
&= E[X_1] + E[X_2] + \cdots + E[X_k] \\
&= \frac{1}{p} + \frac{1}{p} + \cdots + \frac{1}{p} = \frac{k}{p}
\end{aligned} \tag{2.3.63}$$

The variance of N is found similarly:

$$\begin{aligned}
Var[N] &= Var[X_1 + X_2 + \cdots + X_k] \\
&= Var[X_1] + Var[X_2] + \cdots + Var[X_k] \\
&= \frac{q}{p^2} + \frac{q}{p^2} + \cdots + \frac{q}{p^2} = \frac{kq}{p^2}
\end{aligned} \tag{2.3.64}$$

Equations (2.3.63) and (2.3.64) give the mean and variance of the Pascal random variable of order k.

In summary, the algebra of expectations is an analysis tool that often yields useful results with a minimum of mathematical effort.

2.3.8 A Retrospective on the Definition and Rules of Probability

Review of the definition of probability.   We defined probability in the context of a repeatable experiment with a known set of outcomes and events defined on those outcomes. Consider that the experiment is done n times and event A occurs N_A times. We use a capital N now because we recognize that we are dealing with a random variable. The relative frequency of event A in a given set of trials is the random variable $\frac{N_A}{n}$. Probability is defined as a mathematical model for such relative frequencies, and the rules of probability are modeled on the arithmetic properties of relative frequencies plus our intuitive concept of independence. Thus from this point of view we created probabilities from relative frequencies:

$$\frac{N_A}{n} \longrightarrow P[A] \tag{2.3.65}$$

The probability of event A makes a statement about a single performance of the experiment, but it gives information that can be confirmed only through repetition of the experiment.

The binomial model for a repeated experiment.   We now can model a repeatable experiment as a sequence of Bernoulli trials. Consider a trial in which the probability of event A is $P[A] = p$, and we perform the experiment n times. The number of times that event A occurs is then given by the binomial distribution, with N_A being the random variable we have been calling K. Thus here we derive a relative frequency from a probability:

$$P[A] \longrightarrow \frac{N_A}{n} = \frac{K}{n} \tag{2.3.66}$$

We thus have probabilities associated with the various relative frequencies that might arise out of the experiment. These probabilities are simply those of the binomial distribution. For example, we derived the most likely successes [Eq. (2.1.12)] for the binomial distribution to be

$$K = \text{integer part of } (n+1)p \approx np \tag{2.3.67}$$

For the random variable representing the relative frequency, $\frac{K}{n}$, the most likely value would therefore be $\approx p$. Our model is thus behaving well. Figure 2.3.5 shows the distribution of experimental relative frequencies for $n = 40$ and $p = 0.5$.

Figure 2.3.5 looks as we hoped it would. The most likely relative frequencies cluster around $P[A]$, but not too closely. It looks better if we use 400 trials, as shown by Fig. 2.3.6.

Figure 2.3.6 shows less spread and we become confident that with n increased even further the relative frequencies resulting from the repeated experiment will become more tightly clustered around the underlying probability.

The average relative frequency.   We now use the algebra of expectation to find the mean and variance of $\frac{N_A}{n}$, our experimental estimate of the probability, p. Because $K = N_A$ is binomially distributed and n is a constant, it follows that

$$E\left[\frac{N_A}{n}\right] = \frac{1}{n} \times E[N_A] = \frac{np}{n} = p \tag{2.3.68}$$

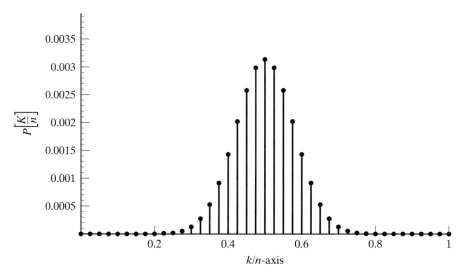

Figure 2.3.5   Probabilities for various relative frequencies with $n = 40$ trials and a probability of success of $p = 0.5$.

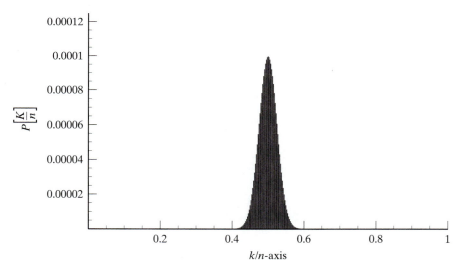

Figure 2.3.6   Probabilities for various relative frequencies with $n = 400$ trials and a probability of success of $p = 0.5$. The peak is now more concentrated around the most likely value. The lines are so close together here that they appear as a continuum, but that is an artifact of the plotting scale.

Thus the expected value of the relative frequency is the probability. Again, we observe that this is the way we want our model to behave.

How close?   The variance of the model of the relative frequency is

$$Var\left[\frac{N_A}{n}\right] = \frac{1}{n^2} \times Var[N_A] = \frac{npq}{n^2} = \frac{pq}{n} \tag{2.3.69}$$

Because $0 \le p \le 1$ and $q = 1 - p$, the variance has a maximum value of $\frac{1}{4n}$ at $p = \frac{1}{2}$. Thus as n increases we are assured that the estimate of the probability converges to the true value in the sense that its mean is the true value and its variance approaches zero. Again, we conclude that our model is behaving consistently.

Summary.   We started out modeling real-world relative frequencies by probabilities. We defined the rules of probability from the arithmetic of relative frequencies, plus our intuitive sense of independence. Our probability model has been developed to the point that we can model repeated experiments through Bernoulli trials, and we used the binomial distribution to describe the number of successes out of n trials. We then divided by n to model the relative frequency. We found that the expected value of this model is the theoretical probability of success. This is reassuring in that expectation models taking an average in the real world, so we conclude that if we perform an experiment a large number of times and average the results we should converge to a stable value. This is a self-consistency check on our model. If our model of a repeated experiment behaved otherwise, it would indicate serious problems with the model.

Further, we calculated the variance of the random variable modeling the relative frequency. Because this variance goes to zero as the number of trials goes to infinity, we have assurance that the scatter of the estimates gets small as the number of trials gets large. This also shows that our probability model is behaving well.

The argument we have given to show the internal consistency of our probability model can be made much more general and rigorous in several mathematical theorems that are called *laws of large numbers*. These laws show that under conditions of statistical regularity a relative frequency converges to a constant, which is the probability, as the number of trial increases without limit. Essentially the laws of large numbers tell us that our intuitive sense of the reasonability of the probability model is consistent with rigorous mathematical logic, which is good to know.

Analysis tools for probability calculations.   To *analyze* is to divide a problem into smaller parts so that it is easier to solve. In probability analysis we have four tools to use in taking problems apart:

1. *Partitions.* A partition divides a space into disjoints sets. The probability of any event can be expressed in terms of the partition in the manner given in Eq. (1.5.7). Therefore a good question one can ask in computing a probability is, Is there a partition I can use in calculating this probability?
2. *Conditional probabilities.* A conditional probability allows a complex event to be analyzed in terms of a sequence of simpler events, in the manner of Eq. (1.5.9). Another good question to ask is, Can I express this probability in terms of conditional probabilities.

3. *Independent events.* As shown in Eq. (1.5.22) we can express the probability of the intersection of independent events as the product of the probabilities of single events. Our intuition of independence is a great tool in analyzing complex probabilities.

4. *Sums of random variables.* We just demonstrated the calculation of expectations of complex events by using sums of random variables. We expressed the binomial random variable as the sum of the simpler Bernoulli random variables, and we expressed the Pascal random variable as the sum of the simpler geometric random variables.

5. *Combinations.* The four analysis tools given here can be combined in analyzing probability problems. Familiarity with the analysis tools, plus practice, will increase your skill in solving probability problems.

2.4 PROBLEMS

2.4.1 Bernoulli Trials, the Binomial and Pascal Models

Exercises on Bernoulli trials, the binomial and Pascal models

P2.1.1   A computer has a 32-bit register. The current drawn from the power supply is $i = 0.1 + 0.05\,k\,\mu A$, where k is the number of 1s in the register. Under normal operating conditions, 1s and 0s are equally likely and independent throughout the register. Find the probability that the current falls between 1.2 and 1.4 μA, inclusive.

   A2.1.1 0.0250

P2.1.2   A sequence of three Bernoulli trials is performed in a chance experiment.
   a. Let the probability of success be 0.2 for all trials, and consider the trials independent. Find the probability that two or more of the trials are successes, given that the last is a success.
   b. Let the probabilities of success be 0.2 for the first trial, 0.3 for the second trial, and 0.4 for the third trial. Consider the trials independent. Find the probability that two or more of the trials are successes, given that the last is a success.

   A2.1.2 (a) 0.360; **(b)** 0.440

P2.1.3   A manufacturer has a probability of 0.8 of producing a system that meets specifications.
   a. On a given day 12 systems were manufactured. What is the probability that 10 or more met specifications?
   b. If 10 systems are ordered, how many have to be manufactured to have a probability of at least 0.75 that 10 or more systems will meet specifications?

   A2.1.3 (a) 0.5583; **(b)** 14

P2.1.4   A fair die is rolled until a 6 occurs.
   a. What is the probability that the series terminates on the third roll?
   b. Given that the series terminates on the third roll, what is the probability that the sum of the three rolls, including the final roll of 6, is 12 or more?

c. Given that the series terminates on the third roll and the sum is 12 or more, what is the probability that 5 does not occur in any of the three rolls?

d. Find the probability that the experiment ends on the third roll and the sum is greater or equal to 12 and no 5 is rolled.

A2.1.4 (a) $\frac{25}{216}$; (b) $\frac{15}{25}$; (c) $\frac{6}{15}$; (d) $\frac{1}{36}$

P2.1.5 An office has three telephone lines. At any given time, the probability that at least one line is in use is 0.8. Find the probability that, at any given time, all three are in use.

A2.1.5 0.07157

P2.1.6 A series of three binomial trials are performed and the probability of two successes is 0.4. What is the probability of three successes?

A2.1.6 two roots: 0.5361 and 0.7819, which give 0.1541 and 0.4781, respectively.

P2.1.7 Assume that the post office loses one in 200 letters. You pay 10 bills/month. Assume that the delivery of a payment can be represented as a series of binomial trials. Find the following:

a. The probability that exactly one of your payments is lost in a year's time.

b. The probability that one or more of your payments are lost in 2 years' time.

A2.1.7 (a) 0.330; (b) 0.700

P.2.1.8 In baseball the *batting average* can be interpreted as the probability of a hit each time a player is at bat. Assume a batter has a batting average of 0.280 and bats five times in a certain game. Assume each time at bat can be represented as a binomial trial.

a. What is the probability that he gets three hits in a game?

b. What is the probability that his first hit occurs on the fourth trial?

c. What is the probability that he will get his first hit before he comes to bat the fifth time?

A2.1.8 (a) 0.114; (b) 0.105; (c) 0.731

P2.1.9 Consider a series of binomial trials in which the probability of a success is p and the probability of a failure is q, where $q = 1 - p$. The chance experiment is to perform trials until the same result comes up twice in a row, either two successes or two failures. Thus the experiment can end on the second, third, ... trial. For simplicity let pp stand for success on the first trial and success on the second trial, and so on.

a. Describe the sample space. That is, what are the outcomes of this experiment?

b. Show that the sample space is normalized for all values of p.

c. Find the probability that the sequence ends on a success, given that it begins with a success.

A2.1.9 (a) $S = \{pp, qpp, pqpp,$ etc., and also $qq, pqq, qpqq,$ etc.$\}$. (b) Proof: summing the series (four of them) and putting in $p + q = 1$. (c) $\frac{p}{1-p+p^2}$

P2.1.10 Consider a series of 10 binomial trials with $P[\text{success}] = 0.4$. Let k indicate the number of successes.

    a. Find $P[k = 4]$.

    b. Let $F = \{$exactly three of the first four trials are successes$\}$. Find $P[k = 5|F]$.

    c. Find the probability that the first success occurs on the fourth trial.

    d. What if the trials are done with n, the number of trials, unspecified, except that n is at least 5. For each success, n is increased by 1. The trials end when five failures have been recorded. What is the probability that the trials end on the tenth trial?

A2.1.10   **(a)** 0.2508;   **(b)** 0.311;   **(c)** 0.0864;   **(d)** 0.1003

Modeling problems on Bernoulli trials, the binomial and Pascal models

P2.1.11   A professor has a True/False daily test with five questions. Sam studied only a little, so his probability of knowing the right answer is 0.6. George did not study at all but relied rather on his lucky coin. What is the probability that George scored more than Sam? Assume independent binomial trial for Sam and George.

         A2.1.11   0.260

P2.1.12   A certain class of highway bridge has 12 supporting columns, each of which is inspected annually for weakness. Experience shows that, with annual inspection, the probability of a column weakening seriously during the year is 10^{-4}, independent of the condition of the other columns. What is the probability that two bad columns would occur?

         A2.1.12 6.59×10^{-7}

P2.1.13   A deer hunter is a poor shot, having a probability of 0.4 of shooting his deer on any given shot. Assume conditions for binomial trials are satisfied.

    a. If he takes three cartridges with him, find the probability that he gets his deer on the second shot.

    b. If he takes three cartridges with him, find the probability that he gets a deer at all.

         A2.1.13   **(a)** 0.24;   **(b)** 0.784

P2.1.14   A baseball player has a probability of 0.2 of walking, 0.3 of striking out, and 0.5 of hitting the ball. If he hits the ball, he has a 50% chance of getting a hit and a 50% change of being put out. Thus his batting average is 0.250. How many times does he have to come to bat before he has at least a 60% chance of getting at least one hit?

         A2.1.14   4

P2.1.15   A digital transmission system sends a kilobyte (1024 8-bit words) of digital information over a noisy channel. The error rate is 10^{-6}, meaning that one in a million bytes is bad, on average. Assume all bit errors are independent.

    a. Find the probability of exactly one incorrect byte out of 1024.

    b. Find the probability that a given bit is incorrect.

         A2.1.15   **(a)** 1.023×10^{-3};   **(b)** $1.250000546875 \times 10^{-7}$

P2.1.16   A target has a bull's eye ($i = 1$) and three concentric rings ($i = 2, 3$, and 4). For a given player, the probabilities for hitting in each of the four areas are $p_1 = 0.10$, $p_2 = 0.15$, $p_3 = 0.20$, $p_4 = 0.30$.

   a. The player throws 10 darts. What is the probability that all miss the target?
   b. The player throws 10 darts. What is the probability that at least 3 darts hit in the bull's eye or next ring ($i = 1$ or 2)?
   c. How many throws does the player have to make before the probability of two or more hits in the bull's eye is 0.3 or greater?

   A2.1.16 **(a)** 9.537×10^{-7}; **(b)** 0.4744; **(c)** 11

P2.1.17   At the hardware store the nuts and screws get mixed up because customers are careless. I went to buy twelve #8 screws, 1 in. long. The bin consisted of about 100 screws, of which about 6 were the wrong size. What is the probability that, choosing at random, I would end up with all the right size?

   A2.1.17 0.6899 based on the binomial distribution; 0.6830 exact, based on combinatorials.

P2.1.18   The campus pizza booth serves cheese and pepperoni pizza slices. They serve 50 customers each day, and 80% of these want pepperoni. How many slices of pepperoni should they have delivered at the beginning of the day to have a 90% probability of not running out?

   A2.1.18 44 gives 95.2%

P2.1.19   A digital communication system sends information in 8-bit words. No check bit is provided, and the probability of an error on a given bit is constant, regardless of position in the word. On one occasion when conditions were poor, 10 out of 100 words transmitted were detected incorrectly. Estimate the probability that a given word contained exactly two errors.

   A2.1.19 4.43×10^{-3}

P2.1.20   The suitors of a princess bride take part in a high-stakes Easter egg hunt for her hand. Our hero, who truly loves the princess, hires short actors and dresses them as children to represent him in the hunt. He must acquire two golden eggs to get the princess, and each "child" is allowed one golden egg and has a probability of 0.4 of finding such an egg. What is the minimum number of actors that he has to hire to have a probability of at least 0.95 of getting at least two golden eggs?

   A2.1.20 10

P2.1.21   An engineer drives to work along the same route every day, at a speed much greater than the legal limit. The police radar is set up once every four weeks on work days along that route, but at random times during the time when people are commuting. Assume 240 work days per year. If the police are out, there is a 0.2 chance the engineer will get a ticket. Find the probability that she will get fewer than two tickets in a year.

   A2.1.21 0.2749

P2.1.22 An automobile has four tires and one spare. A 3000-mile trip is undertaken. Assume that in each 500-mile stretch, the car has a probability of 0.05 of having one tire failure. Find the probability of completing the trip with no tires repaired along the way. Use a binomial model, but clearly, the model has to be undertaken with caution. We will develop a better model in Chapter 5.

A2.1.22 0.967

P2.1.23 A telemarketer gets paid $1 for each sale he makes. He can make six calls/hour, and each call has a probability of 0.6 of making a sale.
a. Find the probability that he makes at least $18 in working four 1-hour sessions.
b. Find the probability that he makes at least three sales in each of the four 1-hour periods he works.

A2.1.23 (a) 0.960; (b) 0.454

P2.1.24 An experienced fly fisherman gets a fish to strike his lure about 20% of the casts he makes, but an inexperienced fisherman gets a strike on only 10% of his casts. An experienced and an inexperienced fisherman go fishing together. What is the probability that the experienced fisherman has a strike before the inexperienced, considering the strikes independent events? Consider that they fish a long time and cast simultaneously.

A2.1.24 0.643

P2.1.25 A duck hunter has a limit of three ducks. She has a probability of 0.6 of hitting a duck. How many shells should she take to have a probability of 0.9 or greater of getting her limit and not running out of shells?

A2.1.25 Seven shells gives 0.9037

P2.1.26 A medical practice has 50 appointment slots per day. Experience has shown that 20% of the appointments will not show up. Of these broken appointments, 75% will call and cancel, and 25% will simply be no-shows.
a. How many can be expected to phone in to cancel during a typical day?
b. If on a given day 12 people fail to keep their appointments, what is the probability that 10 or more called to cancel?
c. On a day when the first 10 appointments show up, what is the probability that more than 2 appointments are not kept?

A2.1.26 (a) ≈7.5; (b) 0.3907; (c) 0.9921

P2.1.27 A door-to-door salesman gets to give his presentation on one out of every three doors he knocks on. If he gives the presentation, he makes a sale one time out of two. It takes 1 hour to make the presentation, regardless of whether a sale is made.
a. What is the probability that he will make only one presentation out of the first five homes he visits?
b. The salesman must make two sales simply to cover his daily expenses. After that he makes profit to live on, buy food and other necessities, and so on. What is

the probability that he will cover his expenses after he has spent the first 4 hours selling? Neglect knocking and walking time.

A2.1.27 **(a)** 0.329; **(b)** 0.6875

P2.1.28 The corporate jet of FatCats, Inc., offers steak or chicken for the executive traveling in style. Experience has shown that 60% of the passengers prefer steak. If there are nine passengers, how may steaks should the jet carry to have at least a 90% probability of giving a passenger a steak if he or she requests it. (Ignore chicken orders and vegetarians.)

A2.1.28 7 gives $P[\text{not run out}] = 0.929$

P2.1.29 It is said that 90% of small-company start-ups fail in 3 years or less. Assume the failures are described as binomial trials on a yearly basis.
a. An engineer started a company in 2004. What is the probability it will be operating in 2006 (2 years)?
b. If the company lasts 2 years, what is the probability it will last 3 more years?

A2.1.29 **(a)** 0.215; **(b)** 0.1

P2.1.30 If Sam studies, ST, for a test, the probability of getting a question correct is 0.8. If Sam does not study for the test, $\overline{ST}$, the probability that Sam will get the question correct is 0.6. There are 10 questions on the test, and we assume the conditions for independent trials. There is a 70% chance that Sam will study and a 30% chance that he will not study.
a. If Sam studies, find the probability that he makes 70 or more on the test.
b. What is the probability that Sam makes 70 or more on the test?
c. Given that Sam made 70 or more on the test, what is the probability that he studied?

A2.1.30 **(a)** 0.8791; **(b)** 0.7301; **(c)** 0.8429

P2.1.31 I went to graduation last Saturday. The faculty's role was to walk in at the beginning, stand up near the end, and walk out at the end, wearing colorful attire. As I was reading the names of the graduates in the program I made the following observations:
a. There were nine petroleum engineers graduating. I noticed that only three had names beginning with letters from the first half of the alphabet (A–M), whereas six had names beginning with letters from the last half of the alphabet (N–Z). What is the probability that three or fewer had names beginning with letters from the first half of the alphabet? To get an idea of the distribution of names in Austin, I consulted the white pages of the Austin phone book. The As begin on page 1, the Ns begin on page 549.6 (6/10 of page 550), and the Zs end on page 864.9 (9/10 of page 865).
b. There were 60 EEs with names beginning with A–M, and 50 with names beginning with N–Z. What is the probability that 60 or fewer EEs had names beginning with A–M?

A2.1.31 **(a)** 0.06493; **(b)** 0.03326 (used Mathematica to sum 51 terms)

P2.1.32 An experienced fly fisherman gets a fish to strike his lure about 20% of the casts he makes, but an inexperienced fisherman gets a strike on only 10% of his casts. An experienced and an inexperienced fisherman go out together to fish. After each makes three casts, what is the probability that the inexperienced fisherman has more strikes than the experienced, considering these independent events and that they cast simultaneously.

A2.1.32 0.1402

P2.1.33 Consider the design of a telephone exchange to serve 1000 customers. Consider that the lines are modeled as binomial trials with a probability of 0.01 of being in use at the peak time. Find the number of lines the exchange must service simultaneously if we require a probability of 0.98 that the load does not exceed the capacity. In other words, we want a probability of 0.02 that one of the 1000 customers picks up a phone and cannot get a line through the exchange. A trial-and-error approach is a good idea.

A2.1.33 17 lines give $P[\text{get line}] = 0.986$

P2.1.34 A book-of-the-month club sends out a letter to each member offering the selected book. If the member does not want the book, he or she returns the enclosed card; if the card is not returned, the book arrives in about 10 days. The experience of the company is as follows:

- On average 60% return the card, and 40% do not return the card.
- Of the 40% who do not return the card, 75% want the book, and 25% lost or misplaced the card, or forgot.
- Of the ones who failed to return the card by accident or neglect, 50% will keep and pay for the book, and 50% will refuse the book and return it to the club.

You visit a member of the club, who has been a member for 1 year, and observe the books she has acquired in that period of time. Assume your friend is typical of the club membership, and book choices are independent. For the sake of uniformity of notation, consider the following events: L = returned the postcard, W = wanted to buy the book, K = kept and paid for unwanted book, and B = paid for book (on purpose or by default).
a. Interpreting the percentages as probabilities, give $P[L]$, $P[W]$, $P[K]$, and $P[B]$.
b. What is the probability that your friend acquired three or more books from the club during the 12-month period she has been in the club? (*Note:* The events defined may or may not help you from now on. Their use is optional.)
c. Assume your friend acquired at least one book, and you select a book at random. What is the probability that your friend bought the selected book on purpose?

A2.1.34 **(a)** $P[L] = 0.6$, $P[W] = 0.3$, $P[K] = 0.05$, $P[B] = P[W \cup K] = P[W] + P[K] = 0.35$, since $W \cap K = \emptyset$; **(b)** $B_{12}(\leq 3, 0.35) = 0.849$; **(c)** 0.857

P2.1.35 A used-car salesman knows from experience that only one out of 20 people who walk onto the lot to look at cars will buy a car. Assume he talks to 20 customers on a particular day.

a. What is the probability that he sells at least two cars that day?
b. How many customers does he have to see before he has a probability of at least 0.5 of making his first sale?
c. What is the probability that he makes his second sale to the twentieth customer?
d. If we know that he sold at least two cars, find the probability that he sold his first car to one of the first two customers. *Hint:* Use the definition of conditional probability, and partition the numerator.

A2.1.35 **(a)** 0.264; **(b)** 14; **(c)** 0.0189; **(d)** 0.226

P2.1.36 A merchant has learned by experience that 1 in 10 customers will buy something he or she likes if it is not "on sale," but 1 in 5 will buy the wanted item if it is "on sale." Consequently the merchant keeps 25% of her merchandise on sale at all times. For simplicity, assume that all items in the store are of equal interest to shoppers, customers are interested in only one item, and that each customer's choice is independent of all others. Consider the following events: $B = $ {customer buys an item}, and $S = $ {item is on sale}.
a. Find the probability that a customer who enters the shop buys something.
b. If a customer buys an item what is the probability it was not on sale?
c. If 100 customers enter the shop in a day, what is the probability that exactly 10 items were bought?

A2.1.36 **(a)** 0.125; **(b)** 0.600; **(c)** 0.0973

P2.1.37 Screws from Company A come 100 in a box. Some of the screws are defective, with a probability of 0.02 for each screw drawn at random from any box from this company. Company B also puts 100 screws in a box, but owing to a quality program the probability that any screw is bad is 0.005.
a. Find P[two bad screws in a box of A screws].
b. Find P[two bad screws in a box of B screws].
c. If a person has one box from each company, selects a box at random, and selects a screw from the box, at random, what is the probability that the screw selected is bad.
d. If a box is chosen at random and that box proves to have two defective screws in it, what is the probability that the box was from Company A?
e. If five boxes from each company are dumped into a bin, and a screw is selected from the bin, what is the probability that the screw is bad?
f. If the screw selected in part e is bad, what is the probability that the bad screw is from Company A?

A2.1.37 **(a)** 0.2734; **(b)** 0.07527; **(c)** 0.0125; **(d)** 0.7831; **(e)** 0.0125; **(f)** 0.800

P2.1.38 Manufacturer A is known to have a defect rate of 1%, meaning that on average 1 of 100 parts does not meet specifications. Manufacturer B has a defect rate of 0.6%.
a. In a box of 100 parts from manufacturer A, find the probability that 2 or more parts are bad.

     b. If parts from manufacturer B are tested, how many will have to be tested to have a probability of at least 0.95 of finding at least one bad part?

     c. A box of 100 parts from A is mixed with a box of 200 from B. A sample of 10 parts is taken at random and tested. Find the probability that all are good.

A2.1.38 **(a)** 0.264; **(b)** 498; **(c)** 0.929

P2.1.39   A *learning curve* describes the process of decreasing the probability of failure and increasing the probability of success with each trial. Let's say the probability of failure is 0.8 on the first trial, but drops to half the previous value with each trial (0.4, 0.2, etc.). These are thus Bernoulli trials in which the probability of success changes with every trial. Thus, $P[$success on second trial|failure on first trial$] = 0.6$, and so on. How many trials do we have to perform to have a 99% probability of at least one success? *Hint:* There's no magic formula for this. You have to work it out.

A2.1.39 Four trials give 0.9936.

P2.1.40   My grandson, Noah (N), and $I(G)$ sometimes shoot baskets together. I'm slightly better than he is; the probabilities of our hitting a shot are $P[G] = 0.3$ and $P[N] = 0.25$, assuming conditions of binomial trials. I always let him go first, and we alternate until someone hits a basket.

     a. What is the probability that Noah wins?

     b. Assuming that I hit the first basket, what is the probability that I hit it on my first shot?

     c. Sometimes we play a game in which the first to hit three shots (not necessarily in a row) wins. Now, the game can end in five, six, ... shots. If it ends on an odd number, Noah wins, and if even, I win. Find the probability that the game ends on the ninth shot.

A2.1.40 **(a)** 0.526; **(b)** 0.475; **(c)** 0.0483

P2.1.41   My grandson and I sometimes shoot baskets together. I'm actually slightly better than he is, making 27% of my shots, to his 22%. We play the game called *PIG,* in which we shoot until someone makes a shot, and then the other must make the same shot or get a P or I or G. Assume he shoots first. Assume that the shots may be modeled as binomial trials.

     a. Given that he hits the first basket, what is the probability that I will get P on my first shot?

     b. What is the probability that I have P after my first shot?

     c. What is the probability that he hits a basket before I do? *Hint:* This involves summing an infinite geometric series.

A2.1.41 **(a)** 0.73; **(b)** 0.161; **(c)** 0.511

P2.1.42   A company is considering selecting a new computer system from the four equally promising systems in its price range. Let A be the event that system A was selected, and likewise for systems B, C, and D. The company has three individuals studying the specifications. Each has a probability of 0.7 of selecting the best system. When their independent choices are reported, it is found that two of them selected A, and one selected B. Assume that all systems except the best are equally likely to be selected.

a. What is the probability that A is best?
b. What is the probability that B is best?
c. What is the probability that C is best?

A2.1.42 (a) 0.6447; **(b)** 0.2763; **(c)** 0.0394

P2.1.43   A basketball coach ends practice by making every player shoot free throws until he hits three in a row. Consider a player who is a 70% free throw shooter and use a model of binomial trials.

a. What is the probability that the player ends on his seventh shot?
b. Given that the player finishes on the seventh shot, what is his expected number of free throws in the sequence?

A2.1.43 (a) 0.0676; **(b)** 4.63

P2.1.44   A marksman has two target rifles. With the better one (B), he has a probability of 0.85 of hitting the bull's eye. With the other (O), his chances are 0.78; however the better rifle needs a lot of maintenance and spends 60% of the time at the gunsmith's shop. The other rifle spends only 10% of the time at the gunsmith's, and these are independent events.

a. What is the probability that he will have a rifle available on the day of the shooting match?
b. If the better rifle is available, what is the probability he hits eight or more bull's-eyes out of 10 shots?
c. In general, what is the probability he will shoot eight or more bull's-eyes out of 10 attempts on the day of the shooting match? Assume he uses the best rifle on hand, including the possibility that neither rifle is available.

A2.1.44 (a) 0.940; **(b)** 0.820; **(c)** 0.661

P2.1.45   A man plants 10 trees along the lane leading to his house, six Wichita pecan trees (W) and four Native pecans (N). The Wichitas survive transplant with 80% probability and the Natives with 60%. Let $k =$ the number of trees that survive transplantation. Assume independence of survival.

a. What is the probability that all trees survive, $k = 10$?
b. What is the probability that $k = 5$ trees survive?
c. If exactly five trees survive, what is the probability that at least three of the survivors are Wichita pecans?

A2.1.45 (a) 0.0340; **(b)** 0.0816; **(c)** 0.933

P2.1.46   In a digital transmission system, an 8-bit binary word is transmitted. Because of the logic levels, there is a probability p_1 that a ONE $\rightarrow$ ZERO in transmission and a probability p_0 that a ZERO $\rightarrow$ ONE, for each bit in the word, and errors are independent. To standardize notation, let $R = \{$ONE received$\}$ and $T = \{$ONE transmitted$\}$.

In all cases assume that before transmission a ONE or ZERO is equally likely in any position and independent of other bits.

a. Find the probability of an error in transmission on a single-bit basis.

b. If a ONE is received, what is the probability that a ONE was transmitted?

c. What is the *a priori* probability that an entire word will be transmitted with no error, assuming errors are independent?

d. What is the probability that at least 1 bit is received incorrectly?

A2.1.46 **(a)** $\frac{p_1+p_0}{2}$; **(b)** $\frac{1-p_1}{1-p_1+p_0}$; **(c)** $\left(1-\frac{p_1+p_0}{2}\right)^8$; **(d)** $1-\left(1-\frac{p_1+p_0}{2}\right)^8$

2.4.2 Random Variables

Exercises on random variables

P2.2.1　You are given a pair of fair dice, which are rolled. Let X be the sum of the values appearing.

a. Find the PMF, $P_X(x)$.

b. Find $P[X \leq 9]$.

c. Find $P[X$ is even or $\geq 9]$.

A2.2.1 **(a)** $P_X(2) = \frac{1}{36}$, $P_X(3) = \frac{2}{36}$, $P_X(4) = \frac{3}{36}$, $P_X(5) = \frac{4}{36}$, $P_X(6) = \frac{5}{36}$, $P_X(7) = \frac{6}{36}$, $P_X(8) = \frac{5}{36}$, $P_X(9) = \frac{4}{36}$, $P_X(10) = \frac{3}{36}$, $P_X(11) = \frac{2}{36}$, $P_X(12) = \frac{1}{36}$, zow; **(b)** $\frac{30}{36}$; **(c)** $\frac{24}{36}$

P2.2.2　An integer is chosen at random between 0 and 4, inclusive. A random variable is assigned to each outcome according to the following rule: $X = \sin\left(\frac{i\pi}{4}\right)$, where i is the outcome. Find and sketch the PMF for X.

A2.2.2

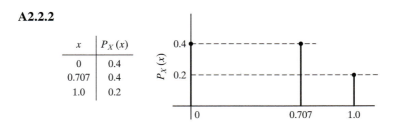

x	$P_X(x)$
0	0.4
0.707	0.4
1.0	0.2

P2.2.3　A series of binomial trials is performed with $P[A] = 0.8$. We are interested in the occurrence of the third success, $k = 3$. Let $N =$ the number of trials.

a. Plot the PMF of N, $P_N(n)$. This is the PMF of the Pascal random variable of order 3.

b. Plot the conditional PMF of N with the condition that failures occurred on the first three trials, $P_N(n \mid$ no success in first three trials).

A2.2.3 **(a)** The plot follows. **(b)** This is no different, except $n' = n - 3$.

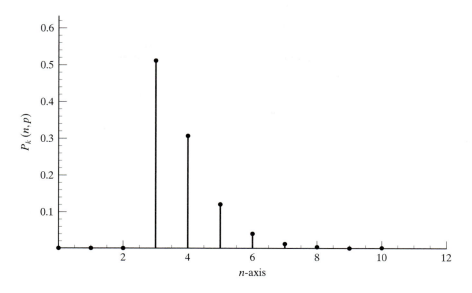

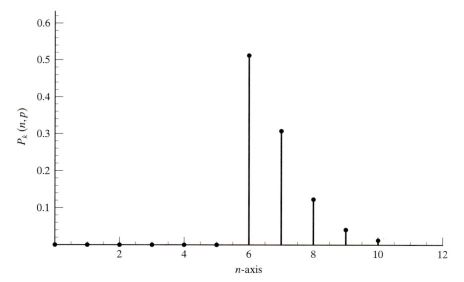

P2.2.4   Calculate and plot the probability mass functions for the following:
a. Binomial for $n = 5$, $p = 0.3$: $K = k$, the number of successes.
b. $S = \{1, 2, 3, 4, 5, 6\}$: $X = \sin\left(\frac{\pi}{6} \times s_i\right)$, where $s_i = 1$, 2, 3, 4, 5, and 6, all equally
likely.

A2.2.4 (a) The first output is the PMF values, followed by the graph.

{{0, 0.16807}, {1, 0.36015}, {2, 0.3087},
{3, 0.1323}, {4, 0.02835}, {5, 0.00243}}

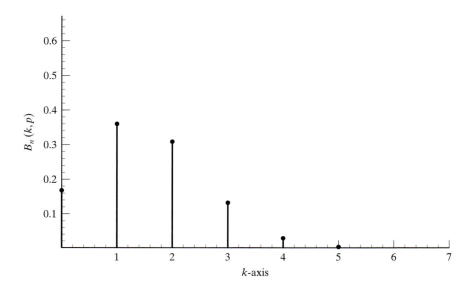

(b) To generate the data, we must compute the value of X for each outcome and attribute the probability that falls on each value. The following table gives the basic information:

s_i	$X(s_i)$	$P[s]$
1	$\frac{1}{2}$	$\frac{1}{6}$
2	$\frac{\sqrt{3}}{2}$	$\frac{1}{6}$
3	1	$\frac{1}{6}$
4	$\frac{\sqrt{3}}{2}$	$\frac{1}{6}$
5	$\frac{1}{2}$	$\frac{1}{6}$
6	0	$\frac{1}{6}$

The PMF comes from the fact that 0 and 1 occur once, and thus have a probability of $\frac{1}{6}$, but $\frac{1}{2}$ and $\frac{\sqrt{3}}{2}$ occur twice and so have a probability of $\frac{1}{3}$.

$$\{\{0, \tfrac{1}{6}\}, \{\tfrac{1}{2}, \tfrac{1}{3}\}, \{\tfrac{\sqrt{3}}{2}, \tfrac{1}{3}\}, \{1, \tfrac{1}{6}\}\}$$

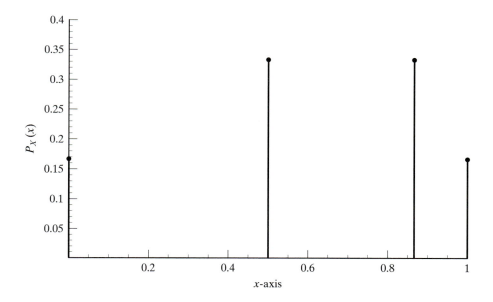

P2.2.5   A number is chosen at random from the space $S = \{-1, 0, 1, 2, 3\}$
a. Plot the PMF, $P_X(x)$, for the random variable $X = s_i$.
b. Plot the PMF, $P_Y(y)$, for the random variable $Y = s_i^2$.
c. Find the probability that on any performance of the experiment the random variable $Y \leq 3$ using the PMF.
d. By means of an array similar to the array in Table 2.2.1, give the joint PMF between X and Y, $P_{XY}(x, y)$.

A2.2.5 (a) $P_X(x) = \frac{1}{5}, x = -1, 0, 1, 2, 3,$ zow

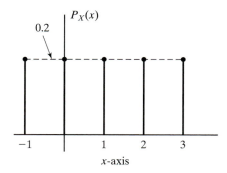

(b) $P_Y(y) = \frac{1}{5}, y = 0, 3, 9, = \frac{2}{5}, y = 1,$ zow.

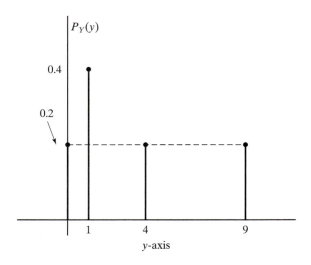

(c) $P[y \le 3] = \frac{3}{5}$

(d)

$Y\backslash X$	-1	0	$+1$	$+2$	$+3$
0	0	$\frac{1}{5}$	0	0	0
1	$\frac{1}{5}$	0	$\frac{1}{5}$	0	0
4	0	0	0	$\frac{1}{5}$	0
9	0	0	0	0	$\frac{1}{5}$

P2.2.6   In a series of three binomial trials with $p = 0.4$, a random variable, X, is assigned to the outcomes to form a base 2 number, with 1 associated with success and 0 associated with failure on each of the three trials. For example, $\bar{A}AA \Rightarrow X = 011_2 = 3_{10}$.
a. Derive and plot the PMF of X, $P_X(x)$, with X in decimal.
b. Find and plot the conditional distribution of X with the condition of an even number of successes, $P_{X|\text{Even}}(x)$. Consider zero to be even.

A2.2.6 (a) $P_X(x) = 0.216, 0.144, 0.144, 0.096, 0.144, 0.096, 0.096, 0.064,$ for $x = 0,$ 1, 2, 3, 4, 5, 6, and 7, respectively. The plot follows.
(b) $P_{X|\text{Even}}(x) = 0.429$ for $x = 0$, and 0.190 for $x = 3, 5,$ and 6, zow. The plot follows.

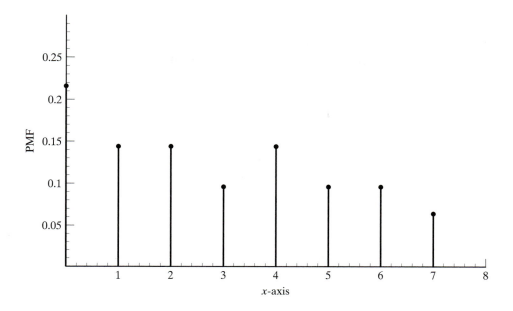

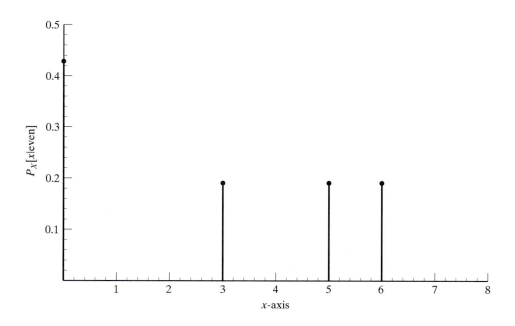

P2.2.7   A series of binomial trials is performed with $P[\text{success}] = 0.8$. Let $X = $ trial number of first success and $Y = $ trial number of second success.

a. Find the conditional PMF $P_{Y|X}(x, y)$ over the range $1 \leq x, y \leq 4$. This is best presented in a table.

b. Derive the joint PMF over the range $1 \leq x, y \leq 4$, which is best presented in a table.

$y \backslash x$	1	2	3	4
1	0	0	0	0
A2.2.7 (a) 2	0.8	0	0	0
3	0.16	0.8	0	0
4	0.032	0.16	0.8	0

$y \backslash x$	1	2	3	4
1	0	0	0	0
(b) 2	0.64	0	0	0
3	0.128	0.128	0	0
4	0.0256	0.0256	0.0256	0

P2.2.8   A chance experiment has outcomes that we may associate with a sequence of integers, $S = \{s_1, s_2, \ldots, \text{to } \infty\}$. Probabilities are assigned to these outcomes according to the rule $P[s_i] = 2^{-i}$.

a. Show that $P[S] = 1$, that is, that the space is properly normalized. This involves summing an infinite geometric series.

b. Let a random variable be assigned to each outcome, where $X = $ the subscript. Thus, $X(s_i) = i$, with $i = 1, 2, 3, \ldots$. Find the probability that X is odd.

c. Given that X is odd, what is the probability that X is less than 5?

d. Given that X is less than 5, what is the probability that X is odd? Are these two events independent?

A2.2.8 (a) It sums to 1; **(b)** $\frac{2}{3}$; **(c)** $\frac{15}{16}$; **(d)** $\frac{2}{3}$; yes, independent

P2.2.9   Two random variables are generated in the following manner: (1) An event of probability $p = 0.7$ is repeated $n = 3$ times. The number of successes is K. Then (2) a number between 0 and K, inclusive, is picked at random. Call this random variable X.

a. What is the PMF of K, $P_K(k)$?

b. What is the joint PMF, $P_{XK}(x, k)$?

c. Find the marginal PMF on X, $P_X(x)$.

A2.2.9 (a) $P_K(k) = B_3(k, 0.7)$, $k = 0, 1, 2, 3$, zow. **(b)** $P_{XK} = \frac{1}{k+1} B_3(k, 0.7)$, $x = 0, 1, \ldots, k$, $k = 0, 1, 2, 3$, zow. **(c)** $P_X(x) = 0.3543, 0.3273, 0.2378$, and 0.08575 for $x = 0, 1, 2,$ and 3, zow.

P2.2.10   Consider a series of binomial trials in which the probability of success is a random variable, P, with a PMF $P_P(p) = \frac{1}{2}$, $p = \frac{1}{3}, \frac{2}{3}$, zow. The chance experiment is to select P and perform a series of trials with that P until the first success occurs. Let $N = $ the trial number of the first success.

a. If the first success occurs on the third trial, what is the probability that $P = \frac{1}{3}$?

b. What range of N favors $P = \frac{1}{3}$, and what range favors $P = \frac{2}{3}$?

A2.2.10 (a) $\frac{2}{3}$, **(b)** $N \geq \frac{1}{3}$, $P = \frac{1}{3}$ is favored; for $N = 2$, neither is favored; and for $N < 2$, $P = \frac{2}{3}$ is favored.

P2.2.11   A integer, between 1 and 10 inclusive is chosen. The probability of choosing a number is inversely proportional to the number, $P_I(i) = \frac{c}{i}, i = 1, 2, \ldots, 10$. Then a fair coin is flipped I times, producing K heads.
a. Find the joint PMF, $P_{IK}(i, k)$.
b. Find $P[I^2 + K^2 \leq 16]$.
c. Find $P_K(7)$, the marginal PMF of K, evaluated at $k = 7$.

A2.2.11 (a) $\binom{i}{k} \left(\frac{1}{2}\right)^i \times \frac{0.3414}{i}, i = 1, 2, \ldots, 10, 0 < k \leq i$, zow; **(b)** 0.617; **(c)** 0.008383

Modeling problems on random variables

P2.2.12   There are three types of soft-drink machines on campus. Those that cost 75¢, those that cost 60¢, and those that cost 50¢. Consider that there are roughly equal numbers of these machines, such that the probability of picking any type is $\frac{1}{3}$. Let the experiment be to pick a machine at random, insert a dollar bill, purchase a drink, and observe the change that comes out of the machine. Assume the machine gives the minimum number of coins in change. Let Q = the number of quarters, D = the number of dimes. (We will ignore nickels.) Describe the PMFs for Q and D.

A2.2.12 $P_Q(q) = 0, \frac{2}{3}, \frac{1}{3}$ for $q = 0$, 1, and 2, respectively, zow; $P_D(d) = \frac{2}{3}, \frac{1}{3}$, for $d = 0$, 1, respectively, zow.

P2.2.13   A student throws darts. He has a 90% chance of hitting the target. If he hits the target, he has a 20% chance of a bull's eye (10 points), a 30% chance of hitting the second ring (5 points), and a 50% chance of hitting the outer ring (2 points). Zero points are awarded when the target is missed. Let X = the points awarded on a throw. Determine and sketch the PMF, $P_X(x)$.

A2.2.13 $P_X(x) = 0.18, 0.27, 0.45, 0.1$, for $x = 10, 5, 2$, and 0, respectively, zow.

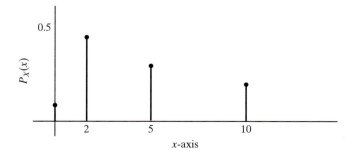

P2.2.14   A man takes his wife to dinner in a restaurant where meals cost \$6, \$8, or \$10. His wife has good taste and is more likely to pick the more expensive dishes. Let $\frac{6}{24}$, $\frac{8}{24}$, and $\frac{10}{24}$ be the probabilities of her choosing the \$6, \$8, or \$10 meals, respectively. He, being from a small town in North Texas, is equally likely to choose any of the \$6, \$8, or \$10 meals. Their choices are independent.

    a. Describe the sample space and give the probabilities of all the various outcomes.

    b. Let the random variable C = the total cost of the two meals. What is the range of C, S_C?

    c. Derive the PMF of C, $P_C(c)$.

    d. The man has only \$22 in his pocket and figures that, considering tax and tip, the total cost should be at most \$18. Find $P_{C|C \leq 18}(c)$, the conditional PMF given that the cost is not more than \$18.

A2.2.14 (a)

He\She	\$6 $\left(\frac{6}{24}\right)$	\$8 $\left(\frac{8}{24}\right)$	\$10 $\left(\frac{10}{24}\right)$
\$6 $\left(\frac{1}{3}\right)$	$\frac{1}{12}$	$\frac{8}{72}$	$\frac{10}{72}$
\$8 $\left(\frac{1}{3}\right)$	$\frac{1}{12}$	$\frac{8}{72}$	$\frac{10}{72}$
\$10 $\left(\frac{1}{3}\right)$	$\frac{1}{12}$	$\frac{8}{72}$	$\frac{10}{72}$

    (b) $S_C = \{12, 14, 16, 18, 20\}$; **(c)** $P_C(c) = \frac{1}{12}, \frac{14}{72}, \frac{1}{3}, \frac{1}{4}, \frac{10}{72}$ for $c = 12, 14, 16, 18, 20$, zow; **(d)** $P_{C|C \leq 18}(c) = \frac{6}{62}, \frac{14}{62}, \frac{24}{62}, \frac{18}{62}$ for $c = 12, 14, 16, 18$, respectively, zow.

2.4.3 The Definition and Algebra of Expectation

Exercises on Expectation

P2.3.1   A container contains balls with numbers, $1, 2, 3, \ldots, m$ written on them. There is one ball with 1 on it, two balls with $2, \ldots$, up to m balls with m written on them. The balls are drawn one at a time, with replacement, until a 4 is drawn. On average it takes seven draws to get a 4. What is m?

    A2.3.1 7

P2.3.2   A random variable takes on five values. The PMF is

$$P_X(1) = 0.1$$
$$P_X(2.1) = 0.2$$
$$P_X(2.6) = 0.2$$
$$P_X(3) = 0.15$$
$$P_X(3.7) = 0.35$$

    a. Show that the PMF is normalized.

    b. Find the mean of X.

    c. Find the variance of X.

   d. Find the probability that on a given performance of the experiment X falls within one standard deviation of the mean.

   A2.3.2 (a) The probabilities add to 1.0; **(b)** 2.79; **(c)** 0.7193; **(d)** 0.55

P2.3.3   A integer is chosen at random in the range $S = \{1, 2, 3, 4, 5, 6, 7, 8, 9\}$. A random variable is defined on the outcomes $X = \frac{1}{i}$, where i is the outcome of the chance experiment.
   a. Give the PMF of X.
   b. Determine the mean of X.
   c. Determine the standard deviation of X.
   d. Find the probability that X falls within one standard deviation of its mean.

   A2.3.3 (a) $P_X(x) = \frac{1}{9}$, $x = 1, \frac{1}{2}, \frac{1}{3}, \frac{1}{4}, \frac{1}{5}, \frac{1}{6}, \frac{1}{7}, \frac{1}{8}, \frac{1}{9}$, zow; **(b)** 0.314; **(c)** 0.269; **(d)** $\frac{8}{9}$

P2.3.4   Consider a series of binomial trials with $n = 7$ and $p = 0.4$. Let K be a random variable that counts the number of successes in the seven trials.
   a. Find the mean of K.
   b. Find the mean square value of K.

   A2.3.4 (a) 2.80; **(b)** 9.52

P2.3.5   The PMF of a random variable is given by $P_X(x) = \frac{c}{x}$, where x takes on the integer values $x = 1, 2, 3, 4, 5$, zow.
   a. Find c.
   b. Find the mean.
   c. Find the standard deviation.
   d. A new random variable is defined by the relationship $Y = (X - 2)^2$. Find the variance of Y.

   A2.3.5 (a) 0.4380; **(b)** 2.190; **(c)** 1.332; **(d)** 6.154

P2.3.6   A PMF is given by the following function:

   $$P_X(0) = 0.1, \; P_X(2) = 0.1, \; P_X(3) = 0.5, \; P_X(5) = 0.3, \; \text{zow}$$

   a. Find the mean and variance of X.
   b. Find the conditional PMF, $P_{X|X\leq4}(x)$.
   c. If $Y = |2.5 - X|$, find the PMF of Y.
   d. Give the expected value of $5 + Y$.

   A2.3.6 (a) $\mu_X = 3.20$, $\sigma_X^2 = 2.16$; **(b)** $P_{X|X\leq4}(0) = \frac{1}{7}$, $P_{X|X\leq4}(2) = \frac{1}{7}$, $P_{X|X\leq4}(3) = \frac{5}{7}$, zow; **(c)** $P_Y(0.5) = 0.6$, $P_Y(2.5) = 0.4$, zow; **(d)** 6.30

P2.3.7   For problem P2.2.13
   a. What is the expectation of X?
   b. What is the expectation of X, given that the target is hit?

   A2.3.7 (a) 4.05; **(b)** 4.50

P2.3.8   For problem P2.2.12
a. Find the expected number of quarters in change.
b. Find the expected number of quarters, given that $D = 0$.

A2.3.8 (a) $\frac{4}{3}$; **(b)** $\frac{3}{2}$

P2.3.9   A telemarketer calls people on the telephone to make appointments for an insurance salesman. The average number of calls that need to be made to make one appointment is 10. Find the probability that the second successful call will occur before the tenth call.

A2.3.9 0.226

P2.3.10   An experiment consists of picking an integer at random between 0 and 5, inclusive: $S = \{0, 1, 2, 3, 4, 5\}$. A random variable is defined as $X = \sin\left[\frac{\pi s_i}{10}\right]$.
a. Find $E[X]$.
b. Find $Var[X]$.
c. Find $P[\mu_X - \sigma_X < X < \mu_X + \sigma_X]$.

A2.3.10 (a) 0.6095; **(b)** 0.1285; **(c)** 0.667

P2.3.11   a. The mean of a random variable described by the binomial distribution is np, and the variance is npq. Find $P[\mu_X - \sigma_X < X \leq \mu_X + \sigma_X]$ if $n = 10$ and $p = 0.32$.
b. The mean of a random variable described by the geometric distribution is $1/p$, and the variance is q/p^2. Find $P[\mu_X - \sigma_X < X \leq \mu_X + \sigma_X]$ if $p = 0.32$.

A2.3.11 (a) 0.693; **(b)** 0.5346

P2.3.12   A chance experiment consists of four binomial trials with $p = 0.4$. A Bernoulli random variable, X, is 0 or 1, depending on the failure or success of the first trial, respectively. The random variable, Y, depends on the remaining three trials: if $X = 1$, then $Y =$ the number of successes in the three trials; if $X = 0$, then $Y =$ the number of failures in the three trials.
a. Find the joint PMF of X and Y.
b. Find the expected value of XY, $E[XY]$.
c. Find the marginal PMF of Y, $P_Y(y)$.

A2.3.12 (a) $P_{XY}(x, y) = 0.6B_3(y, 0.6), x = 0, y = 0, 1, 2, 3$; and $P_{XY}(x, y) = 0.4B_3(y, 0.4), x = 1, y = 0, 1, 2, 3$; **(b)** 0.480; **(c)** $P_Y(0) = 0.125, P_Y(1) = 0.346, P_Y(2) = 0.374, P_Y(3) = 0.155$, zow

P2.3.13   Abe tosses a fair coin twice, and Bert tosses a fair coin three times. Let X_A be the number of heads for Abe and X_B be the number of heads for Bert.
a. Give the bivariate PMF for the two random variables in the form of a 3×4 table.
b. Find the probability that Abe had more heads than Bert.
c. Find $E[X_A - X_B]$.
d. Find $Var[X_A - X_B]$.

$X_B \backslash X_A$	$0(\frac{1}{4})$	$1(\frac{1}{2})$	$2(\frac{1}{4})$
$0(\frac{1}{8})$	$\frac{1}{32}$	$\frac{1}{16}$	$\frac{1}{32}$
$1(\frac{3}{8})$	$\frac{3}{32}$	$\frac{6}{32}$	$\frac{3}{32}$
$2(\frac{3}{8})$	$\frac{3}{32}$	$\frac{6}{32}$	$\frac{3}{32}$
$3(\frac{1}{8})$	$\frac{1}{32}$	$\frac{1}{16}$	$\frac{1}{32}$

A2.3.13 (a) [table above] ; **(b)** $\frac{6}{32}$; **(c)** $-\frac{1}{2}$; **(d)** $\frac{5}{4}$

P2.3.14 Consider two independent random variables, X and Y. The random variable X is an integer uniformly distributed between 0 and 2, inclusive (three values), and Y is a geometric random variable with an expectation of 2. A new random variable is formed as $Z = X + Y$.
a. Find the expected value of Z.
b. Find the variance of Z.
c. Find the PMF of Z.

A2.3.14 (a) 3; **(b)** $\frac{8}{3}$; **(c)** $P_Z(1) = \frac{1}{6}$, $P_Z(2) = 0.25$, $P_Z(3) = 0.2917$, $P_Z(z) = 2.333(\frac{1}{2})^z$, $z > 3$, zow

P2.3.15 In a series of three binomial trials with $p = 0.4$, a random variable, X, is assigned to the outcomes to form a base 2 number, with 1 associated with success (A), and 0 associated with failure $(\bar{A})$. For example, $A\bar{A}A \rightarrow 101_2 = 5_{10}$.
a. Find the expected value of X, $E[X]$.
b. Find the expected value of X if $P[A] = 0.5$. (*Hint:* Don't do any calculations.)

A2.3.15 (a) 2.80; **(b)** 3.5

P2.3.16 A discrete random variable has values at $x_i = 1 + 0.5^{i-1} = 2, 1.5, 1.25, 1.125, \ldots$ where $i = 1, 2, 3, \ldots$. The probabilities of these values are $P[X = x_1] = a$ and $P[X = x_i] = (\frac{1}{3})^{i-1}$, $i > 1$.
a. What is a? *Hint:* The series is a geometric series and can be summed.
b. What is the PMF for X?
c. Find the expected value of X, $E[X]$.

A2.3.16 (a) $\frac{1}{2}$; **(b)** $P_X(x) = \frac{1}{2}$ for $x = 2$, $(\frac{1}{3})^{i-1}$ for $x = 1 + (\frac{1}{2})^{i-1}$, zow; **(c)** $E[X] = 1.7$

P2.3.17 A man is sent to the store to buy groceries, instructed to purchase four apples "without blemish" for an apple dessert. He examines apples for blemishes and finds the probability to be 0.4 of rejecting an apple. That is, $P[\text{good apple}] = 0.6$. Let N be a random variable, the number of apples he must inspect to find the required four perfect apples.
a. Find and plot $P_N(n)$, the PMF for N. (Go to $n = 10$ at least.)
b. Find $E[N]$, the expected number of apples he must examine to find four perfect apples.

A2.3.17 **(a)** $P_N(n) = 0.130, 0.207, 0.207, 0.166, 0.116, 0.0743, 0.04459$, for $N = 4$, 5, 6, 7, 8, 9, and 10; the plot follows; **(b)** The theoretical expectation is $k/p = 4/0.6 = 6.67$; the answer is approximately 6.01, based on $4 \leq n \leq 10$.

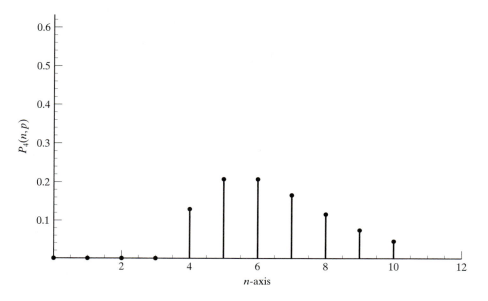

P2.3.18 Consider a series of eight binomial trials. Let X = number of successes on the first four trials and Y = the number of successes on the last four trials. Let $P[\text{success}] = p$.
a. Find $P_{XY}(x, y)$.
b. Find $E[X - Y]$.
c. Find $Var[X - Y]$.

A2.3.18 **(a)** $P_{XY}(x, y) = B_4(x, p) \times B_4(y, p)$; **(b)** 0; **(c)** $8(p - p^2)$

P2.3.19 A sample space consists of all the integers from 1 to ∞. The probability assigned to each is proportional to the reciprocal of the integer's factorial, i.e., $P[s_i] = \frac{c}{i!}$, where c is a constant.
a. Find c.
b. Find the probability that an odd number is chosen in any performance of the experiment.
c. Find the probability that a number less than or equal to 6 is chosen, given that the number is odd.
d. Letting a random variable I = the number chosen, find the expectation of I.

A2.3.19 **(a)** $c \approx 0.582$; **(b)** ≈ 0.684; **(c)** ≈ 0.999829; **(d)** ≈ 1.582. These answers are based on summing terms until they are extremely small, which does not take long.

P2.3.20   A markswoman shoots at a target. The probability of her hitting at least one bull's-eye on the first three shots is 0.7. Assume the conditions of binomial trials are satisfied.
a. What is the probability that she will hit a bull's-eye on the fourth shot?
b. What is the probability that she will hit her first bull's eye on the fourth shot?
c. What is the probability that she will hit her third bull's eye on the tenth shot?
d. If she shoots 10 times, what is the expected number of bull's-eyes?

A2.3.20 (a) 0.3306; (b) 0.09917; (c) 0.07835; (d) 3.306

P2.3.21   A freight elevator in a four-story building can carry one, two, three, or four pieces of equipment. Let X = the number of boxes of equipment, and Y = the floor on which the elevator stops. The joint PMF for these random variables is given in the following table. For example, the probability of unloading three boxes on the second floor is 0.050.

$Y \backslash X$	1	2	3	4
1	0.175	0.075	0.050	0.025
2	0.075	0.025	0.050	0.100
3	0.050	0.100	0.025	0.050
4	0.025	0.100	0	0.075

a. Show that the joint PMF is properly normalized.
b. Are X and Y independent? Explain.
c. Find $P_X(X)$, the marginal distribution of X, the number of boxes.
d. Find $E[X]$.
e. Find $E[X + Y | X + Y \le 3]$, the expected value of the sum of X and Y, given that their sum is less than or equal to 3.

A2.3.21 (a) The entries add to 1; (b) They are not independent, since the entries in the table are not equal to the product of the marginal probabilities; (c) $P_X(x) = 0.325, 0.300, 0.125, 0.250$ for $x = 1, 2, 3$, and 4, respectively, (d) 2.30; (e) 2.46

Modeling Problems on Expectation

P2.3.22   A producer of breakfast cereals puts prizes in Yummies boxes to entice children to beg their parents to buy Yummies. A ring goes into one of every 10 boxes and a small ball into one of every 12 boxes. Assume prizes are placed at random and independently.
a. If a family buys Yummies, what is the probability that their first prize comes in the third box?
b. If at least one prize is in the third box, what is the probability that the third box contains two prizes?
c. On average, how many boxes would they have to buy to get at least one prize?

A2.3.22 (a) 0.119; (b) 0.0476; (c) 5.71

P2.3.23 The state of Quadtana is perfectly square, 300 miles on a side. It has 36 counties, all equally square and each with its county seat at the exact center. The capital of Quadtana, Centerville, is at the exact center of the state. Citizen Jones of another state moves to Quadtana, picking a county in the state at random. Let Z be a random variable describing the distance from Centerville to the county seat of the county where Jones lives.

a. Find and plot the PMF of Z.
b. Find the expected distance from Centerville to Citizen Jones's county seat.
c. Find the standard deviation of this distance.

A2.3.23

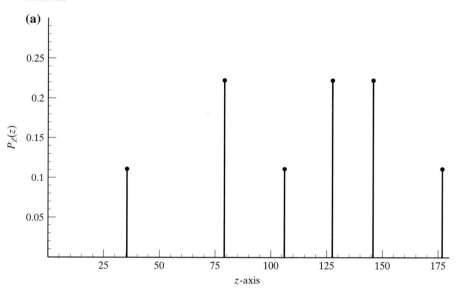

(b) 114 miles; **(c)** 41.0 miles

P2.3.24 A bakery bakes 300 apple muffins/day. These sell for $1.25 each before 5 P.M. and half price afterward until they are sold out. On average the bakery sells a day's output for $350. Find the probability that a given muffin will be sold for full price.

A2.3.24 0.867

P2.3.25 The short-term parking lot at the airport fills up at certain times and has open spaces as people come and go at random times. On average about 6% of the spaces are open at any given time. Assume these spaces are randomly distributed.

a. On average, how many filled spaces does one drive past before finding a place to park?
b. What is the probability that no space will appear in the first 50 spaces passed?

A2.3.25 **(a)** 15.7; **(b)** 0.04533

P2.3.26   A hunter goes out to shoot at ducks. He takes plenty of shells because he's a poor shot. On average he has to shoot 10 times to get one duck.
a. What is the probability that after eight shots he still has no duck?
b. What is the probability that he gets his second duck on the twentieth shot?

A2.3.26 (a) 0.430; **(b)** 0.0285

P2.3.27   A student walks into a drugstore with a $20 bill and buys something. The item bought could cost 1¢ up to the full $20, all values considered equally likely in the absence of information to the contrary. Let $X =$ the number of bills given in change (neglect coins), assuming that the minimum number of bills are given.
a. Find the PMF of X.
b. Find the probability that X is more than three.
c. Find the conditional expected value $E[X|X \neq 2]$.

A2.3.27 (a) $P_X(0) = \frac{1}{20}$, $P_X(1) = \frac{3}{20}$, $P_X(2) = \frac{4}{20}$, $P_X(3) = \frac{4}{20}$, $P_X(4) = \frac{4}{20}$, $P_X(5) = \frac{3}{20}$, $P_X(6) = \frac{1}{20}$, zow; **(b)** 0.4; **(c)** 3.25

P2.3.28   An exam has four problems in it, each worth 25 points. Let N be the number of problems a student answers correctly (no partial credit). The PMF of N is $P_N(0) = 0.05$, $P_N(1) = 0.20$, $P_N(2) = 0.35$, $P_N(3) = 0.25$, $P_N(4) = 0.15$, zow.
a. Express the grade G as a function of N.
b. Find the PMF of G.
c. What is the expected value of G, given that the student answered at least one question correctly?
d. What is the variance of G, given that the student answered at least one question correctly?
e. What is the probability that the student's grade is greater than the mean plus or minus half the standard deviation, all with the condition that the student answered at least one question correctly?

A2.3.28 (a) $G = 25N$; **(b)** $P_G(0) = 0.05$, $P_G(25) = 0.2$, $P_G(50) = 0.35$, $P_G(75) = 0.25$, $P_G(100) = 0.15$, zow; **(c)** 59.2; **(d)** 606; **(e)** 0.368

P2.3.29   Two basketball players shoot from 3-point range until one hits. The first to shoot (A) has a probability of 0.5 of hitting on any given shot, and the second (B) has a probability of 0.6 of hitting on any given shot.
a. What is the probability that A wins?
b. Estimate the average number of shots before a winner is determined.

A2.3.29 (a) 0.625; **(b)** $\approx$1.8 shots

P2.3.30   A parking lot that is not full will have most of the open spaces at the far side, away from the entrance, but a lot that is full will have open spaces more or less uniformly distributed. Assume a lot that is full has 100 spaces, and the probability that any space is open at any time is 0.02.
a. You drive in and cruise down the rows looking for a space. What is the probability that you will find a space in the first 25 spaces you pass?

b. On average, how many spaces will you have to pass to find a space?

c. What is the probability that there are exactly 2 spaces open in the lot at a given time?

A2.3.30 **(a)** 0.3965; **(b)** 49 (based on an infinite parking lot, 42.4 based on 100 spaces; **(c)** 0.2734

P2.3.31 A basketball player who hits 60% of her free throws plays the following game: She takes two shots and then K more shots, where K is the number she makes out of the first two. Thus she takes two, three, or four shots. Let $X =$ the total number she hits. Find the expected value of X.

A2.3.31 1.920

P2.3.32 A stockbroker calls faculty at random to see if they are interested in "learning about our services." From much experience, he knows the following: 30% hang up rudely when they find that he is trying to sell something; 50% listen to his speech and then politely say they are not interested; and 20% ask for printed information. Of those who ask for printed information, one in 10 actually becomes a customer. In the first case, it takes about 15 seconds; in the second, about 1 minute; and in the third, 1.5 minutes to complete the call.

a. Assume our caller works for 30 minutes and makes 30 calls. Find the probability that the first receptive contact is the eighth call. By *receptive* we mean someone in the third category, asking for printed information.

b. Given that the first receptive contact is on the eighth call, what is the probability that four receptive contacts are made among the 30 calls?

c. Given that both conditions of the previous parts are satisfied, what is the probability that the last call is a success, that is, a receptive contact?

d. Find the average time spent on a call.

A2.3.32 **(a)** 0.0419; **(b)** 0.178; **(c)** 0.0242; **(d)** 52.5 seconds

P2.3.33 A chance experiment produces a voltage that is measured at different times. The voltages are discrete, with three values that are on the meter scale and one that is off scale on the high side. The PMF for the voltages on scale are $P_X(1) = 0.2$, $P_X(3) = 0.4$, and $P_X(8) = 0.1$. It is known that the variance is 20. Find the true mean of the voltage random variable.

A2.3.33 5.819 V

P2.3.34 An industrial customer purchases an expensive item that is critical to the company business plan. If the item passes the acceptance tests the customer pays the manufacturer $10M (event A). If the item fails the acceptance tests, the customer sues the manufacturer for $5M (event B). If the manufacturer proves in court that the acceptance tests were defective and that the item met specifications after all, the judge will award the manufacturer $3M as a punitive judgment, plus the customer must accept and pay for the item (event C). The engineers and lawyers make the following estimates: $P[A] = 0.8$, $P[C|B] = 0.6$.

a. Which events constitute a partition?

b. Find the probability that the company pays the punitive judgment.

c. Find the expected cost to the industrial customer.

A2.3.34 (a) A, $B \cap C$, and $B \cap \overline{C}$ partition the space; (b) $P[C] = 0.12$; (c) $9.16M

P2.3.35 In a gambling situation, the odds are set such that the house will come out ahead on average. Let $P[\text{house wins}] = p$, and $P[\text{customer wins}] = 1 - p$. The house wants to realize a 1% profit, meaning that for each $100 bet, the house will on average make $1. Assume that a customer bets $100. How much should the house pay the customer, in addition to giving him back his $100, if the customer wins? (The answer is a function of p.)

A2.3.35 House pays $\frac{100p-1}{1-p}$ on a $100 bet.

P2.3.36 You are in line at the county clerk's office, specifically the line to register automobiles. There are 10 people in front of you. Some people are renewing their registrations, which takes 2 minutes, and others are registering new vehicles, which takes 5 minutes. A sign on the wall informs you that the office takes, on average, 3 minutes to serve a customer. Find the probability that you have to wait more than 36 minutes to be served.

A2.3.36 0.0766

P2.3.37 A recruiter has a mandate to hire 10 engineers. He visits Superior University first and interviews only 10 students because there is such demand for SU engineers he can't get more students to sign up for an interview. He knows that the probability of hiring any given SU engineer is 0.4, because there is such competition for these excellent engineers. He then goes on to Ho-Hum University and keeps interviewing until his quota is filled. At HHU the probability of success on any given interview is 0.8, and plenty of students are looking for jobs. Let $X =$ the number of engineers hired at SU, $Y =$ the number hired at HHU, and $N =$ the number of interviews required to fill his quota.

a. Find $P_X(x)$.

b. Find $E[X]$.

c. Find $E[Y]$.

d. Find $E[N]$.

A2.3.37 (a) $P_X(x) = B_{10}(x, 0.4)$; (b) 4.0; (c) 6.0; (d) 17.5

P2.3.38 A shot-putter expends so much effort on each put that the conditional probability of reaching the target distance, given failure on all previous attempts, is halved with each effort. Assume his probability of success on the first trial is $p_1 = 0.4$. Thus $q_1 = 0.6$, $p_2 = 0.2$, etc. Let $X =$ the trial on which success occurs. Find $E[X|\text{success does occur}]$, the expected trial number for success, given that success occurs on some trial. Consider only three tries.

A2.3.38 1.38

P2.3.39   A calculator has a problem that one time out of 10, on average, when a 4 is keyed, the number actually entered into the calculator is 6. A series of 100 single integers are summed in the calculator, in which all integers, including 0, are equally likely.
a. What is the probability that an error is introduced on any given integer?
b. What is the probability that the sum is incorrect?
c. What is the expected error due to that problem?

A2.3.39 (a) 0.0100; **(b)** 0.634; **(c)** 2

P2.3.40   According to a *learning curve,* experience increases probability of success in an endeavor. Here the chance experiment is a series of independent trials in which the probability of success is $P[A_i \mid \text{failed on previous trial}] = \frac{i}{10}$, where $i = $ trial number. Thus the probability of success on the first trial is 0.1, and the probability of success on the second trial is 0.2, and so on. The experiment is to try until you succeed. Trials beyond 10 never occur, since success is sure on the tenth trial.
a. Find the probability of success on or before the third trial.
b. Given that success is achieved on or before the third trial, what is the probability that success occurred on the third trial?
c. Let $I = $ the trial on which success occurred. Find the PMF of I.
d. Find the average trial on which success occurs.

A2.3.40 (a) 0.216; **(b)** 0.435; **(c)** see the following table; **(d)** 3.66

i	$P_I(i)$
1	0.1
2	$0.9 \times 0.2 = 0.18$
3	$0.9 \times 0.8 \times 0.3 = 0.216$
4	$0.9 \times 0.8 \times 0.7 \times 0.4 = 0.2016$, etc., until
10	0.00036

P2.3.41   Two basketball players shoot baskets. The first to hit a basket wins. The first to shoot has a probability of p_1 of making a basket and the second $p_2 > p_1$.
a. Find the relationship between p_1 and p_2 if the game is fair; that is, each has an equal chance of winning.
b. Find the average length of a (fair) game in terms of p_1. Let $N = $ the number of shots and find $E[N]$. *Note:* The series is not easy to sum. You can give the first four terms if you can't sum it.

A2.3.41 (a) $p_2 = \frac{p_1}{1-p_1}$; **(b)** $p_1 + 2p_1 + 3p_1 \times \frac{1-2p_1}{1-p_1} + 4p_1 \times (1-2p_1) + \cdots + = \frac{4-2p_1}{4p_1}$ (summed by Mathematica).

P2.3.42   An electronic system comes into the shop for repair with one or more of the following problems: About 20% of the time there are power supply problems (let V represent this event); about 30% of the time there are faulty components (let F represent this event); and 60% of the time there are connector or internal cabling problems (let C represent this event). Sometimes nothing is wrong. Cabling problems are independent of power supply and component problems, but power supply and component problems couple in the following fashion: if there is a component problem, there is a 35% chance that there is also a power supply problem.

a. Find $P[F|V]$, the conditional probability that there is a component problem, given that there is a power supply problem.

b. Find $P[V|F \cup C]$, the probability that there is a power supply problem, given that there is either a component or connector (or both) problems.

c. Let the repair cost be the following: $10 + $50 for one problem, $10 + $90 for two problems, and $10 + $120 for three problems. Find the expected repair cost.

A2.3.42 **(a)** 0.525; **(b)** 0.225; **(c)** $50.97, considering that about 37% of the time the cost is zero because there are no problems.

P2.3.43 A basketball coach ends practice by making every player shoot free throws until he hits three in a row. Consider a player who is a 70% free-throw shooter and use a model of binomial trials.

a. What is the probability that the player ends on his fourth shot?

b. What is the probability that the player ends on his seventh shot?

A2.3.43 **(a)** 0.1029; **(b)** 0.0676

P2.3.44 You have rented a car for the day from Wrent a Reck car rental company, whose cars are known to have problems now and then. Let M represent the distance in miles beyond 100 miles that you will be able to drive before the engine overheats. If the car has a good radiator, denoted as event G, then M is a geometric random variable with $p = 0.03$. If the car has a bad radiator, denoted as event B, then M is a geometric random variable with $p = 0.1$. Assume further that $P[G] = 0.6$.

a. What is the PMF of M, given that the radiator is bad?

b. What is the PMF of M generally?

c. If your round trip is 120 miles, what is the probability of getting back without an overheated radiator?

d. What is your expected distance to travel before having radiator trouble?

A2.3.44 **(a)** $(0.9)^{m-1} \times 0.1$; **(b)** $0.04 \times 0.9^{m-1} + 0.018 \times 0.97^{m-1}$; **(c)** 0.3904; **(d)** 124 miles

P2.3.45 Consider a binary communication channel that sends a 2-bit word, $X_1 X_0 = 00,01,10$, or 11. Let X represent a bit sent and Y represent a bit received. Thus X_1 represents the most significant bit sent, and so on. The sent bits are equally likely to be 0 or 1, and values are independent, but errors in transmission are not equal, but have the following transitional probabilities: $P[Y_0 = 1|X_0 = 0] = 0.05$, $P[Y_0 = 0|X_0 = 0] = 0.95$, $P[Y_0 = 0|X_0 = 1] = 0.10$, $P[Y_0 = 1|X_0 = 1] = 0.90$, and the same for X_1 and Y_1.

a. Letting X (no subscript) represent the numerical value of the transmitted word (0,1,2,3) and Y the same for the received word, find the transitional probabilities for X and Y. This is perhaps best expressed in a table of 16 cells.

b. Find the marginal PMF of Y.

c. Let $E = Y - X$ be the numerical value of the error between Y and X. Find the expected value of E.

$Y\backslash X$	0(00)	1(01)	2(10)	3(11)
0(00)	0.9025	0.095	0.095	0.010
1(01)	0.0475	0.855	0.005	0.090
2(10)	0.0475	0.005	0.855	0.090
3(11)	0.0025	0.045	0.045	0.810

A2.3.45 (a) (table above)

(b) $P_Y(0) = 0.2756$, $P_Y(1) = 0.2494$, $P_Y(2) = 0.2494$, $P_Y(3) = 0.2256$, zow; **(c)** -0.0750

ENDNOTES

1. **Answer to you do it on p. 90.** The event $\{k = 3 \text{ or } 4\}$ partitions into the events $\{k = 3\}$ and $\{k = 4\}$, so we can add the probabilities $B_5(3, 0.8) + B_5(4, 0.8) = 0.205 + 0.410 = 0.614$.

2. **Answer to you do it on p. 91.** For a direct calculation of two or more failures, we need $\sum_2^{100} B_{100}(k, 0.005)$, but the sensible calculation is

$$1 - B_{100}(0, 0.005) - B_{100}(1, 0.005) = 1 - 0.606 - 0.304 = 0.090$$

3. **Answer to you do it on p. 92.** Of course, you can proceed by trial and error, as in the example, and if you do it right, you should decide that $n = 5$ gives a probability of 0.530, but $n = 4$ gives 0.453. This problem can be solved analytically as well. The equation is $1 - B_n(0, 0.14) = 1 - (0.86)^n = 0.5$, which yields $n = 4.60$. We must round up to $n = 5$ to have a greater than 50% chance for one or more women in the class.

4. **Geometric series.** We give, without proof, the sums of the finite and the infinite geometric series. The finite geometric series is

$$S_n = 1 + a + a^2 + \cdots + a^n = \frac{1 - a^{n+1}}{1 - a} \quad \text{for all } a$$

For $n \to \infty$ and $a^2 < 1$, the series converges to

$$S = 1 + a + a^2 + \cdots = \frac{1}{1 - a}$$

Note that

$$a^k + a^{k+1} + a^{k+2} + \cdots = a^k(1 + a + a^2 + \cdots) = \frac{a^k}{1 - a}$$

Series related to the geometric series. We also will need the following:

$$\sum_0^\infty ka^k = (a + 2a^2 + 3a^3 + \cdots) = a\frac{d}{da}(1 + a + a^2 + a^3 + \cdots)$$

$$= a\frac{d}{da}\left(\frac{1}{1 - a}\right) = \frac{a}{(1 - a)^2}$$

and the following as well, which extends the same trick:

$$\sum_0^\infty k^2 a^k = (1^2 a + 2^2 a^2 + 3^2 a^3 + \cdots) = a \frac{d}{da}\left(a \frac{d}{da}\left(\frac{1}{1-a}\right)\right)$$

$$= \frac{a(1+a)}{(1-a)^3}.$$

Notice that in the previous two summations, the lower limit can be either $k = 0$ or $k = 1$.

5. **Answer to you do it on p. 94.** The event $n = 5$ through 10, inclusive, partitions into the events $n = 5, n = 6, \ldots, n = 10$. Thus the answer is the sum $P[n = 5 \text{ through } 10] =$

    $$\sum_5^{10} P_1\left(n, \frac{1}{3}\right) = q^4 p + q^5 p + \cdots + q^9 p = q^4 p(1 + q + q^2 + \cdots + q^5) = q^4 - q^{10} = 0.180. \text{ Note}$$

    this probability is easily interpreted as $P[\text{no lights in first four}] - P[\text{no lights in first 10}]$.

6. **Answer to you do it on p. 95.** For the second good potato to be found on the fifth trial exactly, we need $P_2(5, 0.45) = 0.135$.

7. **Zow.** The term *zero otherwise* is used so often that we substitute this acronym, but we read it as "zero otherwise," not the phonetic pronunciation.

8. **Answer to you do it on p. 108.** If all resistor values are equally likely, then 70 Ω has a probability of $\frac{1}{6}$, $P_R(70) = \frac{1}{6}$. Because 70 Ω corresponds to 1.43 W, it follows that $P_W(1.43) = \frac{1}{6}$.

9. **Answer to you do it on p. 109.** If probability is proportional to resistance, $P_R(r) = ar$, where a is a constant. Normalization requires that $a(50 + 60 + 70 + 80 + 90 + 100) = 1$. Because resistor values of 50 Ω and 60 Ω correspond to $W > 1.6$ W, the resulting probability is $P[W > 1.6] = \frac{(50+60)}{50+60+70+80+90+100} = 0.244$.

10. **Answer to you do it on p. 111.** This is rather like Example 2.2.5. The outcome that leads to $X = 0$ is $s = 4$, which has a probability of $\frac{1}{6}$. Because $P[\text{Even}] = \frac{1}{2}$, it follows that $P_{X|E}(0) = \frac{1/6}{1/2} = \frac{1}{3}$.

11. **Answer to you do it on p. 112.** Because only 9 and 16 meet the condition, and they are equally likely, the answer must be $\frac{1}{2}$.

12. **Answer to you do it on p. 113.** This is an instance of Bayes' rule. Let $G =$ the event of a good part. Then Bayes' rule states that $P[M|G] = \frac{P[G|M] \times P[M]}{P[G]} = \frac{0.98 \times 0.4}{0.98 \times 0.4 + 0.99 \times 0.6} = 0.3976$.

13. **Answer to you do it (a) on p. 118.** The answer is 27.

14. **Answer to you do it (b) on p. 118.** Binomial is correct.

15. **The *NK* PMF.** The binomial part is $P[K = k|N = n] = B_n(k, 0.5)$, $k = 0, 1, \ldots, n$, and the uniform part is $P_N(n) = \frac{1}{6}$, $n = 1, 2, \ldots, 6$. Combining them we have

    $$P_{NK}(n, k) = B_n(k, 0.5) \times \frac{1}{6} = \binom{n}{k}\frac{1}{6 \times 2^n} \quad k = 0, 1, \ldots, n, n = 1, 2, \ldots, 6$$

16. **Answer to you do it on p. 123.** The Bernoulli random variable was introduced in Sec. 2.2. Introducing the definition in Eq. (2.3.5), we have $E[X] = 0 \times q + 1 \times p = p$.

17. **Answer to you do it on p. 127.** Using Eq. (2.3.21) and the mean and mean squared values of the binomial random variable, we get

    $$Var[K] = E[K^2] - \mu_K^2 = (np)^2 + np(1-p) - (np)^2 = np(1-p) = npq$$

18. **Calculating the 12.2%.** Basically we want the sum of the geometric distribution from 20 to ∞, which is

$$pq^{20} + pq^{21} + \cdots = pq^{20}(1 + q + q^2 + \cdots) = pq^{20}\left(\frac{1}{1-q}\right) = q^{20}, \text{ since } 1 - q = p$$

For $q = 0.9$ this is $(0.9)^{20} = 0.122 = 12.2\%$.

19. **Answer to you do it on p. 129.** The mean square value of the Bernoulli random variable is $E[X^2] = 0^2 \times q + 1^2 \times p = p$, so the variance is $Var[X] = p - p^2 = pq$. For $p = 0.4$, the answer is 0.24.

20. **Answer to you do it on p. 131.** The requirement $\sqrt{X} > 2.4$ leaves in only $X = 6, 7, 8, 9$, all equally likely. The required conditional expectation is therefore $(6^2 + 7^2 + 8^2 + 9^2) \times \frac{1}{4} = 57.5$.

21. **Answer to you do it on p. 133.**

$$E[e^X] = (e^0 + e^1 + e^2) \times \frac{1}{3} = 3.702 \text{ and } 2E[X] = 2$$

The answer is 1.702.

3

Continuous Random Variables and the Gaussian Model

3.1 CONTINUOUS RANDOM VARIABLES

To this point we have described sample spaces and random variables that are discrete, involving either a finite or a countably infinite number of outcomes. In this chapter we introduce sample spaces and random variables of a continuous nature, involving an uncountable infinity of outcomes. In Sec. 3.1.1 we discuss differences between discrete and continuous spaces and define appropriate means to describe how probability is distributed to a continuous random variable.

3.1.1 Continuous Sample Spaces

Discrete and continuous number systems in engineering

Measured data. All real-world probability spaces are discrete. For example, all measured values have limited accuracy and hence are meaningful only out to, say, the fourth place. This means that, in effect, only discrete values can result from a measurement.

Computer output. Another example is any number produced by a computer or any other digital system. There exists a least significant bit somewhere in the system that limits the output to a discrete set of numbers.

A useful model. Often, a discrete sample space is well modeled as a continuum. If, for example, the accuracy of the data is good, one may have thousands of possible outcomes from a measurement. In such instances, using continuous numbers can offer real advantages. One advantage is that we do not have to worry about the details of the computer or measurement system that produced the numbers when we model with a continuous space.

Easy math.   In addition, the math gets easier. Which calculation would you prefer to perform,

$$\sum_{i=0}^{100} i^4 = 0^4 + 1^4 + 2^4 + \cdots + 100^4 \quad \text{or} \quad \int_0^{100} x^4 \, dx \quad ? \quad\quad (3.1.1)$$

These are essentially the same calculation, except the first is discrete and the second continuous. Clearly, you would rather do the integral rather than the sum. Of course, Mathematica has no trouble with either, so perhaps this is not a big advantage, but generally we like easy math. To see the Mathematica results, see endnote 1.

3.1.2 Describing Probabilities in Continuous Sample Spaces

The concept of a continuous sample space.   Mathematicians can prove that there are an infinite number of rational numbers, numbers that can be expressed as a ratio of integers, in any finite interval of the real line, say, from 1.5 to 2.0. Furthermore, they tell us that between any two rational numbers there exists an infinity of irrational numbers. Hence, an uncountable infinity of points lies between 1.5 and 2.0 on the real axis.

Pick a number, any number.   Consider now the sample space $S = \{1.5 < s \le 2.0\}$, where all outcomes are equally likely. Thus the chance experiment is to pick a number at random between 1.5 and 2.0. Clearly we have an infinity of outcomes. It follows that $P[s = 1.75] = 0$, since 1.75 is only one of an infinity of outcomes. We illustrate this in the following way. Evaluating the following expression will generate $k = 25$ numbers from a population uniformly distributed between 1.5 and 2, printed with 10-place accuracy. Although it is possible that 1.750000000 is one of the numbers, this is rather unlikely. If you are running Mathematica, try it a few times and get a feel for how unlikely it is.

```
k=25;
Table[NumberForm[Random[Real, {1.5,2}],10],{k}]
```

{1.754301748, 1.830036463, 1.690279158,
 1.972605016, 1.718271984, 1.672246016,
 1.534970989, 1.955686084, 1.588103819,
 1.933640064, 1.788797722, 1.750123663, 1.826551125,
 1.787069398, 1.989428098, 1.972417095, 1.622214896,
 1.569336222, 1.811659055, 1.790547474, 1.85559485,
 1.851147333, 1.603731846, 1.585718837, 1.601293102}

A simple model for this experiment suggests that the probability of getting exactly 1.750000000 at least once in 25 tries is 5×10^{-8}. Clearly, if we had asked for 20-place accuracy, getting a prescribed answer would be even more unlikely.

Events of zero probability versus the impossible event.   Thus the probability that $s =$ any prescribed number in the space is exactly zero! This follows from common sense, and also from the classical definition of probability, that the probability of an event is the number of outcomes favorable to the event (one outcome) divided by the number of outcomes (an infinity of outcomes). But $\{s = 1.75\}$ is not the impossible event, since it can occur. Some number between 1.5 and 2.0 occurs each time the experiment is performed. We conclude that although the impossible event has zero probability, $P[\emptyset] = 0$, every event with zero probability is not an impossible event. The impossible event has zero probability by definition, whereas the outcome $\{s = 1.75\}$ has zero probability owing to numerical considerations.

Assigning probabilities to the outcomes for this space.   We can assign probabilities to intervals of the sample space. For example, we expect that $P[1.5 < s \leq 2] = 1$, since this covers the entire range, which is the certain event and has a probability of 1. In general, we expect that the probability that the outcome will occur in a prescribed range is proportional to the width of that range, provided that the range lies within the bounds from 1.5 to and including 2. This means that $P[s_1 < s \leq s_2] = K(s_2 - s_1)$, where K is a constant, s_1 and s_2 are in the range between 1.5 and 2, and $s_1 < s_2$. Since with $s_1 = 1.5$ and $s_2 = 2$ we have the certain event, it follows that the constant, K, must be $\frac{1}{2-1.5} = 2$. Therefore we can calculate the probability that the outcome will fall in the region $s_1 < s \leq s_2$ to be $2(s_2 - s_1)$, provided s_1 and s_2 are in the range between 1.5 and 2, and $s_1 < s_2$. This probability is shown by the crosshatched area in Fig. 3.1.1.

You do it.   (a) For the chance experiment just described, find $P[1.5 < s \leq 1.6]$. Enter your answer in the cell box, and click Evaluate for the response.

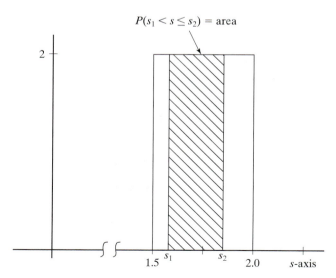

Figure 3.1.1   The crosshatched area gives the probability that s will fall in that range on any performance of the chance experiment.

```
myanswer = ;
```

```
Evaluate
```

For the answer, see endnote 2.

(b) For the same situation, find $P[1.4 < s \leq 1.6]$.

```
myanswer = ;
```

```
Evaluate
```

For the answer, see endnote 3.

Unequal outcomes. If all outcomes in the range are not equally likely, we can represent the distribution of probabilities by a general function rather than a uniform function, as shown in Fig. 3.1.2.

This way of defining probabilities is essentially the same as defining a random variable on the space and describing it by a probability *density* function. In other words, since continuous sample spaces are numerical, with every outcome of the experiment a number or set of numbers, we can simply consider these as random variables defined on the outcomes and discuss how the probability maps into the range of the random variable through a function that is like the probability mass function. We explore these ideas in the next section.

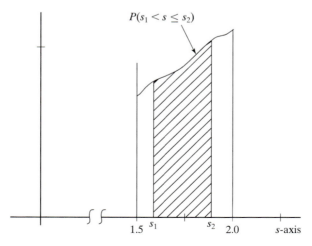

Figure 3.1.2 With outcomes that are not equally likely, we can still represent the probability as an area, which is to say, as an integral of some function.

Summary.   The following are some major points about continuous sample spaces:

- Although all real-world numbers are discrete, the continuous number system offers many theoretical and practical advantages.
- With outcomes in a continuous space, probability is associated with regions of outcomes. A single outcome like $\{s = 1.75\}$ has zero probability.
- Because continuous outcomes are always numerical, the outcomes of a chance experiment and a random variable associated with those outcomes is essentially the same. Therefore, in continuous sample spaces we usually start with a random variable.

3.1.3 The Probability Density Function (PDF)

Probability density functions (PDFs).   Figure 3.1.3 shows how the probability density function is defined.

In Fig. 3.1.3 we see that the sample space maps into the range of the random variable on the real axis, S_X, and the probabilities distribute according to some function, $f_X(x)$. This function is called the *probability density function*, PDF for short. Figure 3.1.3(b) and (c) show the relationship between a PMF, which gives the probability at a point when we have a discrete random variable, and the PDF, which gives the probability that the random variable will lie in an infinitesimal region. The probability that was concentrated at one point in the discrete case (PMF) is spread over a region in the continuous case (PDF).

Definition of probability density function, PDF.   We define the PDF for a continuous random variable as follows:

$$P[x < X \le x + dx] = f_X(x)\,dx, \quad \text{with } dx \ge 0 \tag{3.1.2}$$

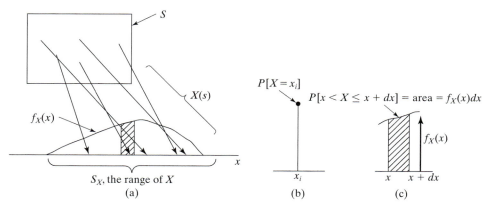

Figure 3.1.3   (a) The random variable is defined in the usual way. (b) With a discrete random variable, all the probability is lumped at one point. (c) With a continuous random variable, probability is distributed to all points. The crosshatched area shows the probability that the random variable, X, will fall in a region between x and $x + dx$.

Thus the PDF is defined in terms of the probability that on any given performance of the experiment the random variable falls in a narrow region in the vicinity of x. Formally, we let $dx \to 0$ according to the conventions of calculus. We may make Eq. (3.1.2) look more like a density by dividing by dx, as in Eq. (3.1.3):

$$f_X(x) = \frac{P[x < X \leq x + dx]}{dx} \tag{3.1.3}$$

which we can interpret as a probability per unit distance in x.

Properties of the probability density function. The PDF has some properties in common with the PMF. Here we list some properties of the PDF.

1. The probability density function, PDF, is nonnegative $f_X(x) \geq 0$. This follows from Eq. (3.1.2) and the rule that probabilities are nonnegative.
2. The probability *mass* function, PMF, is a probability and must be less than or equal to 1, whereas the PDF is a *density* of probability and may be greater than 1. In the previous example $f_X(x) = 2$ in a certain region if $X(s) = s$.
3. The PDF may be used to determine the probability that the random variable, X, will fall in an interval:

$$P[x_1 < X \leq x_2] = \int_{x_1}^{x_2} f_X(x)\,dx, \ \ x_1 \leq x_2 \tag{3.1.4}$$

Discussion of Eq. (3.1.4). To show that Eq. (3.1.4) is true we consider a partition of the event $\{x_1 < X \leq x_2\}$.

In Fig. 3.1.4, we break the region between x_1 and x_2 into many smaller regions of width Δx and label these regions $R_1, R_2, \ldots$. If X is to fall between x_1 and x_2, then it must fall in one and only one of these regions. Thus we may partition the event of interest as follows:

$$\{x_1 < X \leq x_2\} = \{X \in R_1\} \cup \{X \in R_2\} \cup \{X \in R_3\} \cup \cdots \cup \{X \in R_n\} \tag{3.1.5}$$

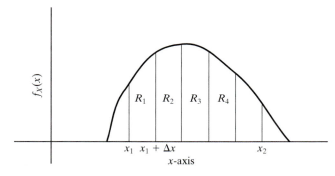

Figure 3.1.4 We break the region between x_1 and x_2 into many smaller regions of width Δx. These allow a partition of the event whose probability is calculated in Eq. (3.1.4).

where n is the number of regions. Because the events on the right of Eq. (3.1.5) are disjoint, we have a partition of the event in question and we may calculate its probability using Eq. (1.5.7) as follows:

$$P[x_1 < X \le x_2] = P[X \in R_1] + P[X \in R_2] + P[X \in R_3] + \cdots + P[X \in R_n] \qquad (3.1.6)$$

But the probabilities of each of the events on the right side can be expressed in terms of the PDF, Eq. (3.1.2). For example,

$$P[X \in R_1] = f_X(x_1)\Delta x \qquad (3.1.7)$$

Thus in Eq. (3.1.6), as $\Delta x \to dx$ the sum becomes the integral in Eq. (3.1.4).

4. The PDF must be normalized. There are no restrictions on x_1 and x_2 in Eq. (3.1.4), so we can set $x_1 = -\infty$, and $x_2 = +\infty$. For these values the event on the left side of Eq. (3.1.4) becomes the certain event, and hence the integral of the PDF must be normalized to unity:

$$P[-\infty < X \le +\infty] = \int_{-\infty}^{+\infty} f_X(x)\,dx = P[S] = 1 \qquad (3.1.8)$$

Thus all PDFs are nonnegative functions with unit area. This is equivalent to the normalization condition for PMFs, Eq. (2.2.3). We might note that the equal sign at the upper limit of the region does not matter for continuous spaces; however, it does matter in discrete spaces and in spaces where continuous and discrete random variables are mixed. We use the less than or equal sign at the top of the interval to develop consistent habits.

5. The PDF has units. If, for example, x was a distance in meters, the PDF would have units of inverse meters. This follows because a probability is a pure number with no units.

6. The PDF is used to compute expectations. The mean is expressed in terms of the PDF as

$$\mu_X = E[X] = \int_{-\infty}^{+\infty} x f_X(x)\,dx \qquad (3.1.9)$$

which follows from the reasoning that was used in defining the mean with the PMF. The integral replaces the sum that was used there, Eq. (2.3.5). For the expectation for functions of the random variable, X, we have

$$E[Y(X)] = \int_{-\infty}^{+\infty} y(x) f_X(x)\,dx \qquad (3.1.10)$$

For example, the mean square value of a random variable and the variance of X would be

$$E[X^2] = \int_{-\infty}^{+\infty} x^2 f_X(x)\,dx$$

and

$$Var[X] = \int_{-\infty}^{+\infty} (x - \mu_X)^2 f_X(x)\,dx = \int_{-\infty}^{+\infty} x^2 f_X(x)\,dx - \mu_X^2 = E[X^2] - \mu_X^2$$

$$(3.1.11)$$

Summary. The PMF and the PDF play similar roles in the development of probability. In discrete spaces, we sum the PMF to normalize and compute probabilities and expectations. In continuous spaces, we integrate the PDF to normalize and compute probabilities and expectations. When we combine discrete and continuous random variables later in this chapter, we will use impulse functions to express the probability on a point in a continuous space.

3.1.4 The Uniform and Exponential PDFs

In Sec. 3.1.2 we used as an example (Fig. 3.1.1) of a continuous sample space a chance experiment in which the outcomes were numbers between 1.5 and 2.0, with all outcomes equally likely. We now have defined PDFs and can develop that example more fully. Our random variable is the outcome itself, $X(s) = s$, where s represents the equally likely outcomes, $\{1.5 < s \leq 2.0\}$. In this example we will find the PDF of X and calculate the mean and variance of this random variable. Because all outcomes are equally likely, we require that the PDF be a constant, C:

$$f_X(x) = C, 1.5 < x \leq 2, \text{ zow} \tag{3.1.12}$$

We can determine C through the normalization condition, Eq. (3.1.8):

$$\int_{-\infty}^{+\infty} f_X(x)\,dx = \int_{1.5}^{2} C\,dx = 0.5\,C = 1, \text{ therefore } C = 2 \tag{3.1.13}$$

This is, of course, the same result that we determined earlier by similar reasoning, in different notation. The mean would be

$$\mu_X = E[X] = \int_{-\infty}^{+\infty} x f_X(x)\,dx = \int_{1.5}^{2} 2x\,dx = x^2\big|_{1.5}^{2} = 1.75 \tag{3.1.14}$$

which is the balance point of the PDF. To calculate the variance, we first calculate the mean square value:

$$E[X^2] = \int_{-\infty}^{+\infty} x^2 f_X(x)\,dx = \int_{1.5}^{2} 2x^2\,dx = \frac{2}{3}x^3\big|_{1.5}^{2} = 3.083 \tag{3.1.15}$$

and hence the variance is

$$Var[X] = E[X^2] - \mu_X^2 = 3.083 - (1.75)^2 = 0.02083 \tag{3.1.16}$$

and the standard deviation is

$$\sigma_X = \sqrt{0.02083} = 0.1443$$

Finally, we find the probability that the random variable, on a given performance of the experiment, falls within one standard deviation of the mean. This is a simple integral, as follows:

$$P[\mu_X - \sigma_X < X \leq \mu_X + \sigma_X] = \int_{\mu_X - \sigma_X}^{\mu_X + \sigma_X} f_X(x)\,dx = \int_{1.606}^{1.894} 2\,dx = 0.577 \tag{3.1.17}$$

We note that this probability is about $\frac{2}{3}$, slightly less in this case, which is typical for symmetric PDFs.

The general properties of a uniform PDF.   Here we want you to generalize the previous example to a uniform PDF between two values, a and b, where $a < b$. Assume that you have the PDF

$$f_X(x) = C, \ a < x \le b, \ \text{zow} \tag{3.1.18}$$

where C is a constant. Your first task is to find C. Because the height can be expressed as 1 over something, we have built that into the form for you to use. Enter your results in the cell box, and click Evaluate. Use an ordinary font (no italics).

```
myanswer = "1/(?)";
```

```
Evaluate
```

For the answer, see endnote 4.

As an example we plot the PDF for $a = 2$ and $b = 4$ in Fig. 3.1.5.

Now, calculate the expected value and the variance. You may follow the preceding example, but use the general case, a and b. Here are some questions you ought to ask yourself about your answer:

- Does the mean you derive look like the balance point of the distribution?

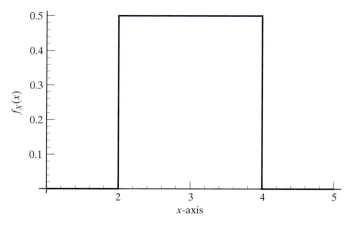

Figure 3.1.5 Plot of the PDF of a uniform distribution between 2 and 4. Note that the height is 1 over the base, such that the area is 1.

- Does the square root of the variance, the standard deviation, bear some relation to the width of the distribution? As a general rule for distributions that are somewhat symmetric, about two-thirds of the area under the PDF curve will lie within one standard deviation on both sides of the mean. A mathematical expression of the previous statement is

$$P[\mu - \sigma < X < \mu + \sigma] \approx \tfrac{2}{3} \tag{3.1.19}$$

Following is a test to see if your results are correct. Calculate the probability given in Eq. (3.1.19). Your answer should be a pure number near $\tfrac{2}{3}$, not dependent on a or b. Enter your answer in the cell box, and click Evaluate for a response.

```
myanswer = ? ;
```

```
Evaluate
```

For the answer, see endnote 5.

Summary of the properties of the uniform PDF.   If the random variable is uniformly distributed between a and b, with $b > a$, it has a PDF of

$$f_X(x) = \frac{1}{b-a}, \ \ a < x \le b, \ \text{zow} \tag{3.1.20}$$

and it has a mean and variance of

$$\mu_X = \frac{b+a}{2} \ \text{ and } \ \sigma_X^2 = \frac{(b-a)^2}{12} \tag{3.1.21}$$

The uniform PDF as a model.   The uniform PDF can successfully model situations in which we know only the range of a random variable. For example, let us say we buy a new car, and the manufacturer guarantees the gasoline mileage to be between 24 and 27 miles per gallon (mpg). If we have no further knowledge, a reasonable model for the PDF of M, a random variable representing the unknown mileage, would be $f_M(m) = \tfrac{1}{3}, 24 < m \le 27$, zow.

Modeling ignorance.   In one sense, use of the uniform PDF is demanded by our ignorance of the true PDF. As such, it is a conservative model. For the car mileage, our intuition might suggest that $M = 25.5$ mpg, being near the middle of the range, is more likely than $M = 24$ mpg. But one also could argue that $M = 24$ mpg is more likely; it all depends on how the manufacturer tests and tinkers with the cars to ensure that the specification is met. In the absence of such detailed knowledge, the uniform PDF is a good model.

The exponential PDF.   Another useful model is the exponential PDF, defined as

$$f_T(t) = ae^{-at}, \ t \ge 0, \ a > 0, \ \text{zow} \tag{3.1.22}$$

which is shown in Fig. 3.1.6 for $a = 1$.

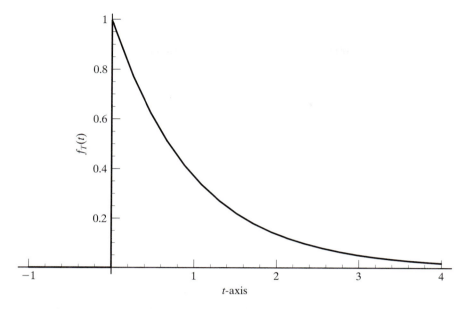

Figure 3.1.6   The exponential PDF is useful for modeling random events in time; hence we use *T* for the random variable. We will derive this distribution from basic assumptions in Chapter 5.

The exponential PDF is useful in describing random events in time; that is why we used *T* for the random variable in Eq. (3.1.22) and in Fig. 3.1.6. We will derive the exponential PDF from basic assumptions in Chapter 5; we introduce it here as a second example to illustrate the properties and uses of PDFs.

- The PDF is nonnegative and is normalized to 1:

$$\int_{-\infty}^{+\infty} f_T(t)\, dt = \int_0^{+\infty} ae^{-at} dt = 1 \tag{3.1.23}$$

- The mean is $\dfrac{1}{a}$:

$$\mu_T = E[T] = \int_{-\infty}^{+\infty} t f_T(t)\, dt = \int_0^{+\infty} tae^{-at}\, dt = \frac{1}{a}\int_0^{+\infty} xe^{-x}\, dx = \frac{1}{a} \tag{3.1.24}$$

- The mean square value is $\dfrac{2}{a^2}$:

$$E[T^2] = \int_{-\infty}^{+\infty} t^2 f_T(t)\, dt = \int_0^{+\infty} t^2 ae^{-at}\, dt = \frac{1}{a^2}\int_0^{+\infty} x^2 e^{-x}\, dx = \frac{2}{a^2} \tag{3.1.25}$$

- The variance is $\dfrac{1}{a^2}$:

$$\sigma_T^2 = E[(T - \mu_T)^2] = E[T^2] - \mu_T^2 = \frac{2}{a^2} - \left(\frac{1}{a}\right)^2 = \frac{1}{a^2} \tag{3.1.26}$$

- The probability that T falls within one standard deviation of the mean is

$$P[\mu_T - \sigma_T < T \leq \mu_T + \sigma_T] = \int_0^{\frac{2}{a}} a e^{-at}\, dt = 1 - e^{-2} = 0.8647 \tag{3.1.27}$$

This is somewhat higher than the $\frac{2}{3}$ mentioned earlier, Eq. (3.1.19), for PDFs with symmetric shapes; the exponential PDF is highly skewed and departs significantly from this rule of thumb.

3.1.5 The Cumulative Distribution Function (CDF)

The cumulative distribution function, CDF.   With continuous random variables we have an alternative way to describe how the probabilities distribute on the real line. This alternative, the cumulative distribution function, CDF, has the advantage that it is a probability.

Definition of the CDF.   The CDF is defined as the probability that the random variable, X, is less than or equal to an independent variable, x: $F_X(x) = P[X \leq x]$. This definition is illustrated in Fig. 3.1.7.

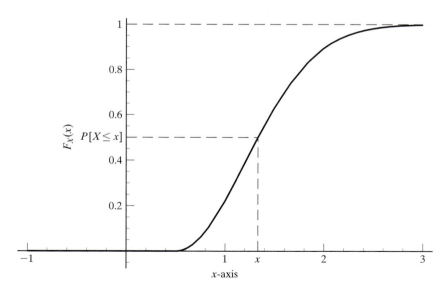

Figure 3.1.7   The height of the CDF is the probability that the random variable, X, is less than or equal to x. The CDF never decreases, because as x increases, more probability is included, and probability never goes away.

The CDF and the PDF. The CDF and the PDF are related through a derivative/integration operation. Comparing the definition of the CDF with Eq. (3.1.4) with $x_1 = -\infty$ and $x_2 = x$, you will realize that

$$F_X(x) = P[X \le x] = \int_{-\infty}^{x} f_X(x')\,dx' \tag{3.1.28}$$

and

$$f_X(x) = \frac{d}{dx}F_X(x) \tag{3.1.29}$$

follows immediately from differentiating Eq. (3.1.28). Note we must use the "dummy" variable, x', since x is the upper limit of the integral.

Comparing the CDF and the PDF. If we have the same information in the CDF as we have in the PDF, why do we need both? As we develop this subject you will see that generally we use the CDF in derivations and in setting up problems. The CDF is a probability, and we have many rules for manipulating, and much experience with, probabilities. The PDF, in contrast, is a probability density and is useful for calculating probabilities and expectations. The PDF is our calculation engine, whereas the CDF is our way out of the woods when we are lost. We need both even though they contain the same information.

In Fig. 3.1.8 we show the CDF for the uniform PDF with limits $a = 2$ and $b = 4$. This is the integral of the PDF in Fig. 3.1.5, provided you use the same a and b, of course.

The properties of the CDF. The properties of the CDF are as follows:

1. The CDF is a probability and hence must lie between 0 and 1: $0 \le F_X(x) \le 1$.

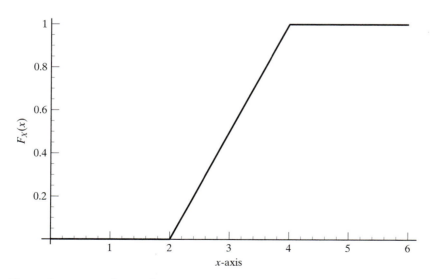

Figure 3.1.8 CDF for uniform PDF between the values of $a = 2$ and $b = 4$.

2. The CDF is nondecreasing, since $P[X \leq x]$ can only gain, and never lose, probability as x increases.
3. The value at $-\infty$ is zero: $F_X(-\infty) = 0$. This represents the probability of an impossible event, $\emptyset = \{X \leq -\infty\}$.
4. The value at $+\infty$ is 1: $F_X(+\infty) = 1$. This represents the probability of a certain event: $S = \{X \leq +\infty\}$.
5. Because $\{X \leq x_2\} = \{X \leq x_1\} \cup \{x_1 < X \leq x_2\}$, and since these two events are disjoint, it follows that

$$P[X \leq x_2] = P[X \leq x_1] + P[x_1 < X \leq x_2] \tag{3.1.30}$$

from which it follows immediately that

$$P[x_1 < X \leq x_2] = P[X \leq x_2] - P[X \leq x_1] = F_X(x_2) - F_X(x_1) \tag{3.1.31}$$

Thus the CDF allows us to determine the probability that a random variable lies in a continuous range by taking the difference between the CDF at the limits of that range. If the CDF is known, this is easier than integrating the PDF.

Example 3.1.1
The CDF of a random variable is $F_X(x) = 1 - e^{-2x}$, $x \geq 0$, zow. Find the probability that on any performance of the experiment the random variable falls between 1 and 1.5.

Solution Using Eq. (3.1.31), we find

$$P[1 < X \leq 1.5] = F_X(1.5) - F_X(1) = 1 - e^{-2 \times 1.5} - (1 - e^{-2 \times 1}) = 0.0855$$

By the way, notice that we always put the less than or equal sign at the top of the range. For a continuous random variable the *or equal* part contributes no probability, since the probability of the event $\{X = 1.5\}$ is zero; nevertheless, it is consistent to include the upper bound of the interval.

You do it. What is the PDF of the random variable described in the previous example? Work out your answer, substitute $x = 1$, enter your answer in the cell box, and click Evaluate for a response.

```
myanswer = ;
```

```
Evaluate
```

For the answer, see endnote 6.

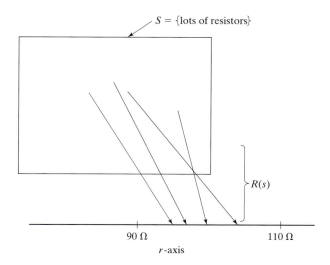

$S = \{\text{lots of resistors}\}$

$R(s)$

90 Ω   110 Ω

r-axis

Figure 3.1.9 The outcomes of the chance experiments are resistors. The random variable is the resistance of the resistors. We are assuming sufficient number of resistors that we model the random variable with a uniform PDF between 90 and 110 Ω, as indicated in Eq. (3.1.32).

3.1.6 Use of PDFs: An Extended Example

We will illustrate these definitions and applications in the context of an extended example. New concepts and definitions will be introduced as required.

Example starting with a resistor chosen at random

The chance experiment is to choose a resistor from a bin containing "100-Ω" resistors. Actually, the bin contains resistors between 90 Ω and 110 Ω, with all values in this range equally likely. The outcome of the experiment is the resistor chosen. The random variable associated with the outcome is the resistance of the resistor, R. We will base a series of examples on this chance experiment. The chance experiment is illustrated in Fig. 3.1.9, and the PDF of the resistors is[7]

$$f_R(r) = 0.05 \ \Omega^{-1}, \ \ 90 < r \le 110, \ \ \text{zow} \tag{3.1.32}$$

Example 3.1.2:   Value of the resistance ─────────────────────────────
Find the probability that the resistance of the chosen resistor is between 100 and 105 Ω.

Solution   We may calculate the probability that the selected resistor falls between 100 and 105 Ω, using Eq. (3.1.4):

$$P[100 < R \le 105] = \int_{100}^{105} f_R(r) \, dr = \int_{100}^{105} 0.05 \, dr = 0.25 \tag{3.1.33}$$

This makes perfect sense because the 5-Ω range is one-fourth of the total range of 20 Ω.

Example 3.1.3: Power range _____

Assume the resistor is a 3-W (watt) resistor. What is the probability that the resistor is thermally stressed by having a power exceeding 3 W, assuming a voltage of 17 V is applied.

Solution We can address this question within the framework of our original experiment, or we can consider this a new chance experiment (choose a resistor and connect it to a 17-V battery) and a new random variable (the resulting power in the resistor). We will regard this as part of the original experiment but define a second random variable that is a function of the original random variable:

$$W(R) = \frac{(17)^2}{R} \tag{3.1.34}$$

This change can be considered a mapping of one random variable to another, from R to $W = (17)^2/R$. This mapping is shown in Fig. 3.1.10. We see that 90 Ω corresponds to 3.21 watts and 110 Ω to 2.63 watts. Hence the range for W will be $2.63 < W \leq 3.21$ watts.

Mapping events. The power 3 watts corresponds to a resistance of 96.3 Ω. The event $\{3 \leq W\}$ contains all values of the power that are greater than or equal to 3 watts. Each of these values corresponds to a resistor in the event $\{R \leq 96.3\}$. Thus we can map an event in W to an event in R.

Calculating the required probability. We may calculate the probability $P[3 \leq W]$ by calculating the probability of the event

$$P[R \leq 96.3] = \text{the area shaded in Fig. 3.1.10} = 0.05 \times (96.3 - 90) = 0.317 \tag{3.1.35}$$

This calculation is based on the mapping of an event in W to a corresponding event in R.

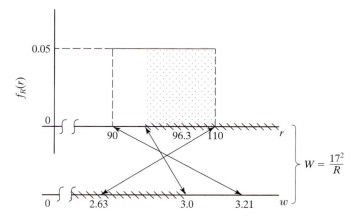

Figure 3.1.10 All the resistor values between 90 and 110 Ω map to powers between 2.63 and 3.21 watts. This can be considered a change in random variables from R to W.

You do it.   What is the probability that the power falls in the range $2.7 < W \leq 2.9$ watts? Enter your answer in the cell box, and click Evaluate for a response.

```
myanswer = ;
```

```
Evaluate
```

For the answer, see endnote 8.

Example 3.1.4:   Expected value of the power
Find the expected value of the power in the resistor: $E[W]$.

Solution   Because the power, W, is a function of a random variable of known PDF, R, we can apply the definition in Eq. (3.1.10):

$$E[W(R)] = \int_{-\infty}^{+\infty} w(r) f_R(r)\, dr = \int_{90}^{110} \frac{17^2}{r} 0.05\, dr = 14.5 \ln\left(\frac{110}{90}\right) = 2.90 \text{ watts} \quad (3.1.36)$$

Thus the resistors connected to 17 V have an average power of 2.90 watts.

3.1.7 Conditional PDFs and Conditional Expectations

As we have stated repeatedly, conditional probabilities provide a powerful analysis tool. We therefore wish to explore the definition and uses of conditional probabilities in the analysis of probabilities in continuous spaces, using PDFs and CDFs. We continue the example with a conditional expectation. This in turn will require the definition and determination of a conditional PDF.

Example 3.1.5:   Expected power of overstressed resistors
Find the expected value of the power in the thermally overstressed resistors: $E[W|W > 3]$.

Solution   Resistors with more power than 3 watts are thermally overstressed. To calculate the average power of all such resistors we need the conditional PDF: $f_{R|W \geq 3}(r)$. The definition requires a slight modification of the definition of an (unconditional) PDF, Eq. (3.1.2).

$$f_{R|W \geq 3}(r)\, dr = \frac{P[(r < R \leq r + dr) \cap (W \geq 3)]}{P[W \geq 3]} \quad (3.1.37)$$

The denominator of Eq. (3.1.37) has been determined to be 0.317. The effect of the conditioning event in the numerator is to limit the domain of resistors to $90 < R \leq 96.3$. The condition thus has two effects on the PDF: (1) it limits the domain (the numerator), and (2) it renormalizes (the denominator). Thus the conditional PDF is

$$f_{R|W \geq 3}(r)\, dr = \frac{0.05}{0.317}\, dr \Rightarrow f_{R|W \geq 3}(r) = 0.158, \quad 90 < r \leq 96.3, \quad \text{zow} \quad (3.1.38)$$

The required conditional expectation can now be determined:

$$E[W(R)|W \geq 3] = \int_{-\infty}^{+\infty} w(r) f_{R|W \geq 3}(r) \, dr = \int_{90}^{96.3} \frac{17^2}{r} \times 0.158 \, dr$$

$$= 45.6 \ln\left(\frac{96.3}{90}\right) = 3.10 \text{ watts}$$

(3.1.39)

Thus the expected power in the thermally overstressed resistors is 3.10 watts.

You do it. Find the expected power of the resistors that yield a power in the range $2.7 < W \leq 2.9$ watts. Calculate the conditional PDF and then the conditional expectation. Enter your answer to at least four-place accuracy, and click Evaluate for a response.

```
myanswer = ;
```

```
Evaluate
```

For the answer, see endnote 9.

In this section we have defined and used conditional PDFs and conditional expectations in a specific context. In endnote 10 we show how to derive a conditional PDF in general.

3.1.8 Transforming Random Variables

Example 3.1.6:   PDF of the power
Find the probability density function, PDF, of the power, $f_W(w)$.

Solution   We are now transforming from one random variable to another, $W \to R$, and from one PDF to another, $f_R(r) \to f_W(w)$. The safest way to perform such a transformation is first to determine the cumulative distribution function of the power and then to determine the PDF from the CDF. By definition, the CDF of W is

$$F_W(w) = P[W \leq w]$$

(3.1.40)

Critical regions.   In general, the form of the CDF will be

$$F_W(w) = (\text{something}), \quad w < \text{some limit}$$

$$= (\text{something else}), \quad \text{lower} < w < \text{upper limit}$$

$$= (\text{something else}), \quad w > \text{another limit, and so on}$$

(3.1.41)

To determine the CDF we first have to identify the various critical regions. Toward that end, examine the mapping of resistance values to power values shown in Fig. 3.1.11.

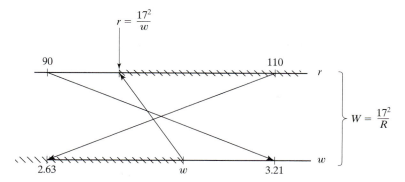

Figure 3.1.11 Here we show a general mapping of the event $\{W < w\}$ to the corresponding event in R, $\{R > 17^2/w\}$. This mapping allows us to calculate the CDF of W from the PDF of R.

In this case, the critical regions are seen to be $w \leq 2.63$, $2.63 < w \leq 3.21$, and $w > 3.21$. (Because the random variable is continuous we have assigned the powers $w = 2.63$ and $w = 3.21$ to the top of the ranges.) Thus our form is

$$F_W(w) = \text{(something)}, \quad w \leq 2.63$$

$$= \text{(something else)}, \quad 2.63 < w \leq 3.21 \qquad (3.1.42)$$

$$= \text{(something else)}, \quad w > 3.21$$

Determining the CDF. We may determine the *somethings* by mapping the event $\{W \leq w\}$ to the identical event $\{R \geq \frac{17^2}{w}\}$, as shown in Fig. 3.1.11. The first *something* is 0 because no values of resistance lead to powers less than 2.63 watts. And the last *something else* is 1 because all values of resistance lead to powers below 3.21 watts. The middle *something else* comes from the mapping and inverse mapping relationship of the function $W(R)$.

We can therefore determine the CDF in this middle region as

$$F_W(w) = P[W \leq w] = P\left[R \geq \frac{17^2}{w}\right]$$

$$= \int_{r = \frac{17^2}{w}}^{r = 110} 0.05 \, dr = 0.05\left(110 - \frac{17^2}{w}\right), \quad 2.63 < w \leq 3.21 \qquad (3.1.43)$$

Thus the final result is

$$F_W(w) = 0, \quad w \leq 2.63$$

$$= 0.05\left(110 - \frac{17^2}{w}\right), \quad 2.63 < w \leq 3.21 \qquad (3.1.44)$$

$$= 1, \quad w > 3.21$$

The plot of this CDF follows.

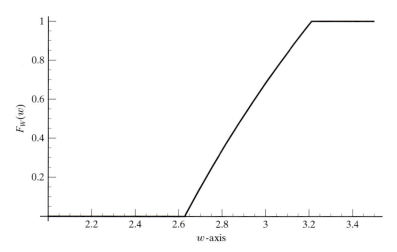

The CDF is 0 below and 1 above the middle range in Eq. (3.1.44), as shown.

Determining the PDF from the CDF.   The PDF is the derivative of the CDF. The PDF is thus zero in the regions where the CDF is 0 or 1. In the middle region, the derivative is

$$f_W(w) = \frac{d}{dw} F_W(w) = \frac{d}{dw} 0.05 \left(110 - \frac{17^2}{w} \right) = \frac{14.5}{w^2}, \ 2.63 < w \le 3.21, \ \text{zow} \qquad (3.1.45)$$

The plot follows.

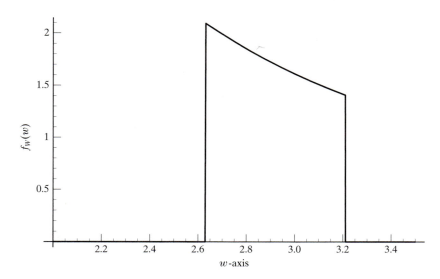

A check of a previous calculation.   We may use this PDF to check the expected power calculated in Eq. (3.1.36):

$$E[W] = \int_{-\infty}^{+\infty} w f_w(w)\, dw = \int_{2.63}^{3.21} w \times \frac{14.5}{w^2}\, dw = 14.5 \ln\left(\frac{3.21}{2.63}\right) = 2.90 \text{ watts} \qquad (3.1.46)$$

Example 3.1.7:   PDF of new mixture of resistors _____
Let us say that someone accidentally dumped some "50-Ω resistors" into the 100-Ω bin, such that 10% of the resistors are 50 Ω, and 90% of the resistors are 100 Ω. The chance experiment is the same as before; namely, pick a resistor at random and note its resistance. Find the resulting PDF.

Solution   We will continue to assume that many resistors of both types are involved and that we may treat the resistance as a continuous random variable. This problem calls for conditional CDFs and PDFs. Let $A = \{$a 50-Ω resistor is chosen$\}$ and $B = \{$a 100-Ω resistor is chosen$\}$. We assume that 50-Ω resistors are uniformly distributed between 45 and 55 Ω. The conditional PDFs would be

$$f_{R|A}(r) = \frac{1}{55 - 45}, \quad 45 < r \le 55, \text{ zow}$$

$$f_{R|B}(r) = \frac{1}{110 - 90}, \quad 90 < r \le 110, \text{ zow} \qquad (3.1.47)$$

We regard these conditional PDFs as given information, based on our model for a 10% resistor. These may be integrated to yield the conditional CDFs.

$$F_{R|A}(r) = \int_{-\infty}^{r} f_{R|A}(r')\, dr' = P[R \le r|A]$$

and

$$F_{R|B}(r) = \int_{-\infty}^{r} f_{R|B}(r')\, dr' = P[R \le r|B] \qquad (3.1.48)$$

These conditional CDFs look similar to Fig. 3.1.8.

We now may formulate the (unconditional) CDF for the random variable R using A and B as a partition of the space of the experiment. Using the law of total probability [Eq. (1.5.7)], we write

$$F_R(r) = P[R \le r] = P[R \le r|A] \times P[A] + P[R \le r|B] \times P[B]$$

$$= F_{R|A}(r) \times P[A] + F_{R|B}(r) \times P[B] \qquad (3.1.49)$$

Thus we may express the CDF of R in terms of the conditional CDFs in Eq. (3.1.48). Using $P[A] = 0.1$ and $P[B] = 0.9$, in Eq. (3.1.49), we obtain the CDF of R. We skip the details. The CDF is plotted in Fig. 3.1.12.

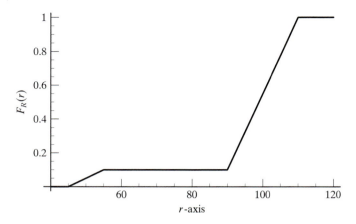

Figure 3.1.12 The CDF of the random variable that consists of 10% 50-Ω resistors and 90% 100-Ω resistors. In both cases we are assuming a uniform distribution over a $\pm10\%$ range centered on the nominal value.

From the CDF in Eq. (3.1.49) we may derive the PDF of R by differentiation:

$$f_R(r) = f_{R|A}(r) \times P[A] + f_{R|B}(r) \times P[B]$$

$$= 0.1 \times 0.1, \ \ 45 < r \leq 55, \ \text{and} \tag{3.1.50}$$

$$= 0.05 \times 0.9, \ \ 90 < r \leq 110, \ \text{zow}$$

This PDF is shown in Fig. 3.1.13.

Example 3.1.8:   Using conditional expectations _____
Find the expected value of R for this modified experiment.

Solution   We apply the definition of expectation (mean), Eq. (3.1.9):

$$\mu_R = E[R] = \int_{-\infty}^{+\infty} r f_R(r)\,dr = P[A] \times \int_{-\infty}^{+\infty} r f_{R|A}(r)\,dr + P[B] \times \int_{-\infty}^{+\infty} r f_{R|B}(r)\,dr$$

$$= P[A] \times E[R|A] + P[B] \times E[R|B] \tag{3.1.51}$$

$$= 0.1 \times 50 + 0.9 \times 100 = 95 \ \Omega$$

Generating random variables

Although we have shown how to transform random variables, we now add a very practical example that relates to calculator and computer simulations of random systems. The following is an instance of the problem we will address:

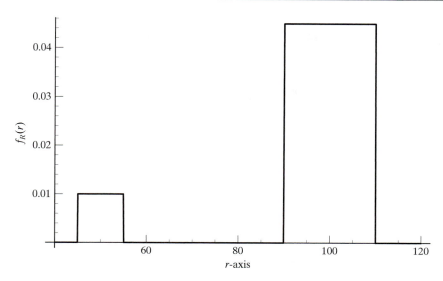

Figure 3.1.13 The PDF of the random variable that consists of 10% 50-Ω resistors and 90% 100-Ω resistors. In both cases we are assuming a uniform distribution over a ±10% range centered on the nominal value. This is the derivative of the CDF in Fig. 3.1.12.

In Eq. (3.1.45) we give the PDF of the power, W, as

$$f_W(w) = \frac{14.5}{w^2}, 2.63 < w \le 3.21, \text{ zow} \qquad (3.1.52)$$

Let us say we wish to generate values of a random variable that has this distribution. Mathematica will generate random numbers of prescribed distributions, provided these are standard distributions. Your calculator will not even do that. Instead, it will generate random numbers that have a uniform distribution between the limits of 0 and 1. Mathematica does the same with the command "Random[ ]", as shown.

```
X = Table[Random[], {10}]
```

{0.926594, 0.336122, 0.390913, 0.544429, 0.57383,
  0.7714, 0.00138949, 0.846951, 0.81984, 0.769131}

Thus we need a method to transform uniformly distributed random numbers to numbers distributed according to some other PDF, such as shown in Fig. 3.1.14. Let us call the uniformly distributed random variable X, as before. We now need $W(X)$ for the transformation. We determine this transformation on the basis of the CDFs of X and W. Fig. 3.1.14 shows the areas corresponding to the CDFs of X and W and indicates an appropriate mapping to make the areas equal, which means the CDFs are equal, $F_X(x) = F_W(w(x))$.

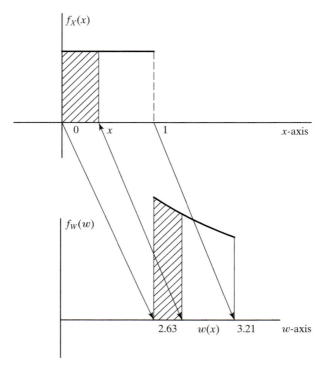

Figure 3.1.14 To transform the uniformly distributed random variable X into another random variable, in this case W, we need $W(X)$ such that the CDFs are equal.

The crosshatched areas should be equal, such that

$$P[X \leq x] = P[W \leq w(x)] \tag{3.1.53}$$

which simply equates the CDFs of X and W. The critical parts of these CDFs are

$$F_X(x) = x, 0 < x \leq 1 \text{ and } F_W(w(x)) = 0.05\left(110 - \frac{17^2}{w(x)}\right), 2.63 < w(x) \leq 3.21 \tag{3.1.54}$$

Setting these equal, we have

$$x = 0.05\left(110 - \frac{17^2}{w(x)}\right) \tag{3.1.55}$$

To obtain the required transformation, we solve for $w(x)$, with the result

$$w(x) = \frac{17^2}{110 - 20x} \tag{3.1.56}$$

We now can generate the required numbers distributed according to the target PDF. The code is

```
X = Table[Random[], {10}];
       17²
W = ─────────── /. x → X
     110 - 20x
```

{2.81238, 2.89968, 3.18438, 2.89623, 3.06527, 2.72755, 3.19802, 3.18 > 2.8656, 2.92151}

To demonstrate how the W values distribute, we execute the following cell for a histogram of 500 samples

```
X = Table[Random[], {500}];
       17²
W = ─────────── /. x → X;
     110 - 20x
Histogram[W];
```

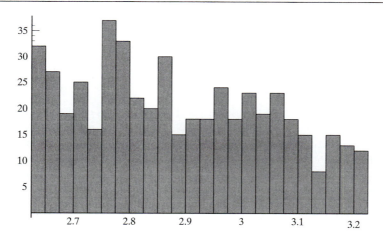

You do it. Derive a transformation $t(x)$ that will transform a uniformly distributed random variable in the range $0 < X \leq 1$ to an exponential random variable with the PDF $f_T(t) = 3e^{-3t}, t \geq 0$, zow. Substitute $t = 0.4$ as myanswer, and click Evaluate for a response.

```
myanswer = ;
```

```
Evaluate
```

For the answer, see endnote 11.

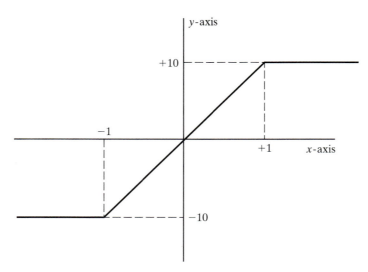

Figure 3.1.15 The amplifier has a gain of 10 over the output region from -10 to $+10$, but those are the limits. Thus all inputs greater in magnitude than 1 will drive the amplifier into the nonlinear region.

3.1.9 Mixed Random Variables

Chapter 2 dealt with discrete random variables, and Chapter 3 has dealt with continuous random variables. Random systems that include both are described by *mixed* random variables. For example, amplifiers have "rails" owing to power supply limits. The gain characteristic of an amplifier with rails is shown in Fig. 3.1.15. This characteristic can produce a mixed random variable, as we now explore.

The input to the amplifier, X, will be uniformly distributed between -1.2 and $+1.3$. Thus the PDF of the input is

$$f_X(x) = \frac{1}{2.5}, \quad -1.2 < x \le +1.3, \quad \text{zow} \qquad (3.1.57)$$

We will use the transformation in Fig. 3.1.15 to find the PDF of the output, Y. First, we determine the CDF of Y. As shown in Eq. (3.1.41), we should first determine the critical regions. The definition of the CDF of Y is

$$F_Y(y) = P[Y \le y] \qquad (3.1.58)$$

The easy regions in this case are (1) $y < -10$, where the CDF is zero, since it is impossible for Y to be less than any y in this region, and (2) $y \ge +10$, where the CDF is 1, since all values of Y are $+10$ and below.

The discrete value $y = -10$ will constitute a region in this case, since this value corresponds to the negative saturation region. Here the result is

$$F_Y(-10) = P[Y \le -10] = P[X \le -1] = \frac{-1 - (-1.2)}{2.5} = \frac{0.2}{2.5} \qquad (3.1.59)$$

Thus the CDF jumps from 0 to 0.08 at exactly $y = -10$, which is indicative of a probability mass at this value of y.

The next critical region is $-10 < y < +10$. Here we do not put an equal sign on the upper end because $y = +10$ is the upper saturation region and is a special case. In this middle region the event $\{Y \le y\}$ is the same as the event $\{X \le \frac{y}{10}\}$. Thus the required probability calculation is

$$F_Y(y) = P[Y \le y] = P[X \le \frac{y}{10}] = \int_{x=-\infty}^{x=y/10} f_X(x)\, dx = \frac{y/10 - (-1.2)}{2.5} \qquad (3.1.60)$$

The next special case is $y = +10$. Because all values of Y fall at or below $+10$, the CDF must be 1, as stated earlier. Thus increasing y beyond $+10$ adds nothing. Note, however, that there is a jump of the CDF at $y = +10$. If we substitute $y = 10$ into Eq. (3.1.60), we find

$$F_Y(+10) = \frac{10/10 + 1.2}{2.5} = \frac{2.2}{2.5} \qquad (3.1.61)$$

Thus the CDF jumps by $\frac{0.3}{2.5}$ at exactly $y = +10$, which indicates finite probability mass at this value of y. We may now plot the CDF of Y in Fig. 3.1.16. The finite jumps at $y = \pm 10$ indicate that the output is a mixed random variable, having both discrete and continuous components.

The PDF of Y.   We must take the derivative of $F_Y(y)$, pictured in Fig. 3.1.16, to obtain the PDF of Y. The discontinuities at ± 10 indicate that no derivative can be defined at these points unless we resort to the use of impulse functions, which is exactly what we will do. If you need a short review on unit step and impulse functions, see endnote 12.

Using the unit step notation, we can express the CDF of Y as

$$F_Y(y) = \frac{y/10 - (-1.2)}{2.5}(u(y - (-10)) - u(y - 10)) + u(y - 10) \qquad (3.1.62)$$

The first unit step function "turns on" the straight line at $y = -10$, and the second unit step turns it off. The third unit step function makes the CDF 1 for all values greater than $+10$. The PDF is the derivative of Eq. (3.1.62). We will call the straight-line function $s(y)$ (the part in front of the unit step functions). With this notation, the derivative is

$$f_Y(y) = s(-10)\delta(y - (-10)) - s(+10)\delta(y - 10) + \delta(y - 10) + \frac{1}{25}(u(y - (-10)) - u(y - 10))$$

$$= s(-10)\delta(y - (-10)) + (1 - s(+10))\delta(y - 10) + \frac{1}{25}(u(y - (-10)) - u(y - 10))$$

$$(3.1.63)$$

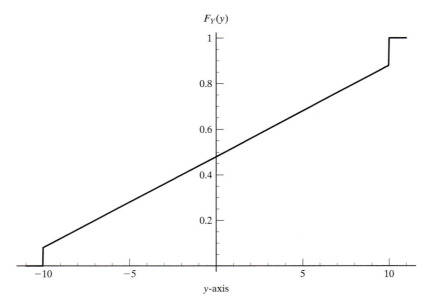

Figure 3.1.16 The CDF of the amplifier output, Y, shows jumps at ± 10 corresponding to the saturation regions of the amplifier. The output will therefore be a mixed random variable, having discrete and continuous components.

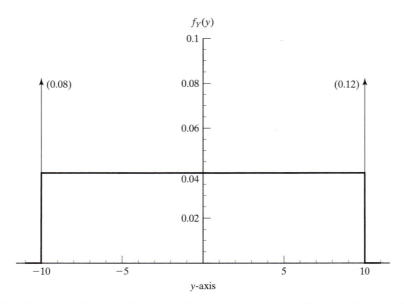

Figure 3.1.17 The PDF of Y has discrete and continuous aspects. The impulse functions indicate the presence of discrete components, and the continuous part, here a constant, indicates the continuous component.

Equation (3.1.63) looks complicated but can be interpreted as two impulses and a continuous section. The first impulse has a magnitude of $s(-10) = \frac{2}{25}$ at $y = -10$, which corresponds to the discontinuity in Fig. 3.1.16 at that point. The second term is an impulse of magnitude $1 - s(+10) = \frac{3}{25}$ at $y = +10$ and corresponds to the discontinuity in Fig. 3.1.16 at that point. The last term in Eq. (3.1.63) has a constant height of $\frac{1}{25}$ over the range $-10 < y < +10$ and corresponds to the straight-line portion in Fig. 3.1.16. The corresponding PDF is shown in Fig. 3.1.17.

The PDF in Fig. 3.1.17 is the derivative of the CDF in Fig. 3.1.16. The discontinuities in the CDF lead to the impulse functions in the PDF. Mixed random variables always lead to these features.

Summary. Section 3.1 presented the basic tools for describing continuous random variables. The major points follow:

- The distribution of probabilities of a continuous random variable may be described by a probability density function, PDF, or a cumulative distribution function, CDF. The PDF and the CDF contain the same information.
- The CDF is a probability and is useful for derivations and for analyzing problems. The PDF is a density of probability and is useful for calculating probabilities and expectations.
- Conditional CDFs and PDFs can be defined and provide useful tools for analysis and calculation.

In Sec. 3.2 we extend these concepts and definitions to the bivariate case, two random variables.

3.2 BIVARIATE RANDOM VARIABLES

3.2.1 Bivariate Probability Density Functions, PDFs

Mapping two random variables into the Cartesian plane. In this section we deal with two continuous random variables, call them X and Y. The two random variables map the sample space into the Cartesian plane, as shown in Fig. 3.2.1(a), that is, for each outcome of the chance experiment there is an associated point X, Y in the x, y plane.

Many physical problems introduce two or more such random variables. For examples, the location of an imperfection on a semiconductor wafer, the height and weight of an individual from a population, or the velocity of a molecule in a gas (three components = three random variables). The definitions and methodologies we introduce for two random variables in this section are routinely extended to three or more random variables.

Definition of bivariate PDF. Definitions are the same as for the discrete bivariate PMF, with appropriate accommodation for continuous space. For example, the bivariate PDF, $f_{XY}(x, y)$, also called the *joint PDF*, is defined as

$$f_{XY}(x, y)\, dx\, dy = P[(x < X \le x + dx) \cap (y < Y \le y + dy)] \tag{3.2.1}$$

and $f_{XY}(x, y)$ is thus a probability per unit area.[13] This definition applies to random variables that are continuous in both X and Y and is illustrated in Fig. 3.2.1(b). The definition requires that dx and dy be positive for the probability to be defined, from which it follows that the bivariate PDF must be positive.

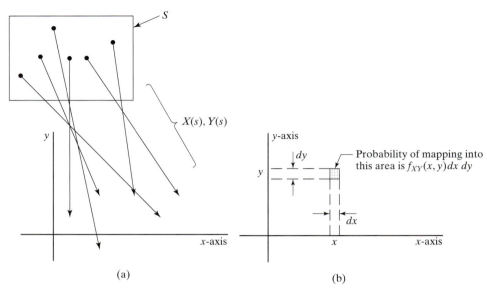

(a)   (b)

Figure 3.2.1   (a) Two random variables map the sample space into the Cartesian plane. Events are expressed as areas in this plane. (b) The bivariate PDF is expressed in terms of the probability that an X, Y point resulting from a single performance of the experiment falls in a small rectangle of area $dx\,dy$, located at x, y.

Independent random variables.   When X and Y are independent random variables, the $\cap$ in Eq. (3.2.1) becomes $\cap \rightarrow \times$ and the result is

$$f_{XY}(x, y)\,dx\,dy = P[x < X \le x + dx] \times P[y < Y \le y + dy] = f_X(x)\,dx \times f_Y(y)\,dy \quad (3.2.2)$$

Because dx and dy are arbitrary in magnitude, it follows that when X and Y are independent the bivariate PDF is the product of the PDFs of the two random variables, as shown in Eq. (3.2.3). In this context, f_X and f_Y are called the *marginal PDFs*.

$$f_{XY}(x, y) = f_X(x) f_Y(y) \text{ for } x \text{ and } y \text{ independent} \quad (3.2.3)$$

If $f_{XY}(x, y)$ is nonzero over a region, then for independence the boundaries of that region must also be factorable into separate dependence on x and y.

Example 3.2.1:   Bivariate PDF _____
Consider two independent random variables: X is uniformly distributed between 0 and 5, and Y is uniformly distributed between 5 and 5.5. Find the bivariate PDF, $f_{XY}(x, y)$.

Solution   The PDFs of X and Y are $f_X(x) = 0.2, 0 < x \le 5$, zow; $f_Y(y) = 2, 5 < y \le 5.5$, zow. From Eq. (3.2.3), it follows that the joint PDF is

$$f_{XY}(x, y) = f_X(x) f_Y(y) = 0.2 \times 2 = 0.4, \ 0 < x \le 5 \cap 5 < y \le 5.5, \text{ zow} \quad (3.2.4)$$

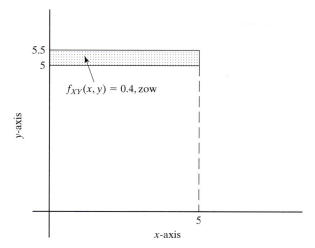

Figure 3.2.2 The joint PDF is a constant over a rectangular area. The area of the rectangle is 2.5, so the PDF has a "height" of 1/2.5 = 0.4, such that the volume under the PDF surface is unity.

This PDF is shown in Fig. 3.2.2. Identification of the region where the PDF is nonzero is fully as important as the value of the PDF in that region. This is the significance of the "zow."

Calculating probabilities. The properties of the bivariate PDF are simple extensions of the single variable case. For example, instead of integrating in one dimension to find the probability that the random variable falls in a prescribed range, we integrate in two dimensions to find out the probability that the random variables fall into a prescribed region in the x, y plane, as indicated in Eq. (3.2.5) and in Fig. 3.2.3.

$$P[X, Y \in A] = \iint\limits_{A} f_{XY}(x, y) \, dx \, dy \tag{3.2.5}$$

Equation (3.2.5) may be justified in the same way that we derived Eq. (3.1.4), except here we must divide the event represented by the area in Fig. 3.2.3 into little rectangles of dimensions $dx \times dy$, as shown in Fig. 3.2.1(b), and sum up, in an integral, the probabilities associated with each small rectangle. These rectangles constitute a partition of the event $\{X, Y \in A\}$.

Normalization. Bivariate PDFs are nonnegative functions that are normalized to unit volume when integrated over the x, y plane. This follows from Eq. (3.2.5) if we let A be the event that X, Y falls somewhere in the plane.

$$A = \{(-\infty < X < +\infty) \cap (-\infty < Y < +\infty)\} = S \tag{3.2.6}$$

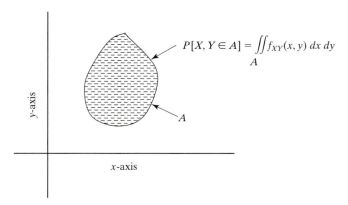

Figure 3.2.3　To calculate the probability of an event, we integrate the bivariate PDF over the area in *x, y* space representing the event.

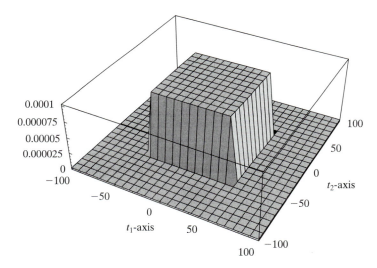

Figure 3.2.4　A bivariate PDF in three dimensions. This is the PDF for the "glitch" example later in this section.

where S is the certain event. Because $P[S] = 1$, Eq. (3.2.5) leads directly to

$$\int_{-\infty}^{+\infty} \int_{-\infty}^{+\infty} f_{XY}(x, y)\, dx\, dy = 1 \tag{3.2.7}$$

Normalized volume.　When the PDF is plotted on an axis normal to the x, y plane, Eq. (3.2.7) can be interpreted as requiring unit volume under the PDF curve, as illustrated by Fig. 3.2.4 for the PDF in Example 3.2.4.

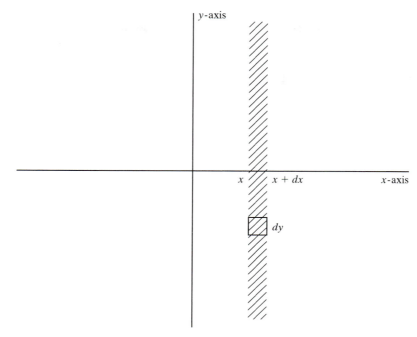

Figure 3.2.5 We can calculate the probability that X falls in a strip by integrating the bivariate PDF over the strip. This leads to the calculation of the marginal PDF on X shown in Eq. (3.2.9).

Marginal PDFs.   Consider the following expression:

$$f_X(x)\,dx = P[(x < X \le x + dx) \cap (-\infty < Y < +\infty)] = \left[\int_{-\infty}^{+\infty} f_{XY}(x, y)\,dy\right] dx \quad (3.2.8)$$

The first term in Eq. (3.2.8) says that X falls in a small increment dx near x. The middle term says the same thing in terms of the definition of the PDF of X but puts in Y to change to the bivariate context, saying in effect that all values of Y are accepted. The last term calculates the probability in the middle term from the bivariate PDF, as shown in Fig. 3.2.5.

Writing Eq. (3.2.8) without the middle term and dropping the dx's on both sides gives

$$f_X(x) = \int_{-\infty}^{+\infty} f_{XY}(x, y)\,dy \quad (3.2.9)$$

In the bivariate context, $f_X(x)$ is called the *marginal* PDF of X. The idea is that we take all the probability in the strip and push it, as with a bulldozer, to the top margin of the plane. We might equally well call it the *axial* PDF if we think of all the probability in the plane heaped up on the x-axis. Often, Eq. (3.2.9) is called *integrating Y out of the distribution*, since in effect we are expressing that all values of Y are acceptable. In the same way we can integrate X out of the bivariate PDF to obtain the marginal distribution on Y:

$$f_Y(y) = \int_{-\infty}^{+\infty} f_{XY}(x, y)\, dx \tag{3.2.10}$$

Example 3.2.2:   Marginal PDFs

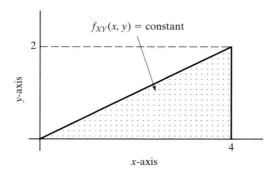

Figure 3.2.6   A point is chosen at random in the triangle shown, which means that the bivariate PDF is constant. We will calculate the marginal PDFs on X and Y.

Consider a point chosen at random in a triangle, as shown in Fig. 3.2.6.

The PDF.   Our first task is to normalize the PDF. Because the bivariate PDF is constant over the triangle, its magnitude must be the reciprocal of the area of the triangle, which is 4. Hence,

$$f_{XY}(x, y) = \frac{1}{\text{area}} = \frac{1}{4} \text{ over the triangle, zow} \tag{3.2.11}$$

The marginal PDF for X.   Using Eq. (3.2.9), we fix x and integrate from $-\infty$ to $+\infty$ in y. The only region in x where we will encounter any probability is in the region $0 < x \leq 4$. In that region the integrand is zero except between $y = 0$ and $y = x/2$, as shown in Fig. 3.2.7. Thus the result is

$$f_X(x) = \int_{y=0}^{y=x/2} \frac{1}{4}\, dy = \frac{1}{4} \times \frac{x}{2} = \frac{x}{8}, \ 0 < x \leq 4, \text{ zow} \tag{3.2.12}$$

This PDF is shown in Fig. 3.2.8, and clearly is appropriately normalized.

Marginal PDF in Y.   We can integrate out X and get the marginal PDF in Y, as shown in Eq. (3.2.10). Here the path is horizontal and yields a nonzero result only in the region $0 < y \leq 2$. The path of integration is shown in Fig. 3.2.9.

The required integration is

$$f_Y(y) = \int_{x=2y}^{x=4} \frac{1}{4}\, dx = \frac{1}{4}(4 - 2y), \ 0 < y \leq 2, \text{ zow} \tag{3.2.13}$$

This PDF is shown in Fig. 3.2.10.

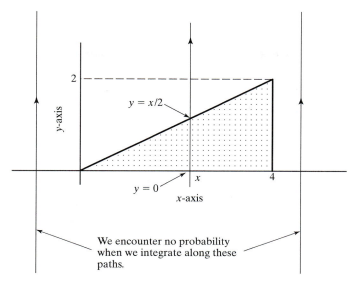

Figure 3.2.7   Integrating the PDF in the positive y direction. The only place in x where probability is encountered is $0 < x \le 4$. All other paths give zero. When probability is encountered it is between $y = 0$ and $y = x/2$.

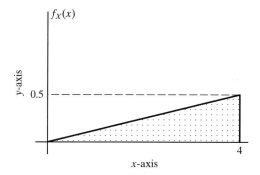

Figure 3.2.8   The marginal PDF for X. Notice the area under the curve is 1, as required for all PDFs.

Interpretation of the marginals.   Look at Fig. 3.2.6 and think of the shaded triangle as so much sand. If you push the sand onto the x-axis, you get excess sand at $x = 4$, as shown by the marginal PDF on X in Fig. 3.2.8. If, however, you push the sand onto the y-axis, you get excess at $y = 0$, as shown for the marginal PDF on Y in Fig. 3.2.10. Of course, you would have the same situation if you pushed the sand to the "margins" at $x = \infty$ or $y = \infty$, but that is so far off that it is more convenient to (mentally) push the sand onto the axes.

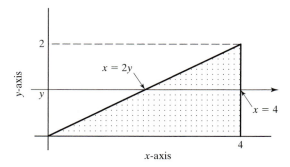

Figure 3.2.9   The integration in x encounters probability only between $x = 2y$ and $x = 4$. Only paths in the range $0 < y \leq 2$ give nonzero results. The integral is evaluated in Eq. (3.2.13).

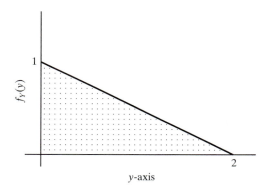

Figure 3.2.10   The marginal PDF in Y. Again, we note that the PDF is properly normalized.

You do it.   Let X, Y be chosen at random in the quarter circle shown in Fig. 3.2.11. Find the marginal PDF in X. Evaluate your answer at $x = 0.5$, and click Evaluate for a response.

```
myanswer = ;
```

```
Evaluate
```

For the answer, see endnote 14.

Conditional PDFs.   The bivariate case also allows the definition of conditional PDFs. These, like conditional probability in general, provide a useful analysis tool. We now define the conditional PDF, $f_{Y|X}(x, y)$. We begin with the definition of the bivariate PDF of Eq. (3.2.1), repeated in Eq. (3.2.14).

$$f_{XY}(x, y)\, dx\, dy = P[(x < X \leq x + dx) \cap (y < Y \leq y + dy)] \qquad (3.2.14)$$

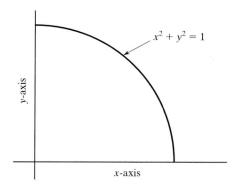

Figure 3.2.11   The PDF is uniform in the quarter circle. You are to find the marginal PDF in X.

The probability on the right side can be expressed as a conditional probability. By definition [Eq. (1.5.2)] of conditional probability,

$$f_{XY}(x, y)\, dx\, dy = \underbrace{P[(x < X \le x + dx)|(y < Y \le y + dy)]}_{f_{X|Y}(x,y)\, dx} \times \underbrace{P[(y < Y \le y + dy)]}_{f_Y(y)\, dy} \quad (3.2.15)$$

Equation (3.2.15) contains the definition of the conditional PDF, except that the conditioning term is usually abbreviated simply as $Y = y$, which is equivalent when the random variables are continuous and dy is infinitesimal. Thus we have

$$f_{X|Y}(x, y)\, dx = P[x < X \le x + dx|Y = y] \quad (3.2.16)$$

In consequence of the definition of the conditional PDF in Eq. (3.2.15), we have, after canceling the differentials

$$f_{XY}(x, y) = f_{X|Y}(x, y) \times f_Y(y) \quad (3.2.17)$$

and since Eq. (3.2.14) is symmetric in X and Y, we can equally derive

$$f_{XY}(x, y) = f_{Y|X}(x, y) \times f_X(x) \quad (3.2.18)$$

Example 3.2.3:   Bivariate PDF _____

Consider the following description of two random variables. We choose X at random between 0 and 4; then we choose Y at random between 0 and $X/2$. We will derive the bivariate PDF. The space for this problem is identical with that shown in Fig. 3.2.6, but the bivariate PDF is no longer constant in the region because of the method used for choosing the values of X and Y. We show in Fig. 3.2.12 the region for these random variables.

   We now derive the PDF. For X, we have

$$f_X(x) = \frac{1}{4}, \quad 0 < x \le 4, \quad \text{zow} \quad (3.2.19)$$

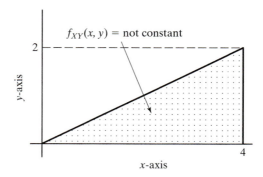

Figure 3.2.12   The region for the random variables is the same as in Fig. 3.2.6, but the joint PDF is no longer uniform because of the manner in which the random variables are defined.

and for Y we have

$$f_{Y|X}(x, y) = \frac{2}{x}, \ 0 < y \le x/2, \ \text{zow} \tag{3.2.20}$$

Note that the appropriate PDF for Y is a conditional PDF, since the PDF of Y depends on X. Using Eq. (3.2.18) we find the bivariate PDF as

$$f_{XY}(x, y) = f_{Y|X}(x, y) \times f_X(x) = \frac{2}{x} \times \frac{1}{4} = \frac{1}{2x}, \ 0 < y \le x/2 \cap 0 < x \le 4, \ \text{zow} \tag{3.2.21}$$

As stated previously, the region of nonzero probability in the x, y plane is identical with the previous example, Fig. 3.2.6; however, the bivariate PDF is different: instead of a constant PDF we have the PDF given in Eq. (3.2.21). Both pick a point in the x, y plane "at random," but they use different methods and lead to different results.

You do it.   Derive the marginal PDF of X for the PDF given in Eq. (3.2.21). Substitute $x = 2$, and click Evaluate for a response.

```
myanswer = ;
```

```
Evaluate
```

If you're having trouble, see endnote 15 for the answer.

Find the marginal PDF for Y.   Find the marginal PDF for Y and substitute $y = 1$. Enter your answer in the cell box, and click Evaluate for a response.

```
myanswer = ;
```

```
Evaluate
```

For the answer, see endnote 16.

If you want to check the normalization and see a plot of this marginal PDF, see endnote 17.

Expectation.   As in the case of a single continuous random variable, the summations used in the discrete case become integrals. For example, the expectation of a function of the two random variables would be computed as follows:

$$E[Z(X, Y)] = \int_{-\infty}^{+\infty} \int_{-\infty}^{+\infty} z(x, y) f_{XY}(x, y) \, dx \, dy \tag{3.2.22}$$

Conditional expectations.   Conditional expectations can be defined and are extremely useful. For example, the expectation conditioned on event A would require the PDF conditioned on A,

$$f_{XY|A}(x, y) \, dx \, dy = \frac{P[(x < X \le x + dx) \cap (y < Y \le y + dy) \cap A]}{P[A]} \tag{3.2.23}$$

and the conditional expectation would be

$$E[Z(X, Y)|A] = \int_{-\infty}^{+\infty} \int_{-\infty}^{+\infty} z(x, y) f_{XY|A}(x, y) \, dx \, dy \tag{3.2.24}$$

Example 3.2.4:   Two pulses _____
We now illustrate the use of the bivariate PDF to calculate probabilities and expectations. Two pulses in a digital system are supposed to arrive at a gate simultaneously but can vary by ± 50 ns owing to varying path delays. The pulses cause a glitch (false signal) whose width is the difference in arrival times. Consider that the delays are independent and uniformly distributed between -50 and $+50$ ns. Find the probability that the resulting glitch is longer than 60 ns, and also find the expected glitch width.

Solution   Let T_1 and T_2 represent the amount of the two delays in nanoseconds. Because both are uniformly distributed between -50 and $+50$ the PDF of T_1 is $f_{T_1}(t_1) = 1/100$, $-50 < t_1 \le +50$, and similarly for T_2. Since the delays are independent, the joint PDF is

$$f_{T_1 T_2}(t_1, t_2) = f_{T_1} \times f_{T_2} = 10^{-4}, \ -50 < t_1, t_2 \le +50, \ \text{zow} \tag{3.2.25}$$

This PDF is nonzero in a square in the t_1, t_2 plane, 100 on a side and centered on the origin, as shown in Fig. 3.2.13.

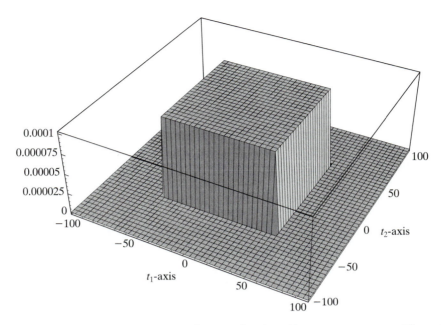

Figure 3.2.13   A three-dimensional plot of a PDF that is uniform over a square. The volume under the PDF curve must be 1. This is the PDF for Example 3.2.5.

Example 3.2.5:   Calculating the required probability and expectation _____

The event.   We are asked to determine the probability of the event $|T_1 - T_2| > 60$. The probability of this event can be determined by integrating the PDF over the regions of the t_1, t_2 plane where $|t_1 - t_2| > 60$. These regions are shown as the shaded triangles in Fig. 3.2.14.

The probability.   To determine the probability of the event represented by the shaded triangles in the figure, we must integrate the joint PDF over these triangular regions. Fortunately, the PDF is a constant, and the regions are simple geometric figures, whose area we may determine from their triangular shape. The results are

$$P[|T_1 - T_2| \geq 60] = 10^{-4} \times \text{area of triangles} = 10^{-4} \times 2 \times \tfrac{1}{2}(40)(40) = 0.16 \qquad (3.2.26)$$

Had the shapes been irregular or the PDF a complicated function, we would have had more mathematical work to do, but the principle would have been the same.

_____

You do it.   What is the probability that the glitch width is less than 20 nanoseconds? Calculate your answer, and click Evaluate for a response.

```
myanswer = ;
```

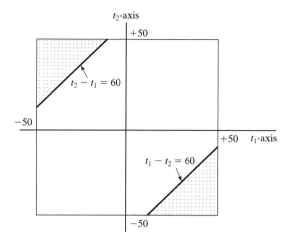

Figure 3.2.14   The region with nonzero probability is a square, 100 on a side. The shaded corners correspond to the event that $|T_1 - T_2|$ is greater than 60 ns. Integration of the PDF over these regions determines the probability.

Evaluate

For the answer, see endnote 18.

The expectation.   The expected glitch width can be calculated from the definition in Eq. (3.2.22):

$$E[|T_1 - T_2|] = \iint\limits_{\text{square}} |t_1 - t_2| f_{T_1 T_2}(t_1, t_2) \, dt_1 \, dt_2$$

$$= 2 \times \iint\limits_{t_1 > t_2} (t_1 - t_2) f_{T_1 T_2}(t_1, t_2) \, dt_1 \, dt_2 \tag{3.2.27}$$

Because of the symmetry of the integrand we can evaluate the integral over the region where $t_1 > t_2$ and double the result. This gets rid of the absolute value bars and reduces the work and confusion. The region of integration is shown in Fig. 3.2.15.

We integrate first in t_2 and then in t_1. The details follow.

$$E[|T_1 - T_2|] = 2 \int_{t_1=-50}^{t_1=+50} \left[\int_{t_2=-50}^{t_2=t_1} (t_1 - t_2) \times 10^{-4} \, dt_2 \right] dt_1$$

$$= 2 \times 10^{-4} \int_{-50}^{+50} \left[t_1 t_2 - \frac{t_2^2}{2} \right]_{-50}^{t_1} dt_1 \tag{3.2.28}$$

$$= 2 \times 10^{-4} \int_{-50}^{+50} \left[\frac{t_1^2}{2} + 50 \, t_1 + \frac{50^2}{2} \right] dt_1 = 33.3 \text{ ns}$$

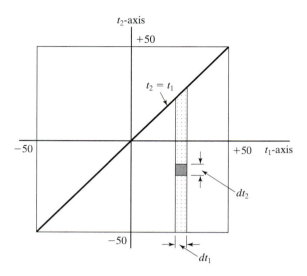

Figure 3.2.15   Integration of Eq. (3.2.27) for the expected glitch width. We integrate first in the vertical direction and then in the horizontal. We integrate only over the bottom triangle and double the result.

This appears to be a reasonable answer, since the maximum delay is 100 nanoseconds, but more delays are near zero (the region near the diagonal) than near the maximum (the corner regions).

You do it.   Find the expectation of T_1, given that $T_1 > T_2$. Enter your answer in the cell box, and click Evaluate for a response.

```
myanswer = ;
```

```
Evaluate
```

For the answer, see endnote 19.

3.2.2 Bivariate Cumulative Distribution Functions, CDFs

Bivariate cumulative distribution functions, CDFs, find some use. For the bivariate case, the joint CDF is defined as

$$F_{XY}(x, y) = P[(X \le x) \cap (Y \le y)] \tag{3.2.29}$$

This corresponds to the probability that X, Y will fall to the left of and below x, y, as shown in Fig. 3.2.16.

From the definition, and the properties of the bivariate PDF, a number of consequences follow:

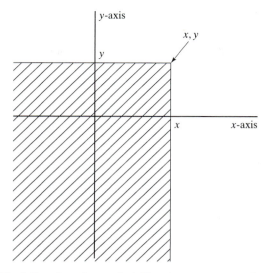

Figure 3.2.16 The CDF is defined as the probability that on one performance of the experiment X, Y will fall left of and below the point x, y, the crosshatched area shown.

- If either x or y is $-\infty$, the CDF must be zero. These represent impossible events, for example,

$$F_{XY}(-\infty, y) = P[(X \leq -\infty) \cap (Y \leq y)] = 0 \qquad (3.2.30)$$

- If both arguments are $+\infty$, these represent the certain event, which has a probability of 1:

$$F_{XY}(+\infty, +\infty) = P[(X \leq +\infty) \cap (Y \leq +\infty)] = P[S] = 1 \qquad (3.2.31)$$

- If one of the variables is $+\infty$, then the bivariate CDF reduces to the marginal CDF of the other variable. For example, if $x = +\infty$, then

$$F_{XY}(+\infty, y) = P[(X \leq +\infty) \cap (Y \leq y)] = P[Y \leq y]$$

$$= F_Y(y), \text{ and likewise for } F_X(x) \qquad (3.2.32)$$

since the condition $X \leq +\infty$ is certain to be satisfied. For this reason $F_Y(y)$ is called the *marginal CDF on Y*, since $x \to +\infty$ takes us to the margin of the plane.
- For independent random variables, the joint CDF factors into the product of the marginal CDFs:

$$F_{XY}(x, y) = P[(X \leq x) \cap (Y \leq y)] = P[X \leq x] \times P[Y \leq y] = F_X(x) \times F_Y(y) \qquad (3.2.33)$$

- The joint PDF is the derivative of the joint CDF:

$$f_{XY}(x, y) = \frac{\partial^2}{\partial x \, \partial y} F_{XY}(x, y) \tag{3.2.34}$$

- Finally, from Eq. (3.2.29) and (3.2.5), we can derive the bivariate CDF from the bivariate PDF:

$$F_{XY}(x, y) = P[(X \leq x) \cap (Y \leq y)] = \int_{-\infty}^{x} \int_{-\infty}^{y} f_{XY}(x', y') \, dx' \, dy' \tag{3.2.35}$$

Use of bivariate CDFs. Having defined the bivariate CDF and shown many of its properties, we now consider its value in solving problems. For one random variable, CDFs are very important in setting up problems. For two or more random variables, CDFs are of limited usefulness except in theoretical developments. The problem is that CDFs can be used to determine probabilities only if the region of interest is some form of rectangle, which seldom occurs in applications. Thus bivariate CDFs are useful conceptually and relate to the bivariate PDF in a straightforward way, but have limited use in setting up and solving problems, which is the focus of this book. The following example illustrates these points. We use the bivariate PDF in dealing with two random variables; the CDF is used only for a single random variable.

Example 3.2.6:   Two delays

A message must be sent over a network through two computers. The delays in each computer are random variables uniformly distributed between 0 and 2 seconds and are independent. Find the expected delay, the standard deviation of the delay, and the PDF of the delay.

Solution   The model for this problem is similar to that of the previous problem. We let T_1 and T_2 represent the two independent delay times and give their joint PDF as

$$f_{T_1 T_2}(t_1, t_2) = f_{T_1} \times f_{T_2} = \tfrac{1}{2} \times \tfrac{1}{2} = \tfrac{1}{4}, \ 0 < t_1, t_2 \leq 2, \ \text{zow} \tag{3.2.36}$$

Here we are interested in the combined delay $T = T_1 + T_2$. We thus are defining a third random variable that is a function of the original bivariate random variables, $T(T_1, T_2)$. We can clearly calculate the expected delay and the standard deviation of the delay using the algebra of expectation, but we will first calculate the PDF of the combined delay and, from that, calculate the mean and the standard deviation. Because this is a derivation, we will begin with the CDF of T and from that derive its PDF. This CDF is

$$F_T(t) = P[T \leq t] = P[T_1 + T_2 \leq t] = \iint\limits_{\text{shaded region}} f_{T_1}(t_1) f_{T_2}(t_2) \, dt_1 \, dt_2 \tag{3.2.37}$$

where the shaded area is that shown in Fig. 3.2.17.

Again the math is easy because the PDF is constant and the area is a triangle. The results are

$$F_T(t) = \frac{1}{2}t^2 \times 0.25 = \frac{t^2}{8}, \ 0 \leq t \leq 2 \tag{3.2.38}$$

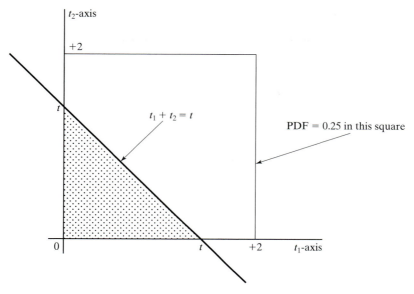

Figure 3.2.17   Calculation of the CDF of T requires integration of the bivariate PDF over the triangular region, which is simply the area times the PDF. For $t > 2$, the easiest calculation takes the area of the entire square and subtracts the area of a triangle.

We can use Eq. (3.2.38) only up to $t = 2$ because the geometric shape is different for $2 \leq t \leq 4$. Sparing you the details, we give the CDF in this region as

$$F_T(t) = \left(4 - \frac{(4-t)^2}{2}\right) \times 0.25, \ 2 \leq t \leq 4 \qquad (3.2.39)$$

The CDF is 0 for $t < 0$, and 1 for $t > 4$, outside the two regions defined in Eqs. (3.2.38) and (3.2.39), and is plotted in Fig. 3.2.18.

The PDF is the derivative of the CDF:

$$f_T(t) = \frac{d}{dt} F_T(t) = \frac{t}{4}, \ 0 \leq t \leq 2$$

$$= \frac{(4-t)}{4}, \ 2 \leq t \leq 4, \ \text{zow} \qquad (3.2.40)$$

which is shown in Fig. 3.2.19.

We now may complete the remaining parts of the example. We may use the PDF to determine the mean:

$$\mu_T = E[T] = \int_{-\infty}^{+\infty} t f_T(t) \, dt = \int_0^2 t \times \frac{t}{4} \, dt + \int_2^4 t \times \frac{(4-t)}{4} \, dt = 2 \qquad (3.2.41)$$

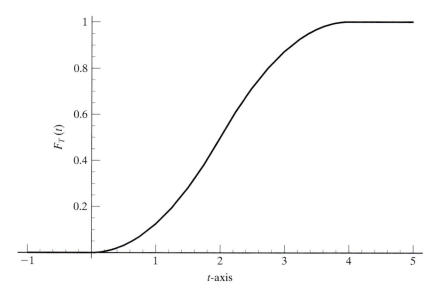

Figure 3.2.18   The CDF of the total delay.

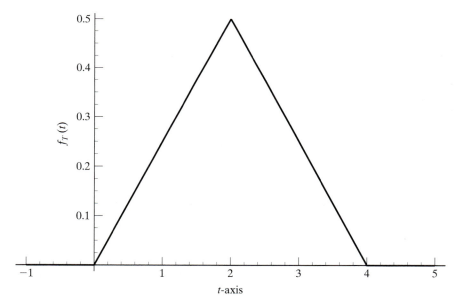

Figure 3.2.19   The PDF of the total delay. Note that the area is unity, as required of all PDFs.

which clearly is the balance point of the distribution. The variance can be computed similarly:

$$Var[T] = E[(T - \mu_T)^2] = \int_0^2 (t-2)^2 \times \frac{t}{4}\, dt + \int_2^4 (t-2)^2 \times \frac{(4-t)}{4}\, dt = 0.667 \quad (3.2.42)$$

The standard deviation of the delay is therefore $\sigma_T = \sqrt{0.667} = 0.816$ second.

Using the algebra of expectation.   We may confirm the mean and standard deviation calculations using the algebra of expectation. The mean is the sum of the means of the two random variables:

$$E[T] = E[T_1 + T_2] = E[T_1] + E[T_2] \tag{3.2.43}$$

Because T_1 and T_2 are uniformly distributed between 0 and 2, their individual means are

$$E[T_1] = E[T_2] = \frac{(0+2)}{2} = 1 \tag{3.2.44}$$

and therefore $E[T] = 2$, as in Eq. (3.2.41). Because T_1 and T_2 are independent, their variances add:

$$Var[T] = Var[T_1 + T_2] = Var[T_1] + Var[T_2] \tag{3.2.45}$$

For a random variable uniformly distributed between a and b, the variance is known to be $\frac{(b-a)^2}{12}$ [see Eq. (3.1.21)] and thus the variance of T is

$$Var[T] = \frac{2^2}{12} + \frac{2^2}{12} = \frac{2}{3} \tag{3.2.46}$$

which agrees with Eq. (3.2.42).

For a simulation of this example, see endnote 20.

You do it.   Now, work out this example to test your understanding of the material in this section.

a. A bivariate CDF is $F_{XY}(x, y) = c(1 - e^{-2x})\tan^{-1}(y/6)$ for $0 < x, y < +\infty$, zow. First, you need to find c. Think about it (no calculation required) and enter your answer as "myanswer" in the cell box, and click Evaluate for a response.

```
myanswer = ;
```

```
Evaluate
```

For the answer, see endnote 21.

b. Now, find the marginal PDF for Y and give its value at $y = 2$.

```
myanswer = ;
```

```
Evaluate
```

For the answer, see endnote 22.

Summary. This section presented the concept of bivariate random variables and showed how probability is described for two variables through PDFs and CDFs. We emphasized the use of the bivariate PDF to calculate probability and expectations. In the next section we extend this type of analysis to more than two random variables.

3.3 INDEPENDENT, IDENTICALLY DISTRIBUTED (IID) RANDOM VARIABLES AND THE CENTRAL LIMIT THEOREM

3.3.1 Independent, Identically Distributed (IID) Random Variables

Overview. In this section we present the concepts of multivariate random variables that are independent and have identical PDFs. These we call *IID* random variables. The first *I* stands for *independent,* the second *I* stands for *identical,* and the *D* stands for *distributed.* We will speak of the "first I" meaning independent, and the "second I" meaning identically distributed.

We will compute the mean, variance, and PDF of sums of such IID random variables. This leads naturally to the presentation of the central limit theorem, which expresses what happens when the number of IID random variables gets very large. Properly normalized, the sum of many IID random variables gives a random variable that has a Gaussian or normal PDF, which we introduce in the last subsection of this section. The full exploration of the Gaussian distribution comes in Sec. 3.4.

Why are we interested in IID random variables? One situation that yields IID random variables is the following. Take a basic experiment that yields a random variable. Repeat it to obtain random variables that are independent yet identical in their characteristics. Examples are repeating a measurement for a fluctuating quantity, measuring bolts out of a bin in a hardware store, or measuring antennae on fruit flies. For two measurements, this suggests the diagram in Fig. 3.3.1.

Note that we are using X_1 and X_2 for the random variables in Fig. 3.3.1. This makes more sense than using X and Y because we must also consider a large number of IID random variables. Besides, this notation suggests the identical characteristics of the random variables.

What is different between this situation and Bernoulli trials? Not much, really, except a Bernoulli trial has a binary result, and here the result is a random variable with its PDF.

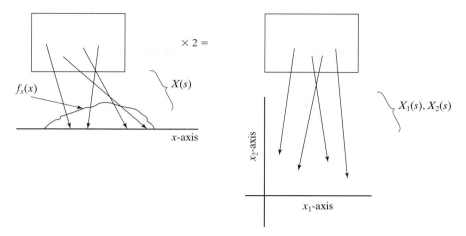

Figure 3.3.1 If we measure a quantity twice and consider the two measurements as separate random variables, we get IID bivariate random variables. If we measure n times, we have n IID random variables and a PDF in n-dimensional space.

We can indeed analyze n Bernoulli trials in terms of n IID random variables (see Sec. 2.3.7). This thought experiment is just one way to envision how one might have IID random variables. There are other ways also.

Why are IID random variables important in practical applications? We have also mentioned that data sets are often modeled as IID random variables. Errors in measurements are often well modeled by IID random variables. Manufacturing suggests another situation that might lead to IID random variables. In the manufacturing process, errors are introduced in dimensions, properties of component parts, and so forth. If n such errors are introduced, all independent and having more or less equal importance, then we might use n IID random variables to model the errors. Indeed, this is a useful model whenever a host of small effects combine to make a large effect. We also can analyze repeated trials in terms of IID random variables, as in Sec. 2.3.7.

But by far the most important use for IID random variables is their use in the central limit theorem. Because this is a major topic near the end of this section, we will delay discussion until we develop the subject further.

The multivariate CDF and PDF for IID random variables

The forms for the multivariate CDF and PDF for IID random variables are easily generalized from the bivariate case. Here we illustrate for two IID random variables and let you generalize in your own mind. Recall the definition of the CDF:

$$F_{X_1 X_2}(x_1, x_2) = P[(X_1 \le x_1) \cap (X_2 \le x_2)] \tag{3.3.1}$$

but since X_1 and X_2 are independent, this equation factors into

$$F_{X_1 X_2}(x_1, x_2) = P[X_1 \le x_1] \times P[X_2 \le x_2] = F_{X_1}(x_1) \times F_{X_2}(x_2) \tag{3.3.2}$$

That makes use of the first I = independent. The second I allows us to drop the subscripts of the two CDFs, since they are identical functions. Thus we have

$$F_{X_1 X_2}(x_1, x_2) = F_X(x_1) \times F_X(x_2) \qquad (3.3.3)$$

Because the PDF can be derived from the CDF, it follows that the PDF also factors:

$$f_{X_1 X_2}(x_1, x_2) = f_X(x_1) \times f_X(x_2) \qquad (3.3.4)$$

Equations (3.3.3) and (3.3.4) can be generalized to n IID random variables by writing more variables. The two Is in the IID random variables, and the forms for the CDFs and PDFs that follow, allow many simplifications and special results in the application of the algebra of expectation to IID random variables.

Examples?   Actually, we just gave two examples in the previous section. Both Examples 3.2.4 and 3.2.6 involved IID random variables. You might want to review those examples to illustrate the concepts.

3.3.2 The Algebra of Expectation for IID Random Variables

The sum of IID random variables.   In this subsection we look at the algebra of expectation applied to functions of n IID random variables. As promised, there are simplifications due to both Is.

The mean.   Let $Y_2 = X_1 + X_2$ be the sum of two IID random variables. The subscript on Y indicates the number of IID random variables being added, two in this case. The expectation of the sum is

$$E[Y_2] = E[X_1 + X_2] = E[X_1] + E[X_2] = \mu_X + \mu_X = 2\mu_X \qquad (3.3.5)$$

where μ_X is the mean of the random variables. Recall that all the Xs have identical PDFs and hence have the same mean. This is the second I of the IID; the first I is not involved in Eq. (3.3.5). Clearly, Eq. (3.3.5) generalizes to n IID random variables:

$$E[Y_n] = n\mu_X \qquad (3.3.6)$$

The variance.   We will derive the variance of Y_2 because this also generalizes for n IID random variables. We begin with the definition of variance:

$$Var[Y_2] = E[(Y_2 - \mu_{Y_2})^2] = E[(X_1 + X_2 - 2\mu_X)^2] = E[((X_1 - \mu_X) + (X_2 - \mu_X))^2] \quad (3.3.7)$$

When we square and distribute the expectation, we get

$$Var[Y_2] = E[(X_1 - \mu_X)^2] + 2E[(X_1 - \mu_X)(X_2 - \mu_X)] + E[(X_2 - \mu_X)^2] \qquad (3.3.8)$$

The first and last terms of Eq. (3.3.8) are by definition the variances of X_1 and X_2, respectively, which are both σ_X^2 due to the second I. The middle term drops out, as shown earlier in Eq. (2.3.54) in the context of discrete random variables. Because this is such an important property, we demonstrate it again here.

We showed in Eq. (3.3.4) that for independent random variables, the bivariate PDF factors into the marginal PDFs of the two random variables. It follows then that the middle term in Eq. (3.3.8) also can be factored:

$$2E[(X_1 - \mu_X)(X_2 - \mu_X)] = 2\int_{-\infty}^{+\infty} \int_{-\infty}^{+\infty} (x_1 - \mu_X)(x_2 - \mu_X) f_{X_1}(x_1) f_{X_2}(x_2)\, dx_1\, dx_2$$

$$= 2\int_{-\infty}^{+\infty} (x_1 - \mu_X) f_X(x_1)\, dx_1 \times \int_{-\infty}^{+\infty} (x_2 - \mu_X) f_X(x_2)\, dx_2$$

$$= 0 \times 0 \tag{3.3.9}$$

since $E[X - \mu_X] = 0$. Thus the middle term in Eq. (3.3.8) drops out, and the final result is

$$Var[Y_2] = Var[X_1 + X_2] = Var[X_1] + Var[X_2] = 2\sigma_X^2 \tag{3.3.10}$$

Notice that both Is were required to derive Eq. (3.3.10). The first I, meaning *independent,* was required to show that the middle term dropped out, and the second I, meaning *identical,* was required to give identical variances to the first and third terms, to yield Eq. (3.3.10).

The result in Eq. (3.3.10) can be generalized through a proof by induction to apply to n random variables;[23] thus in general,

$$Var[Y_n] = Var[X_1 + X_2 + \cdots + X_n] = n\sigma_X^2 \tag{3.3.11}$$

You do it.   Consider that we have the sum of five IID exponential random variables. Because the times between random events in time, such as radioactive decay counts, are exponentially distributed, this sum represents the delay to the fifth event from the beginning. Let $D_5 = T_1 + T_2 + T_3 + T_4 + T_5$ be this delay. Each of the IID random variables is described by the following PDF:

$$f_T(t) = 2e^{-2t}, \quad t > 0, \quad \text{zow} \tag{3.3.12}$$

We ask you to calculate the mean square value of D_5. This is not a simple problem, so let us think about it for a while. First, you may want to review the properties of the exponential PDF, [Eq. (3.1.22)], which were derived in Sec. 3.1. Note that the mean and variance of the exponential PDF are derived there. Also note that we are asking for the mean square value. You may recall that the mean square value can be expressed in terms of the mean and the variance. This is one of the results of the algebra of expectation in Eq. (2.3.41). Now, with these hints and the results of this section, give your value of the mean square value of D_5, and click Evaluate for a response.

```
myanswer = ;
```

```
Evaluate
```

For the answer, see endnote 24.

3.3.3 The Averaging of Measurements

The purpose of this section is to illustrate the relevance of IID random variables to measurements. This will give us a brief introduction to a topic in statistics that we will explore in more depth in Chapter 4.

Measuring noisy data.   All measurements involve noise, whether you can see it or not. Many measurements can be performed only once because the random noise is much less than the uncertainties due to calibration errors and instrument sensitivity; however, when random noise is significant, accuracy can be improved by making many "independent" measurements and averaging. This section models the process of averaging repeated measurements.

Measurement in the presence of noise.   The quantity to be measured consists of a signal, which we assume to be constant, and noise, which we assume varies with time.[25] This situation is suggested by Fig. 3.3.2.

We indicate x_1, x_2, and x_3 as three samples of the quantity to be measured. In general, we will discuss n such measurements, which will be averaged to produce an estimate of s, the unknown quantity we are seeking to measure. The measurements are assumed to consist of a signal, s, which is constant, plus a noise component $n(t)$, which is fluctuating, $x(t) = s + n(t)$.

Reducing the noise by averaging.   One can improve the accuracy of the measurement of s by making a number of independent measurements and averaging the results. This is true

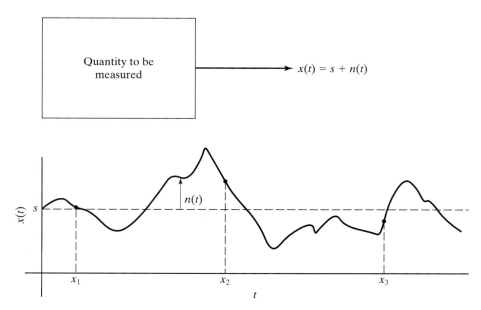

Figure 3.3.2   The signal is s, which is constant, and the random noise adds to it. The sum is x, the measured quantity. We have to wait between measurements to get independent measurements. The first l requires independent measurements.

because the signal is always the same but the noise varies, sometimes positive and sometimes negative. Thus the noise will in part cancel out, but the signal will always add constructively.

The repeated measurements produce a set of numbers, $x_1, x_2, x_3, \ldots, x_n$, which we average to estimate the signal. Thus our estimate of the signal is

$$s \approx \frac{x_1 + x_2 + x_3 + \cdots + x_n}{n} \tag{3.3.13}$$

That is the procedure for measuring s: take n measurements and do an arithmetic average. Our task now is to form a model of this procedure that falls under the probability paradigm, so that we can examine the validity and accuracy of this procedure.

The probability model.   Because we make n measurements, we have our choice of two ways to model the process. We can identify the chance experiment with the making of one measurement, which will be the resulting random variable, and we then must identify the data set with the n-fold repetition of the experiment. Alternatively, we can regard the chance experiment as the taking of the entire data set, which in this view is modeled by n IID random variables. Thus the outcome of the chance experiment maps to the data set, a point in n-dimensional space.

We will use the second viewpoint: The "outcome" of the chance experiment is the taking of n data points, which are modeled by n IID random variables. In this view, if we repeated the experiment, we would get a different set of values for the data. The IID random variables $X_1, X_2, \ldots, X_n$ represent the properties of all such data sets that might be gathered, with their associated distributions.

We *model* this series of measurements by a set of random variables, $X_1, X_2, X_3, \ldots, X_n$. These variables model the "data" that we are going to analyze. The random variables X_i consists of a constant, s, and noise components,

$$X_i = s + N_i \tag{3.3.14}$$

In Eq. (3.3.14), we use lowercase for s, the constant signal, and uppercase for the noise component, N_i, because it is a random variable. Indeed, N_i is an IID random variable, just as X_i is an IID random variable.

What do we mean by "independent" measurement?   We recognize that the signal plus noise is fluctuating on some time scale. We can only accomplish our purpose of getting noise contributions to cancel by waiting long enough between measurements for the sign and magnitude of the noise to randomize. How long that might be depends on the time scale of the fluctuations and can be estimated by observing the data. In Chapter 6 we will develop methods to make this judgment in a quantitative manner.

Analyzing the data

We now have a data set and a probability model for the data set. Our estimate of the signal, s, is to average the data, as given in Eq. (3.3.13). Our model for this process is to average the IID random variables, which gives a random variable, $\hat{S}$, modeling the average:

$$\hat{S} \approx \frac{X_1 + X_2 + X_3 + \cdots + X_n}{n} \tag{3.3.15}$$

The vocabulary of this approach is that the average of the data set in Eq. (3.3.13) is a *statistic* of the data sets, and the random variable $\hat{S}$ models that statistic.

Investigating the statistical properties of $\hat{S}$. We now can do the mental experiment of taking an infinite number of data sets and averaging the results. This is in effect what we do when we take the expectation of $\hat{S}$:

$$E[\hat{S}] = E\left[\frac{X_1 + X_2 + X_3 + \cdots + X_n}{n}\right] = \frac{nE[X]}{n} = \frac{nE[s+N]}{n} = s \qquad (3.3.16)$$

where we have assumed the IID noise random variables, N, have zero mean. Thus the expectation of the estimator is the signal we wish to measure. Thus our "statistic," the simple average, would average to the true value if we repeated the experiment again and again. It is said to be an unbiased statistic, or an unbiased estimator. This is hardly a profound result: it merely says that taking the average of a data set does not skew the results toward the low or the high side.

Uncertainty in the average. The fluctuations, or uncertainty, in the average are associated with the standard deviation of $\hat{S}$. We calculate the variance of the estimator using Eq. (3.3.11):

$$Var[\hat{S}] = Var\left[\frac{X_1 + X_2 + X_3 + \cdots + X_n}{n}\right] = \frac{n\,Var[X]}{n^2} = \frac{\sigma_X^2}{n} \qquad (3.3.17)$$

But the variance of the data is just the variance of the noise, since s is a constant [Eq. (2.3.43)]:

$$\sigma_X^2 = Var[X] = Var[s+N] = \sigma_N^2 \qquad (3.3.18)$$

Combining Eqs. (3.3.17) and (3.3.18) and taking the square root to get the standard deviation, we have

$$\sigma_{\hat{S}} = \frac{\sigma_N}{\sqrt{n}} \qquad (3.3.19)$$

We expand on the meaning of the variance of the noise. Each measurement samples the noise at an independent time. The scatter of these noise samples is indicated by their standard deviation, σ_N. Equation (3.3.19) shows the benefit of taking many data points and averaging. We can improve the accuracy of the measurement by a factor of 2 by taking four measurements and averaging. Equation (3.3.19) also shows the limitations of averaging: we can take 100 measurements to get an improvement by a factor of 10, but to get an improvement of 100 we must take 10,000 measurements. This would be impractical unless somehow the taking and averaging of data were automated.

You do it. Assume you are measuring a voltage that has an error per measurements of 0.2 V (that is, $\sigma_N = 0.2$). How many measurements would you have to average to achieve an accuracy of 0.01 V ($\sigma_{\hat{S}} = 0.01$). Enter your answer in the gray cell box, and click Evaluate for a response.

```
myanswer = ;
```

```
Evaluate
```

For the answer, see endnote 26.

Summary. This subsection applied the algebra of expectation and the concept of IID random variables to the problem of averaging a data set. The benefit of averaging is shown in Eq. (3.3.19) in that the accuracy of the average improves as the square root of the number of values being averaged. To model the process of averaging data, we introduced some basic ideas from statistics. These ideas will be further developed in Chapter 4.

3.3.4 The PDF of the Sum of Independent Random Variables

In this section we are focusing on the sum of random variables. Specifically, we are interested in the PDF of the sum of independent random variables, not necessarily identically distributed. We begin with two random variables and then extend to a large number of independent random variables. The irony is that it is fairly challenging to deal with the sum of two random variables, but dealing with the sum of many random variables is relatively easy. This fortuitous and important result is called the *central limit theorem* (CLT). This development belongs under the heading of IID random variables because the most accessible proof of the CLT is based on the properties of IID random variables.

Two independent random variables. Our goal is to derive the PDF of the sum of two independent random variables. We do not assume IID random variables, so we will use the notation $Z = X + Y$, where X and Y are independent random variables. We assume we know the PDFs of X and Y, $f_X(x)$ and $f_Y(y)$, and we want to determine the PDF of Z, $f_Z(z)$. We will do a general derivation and then give some examples.

First we find the CDF. We will derive $F_Z(z)$ first and then differentiate to get $f_Z(z)$. The definition of the CDF is

$$F_Z(z) = P[Z \le z] = P[X + Y \le z] \tag{3.3.20}$$

where we have expressed Z in terms of X and Y. To determine this probability involving X and Y; we integrate the bivariate PDF over the appropriate portion of the x, y plane, as illustrated in Sec. 3.2. Thus we need the bivariate PDF,

$$f_{XY}(x, y) = f_X(x) \times f_Y(y) \tag{3.3.21}$$

where we have used the independence of X and Y, and we integrate Eq. (3.3.21) over the region of the x, y plane corresponding to the event described in Eq. (3.3.20). The event $X + Y \le z$ is represented by the crosshatched area in Fig. 3.3.3, which also shows how the limits of the integral are set up in Eq. (3.3.22) to cover this area.

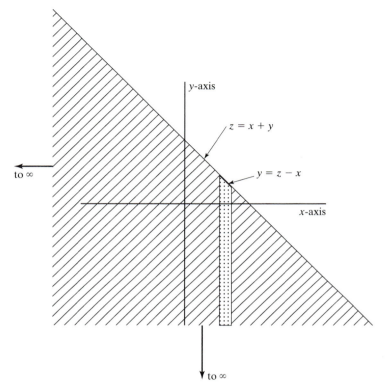

Figure 3.3.3   The triangular shaded area shows the region of integration for determining the probability in Eq. (3.3.20). The triangle should be extended to negative infinity, to the left and below. The vertical strip corresponds to the inner integration in Eq. (3.3.22).

To derive the required probability, we must integrate over the crosshatched area in Fig. 3.3.3, leaving z constant, because the crosshatched region is where the event $\{X + Y \leq z\}$ is satisfied:

$$F_Z(z) = P[X + Y \leq z] = \int_{-\infty}^{+\infty} \left[\int_{-\infty}^{z-x} f_X(x) \times f_Y(y)\, dy \right] dx \qquad (3.3.22)$$

We integrate first in y to get the probability in the vertical strip, and then integrate over the entire range of x to cover the entire crosshatched area. The PDF of x can be brought out of the inner integral, but is best left inside. We cannot evaluate the integral because we have not specified the PDFs of the random variables. We take the derivative of Eq. (3.3.22) to determine the PDF of Z:

$$f_Z(z) = \frac{d}{dz} F_Z(z) = \frac{d}{dz} \int_{-\infty}^{+\infty} \left[\int_{-\infty}^{z-x} f_X(x) \times f_Y(y)\, dy \right] dx \qquad (3.3.23)$$

The form of the PDF of Y may be determined using Leibnitz's rule for differentiation of an integral.[27] This is the simplest case, in which the derivative operates only on the upper limit, and in effect undoes the integration with respect to y. Because the derivative of the upper limit with respect to z is 1, we merely substitute the upper limit for the variable of integration, $y \rightarrow z - x$, and get the result

$$f_Z(z) = \frac{d}{dz} \int_{-\infty}^{+\infty} \left[\int_{-\infty}^{z-x} f_X(x) \times f_Y(y) \, dy \right] dx = \int_{-\infty}^{+\infty} f_X(x) f_Y(z - x) \, dx \qquad (3.3.24)$$

The form of this result is well known from signal analysis as the *convolution integral*. Thus we find that the PDF of the sum of two random variables is the convolution of the PDFs of the individual random variables. This operation often is expressed with the * symbol, as

$$f_Z = f_X * f_Y \qquad (3.3.25)$$

Deriving a convolution integral and writing it symbolically is relatively easy. Having the skill to perform a convolution and get the correct result is not so easy. For this reason, we offer a tutorial on convolution (see Appendix B). We encourage you to review this tutorial even if you are good at convolutions already.

You do it.   Now that you did the tutorial, it is time to show that you can perform convolutions yourself. Let X and Y be IID exponential random variables: $f_X(x) = f_Y(x) = 2e^{-2x}$, $x > 0$, zow. Find $f_Z = f_X * f_Y$ and evaluate at $z = 0.5$. Enter your answer to at least three decimal places in the cell box, and click Evaluate for a response.

```
myanswer = ;
```

```
Evaluate
```

For the answer, see endnote 28.

Applications.   We have shown that the PDF of the sum of two independent random variables is the convolution of the PDFs of the random variables being added. By simple induction this convolution relationship is true for sums with three or more independent random variables. The convolution relationship is very useful in many applications and will appear from time to time in the remainder of this book.

In the remainder of this section we explore the consequences of summing IID random variables. The intention is to lead to, and to make plausible, the central limit theorem.

Multiple convolutions.   Let X be uniformly distributed over the some interval. Figure 3.3.4 shows a uniform PDF.

The convolution of this PDF with itself is a triangle. Figure 3.3.5 shows the PDF for the sum of two IID uniform random variables.

The convolution of two uniform PDFs gives a linear function, as shown in Fig. 3.3.5. If we convolve the triangular PDF with itself, we get a third-order curve, as shown in Fig. 3.3.6.

We now convolve the previous PDF with the triangle. Figure 3.3.7 shows the PDF of the sum of six uniform random variables. It now looks bell shaped.

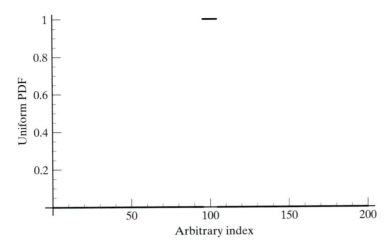

Figure 3.3.4   A uniform PDF. We will convolve this PDF with itself multiple times.

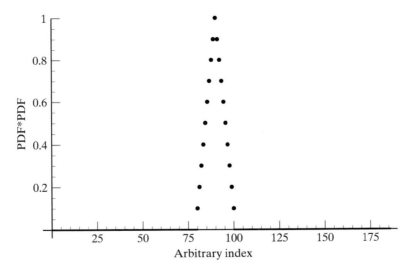

Figure 3.3.5   The convolution of the uniform PDF with itself.

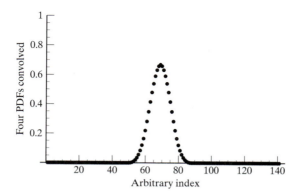

Figure 3.3.6   This is the uniform PDF convolved with itself four times.

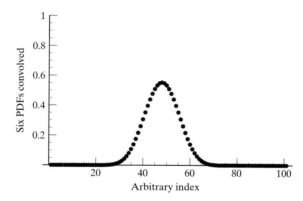

Figure 3.3.7   The convolution of the uniform PDF with itself six times.

To show how close to the Gaussian this PDF in Fig. 3.3.7, we will generate a Gaussian with the same mean and standard deviation and compare the differences. This comparison is a bit complicated, so we show you the code. First, we must normalize the results of the multiple convolutions:

```
g6normalized = g6/Sum [g6[[i]], {i, 1, 100}];
```

To generate the Gaussian, we must calculate the mean and standard deviation of the points:

```
mean6 = Sum [g6normalized [[i]]*i, {i, 1, 100}]
meansquare6 = Sum[g6normalized [[i]]*i^2, {i, 1, 100}]
standev6 = Sqrt[meansquare6 - mean6^2]
48.
```

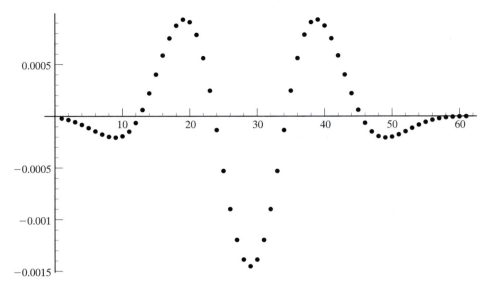

Figure 3.3.8   A plot of the residuals after subtracting a Gaussian from the PDF of six uniform random variables added together.

```
2353.5
7.03562
```

Next, we generate the Gaussian as a table of values.

```
gGauss = Table[PDF[NormalDistribution[mean6, standev6], i],
    {i, 1, 100}];
```

Now, we subtract the Gaussian from the six-fold convolution PDF and plot the result:

```
Residuals =
  Table[g6normalized[[i]] - gGauss[[i]], {i, 20, 80}];
ListPlot[Residuals, ImageSize → 400];
```

Figure 3.3.8 shows the difference between the results of convoluting six uniform random variables and a Gaussian of the same mean and standard deviation. At the center, where the error is maximum, the Gaussian is larger by less than 3%.

The effects of multiple convolutions.   Convolution broadens, smooths out, and lowers the peak of the convolved functions. Here is the important point: you always end up with the same result independent of the function with which you started. Demonstrating this would take a bit more programming than we would ask you to do, but if you want to see it, see endnote 29.

"The" bell-shaped curve. When we perform multiple convolutions, the results get smoother, broader, and more bell shaped. In fact, it can be proven, under a variety of conditions, that as the number of convolutions grows toward infinity, the result approaches "the" bell-shaped curve, meaning the Gaussian PDF.

3.3.5 The Central Limit Theorem (CLT)

The mathematical central limit theorem. As just stated, it has long been known that, under a variety of assumptions, the PDF of the suitably normalized sum of n random variables, as $n \to \infty$, tends to approach the form

$$f_Z(z) \to \alpha e^{-\beta(z-\gamma)^2} \tag{3.3.26}$$

where α, β, and γ are constants. This function is the Gaussian or normal distribution, and we can express the constants in terms of the mean and variance of the random variable, and the normalization condition. We will study the properties of the Gaussian PDF in the next section.

The real-world central limit theorem. Because nature knows no infinities, we need to inquire how many random variables we must add before the Gaussian is an adequate model. This is the appropriate question for the engineer. When we added six uniformly distributed random variables we got a PDF that looks bell shaped. When we compared that result with a true Gaussian, fit to have similar properties, we saw little difference. Our conclusion is that we do not have to add many random variables to have a PDF that is reasonably Gaussian, except for the extreme "tails."

The importance of the central limit theorem. It's comforting to know that the central limit theorem exists. But as engineers that deal with real systems, either natural or human-made, we know that nothing real has an infinite number of components or causes. There are only 10^{80} particles in the universe, an insignificant number compared with infinity.

What matters for us is that when we add random variables the resulting PDF tends toward the Gaussian and gets there quickly in most practical situations. Thus when we consider a situation in which there are a moderately large numbers of "causes" combining to make some "effect" we are justified in assuming a Gaussian model, at least until the model proves to be inadequate. For example, resistor noise consists of the combined effect of the random motion of a large number of carriers in the resistors. We therefore expect resistor noise to be Gaussian, and experiments show this expectation to be valid. In contrast, when effects multiply, or combine in other nonlinear ways, the Gaussian is perhaps not a good model, since it deals with sums. Ultimately, measurement, or a successful design, must justify the Gaussian assumption.

Comparing the Gaussian with the binomial and Pascal PMFs. In Sec. 2.3 we showed that the number of successes in n Bernoulli trials can be determined as the sum of n Bernoulli random variables. When n is large, the familiar bell-shaped curve emerges. Figure 3.3.9 compares the binomial for $n = 20$, $p = 0.4$ (the dots) with a Gaussian of the same mean and variance (the connected lines). The Gaussian is clearly a good approximation to the binomial distribution, even for a mere 20 trials.

The Pascal PMF and the normal PDF. We also showed in Sec. 2.3 that we can express the Pascal random variable as the sum of k geometric random variables. There we used the algebra

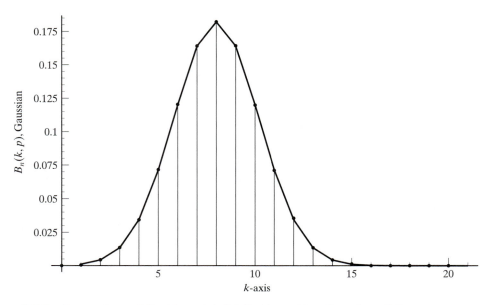

Figure 3.3.9   Comparison of the binomial distribution with a Gaussian of the same mean and variance. The dots are the binomial probabilities and the connected lines a Gaussian with the same mean and variance. The Gaussian points are joined for easy identification.

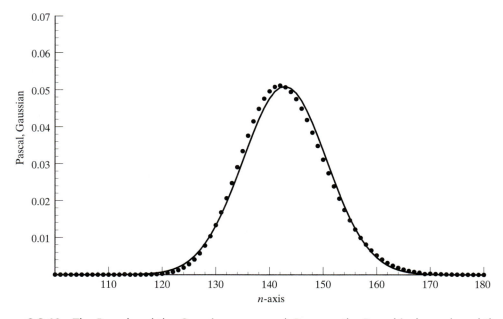

Figure 3.3.10   The Pascal and the Gaussian compared. Because the Pascal is skewed, and the Gaussian is symmetric, the fit is imperfect.

of expectation to calculate the mean and variance of the Pascal random variable, with the results

$$E[N] = \frac{k}{p} \text{ and } Var[N] = \frac{kq}{p^2} \qquad (3.3.27)$$

where N = the number of independent trials to the kth success, and $p = P[\text{success}]$ and $q = 1-p$. In the present discussion of the central limit theorem, we would expect the Pascal random variable for large k to be approximately Gaussian. Let us test this by comparing the free-throw shooter's distribution, Fig. 2.1.4, with a Gaussian of the same mean and variance. Figure 3.3.10 compares the two distributions.

Figure 3.3.10 shows that convergence is slower with nonsymmetric distributions. If you look at the geometric distribution (p. 93), you will see that it is very skewed. Adding many of these gives a result that is still skewed, as shown in Fig. 3.3.10. The Gaussian, being symmetric, has trouble matching the unsymmetric results, as you can see.

The practice of replacing a computationally difficult discrete distribution, such as the binomial or the Pascal, with the Gaussian is a holdover from the time when calculations were done by hand. Now that there is no lack of computational power, techniques that substitute the Gaussian for some other distribution are of less importance than in the past. We present these examples to illustrate one aspect of the CLT.

3.4 THE GAUSSIAN (NORMAL) RANDOM VARIABLE

3.4.1 The Normalized Gaussian Random Variable

Background.   We showed in Sec. 3.3 that the sum of n IID random variables has a PDF that is the n-fold convolution of the PDF of the individual random variables. We asserted and demonstrated that such multiple convolutions tend to approach a stable shape, regardless of the original PDF. This shape is "the" bell-shaped curve, the Gaussian distribution, also called the *normal* distribution. The central limit theorem gives a mathematical foundation for believing that the Gaussian distribution will emerge in situations where complexity of a certain type underlies the randomness. Specifically, where many causes add together to create an effect, that effect will follow a normal distribution. That's why it is called *normal*, because it fits so many situations. Mathematical proof aside, the normal distribution is justified by its success in modeling real random systems.

Although *Gaussian* and *normal* are synonymous in this context, we favor *"Gaussian"* to honor Carl Frederick Gauss, considered by many the most productive mathematician of all time. Earlier workers derived and worked with this distribution, but Gauss was the first to state it clearly and recognize its significance.

Looking ahead.   This section investigates the mathematical properties of the normal distribution and begins the exploration of its use as a model in random systems. We will become familiar with the Gaussian CDF and PDF, both in normalized and in general form. We will show how independent Gaussian random variables add, and give applications in error analysis. We will continue the practice of using the Gaussian to approximate discrete distributions, since this approximation has some use in practical analysis.

The normalized Gaussian PDF

Normalization. Here we assume a Gaussian random variable with zero mean and unit variance. We will use the following notation as a shorthand: $Z = N(0, 1)$ means "The random variable Z is normal (Gaussian) with zero mean and unity variance." The general form for a Gaussian distribution is

$$f_Z(z) = \alpha e^{-\beta(z-\gamma)^2} \text{ for all } z \tag{3.4.1}$$

where α, β, and γ are constants.

We now normalize the distribution for unit area, zero mean, and unity variance.[30] We may achieve zero mean by setting $\gamma = 0$, since that gives the distribution even symmetry about the origin. If a PDF has even symmetry about any point, that point is clearly the balance point and thus the mean. Using standard integral tables, we find for unit area

$$\int_{-\infty}^{+\infty} f_Z(z)\, dz = \int_{-\infty}^{+\infty} \alpha e^{-\beta z^2}\, dz = \alpha \sqrt{\frac{\pi}{\beta}} = 1 \tag{3.4.2}$$

and for unit variance

$$\int_{-\infty}^{+\infty} (z - 0)^2 f_Z(z)\, dz = \int_{-\infty}^{+\infty} \alpha z^2 e^{-\beta z^2}\, dz = \alpha \sqrt{\frac{\pi}{4\beta^3}} = 1 \tag{3.4.3}$$

Simultaneous solution of Eqs. (3.4.2) and (3.4.3) yields

$$\alpha = \frac{1}{\sqrt{2\pi}} \text{ and } \beta = \frac{1}{2} \tag{3.4.4}$$

Thus the normalized Gaussian PDF is

$$f_Z(z) = \frac{1}{\sqrt{2\pi}} e^{-z^2/2} \text{ for all } z \tag{3.4.5}$$

Equation (3.4.5) is another form of what we mean when we write $Z = N(0, 1)$. Figure 3.4.1 shows a plot of the normalized Gaussian PDF.

The square in the exponent causes this function to be fairly flat on top and drop rapidly as z increases. The tails of the distribution for large z in the plus or minus directions get very small. For example, for $z = \pm 7$, they are

```
PDF[NormalDistribution[0, 1], 7.0]
9.13472 × 10⁻¹²
```

The cumulative distribution function (CDF) for the normalized Gaussian random variable

Definition. By definition, the CDF of the normal distribution is

$$F_Z(z) = P[Z \le z] = \int_{-\infty}^{z} \frac{1}{\sqrt{2\pi}} e^{-y^2/2}\, dy \tag{3.4.6}$$

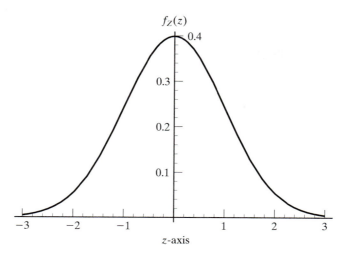

Figure 3.4.1   The PDF for the normalized Gaussian random variable, meaning zero mean and unit variance. This is "the" bell-shaped curve.

where we have used y for the dummy variable of integration, since z is the upper limit on the integral. There is no function whose derivative is the integrand, so this integral must be calculated numerically and tabulated. We have such a table,[31] but in the electronic book we mostly use Mathematica's library of functions. Figure 3.4.2 is a plot of the normalized Gaussian CDF.

Rather than look up the values of this function in a table, we call the CDF function. For example, for $z = +7$, the CDF has the value

```
CDF[NormalDistribution[0, 1], +7];
N[%, 20]
0.99999999999872018746
```

Some practical matters.   Because we cannot count on using Mathematica at all times and places, we introduce the use of tables to determine the CDF of the Gaussian random variable. Because the Gaussian random variable is so important, a special notation is used for its CDF: $\Phi(z)$ is used to designate the CDF of $N(0, 1)$. Thus the following equation defines $\Phi(z)$:

$$\Phi(z) = \int_{-\infty}^{z} \frac{1}{\sqrt{2\pi}} e^{-y^2/2}\, dy \tag{3.4.7}$$

Normally, values are tabulated only for positive z. By symmetry, values for negative z are found as

$$\Phi(-z) = 1 - \Phi(z) \tag{3.4.8}$$

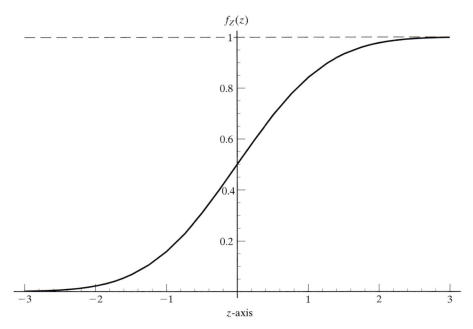

Figure 3.4.2 The CDF for the normalized Gaussian random variable.

The probability that Z is less than z in magnitude is

$$P[-z < Z < +z] = \Phi(z) - \Phi(-z) = 2\Phi(z) - 1 \tag{3.4.9}$$

Also, we note that the CDF approaches 1 as z gets large. To determine the tail probabilities, we need to use the $Q(z)$ function, which is defined as

$$Q(z) = \int_z^{+\infty} \frac{1}{\sqrt{2\pi}} e^{-y^2/2} \, dy \tag{3.4.10}$$

If you do not have a table for $Q(z)$ handy, you can use the asymptotic form:

$$Q(z) \rightarrow \frac{1}{z\sqrt{2\pi}} e^{-z^2/2} \text{ as } z \rightarrow +\infty \tag{3.4.11}$$

which works with less than 0.00002 error for $z > 3.5$. Also, you can use error function tables, since $Q(z) = \frac{1}{2}\text{erfc}\left(\frac{z}{\sqrt{2}}\right)$.

You do it. What is $\Phi(-1.5)$? Look it up in the table,[31] enter your answer in the cell box, and click Evaluate for a response.

```
myanswer = ;
```

```
Evaluate
```

For the answer, see endnote 32.

3.4.2 The General (Unnormalized) Gaussian Random Variable

Changing variables.   We may generalize to arbitrary mean and variance by making a change of variables. We define a random variable, X, in terms of the normalized random variable, Z, by the following linear transformation $X = aZ + b$. We can identify a and b from the algebra of expectation. The mean of X is

$$E[X] = E[aZ + b] = aE[Z] + b = \mu_X \Rightarrow b = \mu_X \qquad (3.4.12)$$

since $E[Z] = 0$. Similarly, the variance of X is

$$Var[X] = Var[aZ + b] = a^2 \, Var[Z] = \sigma_X^2 \Rightarrow a = \sigma_X \qquad (3.4.13)$$

since $Var[Z] = 1$. Note that in Eq. (3.4.13) we drop the additive constant, b, according to Eq. (2.3.43). Therefore the required transformation from a normalized Gaussian, $Z = N(0, 1)$, to a general Gaussian, $X = N(\mu_X, \sigma_X^2)$, is

$$X = \sigma_X Z + \mu_X \qquad (3.4.14)$$

The PDF for X.   We now show that X has a Gaussian PDF. To find the PDF for X, we must formally change random variables. We begin with the CDF for X. By definition, the CDF for X is

$$F_X(x) = P[X \le x] \qquad (3.4.15)$$

In Fig. 3.4.3, we show the plot of Z and X. We want to calculate a probability in X, as required by Eq. (3.4.15), in terms of an event in Z.

Because the event $X \le x$ corresponds to the event $Z \le \frac{x - \mu_X}{\sigma_X}$, we can calculate the probability of the former from the PDF of Z, as follows:

$$F_X(x) = P[X \le x] = P\left[Z \le \frac{x - \mu_X}{\sigma_X}\right] = \int_{-\infty}^{\frac{x - \mu_X}{\sigma_X}} f_Z(z) \, dz = \Phi\left(\frac{x - \mu_X}{\sigma_X}\right) \qquad (3.4.16)$$

For purposes of deriving the PDF of X, Eq. (3.4.16) is merely an intermediate point, but it actually is a very useful result, and we will return to it later. For now, we give a plot, using specific values for $\mu_X = +10$, and $\sigma_X = 4$, in Fig. 3.4.4. This plot looks like $\Phi(z)$, except it reaches 50% at the mean of 10 and is expanded in width by a factor of 4.

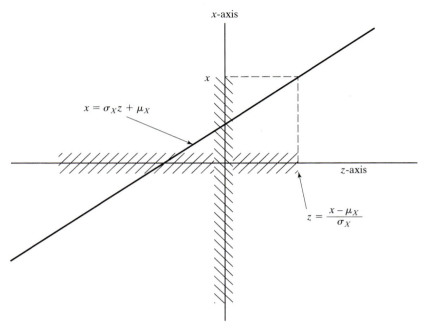

Figure 3.4.3 The mapping of Z into X. We have shaded in the event $X \leq x$ with the vertical crosshatched region and shown how it corresponds to the event $Z \leq \frac{x-\mu_X}{\sigma_X}$ in the horizontal crosshatched region. This event mapping allows us to calculate the CDF of X.

The PDF of X. The PDF of the generalized Gaussian random variable is the derivative of Eq. (3.4.16) with respect to x. To perform the derivative, we use Leibnitz's rule (see endnote 27):

$$
f_X(x) = \frac{d}{dx} \int_{-\infty}^{\frac{x-\mu_X}{\sigma_X}} \frac{1}{\sqrt{2\pi}} e^{-z^2/2} \, dz = \frac{1}{\sqrt{2\pi}} e^{-\frac{1}{2}\left(\frac{x-\mu_X}{\sigma_X}\right)^2} \times \frac{d}{dx}\left(\frac{x-\mu_X}{\sigma_X}\right)
$$

$$
= \frac{1}{\sqrt{2\pi\sigma_X^2}} e^{-\frac{1}{2}\left(\frac{x-\mu_X}{\sigma_X}\right)^2} \quad \text{for all } x
$$

(3.4.17)

The normalization term in front is sometimes expressed as $\frac{1}{\sigma_X\sqrt{2\pi}}$. This PDF is represented by the shorthand $X = N(\mu_X, \sigma_X^2)$ and is read, "X is a Gaussian (or normal) random variable with a mean of μ_X and a variance of σ_X^2." We can show easily that 68.3% of the probability falls within one standard deviation of the mean, and 95.4% falls within two standard deviations of the mean. We show this PDF for a mean of 10 and a variance of 16 ($\sigma_X = 4$) in Fig. 3.4.5.

The general Gaussian PDF in Eq. (3.4.17) is important and will be used frequently from now on, but when we calculate probabilities, we will have to return to the CDF in Eq. (3.4.16). For example, consider the random variable $X = N(10, 16)$, whose PDF is shown in Fig. 3.4.5. Let us say we wish to calculate the probability that X falls in the region between 5 and 20. Of course,

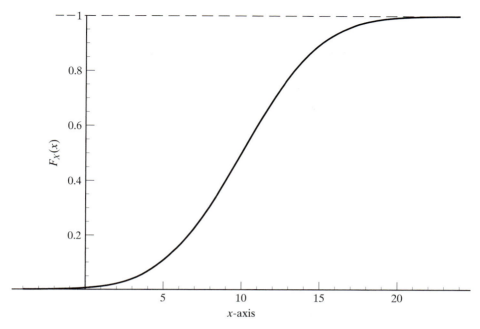

Figure 3.4.4   The CDF for $X = N(10,16)$. This CDF is the same as the CDF for the normalized Gaussian random variable in Fig. 3.4.2, except the 50% point is at $x = +10$, the mean, and the scale is expanded by a factor of 4, which is the ratio of the standard deviations.

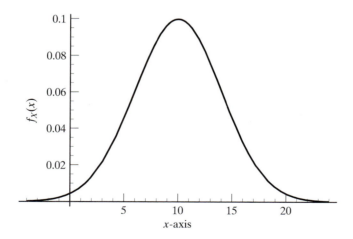

Figure 3.4.5   The PDF for $X = N(\mu_X, \sigma_X^2)$ with $\mu_X = +10$ and $\sigma_X = 4$. Note that the PDF is centered on the mean and is broader and shorter than the normalized PDF in Fig. 3.4.1 by a factor of 4.

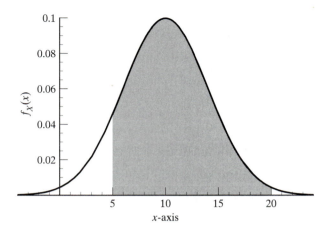

Figure 3.4.6   The probability $P[5 < X \le 20]$ is the shaded area shown.

we can express this as an integral:

$$P[5 < X \le 20] = \int_5^{20} f_X(x)\,dx \tag{3.4.18}$$

where $f_X(x)$ is given in Eq. (3.4.17); however, the antiderivative does not exist in closed form, so we resort directly to the tabulated CDF, $\Phi(z)$. Here is how we can determine this probability:

$$P[5 < X \le 20] = F_X(20) - F_X(5) = \Phi\left(\frac{20 - 10}{4}\right) - \Phi\left(\frac{5 - 10}{4}\right) = \Phi(2.5) - \Phi(-1.25) \tag{3.4.19}$$

When we look up $\Phi(-1.25)$ in a table, we do not find it there and have to use the relationship in Eq. (3.4.8) to obtain

$$P[5 < X \le 20] = \Phi(2.5) - \Phi(-1.25) = \Phi(2.5) + \Phi(+1.25) - 1 \tag{3.4.20}$$

Of course, having Mathematica handy, we can use it for the calculation in Eq. (3.4.19) directly:

```
CDF [NormalDistribution[10, 4], 20.0] -
 CDF [NormalDistribution[10, 4], 5.0]
0.888141
```

The value calculated is represented by the shaded area in Fig. 3.4.6.

Example 3.4.1: A bolt _____

A hole is exactly 0.500 in. in diameter. A bolt is manufactured with an OD of $0.498 \pm 0.003(1\sigma)$ in. Assume that the errors are normal, and let D be the random variable representing the bolt diameter. Thus $D = N(0.498, (0.003)^2)$. Find the probability that the bolt will not fit into the hole.

Solution   The event of interest is $D > 0.500$ if we assume no force is applied to force the bolt into the hole. Thus we calculate the probability

$$P[D > 0.500] = 1 - P[D \leq 0.500] = 1 - \Phi\left(\frac{0.500 - 0.498}{0.003}\right) = 1 - \Phi(0.667) \qquad (3.4.21)$$

Using Mathematica, we calculate

```
1 - CDF[NormalDistribution[0, 1], 0.667]
0.252386
```

You do it.   Let us say there is also a problem if the bolt is too loose, but that we allow for forcing the bolt. Let us assume that a bolt is accepted if its diameter falls in the range $0.495 < D \leq 0.502$. Calculate the probability that a bolt selected at random will be accepted. You can use Mathematica if you are running the full system, or you can use the table in endnote 31. Enter your answer in the cell box, and click Evaluate for a response.

```
myanswer = ;
```

```
Evaluate
```

For the answer, see endnote 33.

Example 3.4.2:   A resistor
Assume resistors as manufactured have a normal distribution. If 9% of a production run are not within $\pm 10\%$ of the nominal value and thus cannot be sold as $\pm 10\%$ resistors, what fraction is within $\pm 5\%$ of the nominal value?

Solution   Assume R is a random variable describing the resistance value chosen from the population of resistors. The mean μ_R is the nominal value, but the standard deviation, σ_R is unknown. Our first task is to find σ_R, which we can determine from the information that 9% of the resistors are outside the $\pm 10\%$ boundary. Thus we must have

$$P[0.9\,\mu_R < R \leq 1.1\,\mu_R] = 0.91 \qquad (3.4.22)$$

Using the normalized Gaussian CDF in Eq. (3.4.16) to evaluate this probability, we have

$$P[0.9\,\mu_R < R \leq 1.1\,\mu_R] = \Phi\left(\frac{0.1\,\mu_R}{\sigma_R}\right) - \Phi\left(\frac{-0.1\,\mu_R}{\sigma_R}\right) = 2\,\Phi\left(\frac{0.1\,\mu_R}{\sigma_R}\right) - 1 = 0.91$$

$$(3.4.23)$$

where we used Eq. (3.4.8) for the negative argument. We solve Eq. (3.4.23) to get the requirement

$$\Phi\left(\frac{0.1\,\mu_R}{\sigma_R}\right) = 0.955 \tag{3.4.24}$$

which we can determine by interpolation in the Φ table in endnote 31. But it is even easier to use an inverse CDF table, $z = \Phi^{-1}(p)$, which we also give.[34] You can see from the table that $\Phi^{-1}(0.955) = 1.6950$. Thus

$$\frac{0.1\mu_R}{\sigma_R} = 1.695 \Rightarrow \frac{\mu_R}{\sigma_R} = 16.95 \tag{3.4.25}$$

Thus from the fact that 9% of the resistors do not meet the $\pm10\%$ specification we derive the ratio of the nominal resistance to the standard deviation of the distribution. The question asks us to determine the probability that a resistor falls within $\pm5\%$ of the nominal value. This question can be interpreted two ways: (1) What is the probability that a resistor chosen at random from the original batch falls within $\pm5\%$ of the nominal? or (2) What is the probability that a resistor chosen at random from the resistors that meet the $\pm10\%$ specification also falls within $\pm5\%$ of the nominal value? The first is unconditioned, and the second is conditioned. We address the first interpretation first. We may write this as

$$P[0.95\,\mu_R < R \le 1.05\,\mu_R] = \Phi\left(\frac{0.05\,\mu_R}{\sigma_R}\right) - \Phi\left(\frac{-0.05\,\mu_R}{\sigma_R}\right) = 2\Phi\left(\frac{0.05\,\mu_R}{\sigma_R}\right) - 1 \tag{3.4.26}$$

Using the result derived in Eq. (3.4.25), we have

$$P[0.95\,\mu_R < R \le 1.05\,\mu_R] = 2\Phi(0.05 \times 16.95) - 1 = 2\Phi(0.8475) - 1 = 0.603 \tag{3.4.27}$$

Thus 60.3% of the resistors meet the 5% specification. If we take the second interpretation, we merely increase this value to $\frac{0.603}{0.91} = 0.663$.

You do it. Let us say the machine that makes resistors is misadjusted one day, and the mean for the resistors that are actually manufactured is $1.03\,\mu_R$; that is, on average, the resistances are 3% too high. What now is the yield of resistors in the $\pm10\%$ range? Calculate the yield (before, it was 91%) to at least three places, and enter your answer in the cell box. Use percentage, but do not enter a % sign. Click Evaluate for a response.

```
myanswer = ;
```

```
Evaluate
```

For the answer, see endnote 35.

Example 3.4.3:   Gas mileage _____

We will offer one more example because it involves slightly different mathematics. An auto manufacturer has certain requirements for the automobiles that it manufactures. The gasoline mileage, as the cars come off the assembly line and are tuned, is a Gaussian random variable, $M = N(25, (2)^2)$ mpg. The manufacturer then tests the mileage and remanufactures any unit that tests below 23 mpg. Determine the average mileage of all autos that meet the mileage specification.

Solution   The problem calls for the conditional expectation $E[M|M \geq 23]$, which calls for the conditional PDF $f_{M|M \geq 23}(m)$. We calculate the probability of the conditioning event as

$$P[M \geq 23] = 1 - P[M < 23] = 1 - \Phi\left(\frac{23 - 25}{2}\right) = \Phi(1) = 0.8413 \tag{3.4.28}$$

The required conditional PDF is therefore

$$f_{M|M \geq 23}(m) = \frac{1}{0.8413} \times \frac{1}{2\sqrt{2\pi}} \exp\left[-\frac{1}{2}\left(\frac{m - 25}{2}\right)^2\right], \ 23 \leq m < +\infty \tag{3.4.29}$$

The expectation is

$$E[M|M \geq 23] = \int_{23}^{+\infty} m \times \frac{1}{0.8413} \times \frac{1}{2\sqrt{2\pi}} \exp\left[-\frac{1}{2}\left(\frac{m - 25}{2}\right)^2\right] dm \tag{3.4.30}$$

We modify this integral by writing the first m as $(m - 25) + 25$ and thus split Eq. (3.4.30) into two integrals; call them I and II. The first is

$$\text{I:} \int_{23}^{+\infty} (m - 25) \frac{1}{0.8413} \times \frac{1}{2\sqrt{2\pi}} \exp\left[-\frac{1}{2}\left(\frac{m - 25}{2}\right)^2\right] dm \tag{3.4.31}$$

We change variables to $w = \frac{m-25}{2}$, which yields

$$\text{I:} \int_{-1}^{+\infty} w \frac{1}{0.8413} \times \frac{2}{\sqrt{2\pi}} \exp\left[-\frac{1}{2}w^2\right] dw = \frac{1}{0.8413} \times \frac{2}{\sqrt{2\pi}} \int_{-1}^{+\infty} \exp\left[-\frac{1}{2}w^2\right] d\left(\frac{1}{2}w^2\right) \tag{3.4.32}$$

which gives the result

$$\sqrt{\frac{2}{\pi}} \frac{1}{0.8413} e^{-0.5} = 0.5752 \tag{3.4.33}$$

The second integral is easier because it reduces to Eq. (3.4.28):

$$\text{II:} \ 25 \times \int_{23}^{+\infty} \frac{1}{0.8413} \times \frac{1}{2\sqrt{2\pi}} \exp\left[-\frac{1}{2}\left(\frac{m - 25}{2}\right)^2\right] dm = 25 \tag{3.4.34}$$

Thus we find $E[M|M \geq 23] = 25.5752$. We did the integral analytically to show you the technique. We can confirm it numerically with Mathematica.

```
NIntegrate[m PDF[NormalDistribution[25, 2], m],
   {m, 23, Infinity}] / CDF[NormalDistribution[0, 1], 1]
25.5752
```

Another way to integrate this is to have a self-normalizing integral. The critical part of the integral is the factor $\exp\left[-\frac{1}{2}\left(\frac{m-25}{2}\right)^2\right]$; the rest is a group of constants. Here, then, is another way to do the calculation.

```
NIntegrate[mExp[-0.5((m - 25)/2)^2], {m, 23, Infinity}]/
   NIntegrate[Exp[-0.5((m - 25)/2)^2], {m, 23, Infinity}]
25.5752
```

Note that we put the m in the numerator but not in the denominator. All the constants cancel, and we get the conditional expectation as required.

3.4.3 The Gaussian Used to Approximate Discrete Distributions

We showed in Sec. 3.3.5 that, as a consequence of the central limit theorem, we expect the Gaussian to approximate discrete distributions that represent the sum of a large number of random variables. We illustrated with some plots that compared the Gaussian with the binomial and the Pascal distributions.

Here we investigate a bit further and use the Gaussian to make calculations related to binomial trials. We introduce the calculation with a story.

Billy Bob Bojangles, having made a fortune in oil, decided to establish West Texas Airlines, headquartered at the Midland/Odessa Airport. Business was great and they sold all 140 seats on every flight. Some months after starting, Billy Bob's operations officer informed him that WTA flights were only 95% full because of last-minute cancellations and changes of plans, and so on. Billy Bob reached for the nearest envelope, turned it over, and made the following calculation: $\frac{140}{0.95} = 147.4$. Being conservative, Billy Bob rounded down and told the ticket people to sell 147 seats on every flight. Our job is to calculate the probability that a flight will be oversold, that is, that more than 140 people will show up to board the flight.

Our model.   We model a flight as a series of 147 binomial trials. The probability of "success" is 0.95, and the random variable $K =$ the number of people that show up. The event $\{$oversold$\} = \{140 < K \le 147\}$. Rather than do the calculation with the binomial distribution, however, we will use the Gaussian as an approximation.

Fitting a Gaussian to a binomial distribution.   We make the two distributions have the same mean and variance. For the binomial, we derived the mean and variance [Eqs. (2.3.55, 2.3.56)] as

$$\mu_K = np = 147 \times 0.95 = 139.7 \text{ and } \sigma_K^2 = npq = 147 \times 0.95 \times 0.05 = 6.983 \qquad (3.4.35)$$

Thus our Gaussian model is $M = N(139.7, 6.983)$. We call this continuous random variable M because it is a continuous model for the discrete random variable K.

The "oversold flight" calculation.   We will calculate the probability that a flight will be oversold, which corresponds to $K > 140$. This corresponds to the probability that $M > 140.5$. Why 140.5? Because M is a continuous random variable replacing a discrete random variable; so all the probability associated with $K = 141$ is modeled by $140.5 < M \leq 141.5$, and likewise for all the other discrete values. This is called a *continuity correction,* since we are approximating a discrete distribution with a continuous distribution. The required calculation is thus

$$P[\text{oversold}] = \int_{140.5}^{147.5} N(139.7, 6.983) \, dm = \Phi\left(\frac{147.5 - 139.7}{\sqrt{6.983}}\right) - \Phi\left(\frac{140.5 - 139.7}{\sqrt{6.983}}\right)$$
(3.4.36)

which is $0.9984 - 0.6133 = 0.3851$. Thus more than 38% of the WTA airlines flights are overbooked owing to Billy Bob's back-of-the-envelope calculation.

The exact calculations.   Because we have the ready ability to make the exact calculation, let us see how accurate the approximate calculation is. The exact calculation is

```
Sum[PDF[BinomialDistribution[147, 0.95], k], {k, 141, 147}]
0.394075
```

In Eq. (3.4.36) we set the upper limit to 147.5, but infinity is more appropriate for calculating the probability above 140.5. Changing that limit to $+\infty$ raises the approximate calculation to 0.3867, which is closer to the true value but still 2% low.

You do it.   You are now Billy Bob for a moment, so reach for the nearest envelope, turn it over, and calculate the number of tickets to be sold to have a 5% or less chance of being oversold. Enter your answer, an integer, in the cell box, and evaluate the cell to see how you did. Use the Gaussian approximation and let n be the unknown. Note that the mean and variance involve n.

```
myanswer = ;
```

```
Evaluate
```

For the answer, see endnote 36.

3.4.4 The Sum of Independent Gaussian Random Variables

The PDF of the sum of two independent normal random variables.   We are concerned in this section with the sum of two or more independent Gaussian random variables. From the previous section we know that the PDF of the sum of two Gaussian random variables is

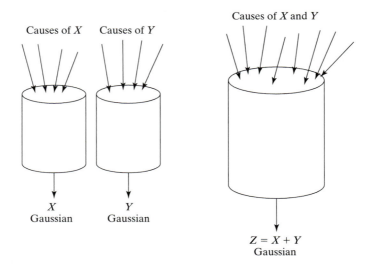

Figure 3.4.7   The central limit theorem leads us to expect that the sum of two Gaussian random variables will be Gaussian.

the convolution of the PDFs of the individual Gaussian random variables. Thus the basic question is, What is the convolution of one Gaussian PDF with another Gaussian PDF?

A mental experiment.   Consider the sum of a large number of IID random variables; think of them as "causes" and the result as an "effect." We expect the PDF of the effect, call it X, to be Gaussian in light of the CLT. Consider the sum of another large number of IID random variables, more and different causes. We expect the PDF of their effect, call it Y, to be Gaussian also. Now, we consider the sum of the two effects, call it $Z = X + Y$. Because this sum essentially adds all the causes of X and Y, by the CLT we expect Z to be Gaussian also. On this basis we expect the convolution of two Gaussians to be Gaussian as well, and this is correct. It follows that the sum of three or more Gaussians remains Gaussian as well. This argument is summarized in Fig. 3.4.7.

We skip the mathematical proof and assert the following as true for independent Gaussian random variables: If

$$X = N(\mu_X, \sigma_X^2) \text{ and } Y = N(\mu_Y, \sigma_Y^2), \text{ then } Z = X + Y = N(\mu_Z, \sigma_Z^2) \qquad (3.4.37)$$

where $\mu_Z = \mu_X + \mu_Y$ and $\sigma_Z^2 = \sigma_X^2 + \sigma_Y^2$

In Eq. (3.4.37) we used the algebra of expectation [Eqs. (2.3.52, 2.3.53)] to add the means and variances. Therefore, adding two or more independent Gaussian random variables is routine: we merely add the means and variances and use these to describe the resulting Gaussian random variable.

Example 3.4.4:   Two resistors _____

We put a $100 \pm 10\%$ Ω resistor in series with a $50 \pm 10\%$ Ω resistor. What is the resulting resistance?

Solution   We assume that the resistors have Gaussian distributions, and the $\pm 10\%$ refers to the standard deviation. (This is not a realistic model for resistor values, just a textbook example.) Thus $R_1 = N(100, (10)^2)$, and $R_2 = N(50, (5)^2)$. The sum is therefore $R = N(150, 125) = N(150, (11.2)^2)$. Thus the series combination is $150 \pm 7.45\%$ Ω.

You do it.   Consider independent random variables $X_1 = N(5, 1)$ and $X_2 = N(5, 1)$. Let $Y = X_1 - X_2$. Find the probability $P[Y \leq 1]$. Enter your answer in the cell box, and click Evaluate for a response.

```
myanswer = ;
```

```
Evaluate
```

For the answer, see endnote 37.

3.4.5 Error Analysis Using Random Variables

Error analysis.   Error analysis plays an important role in both the design and analysis of systems. Experience shows that there are many sources of error in system performance: noise of various types, uncertainties in the properties of many system components, and manufacturing and construction variations of all sorts. These errors must be combined into some overall error in system performance. Typically, errors are assumed independent, for lack of better knowledge, and small relative to nominal values. If these assumptions are shaky, then the engineer generally seeks assistance from a trained statistician or some other expert in error analysis. In this section we show how random variables are used to model errors and how errors are typically combined. Although we speak in the context of Gaussian random variables, that assumption is not essential for much of what follows. The Gaussian assumption will be discussed at the end of this subsection.

Combining linear errors.   Errors combine in either a linear or a nonlinear manner. When errors simply add in a linear fashion, the random variables representing the error are combined by simple addition. The results of such an addition were examined in the previous section: the means and variances add according to the algebra of expectation, and if the errors are Gaussian, then their sum is also Gaussian.

Combining nonlinear errors.   When errors are combined in a nonlinear manner, error analysis usually employs a linearization of the system properties. The following example demonstrates this process. We introduce the main ideas in the context of a low-tech example: a measuring tape used in surveying. The tape is used to measure a distance and we are interested in the manner in which the errors in the tape combine to influence the error in the measured distance.

Sources of error.   One source of error is the calibration of the tape. The tape was manufactured and marked imperfectly, and hence this error is inherent in using this particular tape. The "chance experiment" in this case is picking a tape to make the distance measurement. The outcomes of this experiment are all the tapes that could have been chosen. We assume the calibration errors are normally distributed. We define a random variable C to represent the relative calibration error. Thus if the tape were used perfectly under ideal circumstances the measured distance would be $D = d(1 + C)$, where d is the true distance, and D is the measured distance. This measured distance is a random variable because it depends on the outcome of a chance experiment, namely, the choosing of a tape to make the measurement. We assume that the calibration errors have zero mean (no bias) and 0.5% standard deviation; hence the calibration errors are normal, $C = N(0, (0.005)^2)$.

Measurement errors are a second source of error. The tape is temperature sensitive and stretches owing to the force of pulling. Even if these effects are compensated for, there is some uncertainty due to these measurement errors. We introduce another random variable, M, to describe these errors. Here the experiment is making the measurement. If we repeated the experiment we would get a different measured result. We assume the measurement errors are normally distributed with zero bias and 0.4% (1σ) error; hence $M = N(0, (0.004)^2)$. Because the measurement errors are proportional to the distance measured, we have now

$$D = d(1 + C)(1 + M) \tag{3.4.38}$$

Notice that C and M are normalized errors, not absolute errors. The absolute error due to calibration would be dC. There are yet other errors we might consider, such as the reading of the scale, but we will consider only calibration and measurement errors, since these will illustrate the principle of how errors combine. We may expand Eq. (3.4.38) as

$$D = d + d(C + M) + \underbrace{dCM}_{\text{small}} \tag{3.4.39}$$

The last term is small, as indicated, and will be ignored. This technique keeps only the linear terms and is called *linearization*. We now apply the algebra of expectation. The mean of D is

$$E[D] = E[d + d(C + M)] = d + d(0 + 0) = d \tag{3.4.40}$$

Thus the measurement is unbiased because the errors are unbiased. Because we have expressed the errors in the calibration and measurement in a normalized form, let us introduce a normalized combined error, E. This combined error is defined by the expression

$$D = d(1 + E) \tag{3.4.41}$$

When we substitute Eq. (3.4.41) into Eq. (3.4.39), we find

$$E = C + M \tag{3.4.42}$$

Because C and M are Gaussian, it follows that E is Gaussian also: $E = N(0, \sigma_C^2 + \sigma_M^2)$. We introduce σ_E, the standard deviation of E, as a measure of the total error, and we find

$$\sigma_E = \sqrt{\sigma_C^2 + \sigma_M^2} \tag{3.4.43}$$

We may read Eq. (3.4.43) as follows: "The normalized (or percent) combined error is the Pythagorean sum of the normalized errors of the various components contributing to the measurement."[38] We could have generalized to any number of components rather than the two we used in the derivation. This is an important result and is often used in error analysis. The constraints are that the errors are the linear term in a power series expansion of the contributing term, and that errors must be small.

Example 3.4.5:   Error in a simple system _____

Consider the simple system shown in Fig. 3.4.8. We assume that there are errors in X, Y, and A, and we use the principles of this section to combine these into an overall error in Z. We define the *absolute* errors in X, Y, and A as E_X, E_Y, and E_A. Our goal is to determine the absolute error in Z, E_Z.

The nonlinear term.   First, we look at the nonlinear term, the product AX. Our model is that

$$A = a + E_A \text{ and } X = x + E_X \tag{3.4.44}$$

where a and x are the true values of A and X. Because we assume unbiased errors, we may also describe a and x as the average values of A and X. An alternative description of the variables and errors would be to state that $A = N(a, \sigma_A^2)$ or $E_A = N(0, \sigma_A^2)$, and likewise for X. We linearize the product AX, which becomes

$$AX = (a + E_A)(x + E_X) = ax + aE_X + xE_A + \underbrace{E_A E_X}_{\text{small}} \approx ax + aE_X + xE_A \tag{3.4.45}$$

where we dropped the second-order term, $E_A E_X$. We now normalize Eq. (3.4.45) by introducing the absolute error in the product, E_{AX}, and factoring ax out of both sides.

$$AX = ax\left(1 + \frac{E_{AX}}{ax}\right) = ax\left(1 + \frac{E_X}{x} + \frac{E_A}{a}\right) \Rightarrow \frac{E_{AX}}{ax} = \frac{E_X}{x} + \frac{E_A}{a} \tag{3.4.46}$$

Thus the normalized error in the product is approximated by the sum of the normalized errors in the components. The error in the product is also Gaussian, $AX = N(ax, \sigma_{AX}^2)$, where σ_{AX}^2 is the variance of E_{AX}. According to the results of the previous sections the *normalized* errors add in a Pythagorean sum. Thus the errors add as

$$\frac{\sigma_{AX}}{ax} = \sqrt{\left(\frac{\sigma_A}{a}\right)^2 + \left(\frac{\sigma_X}{x}\right)^2} \tag{3.4.47}$$

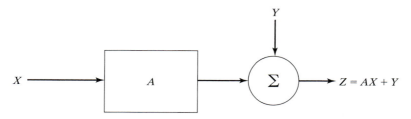

Figure 3.4.8   In this simple system we assume there are errors in X, Y, and A, and we will determine how these combine to produce an error in Z.

Therefore the *absolute* error in the AX term, expressed in terms of its standard deviation, is

$$\sigma_{AX} = ax\sqrt{\left(\frac{\sigma_A}{a}\right)^2 + \left(\frac{\sigma_X}{x}\right)^2} = \sqrt{(x\sigma_A)^2 + (a\sigma_X)^2} \tag{3.4.48}$$

Thus we can express the product as $AX = N(ax, \sigma_{AX}^2)$, bearing in mind the assumption of small errors in A and X.

The linear part.   Having done the product we move to the sum. Adding random variables is routine: the means and variances of the absolute errors add because we are assuming independence. Our means are zero, so we must obtain the Pythagorean sum of the variances of AX and Y, as follows:

$$\sigma_{\text{combined}} = \sqrt{\sigma_{AX}^2 + \sigma_Y^2} = \sqrt{(x\sigma_A)^2 + (a\sigma_X)^2 + \sigma_Y^2} \tag{3.4.49}$$

Let us assume that $a = 10$, $x = 2$, and $E[Y] = 5$. In all cases we assume the standard deviation of all the errors is 10%. Thus $\sigma_A = 10\% \times 10 = 1$, $\sigma_X = 10\% \times 2 = 0.2$, $\sigma_Y = 10\% \times 5 = 0.5$. In this case the mean of the output is $10 \times 2 + 5 = 25$, and the standard deviation is given by Eq. (3.4.49) as

$$\sigma_{\text{combined}} = \sqrt{(2 \times 1)^2 + (10 \times 0.2)^2 + (0.5)^2} = 2.87 \ (11.5\%) \tag{3.4.50}$$

Comments.   The overall error generally increases on a percentage basis owing to the addition of errors. The Pythagorean sum favors the larger contributors.

The Gaussian assumption.   We described the random variables as Gaussian random variables, but the results in this section depend solely on independence and well-known results from the algebra of expectation. Why the Gaussian model? There are several reasons: (1) error-producing processes are complex, and thus errors are often well modeled by the Gaussian PDF; (2) by the time many errors have been combined in an overall error analysis, the results should approach the Gaussian according to the CLT; and (3) the assumption is traditional and thus may go unchallenged.[39]

As a consequence of the Gaussian assumption, the results of an error analysis are often presented in statements like $w = 25 \pm 2.87 (1\sigma)$, meaning that the 2.87 is the standard deviation, or rms error, and the expression is interpreted as a 68% chance that the true value will fall in the range 25 ± 2.87. This probability of 68% assumes the Gaussian distribution.

Summary.   In this section we modeled the combination of errors in a complex system. Such error analysis is not dependent on the Gaussian assumption, but in practice this assumption is usually made for the individual errors and for their sum. When factors are multiplied or divided, their *relative* errors (normalized errors) add in a Pythagorean sum. When factors are added or subtracted, their absolute errors add in a Pythagorean sum.

You do it.   Assume that the output of a system is $A(X + Y)$, where $A = N(10, 1^2)$, $X = N(2, 0.2^2)$, and $Y = N(5, 0.5^2)$. These are the same numbers as in Example 3.4.4. The mean of the output is $10 \times (2 + 5) = 70$. Find the standard deviation of the output in percent (but do not enter the % sign). Note that you need to combine X and Y before you consider A. If you multiply out the expression, you will get the wrong answer, since errors will not be independent in the resulting terms.

```
myanswer = ;
```

```
Evaluate
```

For the answer, see endnote 40.

3.5 THE RAYLEIGH AND BIVARIATE GAUSSIAN RANDOM VARIABLES

In this section we introduce two new distributions. The Rayleigh is closely related to the Gaussian and is important in many physics and engineering problems, and the bivariate is important in signal processing and in many other contexts. We also introduce concepts such as correlation to express a linear relationship between random variables.

3.5.1 The Rayleigh Distribution

The Rayleigh distribution describes the random variable resulting from the Pythagorean sum of two IID Gaussian random variables. Let $R = \sqrt{X^2 + Y^2}$, where $X = N(0, \sigma^2)$ and $Y = N(0, \sigma^2)$. We choose zero means for convenience. We will derive the PDF of R.

Applications of the Rayleigh model.   The following three situations are well modeled by the Rayleigh distribution.

1. In a dart game, we throw at the center of the target, so presumably the center (the origin of the coordinate system) is our average position in both horizontal (x) and vertical (y) directions. If our errors in the two planes are Gaussian, equal in variance, and independent, then our miss distance from the center (the bull's-eye) will be Rayleigh distributed. The same applies for miss distances for bombs, guns, and other "aimed" items.
2. The motion of star images owing to refraction in the atmosphere is due to random variations in the optical properties of the air. The distance of the star image from the true location of the star will be Rayleigh distributed.
3. Tracking errors from radars and other locating systems can be Rayleigh distributed.

The model.   Because X and Y are independent, their bivariate PDF is the product of the marginal PDFs. Thus

$$f_{XY}(x, y) = f_X(x) \times f_Y(y) = \frac{1}{\sigma\sqrt{2\pi}} e^{-\frac{1}{2}\left(\frac{x}{\sigma}\right)^2} \times \frac{1}{\sigma\sqrt{2\pi}} e^{-\frac{1}{2}\left(\frac{y}{\sigma}\right)^2} \qquad (3.5.1)$$

where we used the Gaussian PDFs [Eq. (3.4.17)] for X and Y with zero means and the same variance. We can collect terms in Eq. (3.5.1) to have

$$f_{XY}(x, y) = \frac{1}{2\pi\sigma^2} e^{-\frac{1}{2}\frac{x^2+y^2}{\sigma^2}} \tag{3.5.2}$$

The striking feature of Eq. (3.5.2) is the $x^2 + y^2$ term in the exponent. A circle of radius r is described by $x^2 + y^2 = r^2$, so this tells us that the distribution has circular symmetry about the origin. This pattern suggests a change of variables from rectangular to cylindrical.

The Rayleigh CDF.   Let the random variable $R = \sqrt{X^2 + Y^2}$ be the distance from the origin to the point X, Y, as shown in Fig. 3.5.1.

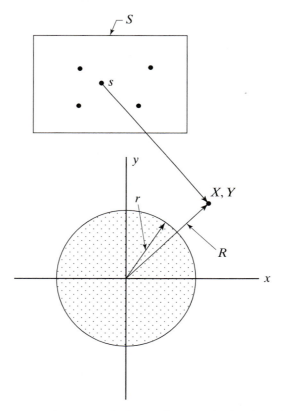

Figure 3.5.1   The chance experiment results in a value X, Y in the Cartesian plane a distance R from the origin. We will calculate the probability, $P[R \leq r]$, which is the probability that the point X, Y falls in a circle of radius r.

The CDF is defined as $F_R(r) = P[R \leq r] = P[X, Y \in$ circle of radius $r]$. We calculate this probability by integrating f_{XY} over the circle:

$$F_R(r) = \iint\limits_{\text{circle}} \frac{1}{2\pi\sigma^2} e^{-\frac{1}{2}\frac{x^2+y^2}{\sigma^2}} \, dx \, dy \tag{3.5.3}$$

This integral is best evaluated in cylindrical coordinates, since the integrand and limits have circular symmetry. If we let r' be the variable of integration, the differential area transforms as $dx \, dy \to r' \, dr' \, d\phi$, where ϕ is the angle measured counterclockwise from the x-axis. Thus the integral in Eq. (3.5.3) becomes

$$F_R(r) = \int_0^{2\pi} d\phi \int_0^r \frac{1}{2\pi\sigma^2} e^{-\frac{1}{2}\frac{r'^2}{\sigma^2}} r' \, dr' \tag{3.5.4}$$

We have separated the two integrals, since ϕ does not appear in the integrand due to the symmetry. The ϕ integration removes the 2π, and the r' integration is routinely performed to give

$$F_R(r) = 1 - e^{-\frac{1}{2}\left(\frac{r}{\sigma}\right)^2}, \quad r > 0, \text{ zow} \tag{3.5.5}$$

Equation (3.5.5) describes the Rayleigh CDF. We derived this CDF as a means to obtain the Rayleigh PDF, but the CDF is quite useful in solving problems. Figure 3.5.2 gives a plot for $\sigma = 10$.

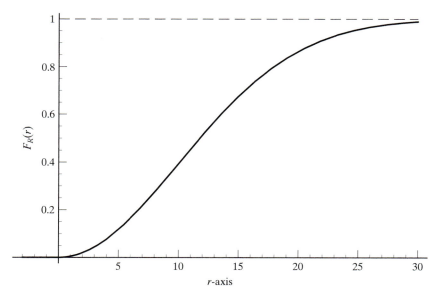

Figure 3.5.2   The Rayleigh CDF for $\sigma = 10$. Here σ is not the standard deviation of the Rayleigh distribution but the standard deviation of the underlying Gaussian distributions.

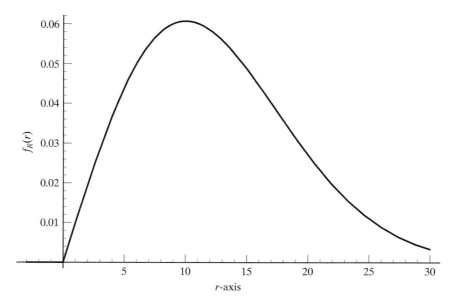

Figure 3.5.3 The Rayleigh PDF for $\sigma = 10$. The mean is 12.53, and the standard deviation is 6.55.

The Rayleigh PDF. We obtain the Rayleigh PDF by differentiating the Rayleigh CDF, Eq. (3.5.5).

$$f_R(r) = \frac{d}{dr} F_R(r) = \frac{r}{\sigma^2} e^{-\frac{1}{2}\left(\frac{r}{\sigma}\right)^2}, \quad r \geq 0, \quad \text{zow} \tag{3.5.6}$$

We plot this result in Fig. 3.5.3 for $\sigma = 10$.

The mean and variance of the Rayleigh distribution. We may work out the mean as

$$\mu_R = E[R] = \int_{-\infty}^{+\infty} r f_R(r)\, dr = \int_0^{\infty} r \frac{r}{\sigma^2} e^{-\frac{1}{2}\left(\frac{r}{\sigma}\right)^2}\, dr = \sqrt{\frac{\pi}{2}}\,\sigma \tag{3.5.7}$$

The variance of the Rayleigh is

$$\sigma_R^2 = E[R^2] - \mu_R^2 = \int_0^{\infty} r^2 \frac{r}{\sigma^2} e^{-\frac{1}{2}\left(\frac{r}{\sigma}\right)^2}\, dr - \frac{\pi}{2}\sigma^2 = (4 - \pi)\frac{\sigma^2}{2} \tag{3.5.8}$$

For the example plotted for $\sigma = 10$, the mean is 12.53 and the standard deviation is 6.551. The probability that R falls within one standard deviation of the mean is

```
CDF [RayleighDistribution [10], 12.53 + 6.551] -
 CDF [RayleighDistribution [10], 12.53 - 6.551]
0.674364
```

This is very close to our two-thirds rule of thumb [Eq. (3.1.19)], but we have no reason to expect such good success, since the Rayleigh PDF is somewhat nonsymmetric.

Example 3.5.1:   Throwing darts

A man throws darts at a circular target and hits the target 80% of the time. How often does he hit the target in the center bull's-eye, which contains one-fourth of the target area?

Solution   We assume that the hit positions of the dart are Rayleigh distributed. We are not given the radius of the target, so we will call it r_0. Hitting the target 80% of the time translates into a probability of

$$P[R \leq r_0] = F_R(r_0) = 1 - e^{-\frac{r_0^2}{2\sigma^2}} = 0.8 \Rightarrow \sigma = 0.557 r_0 \tag{3.5.9}$$

If the bull's-eye occupies one-fourth of the target area, then the radius of the bull's-eye must be half the radius of the target. The probability of hitting the bull's-eye is therefore

$$P\left[R \leq \frac{r_0}{2}\right] = F_R\left(\frac{r_0}{2}\right) = 1 - e^{-\frac{1}{2}\left(\frac{r_0/2}{0.557 r_0}\right)^2} = 0.331 \tag{3.5.10}$$

You do it.   What if the bull's-eye has a radius one-third of the target radius. What then will be the probability of hitting the bull's-eye, given that you hit the target? Calculate your answer to at least three decimal places, enter your answer in the cell box, and click Evaluate for a response.

```
myanswer = ;
```

```
Evaluate
```

For the answer, see endnote 41.

Summary.   We took two IID Gaussian random variables and derived the Rayleigh distribution. In the last section of this chapter we begin with independent Gaussian random variables and derive the general bivariate Gaussian distribution. Before we can understand this important distribution, we must understand about the correlation between random variables.

3.5.2 Correlation between Random Variables

Relating random variables. Section 3.2 introduced bivariate continuous random variables and discussed how the bivariate PDF describes how probability is distributed in the Cartesian plane. The bivariate PDF gives exhaustive information about the relationship between the two random variables.

Sometimes, however, less information is valuable even if the bivariate PDF is unknown. *Correlation* indicates the degree to which a *linear* relationship exists between two random variables. Before we define correlation, we give an example to illustrate the concept.

An example of correlation. Suppose we take data on students' height and weight. Generally we expect the weight to increase with height. If people were strictly scaled versions of one another, the weight would increase as the third power of the height, but since these properties vary over a limited range, the dependence can be approximated by a linear relationship. To illustrate, we consider the following "data." Here we have assumed heights $N(70, 6^2)$ inches and weights that on average are proportional to height cubed but have a Gaussian distribution with a standard deviation of 20; that is, $W \propto H^3 \pm 20(1\sigma)$. Figure 3.5.4 shows 100 points generated with this pattern.

How do we describe this trend? Figure 3.5.4 suggests a linear relationship. We can represent that relationship through certain expectations. We give three measures that characterize the linear relationship with increasing precision: the correlation, the covariance, and the correlation coefficient. In the following paragraphs we first define the concept, then we give two extremes, and finally we give the measure for the data in Fig. 3.5.4.

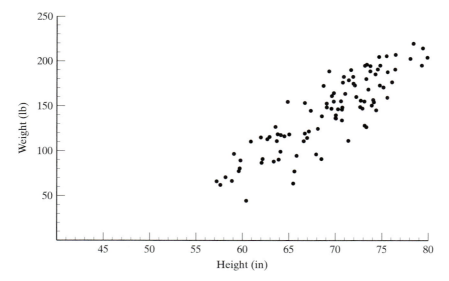

Figure 3.5.4 Height–weight data generated with weight proportional to the cube of the height, plus a random component.

The correlation.   We use X and Y to represent the two random variables of interest. These are not necessarily Gaussian random variables. The correlation between X and Y, R_{XY}, is defined as

$$R_{XY} = E[XY] = \iint\limits_{-\infty}^{+\infty} xy f_{XY}(x, y)\, dx\, dy \qquad (3.5.11)$$

We consider two extremes, X and Y independent, and $Y = aX$, where a is a constant.

- For X and Y independent, the algebra of expectation tells us that

$$R_{XY} = E[XY] = E[X] \times E[Y] = \mu_X \mu_Y \qquad (3.5.12)$$

  Thus in this case the correlation is the product of the means.
- For the second extreme, where X and Y are related through a known constant, the correlation is

$$R_{XY} = E[XY] = E[X \times aX] = aE[X^2] = a(\sigma_X^2 + \mu_X^2) = \pm \sigma_X \sigma_Y + \mu_X \mu_Y \quad (3.5.13)$$

  Because $Y = aX$, it follows that $\mu_Y = a\mu_X$, and $\sigma_Y = \pm\, \sigma_X$. The reason we use "$\pm$" is that the standard deviation of Y must be a positive number; hence if a is negative, $\sigma_Y = -a\sigma_X$. When we compare Eqs. (3.5.12) and (3.5.13), we see that the term $\pm\sigma_X\sigma_Y$ appears as an indication of the linear relationship between X and Y.

We may calculate an experimental correlation for the height–weight data by the following cell:

```
corr = Sum [height [[i]] * weight [[i]], {i, 1, 100}]/100
10392.9
```

And what does that result tell us? Not much. We have to go to the next definition to increase our precision.

The covariance.   The covariance of X and Y is defined as

$$Cov[XY] = E[(X - \mu_X)(Y - \mu_Y)] = E[XY] - \mu_X \mu_Y = R_{XY} - \mu_X \mu_Y \qquad (3.5.14)$$

The logic of this definition should be clear: we are removing the means of X and Y to focus more on the relationship between variations in these random variables. Again we look at the covariance in the two extremes.

- For X and Y independent, we have

$$Cov[XY] = E[XY] - \mu_X \mu_Y = E[X]E[Y] - \mu_X \mu_Y = 0 \qquad (3.5.15)$$

  Thus for independent random variables, the covariance is zero, indicating no linear relationship. Of course, independent random variables should not exhibit a relationship of any kind, including a linear relationship.

- For X and Y linked in a linear relationship, $Y = aX$, a a constant, the covariance becomes

$$Cov[XY] = E[XY] - \mu_X\mu_Y = E[X \times aX] - \mu_X\mu_Y = a(\sigma_X^2 + \mu_X^2) - \mu_X\mu_Y$$
$$= \pm\sigma_X\sigma_Y + \mu_X\mu_Y - \mu_X\mu_Y = \pm\sigma_X\sigma_Y \tag{3.5.16}$$

where, as before, we use "+" if a is positive and "−" if a is negative. Again, we find the $\sigma_X\sigma_Y$ term signaling that changes in the random variables are related.

For our height–weight data we calculate the covariance to be

```
Off[General::spell1]
covariance = Sum[(height[[i]] - Mean[height]) *
    (weight[[i]] - Mean[weight]), {i, 1, 100}]/100
223.462
```

Again we ask, What does this mean? The answer is that we don't know what it means until we compare it with the standard deviations of X and Y. This leads to the definition of the correlation coefficient, which is the most precise measure of linear relationship.

The correlation coefficient.   The correlation coefficient is defined as

$$\rho_{XY} = \frac{Cov[XY]}{\sigma_X\sigma_Y} = \frac{E[XY] - \mu_X\mu_Y}{\sigma_X\sigma_Y} \tag{3.5.17}$$

Again we consider the extremes:

- If X and Y are independent, the correlation coefficient is zero because the numerator of Eq. (3.5.17) is zero, and the denominator of Eq. (3.5.17) cannot be zero.
- If X and Y are dependent in a linear way, comparison of Eqs. (3.5.17) and (3.5.16) shows that the correlation coefficient becomes $\rho = \pm 1$.

For the height–weight data in Fig. 3.5.4, the correlation coefficient is

```
Off[General::spell1]
Correlation[height, weight]
0.886513
```

Interpreting the correlation coefficient.   The interpretation of $\rho = +1$ is that X and Y have perfect positive correlation, that is, that Y increases with X in a linear fashion with no scatter. The interpretation of $\rho = -1$ is that X and Y have a perfect negative correlation, that is, that Y decreases as X increases, but still in a linear fashion and with no scatter. You can get a feel for the effect of the correlation coefficient if you are running full Mathematica, by opening the next cell, entering different values for rho, and seeing the effect on the scatter

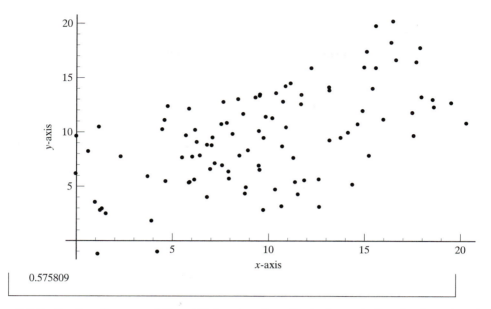

0.575809

Figure 3.5.5 Scatter diagram of X and Y showing the effect of correlation. By changing rho you can confirm that for positive correlation there is an upward trend, and for negative correlation there is a downward trend. For correlations near ± 1, the data lie close to a straight line. Zero correlation shows no pattern. For this plot, $\rho = 0.5$.

diagram. In Fig. 3.5.5 there are 100 random values for the bivariate Gaussian distribution with fixed values for the mean and standard deviations for X and Y. You can change any of the values of the five parameters defining the Gaussian random variables.[42] The last number printed is the actual correlation coefficient between the generated values, to compare with $\rho = 0.5$, which is a theoretical parameter in the distribution.

Example 3.5.2:   Correlation _____

Consider two independent Gaussian random variables, $X = N(2, 1)$ and $Y = N(3, 2)$, from which we create a third Gaussian random variable, $Z = \frac{1}{2}X + \frac{1}{3}Y$. The purpose of this combination is to create random variables that are correlated. We will work out the correlation properties between X and Z, specifically the correlation coefficient, ρ_{XZ}. The properties of X we know: $\mu_X = 2$ and $\sigma_X = \sqrt{1}$. The mean of Z is

$$\mu_Z = E\left[\tfrac{1}{2}X + \tfrac{1}{3}Y\right] = \tfrac{1}{2} \times 2 + \tfrac{1}{3} \times 3 = 2 \qquad (3.5.18)$$

and the variance of Z is

$$Var[Z] = Var\left[\tfrac{1}{2}X + \tfrac{1}{3}Y\right] = \left(\tfrac{1}{2}\right)^2 \times 1 + \left(\tfrac{1}{3}\right)^2 \times 2 = \tfrac{17}{36} \qquad (3.5.19)$$

where we used the independence of X and Y to add their variances. The correlation between X and Z is

$$E[XZ] = E\left[X\left(\tfrac{1}{2}X + \tfrac{1}{3}Y\right)\right] = \tfrac{1}{2}E[X^2] + \tfrac{1}{3}E[XY] = \tfrac{1}{2}(2^2 + 1) + \tfrac{1}{3} \times 2 \times 3 = \tfrac{9}{2} \quad (3.5.20)$$

The calculations in Eqs. (3.5.19) and (3.5.20) involve several identities from the algebra of expectation, specifically, Eqs. (2.3.39), (2.3.41), (2.3.46), and (2.3.51). The covariance of X and Z is

$$Cov[XZ] = E[XZ] - \mu_X \mu_Z = \tfrac{9}{2} - 2 \times 2 = \tfrac{1}{2} \quad (3.5.21)$$

Thus the correlation coefficient is

$$\rho_{XZ} = \frac{Cov[XZ]}{\sigma_X \sigma_Z} = \frac{\tfrac{1}{2}}{\sqrt{1} \times \sqrt{\tfrac{17}{36}}} = 0.7276 \quad (3.5.22)$$

You do it.   If $Z = X + Y$, with X and Y defined as in the previous example, find ρ_{YZ}.

```
myanswer = ;
```

```
Evaluate
```

For the answer, see endnote 43.

Why all three?   If the correlation coefficient is the only measure of relationship readily interpreted, why do we need the correlation defined in Eq. (3.5.11) and the covariance defined in Eq. (3.5.14)? The answer is that we need to know more than the degree of relationship between X and Y: we need to know about the scatter in their values, which are given by the covariance, and we need to know about their means also, as included in the correlation. When we deal in Chapter 6 with random processes, we will find correlation to be extremely useful.

Correlation and independence.   As stated earlier, independence is a stronger condition than lack of correlation. If two random variables are uncorrelated, it means that there is no *linear* relationship between them, but there can still be a nonlinear relationship. If two random variables are independent, this means that there is no relationship between them whatever, linear or otherwise.

Uncorrelated but not independent.   Figure 3.5.6 shows an example of random variables X and Y that have a nonlinear coupling. We generate the plot and then the numerical correlation coefficient between the values of X and Y. The theoretical correlation for this distribution is zero. The calculated correlation values vary a lot, both plus and minus, but generally average zero as we repeat the process.

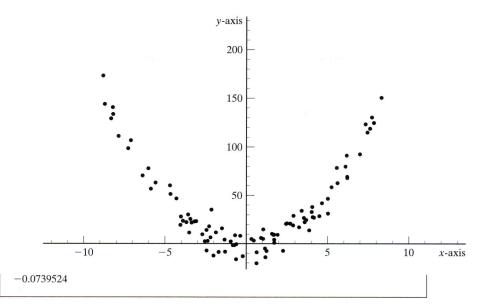

Figure 3.5.6   The *X* and *Y* values have a parabolic relationship, plus a random component, but are uncorrelated because there is no *linear* relationship.

Correlation and the Gaussian distribution.   The definitions for the various expressions of correlation apply to all random variables, but for convenience, we have used the Gaussian in examples. For the bivariate Gaussian distribution in the next section, the correlation coefficient appears explicitly in the PDF.

3.5.3 The Bivariate Gaussian Distribution

In this section we present the general form of the PDF of the bivariate Gaussian random variable, which we used to generate Fig. 3.5.5. We start with two independent, identically distributed, normalized Gaussian random variables $V = N(0, 1)$ and $W = N(0, 1)$. Because these are independent, we can write their joint PDF as

$$f_{VW}(v, w) = f_V(v) \times f_W(w) = \frac{1}{\sqrt{2\pi}}e^{-\frac{1}{2}v^2} \times \frac{1}{\sqrt{2\pi}}e^{-\frac{1}{2}w^2} = \frac{1}{2\pi}e^{-\frac{1}{2}\left(v^2+w^2\right)} \qquad (3.5.23)$$

From *V* and *W* we create two new random variables, *X* and *Y*, that are not independent but have a linear relationship. Let

$$X = V \text{ and } Y = aV + bW, \text{ where } a \text{ and } b \text{ are constants} \qquad (3.5.24)$$

We require that *X* and *Y* also be normalized. This is automatic for *X* and also for the mean of *Y*, but normalizing the variance of *Y* requires

$$\sigma_Y^2 = 1 = Var[aV + bW] = a^2 \, Var[V] + b^2 \, Var[W] \Rightarrow a^2 + b^2 = 1 \qquad (3.5.25)$$

since $Var[V] = Var[W] = 1$. We now express a and b in terms of the correlation coefficient, ρ. By definition,

$$\rho = \frac{Cov[XY]}{\sigma_X \sigma_Y} = E[XY] = E[V(aV + bW)] = a \tag{3.5.26}$$

The ready simplification of Eq. (3.5.26) into the form $\rho = a$ follows from the normalized nature of X, Y, V, and W. Using Eq. (3.5.25) we find that

$$b = \sqrt{1 - a^2} = \sqrt{1 - \rho^2} \tag{3.5.27}$$

In summary, our change of random variables is

$$X = V$$
$$Y = \rho V + \sqrt{1 - \rho^2}\, W \tag{3.5.28}$$

which may be inverted to give

$$V = X$$
$$W = -\frac{\rho}{\sqrt{1 - \rho^2}} X + \frac{1}{\sqrt{1 - \rho^2}} Y \tag{3.5.29}$$

Recall that X and Y are both normalized Gaussian random variables. This means that the *marginal* PDFs are normalized Gaussian random variables, but the bivariate PDF of X and Y will depend on the correlation coefficient. Our next step is to derive the bivariate PDF. Normally we would do this through the bivariate CDF, but in this case we will perform a formal transformation of variables. This is safe, since Eq. (3.5.23) is continuous everywhere, and the transformation is linear. Thus we substitute (3.5.29) into (3.5.18) and multiply by the Jacobian of the transformation, which is $\frac{1}{\sqrt{1-\rho^2}}$. We have after some simplification

$$f_{XY}(x, y) = \frac{1}{2\pi\sqrt{1 - \rho^2}} \exp\left[-\frac{x^2 - 2\rho xy + y^2}{2(1 - \rho^2)}\right] \tag{3.5.30}$$

This is the normalized bivariate Gaussian PDF.

A robust PDF. Here's the surprise. The PDF in Eq. (3.5.30) is robust with respect to the details of the linear transformation that we use to obtain the correlated random variables. For example, instead of the transformation in Eq. (3.5.28), we might have used a rotational transformation:

$$X = V \cos\phi + W \sin\phi$$
$$Y = -V \sin\phi + W \cos\phi \tag{3.5.31}$$

This transformation also produces normalized Gaussian random variables, and the correlation coefficient is $\rho = \cos 2\phi$. Nonetheless, had we carried through the details, we would have obtained

Eq. (3.5.30) for the bivariate PDF. Our assertion is that Eq. (3.5.30) is valid no matter how the bivariate Gaussian random variables are produced.

Another surprise.   Here's a second surprise. If we set $\rho = 0$ in Eq. (3.5.30), the bivariate PDF factors into the marginal PDFs in X and Y. This shows that *uncorrelated* Gaussian random variables are *independent*.

$$f_{XY}(x, y) \underset{\rho \to 0}{\to} \frac{1}{2\pi} \exp\left[-\frac{x^2 + y^2}{2}\right] = f_X(x) \times f_Y(y) \tag{3.5.32}$$

In general, independence entails lack of correlation, but lack of correlation does not entail independence. Independence is a stronger condition than correlation. For Gaussian random variables, however, lack of correlation entails independence. In other words, if there is no *linear* relationship between Gaussian random variables, then it follows that there is no relationship whatever.

The general bivariate Gaussian.   We will now generalize X and Y. With the risk of some notational confusion, we make the substitution

$$X \to \frac{X - \mu_X}{\sigma_X}$$
$$Y \to \frac{Y - \mu_Y}{\sigma_Y} \tag{3.5.33}$$

Again, we can make a formal transformation, since Eq. (3.5.30) is continuous everywhere. This transformation involves substituting the new variables into Eq. (3.5.30) and multiplying by the Jacobian, which is $\frac{1}{\sigma_X \sigma_Y}$. The result is

$$f_{XY}(x, y) = \frac{1}{2\pi \sigma_X \sigma_Y \sqrt{1 - \rho^2}} \exp\left[-\frac{1}{2(1 - \rho^2)}\left[\left(\frac{x - \mu_X}{\sigma_X}\right)^2\right.\right.$$
$$\left.\left. - 2\rho \left(\frac{x - \mu_X}{\sigma_X}\right)\left(\frac{y - \mu_Y}{\sigma_Y}\right) + \left(\frac{y - \mu_Y}{\sigma_Y}\right)^2\right]\right] \tag{3.5.34}$$

Before summarizing the properties of the general bivariate Gaussian PDF given in Eq. (3.5.34) we will plot it in three dimensions in Fig. 3.5.7 to see what it looks like. You also can see a plot of a bivariate Gaussian in the form of a scatter diagram in Fig. 3.5.5.

The properties of the bivariate Gaussian PDF.   The general bivariate Gaussian PDF is given in Eq. (3.5.34). It has the following properties

1. The marginal PDFs are Gaussian:

$$X = N(\mu_X, \sigma_X^2) \text{ and } Y = N(\mu_Y, \sigma_Y^2) \tag{3.5.35}$$

2. The correlation coefficient is

$$\rho = \frac{E[XY] - \mu_X \mu_Y}{\sigma_X \sigma_Y} \tag{3.5.36}$$

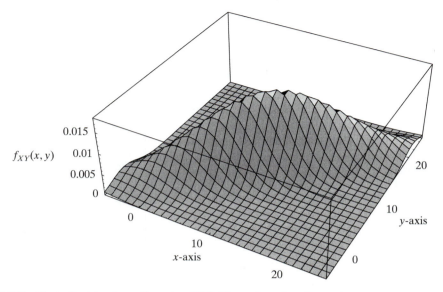

Figure 3.5.7   Plot of a bivariate Gaussian PDF. The values for the various parameters $\rho = +0.9$, $\mu_X = 10$, $\sigma_X = 5$, $\mu_Y = 10$, and $\sigma_Y = 4$. You are invited to change the correlation coefficient, rho, and observe the effects.

3. The conditional PDF, $f_{Y|X}(x, y)$, depends on the conditional mean and variance of Y, given X. These are

$$\mu_{Y|X}(x) = \mu_Y + \rho \frac{\sigma_Y}{\sigma_X}(x - \mu_X) \text{ and } \sigma_{Y|X}^2 = \sigma_Y^2(1 - \rho^2) \tag{3.5.37}$$

In these terms the conditional PDF is

$$f_{Y|X}(x, y) = \frac{1}{\sigma_{Y|X}\sqrt{2\pi}} \exp\left[-\frac{1}{2}\left(\frac{y - \mu_{Y|X}}{\sigma_{Y|X}}\right)^2\right] \tag{3.5.38}$$

You might observe that this conditional PDF was used in generating the scatter diagram in Fig. 3.5.5. Proving the relationships in Eqs. (3.5.35)–(3.5.38) is something of a chore and will be omitted here. The key, in case you want to derive these properties, is completing the square in the exponent.

The final surprise.   The final surprise is that, having invested much effort in deriving and investigating the bivariate Gaussian PDF, we will make little use of it here or later in this book. Our situation is that of a mountain climber who, having climbed the mountain, looks around and then descends. The bivariate, and the multivariate, Gaussian PDFs are important in advanced work in many areas, but our interest is in modeling of random systems at a basic level. Besides, this PDF becomes analytically difficult, and there are few problems that serve our present purposes apart from mathematical exercises.

3.6 PROBLEMS

3.6.1 Continuous Random Variables

Exercises on continuous random variables

P3.1.1   A random variable, X, has a PDF of the form shown in the figure.

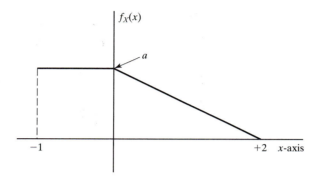

a. Find a.
b. Find the mean of X.
c. Find the variance of X.

A3.1.1 (a) $\frac{1}{2}$; **(b)** $\frac{1}{12}$; **(c)** 0.4931

P3.1.2   A random variable is described by the CDF shown in the figure.

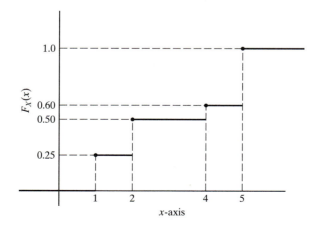

a. Is this a continuous or a discrete random variable?
b. Find the mean, μ_X, and the standard deviation, σ_X.
c. Calculate the probability $P[\mu_X - \sigma_X < X \le \mu_X + \sigma_X]$.

A3.1.2 (a) discrete; **(b)** $\mu_X = 3.13$, $\sigma_X = 1.71$; **(c)** 0.35

P3.1.3   The PDF of a random variable has the form shown in the figure.

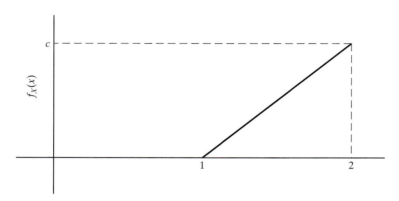

a. Find c.
b. Find the probability that X is greater than 1.2.
c. Find the mean of X.
d. Find the variance of X.

A3.1.3 (a) 2; **(b)** 0.96; **(c)** $\frac{5}{3}$; **(d)** 0.0556

P3.1.4   A random variable has a bimodal distribution, as shown.

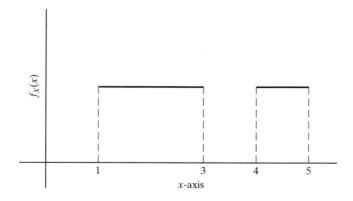

a. Find the mean of this random variable.
b. Calculate $P[\mu_X - \sigma_X < X < \mu_X + \sigma_X]$.

A3.1.4 (a) 2.833; **(b)** 0.5201

P3.1.5   The shape of the PDF of a random variable is shown in the figure. Find the probability that a given performance of the basic experiment produces a value within one standard deviation of the mean.

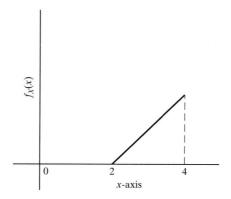

A3.1.5 0.6287

P3.1.6   A random experiment yields a number, Y, between 8 and 10, all values in the continuous range being equally likely. A random variable, $X(Y) = Y(Y - 8)$, is defined on
the outcome.
a. Find the range of X.
b. Find the expectation of X.
c. Find the CDF of X, $F_X(x)$.

A3.1.6 (a) $0 < X < 20$; **(b)** 9.33; **(c)** $F_X(x) = 0,\ x < 0;\ = 0.5\left[4 + \sqrt{16 + x} - 8\right]$,
$0 < x \le 20;\ = 1,\ x > 20$

P3.1.7   Develop a transformation to take a random number, Y, uniformly distributed between
0 and 1, and produce a random number with an exponential distribution, $f_X(x) =
12e^{-12x}$, $x > 0$, zow.

A3.1.7 $x(y) = -\frac{1}{2}\ln(1 - y)$ or $-\frac{1}{2}\ln(y)$ or $y(x) = 1 - e^{-12x}$

P3.1.8   Develop a transformation to take a random number, Y, uniformly distributed between
0 and 1, and produce a random number with a Rayleigh distribution, $f_X(x) =
0.01xe^{-0.005x^2}$, $x > 0$, zow.

A3.1.8 $y(x) = 1 - \exp\left[-\frac{1}{2}\left(\frac{x}{10}\right)^2\right]$ or $x(y) = 10\sqrt{-2\ln(1 - y)}$ or $10\sqrt{-2\ln(y)}$

P3.1.9   The CDF of a random variable is given as

$$F_X(x) = 0,\ x \le -10$$
$$= 0.01(x + 10)^2,\ -10 < x \le 0$$
$$= 1,\ x > 0$$

a. Plot $f_X(x)$, the PDF.
b. Find $P[-5 < X \le 5]$.
c. Find the expected value of X.

A3.1.9 (a) see the figure; **(b)** 0.75; **(c)** −3.33

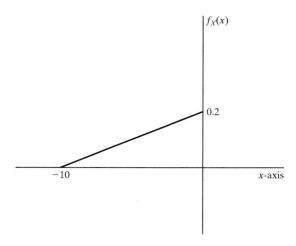

P3.1.10   A modified Laplace random variable is given by the formula

$$f_X(x) = ae^{+2x}, \ x < 0$$

$$= ae^{-x}, \ x \geq 0$$

and shown in the plot.

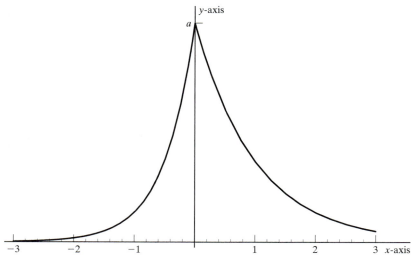

a. Find a.
b. Find the mean of the random variable.
c. Find the standard deviation of the random variable.

A3.1.10 (a) $\frac{2}{3}$; **(b)** $\frac{1}{2}$; **(c)** 1.118

P3.1.11   A time, X, is chosen at random out of some period of time, with all values equally likely. Find the probability that the random variable falls within one standard deviation of its mean.

A3.1.11 0.577

P3.1.12   A random variable is distributed with a triangular PDF, as shown in the figure.
a. Find the height of the triangle for proper normalization.
b. Find the expected value of X. (*Hint:* Use the symmetry of the function.)
c. Find the variance of X.
d. Find the probability that on any given performance of the experiment the random variable will fall within one standard deviation of the mean.

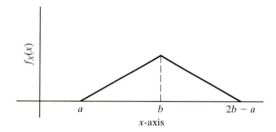

A3.1.12 (a) $1/(b-a)$; **(b)** b; **(c)** $(b-a)^2/6$; **(d)** 0.650

P3.1.13   A random variable is $0 < X \le 3$ and is distributed as shown in the figure.
a. Find $f_X(x)$.
b. Find $E[X]$.
c. Find $E[X^2]$.
d. Find $Var[X]$.

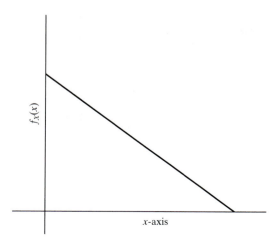

A3.1.13 **(a)** $f_X(x) = \frac{2}{3} - \frac{2}{9}x, \ 0 < x \le 3$, zow; **(b)** 1; **(c)** 1.5; **(d)** 0.5

P3.1.14   Two random variables, X and Y, are related as $Y(X)$. The PDF of X is triangular between 0 and 2, and the PDF of Y is uniform between 1 and 1.5, as shown in the figure. Find $Y(X)$. Of the two possible continuous solutions choose the one in which Y increases as X increases.

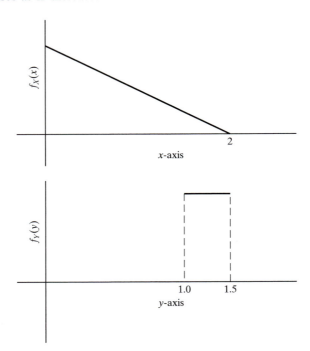

A3.1.14 $y(x) = \frac{x}{2} - \frac{x^2}{8} + 1$

P3.1.15   A PDF is of the form $f_X(x) = a(1 - x^2), 0 < x < 1$, zow, where a is a constant.
a. Find a.
b. Find $Var[X]$.
c. Find the probability that on any given performance of the experiment X will be greater than the mean.

A3.1.15 **(a)** 1.5; **(b)** 0.0594; **(c)** 0.464

P3.1.16   The CDF of a discrete random variable is shown in the figure.
a. Find $P[X > 0]$.
b. Find $P[X = 1]$.
c. Find $P[(-10 < X \le -2) \cup (X > 3)]$.

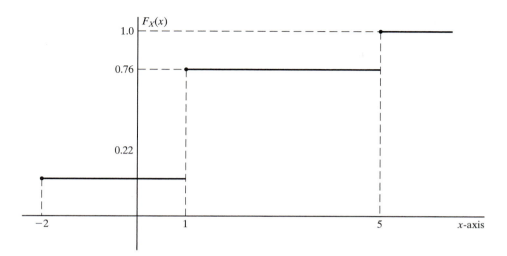

A3.1.16 **(a)** 0.78; **(b)** 0.54; **(c)** 0.460

P3.1.17   A random variable is described by an exponential distribution, $f_X(x) = ae^{-0.01x}$, $x \geq 0$, zow.
a. Find a.
b. Let $Y = 2X + 12$. Find $E[Y]$.
c. Find $P[Y < 50]$.
d. Find $f_Y(y)$.

A3.1.17 **(a)** 0.01; **(b)** 212; **(c)** 0.173; **(d)** $f_Y(y) = \frac{1}{200}e^{(y-12)/200}$, $y \geq 12$, zow.

P3.1.18   A PDF is shown in the figure.

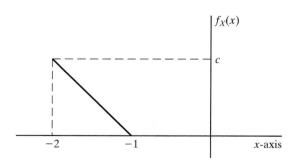

a. Find c.
b. Find the CDF for this random variable.

c. Find the mean of the random variable.

d. Find the variance of the random variable.

A3.1.18 (a) 2; **(b)** $F_X(x) = 0$, $x < -2$, $= 1 - (x+1)^2$, $-2 < x < -1$, zow; **(c)** -1.667; **(d)** 0.0556

P3.1.19   A mixed random variable has $P[X = 0] = 0.4$ and $P[1 < X \leq 3] = 0.6$, where all values of X between 1 and 3 are equally likely.

a. Give the PDF of X as a mathematical function, using impulse and unit step functions.

b. Plot the CDF of X.

c. Find the mean of X.

d. Find the variance of X.

A3.1.19 (a) $f_X(x) = 0.4\delta(x) + 0.3(u(x-1) - u(x-3))$; **(b)** The CDF is given in the figure; **(c)** 1.2; **(d)** 1.16

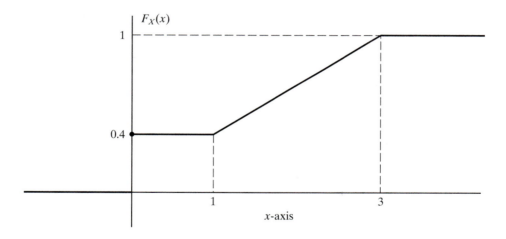

P3.1.20   The Laplace random variable has a PDF that is a double exponential, $f_T(t) = ae^{-|t|/2}$, for all values of t and a, a constant to be determined.

a. Find a.

b. Find the expected value of T, given that $T \geq -1$.

c. Let $W = T^2$. Find the PDF of W.

A3.1.20 (a) $\frac{1}{4}$; **(b)** 1.31; **(c)** $f_W(w) = \frac{\exp[-\sqrt{w}/2]}{4\sqrt{w}}$, $w \geq 0$, zow

P3.1.21   The bimodal PDF has two sections, $A = \{a < X \leq b\}$ and $B = \{c < X \leq d\}$, as shown. Note that $a < b < c < d$ and all values are equally likely within the two ranges.

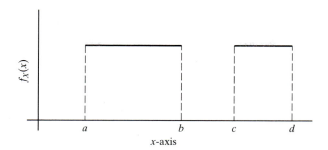

a. What is $f_X(x)$?

b. Find $P[A]$.

c. Find $E[X|A]$.

d. What, if any, are the values of a, b, c, and d that make A and B independent?

A3.1.21 **(a)** $\frac{1}{(b-a)+(d-c)}$, $A \cup B$, zow; **(b)** $\frac{b-a}{(b-a)+(d-c)}$; **(c)** $\frac{a+b}{2}$; **(d)** since $A \cap B = \emptyset$, they cannot be independent

P3.1.22   A random variable has a CDF given as

$$F_X(x) = e^{+20x}, \ x < 0,$$

$$= 1, \ x \geq 0$$

a. Find $E[X]$.

b. Find $Var[X]$.

c. If $Y = \tan^{-1} X$ (Y in radians), find $P[Y < -0.1]$.

A3.1.22 **(a)** $-\frac{1}{20}$; **(b)** $\frac{1}{400}$; **(c)** 0.134

P3.1.23   A random variable, X, is uniformly distributed between 0 and 10. Let A be the event that X lies more that one standard deviation from the mean.

a. Find the probability $P[A]$.

b. Find $F_{X|A}[x]$, the CDF conditional on A.

A3.1.23 **(a)** 0.4226; **(b)** see the figure

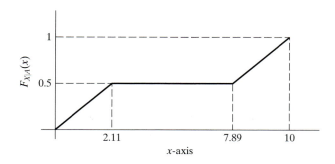

P3.1.24   A random variable has a PDF of the form $f_X(x) = \alpha(x + 1)$ for $-1 < x \le 0$ and $f_X(x) = \alpha\left(1 - \frac{x}{2}\right)$ for $0 < x \le 2$, zow.
a. Find α.
b. Find $E[X]$.
c. Find $Var[X]$.
d. Let $Y = |X|$. Find $f_Y(y)$.

A3.1.24 **(a)** 2/3; **(b)** 0.333; **(c)** 0.389; **(d)** $f_Y(y) = \frac{2(2-1.5y)}{3}$, $0 < y \le 1$;
$= \frac{2(1-0.5y)}{3}$, $1 < y \le 2$, zow

P3.1.25   The exponential PDF is often successful in modeling the time between random events, such as the times between automobile accidents at a prescribed intersection. Let $f_T(t) = 0.05e^{-0.05t}$, $t \ge 0$, zow, describe the PDF of the random variable, $T = $ time between accidents.
a. Find the expected value of T.
b. Find $P[T < t | T < 10]$ for all values of t.
c. Find the expected value of T, given that T is less that 10.
d. Consider the random variable, X, where $X = 0$, $T < 0$; $= T$, $0 < T \le 10$; $= 10$, $T > 10$. Find the expected value of X.

A3.1.25 **(a)** 20; **(b)** $P[T < t | T < 10] = 0$, $t < 0$, $= \frac{1-e^{-0.05t}}{1-e^{-0.5}}$, $0 < t \le 10$, $= 1$, $t > 10$; **(c)** 4.585; **(d)** 7.869

P3.1.26   A random variable X has the PDF shown in the figure. The PDF is $f_X(x) = Ae^{-x/2}$, $x \ge 0$, zow.
a. Find A.
b. Find the probability that X is less than 1.
c. Another random variable Y is defined in terms of X in the manner given in the figure. Note that $Y(X)$ is zero for $X > 2$. Find $E[Y]$.
d. Find the PDF of Y, $f_Y(y)$.

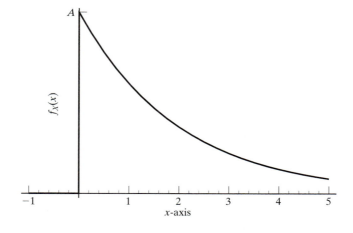

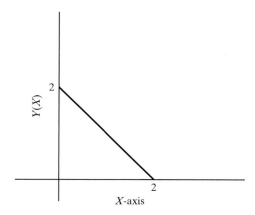

A3.1.26 **(a)** 0.5; **(b)** 0.3935; **(c)** 0.736; **(d)** $f_Y(y) = e^{-1}\delta(y) + (e^{-1}/2)e^{+y/2}$,
     $0 \le y \le 2$, zow.

P3.1.27   A random variable, X, is uniformly distributed over $1 < X \le 3$. A second random
     variable, Y, is defined as $Y = e^X$.
     a. Find the mean of Y.
     b. Find the standard deviation of Y.
     c. Find the PDF of Y.
     d. Find the probability that Y falls within $\pm$ one standard deviation of its mean.

A3.1.27 **(a)** 8.684; **(b)** 4.86; **(c)** $f_Y(y) = \frac{1}{2y}$, $e^1 < y < e^3$, zow; **(d)** 0.6321

P3.1.28   A random variable has a constant PDF that is bimodal, as shown in the figure, where
     $a > 1$.

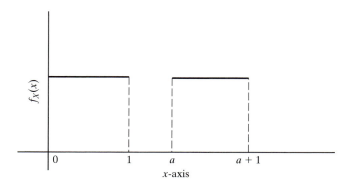

     a. Find the mean as a function of a.
     b. Find a to give a variance of 0.4.

A3.1.28 **(a)** $\frac{a}{2} + \frac{1}{2}$; **(b)** 1.125

P3.1.29   A random variable, X, has an exponential PDF, $f_X(x) = ae^{-ax}$, $x \geq 0$, zow.

a. Find a such that the mean square value of X is 4.

b. A new random variable, $Y(X)$, is related to X as shown in the figure. Find and plot the CDF of Y.

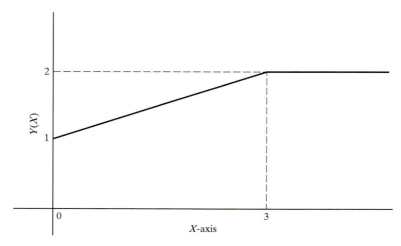

c. Find the PDF of Y.

d. Find the mean value of Y.

A3.1.29 **(a)** 0.707; **(b)** $F_Y(y) = 0$, $y \leq 1$, $= 1 - e^{-\frac{3}{\sqrt{2}}(y-1)}$, $1 < y < 2$, $= 1$, $y \geq 2$, the plot follows; **(c)** $f_Y(y) = 0.120\delta(y - 2) + \frac{3}{\sqrt{2}}e^{-\frac{3}{\sqrt{2}}(y-1)}$, $1 \leq y \leq 2$, zow; **(d)** 1.41

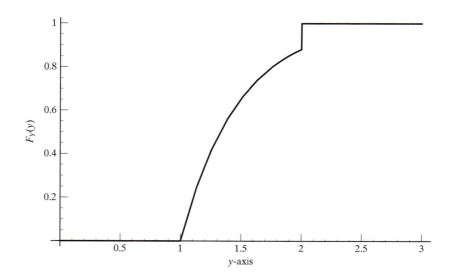

P3.1.30   A random variable, X, has a continuous part, uniformly distributed between 0 and 2, and a discrete part, which is unknown in value, x_1, and probability, p. The mean of the random variable is 1.25, and its variance is 0.5.

a. Find the value and probability of the discrete part of the random variable.
b. Find the expectation $E[e^X]$.

A3.1.30 (a) $x_1 = 2.195$, $p = 0.2091$; **(b)** 4.40

P3.1.31   Let X be uniformly distributed between -3 and $+3$. Let Y be related to X by the piecewise linear transformation shown in the graph.

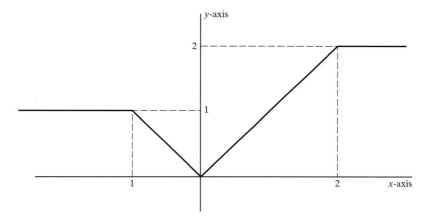

a. Find and plot the CDF of Y.
b. Find the PDF of Y.
c. Find the mean of Y.

A3.1.31 (a) $F_Y(y) = 0$, $y < 0$, $= \frac{y}{3}$, $0 < y < 1$, $= \frac{2}{3}$, $y = 1$, $= \frac{y+3}{6}$, $1 < y < 2$, $= 1$, $y \geq 2$, the plot follows; **(b)** $f_Y(y) = \frac{2}{6}\delta(y-1) + \frac{1}{6}\delta(y-2) + \frac{1}{3}(u(y) - u(y-1)) + \frac{1}{6}(u(y-1) - u(y-2))$; **(c)** 1.083

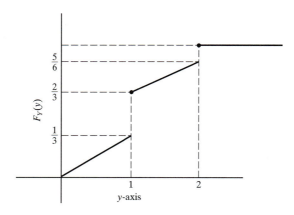

P3.1.32   A PDF is shown in the figure.

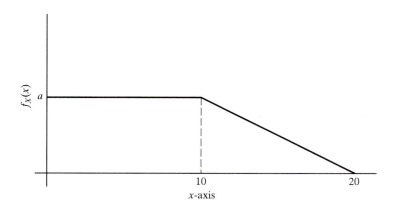

a. Find a.
b. Find the CDF, $F_X(x)$. Be sure to define for all values of x.
c. Find x such that $F_X(x) = 1.6 F_X(x/2)$, $x > 0$.

A3.1.32 (a) $\frac{1}{15}$; **(b)** $F_X(x) = 0$, $x < 0$; $= \frac{x}{15}$, $0 < x \le 10$; $= -\frac{1}{3} + \frac{x}{7.5} - \frac{x^2}{300}$, $10 < x \le 20$; $= 1$, $x > 20$; **(c)** 18.63

P3.1.33   A mixed random variable (part discrete and part continuous) is $X = 1$ with probability y, and X is uniformly distributed between 1 and 2 with probability $1 - y$.
a. Find $\mu_X(y)$, the mean of X as a function of y.
b. Find y such that the variance of X is at a maximum.

A3.1.33 (a) $1.5 - 0.5y$; **(b)** $\frac{1}{3}$

P3.1.34   Let X be a random variable uniformly distributed between 0 and 4. Let A be the event $\{0 < X \le x_0\}$ and B the event $\{x_0/2 < X \le x_0/2 + 1\}$, with the restriction that $x_0 \le 4$.
a. Find $P[A]$.
b. Find $P[B]$.
c. Can A and B be independent for any $x_0 \le 4$? Explain your answer.

A3.1.34 (a) $\frac{x_0}{4}$; **(b)** 0.25; **(c)** not independent except for $x_0 = 4$, when A is the certain event.

P3.1.35   The gain of a satellite front-end receiver is $G_{dB} = 10 \pm 1$ dB, with all values within that range equally probable. The relationship between gain in decibels and the power gain is $G_{dB} = 10\log G_P$ or $G_P = 10^{(G_{dB}/10)}$, where G_P is the power gain.
a. Find the cumulative distribution function of the power gain, $F_{G_P}(g_P)$.
b. Find the PDF of the power gain, $f_{G_P}(g_P)$.
c. Write an expression for the expected value of the power gain, $E[G_P]$, and determine a numerical value.

A3.1.35 **(a)** $F_{G_P}(g_P) = 0$, $g_P < 10^{0.9}$, $= 0.5(10\log_{10}(g_P) - 9)$, $10^{0.9} < g_P \leq 10^{1.1}$, $= 1$, $g_P > 10^{1.1}$; **(b)** $f_{G_P}(g_P) = \frac{2.17}{g_P}10^{0.9} < g_P \leq 10^{1.1}$, zow; **(c)** 10.09

P3.1.36 In the following, parts a and b are based on one chance experiment and parts c and d on another.

    a. Assume that a point is chosen at random within a circle of radius 1, centered at the origin. Let R = the distance from the origin to the point. Find the PDF of R.

    b. Let X = the projection of the point on the x-axis. Find the PDF of X.

    c. Assume that a point is chosen at random in a square centered on the origin. The square is 2 on a side. Let X be the projection of the point on the x axis. Find the PDF of X.

    d. For the square, let R = the distance from the origin to the point. Find the PDF of R.

A3.1.36 **(a)** $f_R(r) = 2r$, $0 < r \leq 1$, zow; **(b)** $f_X(x) = \frac{2}{\pi}\sqrt{1 - x^2}$, $-1 < x \leq +1$, zow; **(c)** $f_X(x) = 0.5$, $-1 < x \leq +1$, zow; **(d)** $f_R(r) = \frac{\pi}{2}r, 0 < r < 1$, $f_R(r) = r(\frac{\pi}{2} - 2\cos^{-1}(1/r))$, $1 < r \leq \sqrt{2}$, zow

Modeling Problems on Continuous Random Variables

P3.1.37 A sinusoidal voltage of peak value V_p volts is connected by a switch to an ideal half-wave raw rectifier (no filter or capacitor, just rectification). If the switch is closed at a random time, what is the expected value of the output voltage of the rectifier at the instant of switch closure, ignoring any delays in the circuit?

A3.1.37 V_p/π

P3.1.38 A student lives a 10-minute walk from campus. The bus comes by every 12 minutes and takes 1 minute to get to campus from his stop. Let T = the time to campus on the bus, a random variable.

    a. What is the PDF of T?

    b. What is the probability that walking is faster than riding the bus?

    c. What is the student's expected time saving if he rides the bus?

A3.1.38 **(a)** $f_T(t) = \frac{1}{12}$, $1 < t \leq 13$, zow; **(b)** 0.25; **(c)** 3 minutes

P3.1.39 A student needs to get permission from a professor to register for a course. He goes at random times to the professor's office to gain the required permission. During weekday work hours, 8 A.M.–5 P.M., the professor spends 1.5 hours on personal matters such as eating and socializing, is in class 2 hours, is in her office 1 hour, and does research, class preparation, and administrative work the remainder of the time.

    a. What is the probability that the student will be able get the permission on or before the third visit?

    b. What is the average number of times the student can expect to go to find the professor in her office?

A3.1.39 **(a)** 0.298; **(b)** 9

P3.1.40 A man drives to work along a route with one traffic light. He drives on a major road, so the light is green for him three times as long as it is red: specifically, it is green for

45 seconds and red for 15 seconds (ignore yellow). Assume he approaches the light at a random time.

a. Find the probability of his having to stop at the light.

b. Find his expected delay time due to the light.

A3.1.40 (a) 0.25; **(b)** 1.875 s

P3.1.41   A woman drives to work along a route with three traffic lights. All lights are green for 30 s and red for 30 s (ignore yellow). Assume she hits all lights at random, independent times.

a. Find the probability of her having to stop at two or more lights.

b. Find her expected delay time due to the lights.

A3.1.41 (a) 0.5; **(b)** 22.5 s

P3.1.42   A driver drives north from Austin on I-35, turns right somewhere in the first 100 mi, and drives until she reaches her destination. If the total distance traveled is 120 mi, what is the expected distance from Austin to the destination if both roads are modeled as perfectly straight and as intersecting at a 90° angle?

A3.1.42 94.7 miles

P3.1.43   A laboratory purchasing agent must buy a set of weights to measure mass in the range $0 \leq M \leq 10$ g. The balance has a graduated scale to measure the fractions of a gram. Thus the scale weighs 0–1 g without any weights, 1–2 g with a 1-g weight, and so on. Consider the following sets: 1, 2, 2, 5 and 1, 2, 3, 4 g. Which set on average will require fewer weights on a measurement, and what is the average number of weights used? Consider all values of M equally likely.

A3.1.43 Set #2 is better with an average of 1.6 weights

P3.1.44   A parking garage is simply a long parking lot. Open spaces are more likely as one drives farther from the entrance. Consider a parking garage that is 130 yd long. In the figure is shown the conditional PDF of the distance from the entrance to find a space, given the event $A = \{$a space is found$\}$, where $P[A] = 0.8$.

a. Find the probability that a parking place is found in the region from the entrance to 60 yd. This is probability unconditioned by event A.

b. Given that a parking place is found, find the average distance into the garage where the place is located.

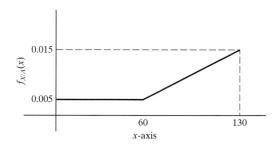

A3.1.44 (a) 0.24; **(b)** 79.6 yd

P3.1.45 A bird lands on a power line. The maximum height of the line is 100 ft above the ground, and the minimum height is 90 ft. Find the PDF of the bird's height above the ground. You may model the height of the line as a parabola or as an arc of a circle. The parabola is easier.

A3.1.45 (a) $f_H(h) = 0.05\sqrt{\dfrac{10}{h-90}}$, $90 < h \le 100$, zow

P3.1.46 A small ball coming to rest in a circular pit will be located from the center with a probability proportional to the distance from the center, because there is more area at the larger radii. This means that the PDF of the radius to the ball, R, is of the form $f_R(r) = \alpha\left(\dfrac{r}{r_0}\right)$, where r_0 is the radius of the pit, as shown in the figure, and α is a constant.

a. Find α.
b. Find the CDF, $F_R(r)$.
c. Find the expected value of R.
d. Find the expected value of the shortest chord, C, passing through the ball's center, as shown.

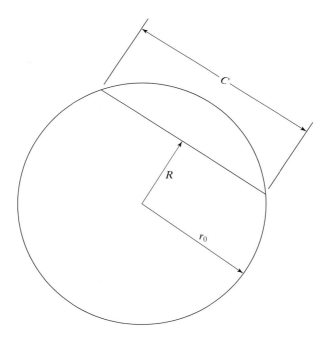

A3.1.46 (a) $\dfrac{2}{r_0}$; **(b)** $F_R(r) = 0$, $r \le 0$, $= \left(\dfrac{r}{r_0}\right)^2$, $0 < r \le r_0$, $= 1$, $r > r_0$; **(c)** $\dfrac{2}{3}r_0$; **(d)** $\dfrac{4}{3}r_0$.

P3.1.47   A line is drawn at random on a piece of paper. Also a circle of radius r_0 is drawn on the paper. Find $E[\Theta|\text{intersects}]$, where Θ is the magnitude of the angle created as shown. The event "intersects" is the event that the line intersects the circle. *Hint:* There are many ways to model this problem. We assume that the random variable R, the shortest distance between the line and center of the circle, is uniformly distributed between 0 and r_o, and define $0 < \Theta \leq \pi$. The geometry is given in the figure.

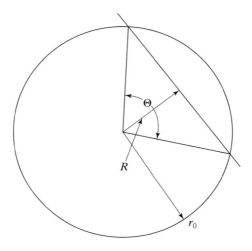

A3.1.47 2 rad

P3.1.48   The traffic light at 30th and Guadalupe is green for Guadalupe for 60 seconds, gives a left turn for southbound traffic on Guadalupe for 30th east for 10 seconds, allows a green for eastbound traffic on 30th for 25 seconds, and allows a green for westbound traffic on 30th for 25 seconds, as shown in the figure. When I leave my home on 31st Street to come to campus, I have a choice of two routes: I can drive to Guadalupe, drive south, and turn left onto 30th east; or I can go to 30th and drive east, crossing Guadalupe at the light. Assume I hit the light at a random time during its cycle, which is shown in the figure.

a. If I take the Guadalupe route, what is my expected wait time (W) at the light? Let T = the time I arrive at the light.

b. If I take the 30th east route, what is my expected wait time (W), again assuming T = time I arrive at the light?

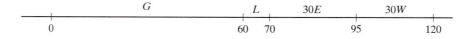

A3.1.48 (a) 50.4 s; **(b)** 37.6 s

P3.1.49 A battery-operated analog clock is hung on a wall, with its axis of rotation 6 ft from the floor, as shown in the figure. A fresh battery is put in the clock, and it runs for many months before the battery runs down. A random variable is defined as follows: if the clock stops between 4 o'clock and 8 o'clock, $X =$ the magnitude, always positive, of the distance from the point beneath the clock axis to the point on the floor at which the hour hand was pointed, as shown; between 8 o'clock and 4 o'clock, $X = 0$.
a. Find the PDF for X.
b. Find the expected value of X.

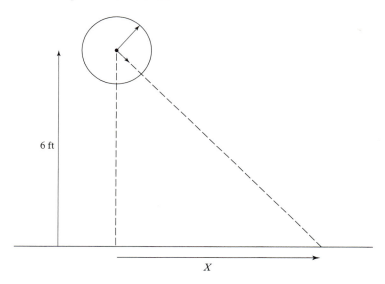

A3.1.49 (a) $\frac{2}{3}\delta(x) + \frac{6}{\pi}\frac{1}{x^2+36}$ for $0 < x < 6\tan 60°$, zow; **(b)** 1.324 ft

P3.1.50 A company brings a new product to market. According to its marketing models, the probability of making a profit is 80%, and the probability of losing money is 20%. The projected profit is anywhere between 0 and $1M, whereas the projected loss is anywhere between 0 and $100K. (Assume all values equally likely in these ranges.)
a. Find the probability that profits exceeds $600K.
b. Find the expected profit. Count loss as negative profit.
c. Find the standard deviation of the profit.

A3.1.50 (a) 0.320; **(b)** $390K; **(c)** $339K

P3.1.51 The movement of a certain antelope is approximated by the CDF shown. The equation of the curve between 0 and 10 is the parabola

$$F_X(x) = 0, \ x < 0$$
$$= 0.5 + (0.1 - 0.005x)x, \ 0 < x \leq 10$$
$$= 1, \ x \geq 10, \ \text{zow}$$

where X is the speed of the antelope in meters/second.

a. Find the PDF of the antelope speed.

b. Let the kinetic energy be $K = 80X^2$. Find the expected value of K.

c. Find the CDF and PDF of K.

d. Find the conditional PDF $f_{X|K>2000}(x)$.

A3.1.51 **(a)** $0.5\delta(x) + 0.1 - 0.01x$, $0 < x \le 10$, zow; **(b)** 667; **(c)** $F_K(k) = 0$, $k < 0$, $= 0.5$, $k = 0$, $= 0.5 + 0.1\sqrt{\frac{k}{80}} - 6.25 \times 10^{-5}k$, $0 < k \le 8000$, $= 1$, $k > 8000$, $f_K(k) = 0.5\delta(k) + \frac{5.59 \times 10^{-3}}{\sqrt{k}} - 6.25 \times 10^{-5}$, $0 < k \le 8000$, zow; **(d)** $\frac{0.1 - 0.01x}{0.125}$, $5 < x \le 10$, zow

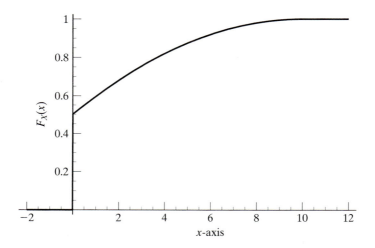

P3.1.52   Two cowboys were drinking in a saloon. The first bragged that he could shoot a hole in a ball that was thrown in the air, and the second bet him some money that he couldn't hit it once in 100 tries. They adjourned to the street, found a 3-in. diameter ball, and the contest began. The shooter missed again and again, until he hit the ball on the 89th try and thus won the bet. Afterward, the ball was examined, and the length of the hole through the ball was measured. From a probability point of view, what is the expected length of the hole? *Hint:* The fact that he took so many shots shows that he was lucky to hit the ball and that, therefore, all points on the ball cross section are equally likely.

A3.1.52 2.0 in.

P3.1.53   In the digitization process, errors occur owing to the continuous nature of the input and the discrete nature of the output. In the figure, we show the problem, with an error, X, between the output voltage level and the input voltage level. The maximum value of the error is half the least significant bit, LSB/2. We model the randomness of the error by defining a random variable, V, a random voltage between $-$LSB/2 and $+$LSB/2. Clearly, the error is a function of the random variable, $X(V)$. Find

a. The PDF for V.

b. The CDF for V.

c. The expected error, $E[X]$.

d. The expected magnitude of the error, $E[|X|]$.

e. The standard deviation of the error, σ_X.

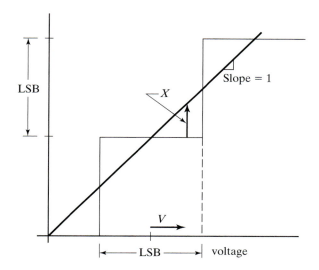

A3.1.53 **(a)** $f_V(v) = \frac{1}{\text{LSB}}$, $-\frac{\text{LSB}}{2} < v \le +\frac{\text{LSB}}{2}$, zow; **(b)** $F_V(v) = 0$, $v < -\frac{\text{LSB}}{2}$, $= \frac{1}{2} + \frac{v}{\text{LSB}}$, $-\frac{\text{LSB}}{2} < v < \frac{+\text{LSB}}{2}$, $= 1$, $v > +\frac{\text{LSB}}{2}$; **(c)** 0; **(d)** $\frac{\text{LSB}}{4}$; **(e)** 0.2887 LSB

P3.1.54 You borrow your friend's car to drive to San Marcos (45 mi) to see your high school friend. The gas gauge is broken, so you don't know how much gas is in the car. The tank holds 16 gal and the car gets 30 mpg, so you decide to take a chance.

a. What is the probability that you will not run out of gas on the way?

b. If you don't run out of gas on the way, what is the probability that you will not run out of gas on the way back if you decide to take a chance again?

c. Assuming that you make it back and return the car to your friend, what is his expected distance to run out of gas if he puts no gas in the car?

A3.1.54 **(a)** 0.9063; **(b)** 0.8966; **(c)** 195 mi

P3.1.55 A string 1 m long is cut into two pieces. A right triangle is formed, with the shorter piece a leg, and the longer piece the other leg and the hypotenuse stretched, to form the triangle. Find the expected area of the triangle.

A3.1.55 0.0284 m^2

P3.1.56   A parking garage is, as we've all experienced, simply a long parking lot. Because people park as soon as possible, the PDF of the distance, X, to the first available space tends to increase with distance from the entrance. Consider the following model. Let the length of the parking garage $= 300$ yd. Let $f_X(x) = ae^{x/300}$, $0 < x \le 300$, where X is in yards. The probability that you will find a space in the garage is 0.9, and the probability that the garage is full is 0.1.

a. Find a.

b. Assume you drive into the garage and drive the first 200 yd without finding a space. What is the probability that you will find a space in the garage?

A3.1.56 (a) 0.001746; **(b)** 0.8014

P3.1.57   A digital multimeter measures to high accuracy but displays only to millivolts, such as 5.217 V. The display is rounded from the true voltage, which is measured with great accuracy (assume a uniformly distributed continuous random variable). The error is defined as $E = |V_{\text{measured}} - V_{\text{displayed}}|$.

a. Find the expected error.

b. Find the standard deviation of the error.

A3.1.57 (a) 0.25 mV; **(b)** 0.1443 mV

P3.1.58   Seventy percent of the people who pay the entrance fee finish a marathon race. Ten percent of the people who pay the entrance fee do not show up for a variety of reasons. The remaining 20% drop out somewhere between 13 and 26 mi (assume a uniform distribution and assume the race is 26 mi.)

a. Find the probability that a person who paid the entrance fee, picked at random, goes beyond the 20-mi marker.

b. What is the average distance a runner runs, given that he or she shows up and runs?

A3.1.58 (a) 0.792; **(b)** 24.6 mi

P3.1.59   Abe and Bert play tennis. Abe is better than Bert. That's all we know, so we'll assume that $P[\text{Abe wins a set}] = P$, where P is a random variable uniformly distributed in the range $0.5 < P \le 1$. Because the probability that Abe wins a set is a random variable, the probability that Abe wins the match is also a random variable. The expectation of that random variable is an appropriate estimate of Abe's prospects for winning the match.

a. What is the expectation of Abe's winning the match if they play best two out of three sets?

b. What is the expectation of Abe's winning the match if they play best three out of five sets?

Note: We assume conditions of binomial trials. Not all sets are played if any player gets two sets in part a or three sets in part b.

A3.1.59 (a) 0.8125; **(b)** 0.8438

3.6.2 Bivariate Continuous Random Variables

Exercises on bivariate continuous random variables

P3.2.1   Two random variables are uniformly distributed in a quarter circle in the first quadrant of the x, y plane, as shown in the figure.

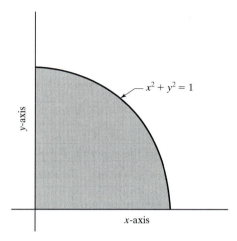

Find
a. The joint PDF.
b. The marginal PDFs on X and Y.
c. The means of X and Y.
d. The conditional expectation, $E[Y|X = x]$.

A3.2.1   **(a)** $f_{XY}(x, y,) = \frac{4}{\pi}$, over the quarter circle; **(b)** $f_X(x) = \frac{4}{\pi}\sqrt{1 - x^2}, 0 < x <$
1, zow, $f_Y(y) =$ the same formula with y; **(c)** $\frac{4}{3\pi}$; **(d)** $\frac{\sqrt{1-x^2}}{2}, 0 < x < 1$, zow

P3.2.2   A circle is inscribed in a square, as shown. If points are chosen at random in the square, what is the probability that the sixth point chosen will be the first outside the circle? *Hint:* This problem combines a continuous probability model with a well-known discrete distribution.

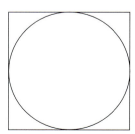

A3.2.2   0.0641

P3.2.3   Two random variables are described by the bivariate PDF $f_{XY}(x, y) = Ae^{-2x}(2 - |y|), x \geq 0, -2 < y \leq +2$, zow.
a. Find A.
b. Find the marginal PDFs, f_X and f_Y.
c. Are X and Y independent? Explain.
d. Find $P[X \leq Y]$.

A3.2.3   (a) $\frac{1}{2}$; (b) $f_Y(y) = \frac{2-|y|}{4}, -2 < y \leq +2$, zow, $f_X(x) = 2e^{-2x}, x \geq 0$, zow;
(c) independent, since $f_{XY} = f_X \times f_Y$; (d) 0.3114

P3.2.4   Two random variables, X and Y, are uniformly distributed in the triangular area shown in the figure.

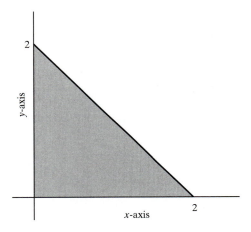

a. Find the joint PDF of X and Y.
b. Find the marginal PDF of X.
c. Are X and Y independent? Explain.
d. Determine $E[X + 2Y]$.

A3.2.4   (a) $f_{XY}(x, y) = \frac{1}{2}$ in triangular region, zow; (b) $f_X(x) = \frac{1}{2}(2 - x), 0 < x \leq 2$, zow, and f_Y is the same form by symmetry; (c) no, because $f_{XY} \neq f_X f_Y$;
(d) 2

P3.2.5   A bivariate PDF is $f_{XY}(x, y) = c(x + y), 0 < x \leq 2, 0 < y \leq 1$, zow, where c is a constant.
a. Find c.
b. Find the marginal PDF of X.
c. Find the conditional PDF, $f_{Y|X}(x, y)$.
d. Find the conditional expectation, $E[Y|X]$.

A3.2.5   (a) $\frac{1}{3}$; (b) $f_X(x) = \frac{1}{3}(x + \frac{1}{2}), 0 < x \leq 2$, zow; (c) $\frac{(x+y)}{(x+\frac{1}{2})}, 0 < x \leq 2, 0 < y \leq 1$; (d) $E[Y|X] = \frac{\frac{x}{2}+\frac{1}{3}}{x+\frac{1}{2}}, 0 < x \leq 2$, zow

P3.2.6   Bivariate random variables, X and Y, are uniformly distributed in a quarter circle of radius 1, as shown in the figure. That is, $f_{XY}(x, y) = c$ in the quarter circle, zow.

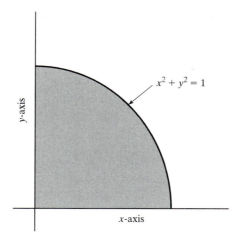

a. Find the marginal PDF of X.
b. Find $P[X < Y/2]$.
c. Find $f_{Y|X}(x, y)$ at $x = 0.5$.

A3.2.6   **(a)** $\frac{4}{\pi}\sqrt{1 - x^2}, 0 < x < 1$, zow; **(b)** 0.2952; **(c)** 1.155, $0 < y < \sqrt{0.75}$, zow, $x = 0.5$

P3.2.7   The CDF of a bivariate X and Y is defined as $F_{XY}(x, y,) = c(y \sin x + x \sin y), 0 < x \leq \frac{\pi}{2}$ and $0 < y < \frac{\pi}{2}$. The CDF is 1 above and to the right of the top right corner of the square region and 0 below and to the left of the square region. Its value above the square region and to the right of the square region can be deduced.
a. Find c.
b. Calculate the bivariate PDF.
c. Are X and Y independent? Explain.
d. Find the mean of X.

A3.2.7   **(a)** $\frac{1}{\pi}$; **(b)** $\frac{1}{\pi}(\cos x + \cos y), 0 < x \leq \frac{\pi}{2}$ and $0 < y < \frac{\pi}{2}$, zow; **(c)** no, the PDF cannot be factored (although the boundary can); **(d)** 0.6781

P3.2.8   Two numbers, X_1 and X_2, are selected independently and at random between 0 and 1.
a. Find $P[X_1 < \pi X_2]$.
b. Find $P[|X_1 - X_2| < 0.3]$.

A3.2.8   **(a)** $\frac{1}{2\pi}$; **(b)** 0.51

P3.2.9   Assume a value of X is chosen at random between 0 and a, then a value of Y is chosen at random between X and $2a$.
a. Find the bivariate PDF, $f_{XY}(x,y)$.
b. Find the marginal PDF for Y, $f_Y(y)$.

A3.2.9 **(a)** $f_{XY}(x, y) = \frac{1}{a(2a-x)}, 0 < x \leq a, x < y \leq 2a$, zow; **(b)** $f_Y(y) = -\frac{1}{a} \ln\left[1 - \frac{y}{2a}\right), 0 < y \leq a$, $f_Y(y) = \frac{1}{a}\ln 2, a < y \leq 2a$, zow

P3.2.10 Two points are chosen at random on a line of unit length. Let X_1 be the distance from the origin to the nearer point and X_2 be the distance to the farther point.
a. Find the expected separation between the points, $E[X_2 - X_1]$.
b. Find the variance of the separation between the points.
c. Find the probability that X_2 is at least twice X_1.

A3.2.10 **(a)** $\frac{1}{3}$; **(b)** $\frac{1}{18}$; **(c)** $\frac{1}{4}$

P3.2.11 A point is chosen at random in a 3-4-5 triangle. Find the probability that the closest side of the triangle is the hypotenuse.

A3.2.11 0.417

P3.2.12 Two independent random variables, X and Y, have PDFs as shown in the figure.
a. Find $E[Y]$.
b. What is $F_{XY}(0.5, 0.5)$?
c. What is $E[X + XY]$?
d. Find $P[X + Y \geq 3]$.

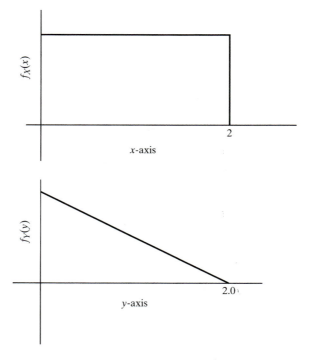

A3.2.12 **(a)** $\frac{2}{3}$; **(b)** 0.109; **(c)** $\frac{5}{3}$; **(d)** 0.0417

P3.2.13 A random variable, X, is chosen at random in the range 0 to 1. A second random variable, Y, is chosen at random in the range 0 to e^{+X}.
a. Find the bivariate PDF, $f_{XY}(x, y)$.
b. Find the marginal PDF for Y.
c. Find the expected value of Y.

> **A3.2.13 (a)** $f_{XY}(x, y) = e^{-x}, 0 < x \leq 1, 0 < y \leq e^{+x}$, zow; **(b)** $f_Y(y) = 0.632, 0 < y \leq 1, \frac{1}{y} - e^{-1}, 1 < y \leq e^1$, zow; **(c)** 0.859

P3.2.14 Three points are selected at random on a unit circle, to form a triangle. Let $L =$ the perimeter (sum of the sides) of the triangle. Find $E[L]$. *Hint:* Let the first point be at an angle of zero, and the other two be at random angles. This reduces the problem to two random variables.

> **A3.2.14** $\frac{12}{\pi}$

P3.2.15 A point is chosen at random in a unit square as shown in the figure.

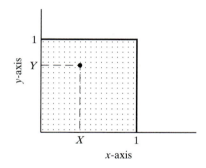

a. Find the probability that the point is within one unit from the origin.
b. Find the probability that the right triangle formed with the x-axis as a base has an area less than 0.1.
c. Let $D =$ the distance to the nearest axis (x- or y-axis). Find $E[D]$.
d. Let $C =$ the distance to the nearest corner. Find $E[C]$.

> **A3.2.15 (a)** 0.785; **(b)** 0.522; **(c)** $\frac{1}{3}$; **(d)** 0.383 by numerical integration

P3.2.16 A marble is tossed into a square box 1 m on a side. It comes to rest at a random position in the box.
a. Find the PDF of the marble's position, drawing a picture to show your coordinate system.
b. Find the probability that the marble is more than 30 cm from the center.
c. Find the expected distance of the marble from the center of the box.

> **A3.2.16 (a)** $f_{XY}(x, y) = 1$ in. square, zow; **(b)** 0.717; **(c)** 0.3826 by numerical integration

P3.2.17   An experiment produces random variables, X and Y, that are distributed such that the outcome falls in the trapezoidal area shown in the figure, with all points equally likely.

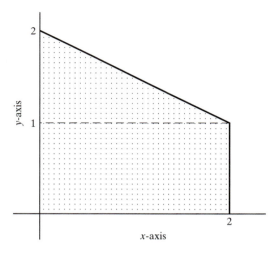

a. What is $f_{XY}(x, y)$?
b. What is the marginal distribution on X, $f_X(x)$?
c. Find the expected value of X.
d. Find $Var[X]$.

A3.2.17 (a) $\frac{1}{3}$ in shaded area, zow; **(b)** $f_X(x) = \frac{1}{3}\left(2 - \frac{x}{2}\right), 0 < x \le 2$, zow; **(c)** 0.889; **(d)** 0.321

P3.2.18   A point is chosen at random in a square 1 unit on a side in the x, y plane, as shown in the figure.

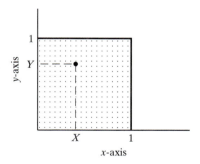

Let the position of the point be described by two random variables, X and Y. A new random variable is then generated as $Z = Y + X^2$.
a. Find $E[Z]$.
b. Find the CDF of Z.

A3.2.18 **(a)** $\frac{5}{6}$; **(b)** $F_Z(z) = 0$, $z < 0$, $= \frac{2}{3}z^{3/2}$, $0 < z \leq 1$, $= 1 - (\frac{2}{3} - z) + \sqrt{z-1} - z\sqrt{z-1} + \frac{1}{3}(z-1)^{3/2}$, $1 < z \leq 2$, zow

P3.2.19 The random variable X is uniformly distributed between 1 and 2. The random variable Y has a PDF that depends on X; namely, $f_{Y|X}(x, y) = xe^{-xy}$, $y \geq 0$, zow.
a. Find the joint PDF. Be sure to indicate the value throughout the x,y plane.
b. Find the marginal PDF on Y.
c. Find the probability that Y is greater than $X : P[Y > X]$.

A3.2.19 **(a)** $f_{XY}(x, y) = xe^{-xy}$, $1 < x \leq 2$, $y \geq 0$, zow; **(b)** $f_Y(y) = (\frac{1}{y} + \frac{1}{y^2})e^{-y} - (\frac{2}{y} + \frac{1}{y^2})e^{-2y}$, $y \geq 0$, zow; **(c)** 0.1353

P3.2.20 Consider two independent random variables, X_1 and X_2, each uniformly distributed between 0 and a. Let a random variable, $Y = (X_1 + X_2)^2$, be defined. Find the PDF of Y.

A3.2.20 $f_Y(y) = \frac{1}{2a^2}$, $0 < y \leq a^2$, $= \frac{1}{a\sqrt{y}} - \frac{1}{2a^2}$, $a^2 < y \leq 4a^2$, zow

P3.2.21 Consider the CDF $F_{XY}(x, y) = (a + b \tan^{-1}x)(1 - e^{-y})$, with $-\infty < x < +\infty$ and $0 < y < \infty$, zow.
a. Find a and b such that $F_{XY}(x, y)$ has the properties of a CDF.
b. Find the joint PDF.
c. Are X and Y independent random variables? Give a reason for your answer.
d. Consider X and Y as the coordinates of a point in the Cartesian plane. Write an expression for the probability that both X and Y are positive and within 1 unit of the origin. No calculation is required.

A3.2.21 **(a)** $a = \frac{1}{2}$, $b = 1/\pi$; **(b)** $f_{XY}(x, y) = \frac{1}{\pi(1+x^2)}e^{-y}$ for $-\infty < x < +\infty \cup 0 < y < +\infty$; **(c)** yes, both PDF and boundaries factor; **(d)** $P[X$ and Y in area$] = \frac{1}{\pi} \int_0^1 \tan^{-1}\sqrt{1 - y^2}\ e^{-y}dy$

P3.2.22 A point is chosen at random in a square that is d on a side.
a. Find the expected distance to the nearest corner.
b. Find the expected distance to the farthest corner. *Hint:* Give careful thought to how you define the basic experiment and the random variables you define. You can save a lot of time by using the symmetry of the problem.

A3.2.22 **(a)** $0.383d$; **(b)** $1.07d$ Mathematica does these integrals readily, provided you use the NIntegrate command to make it faster.

P3.2.23 Two random variables, X and Y, are uniformly distributed in the triangle shown in the figure.
a. What is $f_{XY}(x,y)$?
b. What is $f_{X|Y}(x, y)$, the conditional density on X, given that Y is specified?
c. Find $E[XY]$.
d. Let $Z = X + Y$. Find $F_Z(z)$, the CDF of Z.

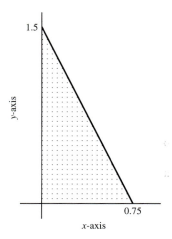

A3.2.23 (a) 1.778; **(b)** $f_{X|Y}(x, y) = \frac{2}{1.5-y}, 0 < x < \frac{1.5-y}{2}, 0 < y < 1.5$, zow;
(c) 0.0937; **(d)** $F_Z(z) = 0, z \leq 0, = \frac{1.778}{2}z^2, 0 < z \leq 0.75, = 1 - \frac{1.778}{2}(1.5 - z)^2, 0.75 < z \leq 1.5, = 1, z > 1.5$

P3.2.24 A point is chosen at random on the arc of radius r_0, which is equivalent to choosing a random variable Θ to describe the angle, where $0 < \Theta \leq \pi/2$ as shown in the figure.
  a. Find $f_\Theta(\theta)$, the PDF of the angle.
  b. If the random variable, X, describes the projection of the point on the horizontal axis, find $E[X]$.
  c. Find the CDF and PDF of X, $F_X(x)$ and $f_X(x)$.
  d. We now introduce a new random variable, R, to describe the distance from the origin. R is uniformly distributed between $0 < R \leq r_0$ and independent of Θ. Letting X be the projection as before, find $E[X(\Theta, R)]$.
  e. If we now make all points in the quarter circle equally likely, what is $E[X(\Theta, R)]$? *Hint:* This value will be larger than for part d, because there are many more points at large R.

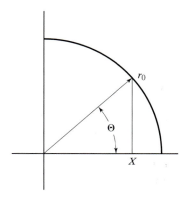

A3.2.24 **(a)** $f_\Theta(\theta) = \frac{2}{\pi}, 0 < \theta \leq \frac{\pi}{2}$, zow; **(b)** $\frac{2r_0}{\pi}$; **(c)** $F_X(x) = 0, x < 0, = 1 - \frac{2}{\pi}\cos^{-1}\frac{x}{r_0}, 0 < x \leq r_0, = 1, x > r_0$, and $f_X(x) = \frac{2}{\pi\sqrt{r_0^2 - x^2}}, 0 < x \leq r_0$, zow; **(d)** r_0/π; **(e)** $4r_0/3\pi$

Modeling problems on bivariate continuous random variables

P3.2.25 Two motorists set out from Centerville, one going north and one west. Each had an automotive breakdown before reaching the next town, which was 20 miles north and 25 miles west, respectively. Find the probability that the two stranded motorists were more than 18 mi apart. Assume independence of the random distances of the breakdowns.

A3.2.25 0.4911

P3.2.26 A wealthy student, who carries anywhere from 0 to $50 in his pocket at any time, and a poor student, who carries from 0 to $10, are walking down the street one dark night and a robber stops them and takes all their money.
a. What is the expected "take" of the robber?
b. What is the variance of the "take" of the robber?
c. What is the probability that the robber got more than $40?

A3.2.26 **(a)** $30; **(b)** 216.67 ^{2}; **(c)** $P[\text{take} > \$40] = 0.3$

P3.2.27 A trucking company owns two trucks, which it runs continually between Austin and Dallas (200 mi) on uncoordinated schedules. Each truck has a citizen's band radio with a range of 50 mi. What is the probability that at a random time the two trucks are within radio range?

A3.2.27 0.438

P3.2.28 An inverting op-amp amplifier has a gain of $A_V = -R_F/R_1$. Assume that the feedback resistance is $R_F = 10$ kΩ and the input resistance $R_1 = 1$ kΩ, with both resistors 10% resistors. Assume resistor values independent and within 10% of the nominal values, with resistor values equally likely within that range. Find the expected value of the gain.

A3.2.28 -10.03

P3.2.29 Two birds sit on a power line, 100 ft between poles. The bird positions are random and independent.
a. What is the average distance between the birds?
b. The line runs north-south. Another bird lands on the line. What is the expected position of the northmost bird from the southmost pole?

A3.2.29 **(a)** 33.3 ft; **(b)** 75 ft

P3.2.30 I just took my old car to the shop again: $260 to replace the water pump. The cost didn't surprise me, since it costs $100–$400 when I take the car in for repair. They charge me \$75/hour for the mechanic's time, but that is calculated on the basis of the "book time" it takes to fix the different problems. I'm told a good mechanic can fix a car in 60–80% of the book time. Thus we have two random variables here, C = the cost of repair (\$260 in this instance, but varies with each repair) and F = the fraction of the book time it takes the mechanic to fix the various problems. We will consider these random variables independent and uniformly distributed within the bounds given.

a. What is the average gain to the shop for an hour of the mechanic's time?
b. What is the expected time it will take the mechanic to fix my water pump problem?
c. How much time does it take the mechanic on a typical repair on my car?

A3.2.30 (a) \$107.88; **(b)** 2.43 hr; **(c)** 2.33 hr

P3.2.31   A telephone receives a call at a random time during $0 < X \le 60$ minutes. The duration of the call, Y, is exponentially distributed, $f_Y(y) = \frac{1}{30}e^{-y/30}$, $y \ge 0$, zow. Consider the time and the duration of the call independent.

a. Find the bivariate PDF. Be sure to give its value for all values of x and y.
b. Find the probability that the phone is in use at the end of the hour.

A3.2.31 $\frac{1}{1800}e^{-y/30}$, $0 < x \le 60$, $y \ge 0$, zow; **(b)** 0.432

P3.2.32   The waiting time until a phone call arrives is exponentially distributed with an average wait of 5 minutes. The length of a phone conversation is uniformly distributed from 1 to 3 minutes, independent of the wait time. Let W = time to wait for a call, and T = time of talking.

a. Find the probability that the first call is completed before 4 minutes elapses from a time when the phone is not in use.
b. Given that a call comes in, what is the probability that another call does not come in before the first conversation ends?

A3.2.32 (a) 0.3252; **(b)** 0.6748

P3.2.33   Cold fronts that cause rain travel through central Texas. The widths of the fronts vary between 0 and 20 mi, and the velocities of the fronts perpendicular to their lengths vary between 10 and 25 mph. Represent these two variables by two independent uniform random variables, W and V.

a. Give the bivariate PDF throughout the w, v plane.
b. Find the probability that it rains more than 1 hour on one of these fronts.
c. Find the expected duration of the rain.

A3.2.33 (a) $f_{WV}(w, v) = \frac{1}{300}$, $0 < w \le 20 \cap 10 < v \le 25$, zow; **(b)** $\frac{1}{6}$; **(c)** 0.6109 hr

P3.2.34   An air traffic controller must deal with aircraft that arrive close together in time. Flight A arrives at 10:05 ± 5 minutes and Flight B arrives at 10:12 ± 10 minutes. Find the probability that the two flights will arrive within 2 minutes of each other, assuming independence and uniform distributions within the limits stated.

A3.2.34 0.160

P3.2.35   An engineer has two ways for measuring a physical parameter, but one is more accurate that the other. Let the two measurements be modeled by independent random variables X and Y, with each having the same mean (the true value of the parameter) $\mu = \mu_X = \mu_Y$, but with different variances $\sigma_X^2 \neq \sigma_Y^2$. Rather than throw out the less accurate data, the engineer decides to make a weighted average, $Z = aX + bY$.

   a. Find the relationship between a and b such that Z is an unbiased estimator of the true mean, μ, that is, that $E[Z] = \mu$.

   b. Find the relationship between a and b such that Z is the most accurate estimator of the mean, μ. This requires that $Var[Z] = $ minimum.

   c. Find a and b in terms of μ, σ_X, and σ_Y, to satisfy both conditions.

   A3.2.35 (a) $a + b = 1$; (b) $2a\sigma_X^2 + 2b\sigma_Y^2 \frac{db}{da} = 0$; (c) $a = \frac{\sigma_Y^2}{\sigma_X^2 + \sigma_Y^2}$, $b = \frac{\sigma_X^2}{\sigma_X^2 + \sigma_Y^2}$

P3.2.36   In Rhombean society, all boys marry between 20 and 30 years of age, and all girls between 15 and 25. Assume equally likely times to marry and independence between boys' and girls' ages of marriage.

   a. What is the probability that a girl marries a boy younger than herself?

   b. On average, how much older is the husband than the wife?

   c. Find the average difference in age between husbands and wives, given that the husband is younger than the wife.

   A3.2.36 (a) 0.125; (b) 5 yrs; (c) 1.67 yrs

P3.2.37   A wooden rod is divided at random into three segments by marking the rod at two random and independent points and cutting the rod at those points. What is the probability that a triangle can be formed from the three segments?

   A3.2.37 0.25

P3.2.38   A beer company owns two trucks, A and B, that travel continually between San Antonio and Austin, 90 mi, with no coordination. Find the probability that at a random time truck A is closer to Austin than it is to truck B.

   A3.2.38 0.25

P3.2.39   A homeowner has a square yard that is 100 ft on a side. He mows it with a gasoline mower. When he starts he fills up the gas tank and puts the cap back on the gas tank. When he finishes and is standing in the center of the square, he notices that the gas cap has fallen off somewhere. What is the expected distance between the homeowner and the gas cap, assuming all points in the square are equally likely?

   A3.2.39 38.26 ft

P3.2.40   A trucking company owns two trucks. One travels continually between Austin and Waco (100 miles), and the other between Austin and San Antonio (85 miles, in the opposite direction). At any time, these trucks can be anywhere on their respective routes and are totally uncoordinated. For simplicity assume that I-35 is perfectly straight between Waco and San Antonio.

a. Let W be the distance from Austin to the Waco truck and S be the distance from Austin to the San Antonio truck. Find the bivariate PDF, $f_{WS}(w, s)$.

b. Find the probability that the two trucks are within 100 mi of each other and going in the same direction.

A3.2.40 **(a)** $f_{WS} = 1/(100 \times 85)$ for $0 < w < 100, 0 < s < 85$, zow; **(b)** 0.288

P3.2.41   Assume a 10-Ω resistor can be any value between 9 and 11 Ω with equal probability.

a. What is the PDF of the resistance, R?

b. What is the CDF of the conductance, $G = 1/R$?

c. What is the PDF of the conductance?

d. What is the expected value of the resistance?

e. What is the expected value of the conductance?

f. Is $E[R] = 1/E[G]$ exactly?

g. If two such resistors are connected in series, what is the PDF of their equivalent resistance? Assume independence.

h. If connected in parallel, what is the probability that the parallel resistance will be greater than 5 Ω? Assume independence.

A3.2.41 **(a)** $f_R(r) = 0.5$, $9 < r \leq, 11$, zow; **(b)** $F_G(g) = 0$, $g < 0.0909$; $= 0.5 \times \left(11 - \frac{1}{g}\right)$, $0.0909 < g \leq 0.1111$; $= 1$, $g > 0.1111$; **(c)** $f_G(g) = \frac{0.5}{g^2}$, $0.0909 < g \leq 0.1111$, zow; **(d)** 10 Ω; **(e)** 0.1003 $\mho$; **(f)** no, but close; **(g)** see the figure; **(h)** 0.471

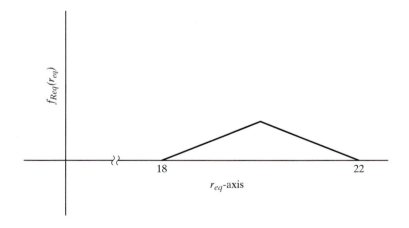

P3.2.42   A bug is placed on a table in the center of a 1-m square. The bug then starts off in an arbitrary direction at a speed somewhere between 1 and 2 cm/s. Let $T = $ the time required to reach the edge of the box. Assume the direction is independent of the speed. Note the eight-fold symmetry of the geometry. Find $E[T]$.

A3.2.42 38.9 s

P3.2.43 A person empties the change out of his pocket every evening, and so begins each day with only folding money in his pocket.

    a. Assume he makes one purchase per day. Let $X =$ the fractional part of the price. For example, for a price of \$1.29, $X = 29$. Let $C =$ the change in his pocket at the end of the day in cents ($C = 71$ for the \$1.29 purchase.) Assume that X is a continuous random variable. Find the PDF of C. *Hint:* Although this is a discrete distribution, it works fine to model C as a continuous random variable with $0 < C \leq 100$. (Yes, we know 99 would be right for the discrete case, but it works out all right and doesn't make that much difference.)

    b. Find the expected value of C.

    c. Now, assume two purchases per day, with X_1 and X_2 being independent random variables describing the amounts of the purchases. Again, let C be the change in the pocket at the end of the day. Find the expected value of C for two purchases.

A3.2.43 **(a)** $f_C(c) = 0.01$, $0 < c \leq 100$, zow; **(b)** 50; **(c)** 50

P3.2.44 A tornado blows a yardstick onto a football field. What is the probability that the yardstick comes to rest across a yardline? Assume a yardline every 5 yd and a location somewhere near the center of the field such that the sidelines are not a factor.

A3.2.44 $\frac{2}{5\pi}$ (This is a Texas version of the famous Buffon's needle problem)

P3.2.45 A mother has two children, a 1-year-old who takes a 1-hour nap every afternoon and a 2-year-old who takes a 30-minute nap every afternoon. Assume the beginning of the nap times are independent and uniformly distributed during the period between 1 P.M. and 4 P.M. Find the probability that the mother has both children sleeping at the same time.

A3.2.45 0.431

P3.2.46 A 100-kHz sinewave oscillator puts out a voltage with a peak amplitude between 2 and 4 V, with all values equally likely. Find the probability that the output voltage is greater than $+2$ V at a random time if the oscillator is operating.

A3.2.46 0.2475

P3.2.47 A soccer team makes two goals in a game, which lasts 80 minutes. What is the probability that the goals occur in the same half and at least 10 minutes apart?

A3.2.47 0.281

P3.2.48 You borrow your roommate's car and she warns you, "The gas gauge shows empty, but there are somewhere between three and four gallons left." Since you must drive 40 mi and return, you ask, "What kind of mileage does your car get?" "Twenty to twenty-five miles per gallon," is the reply. Find the probability of getting back without running out of gas, assuming you put no gas in the car and the information given by your roommate is valid. Assume independence and, for lack of better information, uniform distributions for the gas and mileage.

A3.2.48 0.430

P3.2.49 A student studies hard for a quiz, mastering 80–100% of the anticipated material; however, only 60% of the quiz is the expected material. On the unanticipated material, the student can expect to get from 0 to 100%, depending on luck and innate problem-solving skill. Assume these are independent.

     a. Find the probability that the student made 90 or greater on the exam.

     b. What is his expected grade?

     c. What is his expected grade, given that he did worse on the unexpected than the expected material?

     A3.2.49 (a) 0.104; **(b)** 74; **(c)** 72.3

P3.2.50 A gallon of paint is somewhere between a quarter and half full, estimated by weight and the shaking technique. A gallon will cover 300–400 ft^2. For uniformity of notation, let F be a random variable representing how full the can is, C represent the coverage in square feet/can, and A be the area covered, where $A = FC$. Assume that F and C are independent.

     a. Find the joint PDF, $f_{FC}(f, c)$.

     b. If your project requires 100 ft^2 to be painted, what is the probability that you have enough paint?

     c. What is the expected area you can paint?

     A3.2.50 (a) $f_{FC} = 0.04$ for rectangle bounded by $f = 0.25$ and 0.5 and $c = 300$ and 400, zow; **(b)** 0.8493; **(c)** 131.3 ft^2

P3.2.51 You are driving down the highway and it is sprinkling lightly, so you have your windshield wipers on. The wipers complete their cycle in 2 seconds, and for simplicity we assume that they move at a uniform rate.

     a. Assume a raindrop hits the windshield at a random time and that the wiper is moving toward the raindrop at the time it hits. Find the expected time between the time when the drop hits and when it gets wiped away.

     b. Assume a raindrop hits the windshield at a random time and that the wiper is moving away from the raindrop at the time it hits. Find the expected time between the time when the drop hits and when it gets wiped away.

     c. Assuming the conditions in parts a and b are equally likely, find the expected time between the time a drop hits and when it gets wiped away.

     A3.2.51 (a) $\frac{1}{3}$ s; **(b)** 1 s; **(c)** $\frac{2}{3}$ s

P3.2.52 A power line is 100 ft between poles and has 10 birds in one section, perched at random positions independent of one another.

     a. What is the probability that three or more birds are in the central 20-ft section of the line?

     b. Two of the birds are crows. What is the probability that they are within 20 ft of each other?

     A3.2.52 (a) 0.3222; **(b)** 0.36

P3.2.53   A string is marked at two independent, random points, where all points are equally likely for X and Y, the two points. The string is then cut at the two points. Find the probability that the smallest of the three resulting pieces is greater than one-tenth the original length of the string. *Hint:* No generality is lost if X is the closer of the original points to the origin, provided the bivariate PDF is adjusted appropriately.

   A3.2.53 0.49

P3.2.54   A successful painter charges $P = 1000 + 1000A$ dollars for painting, where A is the area in square feet. The area of a painting is negotiated with the customer and is anywhere from 2 to 4 ft^2 (assume uniform distribution). The rate at which the painter works is $0.1 < R \leq 0.2$ ft^2/hour, where R is the rate, depending on the nature of the painting (again, assume uniform distribution and independent of A.) One day, the painter's CPA asked him three questions. Give your answers.
   a. What do you make per painting, on average?
   b. How long, on average, does it take to complete a painting?
   c. What is your average gain in dollars/hour for your work?

   A3.2.54 **(a)** \$4000; **(b)** 20.8 hr; **(c)** \$202/hr

P3.2.55   This problem concerns a drunken cannoneer and requires that you have the following formula from ballistic mechanics. A cannon with an elevation angle e will shoot a distance of $r = r_m \sin 2e$, where r_m is the maximum range of the cannon. The drunken cannoneer sets the elevation angle of the cannon at random between 0 and $\frac{\pi}{2}$. Let this angle be a random variable, E. The range the cannon shoots is then a random variable, R.
   a. Find the PDF of R.
   b. The drunken cannoneer then sets the azimuthal angle, θ, at a random angle between $-\frac{\pi}{2}$ and $+\frac{\pi}{2}$. Let this be a random variable, Θ. Considering the two angles to be independent, find the joint PDF, $f_{R\Theta}(r, \theta)$.
   c. If the cannon is then fired, what is the probability that the shell will fall within $\frac{r_m}{2}$ of his own troops. This amounts to falling in the dotted area shown in the figure.

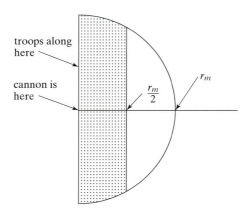

A3.2.55 **(a)** $f_R(r) = \frac{2}{\pi r_m} \times \frac{1}{\sqrt{1-\left(\frac{r}{r_m}\right)^2}}$, $0 < r \le r_m$, zow; **(b)** $f_{R\theta} = \frac{2}{\pi^2 r_m} \times \frac{1}{\sqrt{1-\left(\frac{r}{r_m}\right)^2}}$

in the semicircle; **(c)** 0.6304, done numerically in Mathematica.

P3.2.56   When my wife shops at the grocery store the time (T) she typically takes varies from 15 to 45 minutes, depending on the length of her list and how crowded the store is. The rate (R) at which she spends money varies between 50\$/hr and 100\$/hr, depending what's on the list and how much "impulse shopping" she engages in. In the absence of better information, we will assume both these random variables to be uniformly distributed and independent.

  a. What is the probability that she spents more than 25 minutes on a typical trip to the store?

  b. What is the average cost of a visit to the grocery store?

  c. What is the probability that she spends \$50 or more when the shops?

  d. Given that she spends exactly \$50, what is the expected time she spent shopping?

A3.2.56 **(a)** 0.667; **(b)** \$37.50; **(c)** 0.189; **(d)** 0.625 hour

P3.2.57   A string is cut in two at a point chosen at random, then the longer piece of the two is cut in two at a random point. Find the probability that the longest of the three resulting pieces is greater than half the original length of the string. *Hint:* It's helpful to define X as the longer piece from the first cut and Y as the longer piece from the second cut.

A3.2.57 0.6137

P3.2.58   I'm babysitting my three grandchildren that live in Austin, and part of my job is to put them to bed. The youngest, Justus, goes to bed at 8:30 and the two older ones, Noah and Peggy, go to bed at 8:45. The time for Justus to go to sleep, T_1, is an exponential random variable with an average time of 15 minutes. The time for Noah and Peggy to go to sleep, T_2, is also an exponential random variable with an average time of 10 minutes. We assume that these are independent random variables.

  a. What is the probability that Justus goes to sleep before I put Noah and Peggy to bed?

  b. What is the probability that Justus goes to sleep before Noah and Peggy go to sleep? That is, find $P[T_1 < T_2 + 15]$. *Hint:* A useful partition of the experiment is $T_1 < 15$ and $T_1 \ge 15$.

A3.2.58 **(a)** 0.6321; **(b)** 0.7793

P3.2.59   A student lives on a university bus route that also has a city bus that comes by. The university buses come every 10 minutes and the city buses every 20 minutes. Assume that the arrival times of the two types of buses are independent. The student arrives at the bus stop at a random time. Let $U = $ the time to the next university bus, and $C = $ the time to the next city bus.

  a. Find the bivariate PDF for the two independent random variables.

  b. Find the probability that the city bus arrives first.

A3.2.59 **(a)** $\frac{1}{200}$, $0 < u \le 10 \cap 0 < c \le 20$, zow; **(b)** 0.25

3.6.3 IID Random Variables

Exercises on IID random variables

P3.3.1 Two independent random variables are uniformly distributed, with X between 1 and 1.5 and Y between 0.5 and 0.6. Let $Z = X + Y$.

a. Find $E[Z]$.

b. Find $Var[Z]$.

c. Find $P[Z \le 1.8]$.

d. Find and sketch $f_Z(z)$, the PDF for Z.

A3.3.1 **(a)** 1.8; **(b)** 0.02167; **(c)** 0.5; **(d)** see figure

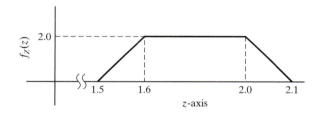

P3.3.2 The Laplace random variable X has a PDF given by $f_X(x) = 2e^{-4|x|}$, $-\infty < x < +\infty$. Consider $W = X + Y$, where Y is uniformly distributed between 0 and 2.

a. On any given performance of the experiment, what is the probability that $W > 2|Y|$?

b. Find the PDF of W.

A3.3.2 **(a)** 0.06248; **(b)** $f_W(x) = \frac{1}{4}(e^{4w} - e^{4(w-2)})$, $w < 0$, $= \frac{1}{4}(1 - e^{+4(w-2)}) + \frac{1}{4}(1 - e^{-4w})$, $0 < w \le 2$, $= \frac{1}{4}(e^{-4(w-2)} - e^{-4w})$, $w > 2$

P3.3.3 Consider two independent random variables, A and T, where A is uniformly distributed between 0 and 1, and T is exponential with an average value of 1. These random variables are added to produce a new random variable, $Y = A + T$.

a. Find the mean of Y.

b. Find the variance of Y.

c. Find the PDF of Y using convolution.

A3.3.3 **(a)** $\frac{3}{2}$; **(b)** $\frac{13}{12}$; **(c)** $f_Y(y) = 0$, $y < 0$, $= 1 - e^{-y}$, $0 < y \le 1$, $= (e - 1)e^{-y}$, $y > 1$

P3.3.4 Consider a sequence of IID random variables, $X_1, X_2, \ldots, X_7$, each of which has a mean of 2 and a variance of 3.

a. Calculate the mean of the sum of the random variables.

b. Calculate the variance of the sum of the random variables.

c. Calculate the mean of the product of the random variables.

d. Calculate the variance of the product of the random variables.

A3.3.4 **(a)** 14; **(b)** 21; **(c)** 128; **(d)** 807,159

P3.3.5   A random variable, X, has a triangular PDF as shown in the figure.

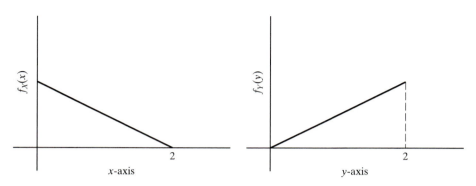

An independent random variable, Y, has a similar PDF as shown in the figure. A third random variable is formed, $Z = X + Y$.

a. Find $E[Z]$ and $Var[Z]$.

b. Sketch $f_Y(y - z)$ and $f_Y(z - y)$, where z is an independent parameter.

c. Find the PDF of z using convolution. Be sure to consider all values of z.

A3.3.5   **(a)** 2, $\frac{4}{9}$; **(b)** plots for $f_Y(y)$, $f_Y(y - z)$, and $f_Y(z - y)$ for $z = 0.5$ follow; **(c)** $f_Z(z) = 0$, $z \le 0$, $= \frac{1}{4}\left(z^2 - \frac{1}{6}z^3\right)$, $0 < z \le 2$, $= \frac{1}{4}\left(\frac{16}{3} - z^2 + \frac{z^3}{6}\right)$, $2 < z \le 4$, $= 0$, $z > 4$

```
fY[y_] : = If [y < 0, 0, If[y > 2, 0, y/2]]
Plot[fY[y], {y, -1, + 3}, AxesLabel → {"y-axis", "fY(y)"}];
```

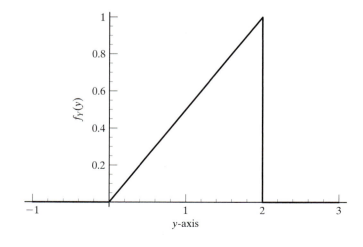

```
z = 0.5 ;
Plot[fY[y - z], {y, -1, +3},
   AxesLabel → {"y-axis", "fY(y-z)"}];
```

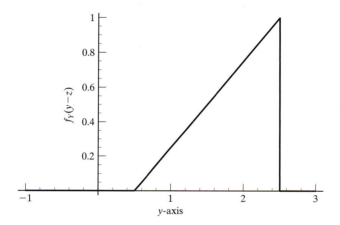

```
z = 0.5 ;
Plot[fY[z - y], {y, -2, +2},
   AxesLabel → {"y-axis", "fY(z-y)"}];
```

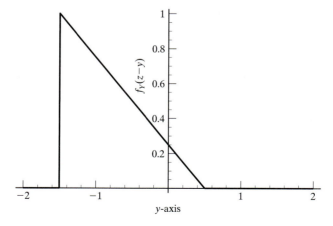

P3.3.6   A fair die is rolled repeatedly until a 6 is rolled. Let R = the sum of the numbers rolled up to and including the last roll of 6. Find the expected value of R. *Note:* This problem can be analyzed in terms of conditional expectation, where the condition is related to the number of trials. The last random variable is not random, since it must be a 6.

A3.3.6   21

Modeling problems on IID random variables

P3.3.7   When an analog signal is converted to a digital signal, quantization errors are introduced. The average quantization error is zero and the variance of the quantization error is $\frac{1}{12} \times$ the width of the quantization region. For example, a voltmeter that gives only two places, such as 32 volts, will have a quantization error with zero bias but an rms error of $\sqrt{\frac{1}{12}} \times 1$ volt, since 1 volt is the width of the region for rounding. In this problem, consider the series of voltage measurements, $x_1 + E_1, x_2 + E_2, \ldots, x_n + E_n$, where the lower case values, x_1, etc., are the values rounded to the nearest volt, and the upper case letters, E_1, etc., represent the quantization errors.

a. Let Y be the sum of the voltage measurements. This will be of the form of a number to the nearest volt $x_1 + x_2 + \cdots + x_n +$ an error, $E = E_1 + E_2 + \cdots + E_n$. Find the variance of Y.

b. If $n = 30$, find the probability that the total quantization error, E is greater in magnitude than 1 volt.

c. Consider now the average of n voltage measurements. How many measurements would have to be averaged before the quantization error is less than 10 mV with a probability of 0.5. In other words, $P[|\text{quantization error of average}| < 10 \text{ mV}] = 0.5$.

A3.3.7   **(a)** $\frac{n}{12}$ V^2; **(b)** 0.527; **(c)** 379 samples to average.

P3.3.8   A courier must take a folder of important papers from one office to another. Depending on the traffic and how she catches the lights, it takes 20 ± 3 minutes between buildings and, depending on the elevator, 2 ± 1 minutes to reach the 26th-floor destination. Assume uniform distributions on the uncertainties of times.

a. Find the average time required to deliver the papers.

b. Derive the PDF of the total delivery time.

A3.3.8   **(a)** 22 min; **(b)** see the figure

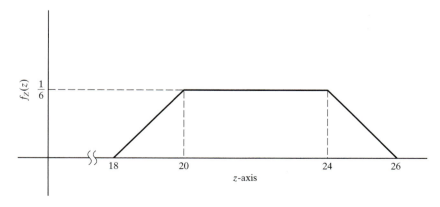

3.6.4 Gaussian Random Variables

Exercises on Gaussian random variables

P3.4.1 A Gaussian random variable, $X = N(4, 2^2)$ is generated by a certain process. We wish to perform a transformation $Y(X)$ that maps X into a uniform distribution, $f_Y(y) = 0.5$, $2 < y \leq 4$, zow.
a. Find the required transformation.
b. Give a second solution that also satisfies the criterion.
c. Does the mean of X correspond to the mean of Y? That is, is $E[Y] = y(\mu_X)$?
d. Is the standard deviation of X greater than, equal to, or less than the standard deviation of Y? Demonstrate your answer.

A3.4.1 **(a)** $y(x) = 2 + 2\Phi\left(\frac{x-4}{2}\right)$; **(b)** $y(x) = 4 - 2\Phi\left(\frac{x-4}{2}\right)$; **(c)** they do not correspond, since $E[X] = 4$, but $y(4) \neq \mu_Y = 3$; **(d)** $\sigma_X = 2$, $\sigma_Y = \frac{2}{\sqrt{12}} = 0.577 < \sigma_X$

P3.4.2 A Gaussian random variable, X, has an unknown mean but a standard deviation of 4.
a. The random variable is positive on 32% of the trials. What is the mean value?
b. This random variable is changed to another Gaussian random variable through the linear transformation $Y = \frac{X}{2} + 1$. Find the expected value of Y.
c. Find the variance of Y.
d. Find the mean of the square of Y.

A3.4.2 **(a)** -1.871; **(b)** 0.06460; **(c)** 4; **(d)** 4.00417

P3.4.3 Let X be a Gaussian random variable with a mean of 0 and a variance of 2: $X = N\left(0, (\sqrt{2})^2\right)$. We define a new random variable, Y, as the absolute value of X: $Y = |X|$.
a. Find the PDF of Y.
b. Find the mean of Y.
c. Find the variance of Y.

A3.4.3 **(a)** $f_Y(y) = \frac{1}{\sqrt{\pi}} \exp\left[-\frac{1}{2}\left(\frac{y}{\sqrt{2}}\right)^2\right]$, $y \geq 0$, zow; **(b)** 1.28; **(c)** 0.8525

P3.4.4 Consider a random variable, $X = N(10, 20)$. We take n independent samples of X. Let N_X count the number of times X falls between 8 and 9.
a. If $n = 30$, find the probability that N_X is less than 3.
b. If $n = 300$, find the probability that N_X is less than 30.

A3.4.4 **(a)** 0.5278; **(b)** 0.8129 using Gaussian, 0.816 based on the binomial

P3.4.5 An electronic manufacturer advertises "six sigma" reliability on a certain product. Because the company has made millions of this part and performed many tests, there is some credibility to the claim. Assume that "quality" is modeled as a Gaussian and any part outside $\pm 6\sigma$ is considered flawed. How many parts will have to be tested before one failure can be expected with probability 0.5?

A3.4.5 Because the area outside 6σ is approximately 2×10^{-9}, approximately 500 million parts would have to be manufactured to have one expected failure. Thus it is extremely unlikely that so many parts were made and tested. Manufacturers do, however, perform accelerated life tests, by which they stress the part through excessive temperature, voltage, or some other critical parameter to produce a significant number of failures. They determine a model for the failures, extrapolate back to rated conditions, and base reliability claims on the model.

P3.4.6 Consider two independent Gaussian random variables: X_1 is $N(2, 1)$, and X_2 is $N(1, 2^2)$. A third random variable is formed: $Y = X_1 - X_2$.
a. Find $E[Y]$.
b. Find $Var[Y]$.
c. Find $P[Y \leq 0]$.

A3.4.6 **(a)** 1; **(b)** 5; **(c)** 0.327

P3.4.7 A Gaussian random variable, X, has a mean of 10 and a variance of 12.
a. Find the probability that on any given performance of the experiment X is less than 13.
b. If $Y = 2X + 3$, find the mean and variance of Y.
c. Find $P[0 < Y \leq 80]$.

A3.4.7 **(a)** 0.8068; **(b)** 23, 48; **(c)** 0.9995

P3.4.8 A Gaussian random variable, X, has a mean of 12 and a variance of 10.
a. Find the probability that on any given performance of the experiment X is less than 11.
b. If $Y = 2X - 3$, find the mean and variance of Y.
c. Find $P[0 < Y \leq 80]$.

A3.4.8 **(a)** 0.3760; **(b)** 21, 40; **(c)** 0.9995

P3.4.9 A Gaussian random variable, X, has a mean of 1 and a variance of 4.
a. Write the PDF, $f_X(x)$.
b. Find the probability that on any given trial of the experiment X is positive.
c. Find the probability that on any given trial of the experiment X falls between $+3$ and $+5$.
d. Find the conditional PDF of X, conditioned that x is positive.

A3.4.9 **(a)** $f_X(x) = \frac{1}{\sqrt{8\pi}} \exp\left[-\frac{1}{2}\left(\frac{x-1}{2}\right)^2 \right]$; **(b)** 0.6915; **(c)** 0.1498; **(d)** $f_{X|X>0}(x) = \frac{1}{0.6915} \frac{1}{\sqrt{8\pi}} \exp\left[-\frac{1}{2}\left(\frac{x-1}{2}\right)^2 \right]$, $x > 0$, zow

P3.4.10 Let X be a Gaussian random variable, $N(1, (2)^2)$, with a mean of 1 and a standard deviation of 2.
a. Find $P[X \leq 0]$.
b. Find $P[X > 5]$.
c. Find $P[|X| < 0.5]$.
d. Find $P[|X| > 1.5]$.

A3.4.10 **(a)** 0.3085; **(b)** 0.0228; **(c)** 0.1747; **(d)** 0.5069

P3.4.11   A Gaussian random variable, X, has a mean of 2 and a variance of 3.
a. Write the PDF.
b. Find the probability that the random variable will be less than 3 on any given performance of the chance experiment.
c. Find $E[X^2]$ for this random variable.

A3.4.11 **(a)** $f_X(x) = \frac{1}{\sqrt{6\pi}} \exp\left[-\frac{1}{2}\left(\frac{x-2}{\sqrt{3}}\right)^2\right]$; **(b)** 0.7181; **(c)** 7

P3.4.12   A Gaussian random variable has a mean of 100 and a standard deviation of 12.
a. Find $P[X < 105]$.
b. Find $P[|X - 101| < 5]$.
c. Find $P[104 < X \leq 104.001]$.
d. Find $P[(X \leq 90) \cup (X > 110)]$.

A3.4.12 **(a)** 0.6616; **(b)** 0.3221; **(c)** 3.145×10^{-5}; **(d)** 0.4047

P3.4.13   A random variable has a PDF as shown in the figure.

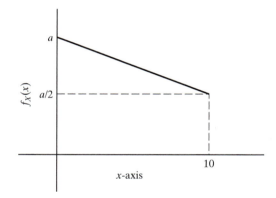

a. Find a.
b. Find the CDF of this random variable.
c. Find the expectation of this random variable.
d. Find the variance of this random variable.
e. Find a transformation $Y(X)$ that gives a random variable, Y, that has a Gaussian distribution $N(1, 4)$. Assume Y increases with increasing X.

A3.4.13 **(a)** $\frac{1}{7.5}$; **(b)** $= 0$, $x \leq 0$, $= \frac{1}{7.5}\left(x - \frac{x^2}{40}\right)$, $0 < x \leq 10$, $= 1$, $x > 10$;
(c) 4.44; **(d)** 8.025; **(e)** $y(x) = 2\Phi^{-1}\left(\frac{1}{7.5}\left(x - \frac{x^2}{40}\right)\right) + 1$

P3.4.14   A bivariate random variable is generated by selecting Y at random between 0 and 2 and then letting $X = N(Y, 1^2)$; that is, X is a normal random variable with a mean of Y and unity variance.
a. Find the joint PDF.
b. Find $P[X \leq 1 | Y = 1.5]$.

c. Find the marginal PDF for X.

d. Find $E[X]$.

A3.4.14 **(a)** $f_{XY}(x, y) = \frac{1}{2} \times \frac{1}{\sqrt{2\pi}} \exp\left[-\frac{1}{2}(x-y)^2\right]$, $0 < y \leq 2$, all x; **(b)** 0.3085; **(c)** $\frac{1}{2}[\Phi(2-x) - 1 + \Phi(x)]$; **(d)** 1

P3.4.15   A normal (Gaussian) random variable, X, has a mean of 1 and a variance of 1. A new random variable, Y, is created by the transformation shown in the graph.

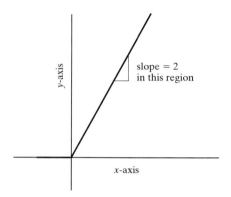

a. Find the CDF of Y.

b. Find the PDF of Y.

c. Find the expected value of Y.

A3.4.15 **(a)** $F_Y(y) = 0$, $y < 0$, $= 0.1587$, $y = 0$, $= \Phi\left(\frac{y}{2} - 1\right)$, $y > 0$; **(b)** $f_Y(y) = 0.1587\delta(y) + \frac{1}{\sqrt{8\pi}} \exp\left[-\frac{1}{2}\left(\frac{y-2}{2}\right)^2\right]$, $y \geq 0$, zow; **(c)** 2.167

P3.4.16   We have a random variable $X = N(5, 12)$. We have also a random variable $Y(X)$, as shown in the figure.

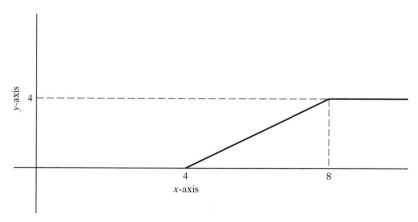

a. Find $P[4 < X \leq 8]$.

b. Find $P[Y > 1.5]$.

c. Find the CDF of Y.

d. Find the PDF of Y.

A3.4.16 (a) 0.4205; **(b)** 0.2820; **(c)** $F_Y(y) = 0$, $y < 0$, $= 0.3863$, $y = 0$, $= \Phi\left(\frac{2y-1}{\sqrt{12}}\right)$, $0 < y < 4$, $= 1$, $y \geq 4$; **(d)** $f_Y(y) = 0.3863\, \delta(y) + \frac{2}{\sqrt{24\pi}} \exp\left[-\frac{1}{2}\left(\frac{2y-1}{\sqrt{12}}\right)^2\right] + (1 - 0.8068)\delta(y - 2)$, $0 \leq y \leq 2$, zow

P3.4.17   Consider two independent random variables, $X = N(\mu_X, \sigma_X^2)$ and Y is uniformly distributed between 0 and μ_X. Let $Z = X + Y$.

a. Find the expectation of Z.

b. Find the variance of Z.

c. Find the PDF of Z.

A3.4.17 (a) $\frac{3}{2}\mu_X$; **(b)** $\sigma_X^2 + \frac{1}{12}\mu_X^2$; **(c)** $\frac{1}{\mu_X}\Phi\left(\frac{z-\mu_X}{\sigma_X}\right) + \frac{1}{\mu_X}\Phi\left(\frac{z-2\mu_X}{\sigma_X}\right)$

P3.4.18   A normalized Gaussian random variable, $Z = N(0, 1)$, is transformed with the relationship $X = 1 - 2Z$.

a. What is the PDF of X?

b. The same X is now transformed to $Y(X)$ by the function shown in the graph. Find the CDF of Y.

c. Find the PDF of Y.

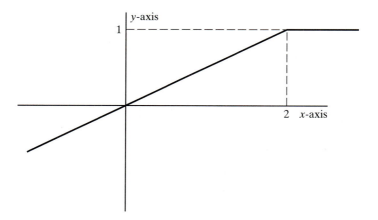

A3.4.18 (a) $f_X(x) = \frac{1}{\sqrt{8\pi}} \exp\left[-\frac{1}{2}\left(\frac{x-1}{2}\right)^2\right]$; **(b)** $F_Y(y) = \Phi(y - 0.5)$, $z < 1$, $= 1$, $y \geq 1$; **(c)** $f_Y(y) = 0.3085\, \delta(y - 1) + \frac{1}{\sqrt{2\pi}} \exp\left[-\frac{1}{2}(y - 0.5)^2\right]$, $y \leq 1$, zow

P3.4.19   A random variable, X, has the PDF shown in the figure.

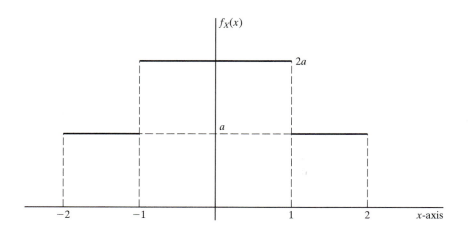

    a. Find a.

    b. Find the mean and standard deviation.

    c. Let Y be the average of 20 IID Xs. Find the probability that Y falls in the range between $+0.1$ and $+0.2$.

    A3.4.19 **(a)** $\frac{1}{6}$; **(b)** $\mu_X = 0$, $\sigma_X = 1.0$; **(c)** 0.1418, using the CLT

P3.4.20   Consider 10 independent random variables, $X_1, X_2, \ldots, X_{10}$. Each is uniformly distributed between 0 and A, where A is a random variable uniformly distributed between 0 and 100. Let Y be the sum of the Xs. Approximate $P[Y > 300]$.

    A3.4.20 0.2367, using the CLT

P3.4.21   Occasionally, a professor will drop the lowest quiz grade. This problem explores what that practice does to the class average. Specifically, consider that the course has two quizzes that are IID with mean μ and standard deviation σ, and for each student the lower of his or her two quiz grades is dropped. What is the resulting class average? Consider two possibilities:

    a. The PDF of the grades is uniform.

    b. The PDF of the grades is normal.

    Hints: (1) Start with the CDF. (2) Let X be the higher of X_1 and X_2. Then $\{X \leq x\} = \{X_1 \leq x \cap X_2 \leq x\}$.

    A3.4.21 **(a)** $\mu + \frac{\sigma}{\sqrt{3}}$; **(b)** $\mu + \frac{\sigma}{\sqrt{\pi}}$

P3.4.22   Consider 100 IID random variables, each uniformly distributed between a and b, and Y their sum: $Y = X_1 + X_2 + \cdots + X_{100}$. We know the probability that Y is less than 21 to be 0.96, and the probability that Y is less than 19.5 to be 0.19. Find a and b.

    A3.4.22 $a = 0.1012$, $b = 0.2988$

P3.4.23   Consider a normalized Gaussian random variable, Z. The mean of Z is 0, and the variance is 1.
a. Find the probability that Z is greater than -0.2.
b. Let $X = aZ + 1$. Find the constant a such that $P[X \leq 2] = 0.6$

A3.4.23 (a) 0.5793; **(b)** 3.948

P3.4.24   A Gaussian random variable, X, has a mean of 2 and a variance of 7.
a. Write the PDF, $f_X(x)$.
b. Find the probability that on any given trial of the experiment X is positive.
c. Find the probability that on any given trial of the experiment X falls between $+2$ and $+5$.
d. Find the conditional PDF of X, conditioned that X is positive.
e. Find the expected value of X, given that X is positive.

A3.4.24 (a) $f_X(x) = \frac{1}{\sqrt{14\pi}} \exp\left[-\frac{1}{2}\left(\frac{x-2}{\sqrt{7}}\right)^2\right]$; **(b)** 0.7752; **(c)** 0.1473; **(d)** $f_{X|X>0}(x) = \frac{1}{0.7752} \frac{1}{\sqrt{14\pi}} \exp\left[-\frac{1}{2}\left(\frac{x-2}{\sqrt{7}}\right)^2\right], x > 0$, zow; **(e)** $E[X|x > 0] = 3.023$

P3.4.25   Two Gaussian random variables, X_1 and X_2, are independent but not identically distributed because they have different means and different standard deviations: $\mu_1 = 1$ and $\mu_2 = 2$, and $\sigma_1 = 0.8$ and $\sigma_2 = 0.6$. Consider a new random variable, Y, which is their sum: $Y = X_1 + X_2$.
a. Find $E[Y]$.
b. Find $E[Y^2]$.
c. Find the probability that $Y < 4$.

A3.4.25 (a) 3; **(b)** 10; **(c)** 0.8413

P3.4.26   A random variable, $X = N(10, 100)$, is sampled repeatedly until a value between 10 and 12 is obtained, at which point the chance experiment ends. Let N be the trial number upon which the experiment ends (a random variable). Thus the results of the experiment are a series of $N - 1$ numbers that do not include anything between 10 and 12, followed by a number between 10 and 12, such as 9.6, -3.2, 12.7, 11.5, giving $N = 4$.
a. Find $P[10 < X \leq 12]$.
b. Find $P[N \geq 6]$.
c. Find $E[X_N]$, the expected value of the number that terminates the experiment.

A3.4.26 (a) 0.0793; **(b)** 0.6616; **(c)** 10.9962

P3.4.27   Let X be an exponential random variable with a mean of 1, and $Y = N(0, 1)$. A third random variable is formed, $Z = X + Y$. Assume X and Y are independent.
a. Find the expectation of Z.
b. Find the standard deviation of Z.
c. Find the bivariate PDF of X and Y, $f_{XY}(x, y)$.
d. Find the PDF of Z.

A3.4.27 (a) 1; (b) $\sqrt{2}$; (c) $\frac{1}{\sqrt{2\pi}} \exp\left[-\frac{1}{2}y^2 - x\right]$; (d) $e^{z+\frac{1}{2}} \Phi(z-1)$

P3.4.28 A chance experiment produces a random variable $X = N(10, 2^2)$. The chance experiment is repeated until a value of X exceeding 12.5 occurs.
  a. Find the expected number of trials to complete the experiment, including the trial on which 12.5 is exceeded.
  b. Find the expected sum of the values of X up to and including the value that exceeds 12.5.
  c. Find the expected sum of the values of X excluding the value that exceeds 12.5.

A3.4.28 (a) 9.465; (b) 94.65; (c) 81.19

P3.4.29 A chance experiment produces two independent random variables, X and Y. The first, X, is Gaussian with zero mean and unity variance. The second, Y, is exponential with a mean of one.
  a. Find the probability that on any performance of the experiment (X, Y) falls in the square $0 < x \leq 1 \cap 0 < y \leq 1$.
  b. Let $Z = X + Y$. Find $E[Z]$.
  c. Find $E[Z^2]$.
  d. Find the PDF of Z.

A3.4.29 (a) 0.2157; (b) 1; (c) 3; (d) $e^{-(z-0.5)} \Phi(z-1)$

Modeling problems on Gaussian random variables

P3.4.30 Gravel as it comes from a certain gravel pit has a Gaussian distribution of radii, $R = N(1, (0.5)^2)$, measured in centimeters; however, the distribution as stated cannot be correct, since it gives finite probability to negative radii, which is impossible. The true distribution has a Gaussian shape for positive radii but is conditional on $R > 0$ and is renormalized accordingly. In other words, the negative tail is chopped off, and the total area is readjusted to unity.
  a. Give the correct distribution for the radii, which is $f_{R|R\geq0}(r)$.
  b. Find the expected radius of a piece of gravel picked at random.

A3.4.30 (a) $f_{R|R\geq0}(r) = \frac{1}{0.9772 \times 0.5\sqrt{2\pi}} \exp\left[-\frac{1}{2}\left(\frac{r-1}{0.5}\right)^2\right]$, $r \geq 0$, zow; (b) 1.02762 by numerical integration; the integral can be evaluated analytically with the use of the $\Phi(z)$ table

P3.4.31 A student takes a true/false test of 50 questions. Not having attended class nor studied the book, and also having a commitment for 15 minutes after the test begins, the student, without even reading the questions, puts random answers on the (machine-graded) answer blank. What is the probability that the student passed the test (60 or more)? There is no penalty for wrong answers.

A3.4.31 0.1015 using the central limit theorem; 0.1013 with the binomial

P3.4.32   A mile relay team consists of four runners. Considering a number of variables, the time each takes to run his part of the race is $N(52, (0.8)^2)$ with time in seconds. Find the probability that the team will complete the race in less than 3 minutes, 26 seconds.

   A3.4.32 0.1056

P3.4.33   A computer biology experiment searches gene space for the right genes to make up the characteristics of the phenotype of the species. It takes 10 μs for each trial, and the probability of finding the right gene is 10^{-4} on each trial. If there are 60 genes that have to be determined for the match, we have binomial trials and the Pascal distribution.
   a. Calculate the time and the standard deviation of the time required for this experiment.
   b. Using the Gaussian to approximate the Pascal distribution, find the probability that the computer experiment will last more than 5 seconds.

   A3.4.33 **(a)** 6 s, 0.775 s; **(b)** 0.9015

P3.4.34   The noise in a digital communication system is Gaussian with zero mean and a standard deviation of 50 mV. A pulse of height v has the noise added to it and must be detected. The threshold for detection is $v/2$. Find v such that the probability of not detecting a pulse is 10^{-3}.

   A3.4.34 0.309 V

P3.4.35   A drinking-straw manufacturing machine must cut the straws to length. On average the straws are the correct length, but there is a random error due to a variety of causes. The average error, neglecting sign, is 0.05 mm. Find the probability that a given straw has greater than average error. Assume a Gaussian model for the errors.

   A3.4.35 0.425

P3.4.36   The average person's reaction time is 0.6 s. Assume that reaction times are normally distributed as $N(0.6, (0.1)^2)$. Nine persons stand in a circle holding hands, and a "squeeze" is sent around the circle. What is the probability that the person who starts the squeeze has to wait more than 5 seconds for the return. *Note:* The beginning person starts a stopwatch when he or she squeezes the first person's hand so nine reaction times are added.

   A3.4.36 0.9085

P3.4.37   A digital system defines a zero as between 0 and 1 V and a one as between 3 and 5 V. The standard deviation of the noise is 0.8 V and is normally distributed.
   a. Find the probability of an error in the worst case, with 1 V for a zero and 3 V for a one.
   b. Find the probability of an error (one or more errors) in an 8-bit word in this worst case.

   A3.4.37 **(a)** 0.0062; **(b)** 0.02532

P3.4.38   A manufacturing process makes resistors with an average resistance 10 kΩ. If 95% of the resistors are within 10% of the average value, what percent are within 1%? Assume a Gaussian PDF for the resistor values.

A3.4.38 15.54%

P3.4.39   Bolts are manufactured to have a nominal diameter of 0.5 in. Actually, they come off the assembly line normally distributed $N(0.498, (0.0012)^2)$, and by test those with a diameter greater than 0.500 in. are melted down and remanufactured. Write the PDF of the bolts that pass inspection and are shipped. Let X = the bolt diameter.

A3.4.39 $f_X(x) = \frac{1}{0.9522} N(0.498, (0.0012)^2),\ x \leq a$

P3.4.40   The Texas State Highway Department sets the speed limits on new roads by the following procedure: (a) No speed limit is posted; (b) the speeds of a large number of vehicles are measured by radar; (c) the speed below which 85% of the cars are driving is determined; that is, the CDF = 0.85; and (d) that speed is rounded up to the next 5 mph. (The assumption seems to be that 85% of the public drive a reasonable speed.) Assuming a normal distribution of speeds and a standard deviation of 6 mph, find the range of mean speeds that give a speed limit of 55 mph.

A3.4.40 43.8 to 48.8 mph

P3.4.41   Joe finally retires, and the office staff take up a collection to buy him a present. All 10 people contribute one bill, and in a situation like this $1, $5, $10, and $20 bills are equally likely to be contributed. Using the central limit theorem, estimate the probability that the contributions exceed $100.

A3.4.41 0.3362 using CLT; 0.3257 exact. This problem is hard to model because with 10 random discrete random variables, and the wide variation in values from $1 to $20, the convolution is not very "Gaussian" at this upper tail. That the CLT answer comes out so close to the exact answer shows something of the robustness of this approach; or maybe it was luck.

P3.4.42   According to the Texas map, we have the following information:

> Austin to Elgin is 25 mi
> Elgin to Paige is 16 mi
> Paige to Giddings is 13 mi
> Giddings to Burton is 19 mi
> Burton to Brenham is 16 mi
> Brenham to Hempstead is 22 mi

Assuming these are true distances between fixed points in these towns, rounded to the nearest mile, estimate the probability that it is more than 112.0 miles from Austin to Hempstead.

A3.4.42 0.0787

P3.4.43 An airline makes more money if it oversells the seats on its flights (obviously). Assume 160 seats on the airplane and a no-show rate of 5%. How many tickets should the airline sell to have a 90% probability of accommodating all the passengers?

 A3.4.43 Using Gaussian approximation to the binomial, $n = 165.2$. Exact binomial: for $n = 165$ probability is 0.919 and for $n = 166$, 0.841.

P3.4.44 A voltage divider has nominal values of $R_1 = 1$ kΩ and $R_2 = 2$ kΩ, as shown in the figure.

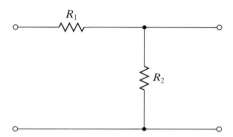

We assume that the resistor values are independent Gaussian random variables, $R_1 = N(1000, 2500)$ and $R_2 = N(2000, 4 \times 10^4)$. The gain of the voltage divider will approximately be a Gaussian random variable also.

a. What fraction of the values of R_1 fall in the range $1000 \pm 10\%$?

b. Find the mean and standard deviation of the gain of the voltage divider, making a linear expansion in the error variables. For uniformity of notation, let $R_1 = 1000(1 + X_1)$ and similarly for R_2.

 A3.4.44 (a) 95.4%; **(b)** $\mu = \frac{2}{3}$, $\sigma = 0.014$

P3.4.45 A travel agent is trying to put together a charter flight to Scotland. She needs 100 passengers to break even and will cancel if less than 100 people sign on, and makes $125 for each additional passenger. Her approach is to mail brochures to people with Scottish names chosen at random from the phone book. Her experience is that 1 in 100 will join the flight.

a. How many should she contact to have an 85% chance of having the flight occur?

b. Given that the flight occurs, what is her expected profit?

 A3.4.45 (a) $\approx 10,993$; **(b)** $1642.57 using Mathematica to sum the binomial, $1599.78 integrating the normal approximation with Mathematica

P3.4.46 The books on a shelf in my study vary from 0.4 cm to 5.6 cm in wide. The shelf is 150 cm wide. Assume a uniform PDF for the book width. Find n such that there is a 60% probability that n books will fit on the shelf.

 A3.4.46 49, using the CLT

P3.4.47 It takes time to count out pennies, so some stores simply round up and do not give pennies in change. Presumably the loss in revenue is recovered by a gain in employee efficiency.

    a. Give the PDF of the random variable $L =$ loss in pennies on a simple transaction.

    b. Find the mean and variance of L.

    c. If the store makes 1000 transactions in a day, what is the probability that its loss exceeds \$21?

    A3.4.47 **(a)** $f_L(l) = \frac{1}{5}\{\delta(l) + \delta(l-1) + \delta(l-2) + \delta(l-3) + \delta(l-4)\}$; **(b)** 2, 2; **(c)** 0.0123, using the CLT

P3.4.48 A NASA computer is charged with the calculation of orbit positions of a satellite. A day's calculation consists of 10^7 calculations of incremental changes in position that are added to give the position of the satellite at the end of the day. The calculations are accurate to 2 ft, so the round-off error on any such calculation is ± 1 ft maximum. Thus we have a rounding error for the day's calculation of $E = \sum_{1}^{10^7} X_i$, where E is the total error and X_i are IID random variables representing the errors on a single rounding operation.

    a. Find the PDF of X.

    b. What is the standard deviation for the total error in a day?

    A3.4.48 **(a)** $f_X(x) = \frac{1}{2}$, $-1 < x < +1$, zow; **(b)** 1826 ft

P3.4.49 A machine that makes resistors produces resistors that are distributed with a Gaussian PDF. When the machine is adjusted correctly, the mean of the resistors that are produced is the nominal value desired, and 80% of the resistors are within $\pm 5\%$ of the nominal value. For example, if the machine is adjusted to produce 100-Ω resistors, then the mean is 100 Ω, and 20% fall outside the range 95 to 105 Ω. Assume these numbers in the following.

    a. If the machine is adjusted correctly, what percentage fall outside $\pm 10\%$ of the nominal value?

    b. Find the conditional PDF $f_{R|G}(r)$, where $G = \{$within $\pm 5\%\}$.

    c. If the machine is misadjusted such that the mean of the manufactured resistors is 3% high, 103 Ω, what percentage now fall within the $\pm 5\%$ range, assuming the standard deviation does not change due to the misadjustment?

    A3.4.49 **(a)** 1.046%; **(b)** $\frac{1}{0.8}\frac{1}{3.906\sqrt{2\pi}}\exp\left[-\frac{1}{2}\left(\frac{r-100}{3.906}\right)^2\right]$, $95 < r < 105$, zow; **(c)** 67.5%

P3.4.50 The cost of medical treatment for a certain condition is described by the random variable $M = N(400, 50^2)$. The insurance company pays 85% up to $M = 425$ and nothing of costs exceeding $M = 425$. Find the PDF of the customer's cost for that treatment. Let $C =$ customer's cost $= M$ minus what the insurance pays.

A3.4.50

$$f_C(c) = \frac{1}{7.5\sqrt{2\pi}} \exp\left[-\frac{1}{2}\left(\frac{c-60}{7.5}\right)^2\right], c \leq 63.75$$

$$= \frac{1}{50\sqrt{2\pi}} \exp\left[-\frac{1}{2}\left(\frac{c-38.75}{50}\right)^2\right], c > 63.75$$

P3.4.51 A shopper goes to a grocery store. The time to buy is a normal random variable, $B = N(20, 100)$, time in minutes. (Throughout the problem, ignore the fact that this indicates a finite probability of a negative time.) The time to check out, C, is an exponential random variable with an average of 3 minutes. Assume B and C to be independent random variables.
a. Find the expected time to complete the shopping and checkout, $T = B + C$.
b. Find the variance of T.
c. Find the PDF of T.
d. Critique the assumption of the independence of B and C.

A3.4.51 (a) 23 minutes; (b) 109; (c) requires a convolution, with the result $f_T(t) = \frac{1}{3}\exp[-t/3 + 12.22]\Phi\left(\frac{t-53.3}{10}\right)$, $t \geq 0$, zow; (d) B and C would probably be correlated in practice, since the longer the shopping time, the longer the checkout time.

P3.4.52 A machine makes resistors with errors in resistor values that are Gaussian in distribution. The mean is the nominal value of $\mu_R = 100 \ \Omega$ and the variance is such that 92% of the resistors are within ±10% of the nominal value.
a. Find the standard deviation of the resistors as manufactured.
b. If resistors outside the ±10% range are removed from the population, what is the PDF of those resistors that remain? This is $f_{R|90<R<110}(r)$.
c. One day the operator noticed that only 88% of the resistors were falling within ±10% of the nominal value of 100 Ω. Her assumption was that the machine had become misadjusted such that the mean was greater than 100 Ω, since more of the resistors were rejected for being greater than 110 Ω. Assuming that the standard deviation was unchanged, find the new value of the mean in this misadjusted state.

A3.4.52 (a) 5.711 Ω; (b) 0.07593 $\exp\left[-\frac{1}{2}\left(\frac{r-100}{5.711}\right)^2\right]$, $90 < r \leq 110$, zow; (c) $\approx 103 \ \Omega$, by trial and error

P3.4.53 Assume that resistors are mass-produced and then sorted and marked according to their tolerances. Assume further that resistor values are distributed normally. Assume further that for a 1000-Ω resistor 7% of the manufactured resistors are not within ±100 Ω (±10%) of the nominal 1000-Ω value.
a. Find σ_R.
b. What fraction of the resistors is not within ±50 Ω (5%) of the nominal 1000-Ω value?
c. Give the conditional PDF of the ±5% resistors, $f_{R|950<R<1050}(r)$. Be sure to give the range and the "zero otherwise" part.

d. If a $\pm 5\%$ resistor is selected at random, what is the probability that it is within $\pm 2\%$ of the nominal 1000-Ω value?

A3.4.53 (a) 55.2; (b) 0.3650; (c) $N(1000, 55.2^2)/0.6350$, $950 < R < 1050$ zow; (d) 0.4456. By the way, this is not a realistic model for the errors in resistors. I once had a student measure $\pm 10\%$ resistors and they were slightly biased, but the σ was quite small. The tails of the distribution did not exceed the range by much. They were fairly Gaussian in their distribution.

P3.4.54   The voltage across a *pn*-junction diode is a Gaussian random variable, $V = N(0, (100 \text{ mV})^2)$. The current in the diode is $I(V) = 10^{-8} \exp[+V/40 \text{ mV}]$ A.
a. Find the probability that the random variable, I, is less than 0.1 μA.
b. Find the expected value of the current. *Hint:* Use the PDF of V and complete the square in the exponent.
c. Find the PDF of I.

A3.4.54 (a) 0.8215; (b) $10^{-8}e^{100/32}$; (c) $\frac{1}{100\sqrt{2\pi}} \exp\left[-\frac{1}{2}\left(0.4\ln\left(10^{+8}i\right)^2\right)\right] \times \frac{40}{i}$, $i > 0$, zow

P3.4.55   In order to get a phone installed in Taos, New Mexico, you have to wait your turn. The crew takes from 2 to 3 hours to get the job done. If you are sixth in line,
a. What is your expected waiting time.
b. Estimate the probability that you will wait more than 16 hours.

A3.4.55 (a) 15 hours; (b) 0.07865, using the CLT

P3.4.56   As part of a party game, 30 guests independently pick an integer between 1 and 9, inclusive, and write it on a piece of paper. The host adds the numbers. Estimate the probability that the sum is less than 143. (Now, who said that engineers don't know how to have fun?)

A3.4.56 0.2321, using the CLT

P3.4.57   A fair coin is flipped 100 times. Use the central limit theorem to estimate the probability that the number of heads resulting is greater than 55.

A3.4.57 0.1357

P3.4.58   A team of 10 telemarketers calls 120 potential donors each between the hours of 6 and 7:30 in the evening. The probability of success on any given call is 0.06. If anyone gets more than 10 donations during an evening, he or she gets a bonus.
a. Find the probability that any one of the callers gets a bonus on any given evening.
b. Find the probability that two or more of the callers get a bonus on any given evening.

A3.4.58 (a) 0.1024 using a Gaussian; exact is 0.1066 using a binomial; (b) 0.2740

P3.4.59   Let's consider a student's numerical grade (on the A = 3.5–4.5, B = 2.5–3.5, C = 1.5–2.5, D = 0.5–1.5, and F =< 0.5 scale). Basically, 3.5 corresponds to 90, 2.5 to 80, and so forth. Assume the grade obtained in a class is a Gaussian random variable,

$G = N(\mu_G, \sigma_G^2)$, where μ_G is the grade the student deserves on the basis of mastery of course content during study, homework activities, and being attentive in class. The standard deviation of G arises because of inaccuracies in the evaluation process; for example, tests do not fully encompass course material, papers are misgraded, a student does not feel well during the final exam. Assume $\sigma_G = 0.2$. X is the grade the student actually gets: $X = 0, 1, 2, 3,$ or 4 for F, D, C, B, or A, respectively.

a. If $\mu_G = 3.6$, find the bias of X as an estimator of μ_G. The bias is $E[X] - \mu_G$.

b. At what value or values of μ_G does the bias vanish?

A3.4.59 **(a)** bias = $+0.0915$; **(b)** bias vanishes at $\mu_G = 3.5, 2.5, 1.5,$ and 0.5

P3.4.60 A delivery person was given the following directions: "Go 6 miles south on Highway 25 and turn right on County Road 260. Follow this road for 4 miles to Fitzgerald Road and turn left. After 3 miles you will see a mailbox and gate with "Preston Ranch" over it. Turn in and the ranch house is 5 miles down that road." We note that the distances are integer miles and we assume that all distances were rounded to the nearest mile. Let X_1, X_2, X_3, and X_4 be random variables representing the exact but unknown distances that are rounded to an integer.

a. Sketch the PDF for X_1.

b. Let $D = X_1 + X_2 + X_3 + X_4$ be the total distance to the ranch house. Find $E[D]$ and $Var[D]$.

c. Estimate $P[D \geq 18.6]$, assuming that the resulting PDF can be approximated by a Gaussian.

A3.4.60 **(a)** See the figure; **(b)** 18, $\frac{1}{3}$; **(c)** 0.9582

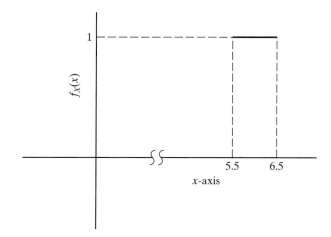

P3.4.61 I am driving from Austin to Electra, Texas, this weekend. On the way, there are 12 traffic lights, each with a delay from 0 to 30 seconds, and there are 12 stop signs or blinking red lights, each of which gives a delay of 2–10 seconds. Assume independent, uniform distributions.

a. What is my expected delay, D, due to all traffic lights and stop signs?

b. What is the standard deviation of my delay?

c. What is the approximate PDF of D, the total delay time, assuming that the result of combining the individual PDFs is approximately Gaussian.

A3.4.61 **(a)** 252 s; **(b)** 31.0 s; **(c)** $f_D(d) = \frac{1}{\sqrt{2\pi \times 964}} \exp\left[-\frac{1}{2}\left(\frac{d-252}{31.0}\right)^2\right]$

P3.4.62   Assume that you have a 32-bit register. If a bit is 0, the stage uses 1 μA, but if a 1, it uses 5 μA. We assume that every bit has a 50% chance of being 0 or 1. The current to the 32 bit-register is thus $I = 32\ \mu$A $+ K \times 4\ \mu$A, where K is the number of bits that are 1 at any given time, a binomial random variable. In fact, the PMF of K is $P_K(k) = B_{32}(k, 0.5)$. Because we have, in effect, 32 binomial trials, K will behave much like a Gaussian random variable; thus the current is also a Gaussian random variable.

a. Find the mean and variance of I.

b. Estimate the probability that at any given time the current will exceed 120 μA.

A3.4.62 **(a)** 96, 128; **(b)** 0.0107, exact is 0.01003

P3.4.63   Assume that resistors, as manufactured, have a Gaussian distribution about the nominal value. Testing eliminates 10% of the resistors, since these fall outside the allowed $\pm 10\%$ range, leaving a Gaussian distribution without the tails. Assume a nominal 100-Ω value.

a. What is the PDF of the "good" resistors? This is a conditional PDF.

b. Find the mean and variance of this distribution. The variance requires numerical integration.

A3.4.63 **(a)** $f_{R|90<R\le110}(r) = \frac{1}{0.9} \times \frac{1}{6.079\sqrt{2\pi}} \exp\left[-\frac{1}{2}\left(\frac{r-100}{6.079}\right)^2\right]$, $90 < r \le 110$, zow; **(b)** mean is 100, variance is 23.03

P3.4.64   An automobile company is designing a car. One important design parameter is gasoline mileage. Let X = gasoline mileage in mpg. The EPA requires that the average of all cars shipped be 25 mpg. The company experience is that the actual mileage has a standard deviation of 2 mpg, so X is $N(\mu_X, (2)^2)$, where μ_X is the design mean. The company policy is not to ship cars with mileage less than 23 mpg. Any car below that value is reworked and retested before shipping. Find the minimum design mean to meet EPA and company standards.

A3.4.64 24.7 mpg

P3.4.65   A private school has competitive admissions; however, the students also are looking at other schools, so even if a student is admitted, there is a good chance he or she will not enroll. Indeed, experience has shown that on average 65% of the admitted students enroll. If the school wants to enroll 100 students, what is the maximum number of students (n) that it should admit to have at least a 90% chance that no more than 100 will enroll?

a. Express the requirement in terms of the binomial distribution. With Mathematica you can find n by trial and error.

b. Use the Gaussian to approximate the binomial to find n.

A3.4.65 **(a)** max n such that $\sum_{k=0}^{100} B_n(k, 0.65) \geq 0.9$ or $\sum_{k=101}^{n} B_n(k, 0.65) < 0.1$; **(b)** 143, using either method

P3.4.66   A system designer has an overall specification of $\pm 10\%$ with 99% probability. She figures there are 10 independent subsystems that contribute equally to this overall error, and she must specify 1σ specifications to the subsystem designers. This problem assumes a linearization of the overall system performance in terms of the errors in the subsystems.

a. What is the 1σ of the overall system to meet the required probability? State assumptions.

b. What must she specify to the subsystem designers, 1σ, for the errors of their subsystems?

A3.4.66 **(a)** assuming Gaussian, $1\sigma = 3.88\%$; **(b)** 1.23% from each subsystem

P3.4.67   Resistors are manufactured with a design mean of 1000 Ω and a standard deviation such that 20% fall outside the range ± 100 Ω, for a yield of 80% "good" resistors. One day the machine was misadjusted, such that the mean became 1050 Ω. The standard deviation remained the same as before. What was the new yield? Assume that the resistors have a Gaussian distribution prior to sorting.

A3.4.67 **(a)** 71.2%

P3.4.68   The gain of an inverting op-amp voltage amplifier is $A_F = -R_F/R_1$ where R_F is the feedback resistance and R_1 is the input resistance. Assume R_1 is a 1000-Ω 5% resistor, where the 5% value is such that 98% of all such resistors are within 5% of the nominal value. The feedback resistor, R_F, is a sensor that is measured with a voltmeter and ammeter, with the following results: $v = 7.2$ V $\pm$ 3% and $i = 2.1$ mA $\pm$ 6%. In all cases the errors have 98% probability error bars. Using a first-order expansion, find the gain and rms error in the gain (1σ), assuming independent Gaussian distributions for all variables.

A3.4.68 $-3.43 \pm 0.1234(1\sigma) = -3.43 (1 \pm N(0, (0.03597)^2))$

P3.4.69   In this problem we develop a model for a true/false test. We assume that there are 20 questions and that the average grade is 80. We assume that on any given question an individual student either knows the answer and answers correctly with 100% accuracy or else guesses and has a 50% chance of guessing correctly. Let $X =$ the number known for certain, $P[\text{correct}] = 1$, and $K =$ the number guessed correctly, $P[\text{correct on guess}] = 0.5$. The grade will be $G = 5(X + K)$. There is no penalty for wrong answers.

a. The simplest model is to assume all students know the same number for sure ($X = x =$ constant, not a random variable), and guessing is the only reason the grades vary. Under this assumption, find x and the standard deviation of the grades, σ_G. *Hint:* K will be described by the binomial distribution, where "n" = the number guessed $= 20 - x$.

b. We now consider that the students vary in their knowledge, such that X becomes a random variable. We assume a Gaussian distribution for X: $X = N(12, (4)^2)$. With this assumption, find the expected value and standard deviation of the grades, $E[G]$ and σ_G. *Another hint:* X and K are not independent, because the number of guesses depends on the number known, X, but conditional distributions are useful. You may have to use the expected values of K and K^2 for the binomial distribution, from Chapter 2.

A3.4.69 (a) 12, $\sqrt{50}$; **(b)** 80, $\sqrt{150}$

P3.4.70 The voltage of a power supply is a random variable described by the PDF shown in the figure. A resistor has a Gaussian PDF, with a mean of 10 Ω and a standard deviation of 0.5 Ω. The resistor is connected across the power supply. Ignore second- and higher-order effects.

a. Find the variance of the voltage.
b. What is the mean of the resulting current?
c. What is the variance of the resulting current?
d. Estimate the probability that the current will exceed 1.1 A.

A3.4.70 (a) 0.167 V^2; **(b)** 1 A; **(c)** 0.00417 A^2; **(d)** 0.0606

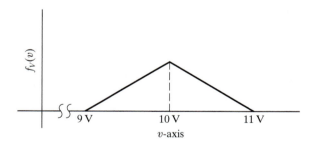

P3.4.71 An amplifier is used to amplify a Gaussian noise signal with a mean of 0.1 V and a standard deviation of 0.4 V. The voltage gain of the amplifier is $\times 10$, but the amplifier saturates at ± 10 V.

a. Find the PDF of the output.
b. Find the expected value of the output.

A3.4.71 (a) $f_X(x) = 0.003\delta(x + 10) + 0.0122\delta(x - 10) + \frac{1}{\sqrt{32\pi}} \exp\left[-\frac{1}{32}(x - 1)^2\right]$
$(u(x + 10) - u(x - 10))$; **(b)** 0.9867

P3.4.72 The following is a model for the weather bureau's rain predictions. Let's assume that, given certain conditions, the bureau can predict the amount of rain with a standard deviation of 0.5 in., assuming a Gaussian model. The random variable is $R = N(\mu_R, (0.5)^2)$, where R is a random variable describing the rainfall and μ_R is the predicted amount. The predicted chances of rain are $P[R > 0]$. The predicted amount is thus negative for chances of rain below 50%.

a. What is μ_R for a 40% chance of rain?

b. If there is an 80% chance of rain, what is the probability that it will rain more than 1 in.?

A3.4.72 **(a)** -0.127; **(b)** 0.123

P3.4.73 In the figure we show a voltage divider with two nominal 1000-Ω resistors and 100 V at the input. In this problem we model the output as a random variable, considering the resistances to be random variables. Here the experiment is to select two resistors and construct the voltage divider. We assume the resistors are described by Gaussian distributions, so let $R_1 = 1000(1 + X_1)$, where $X_1 = N(0, (0.051)^2)$ and $R_2 = 1000(1 + X_2)$, where $X_2 = N(0, (0.0510)^2)$, with the variations in the resistances independent random variables.

a. What fraction of R_1 fall within $\pm10\%$ of the nominal value?

b. Assume $V_0 = 50(1 + X_3)$ V, where X_3 is another normal random variable, found from a first-order expansion of the voltage-divider relationship. Find the mean and standard deviation of X_3.

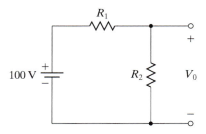

A3.4.73 **(a)** 95%; **(b)** $X_3 = N(0, (0.036)^2)$

P3.4.74 A noninverting op amp has a gain that depends on its feedback and input resistors, R_F and R_1, respectively. Let these be modeled by random variables as $R_F = 10,000(1 + X_F)$ and $R_1 = 1000(1 + X_1)$, where X_F and X_1 are Gaussian random variables, $N(0, \sigma_R^2)$. The variance of the resistors is such that 98% of the resistors fall within $\pm10\%$ of the nominal value.

a. Find σ_R^2.

b. Let the voltage gain be represented as $A = (1 + R_F/R_1) = (1 + R_{FN}/R_{1N})(1 + X_A)$, where the subscript N stands for the nominal values. Determine X_A in terms of X_F and X_1 using a linearized analysis.

    c. The normalized error in the voltage gain, X_A, will be Gaussian if we ignore higher-order effects. Find its mean and variance.

    d. Find the probability that the gain will be within $\pm 5\%$ of its nominal value of 11.0.

A3.4.74   **(a)** $(0.04299)^2$; **(b)** $\frac{10}{11}(X_F - X_1)$; **(c)** $X_A = N(0, (0.05527)^2)$; **(d)** 0.6322

P3.4.75   The figure shows a simple circuit containing a battery and a nonlinear device, with the following terminal characteristic:

$$I = 0, V < 0$$
$$= 12V^2 \text{ mA}, V \geq 0$$

with V in volts. The voltage of the battery is modeled by a random variable, $V = N(12, (0.2)^2)$. (Note that the standard deviation is small compared with the mean voltage, so a linearized analysis is appropriate.)

    a. Find the mean of the current.

    b. Find the variance of the current.

    c. Write the PDF of the current.

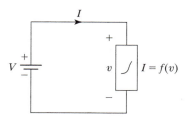

A3.4.75   **(a)** 1.728 A; **(b)** 3.318×10^{-3} A^2; **(c)** $f_I(i) = \dfrac{1}{\sqrt{2\pi \times (0.0576)^2}}$
$\exp\left[-\frac{1}{2}\left(\frac{i-1.728}{0.0576}\right)^2 \right]$

P3.4.76   A shooter has 10 shots at a bull's-eye, B. Her aim is best on the first shot, $P[B_1] = 0.9$, but decreases in a linear fashion, 0.85, 0.8, 0.75, 0.70, 0.65, 0.6, 0.55, 0.5, and 0.45, on shots 2 through 10, respectively. Assume these are independent events.

    a. Find the probability that she hits a bull's-eye on each of her first three shots.

    b. Find the probability that her first success comes on the fourth shot.

    c. Estimate the probability that she hits more than six bull's-eyes. *Hint:* Represent the results of each shot by a Bernoulli random variable, with the sum being the number hit. According to the CLT, this sum will tend toward the Gaussian.

A3.4.76   **(a)** 0.612; **(b)** 0.00225; **(c)** 0.5703

P3.4.77   A large bank makes 10,000 interest calculations per workday. The results are computed to great accuracy but rounded to the nearest cent for recording of the transaction. Assume that the calculated number is a uniform random variable, $0 < X < 1$, with anything below 0.5 rounded down and anything equal to or greater than 0.5 rounded up to the nearest cent.

a. At the end of the day, there is an accumulated round-off error that is the difference between the exact sum of the calculated interest and the sum of the posted values. Let that error be Y. Find the mean and variance of Y.

b. Find the expected value of the absolute value of the round-off error, $E[|Y|]$.

c. The programmer who wrote the software was a crook. He wrote the software to round down if $X < 0.5$, to round up if $X > 0.53$, and to round down if $0.5 < X < 0.53$ and put a penny into his account in a Swiss bank. Estimate his daily take on this system.

A3.4.77 **(a)** $\mu_Y = 0$, $\sigma_Y^2 = \frac{10^4}{12}$; **(b)** 23.03¢; **(c)** 300¢

P3.4.78 A well-known passage from the Bible is in the Gospel of John, Chapter 2, in which Jesus turns water into wine. The passage reads as follows:

[1] On the third day a wedding took place at Cana in Galilee. Jesus' mother was there; [2] and Jesus and his disciples had also been invited to the wedding. [3] When the wine was gone, Jesus' mother said to him, "They have no more wine." [4] "Dear woman, why do you involve me?" Jesus replied. "My time has not yet come." [5] His mother said to the servants, "Do whatever he tells you." [6] Nearby stood six stone water jars, the kind used by the Jews for ceremonial washing, each holding from twenty to thirty gallons. [7] Jesus said to the servants, "Fill the jars with water"; so they filled them to the brim. [8] Then he told them, "Now draw some out and take it to the master of the banquet." They did so, [9] and the master of the banquet tasted the water that had been turned into wine. . . .

Based on this information, answer the following questions:

a. Propose a model for the wine contained in one of the jars.

b. Estimate the probability that more than 160 gallons of wine were produced.

c. Good wine is valued at between $15 and $25 per bottle, which is one-fifth of a gallon. On this basis, estimate the probability that the value of the wine produced was more than $13,500. (This requires a numerical integral.)

A3.4.78 **(a)** $f_X(x) = \frac{1}{10}$, $20 < x \le 30$, for each of the jars; **(b)** by the central limit theorem, ≈ 0.0787; **(c)** 0.6960

3.6.5 Correlation, and the Rayleigh and Bivariate Gaussian Random Variables

Exercises on correlation, and Rayleigh and bivariate Gaussian random variables

P3.5.1 The random variable R is Rayleigh, $F_R(r) = 1 - e^{-10r^2}$, $r > 0$, zow.

a. Give the mean square value of R.

b. Give a transformation, $r(y)$ or $y(r)$, that transforms R into a random variable that is exponential with a mean value of 0.5.

A3.5.1 **(a)** 0.1; **(b)** $y = 5r^2$

P3.5.2 A certain yield in a chemical plant, X, has a correlation coefficient with temperature of $\rho_{XF} = +0.27$ when the temperature, F, is expressed on the Fahrenheit scale. What is the correlation coefficient, ρ_{XC}, when the temperature is expressed on the Centigrade scale?

A3.5.2 There is no change.

P3.5.3 Two independent random variables, X and Y, are uniformly distributed between 0 and 2.
a. What is $P[X > 2Y]$?
b. Find $E[X + Y^2]$.
c. Find the correlation, R_{XY}.

A3.5.3 (a) $\frac{1}{4}$; (b) $\frac{7}{3}$; (c) 1

P3.5.4 Consider two IID Gaussian random variables, X and Y. Both are $N(1, 2^2)$. From these we form a third random variable, $Z = X + 3Y$.
a. Find the mean and variance of Z.
b. Find $P[Z > 5]$.
c. Find the correlation coefficient between X and Z.
d. Write the bivariate PDF for X and Z, $f_{XZ}(x, z)$.

A3.5.4 (a) $Z = N(4, 40)$; (b) 0.4372; (c) 0.316; (d) $f_{XZ}(x, z) = \frac{1}{2\pi \times 2 \times \sqrt{40} \times \sqrt{1-0.1}} \times$

$$\exp\left[-\frac{\left(\frac{x-1}{2}\right)^2 - 2\sqrt{0.1}\left(\frac{x-1}{2}\right)\left(\frac{z-4}{\sqrt{40}}\right) + \left(\frac{z-4}{\sqrt{40}}\right)^2}{2(1-0.1)}\right]$$

P3.5.5 We are given two random variables, X and Y, that have a bivariate PDF, $f_{XY}(x, y) = \frac{1}{\pi}\exp\left[-\frac{1}{2}(x^2 + 4y^2)\right]$.
a. Find the marginal PDFs, $f_X(x)$ and $f_Y(y)$.
b. From these random variables, construct two new random variables, V and W, such that $V = N(0, 1)$ and $W = N(0, 1)$ and $\rho_{VW} = 0.9$.

A3.5.5 (a) $f_X(x) = \frac{1}{\sqrt{2\pi}}\exp\left[-\frac{1}{2}x^2\right]$ and $f_Y(y) = \sqrt{\frac{2}{\pi}}\exp\left[-\frac{1}{2}(4y^2)\right]$; (b) $V = X$, and $W = 0.9X + 0.872Y$

P3.5.6 Two Gaussian random variables, X and Y, have zero means, variances of 1 and 0.25, respectively, and a correlation coefficient of $\rho_{XY} = -\frac{1}{\sqrt{10}}$.
a. Write the bivariate PDF.
b. Write the marginal PDF of Y.
c. Find $E[(X + Y)^2]$.
d. Find $Z = aX + bY$ such that X and Z are independent, and $Z = N(0, 1)$. That is, find the constants a and b.

A3.5.6 (a) by inspection $f_{XY}(x, y) = \frac{1}{\pi\sqrt{1-0.1}}\exp\left[-\frac{x^2 + 2(1/\sqrt{10})2xy + (2y)^2}{2(1-0.1)}\right]$; (b) by inspection $f_Y(y) = N\left(0, \frac{1}{4}\right)$; (c) $-\frac{1}{\sqrt{40}}$; (d) $a = \frac{1}{3}$, $b = +2.11$

P3.5.7   We have two IID Gaussian random variables, X and Y, both $N\left(0, \sigma^2\right)$. We then create from these a third random variable, $Z = X \cos \theta - Y \sin \theta$, where θ is an angle, not a random variable.

a. Write the PDF of Z.

b. Find the correlation coefficient between Y and Z.

A3.5.7 (a) $f_Z(z) = \frac{1}{\sigma \sqrt{2\pi}} \exp \left(-\frac{1}{2} \left(\frac{z}{\sigma} \right)^2 \right]$; **(b)** $-\sin \theta$

P3.5.8   Consider two IID Gaussian random variables, $X = N(1, 4)$ and $Y = N(1, 4)$. From these form a third random variable $Z = aX + bY$, where a and b are constants.

a. Find a and b such that $Z = N(1, 8)$ and there is positive correlation between X and Z.

b. Find the correlation coefficient between X and Z.

A3.5.8 (a) $a = 1.366$ and $b = -0.366$; **(b)** 0.9659

P3.5.9   Two random variables, X and Y, are uniformly distributed in the triangular area shown in the figure.

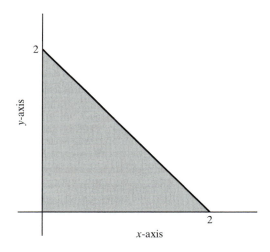

a. Find the variances of X and Y.

b. Calculate the correlation coefficient between X and Y.

A3.5.9 (a) both are $\frac{2}{9}$; **(b)** -0.5

P3.5.10 An experiment results in two random variables: X is exponential with a parameter of λ, and Y is normal with a mean of X and a variance of 1. Note that the PDF of Y depends on X.

a. Give the joint PDF of the two random variables. Be sure to define it over the entire x, y plane.

  b. Find the expected value of Y.

  c. Find the correlation between X and Y.

  A3.5.10   **(a)** $\frac{1}{\sqrt{2\pi}} \exp\left[-\frac{1}{2}(y-x)^2\right] \times \lambda e^{-\lambda x}$, $x > 0$, zow; **(b)** $\frac{1}{\lambda}$; **(c)** $\frac{2}{\lambda^2}$

P3.5.11   Two random variables, X and Y, have a joint CDF of $F_{XY}(x, y) = cxy^2$ over the rectangular region $0 \le x \le 2$ and $0 \le y \le 1$, and outside as required by theory.

  a. Find c.

  b. Find the marginal PDF on Y.

  c. Find the correlation between X and Y.

  d. Find the probability that X is greater than Y.

  A3.5.11   **(a)** $\frac{1}{2}$; **(b)** $2y$, $0 \le y \le 1$, zow; **(c)** $\frac{2}{3}$; **(d)** $\frac{2}{3}$

P3.5.12   A point is selected at random within the shaded triangular area shown in the figure.

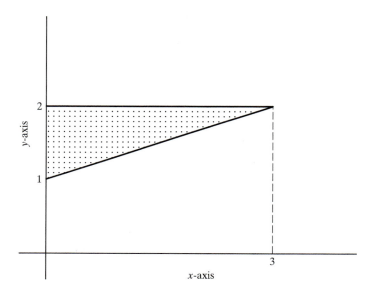

  a. Find the bivariate PDF.

  b. Find the marginal PDF of X.

  c. Find the marginal PDF of Y.

  d. Find the correlation between X and Y, R_{XY}.

  A3.5.12   **(a)** $\frac{2}{3}$ over the shaded area, zow; **(b)** $f_X(x) = \frac{2}{3}\left(1 - \frac{x}{3}\right)$, $0 < x \le 3$, zow; **(c)** $f_Y(y) = 2(y - 1)$, $1 < y \le 2$, zow; **(d)** 1.750

P3.5.13   Two random variables take on values given by the points in the graph, with all points equally likely.

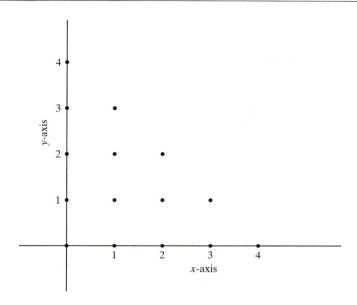

a. Find the marginal PMFs for X and Y.
b. Find the means and variances for X and Y.
c. Find the correlation coefficient between X and Y.
d. Consider a new random variable, $Z = X + 2Y - 1$. Find the mean and variance of Z.

A3.5.13 **(a)** $P_X(x) = \frac{5}{15}$, $x = 0$; $= \frac{4}{15}$, $x = 1$; $= \frac{3}{15}$, $x = 2$; $= \frac{2}{15}$, $x = 3$; $= \frac{1}{15}$, $x = 4$, zow. $P_Y(y)$ is the same except for the change from X to Y, and x to y; **(b)** means $= \frac{4}{3}$ and variances $= \frac{14}{9}$; **(c)** $-\frac{1}{2}$; **(d)** 3, 4.667

P3.5.14 We have two IID Gaussian random variables, X and Y, both $N(0, \sigma^2)$. We then create from these a third random variable, $Z = X \cos \theta + Y \sin \theta$, where θ is a constant.
a. Write the PDF of Z.
b. Find the correlation coefficient between X and Z.

A3.5.14 **(a)** $f_Z(z) = \frac{1}{\sqrt{2\pi\sigma^2}} \exp\left[-\frac{1}{2}\left(\frac{z}{\sigma}\right)^2\right]$; **(b)** $\cos \theta$

P3.5.15 We have two IID Gaussian random variables, X and Y, both $N(0, \sigma^2)$. We then create from these a third random variable, $Z = X \cos \theta + Y \sin \theta$, where θ is a constant.
a. Write the PDF of Z.
b. Find the correlation coefficient between Y and Z.

A3.5.15 **(a)** $f_Z(z) = \frac{1}{\sqrt{2\pi\sigma^2}} \exp\left[-\frac{1}{2}\left(\frac{z}{\sigma}\right)^2\right]$; **(b)** $\sin \theta$

P3.5.16 Consider two random variables, X and Y, that are uniformly distributed in the triangle shown in the figure.

    a. Find f_{XY}.
    b. Find $E[Y|X]$.
    c. Find $E[X]$ and $E[Y]$.
    d. Find $Cov[XY]$.
    e. Find the correlation coefficient between X and Y.

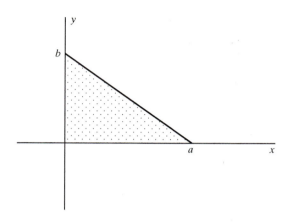

A3.5.16 **(a)** $f_{XY} = 2/ab$ over the triangle, zow; **(b)** $\frac{b}{2a}(a - x)$ $0 < x \leq a$, zow; **(c)** $E[X] = a/3$, $E[Y] = b/3$; **(d)** $Cov[XY] = ab/36$; **(e)** $\rho_{XY} = -\frac{1}{2}$

P3.5.17   Consider two random variables, X and Y, that are uniformly distributed in the triangle shown in the figure.
    a. Find f_{XY}.
    b. Find $f_{Y|X}(x, y)$.
    c. Find $E[X]$ and $E[Y]$.
    d. Find $Cov[XY]$.
    e. Find the correlation coefficient between X and Y.

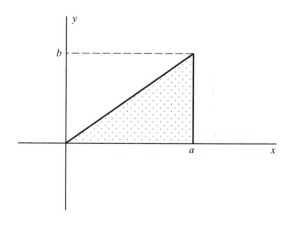

A3.5.17 (a) $f_{XY} = 2/ab$ over the triangle $0 < x \le a$, zow; **(b)** $f_{Y|X}(x, y) = \frac{a}{bx}$, $0 < y \le \frac{bx}{a}$, zow; **(c)** $E[X] = 2a/3$, $E[Y] = b/3$; **(d)** $Cov[XY] = ab/36$; **(e)** $\rho_{XY} = 1/2$;

P3.5.18 Bivariate normalized Gaussian random variables with unity variances and zero means have a correlation coefficient of $\frac{1}{\sqrt{2}}$.
a. Write the joint PDF, $f_{XY}(x, y)$.
b. Write the mathematical expression for the event $\sin(X) + Y < 2$. You do not have to perform the calculation.

A3.5.18 (a) $f_{XY}(x, y) = \frac{1}{\sqrt{2}\pi} \exp\left[-(x^2 - \sqrt{2}xy + y^2)\right]$; **(b)** $P[\sin X + Y < 2] =$
$$\int_{-\infty}^{+\infty} \left[\int_{-\infty}^{2-\sin x} \frac{1}{\sqrt{2}\pi} \exp\left[-(x^2 - \sqrt{2}xy + y^2)\right] dy \right] dx$$

P3.5.19 Consider two independent random variables, X and Y. The mean of X is $\mu_X = 2$, and its standard deviation is $\sigma_X = 1$. The mean of Y is $\mu_Y = 1$, and its standard deviation is $\sigma_Y = 2$. From these form a third random variable: $Z = X + Y$.
a. Find the correlation between X and Z, R_{XZ}.
b. Find the covariance between X and Z, $Cov[XZ]$.
c. Find the correlation coefficient, ρ_{XZ}.

A3.5.19 (a) $E[XZ] = 7$; **(b)** 1; **(c)** $\rho_{XZ} = 0.447$

P3.5.20 Consider two IID Gaussian random variables, X and Y, both $N(1, 2^2)$. From these we form a third random variable, $Z = 2X + Y$.
a. Find the mean and variance of Z.
b. Find $P[Z > 0]$.
c. Find the correlation coefficient between X and Z.
d. Write the bivariate PDF for X and Z, $f_{XZ}(x, z)$.

A3.5.20 (a) $Z = N(3, 20)$; **(b)** 0.749; **(c)** 0.894; **(d)** $f_{XZ}(x, z)$
$$= \frac{1}{2\pi \times 2 \times \sqrt{20} \times \sqrt{1-(0.894)^2}} \times \exp\left[-\frac{\left(\frac{x-1}{2}\right)^2 - 2\sqrt{0.894}\left(\frac{x-1}{2}\right)\left(\frac{z-3}{\sqrt{20}}\right) + \left(\frac{z-3}{\sqrt{20}}\right)^2}{2(1-(0.894)^2)} \right]$$

P3.5.21 Two random variables, V and W, are uniformly distributed between 0 and 1 and are independent. From these, two new random variables, X and Y are formed in the following relationships: $X = V + W$ and $Y = V - W$.
a. Find the means and variances of X and Y.
b. Find the covariance and correlation coefficient of X and Y.
c. Find the CDF of X and Y, evaluated at $(1, 1)$: $F_{XY}(1, 1) =?$

A3.5.21 (a) $\mu_X = 1$, $\mu_Y = 0$, $\sigma_X^2 = \sigma_Y^2 = \frac{1}{6}$; **(b)** both are zero; **(c)** $\frac{1}{2}$

P3.5.22 An experiment produces bivariate random variables, X and Y, that are uniformly distributed in a triangle defined by the points $(x, y) = (0, 0)$, $(2, 0)$, and $(0, 1)$.
a. Find the marginal distributions on X and Y.

    b. Find the means and variances of X and Y.

    c. Find the conditional distribution $f_{Y|X}(x, y)$ and the conditional means and variances, $E[Y|X]$ and $Var[Y|X]$.

    d. Calculate the correlation between X and Y, $E[XY]$.

    e. Find the correlation coefficient between X and Y, ρ_{XY}.

A3.5.22 (a) $f_X(x) = 1 - \frac{x}{2}$, $0 < x \le 2$, zow; $f_Y(y) = 2(y - 1)$, $0 < y \le 1$, zow; (b) $E[X] = \frac{2}{3}$, $E[Y] = \frac{1}{3}$, $Var[X] = \frac{2}{9}$, $Var[Y] = \frac{1}{18}$; (c)

$$f_{Y|X} = \frac{1}{1 - \frac{x}{2}}, \quad E[Y|X] = \frac{1 - \frac{x}{2}}{2}, \quad Var[Y|X] = \frac{\left(1 - \frac{x}{2}\right)^2}{12}, \text{ all } 0 < y \le 1, \text{ zow};$$

(d) $R_{XY} = \frac{1}{6}$; (e) $\rho_{XY} = -\frac{1}{2}$

P3.5.23   The bivariate Gaussian distribution between two correlated random variables is

$$f_{XY}(x, y) = a \exp\left[-\frac{x^2 - 2x - 0.72xy + 0.72y + y^2/4 + 1}{0.963}\right]$$

    a. Find a.

    b. Find $E[X]$.

    c. Find $Var[X]$.

    d. Find $E[XY]$.

    Hint: Do no integrals. The answers all come from Eq. (3.5.34), directly or indirectly.

A3.5.23 (a) 0.1147; (b) 1; (c) 1; (d) -1.44

P3.5.24   The general joint Gaussian bivariate PDF was given in Eq. (3.5.34). Consider the following PDF:

$$f_{XY}(x, y) = \frac{1}{3.2\pi} \exp\left[-\frac{x^2 - 0.6xy + 0.25y^2}{1.28}\right]$$

    a. From the PDF, identify the means and variances of X and Y, and their correlation coefficient.

    b. Find the marginal distribution on X, $f_X(x)$.

    c. Find the conditional expectation on Y, $E[Y|X]$.

    d. Find the conditional density function on Y: $f_{Y|X}(x, y)$.

A3.5.24 (a) $\mu_X = \mu_Y = 0$, $\sigma_X^2 = 1.0$, $\sigma_Y^2 = 4.0$, $\rho_{XY} = 0.6$; (b) $f_X(x) = \frac{1}{\sqrt{2\pi}}$ $\exp\left[-\frac{x^2}{2}\right]$; (c) $1.2x$; (d) $f_{Y|X}(x, y) = \frac{1}{\sqrt{2\pi \times (1.44)^2}} \exp\left[-\frac{(y - 1.2x)^2}{2 \times 1.44}\right]$

P3.5.25   An ellipse, given by the equation $\left(\frac{x}{4}\right)^2 + \left(\frac{y}{2}\right)^2 = 1$, is plotted in the first quadrant in the figure. All points in the quarter ellipse are equally likely.

    a. Find the joint PDF, $f_{XY}(x, y)$.

    b. Find the marginal PDFs, $f_X(x)$ and $f_Y(y)$.

    c. Find the conditional PDF, $f_{Y|X}(x, y)$.

    d. Are X and Y independent? Explain.

e. Find the expected values of X and Y, $E[X]$ and $E[Y]$.

f. Find the correlation between X and Y, $E[XY]$.

g. Find the variances of X and Y, σ_X^2 and σ_Y^2.

h. Find the correlation coefficient between X and Y, ρ_{XY}.

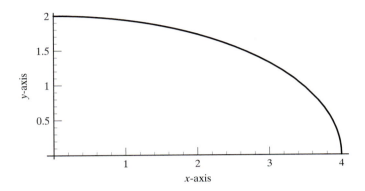

A3.5.25 (a) $f_{XY}(x, y) = \frac{1}{2\pi}$ in region zow; **(b)** $f_X(x) = \frac{\sqrt{1-(x/4)^2}}{\pi}$ for $0 < x \leq 4$,

zow, and $f_Y(y) = \frac{2}{\pi}\sqrt{1 - (y/2)^2}$ for $0 < y \leq 2$, zow; **(c)** $f_{X|Y}(x, y) = $

$\frac{1}{4\sqrt{1-(y/2)^2}}$ for $0 < x < 4\sqrt{1 - (y/2)^2}$, zow; **(d)** not independent; **(e)** $E[X] =$

1.698, $E[Y] = 0.849$; **(f)** $4/\pi$; **(g)** $\sigma_X^2 = 1.118$, and $\sigma_Y^2 = 0.2795$; **(h)** $\rho_{XY} =$
-0.3001

P3.5.26   The Gaussian random variable X has a mean of 2 and a variance of 3^2. The Gaussian
random variable Y is independent of X and has a mean of -2 and a variance of 2^2.
A new random variable is defined as $Z = X + 1.5Y$.

a. Find $P[Z \leq 0]$.

b. Find the correlation coefficient between X and Z.

A3.5.26 (a) 0.5933; **(b)** 0.707

P3.5.27   Consider three IID Gaussian random variables, X, Y, and Z, all $N(1, 2)$. From these,
we form a fourth random variable: $W = X + Y + 2Z$.

a. Find $P[W > 6]$.

b. What is the correlation coefficient between W and X?

A3.5.27 (a) 0.282; **(b)** 0.408

Modeling problems on correlation, and Rayleigh and bivariate Gaussian random variables

P3.5.28   A spinner has a long end, b, and a short end, a, as shown in the figure. As an experiment, the spinner is spun and comes to rest at some angle, with all angles equally

likely. We define two random variables: H = the horizontal projection of the long end, and V = the vertical projection of the short end. Find the following:

a. The mean and variance of H.

b. The CDF of $|V|$.

c. The correlation coefficient between H and V.

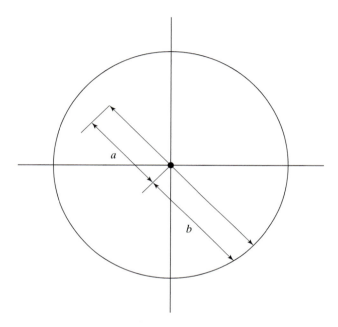

A3.5.28 **(a)** 0, $b^2/2$; **(b)** $F_{|V|}(v) = 0$, $v < 0$, $= \frac{2}{\pi}\sin^{-1}\frac{v}{a}$, $0 < v \le a$, $= 1$, $v > a$; **(c)** 0

P3.5.29   A leaf falling from a tree onto a pavement has a probability of 0.6 of falling within a circle of 1-m radius centered below the leaf's position on the limb, if the wind is calm. What is the probability of its falling in a circle of 2-m radius under the same circumstances?

A3.5.29 0.974

P3.5.30   A courier service carries important documents between two branches of a law firm with offices in Dallas and Austin. To get a document from Dallas to Austin, a courier leaves Dallas and drives to a restaurant in Waco while a courier simultaneously leaves Austin to meet him or her. Let $T_D = N(56, 16)$ be the time from Dallas to Waco, and $T_A = N(60, 25)$ be the time from Austin to Waco.

a. Write the joint PDF of the two times, $f_{T_A T_D}(t_A, t_D)$, assuming independence.

b. Let $W = T_A - T_D$ be the time that the courier from Dallas has to wait at the restaurant. Find the PDF of W.

c. Calculate the probability that W exceeds 5 minutes.

d. A more realistic model would include the correlation between T_D and T_A due to general traffic conditions on I-35. Describe how you would do part c if the random variables were not independent.

A3.5.30 (a) $\frac{1}{40\pi} \exp\left[-\frac{1}{2}\left(\left(\frac{t_A-60}{5}\right)^2 + \left(\frac{t_D-56}{4}\right)^2\right)\right]$; (b) $f_W(w) = \frac{1}{\sqrt{82\pi}} \exp\left[-\frac{(w-4)^2}{82}\right]$; (c) 0.4380; (d) In this case you would use the general bivariate Gaussian PDF and integrate in the region above the line $t_A - t_D = 5$. You would have to know the correlation coefficient between the two variables.

P3.5.31 The Pythagorean sum of two bivariate IID normal random variables leads to the Rayleigh distribution, as shown in the text. This problem extends the analysis from two to three dimensions.

a. Work out the PDF for the Pythagorean sum of three IID normal random variables. Assume $\mu = 0$.

b. A robotic repair satellite is launched to make repairs on a crippled satellite. The inertial navigational system will get the repair satellite to within 500 m, rms error, of the target location in each of three orthogonal directions, say, x, y, and z. Afterward the two have to be docked by remote control. Assume Gaussian errors. Find the expected miss distance between the repair satellite and the crippled satellite on the basis of the inertial navigational system.

A3.5.31 (a) $f_R(r) = \frac{1}{\sigma^3}\sqrt{\frac{2}{\pi}} r^2 e^{-\frac{1}{2}\frac{r^2}{\sigma^2}}$ $r = 0$, zow; (b) 798 m

P3.5.32 A flea will jump a distance of 0 to 1 m with all values equally likely. All directions are also equally likely.

a. Describe the joint PDF, $f_{\Theta R}(\theta, r)$.

b. If the flea is 30 cm from a line on the floor, what is the probability that the flea will jump across the line on the first jump?

c. If the flea jumps 100 times, what is its expected distance from the original position? Use the CCT.

A3.5.32 (a) $f_{\Theta R}(\theta, r) = \frac{1}{2\pi}$, $0 < \theta \le 2\pi \cap 0 < r \le 1$, zow; (b) 0.224; (c) 5.12 m

P3.5.33 Two random variables, X and Y, are uniformly distributed within a quarter circle of radius 1 in the first quadrant, as shown in the graph.

a. Find $f_X(x)$, the marginal distribution on X.

b. Find $E[X] = E[Y]$.

c. Find $Var[X] = Var[Y]$.

d. Find the correlation coefficient between X and Y, ρ_{XY}.

e. The sign of the correlation coefficient is negative. Interpret why this is true in terms of the relationship between X and Y in this geometry.

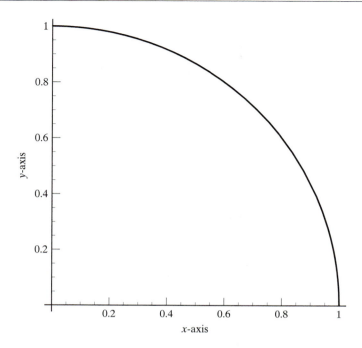

A3.5.33 (a) $\frac{4}{\pi}\sqrt{1-x^2}$, $0 < x \le 1$, zow; (b) $\frac{4}{3\pi}$; (c) 0.0699; (d) $\rho = -0.3001$;
(e) Generally, Y is smaller as X increases, but not strongly so.

P3.5.34   Snow White, while walking through the Pleasant Forest, goes randomly from flower to flower, smelling their fragrance and admiring their beauty. The directions between flowers are uniformly distributed between all angles, $0 < \Theta \le 2\pi$, and the distances between flowers are exponentially distributed, $f_R(r) = 0.05e^{-0.05r}$, $r \ge 0$, zow, where distance is measured in meters. The two random variables are independent.
a. Find $f_{\Theta R}(\theta, r)$ for this experiment.
b. Let $X = R \cos \Theta$ and $Y = R \sin \Theta$ be the distances she moves in rectangular coordinates. Find $E[X]$, $E[Y]$, $Var[X]$, and $Var[Y]$.
c. After Snow White smells 50 flowers, what is her expected distance from where she began? *Hint:* The central limit theorem suggests that the sum of the many moves will be Gaussian in the two orthogonal directions. Because the angles are randomized, the two Gaussians will be independent. Thus we expect a Rayleigh distribution.

A3.5.34 (a) $f_{\Theta R}(\theta, r) = \frac{1}{2\pi} \times 0.05e^{-0.05r}$, $0 < r < \infty$, $0 < \theta \le 2\pi$, zow;
(b) $E[X] = E[Y] = 0$, $Var[X] = Var[Y] = 400$ m^2; (c) 177 m

P3.5.35   A person has a dime and a nickel, both fair coins, which he flips in sequence: first the dime, then the nickel, then the dime again, and so on. If the dime lands heads, he moves 1 m north; if tails he moves 1 m south. If the nickel lands heads, he moves 1 m east; if tails he moves 1 m west. After 200 flips, 100 for each coin, estimate his mean distance from where he began and the standard deviation of that distance. *Hint:* The distances are binomial, but you can use Gaussian, then Rayleigh. Use the indicator random variable $X_i = \pm 1$, depending on the outcome of the ith trial.

A3.5.35 12.53 m (12.5381 exact), 6.551

P3.5.36   The reliability of an automobile, as measured by the time to failure, T, is often modeled as an exponential random variable, $f_T(t) = \lambda e^{-\lambda t}$, $t > 0$ zow, where λ is the average rate of failures in failures/year and is considered a constant. The expected time between failures is, according to this model, $E[T] = \frac{1}{\lambda}$. However, when one buys a used car, the rate of failure becomes a random variable, Λ, due to the unknown history of the vehicle. We will assume that Λ is uniformly distributed between 1 and 1.5 (meaning that expected time between failures is 8 months to 1 year.)
a. Find the bivariate PDF, $f_{T\Lambda}(\lambda, t)$.
b. Find the probability that the time to the first failure exceeds 6 months.
c. What is the expected time to failure?
d. Find the covariance between the failure rate and the time to failure, $Cov[T\Lambda]$.

A3.5.36 **(a)** $f_{T\Lambda}(t, \lambda) = 2\lambda e^{-\lambda t}$, $t \geq 0$, $1 < \lambda \leq 1.5$, zow; **(b)** 0.5367; **(c)** 0.8109 years; **(d)** -0.0137

P3.5.37   Consider a cannon that fires a shell at an angle Θ with a muzzle velocity v. Neglecting air friction and Earth curvature, the shell should follow a parabolic path and hit the ground at a distance $D = \frac{v^2}{g} \sin 2\Theta$, where g is the acceleration due to gravity, assumed independent of height, and Θ is the angle above the horizon at which the cannon is aimed. Assume we set the angle to $30°$ and fire off sufficient munitions to develop a probability model. Let $\Theta = 30° + X$, where $X =$ an error angle $= N(0, \sigma_X^2)$, in radians.
a. Assume that $E[D] = 500$ yd and $\sigma_D = 10$ yd. What is the rms error in the elevation angle Θ if we assume a Gaussian model for X, the errors? We treat the velocity as a constant.
b. It is observed that shells also have errors in direction as well as distance. Indeed, the shells are observed to fall in a circular pattern. What is the rms error in the azimuthal angle Φ, again modeled as a Gaussian random variable.
c. Estimate the average miss distance considering errors in both directions.
d. If the cannon angle is changed to $\theta = 45°$, find the new average distance and the rms miss distance.

A3.5.37 **(a)** 0.0173 rad $= 0.99°$; **(b)** 1.15°; **(c)** 12.5 yd; **(d)** 11.5 yd from the horizontal errors. Errors in elevation do not matter. The model attributes all errors to aiming.

P3.5.38   A "random walk" in two dimensions can be generated in the following process: flip a fair coin and move one unit in the $+x$ direction if heads and one unit in the $-x$ direction if tails; flip another fair coin and move one unit in the $+y$ direction if heads

and one unit in the $-y$ direction if tails. This is one cycle. Repeat the cycle 200 times, always moving from where the previous cycle ended. Let X and Y be the final position.
a. Find the probability that X exceeds $+10$ at the end of the process.
b. Find the probability that both X and Y exceed $+10$ at the end of the process.
c. Estimate the probability that the final position lies outside the circle centered on the origin that goes through $(+10, +10)$.

A3.5.38 (a) 0.2184 using CLT; exact is 0.2188; **(b)** 0.04770 using CLT; exact is 0.04787; **(c)** 0.6065 using Rayleigh; exact is 0.5998

ENDNOTES

1. **Let Mathematica do it.** The following calculates the sum and integral in Sec. 3.1.

```
NSum[i^4, {i, 0, 100}]
NIntegrate[x^4, {x, 0, 100}]
2.05033 × 10⁹
2. × 10⁹
```

2. **Answer to Test your understanding (a) on p. 178.** Because both 1.5 and 1.6 fall in the region where probability is proportional to the range of the base, the answer is the area between 1.5 and 1.6 under the curve in Fig. 3.1.2. Thus $P[1.5 < s \leq 1.6] = 2(1.6 - 1.5) = 0.2$. Try this answer and see if it works.
3. **Answer to Test your understanding (b) on p. 178.** Lowering the lower limit from 1.5 to 1.4 adds no probability, since all points between 1.4 and 1.5 cannot result from the chance experiment. Thus the answer here is the same as before, $P[1.4 < s \leq 1.6] = 0.2$.
4. **Solution to uniform PDF on p. 183.** Because the area under the rectangular PDF is always 1, as required by Eq. (3.1.8), the height must be 1 over the base. Thus the correct answer is $1/(b - a)$. Enter this answer and see if it gives a favorable response.
5. **Solution to $P[\mu - \sigma < X < \mu + \sigma]$ on p. 184.** The mean is $(b + a)/2$, and the variance is $(b - a)^2/12$, so the standard deviation is $(b - a)/\sqrt{12} = 0.289(b - a)$. The required probability is $1/\sqrt{3} = 0.5774$. Try that answer and see if it works.
6. **Answer to you do it on p. 188.** The PDF is the derivative of the CDF, so

$$f_X(x) = \frac{d}{dx}(1 - e^{-2x}) = 2e^{-2x}, x \geq 0, \text{ zow}$$

At $x = 1$, this gives 0.2707.
7. **Resistor PDF.** This is not a good model for the PDF of a 10% tolerance resistor. This model is chosen for convenience.

8. **Answer to you do it on p. 191.** The power range corresponds to a resistor range of $99.66 < R \leq 107.0$. The probability is therefore $0.05 \times (107.0 - 99.66) = 0.3691$.

9. **Answer to you do it on p. 192.** First, we need the conditional PDF, which uses the result in the preceding endnote. The conditional PDF is $f_{R|2.7<W\leq2.9}(r) = \frac{0.05}{0.3691} = 0.1355$, $99.7 < R \leq 107.0$, zow. Thus the conditional expectation is

$$E[W(R)|2.7 < W \leq 2.9] = \int_{99.66}^{107} \frac{17^2}{r} \times 0.1355 \, dr = 2.798 \text{ watts}$$

This result is close to the value you would get if you if you assumed a uniform distribution, so we made the numerical test very fussy about the answer to distinguish between 2.798 and 2.8.

10. **Deriving a conditional PDF.** Here we show a general procedure for deriving a conditional PDF where the condition is that the random variable falls in a certain range. For example, in the following figure we show the condition that X must fall in the range $x_1 < X \leq x_2$.

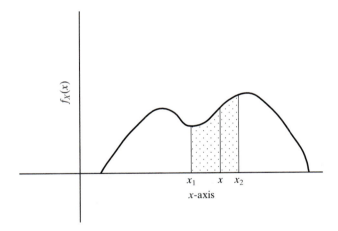

Because this is a derivation, we will first find the conditional CDF and take its derivative to obtain the conditional PDF. The conditional CDF is, by definition,

$$F_{X|x_1<X\leq x_2}(x) = P[X \leq x | x_1 < X \leq x_2] = \frac{P[X \leq x \cap x_1 < X \leq x_2]}{P[x_1 < X \leq x_2]}$$

The event in the numerator can be simplified to $\{X \leq x \cap x_1 < X \leq x_2\} = \{x_1 < X \leq x\}$ with $x_1 < X \leq x_2$, and the probability in the numerator can be expressed in terms of the unconditional CDF, with the result

$$F_{X|x_1<X\leq x_2}(x) = \frac{P[x_1 < X \leq x]}{P[x_1 < X \leq x_2]} = \frac{F_X(x) - F_X(x_1)}{P[x_1 < X \leq x_2]}, \quad x_1 < x \leq x_2$$

When we take the derivative of this equation to obtain the conditional PDF, we obtain

$$f_{X|x_1 < X \le x_2}(x) = \frac{1}{P[x_1 < X \le x_2]} \times f_X(x), \quad x_1 < x \le x_2$$

Thus the conditional PDF is identical with the unconditional PDF except for two changes: (1) the domain is restricted according to the conditions, and (2) the unconditional PDF is divided by the probability of the conditioning event to renormalize the PDF.

11. **Answer to you do it on p. 199.** Because the CDF is $1 - e^{-3t}$, we set $x = 1 - e^{-3t}$ with the result $t(x) = -\frac{1}{3}\ln(1 - x)$. Substitution of $x = 0.4$ gives 0.1703. But note that the PDF of $1 - x$ is the same as the PDF of x, so an alternative formula is $t(x) = -\frac{1}{3}\ln(x)$. This second transformation is easier to implement on your calculator. The second transformation gives 0.3054, which is also an acceptable answer.

12. **The unit step and unit impulse functions.** The unit step function is defined as $u(x) = 0, x < 0$, and $u(x) = 1, x > 1$. The function can be defined as anything we wish at $x = 0$, but $u(0) = 0.5$ is a sensible choice. The unit impulse function, also known as the *Dirac delta function,* is defined as the derivative of the unit step function, $\delta(x) = \frac{d}{dx}u(x)$. The unit step is the definite integral of the impulse function,

$$\int_{-\infty}^{x} \delta(x')\,dx' = u(x)$$

The impulse function can be modeled as a function that has unit area, extremely small base and very large height (in the limit zero width and infinite height). The impulse function has the property of picking out the value of a function when multiplied and integrated, such as

$$\int_{-\infty}^{+\infty} f(x)\delta(x - x_0)\,dx = f(x_0)$$

In a similar way, the derivative of the product of the unit step function times another function picks out the value of the function:

$$\frac{d}{dx}f(x)u(x - x_0) = f(x_0)\delta(x - x_0) + u(x - x_0)\frac{d}{dx}f(x)$$

provided $f(x)$ is continuous at x_0. We will use the impulse function when we deal with mixed random variables to indicate the finite probability mass of a discrete component at a specific value of the random variable.

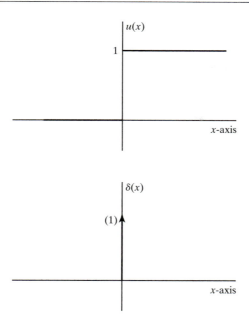

The unit step and unit impulse functions.

13. **Area.** Of course "area" can have any units. If x was distance in centimeters and y was weight in grams, then the units of area would be g-cm. In this case the PDF would have units of g^{-1}-cm^{-1}.

14. **Answer to you do it on p. 210.** The first step is to determine the PDF in the quarter circle. Being uniform, the PDF will be simply 1/area $= 4/\pi$, Now we integrate in the y-direction to integrate Y out of the distribution. Clearly, we will encounter probability only in the range $0 < x \leq 1$. In that range the integral will be simply the value of the PDF times the path length, which is $\sqrt{1 - x^2}$. Therefore the marginal PDF for X is $f_X(x) = \frac{4}{\pi}\sqrt{1 - x^2}$, $0 < x \leq 1$, zow. We require the value at $x = 0.5$, which is 1.103.

15. **Answer to you do it on p. 212.** The marginal PDF on X was given in Eq. (3.2.19), so the answer without any integration is $f_X(x) = \frac{1}{4}, 0 < x \leq 4$, zow. You can, of course, get it by integration, but you don't need to. Integration is required for the PDF on Y, however.

16. **Marginal PDF for Y.** The integration is the same as in Eq. (3.2.13), except we put in $1/2x$ for the PDF. Thus we get

$$f_Y(y) = \int_{x=2y}^{x=4} \frac{1}{2x} dx = \frac{1}{2} \ln\left(\frac{4}{2y}\right) = \frac{1}{2} \ln\left(\frac{2}{y}\right), \quad 0 < y \leq 2, \text{ zow}$$

17. **Normalization and plot of the marginal on Y.** Execute the following cell to check the normalization of the PDF, and execute the second cell to see a plot.

```
Integrate [0.5 Log[2/y], {y, 0, 2}]
1.
```

```
Plot[0.5 Log[2/y], {y, 0, 2},
   AxesLabel → {"y-axis", "f(y)"}];
```

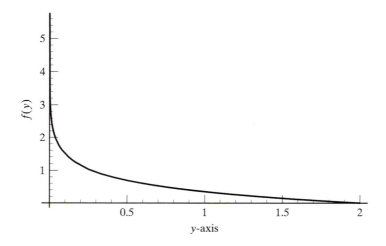

18. **Answer to you do it on p. 215.** The area looks like a sword blade, symmetric about the diagonal to the square. The area is best found by subtracting the corner triangles. The calculated probability is $\left(100^2 - 2 \times \frac{1}{2} \times 80^2\right) \times 10^{-4} = 0.360$.

19. **Answer to you do it on p. 216.** First, we need the conditional PDF. This is the same as before, except the probability is evenly distributed over the part of the space to the right of the diagonal. Since this is half the area, the PDF is 2×10^{-4}. The expectation calculation is very similar to the example, namely,

$$E[T_1 | T_1 > T_2] = \int_{t_1=-50}^{t_1=+50} \left[\int_{t_2=-50}^{t_2=t_1} t_1 \times 2 \times 10^{-4} \, dt_2 \right] dt_1 = 16.67$$

20. **Simulation of Example 3.2.6.** Begin by executing the following cell, and then execute all the cells in order.

```
<< Statistics`ContinuousDistributions`
```

The following generates 100 samples each of T_1 and T_2:

```
t1 = Table[Random[UniformDistribution[0, 2]], {100}];
t2 = Table[Random[UniformDistribution[0, 2]], {100}];
```

This cell plots the scatter diagram of the random numbers

```
cd = Table [{t1[[k]], t2[[k]]}, {k, 1, 100}];
ListPlot[cd, PlotRange → {{-1, +3}, {-1, +3}},
  PlotStyle → {PointSize[0.015]}, ImageSize → 400,
  AspectRatio → 1, AxesLabel → {"t1-axis", "t2-axis"}];
```

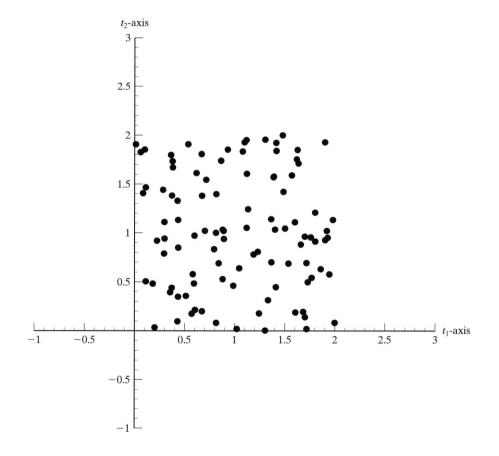

Note the square shape of the scatter diagram and the more or less uniform distribution of the dots. Now let us look at the CDF of the sum of the delay times:

```
Off[General::spell1]
t = Sort[t1 + t2];
h = Table[k/101, {k, 1, 100}];
cdf = Table[{t[[k]], h[[k]]}, {k, 1, 100}];
df = ListPlot[cdf, PlotRange → {{-1, +5}, {0, +1}},
    PlotStyle → {PointSize[0.01]},
    AxesLabel → {"t1-axis", "t2-axis"}];
```

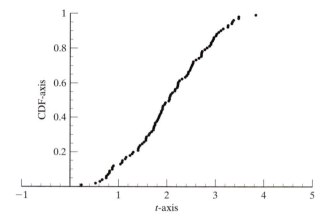

To see how this experimental CDF compares with the theoretical CDF, we reproduce Fig. 3.2.18 on the same scale:

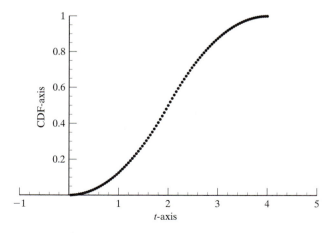

The mean and standard deviation of the sum are

```
<< Statistics`DescriptiveStatistics`
data = Table[t[[k]], {k, 1, 100}];
Mean[data]
StandardDeviation[data]
2.04426
0.797539
```

21. **Answer to you do it (a) on p. 221.** Equation (3.2.31) Requires that $F_{XY}(+\infty, +\infty) = 1$. The limit of the function given is $\pi c/2$. Thus $c = 2/\pi$.

22. **Answer to you do it (b) on p. 222.** The value of c is $\frac{2}{\pi}$. To find the marginal CDF for Y, we let $x \to \infty$ and obtain $F_Y(y) = \frac{2}{\pi}\tan^{-1}(\frac{y}{6})$. The derivative is $f_Y(y) = \frac{1}{3\pi}\frac{1}{1+(y/6)^2}$, which is 0.0955 at $y = 2$.

23. **Proof by induction.** That is, if it works for two, we can show it works for three, and so forth.

24. **Answer to you do it on p. 225.** For one random variable the mean is $\frac{1}{2}$ and the variance is $1/2^2$. These results come from Eqs. (3.1.24) and (3.1.26). When we use Eqs. (3.3.6) and (3.3.11) to find the mean and variance of D_5, we get 2.5 and 1.25, respectively. Then we use the relationship from the algebra of expectation as follows:

$$E[D_5^2] = \mu_{D_5}^2 + \sigma_{D_5}^2 = 2.5^2 + 1.25 = 7.5$$

25. **Random noise.** Measurement of a fluctuating signal in the presence of noise is also an important problem, which will be addressed in Chapter 6. Here we deal with the simpler case of a dc signal in the presence of noise.

26. **Answer to you do it on p. 229.** Because we are expecting the noise to be reduced by a factor of 20, we need 20^2 independent data measurements.

27. **Leibnitz's rule for differentiation of an integral.** Consider an integral of the form

$$f(\alpha) = \int_{g(\alpha)}^{h(\alpha)} i(x, \alpha)\, dx$$

Note that the integral involves α in three ways, in each of the limits and also as a parameter in the integrand. Leibnitz's rule for differentiation of this integral is

$$\frac{d}{d\alpha} f(\alpha) = i(h(\alpha), \alpha)\frac{d}{d\alpha}h(\alpha) - i(g(\alpha), \alpha)\frac{d}{d\alpha}g(\alpha) + \int_{g(\alpha)}^{h(\alpha)} \frac{d}{d\alpha}i(x, \alpha)\, dx$$

The three terms are (1) the integrand with the upper limit substituted for the variable of integration, times the derivative of the upper limit; (2) the same for the lower limit, but with a minus sign; and (3) the original integral with the derivative with respect to α taken inside the integral. The proof is straightforward and found in many math books.

28. **Answer to you do it on p. 231.** The convolution of $2\,e^{-2x}$, $x \geq 0$, zow, with itself is 0 for $z < 0$ and $4ze^{-2z}$ for positive z. At $z = 0.5$ the value is 0.7358.

29. **Convolution of something other than the uniform PDF.** We change the code to give a PDF that is uniform between 9.5 and 10.5, except that it has a hole between 9.8333 and 10.16667. Thus this is a strongly bimodal PDF. First we plot the PDF.

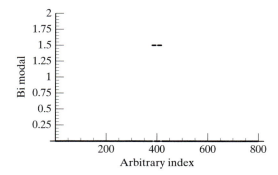

The convolution of this PDF with itself, shown in the following, consists of a large triangle adjoined by smaller "side-lobe" triangles.

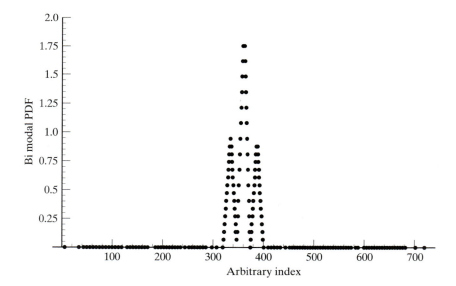

The plot is fairly rough, so let's convolve this with itself, to have the PDF of the sum of 4 IID random variables. The plot keeps looking fairly rough, so we continue the convolution process, to see the results for 4, 6, and 8 IID random variables, as follows.

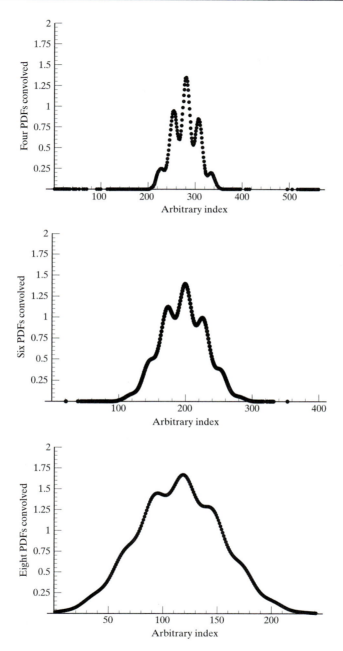

Although the plot still does not look great, the trend toward a bell-shaped curve is clear enough that we are ready to claim victory. The rough appearance occurs partly because of creeping numerical errors, and partly because this PDF is a tough one to tame.

30. **Normalize.** Here "normalize" has the sense of reducing to standard values and has nothing to do with the normal distribution.

31. In the following table you may determine $\Phi(z)$. For example, $\Phi(0.12) = 0.5478$. Note that the 0.00 column is repeated in the 0.100 column as an aid to interpolation.

The Gaussian CDF, $\Phi(z)$

z	0.00	0.01	0.02	0.03	0.04	0.05	0.06	0.07	0.08	0.09	0.10	z
0.0	0.5000	0.5040	0.508	0.5120	0.5160	0.5199	0.5239	0.5279	0.5319	0.5359	0.5398	0.0
0.1	0.5398	0.5438	0.5478	0.5517	0.5557	0.5596	0.5636	0.5675	0.5714	0.5753	0.5793	0.1
0.2	0.5793	0.5832	0.5871	0.5910	0.5948	0.5987	0.6026	0.6064	0.6103	0.6141	0.6179	0.2
0.3	0.6179	0.6217	0.6255	0.6293	0.6331	0.6368	0.6406	0.6443	0.6480	0.6517	0.6554	0.3
0.4	0.6554	0.6591	0.6628	0.6664	0.6700	0.6736	0.6772	0.6808	0.6844	0.6879	0.6915	0.4
0.5	0.6915	0.6950	0.6985	0.7019	0.7054	0.7088	0.7123	0.7157	0.7190	0.7224	0.7257	0.5
0.6	0.7257	0.7291	0.7324	0.7357	0.7389	0.7422	0.7454	0.7486	0.7517	0.7549	0.7580	0.6
0.7	0.7580	0.7611	0.7642	0.7673	0.7704	0.7734	0.7764	0.7794	0.7823	0.7852	0.7881	0.7
0.8	0.7881	0.7910	0.7939	0.7967	0.7995	0.8023	0.8051	0.8078	0.8106	0.8133	0.8159	0.8
0.9	0.8159	0.8186	0.8212	0.8238	0.8264	0.8289	0.8315	0.8340	0.8365	0.8389	0.8413	0.9
1.0	0.8413	0.8438	0.8461	0.8485	0.8508	0.8531	0.8554	0.8577	0.8599	0.8621	0.8643	1.0
1.1	0.8643	0.8665	0.8686	0.8708	0.8729	0.8749	0.8770	0.8790	0.8810	0.8830	0.8849	1.1
1.2	0.8849	0.8869	0.8888	0.8907	0.8925	0.8944	0.8962	0.8980	0.8997	0.9015	0.9032	1.2
1.3	0.9032	0.9049	0.9066	0.9082	0.9099	0.9115	0.9131	0.9147	0.9162	0.9177	0.9192	1.3
1.4	0.9192	0.9207	0.9222	0.9236	0.9251	0.9265	0.9279	0.9292	0.9306	0.9319	0.9332	1.4
1.5	0.9332	0.9345	0.9357	0.9370	0.9382	0.9394	0.9406	0.9418	0.9429	0.9441	0.9452	1.5
1.6	0.9452	0.9463	0.9474	0.9484	0.9495	0.9505	0.9515	0.9525	0.9535	0.9545	0.9554	1.6
1.7	0.9554	0.9564	0.9573	0.9582	0.9591	0.9599	0.9608	0.9616	0.9625	0.9633	0.9641	1.7
1.8	0.9641	0.9649	0.9656	0.9664	0.9671	0.9678	0.9686	0.9693	0.9699	0.9706	0.9713	1.8
1.9	0.9713	0.9719	0.9726	0.9732	0.9738	0.9744	0.9750	0.9756	0.9761	0.9767	0.9772	1.9
2.0	0.9772	0.9778	0.9783	0.9788	0.9793	0.9798	0.9803	0.9808	0.9812	0.9817	0.9821	2.0
2.1	0.9821	0.9826	0.9830	0.9834	0.9838	0.9842	0.9846	0.9850	0.9854	0.9857	0.9861	2.1
2.2	0.9861	0.9864	0.9868	0.9871	0.9875	0.9878	0.9881	0.9884	0.9887	0.9890	0.9893	2.2
2.3	0.9893	0.9896	0.9898	0.9901	0.9904	0.9906	0.9909	0.9911	0.9913	0.9916	0.9918	2.3
2.4	0.9918	0.9920	0.9922	0.9925	0.9927	0.9929	0.9931	0.9932	0.9934	0.9936	0.9938	2.4
2.5	0.9938	0.9940	0.9941	0.9943	0.9945	0.9946	0.9948	0.9949	0.9951	0.9952	0.9953	2.5
2.6	0.9953	0.9955	0.9956	0.9957	0.9959	0.9960	0.9961	0.9962	0.9963	0.9964	0.9965	2.6
2.7	0.9965	0.9966	0.9967	0.9968	0.9969	0.9970	0.9971	0.9972	0.9973	0.9974	0.9974	2.7
2.8	0.9974	0.9975	0.9976	0.9977	0.9977	0.9978	0.9979	0.9979	0.9980	0.9981	0.9981	2.8
2.9	0.9981	0.9982	0.9982	0.9983	0.9984	0.9984	0.9985	0.9985	0.9986	0.9986	0.9987	2.9
3.0	0.9987	0.9987	0.9987	0.9988	0.9988	0.9989	0.9989	0.9989	0.9990	0.9990	0.9990	3.0
3.1	0.9990	0.9991	0.9991	0.9991	0.9992	0.9992	0.9992	0.9992	0.9993	0.9993	0.9993	3.1
3.2	0.9993	0.9993	0.9994	0.9994	0.9994	0.9994	0.9994	0.9995	0.9995	0.9995	0.9995	3.2
3.3	0.9995	0.9995	0.9995	0.9996	0.9996	0.9996	0.9996	0.9996	0.9996	0.9997	0.9997	3.3
3.4	0.9997	0.9997	0.9997	0.9997	0.9997	0.9997	0.9997	0.9997	0.9997	0.9998	0.9998	3.4
3.5	0.9998	0.9998	0.9998	0.9998	0.9998	0.9998	0.9998	0.9998	0.9998	0.9998	0.9998	3.5
3.6	0.9998	0.9998	0.9999	0.9999	0.9999	0.9999	0.9999	0.9999	0.9999	0.9999	0.9999	3.6
3.7	0.9999	0.9999	0.9999	0.9999	0.9999	0.9999	0.9999	0.9999	0.9999	0.9999	0.9999	3.7
4.3	0.9999	0.9999	0.9999	0.9999	0.9999	0.9999	0.9999	0.9999	0.9999	0.9999	0.9999	4.3

32. **Answer to you do it on p. 241.** We must use the identity $\Phi(-z) = 1 - \Phi(z)$. Hence, $\Phi(-1.5) = 1 - \Phi(1.5) = 0.0668$.

33. **Answer to you do it on p. 245.** We require $P[0.495 < D \leq 0.502]$, which is $\Phi\left(\frac{0.502-0.498}{0.003}\right)$ $- \Phi\left(\frac{0.495-0.498}{0.003}\right) = \Phi(1.333) - \Phi(-1) = \Phi(1.333) + \Phi(+1) - 1 = 0.750$, as shown in the following cell:

```
CDF[NormalDistribution[0.498, 0.003], 0.502] -
  CDF[NormalDistribution[0.498, 0.003], 0.495]
0.750134
```

34. **Inverse Gaussian CDF table.** For example, $\Phi(0.0752) = 0.53$. Thus $\Phi^{-1}(0.53) = 0.0752$. For $p < 0.5$, use $-\Phi^{-1}(0.5 - p)$. (See the table on the next page.)

35. **Answer to you do it on p. 246.** We want the probability that $P[0.9\mu_R < R \leq 1.1\mu_R]$ with $R = N(1.03\mu_R, \sigma_R^2)$ and $\frac{\mu_R}{\sigma_R} = 16.95$. This works out to $\Phi(0.07 \times 16.95) - \Phi(-0.13 \times 16.95) = 0.868$, as shown in the following cell. Thus with this misadjustment, the yield drops from 91% to 86.9%.

```
CDF[NormalDistribution[0, 1], 1.187] -
  CDF[NormalDistribution[0, 1], -2.204]
0.868624
```

36. **Answer to you do it on p. 249.** This is the same calculation with n the unknown and the probability known. Using $+\infty$ for the upper limit, we require $\Phi\left(\frac{140.5-n\times0.95}{\sqrt{n\times0.95\times0.05}}\right) = 0.95$. This inverts to $\frac{140.5-n\times0.95}{\sqrt{n\times0.95\times0.05}} = \Phi^{-1}(0.95) = 1.645$, which is a quadratic equation in $\sqrt{n}$. The solution is $\sqrt{n} = +11.97$ and -12.35. The second root is unrealistic, but the first gives the number of tickets to be sold as $(11.97)^2 = 143.4 \rightarrow 143$. Again, we can check the exact probability for 141 or more as follows:

```
Remove [BinomialDistribution]
<< Statistics`DiscreteDistributions`
Sum[PDF[BinomialDistribution[143, 0.95], k], {k, 141, 143}]
0.023909
```

That certainly is within 5%. Let's try 144 to see how that works.

```
Sum[PDF[BinomialDistribution[144, 0.95], k], {k, 141, 144}]
0.0670242
```

Thus our solution is valid.

Inverse Gaussian CDF Function, $z = \Phi^{-1}(p)$

Z	0.000	0.001	0.002	0.003	0.004	0.005	0.006	0.007	0.008	0.009	Z
0.50	0.0000	0.0025	0.0050	0.0075	0.0100	0.0125	0.0150	0.0175	0.0200	0.0225	0.50
0.51	0.0250	0.0275	0.0300	0.0325	0.0351	0.0376	0.0401	0.0426	0.0451	0.0476	0.51
0.52	0.0501	0.0526	0.0551	0.0576	0.0602	0.0627	0.0652	0.0677	0.0702	0.0727	0.52
0.53	0.0752	0.0777	0.0803	0.0828	0.0853	0.0878	0.0903	0.0928	0.0954	0.0979	0.53
0.54	0.1004	0.1030	0.1055	0.1080	0.1105	0.1130	0.1156	0.1181	0.1206	0.1231	0.54
0.55	0.1257	0.1282	0.1307	0.1332	0.1358	0.1383	0.1408	0.1434	0.1459	0.1484	0.55
0.56	0.1510	0.1535	0.1560	0.1586	0.1611	0.1637	0.1662	0.1687	0.1713	0.1738	0.56
0.57	0.1764	0.1789	0.1815	0.1840	0.1866	0.1891	0.1917	0.1942	0.1968	0.1993	0.57
0.58	0.2019	0.2045	0.2070	0.2096	0.2121	0.2147	0.2173	0.2198	0.2224	0.2250	0.58
0.59	0.2275	0.2301	0.2327	0.2353	0.2378	0.2404	0.2430	0.2456	0.2482	0.2508	0.59
0.60	0.2533	0.2559	0.2585	0.2611	0.2637	0.2663	0.2689	0.2715	0.2741	0.2767	0.60
0.61	0.2793	0.2819	0.2845	0.2871	0.2898	0.2924	0.2950	0.2976	0.3002	0.3029	0.61
0.62	0.3055	0.3081	0.3107	0.3134	0.3160	0.3186	0.3213	0.3239	0.3266	0.3292	0.62
0.63	0.3319	0.3345	0.3372	0.3398	0.3425	0.3451	0.3478	0.3505	0.3531	0.3558	0.63
0.64	0.3585	0.3611	0.3638	0.3665	0.3692	0.3719	0.3745	0.3772	0.3799	0.3826	0.64
0.65	0.3853	0.3880	0.3907	0.3934	0.3961	0.3989	0.4016	0.4043	0.4070	0.4097	0.65
0.66	0.4125	0.4152	0.4179	0.4207	0.4234	0.4261	0.4289	0.4316	0.4344	0.4372	0.66
0.67	0.4399	0.4427	0.4454	0.4482	0.4510	0.4538	0.4565	0.4593	0.4621	0.4649	0.67
0.68	0.4677	0.4705	0.4733	0.4761	0.4789	0.4817	0.4845	0.4874	0.4902	0.4930	0.68
0.69	0.4959	0.4987	0.5015	0.5044	0.5072	0.5101	0.5129	0.5158	0.5187	0.5215	0.69
0.70	0.5244	0.5273	0.5302	0.5330	0.5359	0.5388	0.5417	0.5446	0.5476	0.5505	0.70
0.71	0.5534	0.5563	0.5592	0.5622	0.5651	0.5681	0.5710	0.5740	0.5769	0.5799	0.71
0.72	0.5828	0.5858	0.5888	0.5918	0.5948	0.5978	0.6008	0.6038	0.6068	0.6098	0.72
0.73	0.6128	0.6158	0.6189	0.6219	0.6250	0.6280	0.6311	0.6341	0.6372	0.6403	0.73
0.74	0.6433	0.6464	0.6495	0.6526	0.6557	0.6588	0.6620	0.6651	0.6682	0.6713	0.74
0.75	0.6745	0.6776	0.6808	0.6840	0.6871	0.6903	0.6935	0.6967	0.6999	0.7031	0.75
0.76	0.7063	0.7095	0.7128	0.7160	0.7192	0.7225	0.7257	0.7290	0.7323	0.7356	0.76
0.77	0.7388	0.7421	0.7454	0.7488	0.7521	0.7554	0.7588	0.7621	0.7655	0.7688	0.77
0.78	0.7722	0.7756	0.7790	0.7824	0.7858	0.7892	0.7926	0.7961	0.7995	0.8030	0.78
0.79	0.8064	0.8099	0.8134	0.8169	0.8204	0.8239	0.8274	0.8310	0.8345	0.8381	0.79
0.80	0.8416	0.8452	0.8488	0.8524	0.8560	0.8596	0.8633	0.8669	0.8705	0.8742	0.80
0.81	0.8779	0.8816	0.8853	0.8890	0.8927	0.8965	0.9002	0.9040	0.9078	0.9116	0.81
0.82	0.9154	0.9192	0.9230	0.9269	0.9307	0.9346	0.9385	0.9424	0.9463	0.9502	0.82
0.83	0.9542	0.9581	0.9621	0.9661	0.9701	0.9741	0.9782	0.9822	0.9863	0.9904	0.83
0.84	0.9945	0.9986	1.0030	1.0070	1.0110	1.0150	1.0190	1.0240	1.0280	1.0320	0.84
0.85	1.0360	1.0410	1.0450	1.0490	1.0540	1.0580	1.0630	1.0670	1.0710	1.0760	0.85
0.86	1.0800	1.0850	1.0890	1.0940	1.0980	1.1030	1.1080	1.1120	1.1170	1.1220	0.86
0.87	1.1260	1.1310	1.1360	1.1410	1.1460	1.1500	1.1550	1.1600	1.1650	1.1700	0.87
0.88	1.1750	1.1800	1.1850	1.1900	1.1950	1.2000	1.2060	1.2110	1.2160	1.2210	0.88
0.89	1.2270	1.2320	1.2370	1.2430	1.2480	1.2540	1.2590	1.2650	1.2700	1.2760	0.89
0.90	1.2820	1.2870	1.2930	1.2990	1.3050	1.3110	1.3170	1.3230	1.3290	1.3350	0.90
0.91	1.3410	1.3470	1.3530	1.3590	1.3660	1.3720	1.3790	1.3850	1.3920	1.3980	0.91
0.92	1.4050	1.4120	1.4190	1.4260	1.4330	1.4400	1.4470	1.4540	1.4610	1.4680	0.92
0.93	1.4760	1.4830	1.4910	1.4990	1.5060	1.5140	1.5220	1.5300	1.5380	1.5460	0.93
0.94	1.5550	1.5630	1.5720	1.5800	1.5890	1.5980	1.6070	1.6160	1.6260	1.6350	0.94
0.95	1.6450	1.6550	1.6650	1.6750	1.6850	1.6950	1.7060	1.7170	1.7280	1.7390	0.95
0.96	1.7510	1.7620	1.7740	1.7870	1.7990	1.8120	1.8250	1.8380	1.8520	1.8660	0.96
0.97	1.8810	1.8960	1.9110	1.9270	1.9430	1.9600	1.9770	1.9950	2.0140	2.0340	0.97
0.98	2.0540	2.0750	2.0970	2.1200	2.1440	2.1700	2.1970	2.2260	2.2570	2.2900	0.98
0.99	2.3260	2.3660	2.4090	2.4570	2.5120	2.5760	2.6520	2.7480	2.8780	3.0900	0.99

37. **Answer to you do it on p. 251.** Actually, here we subtract, so the means subtract; but the variances add, since $Var[-X] = (-1)^2 Var[X]$. This means that $Y = N(0, 2)$, and $P[Y \leq 1] = \Phi\left(\frac{1-0}{\sqrt{2}}\right) = 0.7794$.

38. **The Pythagorean sum.** The Pythagorean sum is the square root of the sum of the squares. For example, the Pythagorean sum of 1, 2 and 3 is $\sqrt{1^2 + 2^2 + 3^2} = 3.74$.

39. **Error analysis.** Error analysis can be contentious because product acceptance, with attached pride and profit, often rides on error analysis and measurements. These matters sometimes end up in court.

40. **Answer to you do it on p. 255.** The errors in X and Y add absolutely, so $X + Y = N(2 + 5, 0.2^2 + 0.5^2) = N(7, 0.5385^2)$. Thus the normalized error in the sum is $\frac{0.5385}{7} = 7.693\%$. In the multiplication, the percent errors will add in a Pythagorean sense, so the final answer is $\sqrt{10^2 + 7.693^2} = 12.63\%$.

41. **Answer to you do it on p. 259.** We asked for a conditional probability. If there were no condition, then the problem would simply consist of using $r_0/3$ instead of $r_0/2$ in (3.5.10). That would make the answer 0.1637. But the effect of the condition is to divide by the probability of hitting the target, which is 0.8, so the correct answer is 0.2047.

42. **The relationship between correlation and the bivariate Gaussian distribution.** The existence of correlation does not depend on the Gaussian assumption. The bivariate Gaussian is merely a convenient distribution to use to demonstrate the concept. There is, however, a special relationship between correlation and the bivariate Gaussian, which is explained later in this section.

43. **Answer to you do it on p. 264.** The mean and variance of Y are given. The mean of Z is 5, and the variance of 3. The correlation is 17, and the covariance is 2. Thus the correlation coefficient is $\frac{2}{\sqrt{2} \times \sqrt{3}} = 0.8165$.

4

Statistics

4.1 ESTIMATION

4.1.1 What Is Statistics?

Statistics is the art of extracting information from numbers. The beginning point for a statistical study is a set of data, which is to say, some numbers. The word *statistics* is derived from "state," because it was the early European states that began to collect and analyze data on their populations. Of course, early insurance ventures were interested in such facts as mortality information, but much of the early work was done in analyzing scientific measurements, especially in astronomy and what we would call geophysics, and of course games of chance.

Statistics is a major enterprise. Many universities have a department of statistics, separate from the department of mathematics, and award the Ph.D. degree in statistics. Medium and large companies, technical and otherwise, have statisticians on staff, and a basic knowledge of statistics is an accreditation requirement for engineering programs.

Statistics and probability. Many statistical methods do not rely on probability theory. Descriptive statistical techniques involve displaying data and extracting information in ways that are traditional, based on common sense and experience. For example, one needs no knowledge of probability to calculate the average of a series of samples or fit a regression line to a set of data.

In contrast, statistical reasoning based on probability models brings strength to analytical and predictive methods. Thus one makes assumptions about the data source that allow such extensions to be made, and the more one wants to assert, the more one must assume, as we will see.

Looking ahead.   In this chapter we study statistical techniques that relate to data analysis and model testing. It is hoped that engineers will be able to perform basic statistical analysis and know when to call in a trained statistician to consult on more difficult problems. In Sec. 4.1 we study the following problems:

1. Deriving estimators
2. Making spot and range estimation of the mean and variance of a data set, under various conditions

In Sec. 4.2 we study statistical techniques for

1. Performing linear regression under several conditions.
2. Fitting a model to a data set.

In Section 4.3 we introduce basic hypothesis testing concepts. First, we examine a probability model for a set of data.

4.1.2 Data and the Probability Paradigm

Consider that we have a data set such as 24, 69, 67, 45, 17, 60, 76, 28, 15, 15, 65, 67, 19, 23, 12, 90, 78, 94, and 80. These we represent by $x_1, x_2, \ldots, x_n$, where in this case $n = 19$. Let us say we want to determine, as best we can, the mean of these numbers. Of course, this is trivial, as we merely average the numbers, obtaining a result of 49.68. But what if we took another set of data from the same source? Presumably, the second data set would be different from the first and have a different mean. In fact, the following cell generates random numbers and calculates the mean.[1] Execute the cell a few times and you will see that we need to do more than average the data set to determine what we might call the "true mean."

```
Off[General::spell1]
n = 19;
data =
 Table [Floor[Random[UniformDistribution[0, 100]]], {n}]
mean = Sum[data[[i]], {i, 1, n}]/n
N[%]
{24, 69, 67, 45, 17, 60, 76, 28, 15,
 15, 65, 67, 19, 23, 12, 90, 78, 94, 80}
```

$$\frac{944}{19}$$

```
49.6842
```

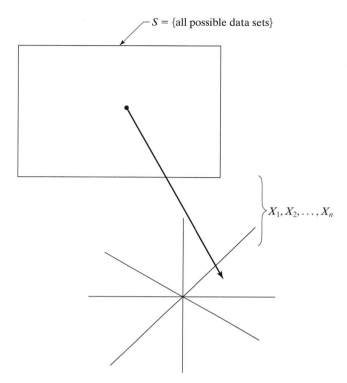

Figure 4.1.1 The chance experiment relating to measuring a data set. The outcomes of the experiment produce all the data sets that might result, which thus become n IID random variables, $X_1, X_2, \ldots, X_n$. The four axes suggest the n-dimensional space.

The probability paradigm. Our probability paradigm is based on a chance experiment with well-defined outcomes and one or more random variables assigned to those outcomes. The preceding cell is a random experiment producing n numerical data values. We may associate the data set with one outcome having n IID random variables defined on that outcome. Thus the chance experiment is to take a data set—one outcome of the experiment results in the data set at hand—and the n IID random variables are the collection of all possible data sets that could have resulted. This is the viewpoint we introduced in Sec. 3.3 on IID random variables in a measurement scenario, to introduce one context (Fig. 3.3.2) in which IID random variables might appear.

Two illustrations will help you understand this point of view. Figure 4.1.1 shows the chance experiment with the n IID random variables symbolized. One outcome maps into a point in n-dimensional space, a data set. The outcomes of the chance experiment produce all possible data sets with their associated probabilities.

The second illustration would be the PDF of the IID random variables. Figure 4.1.2 shows a generic PDF with the mean and standard deviation indicated. These values *define* the meaning of the true mean and true variance (and standard deviation). The PDF is in principle unknowable; we

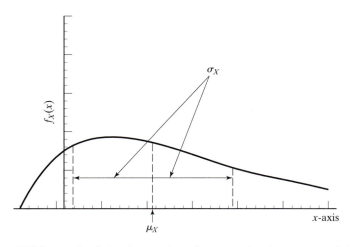

Figure 4.1.2 The PDF for each of the data points. Because the data are modeled as IID random variables, they all have the same PDF (second *I*). The true mean and the true standard deviation are indicated on the PDF. These values define the true mean and standard deviation for the data source. Because the data are real, and the PDF is a model, we can never determine the PDF. We suppose it exists, which is another way of saying that we suppose that the data source is stable in a statistical sense.

suppose that it exists. The PDF is required to exist for our probability model for the data source to have meaning, because we suppose there to be a stable source for the data. That is what we mean by a *repeatable* chance experiment.

The Big Three. We now can present three closely related concepts related to estimation, which we call the Big Three. For the *mean* these are

$$\mu_X = \text{the ``true mean,'' an unknowable number} \tag{4.1.1}$$

$$\bar{x} = \frac{1}{n}(x_1 + x_2 + \cdots + x_n), \text{the ``sample mean''} \tag{4.1.2}$$

This is the simple average of the data set, a known number. The sample mean (the number) is an estimator of the true mean, and its application (the formula for calculating the number) to a data set produces an estimate of the true mean. The estimate is a *statistic* of the data set. Thus an estimator is an algorithm for generating one or more numbers from the data set. The third of the Big Three is

$$\hat{X} = \frac{1}{n}(X_1 + X_2 + \cdots + X_n), \text{the ``estimator model''} \tag{4.1.3}$$

The estimator model is a random variable generated from the IID random variables that generalize the data set. The formula for the estimator model must be identical with the formula of the estimator. The estimator model is a random variable assigned to the outcomes of the chance experiment, calculated from the IID random variables modeling the data set.

The Big Three exist for other aspects of the data set as well. For example, there exists a true variance, a sample variance, and an estimator model for the sample variance. These distinctions, and the associated vocabulary, should clarify our description of the estimation process.

The estimation process.   Assume we want to estimate something about a data source, like its true mean. By some means, such as common sense, we derive an estimator for that parameter. We take data and apply our estimator. We then consider the estimator model and perform probability operations to determine the properties of the estimator model. These properties are then attributed to the estimator. We can say, for example, that the estimator is unbiased. We can say also that the true value lies within a range. We now carry forth this process for the sample mean.

4.1.3 Estimation of the Mean When the Variance Is Known

The problem stated.   Assume we have a data set and we want to estimate the true mean of the source of the data set. Assume further that we know the variance (or standard deviation) of the source of the data set. This second assumption is unrealistic in practice. We deal with this case to illustrate the estimation process. Later we will deal with more realistic estimation methods.

Our data set is $x_1, x_2, \ldots, x_n$. The Big Three are described in Eqs. (4.1.1), (4.1.2), and (4.1.3). We proceed to investigate the properties of the estimator, the sample mean.

The expectation of $\hat{X}$.   Recalling that our probability model for averaging is expectation, we take the expectation of the estimator model in Eq. (4.1.3):

$$E[\hat{X}] = E\left[\frac{1}{n}(X_1 + X_2 + \cdots + X_n)\right] = \frac{1}{n}[E[X_1] + E[X_2] + \cdots + E[X_n]] \qquad (4.1.4)$$

Because we are dealing with IID random variables, all the means are the same and are the true mean: $E[X_i] = \mu_X, i = 1, 2, \ldots, n$. Thus Eq. (4.1.4) becomes

$$E[\hat{X}] = \mu_X \qquad (4.1.5)$$

which indicates that the estimator is unbiased. Here "unbiased" means that the estimate tends to be neither too high nor too low, which is a good property for an estimator to have.

The variance of $\hat{X}$.   The variance gives a measure of the variability or "scatter" of a random variable. The variance of the estimator model is

$$Var[\hat{X}] = Var\left[\frac{1}{n}(X_1 + X_2 + \cdots + X_n)\right] = \left(\frac{1}{n}\right)^2 [Var[X_1] + Var[X_2] + \cdots + Var[X_n]]$$

$$(4.1.6)$$

Because we are dealing with IID random variables, the first I allows us to distribute the variance, as shown in Eq. (2.3.53) in Chapter 2, and the second I gives the same variance for all, $Var[X_i] = \sigma_X^2$, which we will call *the variance of the data*. This is the variance of the PDF of the data points shown in Fig. 4.1.2. Thus Eq. (4.1.6) reduces to

$$Var[\hat{X}] = \sigma_{\hat{X}}^2 = \frac{\sigma_X^2}{n} \qquad (4.1.7)$$

Thus the variance of the sample mean is the variance of the data divided by n. We derived this relationship in Chapter 3 in a similar context and noted there, [Eq. (3.3.17)], the benefits of averaging redundant data. The same applies here, but in this context we are also interested in the limit of the variance of our estimator as $n \to \infty$. We note that the variance of the estimator vanishes as the number of data points in the set increases without limit.

$$\lim_{n \to \infty} \sigma_{\hat{X}}^2 \to 0 \tag{4.1.8}$$

We have shown two properties of the estimator: that it is unbiased and that its variance vanishes as the data set becomes infinite. These properties that we have investigated using the estimator model are attributed to the estimator (the sample mean) and show that the estimator is *consistent*. Taken together, Eqs. (4.1.5) and (4.1.8) indicate that as the size of the data set increases, the sample mean approaches the true value, which is of course what we want.

You will note that this approach generally is to investigate the properties of the estimator model and then attribute these to the estimator, with an appropriate change in vocabulary. This approach is justified by the mental experiment of repeating the data gathering and estimation process a large number of times (in our minds, not actually) and then averaging the estimates, which is what "expectation" models. If this average of the estimates tends toward the true value with increasing accuracy, then we say that estimation based on the first (actually, the one and only) data set is unbiased.

Spot and range estimation of the mean.   The sample mean is a *spot* or *point* estimator of the true mean, meaning that it gives one value but makes no claim as to the accuracy of the estimate. *Range* estimation extends the estimation process to give a range and an associated level of confidence, which is like a probability. We might distinguish the two types of estimates in a situation where a pilot is aiming a bomb at a target. If you are the pilot, you want a spot estimate to tell you when to release the bomb. If you are the target, you want a range estimate to tell you the probability that you will survive. We now develop a range estimate of the mean.

An additional assumption.   To make a range estimate we need to assume that we know the PDF of the estimator model. We will assume that the estimator model is a normal, or Gaussian, random variable, i.e., $\hat{X} = N\left(\mu_X, \frac{\sigma_{\hat{X}}^2}{n}\right)$, where we have used the results of Eqs. (4.1.5) and (4.1.7). What support do we have for this additional assumption? We have two possible answers:

1. The data might be Gaussian. This means that the PDF of the IID random variables modeling the data, shown generically in Fig. 4.1.2, would be a bell-shaped Gaussian PDF. We might know this from experience, from knowledge of the complexity of the physical origin of the data, or from a reasonable statistical test applied to the data. We will develop such a test in Sec. 4.2.
2. The central limit theorem suggests that the PDF of the sum (and average) of a "large" number of random variables tends toward the Gaussian. How "large" depends on the nature of the individual data points, so here judgment is required; but we have seen that random variables with reasonably symmetric PDFs approach a bell-shaped PDF when modest numbers are averaged.

Trade-offs.   Here we might point out the trade-off between the information extracted from a statistical analysis and the risk involved by adding assumptions. If we have a simple data set, we can take the average and be done with the problem. If we want to make some claims about the validity of this procedure, we assume a stable data source, generalize the data as IID random variables, and show that the average, the sample mean, is a consistent estimator. If we want to make stronger statements about the accuracy of the estimate with a range estimation, we must make an additional assumption. In general, the stronger the statements we want to make, the more these statements become vulnerable to the assumptions. As *producers* of statistical analyses we must be aware of these assumptions and cautious of their validity. As *consumers* of the statistical claims of others we must be ready to examine the assumptions underlying any proffered statistical analysis.

The PDF.   We now continue our development of a range estimation of the true mean. The PDF of the estimator model is therefore assumed to be

$$f_{\hat{X}}(x) = \frac{1}{(\sigma_X/\sqrt{n})\sqrt{2\pi}} \exp\left[-\frac{1}{2}\left(\frac{x - \mu_X}{\sigma_X/\sqrt{n}}\right)^2\right] \tag{4.1.9}$$

We may normalize the estimator model by subtracting its mean and dividing by its standard deviation:

$$Z = \frac{\hat{X} - \mu_X}{\sigma_X/\sqrt{n}} = N(0, 1) \tag{4.1.10}$$

Figure 4.1.3 shows the PDF of Z, marked with $1 - \alpha$ in the central region and $\frac{\alpha}{2}$ in each tail of the distribution. The values of z associated with these tail probabilities we will call z_c and $-z_c$.

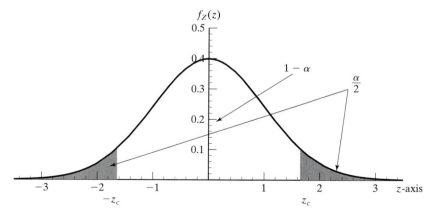

Figure 4.1.3   The normalized Gaussian PDF, with α divided between the tails, and $1 - \alpha$ in the central region. For purposes of this plot, we put 5% in each of the tails and 90% in the middle. For $\alpha = 10\%$, $z_c = 1.645$.

From the fundamental property of a PDF, [Eq. (3.1.4)], it follows that

$$P[-z_c < Z \le z_c] = 1 - \alpha \qquad (4.1.11)$$

Formally, the values of z_c come from the following equations:

$$\Phi(z_c) = 1 - \frac{\alpha}{2} \quad \text{and} \quad \Phi(-z_c) = \frac{\alpha}{2} \qquad (4.1.12)$$

When we substitute Eq. (4.1.10) into Eq. (4.1.11), we have the following probability statement:

$$P\left[-z_c < \frac{\hat{X} - \mu_X}{\sigma_X/\sqrt{n}} < +z_c\right] = 1 - \alpha \qquad (4.1.13)$$

Let us review the nature and origin of the various terms in Eq. (4.1.13). We are free to specify $1 - \alpha$ to give a certain probability, or "confidence," to our range estimate of the mean. From $1 - \alpha$, we look up z_c in an inverse Φ table [see endnote 34 in Chapter 3]. For example, for 90% confidence, we look up $\Phi^{-1}\left(1 - \frac{\alpha}{2}\right) = \Phi^{-1}(0.95)$ and find $z_c = 1.6450$. We know σ_X, the standard deviation of the data (this is the unrealistic assumption), and n, the number of data values. The estimator model, $\hat{X}$, is a random variable about which we are making the probability statement, and μ_X is the unknown mean for which we are deriving a range estimate.

We now manipulate the inequality within the probability statement to convert it into a statement about the unknown mean, μ_X. First, we multiply through by the term in the denominator. Because this term must be positive, the inequalities are unaffected:

$$-z_c \frac{\sigma_X}{\sqrt{n}} < \hat{X} - \mu_X < z_c \frac{\sigma_X}{\sqrt{n}} \qquad (4.1.14)$$

Next, we negate every term, which changes all signs and reverses all inequalities:

$$+z_c \frac{\sigma_X}{\sqrt{n}} > \mu_X - \hat{X} > -z_c \frac{\sigma_X}{\sqrt{n}} \qquad (4.1.15)$$

Finally, we add $\hat{X}$ to all terms, transpose the expression, so that the lower limit is on the left and the upper limit is on the right, and place the probability statement around the results. Thus we have transformed Eq. (4.1.13) into

$$P\left[\hat{X} - z_c \frac{\sigma_X}{\sqrt{n}} < \mu_X < \hat{X} + z_c \frac{\sigma_X}{\sqrt{n}}\right] = 1 - \alpha \qquad (4.1.16)$$

Equation (4.1.16) brackets the unknown mean between a lower limit and an upper limit and assigns a probability of $1 - \alpha$ to the result. Notice that the lower and upper limits are random variables because they include the estimator model, $\hat{X}$.

The interpretation of Eq. (4.1.16).   Recall that we have a data set whose average is the sample mean, $\bar{x}$. The estimator model, $\hat{X}$, represents the average for every possible data set that can result from this source. We replace the estimator model in Eq. (4.1.16) by the sample mean for our particular data set, to obtain an inequality of the form

$$\bar{x} - z_c \frac{\sigma_X}{\sqrt{n}} < \mu_X < \bar{x} + z_c \frac{\sigma_X}{\sqrt{n}} \text{ with a level of confidence } 1 - \alpha \qquad (4.1.17)$$

Equation (4.1.17) gives a range estimate for the unknown mean. Its interpretation follows from the possibility that we could take additional data sets and have for them other values of $\bar{x}$. The probability in Eq. (4.1.16) states that the true mean, μ_X, will fall within the range given by Eq. (4.1.17) with probability $1 - \alpha$. For example, for $1 - \alpha = 90\%$, the true mean will fall in the range 9 times out of 10. Of course, we must know the standard deviation of the data, σ_X, to evaluate the range in Eq. (4.1.17), which is the weak link in this analysis.

Example 4.1.1: Equation (4.1.17) in practice

We will generate random numbers that are uniformly distributed between 0 and 1. Of course, the true mean is 0.5, and the true standard deviation is $\frac{1}{\sqrt{12}} = 0.2887$. You may review the properties of the uniform distribution (Sec. 3.1.4) if you wish. In this example we use our knowledge of the standard deviation but not the mean, except as a check. The code follows to generate the numbers, calculate the sample mean, make the range estimate for a level of confidence $= 90\%$, and test it against the true mean. We begin with $n = 100$, but you can change n if you wish. You are invited to evaluate the cell many times and see if the true mean, 0.5, falls within the lower and upper limits. According to theory, 1 time out of 10 the range should not bracket the true mean. In the following cell, the first output is the sample mean, the second is the lower limit, the third is the upper limit, and the final output checks the lower and upper limits against the true mean, 0.5.

```
n = 100;
TrueMean = 0.5;
TrueStanDev = 1/√12;
zc = 1.645;
data = Table[Random[], {n}];
SampleMean = Sum[data[[i]], {i, 1, n}]/n
LowerLimit = SampleMean - zc * TrueStanDev/√n
UpperLimit = SampleMean + zc * TrueStandDev/√n
If[LowerLimit > TrueMean,
  StylePrint["The true mean is outside the range." "Text"],
  If[UpperLimit < TrueMean, StylePrint[
    "The true mean is outside the range.", "Text"],
  StylePrint["The true mean is within the range.", "Text"]]]
0.524697
0.47721
0.572185
```

The true mean is within the range.

Another way you can learn from the calculations in the preceding cell is to change the value of n to work with larger or smaller data sets. Changing n will not affect the frequency with which the true mean falls outside the limits, but it will change the range of the estimate.

Summary.   In this section we introduced and demonstrated methods of estimation. We investigated the sample mean as a spot estimator and developed a range estimate, assuming that the standard deviation of the data source is known. Although this assumption is not realistic, it leads to a process that well illustrates the methods of estimation. We will address more realistic techniques after we show how to derive estimators.

4.1.4 Deriving Estimators

Although we have illustrated how to evaluate an estimator to see if it is biased and consistent, we have not shown how to derive an estimator. In this section we give three methods for developing estimators. The first is ad hoc, based on common sense, and the second and third are objective and optimum, although still subject to assumption. In Sec. 4.2 we show yet another method.

The sample mean.   The estimator we have worked with to this point was the sample mean, which is an estimator of the true mean. This is simply the average of the data values. How might we "derive" this estimator? Here we give a heuristic method. Then we use maximum likelihood estimation and follow with a method that uses least squares as an error measure.

Let us recall two basic facts: (1) the definition of the mean,

$$\mu_X = E[X] \tag{4.1.18}$$

and (2) that expectation is our method for averaging. We therefore replace the mean in Eq. (4.1.18) with the estimator, the expectation operation by the average, and the random variable by the data values, and we obtain the definition for the sample mean:

$$\mu_X \to \overline{x}, \ E \to \frac{1}{n}\sum \ \text{and} \ X \to x_i \ \Rightarrow \ \overline{x} = \frac{1}{n}\sum_1^n x_i \tag{4.1.19}$$

We will use this approach later to derive an estimator for the variance. Note that we do not have to assume any model for the data.

Maximum likelihood estimation

Maximum likelihood estimation is an objective, optimum mathematical method for estimation. To use this method, however, we must assume that we know the form of the random variable representing the data, that it is Gaussian, Rayleigh, binomial, or some other known PDF. Having made that assumption, we can derive an estimation for some parameter in the distribution using the maximum likelihood method. We illustrate with one discrete and one continuous distribution and then list results for other distributions.

A Bernoulli process.   We illustrate with the simplest possible discrete random variable, the Bernoulli random variable (see Fig. 2.2.6). In this case the data are binary, either 0 or 1, with

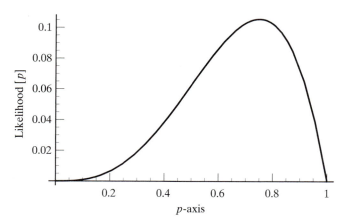

Figure 4.1.4 The likelihood function in Eq. (4.1.20) plotted to show that a maximum was derived.

$P[X = 1] = p$, and $P[X = 0] = q = 1 - p$. Let us say we gather four independent data values, $x_1 = 1, x_2 = 0, x_3 = 1$, and $x_4 = 1$. We will determine p to make this the most likely data set that can result. Replacing the data values with IID random variables, we write the probability of this event to be

$$P[X_1 = 1 \cap X_2 = 0 \cap X_3 = 1 \cap X_4 = 1] = p \times (1 - p) \times p \times p = p^3(1 - p)^1 \qquad (4.1.20)$$

Note that we changed the $\cap$ to $\times$ (first I) and used $P[X = 1] = p$ and $P[X = 0] = 1 - p$. Equation (4.1.20) is called the *likelihood function*. We want to find the value of p that maximizes the likelihood function. This we do by setting to zero the derivative with respect to p:

$$\frac{d}{dp} p^3(1 - p)^1 = 3p^2(1 - p) + p^3(-1) = 0 \implies \overline{p} = \frac{3}{4} \qquad (4.1.21)$$

which is certainly a reasonable estimate. We can show that we have a maximum and not a minimum by plotting the likelihood function against p, as in Fig. 4.1.4.

Note that we changed the notation in Eq. (4.1.21) from p to $\overline{p}$ because the optimum p is our estimate of the probability of a 1. In summary, with three successes out of four trials, our maximum likelihood estimate of the probability of success, p, is $\overline{p} = \frac{3}{4}$. This is not mere common sense but the result of an optimization process.

You do it.   Now, you derive the general formula for n data points, with k ones and $n - k$ zeros. Write the likelihood function, set its derivative to zero, and solve for the estimator for p. Enter your results in the cell box, and click Evaluate for a response. Format fractions in the form "3/4."

```
myanswer = "?"                    ;
```

Evaluate

For the answer, see endnote 2.

A continuous distribution.   We now illustrate the maximum likelihood technique for a Rayleigh random variable. In Sec. 3.5 we derived the PDF of the Rayleigh random variable as

$$f_R(r) = \frac{r}{\sigma^2} e^{-\frac{1}{2}\left(\frac{r}{\sigma}\right)^2}, r \geq 0, \text{ zow} \tag{4.1.22}$$

where σ^2 is the variance of the underlying Gaussian random variables. For the optimization process a convenient form of the Rayleigh is

$$f_R(r) = \frac{2r}{b} e^{-\frac{r^2}{b}}, r \geq 0, \text{ zow} \tag{4.1.23}$$

where $b = 2\sigma^2$. We assume that we take values of r from a source that we know, or suppose, to be Rayleigh distributed, call them $r_i, i = 1, 2, \ldots, n$. We want to derive an estimator for b based on these data. As before, we replace the data set with IID random variables, $R_i, i = 1, 2, \ldots, n$. We imagine a multivariate PDF for all the random variables and evaluate it at the values of the data. Because we assume independent data, the joint PDF (likelihood function) is

$$L(b) = f_{R_1 \ldots R_n}(r_1, \ldots, r_n) = \frac{2r_1}{b} e^{-\frac{r_1^2}{b}} \times \frac{2r_2}{b} e^{-\frac{r_2^2}{b}} \times \cdots \times \frac{2r_n}{b} e^{-\frac{r_n^2}{b}} \tag{4.1.24}$$

As you can see in Eq. (4.1.24), we evaluated the likelihood function at the point corresponding to the data values. We now maximize Eq. (4.1.24) with respect to b to obtain $\bar{b}$, our estimator of the true b. The calculus is easier if we work with the natural log of $L(b)$, which is

$$\ln[L(b)] = \ln\left(\frac{2^n}{b^n} r_1 r_2 \ldots r_n \exp\left[-\frac{1}{b}(r_1^2 + r_2^2 + \cdots + r_n^2)\right]\right)$$

$$= n \ln[2] - n \ln[b] + \ln(r_1 r_2 \ldots r_n) - \frac{1}{b}(r_1^2 + r_2^2 + \cdots + r_n^2) \tag{4.1.25}$$

The derivative of $\ln[L(b)]$ is zero at the same point as the derivative of $L(b)$, so we set the derivative of Eq. (4.1.25) to zero:

$$\frac{d}{db} \ln[L(b)] = 0 - \frac{n}{b} + 0 + \frac{1}{b^2}(r_1^2 + r_2^2 + \cdots + r_n^2) = 0 \Rightarrow \bar{b} = \frac{1}{n}(r_1^2 + r_2^2 + \cdots + r_n^2) \tag{4.1.26}$$

Our estimator of the value of b is the average of the sum of the squares of the data values, or the mean square value of the data set. It can be shown that this is an unbiased estimator.

Example 4.1.2:   Simulation _____

Let's test the success of this result with a simulated data set. In the following cell we generate n data values of a Rayleigh random variable with a known value of $b = 3$, and then use Eq. (4.1.26) to "estimate" b. Execute the cell a few times to see the results.

```
n = 100;
b = 3;
sigma = √(b/2);
data = Table[Random[RayleighDistribution[sigma]], {n}];
bestimate = Sum [data[[i]]², {i, 1, n}]/n
2.96114
```

As you can see, with 100 data points, the results vary quite a bit. Increasing n will reduce the scatter, if you wish to experiment, but on the whole you have to agree that the technique works.

The estimate, however, is vulnerable to the Rayleigh assumption. If, for example, the data are exponential, the prediction is nonsense. In the following cell we use the Rayleigh estimator with a data set generated with an exponential distribution.

```
n = 100;
b = 3;
sigma = √(b/2);
data =
   Table[Random[ExponentialDistribution[sigma]], {n}];
bestimate = Sum [data[[i]]², {i, 1, n}]/n
1.42198
```

Of course, it does predict something, but nothing relative to a Rayleigh distribution. This raises the important question, How do we investigate a data set to see if it is Rayleigh, Gaussian, exponential, uniform, and so on? We will take up this question in Sec. 4.2 and show, in addition, another way to estimate unknown parameters from data sets.

Maximum likelihood estimators (MLE) for common distributions.   The following lists maximum likelihood estimators for some of the common distributions:

1. **The mean of the Gaussian**. The MLE of the true mean for a Gaussian random variable is the sample mean given in Eq. (4.1.2). This is true regardless of whether the variance is known or is an estimate. This estimator is consistent [Eq. (4.1.8)], as we showed previously.
2. **The variance of the Gaussian, when the mean is known.** The MLE is

$$\bar{s}_\mu^2 = \frac{1}{n}[(x_1 - \mu_X)^2 + (x_2 - \mu_X)^2 + \cdots + (x_n - \mu_X)^2] \qquad (4.1.27)$$

   This estimator is consistent, as we will show.
3. **The variance of the Gaussian, when the mean is not known.** When the true mean is not known, we use the sample mean in estimating the variance. The MLE is the same as

Eq. (4.1.27) with the true mean replaced by the sample mean; however this estimator is biased. The consistent, and superior, estimator is

$$\bar{s}_X^2 = \frac{1}{n-1}[(x_1 - \bar{x})^2 + (x_2 - \bar{x})^2 + \cdots + (x_n - \bar{x})^2] \qquad (4.1.28)$$

This is called the *sample variance* and is the square of what a calculator calculates as the sample standard deviation. We will investigate the two variance estimators further.

4. **The probability of success for the binomial distribution.** If you perform n binomial trials [Eq. (2.1.9)], each having a probability p of success, then the results are distributed as a binomial distribution (Sec. 2.1.2).

$$P[k \text{ successes in } n \text{ trials}] = B_n(k, p) = \binom{n}{k} p^k q^{n-k} = \frac{n!}{(n-k)!k!} p^k (1-p)^{n-k}$$
$$(4.1.29)$$

Suppose that we repeat the experiment m times, having successes of $k_i, i = 1, 2, \ldots, m$. We want to use these data values to estimate p. The MLE is

$$\bar{p} = \frac{1}{m} \left(\frac{k_1}{n} + \frac{k_2}{n} + \cdots + \frac{k_m}{n} \right) \qquad (4.1.30)$$

A little reflection will confirm to you that this is the result we obtained in the initial example [Eq. (4.1.21)] using the Bernoulli random variable. The sum of all the ks in the numerator is the total successes, and the product in the denominator, mn, is the total number of trials.

5. **The exponential distribution.** We will derive and explore the exponential distribution in Chapter 5. It is used in reliability studies and models times between random events such as accidents or telephone calls. The exponential distribution is

$$f_T(t) = \lambda e^{-\lambda t}, \quad t \geq 0, \text{ zow} \qquad (4.1.31)$$

Assume we take the data set $t_1, t_2, \ldots, t_n$. The MLE of λ is

$$\bar{\lambda} = \frac{n}{t_1 + t_2 + \cdots + t_n} \qquad (4.1.32)$$

This is the reciprocal of the sample mean of the data. As pointed out previously, the MLE estimator is not always a consistent estimator, but it is still a useful estimator.

Least-mean-square estimation

Least-mean-square error. Another approach to deriving estimators is to minimize the *mean-square error* between the data set and the estimator. This method has a venerable history.[3] Let us say we have a data set, $x_1, x_2, \ldots, x_n$, and we want to estimate with a constant, call it a. The error between a data point, x_i, and the estimate would be

$$\epsilon_i = x_i - a \qquad (4.1.33)$$

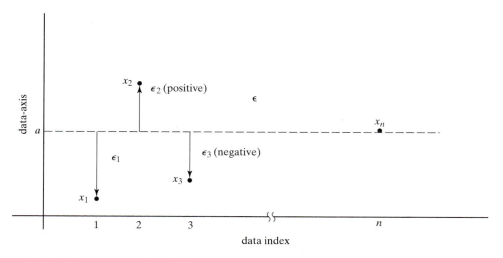

Figure 4.1.5   The errors are the difference between the data points and the constant estimating them. Some of the errors are positive and some negative. The value of *a* that minimizes the sum of the squares of the errors is called the least-mean-square estimator. In this case, this estimator is the sample mean.

The data and errors are shown in Fig. 4.1.5.

We now need to minimize this error in some sense. We use the sum of the squares of the errors as a measure of the total error:

$$E = \sum_{i=1}^{n} \epsilon_i^2 = (x_1 - a)^2 + (x_2 - a)^2 + \cdots + (x_n - a)^2 \qquad (4.1.34)$$

There is no maximum total error, but the minimum total error can be found by differentiating Eq. (4.1.34) with respect to *a*, with the result

$$\frac{dE}{da} = -2[(x_1 - a) + (x_2 - a) + \cdots + (x_n - a)] = 0 \qquad (4.1.35)$$

The value of *a* is

$$a = \frac{1}{n}(x_1 + x_2 + \cdots + x_n) = \bar{x}, \text{ the sample mean} \qquad (4.1.36)$$

Thus the sample mean is the least-mean-square estimator of the data set.[4] We have good grounds for using the sample mean to estimate the true mean: it is supported by common sense; it is the MLE for Gaussian data; and it is the least-mean-square estimator. Having also shown that it is a consistent estimator, we have now laid this problem to rest and can proceed to the estimation of the variance.

4.1.5 Estimation of the Variance, Given the Mean

We turn now to the problem of estimating the variance, given the mean. This is a situation that can occur in practice, although it is rare. For example, let us say we want to estimate the noise level of a radio receiver by sampling the output noise and estimating the standard deviation (or variance) of the samples. If we know that the output is coupled through a capacitor, then we know that the output has zero mean, since a capacitor cannot pass dc. Thus this case can occur in practice, but our main reason for presenting it is to introduce ideas that will be useful later in the more realistic problem of simultaneously estimating the mean and variance of a set of data.

The estimator. Assume we have a data set, $x_1, x_2, \ldots, x_n$, and we know its true mean. We wish to estimate the true variance of the data. The estimator we will investigate is that given in Eq. (4.1.37), called *the sample variance*:[5]

$$\bar{s}_\mu^2 = \frac{1}{n}[(x_1 - \mu_X)^2 + (x_2 - \mu_X)^2 + \cdots + (x_n - \mu_X)^2] \tag{4.1.37}$$

In endnote 6 we give information about using your calculator to calculate this sample variance. We have two reasons for proposing this estimator. First, it follows from the definition of variance and the transformations used in Eq. (4.1.19). The definition of variance is $\sigma_X^2 = E[(X - \mu_X)^2]$, and the transformations are

$$\sigma_X^2 \to \bar{s}_\mu^2, \; E \to \frac{1}{n}\sum \text{ and } X \to x_i \; \Rightarrow \; \bar{s}_\mu^2 = \frac{1}{n}\sum_1^n (x_i - \mu_X)^2 \tag{4.1.38}$$

which is the same as Eq. (4.1.37). The second reason for choosing this estimator is that this is the maximum likelihood estimator for a Gaussian data set. Although we are not ready to restrict ourselves to Gaussian data sets, we will soon have to do so, and this assumption is consistent with that move.

Here our agenda is as before: show that the estimator is consistent as a spot estimator and use it to derive a range estimation. The Big Three for this problem are

$$\sigma_X^2 = \text{the true variance} \tag{4.1.39}$$

$$\bar{s}_\mu^2 = \frac{1}{n}[(x_1 - \mu_X)^2 + (x_2 - \mu_X)^2 + \cdots + (x_n - \mu_X)^2], \text{ the estimator} \tag{4.1.40}$$

$$\hat{S}_\mu^2 = \frac{1}{n}[(X_1 - \mu_X)^2 + (X_2 - \mu_X)^2 + \cdots + (X_n - \mu_X)^2], \text{ the estimator model,} \tag{4.1.41}$$

with the data replaced with IID random variables.

Is the estimator unbiased? To see if the estimator is unbiased, we take the expectation of the estimator model:

$$E[\hat{S}_\mu^2] = \frac{1}{n}[E[(X_1 - \mu_X)^2] + E[(X_2 - \mu_X)^2] + \cdots + E[(X_n - \mu_X)^2]]$$

$$= \frac{1}{n}\underbrace{[\sigma_X^2 + \sigma_X^2 + \cdots + \sigma_X^2]}_{n \text{ times}} = \sigma_X^2 \tag{4.1.42}$$

Equation (4.1.42) follows because, by definition, $\sigma_X^2 = E[(X_i - \mu_X)^2]$, and these are identically distributed (second I). Because the expectation of the estimator model is the true variance, we conclude that the estimator is unbiased. This is true regardless of the PDF of the data; however, to establish that this estimator is consistent, we must assume that the data are Gaussian.

Is the estimator consistent? To show that the estimator is consistent, we must show that the variance of the estimator model approaches zero as $n \to \infty$; however, we cannot in general show that the variance of the estimator model defined in Eq. (4.1.41) vanishes as n increases. We can show this only after assuming a PDF for the IID random variables modeling the data.

Assuming Gaussian data. We assume that the data are Gaussian:

$$X = N(\mu_X, \sigma_X^2), \text{ with } \mu_X \text{ known and } \sigma_X^2 \text{ unknown} \tag{4.1.43}$$

With this assumption, Eq. (4.1.41) becomes the sum of the squares of n independent Gaussian random variables. We may convert our estimator model to a known random variable, and introduce the unknown variance into the mix, by normalizing Eq. (4.1.41) to the sum of the squares of *normalized* Gaussian random variables. We accomplish this conversion by multiplying Eq. (4.1.37) by $\frac{n}{\sigma_X^2}$, with the result

$$V = \frac{n}{\sigma_X^2} \hat{S}_\mu^2 = \left(\frac{X_1 - \mu_X}{\sigma_X}\right)^2 + \left(\frac{X_2 - \mu_X}{\sigma_X}\right)^2 + \cdots + \left(\frac{X_n - \mu_X}{\sigma_X}\right)^2 \tag{4.1.44}$$

where V is a new random variable that is the sum of the squares of n normalized Gaussian random variables.

The chi-square random variable. Our new random variable, V, is called a *chi-square random variable*. Formally, we may define V as

$$V_{\text{dof}} = Z_1^2 + Z_2^2 + \cdots + Z_{\text{dof}}^2 \tag{4.1.45}$$

where V_{dof} is a chi-square random variable with *dof* degrees of freedom, and the Zs are IID normalized Gaussian random variables. We are interested in the PDF of V, its mean, and its variance. We have the tools to derive these results but will skip the details. The formula for the PDF of a chi-square random variable is found in endnote 7. The PDFs for dof $= 1, 3$, and 10 are shown in Fig. 4.1.6.

What we observe with the PDF is that the width increases and the height decreases as the degrees of freedom increase. The mean and variance of the chi-square random variable are

$$E[V_{\text{dof}}] = \text{dof} \quad \text{and} \quad Var[V_{\text{dof}}] = 2 \times \text{dof} \tag{4.1.46}$$

Back to the estimation of the variance. Returning to Eq. (4.1.44), we can now state that $\frac{n}{\sigma_X^2} \hat{S}_\mu^2$ is a chi-square random variable with n degrees of freedom, dof $= n$. From this result

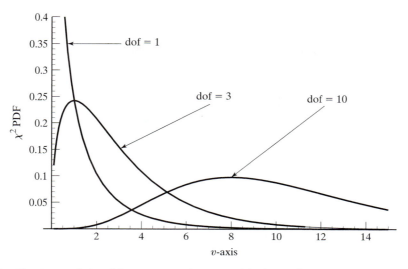

Figure 4.1.6   The PDFs of the chi-square random variable for dof = 1, 3, and 10. As the dofs increase, the PDF becomes wider and lower. The PDF for dof = 3 is the PDF for dof = 1 convolved with itself twice. It takes nine convolutions to produce the PDF for dof = 10.

and Eq. (4.1.46) we derive the mean of the estimator model to be

$$E\left[\frac{n}{\sigma_X^2}\hat{S}_\mu^2\right] = n \Rightarrow E[\hat{S}_\mu^2] = \sigma_X^2 \tag{4.1.47}$$

This is nothing new, since we were able to derive the same relationship in Eq. (4.1.42) without assuming Gaussian data. Similarly, we can determine the variance of the estimator model to be

$$Var\left[\frac{n}{\sigma_X^2}\hat{S}_\mu^2\right] = 2n \Rightarrow \left(\frac{n}{\sigma_X^2}\right)^2 Var[\hat{S}_\mu^2] = 2n \Rightarrow Var[\hat{S}_\mu^2] = \frac{2\sigma_X^4}{n} \tag{4.1.48}$$

This equation is new and just the result we need to confirm that the estimator is consistent [Eq. (4.1.8)], since

$$Var[\hat{S}_\mu^2] \underset{n\to\infty}{\longrightarrow} 0 \tag{4.1.49}$$

Range estimator of the variance.   Having established that the estimator in Eq. (4.1.37) is consistent, we move now to develop a range estimation of the variance for a Gaussian data set when the mean is known. Our method is the same as before: we make a probability statement about the estimator model, manipulate it into a probability statement about the true variance, and convert that statement into a range estimate with a level of confidence.

First, we specify a level of confidence as $1 - \alpha$. This defines two points on the chi-square PDF, as shown in Fig. 4.1.7.

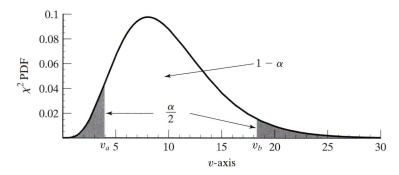

Figure 4.1.7 A plot of the chi-square PDF for dof $= 10$. Two points are marked: the point where the $F_V(v) = \frac{\alpha}{2}$ as v_a, and the point where $F_V(v) = 1 - \frac{\alpha}{2}$ as v_b. This leaves $1 - \alpha$ for the middle region. For the plot, we used $1 - \alpha = 0.9$ for 90% confidence, and $\frac{\alpha}{2} = 0.05$ for 5% in each tail of the distribution. For these values, $v_a = 3.94$ and $v_b = 18.3$.

The probability statement. We now make a probability statement from Eq. (4.1.44) and the properties of a PDF. The probability statement is

$$P\left[v_a < \frac{n}{\sigma_X^2}\hat{S}_\mu^2 < v_b\right] = 1 - \alpha \tag{4.1.50}$$

In Eq. (4.1.50), we know $1 - \alpha$ because we have specified the level of confidence we desire, say, 90%. This leads directly to $v_a = 3.94$ and $v_b = 18.3$. We get these values from a table[8] of values of the inverse of the CDF of the chi-square random variable or have Mathematica calculate them. The code follows for solving for v_a and v_b, given dof and $1 - \alpha$.

```
n = 10;
dof = n;
alpha = 0.1;
va = va/.
   FindRoot[CDF[ChiSquareDistribution[dof], va] == alpha/2,
     {va, 0, dof/2}]
vb = vb/. FindRoot[CDF[ChiSquareDistribution[dof], vb] ==
     1 - alpha/2, {vb, dof, 2 dof}]
3.9403
18.307
```

We know $1 - \alpha$, n, and the resulting values of v_a and v_b in Eq. (4.1.50). We do not know σ_X^2, and $\hat{S}_\mu^2$ is a random variable. We then manipulate the inequality into an inequality with σ_X^2 in the middle. The result is

$$P\left[\frac{n\hat{S}_\mu^2}{v_b} < \sigma_X^2 < \frac{n\hat{S}_\mu^2}{v_a}\right] = 1 - \alpha \tag{4.1.51}$$

which is a range estimate for the unknown variance. We interpret this expression as follows. We can envision taking data sets repeatedly. Each time, we can calculate the estimated value using Eq. (4.1.37). Thus the estimated value is a random variable, since it is a number associated with the outcome of a chance experiment. For each estimated value, we can calculate a range, and the true variance will fall into this range with probability $1 - \alpha$.

Because, in fact, we are not taking multiple data sets but just one, we replace $\hat{S}_\mu^2 \rightarrow \bar{s}_\mu^2$ and state

$$\frac{n\bar{s}_\mu^2}{v_b} < \sigma_X^2 < \frac{n\bar{s}_\mu^2}{v_a} \quad \text{with confidence } 1 - \alpha \tag{4.1.52}$$

The statement also applies to the true standard deviation, which would require the square root of Eq. (4.1.52):

$$\frac{\sqrt{n}\bar{s}_\mu}{\sqrt{v_b}} < \sigma_X < \frac{\sqrt{n}\bar{s}_\mu}{\sqrt{v_a}} \quad \text{with confidence } 1 - \alpha \tag{4.1.53}$$

Example 4.1.3:   Estimation of variance _____

We generate n Gaussian random numbers with a mean of 5 and a variance of 4. Then we calculate the sample variance using Eq. (4.1.37), the lower and upper limits from Eq. (4.1.52), and test these against the true variance. You can execute the cell repeatedly and see that the bounds fail to bracket the true variance about 1 time in 10.

```
n = 10;
TrueMean = 5;
TrueVariance = 4;
data = Table[Random[
      NormalDistribution[TrueMean, √TrueVariance]], {n}];
SampleVariance = Sum[(data[[i]] - TrueMean)², {i, 1, n}]/n
LowerLimit = n * SampleVariance/vb
UpperLimit = n * SampleVariance/va
If [LowerLimit > TrueVariance,
  StylePrint["The true variance is outside the range.",
   "Text"], If[UpperLimit < TrueVariance,
   StylePrint["The true variance is outside the range.",
    "Text"], StylePrint[
   "The true variance is within the range.", "Text"]]]
7.02888
3.83944
17.8384
```

The true variance is within the range.

The four outputs are the sample variance, the lower and upper bounds, and the results of the test against the true variance, which is 4.0. Bear in mind that in the application of this theory the true variance is not known, and we can determine only the range estimate and announce the level of confidence.

Summary and look ahead.   We have now explained procedures for deriving estimators, for modeling estimators, for determining the bias and consistency of estimators, and for developing range estimations. Along the way we used the central limit theorem, assumed at one point that we have Gaussian data, and introduced the chi-square random variable. Unfortunately, the results we obtained can seldom be applied in practice because the assumptions are not met.

We therefore have to retread this ground under more realistic assumptions. Almost always, the problem facing us is that we have a data set $x_1, x_2, \ldots, x_n$ and wish to estimate the mean and the variance, or standard deviation, simultaneously. This is the problem we take up next, and we will find that little new is introduced. In Sec. 4.2 we take up the question of how we determine if a data set can be considered as Gaussian.

4.1.6 Estimation of the Variance, the Mean Unknown

We take up now the estimation of the variance when the mean is unknown. After that we will develop a method for estimating the mean when the variance is unknown. In both cases, we have the Big Three, derive a point estimator, determine its bias and consistency, and develop a range estimate.

Point estimation of the variance.   We call this estimator of the variance when the mean is unknown the *sample variance* and use the symbol $\bar{s}_X^2$ (see endnotes 5). Our estimator will be the same as we used in Eq. (4.1.37), except we will replace the true mean with the sample mean, $\mu_X \to \bar{x}$ and replace n with $n - 1$. Making these changes we have for the Big Three:

$$\sigma_X^2, \text{ the true variance} \tag{4.1.54}$$

$$\bar{s}_X^2 = \frac{1}{n-1}\left[(x_1 - \bar{x})^2 + (x_2 - \bar{x})^2 + \cdots + (x_n - \bar{x})^2\right], \text{ the sample variance} \tag{4.1.55}$$

$$\hat{S}_X^2 = \frac{1}{n-1}\left[(X_1 - \hat{X})^2 + (X_2 - \hat{X})^2 + \cdots + (X_n - \hat{X})^2\right], \text{ the estimator model} \tag{4.1.56}$$

In the estimator model we replaced the sample mean with the estimator model for the sample mean [Eq. (4.1.3)], which is

$$\hat{X} = \frac{1}{n}(X_1 + X_2 + \cdots + X_n) \tag{4.1.57}$$

$$\hat{S}_X^2 = \frac{1}{n-1}\left[(X_1 - \hat{X})^2 + (X_2 - \hat{X})^2 + \cdots + (X_n - \hat{X})^2\right] \tag{4.1.58}$$

The surprising feature in the definition of the sample variance is the "$n - 1$" in Eqs. (4.1.55) and (4.1.56). As we will see, this change is required to produce an unbiased estimator.

Is the sample variance biased? We now determine the bias of the sample variance in Eq. (4.1.55) by taking the expectation of the estimator model in Eq. (4.1.56); however we change the form by subtracting the true mean, which we do not know, from the IID random variables and the estimator model for the sample mean, $(X_1 - \hat{X}) \rightarrow ((X_1 - \mu_X) - (\hat{X} - \mu_X))$:

$$E[\hat{S}_X^2] = \frac{1}{n-1}\left[E\left[((X_1 - \mu_X) - (\hat{X} - \mu_X))^2\right] + \cdots + E\left[((X_n - \mu_X) - (\hat{X} - \mu_X))^2\right]\right]$$

(4.1.59)

where we distributed the expectation operation to the summed terms. Because all the terms in Eq. (4.1.59) are identical, we will work in detail on the first and multiply by n. We expand this first term to get

$$E\left[((X_1 - \mu_X) - (\hat{X} - \mu_X))^2\right] = \underbrace{\frac{E\left[(X_1 - \mu_X)^2\right]}{I}} - \underbrace{\frac{2E\left[((X_1 - \mu_X)(\hat{X} - \mu_X))\right]}{II}}$$
$$+ \underbrace{\frac{E\left[(\hat{X} - \mu_X)^2\right]}{III}}$$

(4.1.60)

The expanded form consists of three terms, which we call I, II, and III. We will deal with each in turn. The first is

$$\text{I:} \quad E\left[(X_1 - \mu_X)^2\right] = \sigma_X^2, \text{ the variance of the data} \qquad (4.1.61)$$

The second term requires a bit of work. Its second expression in parentheses can be written

$$\hat{X} - \mu_X = \frac{1}{n}[(X_1 - \mu_X) + \cdots + (X_n - \mu_X)] \qquad (4.1.62)$$

Then we substitute Eq. (4.1.62) into the middle term of Eq. (4.1.60) and multiply. Thus II takes the form

$$\frac{2}{n}E[(X_1 - \mu_X)^2 + (X_1 - \mu_X)(X_2 - \mu_X) + \cdots] \qquad (4.1.63)$$

Because the random variables are IID, the only nonzero term will come from the X_1 term, which will be the variance of the data multiplied by $\frac{2}{n}$. Hence,

$$\text{II:} \quad 2E\left[((X_1 - \mu_X)(\hat{X} - \mu_X))\right] = \frac{2}{n}\sigma_X^2 \qquad (4.1.64)$$

The third term is by definition the variance of the estimator model for the sample mean, which we dealt with earlier in Eq. (4.1.7). Thus

$$\text{III:} \quad E[(\hat{X} - \mu_X)^2] = Var[\hat{X}] = \frac{\sigma_X^2}{n} \qquad (4.1.65)$$

Combining Eqs. (4.1.61), (4.1.64), and (4.1.65) and multiplying by n, we have the final result:

$$E[\hat{S}_X^2] = \frac{n}{n-1}\left[\sigma_X^2 - \frac{2}{n}\sigma_X^2 + \frac{1}{n}\sigma_X^2\right] = \sigma_X^2 \qquad (4.1.66)$$

Thus the sample variance is an unbiased estimator of the true variance, a result that is independent of the PDF of the data; however, we will have to assume Gaussian data to show that the sample variance is consistent.

Is the sample variance consistent?   To test the consistency of the sample variance as a spot estimator of the true variance, we must assume a PDF for the data. As before, we assume that the data are normal, that each data point would have a Gaussian distribution if we took many data sets and determined the distribution of each data point.[9] The investigation of the variance of Eq. (4.1.58) is similar to the investigation of the sample variance when the mean was known [Eq. (4.1.48)], with one new idea needed. We rearrange Eq. (4.1.58) to the form

$$(n - 1)\hat{S}_X^2 = [(X_1 - \hat{X})^2 + (X_2 - \hat{X})^2 + \cdots + (X_n - \hat{X})^2] \qquad (4.1.67)$$

and divide by the true (but unknown) variance:

$$V = \frac{n - 1}{\sigma_X^2}\hat{S}_X^2 = \left(\frac{X_1 - \hat{X}}{\sigma_X}\right)^2 + \left(\frac{X_2 - \hat{X}}{\sigma_X}\right)^2 + \cdots + \left(\frac{X_n - \hat{X}}{\sigma_X}\right)^2 \qquad (4.1.68)$$

Equation (4.1.68) is identical with Eq. (4.1.44), except n is changed to $n - 1$ and the true mean, μ_X, is changed to the estimator model for the sample mean, $\hat{X}$; but this second change is a big one.

Degrees of freedom.   No longer are the terms on the right side of Eq. (4.1.68) independent because $\hat{X}$ is calculated from the random variables $X_1, X_2, \ldots, X_n$ [Eq. (4.1.3)]. Because of this coupling between terms, we say that the normalized Gaussian random variables, which are squared and added, have lost one degree of freedom. Although the coupling is distributed among all the terms, we can show that the situation is as if one of them, say, the last one, depended on the others. If we add the terms on the right side of Eq. (4.1.68) without the squares, the sum will be zero:

$$\left(\frac{X_1 - \hat{X}}{\sigma_X}\right) + \left(\frac{X_2 - \hat{X}}{\sigma_X}\right) + \cdots + \left(\frac{X_n - \hat{X}}{\sigma_X}\right) = 0 \qquad (4.1.69)$$

That this sum is zero follows from the definition of $\hat{X}$ in Eq. (4.1.3). When we showed that the sample mean was the least-mean-square estimator, we derived $a = \bar{x}$ from Eq. (4.1.36). Because Eq. (4.1.69) is true, it follows that if we know the first $n - 1$ terms, the last term must make the sum be zero. It is said that we have lost one degree of freedom because of this constraint. This loss of one degree of freedom is the reason we divide by $n - 1$ rather than n in calculating the sample variance by Eq. (4.1.55) when the mean is unknown.[10]

Showing that the sample variance is consistent, revisited.   The end result of this discussion of degrees of freedom is that V in Eq. (4.1.68) is a chi-square random variable with $n - 1$ degrees of freedom. This conclusion is proved in advanced texts; we will simply accept it. From this, and the properties of the chi-square random variable in Eq. (4.1.46), two results follow:

$$E\left[\frac{n-1}{\sigma_X^2}\hat{S}_X^2\right] = n-1 \Rightarrow \left(\frac{n-1}{\sigma_X^2}\right)E[\hat{S}_X^2] = n-1 \Rightarrow E[\hat{S}_X^2] = \sigma_X^2 \qquad (4.1.70)$$

$$Var\left[\frac{n-1}{\sigma_X^2}\hat{S}_X^2\right] = 2(n-1) \Rightarrow \left(\frac{n-1}{\sigma_X^2}\right)^2 Var[\hat{S}_X^2] = 2(n-1) \Rightarrow Var[\hat{S}_X^2] = \frac{2\sigma_X^4}{n-1} \qquad (4.1.71)$$

Equation (4.1.70) merely confirms what we already knew, that the sample variance is unbiased. We were able to prove that without assuming Gaussian data. Equation (4.1.71) is what we require to show that the sample variance is consistent, since

$$Var[\hat{S}_X^2] \underset{n\to\infty}{\to} 0 \qquad (4.1.72)$$

Summary.   Our results are that the sample variance defined by Eq. (4.1.55) is a consistent estimator. Along the way, we discussed the concept of degrees of freedom. Otherwise, there is little change from the case in which the mean is known. In the following section we will make use of this similarity to present a range estimation of the true variance.

Range estimation of the variance when the mean is unknown.   In a previous section we derived a range estimate of the variance when the mean was known. The argument followed there is valid in the present case, with small changes, so we merely present the results. Because the sample variance is related to a chi-square random variance with $n-1$ degrees of freedom, the range estimation is merely Eq. (4.1.52) with the one change that we use $n-1$ for n in the range and in determining the values of v_a and v_b. Thus

$$\frac{(n-1)\bar{s}_X^2}{v_b} < \sigma_X^2 < \frac{(n-1)\bar{s}_X^2}{v_a} \text{ with confidence } 1-\alpha \qquad (4.1.73)$$

where the values of v_a and v_b are determined for dof $= n-1$ and our prescribed level of confidence, $1-\alpha$. For example, consider that we have 19 data points and want 90% confidence in our range estimate. The following cell calculates v_a and v_b.

```
n = 19;
dof = n - 1;
alpha = 0.1;
va = va/.
  FindRoot[CDF[ChiSquareDistribution[dof], va] == alpha/2,
    {va, 0, dof/2}]
vb = vb/. FindRoot[CDF[ChiSquareDistribution[dof], vb] ==
      1 - alpha/2, {vb, dof, 2 dof}]
9.39043
28.8693
```

We then use these values and the sample variance from our data set to calculate the lower and upper limits to the range estimate. The following cell does the following: (1) it generates a set of n Gaussian data points with a known mean and variance; (2) it calculates the sample mean; (3) it uses the sample mean to calculate the sample variance; (4) it calculates the lower and upper limits, Eq. (4.1.73); and (5) it tests the range against the known variance. Try it.

```
n = 19;
TrueMean = 5;
TrueVariance = 4;
data = Table[Random[
     NormalDistribution[TrueMean, √TrueVariance]], {n}];
SampleMean = Sum[data[[i]], {i, 1, n}]/n
SampleVariance =
 Sum[(data[[i]] - SampleMean)², {i, 1, n}]/(n - 1)
LowerLimit = (n - 1) * SampleVariance / vb
UpperLimit = (n - 1) * SampleVariance / va
If[LowerLimit > TrueVariance,
 StylePrint["The true variance is outside the range."
   "Text"], If[UpperLimit < TrueVariance,
  StylePrint["The true variance is outside the range."
   "Text"], StylePrint[
   "The true variance is within the range." "Text"]]]

4.86485
4.98544
3.10842
9.55632
```

The true variance is within the range.

The outputs are the sample mean (compare with 5), the sample variance (compare with 4), the lower and upper limits, and the results of the test of the range against the true variance. Execute the cell repeatedly and observe the success of the range estimate. It should bracket the true variance 9 times out of 10, on average.

4.1.7 Estimation of the Mean, the Variance Unknown

The sample mean.   The sample mean is a consistent spot estimator of the true mean from a data set, whether or not the variance is known. We were in fact able to show these results making no assumption about the data or the variance. We move immediately to the range estimation of the true mean, given that the variance is unknown.

Range estimate of the mean.   Earlier when we were making a range estimate of the mean, given the variance, we went through a normalization process in Eq. (4.1.10). That normalization was

$$Z = \frac{\hat{X} - \mu_X}{\sigma_X/\sqrt{n}} = N(0, 1) \tag{4.1.74}$$

No longer can we perform this normalization because we now do not know the true standard deviation, so we use instead the sample standard deviation,

$$T = \frac{\hat{X} - \mu_X}{\hat{S}_X/\sqrt{n}} \tag{4.1.75}$$

where $\hat{S}_X$ is the square root of the estimator model of the sample variance given in Eq. (4.1.58). The random variable T is thus a random variable that is a Gaussian random variable divided by a random variable that is the square root of a chi-square random variable with $n - 1$ degrees of freedom divided by $\sqrt{n}$. Although one would assume that the Gaussian and the chi-square random variables are not independent, since they are calculated from the same set of random variables, the numerator and the denominator in Eq. (4.1.75) contain independent random variables. Investigation of the T random variable, named the Student's t random variable, is beyond the scope of this book. The mathematical expression for the Student's t random variable is given in endnote 11. The PDF of this random variable is bell-shaped, like the Gaussian, and indeed for dof ≥ 30 is so similar to the Gaussian that the Gaussian may be used instead of the Student's t. In Fig. 4.1.8 we give the Student's t for dof $= 6$ with a Gaussian of the same mean and variance.

To make a range estimate we need to specify a level of confidence, $1 - \alpha$, and determine the value of t corresponding to that value of α, as illustrated in Fig. 4.1.9. We may determine t_c by looking it up in a table [endnote 12] or by using Mathematica, as in the following cell, where we assume six degrees of freedom.

```
n = 7; (*The number of data values*)
dof = n - 1;
alpha = 0.1;
tc = tc /. FindRoot[CDF[StudentTDistribution[dof], tc] ==
    1 - alpha / 2, {tc, 0, 8 / dof}]
1.94318
```

The range estimate for the mean follows from the definition of T in Eq. (4.1.75), the definition of t_c, and the PDF of the Student's t random variable

$$P\left[-t_c < \frac{\hat{X} - \mu_X}{\hat{S}_X/\sqrt{n}} < +t_c\right] = 1 - \alpha \tag{4.1.76}$$

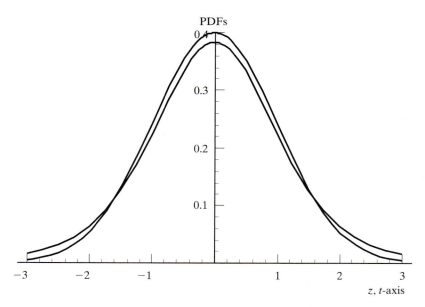

Figure 4.1.8 A plot of the Student's *t* PDF for six degrees of freedom and the Gaussian PDF with the same mean and variance. The Gaussian is taller and more narrow than the Student's *t*, a result of the uncertainty of the variance. If the dof are greater than 30, the two become very close.

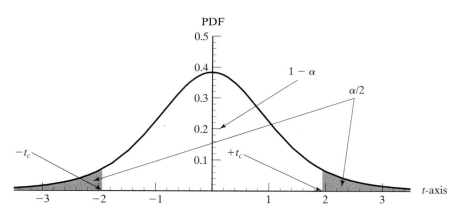

Figure 4.1.9 The Student's *t* distribution with the value of $t_c = 1.943$ corresponding to 90% level of confidence. The values of $-t_c$ and $+t_c$ correspond to the points in the CDF for $\frac{\alpha}{2}$ and $1 - \frac{\alpha}{2}$, respectively.

In the same manner as we followed before in developing a range estimate of the mean [Eq. (4.1.13)], given the variance, we manipulate this estimate into a statement about the mean:

$$P\left[\hat{X} - t_c\frac{\hat{S}_X}{\sqrt{n}} < \mu_X < \hat{X} + t_c\frac{\hat{S}_X}{\sqrt{n}}\right] = 1 - \alpha \qquad (4.1.77)$$

Finally, we replace the estimator model with the sample mean, $\hat{X} \to \bar{x}$; replace the estimator model for the sample standard deviation with the sample standard deviation, $\hat{S}_X \to \bar{s}_X$; change the vocabulary from *probability* to *level of confidence*, and we obtain our range estimate:

$$\bar{x} - t_c\frac{\bar{s}_X}{\sqrt{n}} < \mu_X < \bar{x} + t_c\frac{\bar{s}_X}{\sqrt{n}} \text{ with level of confidence } 1 - \alpha \qquad (4.1.78)$$

The procedure for making a range estimate of the mean is as follows: (1) establish a required level of confidence (we will use 90%, so $\alpha = 10\%$); (2) determine t_c for dof $= n - 1$ from the number of data values (n) and the value of α, either from a table (see endnote 12) or with Mathematica; (3) calculate the sample mean and sample variance (and sample standard deviation, its square root); and (4) calculate the lower and upper limits from Eq. (4.1.78). This procedure is illustrated in the following cell, which does the calculation for $n = 7$ data values and tests the result against the true mean used to generate the data set.

```
n = 7;
dof = n - 1;
tc = 1.9431933238234496 (*from the previous cell*);
TrueMean = 5;
TrueVariance = 4;
data = Table[Random[
    NormalDistribution[TrueMean, √TrueVariance]], {n}];
SampleMean = Sum[data[[i]], {i, 1, n}] / n
SampleVariance =
 Sum[(data[[i]] - SampleMean)², {i, 1, n}] / (n - 1)
LowerLimit = SampleMean - tc * √SampleVariance / n
UpperLimit = SampleMean + tc * √SampleVariance / n
If [LowerLimit > TrueMean,
 StylePrint["The true mean is outside the range.", "Text"],
 If[UpperLimit < TrueMean, StylePrint[
    "The true mean is outside the range.", "Text"],
  StylePrint["The true mean is within the range.", "Text"]]]
4.88735
6.62317
2.99718
6.77751
```

The true mean is within the range.

The outputs are the sample mean (compare with 5), the sample variance (compare with 4), the lower and upper limits of the range estimate, and the results of the test of the range against the true mean. You may execute the cell many times to see how well the test does. It should fail, on average, 1 time out of 10.

4.1.8 Summary of Estimation of Mean and Variance

In this section we developed spot and range estimators for the mean and variance of a data set under a variety of conditions, and we developed a precise notation to denote the various distinctions and cases under study. Along the way, assumptions were made. In the following sections we summarize the various results with assumptions for the four cases studied in Sec. 4.1.

Estimation of the mean when the variance is known. The appropriate spot estimator is the sample mean, defined in Eq. (4.1.2) and repeated in Eq. (4.1.79):

$$\bar{x} = \frac{1}{n}(x_1 + x_2 + \cdots + x_n) \tag{4.1.79}$$

The sample mean is shown to be an unbiased and consistent estimator of the true mean, regardless of the PDF of the data source.

A range estimate of the true mean, given that the variance is known, cannot be given without assuming a PDF for the data source. If the data are Gaussian, then the range estimate of the true mean is given by Eq. (4.1.17) and repeated in (4.1.80):

$$\bar{x} - z_c \frac{\sigma_X}{\sqrt{n}} < \mu_X < \bar{x} + z_c \frac{\sigma_X}{\sqrt{n}} \text{ with a level of confidence } 1 - \alpha \tag{4.1.80}$$

where z_c is defined by the level of confidence, α, and the Gaussian inverse CDF in Eq. (4.1.12). Thus the procedure is to (1) choose the level of confidence; (2) determine z_c from the Φ^{-1} table [endnote 34 in Chapter 3]; (3) calculate the sample mean from the data set; and (4) use Eq. (4.1.80) with the known standard deviation, σ_X, and number of data values, n.

Estimation of the mean when the variance is not known. The appropriate spot estimator is still the sample mean, Eq. (4.1.79). The range estimate of the true mean involves the sample variance, given by Eq. (4.1.55) and repeated in Eq. (4.1.81):

$$\bar{s}_X^2 = \frac{1}{n-1}\left[(x_1 - \bar{x})^2 + (x_2 - \bar{x})^2 + \cdots + (x_n - \bar{x})^2\right] \tag{4.1.81}$$

For Gaussian data, a range estimation of the mean is given by Eq. (4.1.78) and repeated as (4.1.82):

$$\bar{x} - t_c \frac{\bar{s}_X}{\sqrt{n}} < \mu_X < \bar{x} + t_c \frac{\bar{s}_X}{\sqrt{n}} \text{ with level of confidence } 1 - \alpha \tag{4.1.82}$$

where t_c is derived from the inverse CDF of the Student's t distribution; the degrees of freedom, which is $\text{dof} = n - 1$; and the prescribed level of confidence, $1 - \alpha$. The cell that determines t_c is given on page 383, or t_c can be determined from tables [see endnote 12]. Thus the procedure is to (1) choose the required level of confidence; (2) determine t_c from the cited cell or table[12]; (3) calculate the sample mean and sample variance from the data set; and (4) use Eq. (4.1.82) with the number of data values, n.

Estimation of the variance when the mean is known. The appropriate spot estimator is the sample variance given in Eq. (4.1.40) and repeated in Eq. (4.1.83). This sample variance is an unbiased estimator of the true variance:

$$\bar{s}_\mu^2 = \frac{1}{n}\left[(x_1 - \mu_X)^2 + (x_2 - \mu_X)^2 + \cdots + (x_n - \mu_X)^2\right] \qquad (4.1.83)$$

To show that Eq. (4.1.83) gives a consistent estimator, one must assume Gaussian data. Note that we use the subscript μ on the sample variance when the mean is known, to distinguish this sample variance from the sample variance when the mean is not known.

The range estimate of the variance is also based on Gaussian data and is given by Eq. (4.1.52) and repeated in Eq. (4.1.84)

$$\frac{n\bar{s}_\mu^2}{v_b} < \sigma_X^2 < \frac{n\bar{s}_\mu^2}{v_a} \quad \text{with confidence } 1 - \alpha \qquad (4.1.84)$$

where v_a and v_b are derived from the inverse CDF of the chi-square random variable for dof $= n =$ the number of data values, is calculated above (see page 376) or is tabulated (endnote 8). Thus the procedure for making a range estimate of the variance is as follows: (1) calculate the sample variance given by (4.1.83); (2) determine the values of v_a and v_b from a table or from the cell cited in the previous sentence and from the desired level of confidence; (3) calculate the range estimate according to Eq. (4.1.84).

Estimation of the variance when the mean is unknown. The appropriate spot estimator is the sample variance given in Eq. (4.1.55) and repeated in Eq. (4.1.85). This sample variance is an unbiased estimator of the true variance:

$$\bar{s}_X^2 = \frac{1}{n-1}\left[(x_1 - \bar{x})^2 + (x_2 - \bar{x})^2 + \cdots + (x_n - \bar{x})^2\right] \qquad (4.1.85)$$

To show that Eq. (4.1.85) gives a consistent estimator, one must assume Gaussian data. Note that we use the subscript X on the sample variance when the mean is unknown, to distinguish this sample variance from the sample variance when the mean is known, Eq. (4.1.83).

The range estimate of the variance is also based on Gaussian data and is given by Eq. (4.1.73) and repeated in Eq. (4.1.86):

$$\frac{(n-1)\bar{s}_X^2}{v_b} < \sigma_X^2 < \frac{(n-1)\bar{s}_X^2}{v_a} \quad \text{with confidence } 1 - \alpha \qquad (4.1.86)$$

where v_a and v_b are derived from the inverse CDF of the chi-square random variable for dof $= n - 1 =$ one less than the number of data values, which is given near (see page 376) or is tabulated (see endnote 8). Thus the procedure for making a range estimate of the variance is as follows: (1) calculate the sample variance given by Eq. (4.1.85); (2) determine the values of v_a and v_b from a table or from the cell cited in the previous sentence and from the desired level of confidence; (3) calculate the range estimate according to Eq. (4.1.86).

Summary.   In Sec. 4.1 we described how to make spot and range estimations of the mean and variance of a data set under a variety of conditions. The most common situation is that the mean and variance of a data set must be estimated simultaneously. Along the way, we studied one method for deriving estimators, learned how to distinguish the Big Three (the true value, the estimator, and the estimator model), defined and proved consistency for our estimators, learned about degrees of freedom, and became acquainted with two new random variables, the chi-square and the Student's t.

Looking ahead.   In this section we dealt with one-dimensional data sets, values of x. In the next section we deal with two-dimensional data sets, pairs of numbers like $\{x_i, y_i\}$ and learn how to develop models for data of this class. In the process we deal with the problem of fitting a model to a data set. In the present section, for example, we had to assume Gaussian data sets to obtain most of our results. How does one confirm that this is a reasonable assumption? Read on and see.

4.2 LINEAR REGRESSION

In Sec. 4.1, on estimation, we learned how to analyze one-dimensional data sets for the mean and variance of the source of the data. The data were modeled as IID random variables, an estimator was proposed, the estimator was examined for consistency as a spot estimator, and range estimates were developed with a prescribed level of confidence. We now consider two-dimensional data sets.

4.2.1 The Need for Two-Dimensional Models

Two-dimensional data sets.   A one-dimensional data set has independent samples of some random quantity, $x_1, x_2, \ldots, x_n$. By *two-dimensional data sets,* we mean bivariate data sets with associated data points such as $\{x_1, y_1\}, \{x_2, y_2\}$. To illustrate, we will recycle an example from Sec. 3.5.

An illustration of paired data.   Suppose we take data on students' height and weight. Generally, we expect the weight to increase with height. If people were perfectly scaled versions of one another, the weight would increase as the third power of the height, but since these properties vary over a limited range, we can approximate the dependence with a linear relationship. To illustrate, we consider the following "data." Here we have assumed heights $N(70, 6^2)$ in. and weights that have a Gaussian distribution with the mean proportional to height cubed and a standard deviation of 20 lb.

As you can see in Fig. 4.2.1, there appears to be a linear relationship between height and weight, and we might want to model this relationship. The following section develops such a model.

4.2.2 Linear Regression Techniques

The problem stated.   Assume we have a data set consisting of associated values $\{x_i, y_i\}, i = 1, 2, \ldots, n$. We seek the best model of the form

$$y(x) = ax + b \qquad (4.2.1)$$

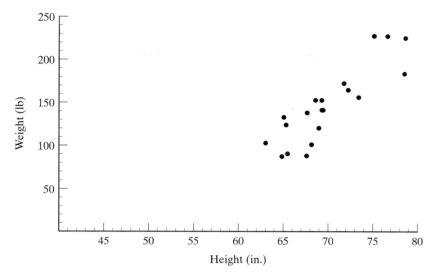

Figure 4.2.1   Height–weight data generated with weight proportional to the cube of the height, plus a random component.

where a and b are to be determined from the data set. We interpret "best" to mean that the mean square error between the data set and the model will be minimum. The error will be

$$\epsilon_i = y_i - y(x_i) = y_i - ax_i - b \tag{4.2.2}$$

The total error is

$$E(a, b) = \sum_{i=1}^{n} \epsilon_i^2 = \sum_{i=1}^{n} (y_i - ax_i - b)^2 \tag{4.2.3}$$

We minimize the total error using standard methods of calculus, setting to zero the partial derivatives of $E(a, b)$ with respect to a and b:

$$\frac{\partial E(a, b)}{\partial a} = \sum_{i=1}^{n} 2(y_i - ax_i - b)(-x_i) = 0, \text{ and} \tag{4.2.4}$$

$$\frac{\partial E(a, b)}{\partial b} = \sum_{i=1}^{n} 2(y_i - ax_i - b)(-1) = 0 \tag{4.2.5}$$

Simultaneous solution of Eqs. (4.2.4) and (4.2.5) leads to the least-mean-square regression line fitting the data. We do not give the formulas here because you have no need to know them, since they are programmed into your calculator. You may examine the formulas in endnote 13 if you wish.

What if *b* is zero?   Some models require the regression line to go through the origin; that is, they require that $b = 0$. In this case your calculator will give the wrong answer, since it fits a two-parameter line to the data. If our model is $y(x) = ax$, we must modify the total error to be

$$E(a) = \sum_{i=1}^{n} \epsilon_i^2 = \sum_{i=1}^{n} (y_i - ax_i)^2 \tag{4.2.6}$$

The total error is minimum when

$$\frac{dE(a)}{da} = \sum_{i=1}^{n} 2(y_i - ax_i)(-x_i) = 0 \Rightarrow a = \frac{\displaystyle\sum_{1}^{n} x_i y_i}{\displaystyle\sum_{1}^{n} x_i^2} \tag{4.2.7}$$

which does you no good unless you know where $\displaystyle\sum_{1}^{n} x_i y_i$ and $\displaystyle\sum_{1}^{n} x_i^2$ are stored in your calculator. For this reason we give in endnote 14 some advice about how to find this information for your own calculator.

Example 4.2.1:   Regression analysis
As an example we will calculate the regression line for the height–weight data we generated. In this case, we may use Mathematica's routine that fits polynomials to data sets, which gives the results that $w(h)$ is

```
-235.683 + 5.56949 h
```

The output is the regression line shown and plotted in Fig. 4.2.2 with the data.

Estimators.   A linear regression line can be considered an estimation. Here we also have a Big Three:

$y(x)$ is the true regression line, unknown but assumed to exist.   (4.2.8)

$\bar{y}(x)$ is an estimate of the true regression line, derived from our data to minimize total error for a specific data set. This estimate uses the values of a and b, given in   (4.2.9) endnote 13, which are estimates of the true slope and true intercept of the true regression line.

$\hat{Y}(x)$ is an estimator model that we may use to examine the properties of the   (4.2.10) estimator.

Serious investigation of the properties of these estimators is beyond the scope of this book. A reference is given in endnote 15. Our goal is to alert you to the strengths and limits of linear regression as a means to characterize a two-dimensional data set.

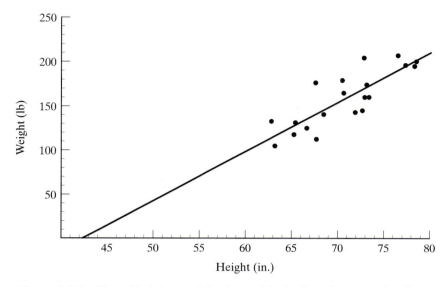

Figure 4.2.2 Plot of height–weight data with the best-fit regression line.

Some real data

Now we examine some real data by analyzing book prices versus book pages from a publisher's catalog. The author examined the "recently published" section of the most recent catalog of the InterVarsity Press and noted the prices and stated lengths of the paperback books. Figure 4.2.3 is a plot of the data.

We may fit a linear regression model as follows:

```
model = Fit[plotdata, {1, p}, p]
r[p_] := model
4.98524 + 0.0455517 p
```

The price intercept of the regression line is about $5, and the slope of the regression line is about 4.6¢/page. Our interpretation of the numbers is that the $5 is something of an overhead figure, a base price for all books, and the 4.6¢/page is the component of the price related to the length of the book. Because the book prices do not fall exactly on a straight line, we conclude that there are other factors influencing the price of the books.[16]

Figure 4.2.4 is a plot of the data with the regression line.

We now have a model: price $= 4.99 + 0.0456 \times$ pages. We might want to know how accurate a predictor it is. One measure would be the correlation coefficient between pages and price.[17] This is calculated by the Mathematica command "Correlation."

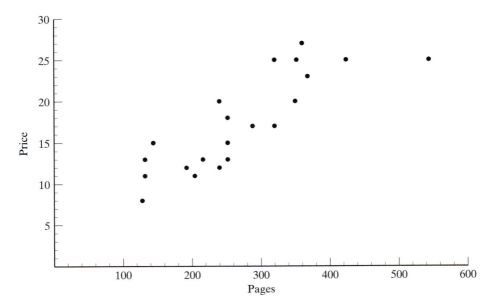

Figure 4.2.3   A plot of price versus number of pages for paperback books published by InterVarsity Press, Spring 2001.

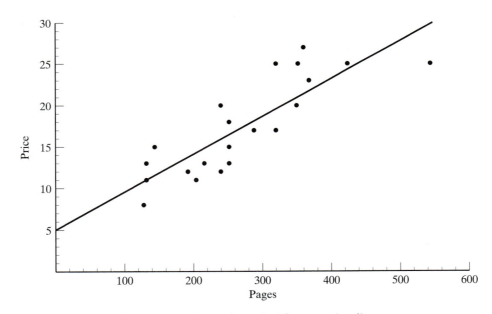

Figure 4.2.4   Data plotted with regression line.

```
Correlation[prices, pages];
N[%]
0.836888
```

This result confirms what our eyes tell us, that the correlation is significant.

A measure of the accuracy of the model.   Another measure of the accuracy of the model would be the sample standard deviation of the errors between the prices and the model. These errors are the differences between the true prices and the predicted prices from the regression line. The regression line is chosen to minimize these errors in the mean square sense. In the following cell, we calculate the predicted values, subtract them from the prices, and calculate the standard deviation as the square root of the sum of the squares divided by the number of data points *minus* 2. We divide by $n - 2$ because we lost two degrees of freedom by fitting a two-parameter model to the data.

```
prediction = r[p] /. p → pages;
errors = prices - prediction;
errorstandeviation =
  Sqrt[Sum[errors[[i]]², {i, 1, n}] / (n - 2)]
3.24306
```

The resulting standard deviation, \$3.24, gives a measure of the accuracy of the model. Thus our model would be

$$\text{price} = \text{estimated price (pages)} \pm 3.24(1\sigma)$$
$$= 4.99 + 0.0456 \times \text{pages} \pm 3.24(1\sigma)$$

(4.2.11)

If the errors are distributed symmetrically, about two-thirds [Eq. (3.1.19)] of the actual prices will fall within \$3.24 of the predicted value.

4.2.3 Fitting a Model to a Data Set

We now take up the question of fitting a model to a data set.[18] The method involves determination of an experimental CDF based on the data by rank ordering the data and then fitting a theoretical CDF, with unknown parameters, to the rank-ordered data. The context is that we have a set of one-dimensional data, $x_1, x_2, \ldots, x_n$, and we wish to determine if the data source is uniformly distributed, Gaussian, exponential, and so on. The issue of whether it is Gaussian is particularly important, since our range estimation techniques rest on the assumption of Gaussian data.

In the process of developing a technique for fitting a distribution to a data set, we develop another method for estimating parameters in distributions. Our method is based on linear regression. Of course, there are more advanced methods of fitting models to data, but we use linear regression because calculators can determine a regression line and also because our eyes can determine and interpret a regression line fairly accurately.

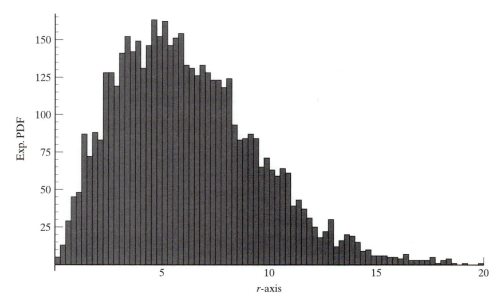

Figure 4.2.5   Histogram of a Rayleigh distribution with $\sigma = 5$, which should peak at $r = 5$. For large numbers of data points, the Rayleigh shape can be identified, but for small numbers (try $n = 50$), a histogram is too rough to be of much use in identifying the PDF.

Should the PDF be used?   If one has many data points, a histogram of the data can show general features. But "many data points" means hundreds and even thousands in this case, certainly too many for hand analysis. But for the record, we will give an example. Let us say we have a data set and we want to determine its PDF. We generate such a data set, using the Rayleigh PDF, and we plot a histogram (Fig. 4.2.5).

```
n = 5000;
data = Table[Random[RayleighDistribution[5]], {n}];
Histogram[data, ImageSize → 400,
   AxesLabel → {"r-axis", "Exp. PDF"}];
```

Should the CDF be used?   Integration tends to smooth fluctuations in signals. For this reason the CDF of the distribution, which is an integration of the PDF, will be used in fitting the data. Specifically, we will match the CDF of a theoretical model to the experimental CDF of the data.

Finding the experimental CDF

The data.   We present our method in the context of a specific problem, fitting a Rayleigh model to a data set. For the data set we looked up cities in Texas with populations exceeding

2500 and names beginning with A, and we measured their distance from Austin on a map. The cities were Abernathy, Abilene, Alamo, Alamo Heights, Aldine, Alice, Alpine, Alvin, Amarillo, Andrews, Angleton, Anson, Aransas Pass, Arlington, Athens, Atlanta, and Azle, 17 cities in all. The distances from Austin are given in the cell in order of the names given.

```
distance = {357, 199, 297, 76, 152, 186, 371, 168,
    435, 333, 165, 222, 182, 183, 182, 297, 189};
n = Length[distance]
17
```

We now develop the experimental CDF. Recall that the CDF is defined as the probability that the random variable falls less than a prescribed value. The experimental CDF will therefore estimate the probability that the distance will fall below a prescribed distance. For this discussion we put the data in rank order, from smallest to largest, tabulated with rank number. Note that one of the distances is repeated, which is no problem.

```
distancesort = Sort[distance];
firstsort =
 Table[{k, distancesort[[k]]}, {k, 1, n}] // TableForm
1       76
2       152
3       165
4       168
5       182
6       182
7       183
8       186
9       189
10      199
11      222
12      297
13      297
14      333
15      357
16      371
17      435
```

Look, for example, at the middle distance, ranked 9, 189 miles. For this data set, about half the distances fall below 189 and about half above. A first guess for the experimental CDF, therefore, would be something like $\frac{k}{n}$, where k is the rank number and n is the number of data points. We show this experimental CDF in Fig. 4.2.6.

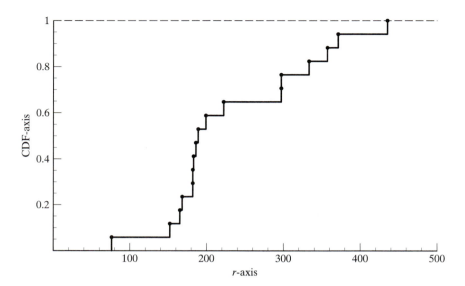

Figure 4.2.6   Plot of the experimental CDF, using $\frac{k}{n}$ for the CDF. The problem with this plot is that it reaches 1, which leads to problems with many models. We change the experiment CDF to $\frac{k}{n+1}$ to remedy this problem.

This certainly looks like a CDF: it starts at 0 and ends at 1. But there is a problem that is not evident at this stage; that is, many probability models *asymptote* to 1 and have no way to accommodate an experimental CDF that reaches exactly 1. We thus make the empirical adjustment of defining the experimental CDF as $F_k(r_k) = \frac{k}{n+1}$. Using this new experimental CDF, the plot looks like the one in Fig. 4.2.7.

Why the $n + 1$?   Think of the $n + 1$ as an empirical correction for a finite data set. This correction has the virtue that it places the data symmetrically between 0 and 1.[19] Note that the first point has a value of $\frac{1}{n+1}$, and the last point falls below 1 by $1 - \frac{n}{n+1} = \frac{1}{n+1}$. The "$n + 1$" ensures that the experimental CDF never reaches 1, which creates a problem with many theoretical CDFs, including the Rayleigh. This technique is known as *mean ranking* the data.

Now that we have an experimental CDF, we can proceed with the problem of fitting the theoretical model. The following table shows the rank number, the distance, and the experimental CDF.

```
ExpCDFunction =
  Table[{k, distancesort[[k]], N[k / (n + 1)]}, {k, 1, n}] //
    TableForm
1        76         0.0555556
2        152        0.111111
3        165        0.166667
```

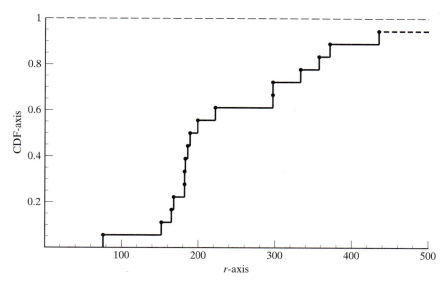

Figure 4.2.7   The experimental CDF with $F_k(r_k) = \frac{k}{n+1}$. The "$n+1$" term corrects for a finite data set and places the plot symmetrically between 0 and 1.

4	168	0.222222
5	182	0.277778
6	182	0.333333
7	183	0.388889
8	186	0.444444
9	189	0.5
10	199	0.555556
11	222	0.611111
12	297	0.666667
13	297	0.722222
14	333	0.777778
15	357	0.833333
16	371	0.888889
17	435	0.944444

Putting the model into the form of a straight line

The basic hypothesis we are testing is that cities are distributed with distances from Austin that are Rayleigh distributed. There is no serious reason for assuming Rayleigh;[20] this is just an example. We are now going to transform our Rayleigh model into the form of a straight line. The Rayleigh

CDF is

$$F_R(r) = 1 - e^{-\frac{r^2}{b}}, r \geq 0, \text{ zow} \tag{4.2.12}$$

where b is an unknown parameter to be determined. To get a straight line, we first rearrange, $1 - F = e^{-\frac{r^2}{b}}$, and take the natural $\log^{21}$: $\ln(1 - F) = -\frac{r^2}{b}$. Finally, we negate and take the square root for the final result:

$$\sqrt{-\ln(1 - F)} = \frac{r}{\sqrt{b}} + 0 \tag{4.2.13}$$

We added the "$+0$" term to emphasize that Eq. (4.2.13) has the form of a straight line, $y = \alpha x + \beta$, where $\beta = 0$. According to Eq. (4.2.13), if the data were Rayleigh, the plot of $y_k = \sqrt{-\ln(1 - F_k)}$ versus r_k would be a straight line going through the origin, having a slope of $\frac{1}{\sqrt{b}}$.

The table, from which we will make a plot, is as follows:

```
tabletoplot = Table[{k, distancesort[[k]], N[k / (n + 1)],
    N[√-Log[1 - k/(n + 1)]]}, {k, 1, n}] // TableForm
1       76      0.0555556       0.239078
2       152     0.111111        0.343195
3       165     0.166667        0.426991
4       168     0.222222        0.501313
5       182     0.277778        0.570458
6       182     0.333333        0.636761
7       183     0.388889        0.701767
8       186     0.444444        0.766672
9       189     0.5             0.832555
10      199     0.555556        0.900517
11      222     0.611111        0.971834
12      297     0.666667        1.04815
13      297     0.722222        1.13178
14      333     0.777778        1.22641
15      357     0.833333        1.33857
16      371     0.888889        1.4823
17      435     0.944444        1.70011
```

We plot distance, the second column, along the x-axis, and the transformation of the experimental CDF, $\sqrt{-\ln[1 - k/(n + 1)]}$ in the fourth column, along the y-axis. The result is

```
yvalues = Table[Sqrt[-Log[1 - k / (n + 1)]], {k, 1, n}];
plotlist =
   Table[{distancesort[[k]], yvalues[[k]]}, {k, 1, n}];
```

```
plot1 = ListPlot[plotlist, PlotRange → {{0, 500}, {0, 2}},
    ImageSize → 400, PlotStyle → PointSize[0.015],
    AxesLabel → {"Data values", "f(Exp. CDF)"}];
```

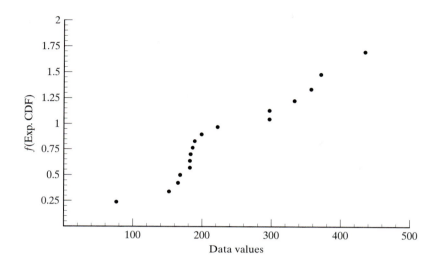

If the model were correct, the dots would fall along a line passing through the origin. The results are not terribly impressive, but not ridiculous either. Certainly, we can fit a line and see how it looks. That is the next step. The regression line for the data is given by

```
yfit = Fit[plotlist, {1, r}, r]
-0.105974 + 0.00416125 r
```

but this is not what we require, since our model must pass through the origin. The best fit *through the origin* is

```
yfit = Fit[plotlist, {0, r}, r]
0.00377111 r
```

Recall that the model is

$$\sqrt{-\ln(1 - F)} = \frac{r}{\sqrt{b}} + 0 \tag{4.2.14}$$

so the slope of the regression line through the origin is identified with $\frac{1}{\sqrt{b}}$. The unknown parameter b is therefore derived from the fit as

```
b = (r / yfit)²
70317.4
```

Thus the PDF, fitted to the data, is

$$f_R(r) = \frac{2r}{70317.4} \exp\left[-\frac{r^2}{70317.4}\right] \tag{4.2.15}$$

Finally, we display the data with the best-fit regression line through the origin to see how it compares.

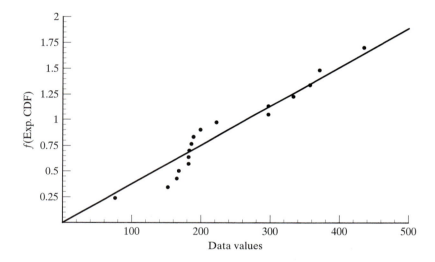

We now can make a judgment as to the suitability of the model. Our eye tells us that the data fit the line fairly well. There is a region of poor fit around 200 mi, but on the whole the model works. We can also judge the excellence of fit by calculating the experimental correlation coefficient:[17]

```
Correlation[distancesort, yvalues];
N[%]
0.96685
```

Another model. We now look at a model that ought to work but does not work as well as the Rayleigh. We might suppose that towns in the category described would be randomly distributed with a more or less uniform density in towns per unit area. We will develop this model and try it against the data. The chance experiment would be to pick a town at random, and the random variable, R, would be its distance from Austin. The theoretical CDF, $F_R(r) = P[R \leq r]$, would be the probability that a town so chosen would be closer to Austin than r. With a uniform density, we would expect that probability to be proportional to the area enclosed, and thus we would expect the form

$$F_R(r) = K \times \pi r^2 \tag{4.2.16}$$

where K is the density of towns per unit area. We will try this model against the experimental CDF developed previously. Transforming Eq. (4.2.16) to a form linear in r and substituting the experimental CDF for the theoretical CDF and the data, r_k, for the independent variable, r, we have

$$\sqrt{F_k} = \sqrt{\pi K} r_k + 0 \tag{4.2.17}$$

which is a straight line through the origin with a slope of $\sqrt{\pi K}$. We recycle the earlier code, substituting $\sqrt{F_k} = \sqrt{\frac{k}{n+1}}$ for the y-values, with the result

```
yvalues = Table[Sqrt[k / (n + 1)], {k, 1, n}];
plotlist =
  Table[{distancesort[[k]], yvalues[[k]]}, {k, 1, n}];
plot1 = ListPlot[plotlist, PlotRange → {{0, 500}, {0, 1}},
   AxesLabel → {"data values", "f(Exp. CDF)"},
   ImageSize → 400, PlotStyle → PointSize[0.015]];
```

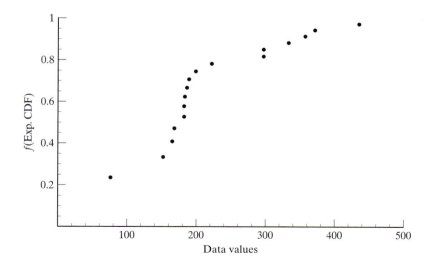

This shows some promise, so let's fit a line and compare it with the Rayleigh results.

```
yfit = Fit[plotlist, {0, r}, r]
K = (yfit / r)²/π
0.00276228 r
2.42877 × 10⁻⁶
```

We now plot the best-fit regression line with the data and examine it for fit and trends.

```
slope = √(π K);
RegressionLine = Table[{r, slope * r}, {r, 0, 500, 100}];
plot2 = ListPlot[RegressionLine,
    PlotJoined -> True, PlotRange → {{0, 500}, {0, 1}},
    DisplayFunction → Identity];
Show[plot1, plot2, AxesLabel →
    {"data values", "f(Exp. CDF)"}, ImageSize → 400];
```

The fit with the uniform-density model in Fig. 4.2.8 is not as good as with the Rayleigh model. An objective measure of the fit is the sample correlation coefficient:

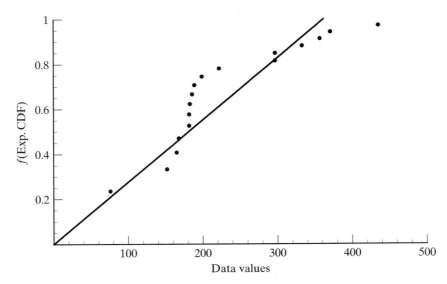

Figure 4.2.8 Data and regression line for city–distance data with a uniform-density model. Although the model works to some degree, the Rayleigh model is better.

```
Correlation[distancesort, yvalues];
N[%]
0.902776
```

Compare this value with 0.96685 for the Rayleigh model.

Summary.   We analyzed a data set against two models. Neither works perfectly, and perfection should not be expected, but the Rayleigh model works better than the uniform-density model. We know this because our eyes tell us, and we know it because the sample correlation coefficient is near 1 for the Rayleigh model and somewhat lower for the uniform-density model.

This analysis technique can be used with the following one-parameter distributions: uniform between the origin and an unknown maximum $(0, a)$, exponential, and Rayleigh. This analysis technique can also be used with the following two-parameter distributions: Gaussian, Weibull, lognormal, and uniform (a, b). Later, we will give examples with the exponential and Weibull in connection with reliability theory. We finish this section with a discussion of the Gaussian distribution.

4.2.4 Fitting the Gaussian Distribution to a Data Set

Importance.   Gaussian data appear often in practice, and we have tools to make spot and range estimates of the mean and variance based on Gaussian data; but the Gaussian CDF has no simple algebraic form, and many calculators do not calculate the Gaussian CDF and its inverse. The following analysis shows how to overcome this difficulty.

The theoretical Gaussian model.   Recall the PDF and the CDF of the normalized Gaussian random variable:

$$f_Z(z) = \frac{1}{\sqrt{2\pi}}\, e^{-\frac{1}{2}z^2} \quad \text{and} \quad F_Z(z) = \Phi(z) = \int_{-\infty}^{z} \frac{1}{\sqrt{2\pi}}\, e^{-\frac{1}{2}z'^2}\, dz' \tag{4.2.18}$$

If we have a general Gaussian random variable, $X = N(\mu_X, \sigma_X^2)$, then its CDF is

$$F_X(x) = \Phi\left(\frac{x - \mu_X}{\sigma_X}\right) \tag{4.2.19}$$

We take the inverse of Eq. (4.2.19) to obtain

$$\Phi^{-1}(F_X) = \left(\frac{1}{\sigma_X}\right) x + \left(-\frac{\mu_X}{\sigma_X}\right) \tag{4.2.20}$$

which is of the form of a straight line

$$y = ax + b, \text{ with } y = \Phi^{-1}(F_X), a = \frac{1}{\sigma_X} \quad \text{and} \quad b = -\frac{\mu_X}{\sigma_X} \tag{4.2.21}$$

In principle, there is no problem in transforming a Gaussian CDF into a straight line.

Fitting the model.   We rank order the data, calculate the experimental CDF, and calculate the y-values using

$$y_k = \Phi^{-1}(F_k) = \Phi^{-1}\left(\frac{k}{n+1}\right), \quad \text{where } n = \text{the number of data points} \qquad (4.2.22)$$

We then plot the y_k-values against the rank-ordered data values, x_k, and the slope and y-intercept give the mean and standard deviation according to Eq. (4.2.21).

The problem.   The only problem is finding the values of $\Phi^{-1}\left(\frac{k}{n+1}\right)$. Your calculator probably does not give these results directly. You can look them up in a $\Phi(z)$ table [see endnote 31 in Chapter 3] or a Φ^{-1} table [see endnote 34 in Chapter 3], or use some solver like Excel or Mathematica to calculate them. We also present a graphical method here.

Example 4.2.2:   Fitting the Gaussian to a data set ─────────────────────────────
First, we give an example using Mathematica to invert the $\Phi(z)$ function. We generate some data with a Gaussian distribution of known mean and variance:

```
Off[General::spell1]
truemean = 20;
truevariance = 3;
number = 30;
gaussiandata = Table[Random[
    NormalDistribution[truemean, √truevariance]], {number}]
{15.8801, 19.0906, 18.9982, 20.3317, 20.4007,
 21.0418, 19.0412, 18.7255, 16.8738, 20.8332,
 22.6731, 17.6425, 16.9638, 20.4359, 20.9032,
 23.9873, 20.8444, 22.1259, 18.6284, 19.4409,
 22.4932, 16.8802, 20.1494, 21.2103, 19.2457,
 20.59,   18.5547, 20.8854, 18.817,  20.9179}
```

We then rank order the data and count the number of points.

```
gaussiansort = Sort[gaussiandata]
n = Length[gaussiandata]
{15.8801, 16.8738, 16.8802, 16.9638, 17.6425,
 18.5547, 18.6284, 18.7255, 18.817,  18.9982,
 19.0412, 19.0906, 19.2457, 19.4409, 20.1494,
 20.3317, 20.4007, 20.4359, 20.59,   20.8332,
 20.8444, 20.8854, 20.9032, 20.9179, 21.0418,
 21.2103, 22.1259, 22.4932, 22.6731, 23.9873}
30
```

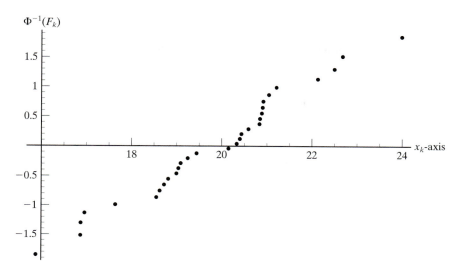

Figure 4.2.9   The inverse of the Gaussian PDF, evaluated at the experimental CDF, $F_k = \frac{k}{n+1}$, plotted against the rank-ordered data values. We expect something like a straight line because we generated the data to have a Gaussian distribution. The slope and intercept allow estimation of the mean and standard deviation of the data set.

We have to generate the y_k-values by inverting the Gaussian CDF. The following cell generates the inverse of the Gaussian CDF for $p = \frac{k}{n+1}$ and plots these values against the rank-ordered data, as shown in Fig. 4.2.9.

```
ysolutions = Table[
    FindRoot[CDF[NormalDistribution[0, 1], z] = k/(n + 1),
    {z, -1, +1}], {k, 1, n}];
yvalues = z / . ysolutions;
plotit =
    Table[{gaussiansort[[k]], yvalues[[k]]}, {k, 1, n}];
ListPlot[plotit, PlotStyle → PointSize[0.015],
    AxesLabel → {"xk-axis", "Φ⁻¹(Fk)"}, ImageSize → 400];
```

We then fit a regression line to the data.

```
gaussianfit = Fit[plotit, {1, x}, x]
-9.56763 + 0.482721 x
```

The mean and standard deviation are derived from the regression line slope and intercept according to Eq. (4.2.21).

```
b = gaussianfit / . x → 0;
a = gaussianfit - b / . x → 1;
meanestimate = -b / a
standevestimate = 1 / a
19.8202
2.07159
```

The first output is to be compared with 20 and the second to $\sqrt{3} = 1.73$, which are the true mean and standard deviation of the generated data set. We might wonder if these are the same as the sample mean and sample standard deviation. These are

```
Mean[gaussiandata]
StandardDeviation[gaussiandata]
19.8202
1.87471
```

A few tries will convince you that the two methods give the same means but different standard deviations. The advantage of the regression line approach is that we have strong assurance from the appearance of Fig. 4.2.9 that we are dealing with a data set that can be treated as Gaussian. This information allows us to make range estimates based on the sample mean and the sample variance.

Fitting to the Gaussian by hand.   What do you do without a table or a mathematical engine to invert the Gaussian CDF? We give here an additional method, "probability paper." *Probability paper* is a nomograph that inverts the Gaussian CDF for the user by using a nonlinear scale. Figure 4.2.10 shows a scanned image of a data analysis plotted on probability paper. The data are rank ordered: the x-values are plotted horizontally, and the experimental CDF plotted vertically. See the caption for more details. The data appear to be reasonably well fitted by a line, which was fitted by eye.

Probability paper is available from stores selling engineering supplies, or you can find sources on the web, or you can generate your own using Mathematica. The paper in Fig. 4.2.10 was generated in Mathematica, exported to Adobe Illustrator for annotation, and printed.

Summary.   In Sec. 4.2 we began by presenting linear regression, using the least-mean-square error criterion. We illustrated with several examples. We then moved to the question of fitting a theoretical model, in this case a PDF, to a data set. We introduced the concept of an experimental CDF and transformed the theoretical CDF into a straight line to use linear regression. We then addressed the special case of a Gaussian data set, in which case the theoretical CDF is a tabulated function. We showed an analytical method and a graphical method based on probability paper. In Sec. 4.3 on hypothesis testing, the chi-square measure will furnish another method to test if a data set can be considered Gaussian.

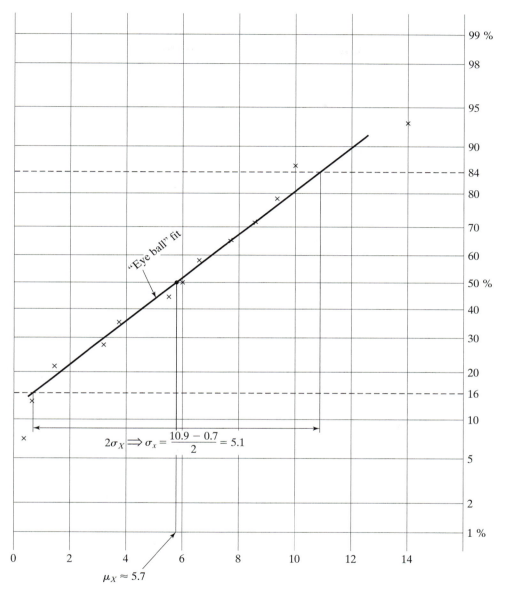

Figure 4.2.10 Scanned image of the analysis of a data set using probability paper. There were $n = 13$ data points, so the experimental CDF is $F_k = \frac{k}{n+1} = \frac{k}{14} = 7\%$, 14%, and so on, up to 93%. The values in the data set rank ordered from -0.4 to $+14$. The data plot reasonably straight, so the data are approximately Gaussian. The line was fitted by eye. Note that the mean can be estimated from where the line crosses 50%, and the standard deviation can be estimated as half the distance between the x-values where the line crosses 16% and 84%.

4.3 HYPOTHESIS TESTING

What is hypothesis testing? A *statistical hypothesis* is a speculation about a population that may or may not be true but may be tested by observation. In one sense, a statistical hypothesis represents a distillation of the complexities of reality to a simple proposition, such as, "this new process is superior to the old process," or "this new process is not superior to the old process." People who hire statisticians need to make decisions on the basis of data, and they want their choices spelled out in terms that are as simple as possible.

When should hypothesis testing be used? Hypothesis testing is used when something changes in an established situation and you wish to see if it made a detectable difference. For example, you drive home by the same route each day and you know that it takes about 25 minutes, plus or minus a few minutes for random effects due to traffic, weather, season of the year, and the like. Then a new road is completed and you want to see if it will get you home quicker, so you start going the new way, recording your travel time. Sooner or later you become convinced that the new way is better, or perhaps that the old way is better. Of course, this experiment would not be conducted with great rigor because the matter is not of great importance.

But when the stakes are high, and when the random aspects of the data sources can be described with probability models, the testing of a hypothesis can be made quite rigorous. Because it costs money and effort to gather data, there must be a serious interest in overthrowing the current understanding and establishing the new. The process and standards for overthrowing an established "truth" are standardized among statisticians by experience and tradition to safeguard the process from manipulation by personal or political bias.

The importance of vocabulary. As an engineer or manager, you might consult with a statistician to help you make a decision on the basis of data; or you might play the role of the statistician, helping your management make a decision on the basis of data. In either event you need to know the vocabulary of this aspect of statistics. This is an important part of statistics, and the definitions, vocabulary, and conventions are well established. We will introduce and define terms as we need them in developing some typical tests of hypotheses.

Looking ahead. We begin with tests based on data modeled as a binomial random variable. We follow with tests for the mean and variance of a data set. Finally, we investigate the chi-square test for testing if a data set fits an assumed PDF, or has some other property, such as independence.

4.3.1 Basic Hypothesis Testing

Did it make a difference? Consider the following situation. You are working for a company, Advancement, Inc., that has a rival, BetterSystems, Inc. Advancement currently owns 30% of the market, and BetterSystems owns 70%. In the effort to improve market share, you engage an advertising agency to develop and test a new line of advertising. Part of the testing of the advertising involves calling citizens at random in the area where the new ads are being circulated, to see what influence the ads have had. You are interested in the following two questions: (1) Have the ads had any influence, positive or negative, over the sales in that region? and (2) Have the ads had a positive influence on sales in that region? Clearly, you are more interested in the second question, because increasing sales is the purpose of the new ads, but for the sake of completeness, we will deal with both questions.

A binomial model.   The test consists of calling citizens at random and asking them if they bought brand A or brand B recently. If they bought, which did they buy? Let us say that we arbitrarily specify that the survey must find 50 customers who have bought recently. We will assume the conditions of binomial trials (see page 87) for the purchases, and thus the binomial distribution will be our model for the results of these trials. Because A's current market share is 30%, we expect 15 of 50 customers to buy A if the ad made no difference. Since we expect some random variation, we specify that the ads made no difference if between 9 and 21, inclusive, bought A, but if fewer than 9 or more than 21 bought A, then the new ads made a difference. The reason for this range will soon be discussed.

The following cell calculates the probability of having fewer than 9 and more than 21 customers purchase brand A, based on the assumptions of binomial trials and $p = 0.3$. According to the result, 4.3% of the probability falls outside the range 9–21, inclusive. This means that *even if the ads made no difference*, 4.3% of the time the responses of 50 callers would indicate a difference due to the new ads. We chose this range to make this probability of making a mistake below 5%, which is an accepted threshold for this sort of test.

```
p = 0.3;
n = 50;
α = 1 - Sum[PDF[BinomialDistribution[n, p], k], {k, 9, 21}]
0.0433404
```

Translation into the vocabulary of statistical hypothesis testing.   We will now review this example and introduce some vocabulary to describe the process. The hypotheses that we are testing are

H_0: The null hypothesis is that $p = 0.3$.

H_1: The alternative hypothesis is that $p \neq 0.3$.

The *null hypothesis* describes the "truth" that has been well established but that we are challenging. Because the ads cost money, and the survey costs money and effort, we frame the null hypothesis such that the data can permit its rejection with some force. For example, if 25 out of 50 persons had bought brand A, we would have evidence to reject the null hypothesis and accept the alternative hypothesis; however, if 16 out of 50 people had bought brand A, then we have scant evidence to reject the null hypothesis, and hence we must retain it. This does not mean that the null hypothesis is true, however; it merely means that we have insufficient evidence to reject it. When the data do not lead to its rejection, the null hypothesis is accepted, not so much because the data support it but because it was accepted in the past.

The *alternative hypothesis* is that $p \neq 0.3$. Later we will test a second alternative hypothesis, namely, $p > 0.3$. These alternative hypotheses shape the nature of the test. In the case in which the alternative hypothesis is $p \neq 0.3$, we consider survey results outside the range 9–21, inclusive, to indicate the rejection of the null hypothesis. Thus if 5 of 50 callers had bought brand A, this would be evidence that would lead to the rejection of the null hypothesis in favor of the alternative hypothesis. Consider, on the other hand, that the alternative hypothesis was $p > 0.3$. In this case 5 of 50 buying brand A would weigh more heavily against the alternative hypothesis than against the null hypothesis. In this second case the null hypothesis would not be rejected.

The *critical region* is the region, defined before any survey results become available, that would lead to the rejection of the null hypothesis. In this case the critical region is all values outside the central region 9–21, inclusive. We thus have two *critical values,* 8.5 on the low end and 21.5 on the high end.[22] These values define the boundary between the regions for accepting or rejecting the null hypothesis.

Type I and type II errors.   Because the result of a hypothesis test is binary, there are two types of errors that can be made:

>   A *type I error* results from rejecting the null hypothesis when it is true.

>   A *type II error* results from accepting the null hypothesis when it is false.

In the previous cell we calculated the probability of a type I error. We showed that

$$\alpha = P[\text{type I error}]$$
$$= P[H_0 \text{ is rejected} \mid H_0 \text{ is true}] = P[K < 9 \cup K > 21 \mid p = 0.3] = 0.04334$$

$(4.3.1)$

The probability of a type I error, α, is called the *level of significance* of the test. If $\alpha = 0.04334$ is unacceptably high, we can broaden the range of acceptance or take more data. For example, if we broadened the acceptance range to 8–22 out of 50, inclusive, then the probability of a type I error would be $\alpha = 0.01954$. As we shall soon see, broadening the acceptance range leads to an increase in the probability of a type II error. In this case we cannot calculate the probability of a type II error because the alternative hypothesis is too general.

Summary.   We defined a null hypothesis and an alternative hypothesis. Our test procedure is to identify 50 people who bought brands A or B. If between 9 and 21 people, inclusive, bought brand A, we accept the null hypothesis and conclude that the new ads made no difference. If fewer than 9 or more than 21 bought brand A, then we reject the null hypothesis and conclude that the new ads made a difference in market share. This procedure has a level of significance of $\alpha = 0.04334$, meaning that this is the probability of rejecting the null hypothesis when it is in fact true. If fewer than 9 bought brand A, this is evidence that the new ads hurt market share. If more than 21 bought brand A, this is evidence that the new ads increased market share.

Did the ads improve our market share?   We have just considered the question, Did the ads make a difference? We now consider the question, Did the ads make a *favorable* difference? Our null hypothesis will be the same, but now we frame the alternative hypothesis to indicate a higher probability that the buyer chose brand A.

> H_0: The null hypothesis is that $p = 0.3$.

> H_1: The alternative hypothesis is that $p > 0.3$.

The possibility that $p < 0.3$ is not being considered. We assume that either H_0 or H_1 must be true. As explained before, the region of acceptance now includes all values below 15, since these favor the null hypothesis over the alternative hypothesis. Values above 15 favor the alternative hypothesis, but we must choose a critical value to keep an acceptable type I error. We specify a type I error less than 5% and find the critical value by trial and error in the following cell:

```
p = 0.3;
n = 50;
cv = 20;  (*The critical value*)
α = 1 - Sum[PDF[BinomialDistribution[n, p], k], {k, 0, cv}]
0.0477638
```

The critical value proves to be 20.5, since a value of 20 gives a type I error probability of $\alpha = 0.04776$. Thus our procedure to test against this alternative hypothesis is to identify 50 people who bought brand A or B, and if more than 20.5 purchased brand A, then we reject the null hypothesis and conclude that the new ads increased market share. If 20 or fewer bought brand A, then we retain the null hypothesis that the ads made no difference at a level of significance of $\alpha = 4.776\%$.

Type II errors.   If we accept the null hypothesis when it is false, we commit a type II error. We have not calculated the probability of a type II error because our alternative hypotheses have been too general. Let us consider the following null and alternative hypotheses:

$$H_0: \text{The null hypothesis is that } p = 0.3.$$

$$H_1: \text{The alternative hypothesis is that } p = 0.5.$$

As before, we assume that either the null hypothesis or the alternative hypothesis is true. This new alternative hypothesis does not change the test procedure, nor does it change the probability of a type I error for the same acceptance region. It does allow us to calculate the probability of a type II error, as follows:

$$\beta = P[\text{type II error}]$$
$$= P[\text{accept } H_0 \mid H_0 \text{ is false}] = P[K \leq 20 \mid H_1] = P[K \leq 20 \mid p = 0.5] \qquad (4.3.2)$$

Equation (4.3.2) expresses the probability that we accept the null hypothesis when it is false, when in fact the market share is 50% owing to the new ads. We compute the probability of a type II error in the following cell:

```
p = 0.5;
n = 50;
cv = 20;
```

```
β = Sum[PDF[BinomialDistribution[n, p], k], {k, 0, cv}]
0.101319
```

The high probability of making a type II error indicates that we have a weak test. We have made the acceptance region for the null hypothesis very broad, such that we will accept it 10.1% of the time when the alternative hypothesis is true.

Because we would like to reject the null hypothesis with some confidence, we set the rejection region to have a low probability; in this case we have $\alpha = 0.04776$, or a 4.776% chance of making an error when we reject the null hypothesis. We then check β, the probability of making a type II error. The *power of the test* is defined as $1 - \beta$, and we want this as near 1 or 100% as reasonable. In this case the power of the test is $1 - 0.101 = 0.899$. This may or may not be acceptable to the management of your company.

To reduce type II error, we have three choices: (1) we can lower the critical value below 20, which will increase α and decrease β; (2) we can get more data (increase n); or (3) some combination of the previous two. The following cell allows a trial-and-error exploration of the effects of the two parameters. Our goal is to render both α and β less than 0.05.

```
cv = 19;
n = 50;
α = 1 - Sum[PDF[BinomialDistribution[n, 0.3], k], {k, 0, cv}]
β = Sum[PDF[BinomialDistribution[n, 0.5], k], {k, 0, cv}]
0.0848026
0.0594602
```

You may confirm the following results. With $n = 50$, we have α and β averaging ≈ 0.07 at a critical value of 19.5. With these values, we will be wrong about 7% of the time. With $n = 71$, we have α and β averaging ≈ 0.04 at a critical value of 28.5. Thus we need more data than the original $n = 50$ if we wish to distinguish between $p = 0.3$ and $p = 0.5$ with an error probability of less than 0.05.

You do it.   What if we want $\alpha = 0.01$ with the same value of β? In that case, how many data points do we require?

```
myanswer =            ;
```

```
Evaluate
```

For the answer, see endnote 23.

Summary.   We used a binomial model to illustrate basic statistical hypothesis testing. We defined a null and three alternative hypotheses, we defined the rejection and acceptance regions, we defined type I and type II errors, and we defined the level of significance and the power of the test. We found that there is a trade-off between the level of significance of the test, α, and the power of the test, $1 - \beta$. To make α and β acceptably small, more data were required.

4.3.2 Testing Hypotheses Concerning the Mean or Variance of a Population

Continuous distributions.   The example in the previous section used a discrete random variable to model the results of a test. In this section we assume a continuous random variable to model the data used to test a hypothesis. Specifically, we will test hypotheses concerning the mean and will assume that the data are Gaussian.

A time study.   Consider a scenario in which the time required to manufacture an item is under study, and changes are proposed in the manufacturing process to reduce the time required. Because this is a complex process, with many contributors to the final time required, we expect the times to vary randomly, and the model will be Gaussian.

The null and alternative hypothesis.   From extensive experience with the current manufacturing process, we know that the mean time is $\mu = 157$ minutes, and the standard deviation is 7 minutes. Our null hypothesis is that the changes in the process do not matter and hence the mean remains unchanged. Thus

$$H_0 : \text{the null hypothesis is that } \mu = 157.$$

For alternative hypotheses we will consider three: that the mean does change (in either direction), that the mean is reduced, and that the mean is reduced to 151 minutes. First, we consider

$$H_1 : \text{the alternative hypothesis is that } \mu \neq 157.$$

The testing procedure.   The proposed changes are made in the process, and data are taken on the time required to manufacture each of 12 items. Let the recorded times be $x_1, x_2, \cdots, x_{12}$.[24] These we model as IID Gaussian random variables: $X_i = N(\mu, \sigma^2)$, where $\mu = 157$ and $\sigma = 7$, and $i = 1, 2, ..., n$. Because the sample mean [Eq. (4.1.2)], $\bar{x}$, is an unbiased estimator of the true mean, values of the sample mean near 157 will favor the null hypothesis, and values far away from 157 will favor the alternative hypothesis. How far away we will decide on the basis of a prescribed level of significance [Eq. (4.3.1)] for the test. In this case, we will use $\alpha = 0.01$ for the level of significance.

The acceptance region.   The acceptance region will thus be symmetric about 157 and will have a width defined by the probability of a type I error. We may calculate the width based on the random variable that models the sample mean, Eq. (4.1.3), repeated in Eq. (4.3.3):

$$\hat{X} = \frac{1}{12}(X_1 + X_2 + \cdots + X_{12}) \tag{4.3.3}$$

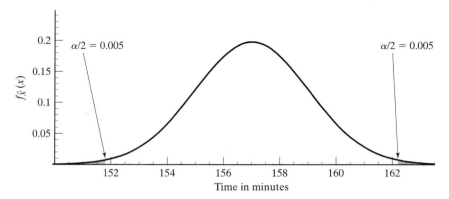

Figure 4.3.1 An illustration of the requirement in Eq. (4.3.5). The shaded tails of the distribution represent the region of rejection of the null hypothesis, and the central lobe the region of acceptance. For $\alpha = 0.01$, the width of the region of acceptance is $2 \times (2.576\sigma/\sqrt{n})$.

The PDF of this random variable, under the assumed null hypothesis is

$$f_{\hat{X}|H_0}(x) = N\left(\mu, \frac{\sigma^2}{n}\right) = N\left(157, \frac{49}{12}\right) \tag{4.3.4}$$

Because the alternative hypothesis is $\mu \neq 157$, the probability of a type I error is

$$P\left[\mu - \frac{w}{2} < \hat{X} < \mu + \frac{w}{2}\right] = 1 - \alpha = 1 - 0.01 \tag{4.3.5}$$

where $\mu = 157$ and w is the width of the region of acceptance. Figure 4.3.1 shows how the 1% probability is distributed between the two tails of the distribution of $\hat{X}$.

From our earlier work on the properties of the normal distribution and its application in estimation of the mean, we know that the half-width of the region of acceptance is defined by

$$\Phi\left(\frac{\mu + w/2 - \mu}{\sigma/\sqrt{n}}\right) = \Phi(z_c) = 1 - \frac{\alpha}{2} = 0.995 \Rightarrow z_c = 2.5760 \tag{4.3.6}$$

which leads to

$$\frac{w}{2} = z_c\frac{\sigma}{\sqrt{n}} = 2.576 \times \frac{7}{\sqrt{12}} = 5.205 \tag{4.3.7}$$

where σ is the standard deviation of the data. Thus if the sample mean of the data comes within 5.2 of 157 on the high or low side, we accept the null hypothesis, and if the sample mean falls outside this range, we reject the null hypothesis and conclude that the changes in the manufacturing process changed the average time it takes to manufacture the product.

Relating to range estimates of the mean. The process we just derived is closely related to the process of making a range estimate of the mean of a data set with a prescribed degree of confidence. The *level of confidence* [Eq. (4.1.17)] for the range estimation turns out to be the complement of the *level of significance* [Eq. (4.3.1)] for a hypothesis test in the following sense: If we estimate the true mean of our 12 data points with a level of confidence of 99% we will define a range about the value of the sample mean. If 157 falls within this range, then the null hypothesis should be accepted, and if 157 falls outside this range then the null hypothesis should be rejected with a level of significance of 1%.

More vocabulary. Customarily, for hypotheses about continuous variables, such as the preceding mean test, levels of significance of 5% and 1% are used for rejecting the null hypothesis. When the null hypothesis is rejected at the 5% level, the test is said to be *significant,* and when the null hypothesis is rejected at the 1% level, the test is said to be *highly significant.* If the alternative hypothesis is definite enough to permit the calculation of the probability of a type II error, then the *power of the test* is also important in describing the value of the test.

Levels of significance of 5% are traditional in the social sciences, where data are hard to come by. In the physical sciences, levels of significance of 1% are also used. These values of 5% and 1% are customary for two reasons. First, tables of the CDF of the random variables used in hypothesis testing do not support testing at arbitrary significance levels, and this was quite important when such tables were derived by hand calculations. Second, standard values of α eliminate the possibility that a statistician will pick a level of significance from personal or political bias to favor or disfavor a hypothesis. Indeed, the statistician should not pick the α value at all, but this is an executive decision, made before data are analyzed.

More on the connection between range estimation and hypothesis testing. We have just presented the close relationship between a range estimation of the mean, developed in Sec. 4.1, and a test of a hypothesis about the mean. This relationship is not incidental but is in fact fundamental to the logic of the two subjects. This logic and the concomitant relationship extends to many aspects of hypothesis testing. In the previous example, for example, we investigated a hypothesis about the mean, $H_0 : \mu = 157$, with an alternative hypothesis, $H_1 : \mu \neq 157$, when the standard deviation of the data was known, $\sigma = 7$. If the standard deviation is not known, then the sample mean of the data is modeled as a Student's t random variable, Eq. (4.1.75), just as in estimating the mean, and the final result of the hypothesis test uses the sample standard deviation [Eq. (4.1.28)] instead of the true standard deviation, and the value of t_c from CDF of the Student's t random variable for $n - 1 = 11$ degrees of freedom. Thus Eq. (4.3.7) becomes

$$\frac{w}{2} = t_c \bar{s}_X = 3.105 \times \frac{\bar{s}_X}{\sqrt{12}} \tag{4.3.8}$$

where $\bar{s}_X$ is the sample standard deviation of the data, and $t_c = 3.105$ for dof $= 11$ and $\alpha = 0.01$.[12] Notice that the region of acceptance is about 20% broader owing to the uncertainty of the standard deviation. For a large data set, $n \geq 30$, the values of t_c are sufficiently close to z_c and the Gaussian values may be used.

In a similar way hypotheses concerning the variance may be tested. In general, the procedure is to make a range estimate to a certain level of confidence, say, $1 - \alpha = 99\%$, of the true variance using the methods presented in Sec. 4.1. If the value of variance being tested as the null hypothesis falls within the region, then the null hypothesis is accepted with a level of significance of $\alpha = 1\%$.

Two-tailed and one-tailed tests. When the alternative hypothesis is $H_1 : \mu \neq 157$, values far away from 157 on both sides favor the alternative hypothesis. This alternative hypothesis leads to a two-tailed test. If the alternative hypothesis is $H_1 : \mu < 157$, then values on the high side favor the null hypothesis over the alternative hypothesis. This alternative hypothesis is that the new process takes less time than the old process, and it leads to a one-tailed test. We now test the null hypothesis against this alternative hypothesis.

Let us prescribe a level of significance of $\alpha = 0.01$, which translates to Eq. (4.3.9):

$$P[H_0 \text{ is rejected} \mid H_0 \text{ is true}] = P[\hat{X} < cv \mid \mu = 157] = \Phi\left(\frac{cv - \mu}{\sigma/\sqrt{n}}\right) = \alpha \qquad (4.3.9)$$

where $\hat{X}$ is the random variable modeling the mean of the data, σ is the standard deviation of the data, $\frac{\sigma}{\sqrt{n}} = \frac{7}{\sqrt{12}}$, and cv is the critical value separating the region of acceptance on the high side from the region of rejection on the low side. From the tables of the inverse CDF [see endnote 34 in Chapter 3] of the Gaussian PDF we find that

$$\Phi\left(\frac{cv - \mu}{\sigma}\right) = 1 - \Phi\left(\frac{\mu - cv}{\sigma}\right) = \alpha \Rightarrow \Phi\left(\frac{\mu - cv}{\sigma}\right) = \Phi(z_c) = 1 - \alpha = 0.99 \qquad (4.3.10)$$

From the inverse CDF of the Gaussian random variable, we find $z_c = 2.326$, and it follows that

$$cv = \mu - z_c \frac{\sigma}{\sqrt{n}} = 157 - 2.326 \times \frac{7}{\sqrt{12}} = 152.3 \qquad (4.3.11)$$

The regions of acceptance (white) and rejection (shaded) are shown in Fig. 4.3.2.

Type II errors. We are unable to calculate the probability of type II errors [Eq. (4.3.2)] in the previous two tests because the alternative hypotheses are too general. A type II error occurs when the null hypothesis is affirmed although it is false, that is, when the alternative hypothesis is

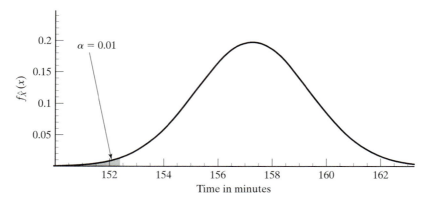

Figure 4.3.2 A one-tailed test with a level of significance of 0.01. The shaded region is the region for rejecting the null hypothesis that the mean remains at $\mu = 157$ for the alternative hypothesis that the mean is smaller than 157.

true. Of course, type II errors can occur under the previous alternative hypotheses, but to calculate the *probability* of a type II error, we need a suitable alternative hypothesis.

Consider the following hypotheses:

$$H_0 : \mu = 157, \text{ the null hypothesis}$$

$$H_1 : \mu = 149, \text{ the alternative hypothesis}$$

Here again the null hypothesis is that the process time does not change. The alternative hypothesis, which is assumed true if the null hypothesis is rejected, is that the process time is reduced to 149 by the changes made in the manufacturing process. For the same level of significance, $\alpha = 0.01$, the critical value remains at 152.3. A type II error would occur if the mean was $\mu = 149$ and yet the null hypothesis was affirmed. The probability of a type II error would be

$$\beta = P[H_0 \text{ is affirmed} \mid H_0 \text{ is false}] = P[\hat{X} > 152.3 \mid \mu = 149] \qquad (4.3.12)$$

where again $\hat{X}$ is the random variable modeling the sample mean of the 12 data points. If the standard deviation of the data is known (assume $\sigma = 7$), then the sample mean is modeled by a Gaussian random variable, $\hat{X} = N(149, \frac{7^2}{12})$. If the standard deviation of the data is not known, then the sample standard deviation must be used (assume $\bar{s}_X = 7$, again), and the random variable modeling the sample mean is a Student's t random variable with $n - 1 = 11$ degrees of freedom. We proceed under the first assumption, that $\hat{X} = N(149, \frac{7^2}{12})$. In this case Eq. (4.3.12) calculates to

$$\beta = P[\hat{X} > 152.3 | \mu = 149] = 1 - \Phi\left(\frac{152.3 - 149}{7/\sqrt{12}}\right)$$

$$(4.3.13)$$

$$= 1 - \Phi(1.633) = 0.0513$$

So the probability of a type II error is 0.0513 with this critical value. Put another way, the power of the test is $1 - \beta = 0.9487$.

Strengthening the test. To strengthen the test, we must have more data. The following cell takes two inputs, $n = $ the number of data points and $cv = $ the critical value separating the regions of acceptance and rejection, and gives two outputs, α and $1 - \beta$, the level of significance of the test and the power of the test. The values $n = 17$ and $cv = 153.0$ give a level of significance lower than 1% and a power exceeding 99%. This says that with 17 data points and a critical value of 153.0, we will make a mistake 1 time out of 100 in distinguishing between means of 157 and 149, and the mistake can be in either direction.

```
n = 17;
cv = 153;
α = N[CDF[NormalDistribution[157, 7/√n], cv]]
PowerOfTest = N[CDF[NormalDistribution[149, 7/√n], cv]]
0.00923496
0.990765
```

Our procedure is thus to take 17 data points and average them. If the average is above 153, we affirm that the new process is no better than the old. If the average falls below 153, then we reject the null hypothesis and affirm that the new process has reduced the average time to 149 minutes.

You do it.   What if we do not know the standard deviation and we want a level of significance of 5% and a power of 95%. Assume the sample standard deviation is 7 for all values of n and all data sets. How many data points do we need?

```
myanswer =             ;
```

```
Evaluate
```

For the answer, see endnote 25.

4.3.3 The Chi-Square Goodness-of-Fit Test

Up to this point we have tested hypotheses about parameters in populations, modeled by parameters in probability distributions, μ, p, and σ. In this section we show a standard test for investigating the goodness of fit between a data set and a proposed probability model. This test works for any proposed model. We will use it to test if a data set is Gaussian and to test for independence. The test also has the feature that it expresses a level of significance and is completely objective.

Background.   The reasoning behind the chi-square test is as follows: Let us say we have a set of data, upward of 50 or more data points, and we want to establish if these data are Gaussian (or independent, or have some other PDF). We compute the sample mean and sample variance and thus propose the null hypothesis that our data are generated by a Gaussian process approximately of the form $X = N(\overline{x}, \overline{s}_X^2)$, where we used the standard symbols for the sample mean and sample variance.

Get some regions.   We partition the data space into regions so that every data point falls into one of the regions. We are free to choose the number of regions and how we form their boundaries, but we have some guidelines. The test becomes unreliable if we have too few data points in each, say, five or fewer, so we divide according to that criterion. We also need enough regions to define the shape of the distribution. The more data points we have, the more regions we can support. We will assume that we have 50 data points. Let us aim for about 7 in each region by dividing the range into seven regions, each of which has equal probability. Thus the CDF of the Gaussian should be set to $\frac{i}{7}$, where $i = 1, 2, 3, 4, 5$, or 6 to define the boundaries of the regions. We number the regions $k = 1, 2, \ldots, 7$. For the normalized Gaussian, the upper boundaries of the first six regions are calculated by the following cell:

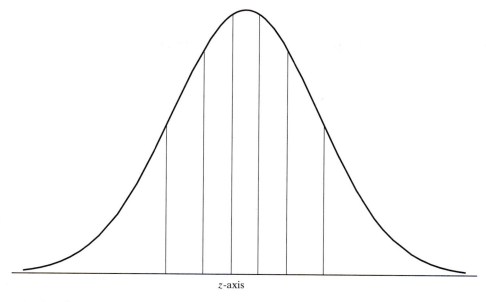

Figure 4.3.3 The PDF of the Gaussian is divided into seven regions of equal probability (area). We thus expect roughly equal numbers of data points to fall into each region if the data are Gaussian.

```
Table[FindRoot[CDF[NormalDistribution [0, 1], z] == i/7,
    {z, -1, +1}], {i, 1, 6}];
regionboundary = z /.%
{-1.06757, -0.565949, -0.180012,
  0.180012, 0.565949,  1.06757}
```

Figure 4.3.3 shows the PDF and these regions.

   We assume that the null hypothesis is correct, that is, that the data are Gaussian. In that case the number of data points that fall into each region should be roughly the same. We illustrate the process by generating some "data" according to a Gaussian distribution.

```
exampledata =
  Table[Random[NormalDistribution [10, 4]], {50}];
(*The true mean and standard deviation are 10 and 4,
 respectively. The sample mean
  and sample standard deviation are now
  calculated and appear after this cell.*)
```

```
samplemean = Mean[exampledata]
samplestandarddeviation = StandardDeviation[exampledata]
(*Here we determine the boundaries of the regions*)
Table[
  FindRoot[CDF[NormalDistribution[
      samplemean, samplestandarddeviation], z] == i/7,
    {z, -1, +1}], {i, 1, 6}];
regionboundary = z/.%
9.84592
3.74942
{5.84315, 7.72393, 9.17098, 10.5209, 11.9679, 13.8487}
```

We now count the number of data points that fall into each region, using the following function.[26]

```
boundaries [exampledata, regionboundary, 7]
```

The number of elements below 5.84315 is 9.

The number of elements between 5.84315 and 7.72393 is 2.

The number of elements between 7.72393 and 9.17098 is 7.

The number of elements between 9.17098 and 10.5209 is 7.

The number of elements between 10.5209 and 11.9679 is 13.

The number of elements between 11.9679 and 13.8487 is 6.

The number of elements above 13.8487 is 6.

Figure 4.3.4 This output gives the number of data values in each region of a Gaussian PDF, divided equally into seven regions of equal probability. These data will be subjected to the chi-square test to test the null hypothesis that the data are Gaussian.

Notice that the data values in Fig. 4.3.4 are distributed more or less equally between the regions. This is what we expect, since we divided the Gaussian PDF into seven regions of equal probability. We could have divided it unequally, however, so there is nothing special about the even distribution.

Binomial trials.   Regardless of how we divide the PDF into regions, the number of data values falling into each region must be a binomial random variable because each trial is independent and the probability of "success" that is, falling in that bin, is the same for each trial. For example, the probability that a data value will fall into the third region is constant, regardless of the PDF of the data or the boundaries of the regions, so long as these do not change. This is the key idea that leads to the chi-square test. Let N_k be a binomial random variable describing the number of data values falling into the kth region, and let p_k be the probability that a data value will fall into the kth region. Then it must be true that $E[N_k] = np_k$ and $Var[N_k] = np_kq_k$, where $q_k = 1 - p_k$ and n is the number of data values.

The central limit theorem. If n is sufficiently large, then N_k will approach a Gaussian random variable. We normalize N_k in the usual way, as follows:

$$Z_k = \frac{N_k - np_k}{\sqrt{np_kq_k}} \tag{4.3.14}$$

and we know that the sum of the squares of independent normalized Gaussian random variables is a chi-square random variable with dof = the number of independent normalized Gaussian random variables added. On this basis we would expect the following sum to be chi-square with i degrees of freedom:

$$\chi^2 = \sum_{k=1}^{k=i} \frac{(N_k - np_k)^2}{np_kq_k} \tag{4.3.15}$$

Despite the logic of this reasoning, Eq. (4.3.15) is not true, even as $n \to \infty$; however, in 1900 Karl Pearson proved that as $n \to \infty$, the expression in Eq. (4.3.15), with the q_k term dropped from the denominator, approaches a chi-square random variable with dof = $i - r - 1$, where r is the number of parameters determined by fitting the theoretical distribution to the data, in our case $r = 2$, since we extracted the mean and variance of the model from the data set.[27] Thus the real chi-square test uses

$$\chi^2 = \sum_{k=1}^{regions} \frac{(N_k - np_k)^2}{np_k} = \sum_{k=1}^{regions} \frac{(\text{experimental} - \text{expected})^2}{\text{expected}}, \quad \text{the chi-square measure}$$
$$\tag{4.3.16}$$

For our case $p_k = \frac{1}{7}$ because we designed the regions to have equal probability, $n = 50$, so the expected number in each region is $\frac{50}{7}$. For the preceding data, the chi-square measure was given by the following cell:

```
chisquaremeasure = (9 - 50/7)²/(50/7) + (2 - 50/7)²/(50/7) + (7 - 50/7)²/(50/7) +

  (7 - 50/7)²/(50/7) + (13 - 50/7)²/(50/7) + (6 - 50/7)²/(50/7) + (6 - 50/7)²/(50/7);

N[%]
9.36
```

Interpreting the chi-square measure. We need to do a bit more work before we are able to interpret this result. Because we have seven regions and fit two parameters to the

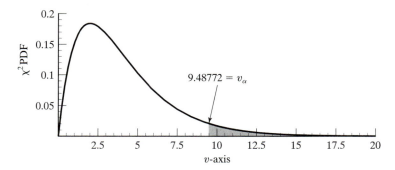

Figure 4.3.5   The upper tail of the chi-square distribution for dof $= 4$. The area of the tail is 5%. A value of the χ^2 measure falling in this region would allow us to reject the null hypothesis at the 5% level of significance.

distribution (the mean and the standard deviation), we compare this result with the chi-square random variable with $7 - 2 - 1 = 4$ degrees of freedom. We will use the chi-square measure to test the null hypothesis, H_0, that the data are compatible with a Gaussian distribution. The alternative hypothesis would be that the data are not Gaussian. The probability of a type I error [Eq. (4.3.1)] is

$$P[\chi^2 > v_\alpha | H_0] = \alpha \qquad (4.3.17)$$

where α is the significance level for the test. In our case we choose $\alpha = 0.05$, or 5% significance. In this case the value of v_α is calculated in the following cell and illustrated by the graph in Fig. 4.3.5. Both use the chi-square distribution for dof $= 4$.

```
alpha = 0.05;
dof = 4;
vα = vα /.
  FindRoot[CDF[ChiSquareDistribution[dof], vα] == 1 - alpha,
    {vα, 0, 1}]
9.48772
```

Interpretation of the test.   Equation (4.3.17) states that if the null hypothesis is true, that is, if the data are Gaussian, then we will reject the null hypothesis only α 5% of the time. Stated positively, the data will pass the chi-square test 95% of the time if the data are Gaussian. In our example $\chi^2(9.36) < v_\alpha(9.48)$, so the data set passes the chi-square test at the 5% significance level.

Misinterpretation of the test.   That the data set passes the chi-square test at the 5% significance level does not mean that we are 95% sure that the data are Gaussian. It means that we have insufficient evidence to conclude otherwise. Data from other distributions might pass the test also. The test assures us that we are not making a big mistake by treating the data as Gaussian, specifically, that 19 out of 20 Gaussian data sets would pass that test. Note that changing the significance level to 1% leads to $v_\alpha = 13.2$,[8] making it easier for the data to pass the test. Thus our confidence in the hypothesis that the data are Gaussian is not increased but rather decreased by using a 1% significance level; however, our confidence in the alternative hypothesis, that the data are not Gaussian, would be strengthened if the data did not pass at the 1% significance level.

Small values of χ^2. If the value of the χ^2 measure is very low, then this also is a low-probability event under the null hypothesis. As an example, consider the lower tail of the chi-square distribution for dof $= 4$. At the 1% level, we have $v_\alpha = 0.2971$. If the χ^2 measure was below this value we would have to consider two alternatives: either we have a data set that happens to fit a Gaussian distribution to an extraordinary degree (luck), or the data were artificially created or modified to be Gaussian (fraud).

4.3.4 Testing Independence with the Chi-Square Test

Earlier (see page 30) in the text we asserted that the number of letters in a person's name is statistically independent of the last digit of their phone number. We made this assertion because we know, or think we know, how phone numbers are assigned, namely, at random. We can now use the χ^2 measure to test this assertion.

The observed data. To get some data, we picked a page in the Austin, Texas, phone book and observed the two quantities in question. Because there are names on this page with $3, 4, \ldots, 12$ letters in the name, and since the last digit of the phone number can be $0, 1, 2, \ldots, 9$, there are 100 combinations that could be observed. We reduced these to 8 by combining names with letters $\leq 5, 6, 7$, and ≥ 8 together because some previous counting led us to expect roughly equal numbers of names in these categories. For each of these categories we observed whether the last digit of the phone number was in the range 0–4 or 5–9. In the first column on page 181 of the 2002 Austin phone book, there are 72 distinct names, and the data are given in Table 4.3.1.

Thus there were seven names with five or fewer letters listed with phone numbers ending in 0–4, and so on. The eight data values in Table 4.3.1 form a 2×4 contingency table. These observed frequencies of occurrence must be compared with the expected data to test the null hypothesis that the phone numbers and the number of letters in a person's name are independent.

The expected data. To calculate what we would expect in the eight places in the contingency table, assuming the null hypothesis, we multiply the marginal frequencies. For example,

Table 4.3.1   A 2×4 contingency table of observed data to be tested for independence. The columns refer to the number of letters in the name, and the rows to the last digit of the phone number

Last digit/letters in name	≤ 5	6	7	≥ 8	Total
0, 1, 2, 3, 4	7	9	10	11	37
5, 6, 7, 8, 9	5	7	8	15	35
Total	12	16	18	26	72

the relative frequency of a person having ≤ 5 letters in his or her name is

$$P[\leq 5] = \frac{12}{72} \tag{4.3.18}$$

and the probability of a person's phone number ending in 0, 1, 2, 3, or 4 is

$$P[0, 1, 2, 3, 4] = \frac{37}{72} \tag{4.3.19}$$

If these are independent events, the probabilities obey the rule

$$P[(\leq 5) \cap (0, 1, 2, 3, 4)] = P[\leq 5] \times P[0, 1, 2, 3, 4] \tag{4.3.20}$$

If we replace the probabilities with the relative frequencies and multiple by the number of trials, 72, we have the expected number of times we expect the event $(\leq 5) \cap (0, 1, 2, 3, 4)$ to occur in 72 names, assuming the null hypothesis of independence. Thus the expected number for this joint event is

$$n_{(\geq 5) \cap (0,1,2,3,4)} = \frac{12}{72} \times \frac{37}{72} \times 72 = 6.167 \tag{4.3.21}$$

which is to be compared with the observed value of 7. Working in this fashion we can create in Table 4.3.2 the expected values.

Table 4.3.2 The expected number of times for the various joint events assuming the null hypothesis of independence

Last digit/letters in name	≤ 5	6	7	≤ 8
0, 1, 2, 3, 4	6.167	8.222	9.250	13.36
5, 6, 7, 8, 9	5.833	7.778	8.750	12.64

The χ^2 test.   We now compare the observed with the expected using the chi-square measure, Eq. (4.3.16). Here the form is

$$\chi^2 = \sum_{i=1}^{8} \frac{(\text{observed} - \text{expected})^2}{\text{expected}} \tag{4.3.22}$$

The calculation in Mathematica follows:

```
observed = {7, 9, 10, 11, 5, 7, 8, 15};
expected =
  {6.167, 8.222, 9.25, 13.36, 5.833, 7.778, 8.75, 12.64};
ChiSquareMeasure = Sum[
  (observed[[i]] - expected[[i]])² / expected[[i]], {i, 1, 8}]
1.36553
```

This result must be compared with the value associated with the tail probability of the chi-square random variable of the appropriate degrees of freedom. For a $r \times c$ contingency table, where $r =$ the number of rows and $c =$ the number of columns, the degrees of freedom is[28]

$$dof = (r - 1)(c - 1) \qquad (4.3.23)$$

which is, for our case, dof = 3. For $\alpha = 5\%$ and dof = 3, we find the critical value in the following cell.

```
alpha = 0.05;
dof = 3;
vα = vα /.
  FindRoot[CDF[ChiSquareDistribution[dof], vα] = 1 - alpha,
    {vα, {0, 1}}]
7.81473
```

Because $1.36553 < 7.81473$, we accept the null hypothesis that the number of letters in a person's name is independent of the last digit in that person's phone number.

Summary. This section on hypothesis testing introduced the testing of hypotheses of the probability of success in a series of binomial trials, of the mean, and of other parameters of a continuous random variable. We used the chi-square measure to test a data set for compatibility with a proposed PDF, such as the Gaussian PDF, and for testing data for independence. Texts that focus on statistics treat many types of hypothesis tests.

4.4 PROBLEMS

4.4.1 Estimation

Exercises on estimation

P4.1.1 For an exponential distribution with a constant rate λ, the expected time to the next event is $\frac{1}{\lambda}$. Because the random variable T is the time between events, to estimate the event rate parameter the following estimator is proposed: $\bar{\lambda} = \frac{1}{n} \sum_{i=1}^{i=n} \frac{1}{t_i}$, where t_i is the measured time between events. Is this a consistent estimator? Explain.

A4.1.1 No, the estimator is biased

P4.1.2 The following set of random data are thought to be Gaussian: -1.00287, 6.44649, 3.55163, 2.61837, -2.32119, 6.09459, -1.57556, -0.0404947, -3.466, 5.59618, 9.08682, 2.88928, -2.51537, 1.78286, -1.40413, -3.34719, 7.11848, -0.0255592, 0.604687 ($n = 19$). Here for your convenience are the numbers sorted: -3.466, -3.34719, -2.51537, -2.32119, -1.57556, -1.40413, -1.00287, -0.0404947, -0.0255592, 0.604687, 1.78286, 2.61837, 2.88928, 3.55163, 5.59618, 6.09459, 6.44649, 7.11848, 9.08682

a. Make a spot estimate of the mean.
b. Make a spot estimate of the standard deviation.
c. Make a range estimate of the mean with 95% confidence.
d. Make a range estimate of the standard deviation with 95% confidence.

A4.1.2 **(a)** 1.584; **(b)** 3.854; **(c)** $-0.2737 < \mu_X < 3.447$; **(d)** $2.912 < \sigma_X < 5.699$

P4.1.3 A data set is taken and the sample mean and sample variance are calculated as 107 and 42, respectively, based on 12 data points.
a. Make a range estimate of the mean at the 98% confidence level.
b. Make a range estimate of the standard deviation at the 95% confidence level.

A4.1.3 **(a)** $101.9 < \mu_X < 112.1$ with 98% level of confidence; **(b)** $4.59 < \sigma_X < 11.0$ with 95% confidence

P4.1.4 A data set is taken and the sample mean and sample variance are calculated as 90 and 22, respectively, based on 13 data points.
a. Make a range estimate of the mean at the 98% confidence level.
b. Make a range estimate of the standard deviation at the 95% confidence level.

A4.1.4 **(a)** $86.5 < \mu_X < 93.5$ with 98% confidence; **(b)** $3.36 < \sigma_X < 7.74$ with 95% confidence

P4.1.5 A data set is taken and the sample mean and sample variance are calculated as 69 and 32, respectively, based on 14 data points.
a. Make a range estimate of the mean at the 98% confidence level.
b. Make a range estimate of the standard deviation at the 95% confidence level.

A4.1.5 **(a)** $65.0 < \mu_X < 73.0$ with 98% confidence; **(b)** $4.10 < \sigma_X < 9.11$ with 95% confidence

P4.1.6 You are given a set of data by the boss: 19.6, 1.88, 12.7, 11.9, 6.85, 12.8, 4.58, 19.0, 2.77, 13.6, 8.31, 11.7, 11.4, 13.8, 8.5, 13.2, 18.6, 8.46, 5.31, 6.99.
a. Calculate the sample mean.
b. Calculate the sample variance.
c. Calculate the sample standard deviation.
d. Make a range estimate of the true variance at the 75% confidence level.
e. Make a range estimate of the true mean at the 90% confidence level.
f. The boss then asks for 5% accuracy and 95% confidence. What is your response?

A4.1.6 **(a)** 10.6; **(b)** 26.2; **(c)** 5.12; **(d)** $19.0 < \sigma_{\bar{X}}^2 < 40.6$; **(e)** $8.62 < \mu_X < 12.6$, **(f)** "Boss, I need about 339 more samples."

P4.1.7 An experiment is known to have data that are distributed according to the Gaussian distribution. The following data were taken to estimate the mean: -8.1, 5.8, 15.0, 2.7, -4.7, 7.4.
a. Give an unbiased point estimate of the mean.
b. Give a range estimate of the mean at the 95% confidence level.

A4.1.7 **(a)** 3.02; **(b)** 3.02 ± 8.83

P4.1.8   Calculate the sample variance of the digits in your own social security number.

> **A4.1.8** There is no unique answer. The variance for random digits is 8.25, but for the $n = 9$ digits for a social security number, the variance can vary widely.

P4.1.9   When I first got my hearing aids, I tested the battery voltages every evening. Here are some of the data on one of the batteries, all in volts: 1.338, 1.318, 1.335, 1.335, 1.345, and 1.339.

> Assume these are normal with a stable mean.
> a. Find the 95% confidence range on the mean.
> b. Find the 95% confidence range on the standard deviation.

> **A4.1.9** **(a)** mean $= 1.335 \pm 0.00955$; **(b)** $0.00057 < \sigma_X < 0.00223$

P4.1.10 A thermocouple is used to measure a constant temperature in the presence of additive noise that is Gaussian. The noise has zero mean, so the mean of the signal-plus-noise is what we are trying to detect. The measurement system produces a series of measurements: 8.6, 7.4, 8.3, 6.7, 8.1, 8.8, and 8.5 mV.
> a. Estimate the range of the signal (the true mean) with 80% confidence.
> b. Estimate the probability that the next measurement in the series will exceed 8.7 mV.

> **A4.1.10** **(a)** $7.652 < \mu_X < 8.466$; **(b)** 0.1969

P4.1.11 Consider the following data: $-0.319, -0.461, -0.201, 0.142, -0.023, -0.029, 0.127, 0.208, 0.477$.
> a. Assume that we know that these data are generated by a process that gives zero mean, like the output of a high-pass filter. Give a range estimate of the variance of the underlying process with 80% confidence.
> b. Assume that we do not know the mean or variance. Give a range estimate of the mean and variance of this data set with 80% confidence.

> **A4.1.11** **(a)** $0.04516 < \sigma_X^2 < 0.1591$; **(b)** $\mu_X = -0.008778 \pm 0.1339, 0.04958 < \sigma_X^2 < 0.1898$

P4.1.12 An experiment consists of a series of n Bernoulli trials. The experiment is performed m times, with $k_1, k_2, \ldots, k_m$ successes on each performance of the experiment. We want to develop an estimator for p, the probability of success on a given trial. Because the relative frequency of success in any performance of the experiment is $\frac{k_i}{n}$, we let $p_i = \frac{k_i}{n}$ be an estimate based on one performance, and $\bar{p} = \frac{1}{m} \sum_{i=1}^{m} p_i$ be the estimator based on all m performances of the experiment. Thus we have trials, an experiment of n trials, and a macroexperiment of m performances of the experiment for modeling the statistics.
> a. Is $\bar{p}$ a biased estimator? Demonstrate your answer.
> b. Is $\bar{p}$ a consistent estimator? Demonstrate your answer.

A4.1.12 (a) The mean of the estimator model is the true mean, since $E\left[\frac{K_i}{n}\right] = \frac{np}{n}$; therefore this is an unbiased estimator; **(b)** $Var[\hat{P}] = \frac{pq}{nm} \to 0$ as $m \to \infty$ and therefore $\bar{p}$ is consistent

P4.1.13   The following data are known to be Gaussian: 88.1, 100, 91.1, 84.2, 92, 68.6, 79.4, 78.4, 79.5, 94.8, 76.4, 76.7, 77.3, 106, 86.1, 87.1, 88.3, 88.5, 84.0, 67.9, 95.2, 74.1, 87.2, 84, 68.5.
   a. Calculate the sample mean.
   b. Calculate the sample variance and sample standard deviation.
   c. Give a range estimate of the standard deviation with a confidence level of 95%.
   d. Give a range estimate of the mean with a confidence level of 95%.
   e. We want to estimate the mean of the process that generated the set of data with an accuracy of ± 0.1 at a confidence level of 98%. That is, $\bar{x} - 0.1 < \mu_X < \bar{x} + 0.1$ with 98% confidence. How many more samples of the process do we need?

A4.1.13 (a) 84.1; **(b)** 93.3 and 9.66, respectively; **(c)** $7.54 < \sigma_X < 13.44$; **(d)** $80.1 < \mu_X < 88.1$; **(e)** we need a total of 50,478, or 50,453 additional samples

P4.1.14   A random variable, X, takes on values $0, 1, 2, \ldots, k$, where k is an unknown positive integer, with equal probability. Since the mean of this distribution is $\frac{k}{2}$, we propose the estimator $\bar{k} = 2\bar{x}$, that is, twice the sample mean of the data, based on n data values. (In practice, this would be rounded to the nearest integer, but we will ignore this part of the process.)
   a. Is $\bar{k}$ an unbiased estimator X? Explain.
   b. Is $\bar{k}$ a consistent estimator X? Explain.

A4.1.14 (a) Yes, $E[\hat{K}] = k$; **(b)** Yes, $Var[\hat{K}] = \frac{a(a-2)}{3n} \xrightarrow{n \to \infty} 0$

P4.1.15   A voltage is measured to be $9.1 < V < 9.7$ with a 90% level of confidence, based on 17 samples. Estimate how many samples would be required to estimate the voltage within ± 0.1 V with a 99% level of confidence. Assume that the data are Gaussian and that the sample variance does not change appreciably.

A4.1.15 334, assuming the sample standard deviation does not change

P4.1.16   A market survey on the price of tea in China shows that, based on 10 samples, the price is $\$326 \pm 32$/ton with 90% confidence.
   a. Find the sample mean and sample variance.
   b. Estimate the probability that the eleventh sample will be less than $\$300$/ton.

A4.1.16 (a) mean $= 326$, var $= 3045$; **(b)** 0.3187

P4.1.17   A statistician is able to bound the mean of Gaussian process to ± 2 and 90% confidence with 10 data points. What is the minimum number of additional data points to bound the mean to ± 1.6 or better with 90% confidence?

A4.1.17 5 *additional* data points

P4.1.18   If 100 data points are required to estimate a constant voltage with an accuracy of ±1 V (1σ), how many data points are required for an accuracy of ±0.5 V (1σ)?

A4.1.18 400

P4.1.19   A statistician took 100 samples of a Gaussian data variable and was able to bound the mean within ±2 mV with a 90% level of confidence. The boss then said she wanted ±1 mV with 95% confidence. How many additional data points were gathered to meet this standard?

A4.1.19 468 additional data points

P4.1.20   A statistician takes data to estimate the mean of a Gaussian process of known standard deviation, $\sigma_X = 24$ μV. The mean must be bounded with a 98% confidence level with ±5 μV. How many samples are required?

A4.1.20 125 samples

P4.1.21   The following numbers are generated by a random-number generator that produces a number uniformly distributed between 0 and 1.0: 0.786, 0.416, 0.547, 0.938, 0.797, 0.018, 0.079, 0.613, 0.405, 0.096, 0.666, 0.339 ($n = 12$).
a. Calculate the sample mean, $\bar{x}$.
b. Calculate the sample variance, $\bar{s}_\mu^2$, given that the mean is known to be 0.5.
c. Calculate the sample variance, assuming that the mean is not known. This calculation will differ from the previous one.
d. Make a 90% confidence level range estimate of the mean, assuming the variance in part c.

A4.1.21 **(a)** 0.475; **(b)** $(0.291)^2$; **(c)** $(0.303)^2$; **(d)** 0.475 ± 0.157 with 90% confidence

P4.1.22   a. If you wanted to determine the average of all the digits in the social security numbers of the student population at a large university (approximately 50,000 students) describe briefly how you would proceed. Note that you do not need to know the SSNs, just the digits in the SSNs.
b. Estimate how many samples you would have to average to have an accuracy of 1%.

A4.1.22 **(a)** The only way would be to make a survey, asking students for their individual sums (not the SSN itself, as this is private.). You should probably take a simple calculator with you, since many do not add numbers without assistance; some candy for rewards would help as well. **(b)** about 450 students

P4.1.23   The following numbers were generated on my calculator as uniformly distributed between 0 and 1: 0.2877, 0.1171, 0.6503, 0.8887, 0.1808, 0.03229, 0.2541, 0.7303, and 0.3910.
a. Develop a transformation that will map the uniform distribution into a random variable that is Rayleigh distributed with a mean of 3.
b. Give the specific values that the given numbers become with this transformation.

c. Using the maximum likelihood estimator, estimate the parameter b in the Raleigh distribution from the numbers in part b.

A4.1.23 (a) $r_i = 2.394\sqrt{-2\ln[1-x_i]}$; (b) {0.288, 1.97}, {0.117, 1.19}, {0.65, 3.47}, {0.889, 5.02}, {0.181, 1.51}, {0.0323, 0.613}, {0.254, 1.83}, {0.73, 3.88}, {0.391, 2.38}; (c) $\bar{b} = 7.6693$; compare with the theoretical value of 11.46

P4.1.24 Consider that X is a continuous random variable uniformly distributed between zero and a. The upper limit of the distribution, a, is a positive but unknown number. Data are taken to estimate a. Because the average value of the random variable is half of a, the following estimator of a is proposed: $\bar{a} = \frac{2}{n}(x_1 + x_2 + x_3 + \cdots + x_n)$.
a. Is this a biased estimator? Explain.
b. Is this a consistent estimator? Explain.

A4.1.24 (a) $E[\hat{A}] = a$, so unbiased; (b) $Var[\hat{A}] = \frac{a^2}{3n} \xrightarrow{n\to\infty} 0$, so consistent

P4.1.25 The Laplace random variable has a PDF of $f_X(x) = \frac{a}{2}e^{-a|x|}$, for all x.
a. Determine a maximum likelihood estimator for the parameter a, based on a data set $x_1, x_1, \ldots, x_n$.
b. Based on your result, estimate a for the following data set: -4.31, -3.71, -0.0201, 1.71, 2.64, 0.936, 1.81, -2.41, 0.271, -0.303, -0.348, 1.22, -0.111, 2.56, 0.253, -1.69, 0.797, -4.64, 0.388, -0.273.

A4.1.25 (a) The estimator is $\bar{a} = \frac{n}{|x_1|+|x_2|+\cdots+|x_n|}$; (b) 0.65793

P4.1.26 In a binomial process, one way to estimate $P[\text{success}] = p$ is to count trials to the first success in a number of separate sequences of trials and estimate p from the results. This trial is of course a geometric random variable. Let the results of m such sequences be $n_1, n_2, \ldots, n_m$, where $n_1 =$ the trial of the first success on the first sequence, and so forth.
a. Derive a maximum likelihood estimator for p, $\bar{p}$, based on $n_1, n_2, \ldots, n_m$.
b. Show, if possible, that your estimator, $\bar{p}$, is unbiased. *Hint:* Try for $m = 1$ and, if successful, prove for $m = 2$, and so on.

A4.1.26 (a) $\bar{p} = \frac{m}{\sum\limits_{1}^{m} n_i}$; (b) for $m = 1$, $E[\hat{P}] = -\frac{p}{1-p}\ln p \neq p$, so it is biased

P4.1.27 Take the data set in the problem P4.1.21 and transform the original uniformly distributed random variable to a Gaussian random variable, $N(2, (1)^2)$. The required transformation is $y = \Phi^{-1}(x) + 2$, where Φ is the normalized Gaussian CDF.
a. Show that this is the required transformation.
b. Calculate the sample mean, $\bar{y}$.
c. Calculate the sample variance, $\bar{s}_Y^2$, assuming that the mean is not known.
d. Make a 90% confidence level range estimate of the mean.
e. Make a 90% confidence level range estimate of the variance.
Note that we have a Gaussian PDF generating the data and hence can use the t and χ^2 distributions.

A4.1.27 (a) equate the CDFs; (b) $\bar{y} = 1.860$; (c) $\tilde{s}_Y^2 = 1.100$; (d) using t distribution, mean $= 1.86 \pm 0.544$; (e) $0.6137 < \sigma_Y^2 < 1.626$

P4.1.28 The following data are assumed to arise from a PDF that is uniformly distributed between $-a$ and $+a$: -2.89, 3.76, -5.75, -0.364, -5.75, 4.79, 0.269, 6.72, 6.21. In this problem we investigate two methods for estimating a.

a. Because the mean is zero, we may estimate a from the sample variance. Here is an estimator: $\frac{(2\bar{a})^2}{12} = \frac{(x_1-0)^2+(x_2-0)^2+\cdots+(x_n-0)^2}{n}$, where the data are designated by the x's. Note that we assumed a true mean of 0 and thus used the appropriate estimator for the sample variance based on that knowledge. Because this estimation deals with the square of a, we will not take the square root. Thus the Big Three are a^2, $\overline{a^2}$, and $\hat{A}^2 = 3 \times \frac{(X_1)^2+(X_2)^2+\cdots+(X_n)^2}{n}$, where $X_1, \ldots, X_n$, are IID random variables uniformly distributed between $-a$ and $+a$. Use the estimator model $\hat{A}^2$ to show that this is an unbiased estimator and use this estimator to estimate a.

b. Another approach would be to deal with only the magnitudes of the data and to use the sample mean. This would lead to the estimator $\frac{\bar{a}}{2} = \frac{|x_1|+|x_1|+\cdots+|x_n|}{n}$. Give the Big Three for this estimator, investigate if it is a biased estimator, and use it to estimate a. For your convenience, here are the numbers without signs: 2.89, 3.76, 5.75, 0.364, 5.75, 4.79, 0.269, 6.72, 6.21.

A4.1.28 (a) Since $E[X_i^2] = \frac{a}{3}$, it is unbiased. The estimator gives 8.0723. (b) The Big Three are the true a, the estimator, $\bar{a} = 2 \times \frac{|x_1|+|x_2|+\cdots+|x_n|}{n}$, the estimator model, $\hat{A} = 2 \times \frac{|X_1|+|X_2|+\cdots+|X_n|}{n}$. This estimator gives 8.11178

Modeling problems on estimation

P4.1.29 Every evening I throw my pocket change into a pint jar in the closet. When the jar is full I take it to the bank, they run the change through a counting machine, and I get back folding money, plus some change. The last four times I went to the bank, the results were $48.62, $51.06, $49.87, and $45.16.

a. Estimate the mean of the cash value of a pint of mixed change.
b. Estimate the variance of the cash value of a pint of mixed change.
c. Stating assumptions, give a 95% confidence range estimate of the variance.
d. Stating assumptions, give a 95% confidence range estimate of the mean.

A4.1.29 (a) The sample mean is 48.68; (b) the sample variance is 6.49; (c) Gaussian assumed, $2.08 < \sigma_X^2 < 90.3$ with 95% confidence; (d) 48.68 ± 4.06, with 95% confidence

P4.1.30 a. Calculate the sample mean and sample variance of the digits in your phone number, including area code, and your SSN, 19 digits in all.
b. Calculate the true mean and variance of 19 random digits, equally likely.

A4.1.30 (a) varies with the individual, but should be close to the results of part b; (b) $\mu = 4.5$, $\sigma^2 = 8.25$

P4.1.31   Some students, for extra credit, counted the number of raisins in a cup of raisins, producing four pieces of data: 355, 380, 361, and 359.
 a. Calculate the sample mean and sample variance of this data set.
 b. Give a range estimate of the average with a confidence level of 80%.
 c. I used a cup of raisins in my cookie recipe that I baked for a class. The recipe makes 9 dozen cookies. What is the probability that the cookie you got in class has exactly three raisins? *Note:* This calls for the Poisson distribution, which comes in Chapter 5, so model it as binomial with a maximum number of raisins $n = 20$ and adjust the probability of success, getting a raisin in a "trial," to give the correct average number of raisins/cookie.

 A4.1.31 (a) 363.75, 123.58; (b) $354.65 < \mu_X < 372.85$; (c) 0.237

P4.1.32   A bank of telemarketers, assisted by a computer that "dials" the number, calls people during the evening to see if they use Twinkies Toothpaste. Using the assumption that the central limit theorem applies, estimate how many responses are required to establish the probability that an average citizen uses the product to ±2% with a confidence of 95%.

 A4.1.32 Using the CLT, about 2400

P4.1.33   The *Austin American-Statesman* publishes weather forecasts 5 days in advance, including predicted high and low temperatures. The following data give the low temperatures, actual and forecasts, for the period from April 1 through April 24 in a recent year. This problem consists of the analysis of these data. You will analyze the accuracy of these predictions for just 1 day, however, depending on the first letter of your last name: A-C, 1-day; D-K, 2-day; L-Q, 3-day; R-V, 4-day; and W-Z, 5-day forecasts.

April	Actual	1-day	2-day	3-day	4-day	5-day
1	48	48	51	51	54	53
2	41	48	52	54	53	52
3	54	56	56	57	58	53
4	64	62	60	58	56	57
5	42	53	55	55	54	50
6	39	42	43	45	51	50
7	41	41	42	40	46	53
8	49	49	48	48	49	50
9	49	53	52	51	51	53
10	55	57	53	57	57	53
11	66	60	63	58	60	60
12	68	64	65	63	60	59
13	56	59	60	62	61	62
14	69	60	61	57	60	64
15	52	49	51	51	53	56

April	Actual	1-day	2-day	3-day	4-day	5-day
16	44	46	49	51	54	55
17	55	56	56	54	54	56
18	67	62	61	60	59	59
19	68	65	66	63	63	63
20	63	67	68	64	63	64
21	70	67	64	66	66	64
22	64	68	66	61	64	64
23	53	57	58	58	60	60
24	48	53	53	53	55	61

a. Give point and range estimates at the 90% confidence level for the average temperature and standard deviation the actual temperatures and the predicted temperatures on your day.

b. Do a sample correlation coefficient between your day's forecasts and the actual. You can do this on your calculator or with Mathematica. If you use Mathematica, realize that you must first load the package Needs["Statistics⌣MultiDescriptiveStatistics⌣"] and use the command "Correlation[list1,list2]", where list1 is the actual and list2 the day based on your name.

A4.1.33 (a,b) The results are in the following table

Day	Sample mean	Sample s.d.	Corr. coeff.
Actual	55.2	10.1	1.0
Day 1	55.9	7.86	0.906
Day 2	56.3	7.22	0.882
Day 3	55.7	6.29	0.810
Day 4	56.7	5.05	0.814
Day 5	57.1	4.91	0.788

Several aspects of this analysis are clear. There is no clear trend in the sample means, but the sample standard deviations get smaller as the forecasts look farther into the future. Also, the accuracy decreases as the forecasts look farther into the future, but in steps: days 1 and 2 are about the same, 90%; and days 3, 4, and 5 are about the same, about 80%. Even so, correlation is good for this data set.

P4.1.34 Some data are taken on the times between phone calls coming into a telephone switch. These data are 0.0347, 0.0585, 0.141, 0.313, 0.403, 0.256, 0.0937, 0.0588, 0.0153, 0.0148, 0.0572, 0.00684, 0.296, 0.0293, 0.0256, 0.0137. These data are known to be exponentially distributed, so the PDF is $f_T(t) = \lambda e^{-\lambda t}$. Use the data to estimate λ, using the MLE for an estimator.

A4.1.34 8.80

P4.1.35 An astronomer observes novas in a distant galaxy that has about a billion stars. In a lifetime of observing, he observed seven novas. Specifically, he observed novas at $t = 2.05$, 4.96, 18.3, 18.4, 41.6, 59.8, and 68.4 years from the time that he started the observations (astronomers are *very* patient). Assume that each nova is an independent event, that is, one nova does not trigger another. The first time period, 2.05 years, is to be included in the data set of time differences. Make an MLE estimate of the rate of supernova production, λ, assuming that times between events are exponentially distributed.

A4.1.35 0.1024 supernova/year

P4.1.36 Pretend that you are a physics professor teaching large freshman physics classes at Weedout University. Your ideal grade distribution is 5% As, 15% Bs, 60% Cs, 15% Ds, and 5% Fs. Assume the class distribution of final grades is $G = N(\mu_G, \sigma_G^2)$.
  a. If the traditional breaks of 90–100 for an A, 80–90 for a B, and so forth, are used, is there any combination of the mean and standard deviation of the class grades that gives the desired distribution?
  b. If not, find the values of the mean and standard deviation that minimize the mean square error between the desired and actual grade distribution. The error criterion is $\epsilon^2 = (\%A - 5)^2 + (\%B - 15)^2 + (\%C - 60)^2 + (\%D - 15)^2 + (\%F - 5)^2$.

A4.1.36 (a) There is no value that works. Because the distribution is symmetric about C, you need to make the mean 75. Then, if you make σ right to give 5% As, the Bs and Cs come out wrong; **(b)** a plot of ϵ^2 versus σ_G shows the minimum to be about $\sigma_G = 5.65$

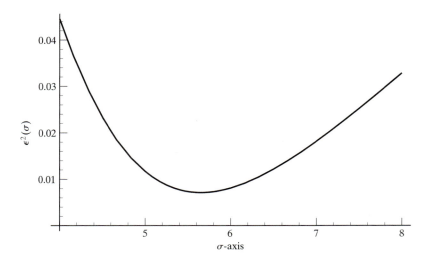

4.4.2 Linear Regression

Exercises on linear regression

P4.2.1 Starting with the beginning of the original test on which this problem appeared, the first 19 full sentences have the following number of words: 20, 21, 23, 13, 6, 24, 25, 6, 33, 20, 21, 27, 15, 22, 11, 12, 8, 16, 16. Sorted into ascending order these become 6, 6, 8, 11, 12, 13, 15, 16, 16, 20, 20, 21, 21, 22, 23, 24, 25, 27, 33.

a. Using probability paper, test whether these might originate from a Gaussian process.

b. Assuming Gaussian data, estimate the mean of the process producing these data. Specifically, we want a range estimation with 80% confidence.

c. Assuming Gaussian data, estimate the standard deviation of the process producing these data. Specifically, we want a range estimation with 80% confidence.

> **A4.2.1** (a) Plot on probability paper looks OK. From the paper, the mean is about 17.8 and the standard deviation about 7. The sample mean is 17.8 and the sample standard deviation is 7.35; **(b)** 15.6 to 20.0; **(c)** 6.12 to 9.46

P4.2.2 The grades from a recent class, sorted into ascending order, are as follows: 60, 66, 72, 74, 74, 74, 75, 75, 77, 77, 77, 77, 78, 78, 78, 78, 80, 81, 81, 82, 82, 83, 83, 83, 85, 85, 85, 85, 86, 87, 87, 87, 89, 89, 90, 91, 91, 92, 95, 95, 95, 95, 97, 100, 100.

a. Fit these data to a Gaussian distribution using probability paper, using the mean ranking technique.

b. Determine the mean and standard deviation from an eyeball-fit line.

> **A4.2.2** (a) The plot is reasonably Gaussian; **(b)** based on the regression line, $\sigma = 9.366$ and $\mu = 83.36$

P4.2.3 The following data are samples of a random variable that is uniformly distributed between 0 and a: 1.29, 1.45, 2.15, 3.05, 3.37, 3.77, 4.23, 5.14, 5.57.

a. Give the experimental CDF for the data in tabular form.

b. Plot the experimental CDF data such that the model is a straight line.

c. Determine a by using linear regression techniques.

d. Estimate the rms error between the experimental CDF and the regression line. Note that 1 dof is removed through the fit.

> **A4.2.3** (a–c) Because the CDF of a uniform distribution is a straight line, plot mean-ranked data on a linear scale and fit a straight line constrained to go through the origin. The slope is 0.1544, and thus the value of a is the reciprocal, 6.475; **(d)** calculate the sample standard deviation by summing the squares of the residuals and dividing by 8, since the fit removes 1 dof. The root of the number thus calculated is 0.051, which is the rms error

P4.2.4 An experiment with noisy data produced the following data: 0.212381, 9.29178, 6.40449, 5.42064, 4.05368, 2.5105, 8.40212, 4.82467, 6.84817. Sorted and rounded to three places these are 0.212, 2.51, 4.05, 4.82, 5.42, 6.4, 6.85, 8.4, 9.29.

a. Plot these data on probability paper and confirm that they might be generated by a Gaussian process.

      b. Estimate the mean of these data with a confidence level of 98%.

      c. Estimate the variance of these data with a confidence level of 98%.

      d. Estimate $P[X > 6]$ two ways and give your judgment as to which is the better estimate.

    A4.2.4 **(a)** Looks OK. Shows a mean of about 5.3 and a standard deviation of about 3.5; **(b)** $2.58 < \mu_X < 8.07$; **(c)** $3.22 < \sigma_X^2 < 39.3$; **(d)** $\frac{4}{9}$ from the experimental CDF, 0.4065 from $N(5.328, 2.842^2)$. The latter estimate is better because it is based on a fit to the entire data set

P4.2.5   The following data are taken from a process that is assumed to be Gaussian: 10.3, 10.2, 6.16, 12.0, 7.31, 13.4, 11.2, 10.9, 9.42, 11.6, 7.08, 3.84, 10.3, 16.3, 8.31, 4.74, 11.1, 9.06, 9.65.

      a. Test for the Gaussian distribution using mean ranking and probability paper.

      b. From the results on the probability paper, estimate the mean and standard deviation of the data.

      c. Using standard statistical techniques, make a range estimate of the mean with 80% confidence

    A4.2.5 **(a)** It looks OK; **(b)** mean about 9.7, standard deviation about 3.2; **(c)** $8.72 < \mu < 10.5$ with 80% confidence

P4.2.6   Random events in time are often modeled by the exponential PDF, $f_T(t) = ae^{-at}, t \geq 0$, zow, with its CDF, $F_T(t) = 1 - e^{-at}, t \geq 0$, zow. The following (sorted) data are taken of times between phone calls arriving at an office: 30.2, 73.1, 87.7, 97.9, 108, 108, 117, 139, 156, and 188 ($n = 10$).

      a. Plot the experimental distribution function. Use the mean-ranking technique, where the relative frequency is approximated by $k/(n+1)$.

      b. Transform the theoretical CDF to the form of a straight line.

      c. Fit a straight line to the transformed data and determine a.

    A4.2.6 **(a)** Plot; **(b)** $-\ln\left(1 - \frac{k}{n+1}\right) = at$; **(c)** if the line is constrained to pass through origin, as the equation requires, $a = 0.00900$

P4.2.7   Random events in time are often modeled by the exponential PDF, $f_T(t) = ae^{-at}, t \geq 0$, zow, with its CDF, $F_T(t) = 1 - e^{-at}, t \geq 0$, zow. The following data are taken of times between phone calls arriving at an office: 0.269, 0.182, 0.143, 0.118, 0.150, 0.353, 0.578, 0.470, 0.667, 0.223 ($n = 10$). Sorted into increasing order, these are 0.118, 0.143, 0.15, 0.182, 0.223, 0.269, 0.353, 0.47, 0.578, 0.667.

      a. Plot the empirical distribution function. However, use the mean-ranking technique, where the experimental CDF is approximated by $k/(n+1)$.

      b. Transform the CDF to the form of a straight line.

      c. Fit a straight line to the transformed data and determine a.

    A4.2.7 **(a)** Plot; **(b)** $-\ln\left(1 - \frac{k}{n+1}\right) = at_k$; **(c)** using a line constrained through the origin, as the equation requires, gives $a = 3.045$

P4.2.8   During an advising period, some advisors advised the following numbers of students:

Day#	Number
1	163
2	208
3	70
4	124
5	100
6	70
7	62
8	105

a. Find the sample mean.
b. Find the sample variance.
c. Find the 90% confidence range on the variance.
d. Find the 90% confidence range on the mean.
e. Fit a line to the data using the least-squares method using day number 1, 2, etc.) as x and the number as y.
f. Find the sample mean of the residuals (should be zero).
g. Find the sample variance of the residuals.
h. Do you conclude that there is a significant time trend to the numbers?
Don't forget that there are $n - 1$ degrees of freedom in the first set of calculations, but $n - 2$ when dealing with the residuals, since we fit a two-parameter model to the data.

A4.2.8   **(a)** 113; **(b)** $(51.0)^2 = 2597$; **(c)** $36.0^2 < \sigma^2 < 91.6^2$ with 90% confidence; **(d)** 113 ± 34.2 with 90% confidence; **(e)** $y = 175 - 13.8x$; this reduces data to 6 dof, since we fit a two-parameter model to the data; **(f)** should be zero; **(g)** $(41.17)^2 = 1694$; **(h)** evidence for a trend is weak

P4.2.9   Some data are taken on a random variable that is known to have a PDF of the form shown in the graph.

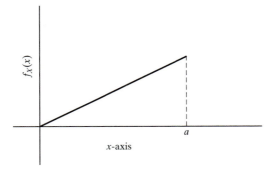

The sorted data are 0.2844, 0.7597, 0.9826, 1.028, 1.072, 1.074, 1.076, 1.232, 1.489, 1.497, 1.641, 1.664, 1.802, 1.980, 1.988.
a. Tabulate the data and the experimental CDF.

b. Put the theoretical CDF into the form of a straight line.

c. Determine a from the data.

A4.2.9 **(a)** $n = 15$, so experimental CDF is $\frac{k}{16}$ at the data values; **(b)** $\sqrt{F_k} = \left(\frac{1}{a}\right)x + 0$; **(c)** 1.96 from fitting a line through the experimental CDF and the origin

P4.2.10 A data set is taken. The raw data are 1.25148, 5.52966, 3.81182, 3.06358, 2.29355, 0.73664, 1.18231, 0.773288, 0.506462, 2.09678, 2.62108, 2.81671, 9.58954, 6.8426, 0.708982, 4.32697, 1.94462, 1.23358, 1.56842. The sorted data are 0.506462, 0.708982, 0.73664, 0.773288, 1.18231, 1.23358, 1.25148, 1.56842, 1.94462, 2.09678, 2.29355, 2.62108, 2.81671, 3.06358, 3.81182, 4.32697, 5.52966, 6.8426, 9.58954.

a. Two models are to be considered. Model 1 is that the data are uniformly distributed over the range $a < x < b$. Model 2 is that the data are exponentially distributed with a PDF of $f_X(x) = c \exp[-c(x-d)]$, $x > d$, zow, where c and d are unknown. Investigate the models and choose the one that better fits the data.

b. With your better model, estimate $P[X > 3]$ on the twentieth data point, if another data point were taken. This estimate should come from your model, not from the data directly.

A4.2.10 **(a)** Use the mean-ranking technique. The plot using the uniform distribution is simply a plot of the mean ranking versus the data and is rather curved. The plot for the exponential distribution is the natural log of the mean ranking versus the data and looks OK. We therefore choose the exponential model. The regression line gives values of $c = 0.3368$ and $d = 0.037$; **(b)** 0.369

P4.2.11 The following data were generated by an experiment: 5.66, 14.8, 10.9, 5.95, 5.08, 7.34, 6.16, 10.1, 5.57, 11.9, 5.1, 7.05, 9.68, 10.7, 11.2, 10.7, 9.67, 12.6, 14.6. We are interested in these numbers for statistical purposes and also are interested in the distribution. The numbers, sorted into ascending order, are 5.08, 5.1, 5.57, 5.66, 5.95, 6.16, 7.05, 7.34, 9.27, 9.68, 10.1, 10.7, 10.7, 10.9, 11.2, 11.9, 12.6, 14.6, 14.8.

a. Estimate the mean of the process that generated these numbers.

b. Estimate the variance of the process that generated these numbers.

c. We wish to examine the hypothesis that these numbers are generated by a process that has a uniform distribution. Using the mean-ranking technique, fit a uniform distribution to these data.

d. Does the hypothesis look plausible? If so, estimate the lower and upper limits of the uniform distribution.

e. Determine the percent error between the variance estimated from the numbers directly and the variance derived from the estimated width of the alleged uniform distribution.

A4.2.11 **(a)** 9.20; **(b)** $9.97 = (3.16)^2$; **(c)** Because CDF is a straight line for a uniform distribution, we plot the mean rank versus the sorted data. **(d)** Looks OK. The regression line is $y = -0.304 + 0.0876x$. The correlation coefficient is 0.982. This implies a lower limit of 3.47 and an upper limit of 14.9 to the uniform distribution. **(e)** From the distribution we get 10.9, versus 9.95 from the sample variance, a difference of 9.5%

P4.2.12   A data set from a process is 0.631, 0.64, 1.64, 2.56, 2.58, 2.8, 3.16, 6.57, 8.58. Note that these data are in rank order. The proposed process that generated these data has a triangular PDF, as shown in the figure.

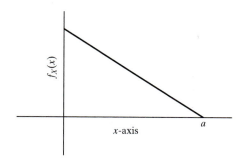

a. Investigate how well these data fit the proposed distribution.

b. Assuming that the distribution is the correct one, estimate a.

A4.2.12 (a) The CDF is quadratic, so the plot is $1 - \sqrt{1 - F} = ax + 0$, where F is the mean-ranked CDF. The plot looks OK, so we accept the hypothesis; **(b)** The line fit through the origin yields a slope of 0.0900699, so the value of a is the reciprocal, 11.1

P4.2.13   A data set is taken. Two possible models for the data are the exponential distribution and the Rayleigh distribution. The data are as follows: 0.023, 0.181, 0.080, 0.377, 0.098, 0.032, 0.109, 0.061, 0.002, 0.035, 0.112, 0.002, 0.090, 0.220, 0.072, 0.201, 0.002, 0.058, 0.036. Sorted, these are 0.002, 0.002, 0.002, 0.023, 0.032, 0.035, 0.036, 0.058, 0.061, 0.072, 0.08, 0.09, 0.098, 0.109, 0.112, 0.181, 0.201, 0.22, 0.377.

a. Analyze the data as if they were exponential to examine that model.

b. Analyze the data as if they were Rayleigh to examine that model.

c. Which model is the better of the two?

d. Based on the best-fit model, estimate the mean of the data.

A4.2.13 (a) looks OK; **(b)** does not look very convincing; **(c)** the exponential model appears better; **(d)** Fitting a line through the origin to the results in part a, we find the slope to be 9.140. The mean, based on the model, would be the reciprocal, 0.1094

P4.2.14   Some random numbers, known to be generated by a uniform distribution (equally likely between a and b) are collected: 13.6, 11.4, 15.4, 12.8, 13.0, 16.5, 18.7, 10.7. Sorted into increasing order these are 10.7, 11.4, 12.8, 13, 13.6, 15.4, 16.5, 18.7.

a. Using the mean-ranking technique to fit a distribution to the data, estimate the upper and lower limits of the distribution, a and b.

b. Using only the sample mean and sample variance, estimate the upper and lower limits, a and b. *Hint:* The standard deviation for a uniform distribution is the width of the distribution divided by $\sqrt{12}$.

A4.2.14 **(a)** fitting the uniform CDF, $a \approx 8.92$ and $b \approx 19.07$; **(b)** $\bar{x} = 14.0$ and $\sigma_X = 2.69$, so width $\approx \sqrt{12} \times 2.69$. Hence $a = 14.0 - \frac{9.32}{2} = 9.3$ and $b = 14.0 + \frac{9.32}{2} = 18.7$

P4.2.15 Some random numbers, known to be generated by a uniform distribution (equally likely between a and b) are collected: 14.2, 21.4, 8.9, 21.3, 8.16, 5.5, 7.8, 14.3.

    a. Using the mean-ranking technique to fit a distribution to the data, estimate the upper and lower limits of the distribution, a and b.

    b. Using only the sample mean and sample variance, estimate the upper and lower limits, a and b. *Hint:* The standard deviation for a uniform distribution is the width of the distribution divided by $\sqrt{12}$.

A4.2.15 **(a)** fitting the uniform CDF, $a = 0.9023$ and $b = 24.49$; **(b)** $\bar{x} = 12.7$ and $\sigma_X = 6.157$ so width ≈ 21.3. Hence $a = 12.7 - \frac{21.1}{2} = 2$ and $b = 12.7 + \frac{21.1}{2} = 23.4$

P4.2.16 Assume the following data: 7.053, -7.325, -1.314, 1.717, 8.625, 0.2063, 5.921, 1.273, -1.291, 7.229, -1.758, -1.051, 1.137, 15.55, -3.819, -7.383, -5.624, -12.23, 0.1281, -3.626. Here are the same numbers, sorted: -12.23, -7.383, -7.325, -5.624, -3.819, -3.626, -1.758, -1.314, -1.291, -1.051, 0.1281, 0.2063, 1.137, 1.273, 1.717, 5.921, 7.053, 7.229, 8.625, 15.55.

    a. Plot a histogram of the data to determine if it is reasonable to assume a Gaussian distribution. The Mathematica command is Histogram[list] but requires the prior command Needs["Graphics‿Graphics‿"] to load in the package that makes histograms.

    b. Plot the CDF of the data on probability paper or use Mathematica to invert the Gaussian CDF to see if the data are approximately Gaussian. From this plot, estimate the mean and variance of the data set.

    c. Give a point estimate of the mean.

    d. Give a point estimate of the variance and standard deviation, assuming the mean is known to be zero.

    e. Give a point estimate of the variance and standard deviation, assuming the mean is unknown.

    f. Give a point estimate of the standard deviation of the estimator model for the sample mean.

    g. Give a 90% confidence range estimate of the standard deviation, making no assumption of the mean.

    h. Give a 90% confidence range estimate of the mean.

A4.2.16 **(a)** looks somewhat bell shaped if plotted with bin size of 5, centered on zero. See the figure for the Mathematica results; **(b)** $\mu_X \approx 0$, $\sigma_X \approx 6.5$; **(c)** 0.171; **(d)** $\bar{s}_\mu = 6.26$, $\bar{s}_\mu^2 = 39.2$; **(e)** $\bar{s}_X = 6.42$, $\bar{s}_X^2 = 41.2$; **(f)** 1.44; **(g)** $5.10 < \sigma_X < 8.80$; **(h)** $\mu_X = 0.171 \pm 2.48$

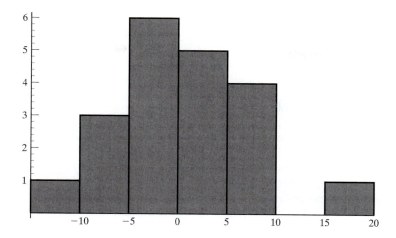

Modeling problems on linear regression

P4.2.17   At www.geo.ed.ac.uk/quakes/magnitude.html we learn that the annual occurrence of earthquakes follows the following pattern:

Richter	Number
8–8.6	0.2
7–7.9	18
6–6.9	120
5–5.9	800
4–4.9	6200
3–3.9	49,000
2–2.9	300,000

Because these numbers vary over a large range, we propose a model $N(R) = \beta e^{\alpha R}$, where $N(R)$ is the number of earthquakes of magnitude R, the Richter number, and α and β are constants.

a. Fit the model to the data using transformation to a straight line and linear regression. Specifically, find the two unknown constants, α and β.

b. Discuss the validity and accuracy of the model.

A4.2.17 **(a)** Make a log-linear plot using natural logs. Fitting a line gives $\ln[\beta] = 18.67$ and $\alpha = -2.258$. Thus the model is $1.3 \times 10^8 e^{-2.258R}$. This fit uses the middle of the various ranges for the Richter number. An argument can be made to use the lower ends of the ranges because of the strong trend in the data. Using the lower ends, we get $N = 4.23 \times 10^7 e^{-2.23\alpha}$; **(b)** The model is good. The 0.2 point is well below the line, and it pulls the line down. Errors are not random. The correlation coefficient is -0.9847. Accuracy can be estimated on a log scale as about 1.54 max error, so $e^{1.54}$ is about $4.66 = 466\%$. That's the worst point

4.4.3 Hypothesis Testing

Exercises on hypothesis testing

P4.3.1   A set of data are taken and sorted into ascending order, with the following results: 9.41, 9.61, 9.76, 9.94, 11.6, 11.7, 11.9, 12.0, and 13.5.
   a. It is alleged that these data are from a source that is $N(\mu, \sigma^2)$. Use the mean-ranking technique and linear regression to estimate the mean and variance, assuming the Gaussian hypothesis.
   b. Using the null hypothesis that $\mu = 10$ and the alternative hypothesis that $\mu \neq 10$, test the null hypothesis at a level of significance $\alpha = 0.05$.

   A4.3.1   (a) The plot is OK. The regression line gives $\mu = 11.0$ and $\sigma = 1.81$; **(b)** The t value is 2.13, since $-2.306 < T < +2.306$ for $\alpha = 0.05$, we retain the null hypothesis

P4.3.2   A chance experiment is performed 100 times. Each performance results in a number: $0, 1, 2, \ldots$. The number of the times that these numbers come up is given by the following table:

i	0	1	2	3	4	5	6	7	8	9	10	11	>11
k	1	1	5	11	18	15	20	12	8	5	2	2	0

Use the χ^2 measure to test the null hypothesis that the tabulated numbers given are derived from 100 repetitions of a binomial experiment with 20 trials. Use a level of significance of $\alpha = 0.05$.

   A4.3.2   The data pass the test and the null hypothesis is not rejected. We have a sample $\bar{p} = 0.273$. We combine $i = 0, 1$, and 2 into one bin and ≥ 9 into one bin. We test against the chi-square random variable with $\alpha = 0.05$ and dof $= 6$, since we have 8 bins but derive two parameters from the data, 100 trials and $\bar{p} = 0.273$

Modeling problems on hypothesis testing

P4.3.3   The random fluctuations in voltage out of an electronic system are dominated by thermal resistor noise. The output has zero mean because it is capacitor coupled. The bandwidth of the system is 100 kHz, and the DVM integrates for 100 ms to measure the voltage. The results of a series of measurements are: 2.30, 3.62, -4.82, 0.93, -1.50, 0.77, 4.26, 3.47, -4.82, and 4.12.
   a. Find the sample mean and the sample variance.

b. The null hypothesis is that the mean is zero. Find the critical values for a two-sided test of a data set against the null hypothesis with a significance of 1%.

c. Apply this test to the data given and either retain or reject the null hypothesis.

A4.3.3 **(a)** $n = 10$, $\bar{x} = 0.833$, and $\bar{s}_X^2 = 3.48^2$; **(b)** The range of acceptance would be $-3.575 < \bar{x} < +3.575$. **(c)** Retain the null hypothesis

P4.3.4 Using the chi-square test, check for independence of the distribution of men and women in the six sections of EE 302 this semester. The degree of significance is $\alpha = 5\%$. The data are as follows;

Gender\Instructor	Holmes	Neal	McCann	Cogdell	Grady	Daniel	Total
F	7	14	13	7	10	9	60
M	47	76	75	58	58	67	381
Total	54	90	88	65	68	76	441

A4.3.4 Since $1.12 < 11.07$, we retain the null hypothesis of independence

P4.3.5 The sales force of the Atlas Corporation is successful in their sales calls 40% of the time. The Better Consultant Group proposes to Atlas that they can train Atlas sales personnel to be more effective. Atlas lets Better run a trial class with four salespersons, who then will go out and make 40 calls the next week.

a. Develop a critical value and regions of acceptance and rejection for the null hypothesis H_0: $p = 0.4$ against the alternative hypothesis H_1: $p > 0.4$. Use a significance level of $\alpha = 5\%$.

b. If Better guarantees $p = 0.6$, what is the probability of a type II error, β, with the test you developed in part a.

A4.3.5 **(a)** reject at 22 and above; **(b)** $\beta = 0.311$

P4.3.6 D. P. Spender, having made a fortune in business, runs for public office. All the recent polls give him 55% of the vote, but during the last week before the election he wonders if he should have additional advertising. He orders a statistical study to investigate two questions:

a. Has his popularity slipped?

b. Is the election a 50–50 toss up at this time?

He requires that the level of significance be 5%, meaning that there is a 5% chance that a mistake will be made. A telephone poll of 1000 voters is ordered, since this is typical for political polls. For each of the questions, determine the critical value for rejecting the null hypothesis of $p = 0.55$.

A4.3.6 **(a)** reject at 523 or fewer; **(b)** using the Gaussian approximation, we can distinguish between $p = 0.55$ and $p = 0.50$ with type I and type II errors $\approx$ 5% with 1120 voters and a critical value of 587.5

P4.3.7 In a scientific experiment a certain unknown parameter is measured repeatedly. The sign of the parameter is the matter of interest: is it $+$ or $-$? The data, which are measurements of the parameter with a lot of noise, are plotted on probability paper and by that test appear to be Gaussian. Let $\bar{x}$ be the sample mean of the data and $\bar{\sigma}_X$ be the sample standard deviation, the square root of the sample variance based on n data points. With these numbers develop a test for the parameter μ_X being positive or negative with significance α.

> **A4.3.7**   Letting t_c be the Student's t value for $1 - \alpha$ confidence in a one-sided test, we have $\bar{x} - t_c \frac{\bar{\sigma}_X}{\sqrt{n}} < \mu_X$ with significance α, and likewise $\mu_X < \bar{x} + t_c \frac{\bar{\sigma}_X}{\sqrt{n}}$ with significance α. If the lower limit is greater than zero, the mean is positive with at a significance level of α, and if the upper limit is less than zero, the mean is negative with significance α

P4.3.8   An EE student contracted with her father to graduate with a 3.0 GPA, the reward being a new car if she succeeded. In the end, she came out with 8 As, 25 Bs, 8 Cs, and 1 D, which calculates to 2.95 (assuming all 3-hour courses, which is an idealization); however, the student, who had studied statistics, attempted to convince the father that there was a fair probability that her true performance was equal to or greater than a GPA of 3.0. Your job is to put together such an argument. A good start would be to distinguish the Big Three.

> **A4.3.8**   The Big Three are the true GPA, the sample GPA, and the estimator model for the sample GPA. Treat the grades as probabilities, the GPA as expectation. The mean is 2.95 and the standard deviation is about 0.7. The null hypothesis is that the true GPA is equal to 3.0, and with a level of significance of 5% the critical value is 2.825. Because the sample GPA of 2.95 is above the critical value, retain the null hypothesis

P4.3.9   A manufacturing process averages $125 \pm 5(1\sigma)$ units produced in a day (assume a normal distribution). A change is proposed in the process that, according to projections, should increase production 7%.

> a. Design a test, based on 2 day's production, that will confirm that the change was effective in increasing production at a significance level of $\alpha = 1\%$. That is, find the critical value of units produced in 2 days to reject the null hypothesis that the new process is no better than the old.
>
> b. For the test in part a, what is the probability of a type II error if the alternative hypothesis is the projected 7% increase? Assume that the standard deviation also increases 7%.

> **A4.3.9**   **(a)** If 267 or more units are produced in the 2 days, we conclude that an improvement has been made at the 1% level of significance; **(b)** However, we have a 47% probability of making a type II error, concluding that no improvement was made when in fact a 7% improvement has been made. More data are needed to distinguish this change

P4.3.10   Your author counted the number of letters in the names on page 181 of the 2002 Austin phone book, skipping hyphenated names like Deans-Smith and two-word names like De Backer. The resulting 132 distinct names are distributed as in the following table:

Letters in name	3	4	5	6	7	8	9	10	11	12
Times occurring	1	3	14	35	36	19	12	5	5	2

a. Calculate the sample mean of the number of letters in the names.
b. Calculate the sample variance of the number of letters in the names.
c. Test the hypothesis that these data fit a Gaussian distribution at a significance level of 5%. Use the sample mean and variance to determine the Gaussian. Combine 3, 4, and 5 into one bin and 10, 11, and 12 into one bin.

A4.3.10 (a) the sample mean is 7.091; (b) the sample variance is 2.862; (c) since 9.69 > 7.81, we reject the hypothesis that the data are from a Gaussian distribution at $\alpha = 5\%$.

ENDNOTES

1. **The random numbers.** From the code you can see that the "data" have a uniform distribution from 0 to 100, so the true mean is 50. With real data, we have no such knowledge.
2. **The predictor for p.** Here the likelihood function is $p^k(1 - p)^{n-k}$. Setting the derivative with respect to p to zero should give $\bar{p} = \frac{k}{n}$.
3. See Stigler, *The History of Statistics,* Chapter 2.
4. **Why *mean*?** This value is called least-*mean*-square estimation for historical reasons. We simply added the squares and did not divide by n to give the average (or *mean*) of the squared errors. Of course, the same results appear whether we divide by n or not.
5. **The name *sample variance*.** We will use the same name for the estimator of the variance for both cases: (1) when the mean is known and (2) when the mean is unknown. The two cases lead to slightly different formulas, and hence different estimators, but we will call them both *sample variance,* since that is really what they are. The two estimators may be distinguished by the different symbols and the context. Incidentally, the sample standard deviation (or variance) that your calculator produces is the one in which the mean is unknown. We show you in endnote 6 how to calculate the sample standard deviation (or variance) when the mean is known.
6. **Calculating the sample variance when the mean is known.** Your calculator can, at a minimum, calculate the sample mean [Eq. (4.1.2)], the sample variance [Eq. (4.1.55)], the slope and the intercept (see endnote 13) of a regression line; however, not all the required statistical calculations one might need are preprogrammed in your calculator. The purpose of this section is to teach you how to do these calculations as well. We will describe how to do these calculations on a Hewlett-Packard calculator; similar methods are available on other calculators.

   Consider calculating the sample variance when the mean is known. The formula [Eq. (4.1.40)] is $\bar{s}_\mu^2 = \frac{1}{n} \sum_{i=1}^{i=n} (x_i - \mu_X)^2$, where we know the mean. Of course, you can simply do the calculation by entering the data point, subtracting the mean, squaring, adding to the previous sum, and finally dividing by the number of data points. There is a better way.

If we square terms in the previous expression, we derive the following form: $\bar{s}_\mu^2 =$
$\frac{1}{n}\left[\sum\limits_{i=1}^{i=n} x_i{}^2 - 2\mu_x \sum\limits_{i=1}^{i=n} x_i + n\mu_X^2\right]$. Thus we need the number of data points, the sum of the
data values, and the sum of the squares of the data values. We can find these easily using the
Σ key. The "sigma" key, Σ, is used in statistical calculations. When values of two related
data points, y and x, are entered in the y and x registers and the Σ key is pushed after each
data entry, the following are summed and stored in your calculator: $n =$ the number of data
points, $\Sigma x =$ the sum of the x-values, $\Sigma x^2 =$ the sum of the squares of x, $\Sigma y =$ the sum
of the y-values, $\Sigma y^2 =$ the sum of the squares of y, and $\Sigma xy =$ the sum of the product of
the x- and y-values. The trick is to find out where these are stored in your calculator. See
the endnote 14 for more information about using your calculator in statistical calculations.

7. **The PDF of the chi-square random variable.** For the record, here is the formula for the
chi-square random variable with dof $= k$: $f_V(v) = \frac{v^{(k-2)/2}e^{-v/2}}{2^{k/2}\Gamma(k/2)}$, where $\Gamma()$ represents the
gamma function. Of course, $v \geq 0$, zow.

8. **The inverse CDF for the chi-square random variable.** Values of v for the probability
$P[V \leq v]$ for the chi-square random variable, where dof $=$ degrees of freedom. For example,
for dof $= 4$, $P[V \leq 7.7794] = 0.900$.

dof	0.005	0.010	0.025	0.050	0.100	0.250	0.500	0.750	0.900	0.950	0.975	0.990	0.995	dof
1	0.0000	0.0001	0.0009	0.0039	0.0157	0.1015	0.4549	1.3233	2.7055	3.8414	5.0238	6.6349	7.8794	1
2	0.0100	0.0201	0.0506	0.1025	0.2107	0.5753	1.3862	2.7725	4.6051	5.9914	7.3777	9.2103	10.596	2
3	0.0717	0.1148	0.2157	0.3518	0.5843	1.2125	2.3659	4.1083	6.2513	7.8147	9.3484	11.344	12.838	3
4	0.2069	0.2971	0.4844	0.7107	1.0636	1.9225	3.3566	5.3852	7.7794	9.4877	11.143	13.276	14.860	4
5	0.4117	0.5542	0.8312	1.1454	1.6103	2.6746	4.3514	6.6256	9.2363	11.070	12.832	15.086	16.749	5
6	0.6757	0.8720	1.2373	1.6353	2.2041	3.4545	5.3481	7.8408	10.644	12.591	14.449	16.811	18.547	6
7	0.9892	1.2390	1.6898	2.1673	2.8331	4.2548	6.3458	9.0371	12.017	14.067	16.012	18.475	20.277	7
8	1.3445	1.6465	2.1797	2.7326	3.4895	5.0706	7.3441	10.218	13.361	15.507	17.534	20.090	21.955	8
9	1.7349	2.0879	2.7003	3.3251	4.1681	5.8988	8.3428	11.388	14.683	16.919	19.022	21.666	23.589	9
10	2.1558	2.5582	3.2469	3.9403	4.8651	6.7372	9.3418	12.548	15.987	18.307	20.483	23.209	25.188	10
11	2.6032	3.0534	3.8157	4.5748	5.5777	7.5841	10.341	13.700	17.275	19.675	21.920	24.725	26.756	11
12	3.0738	3.5705	4.4037	5.2260	6.3038	8.4384	11.340	14.845	18.549	21.026	23.336	26.217	28.299	12
13	3.5650	4.1069	5.0087	5.8919	7.0415	9.2990	12.339	15.983	19.811	22.362	24.735	27.688	29.819	13
14	4.0746	4.6604	5.6287	6.5706	7.7895	10.165	13.339	17.116	21.064	23.684	26.119	29.141	31.319	14
15	4.6009	5.2293	6.2621	7.2609	8.5467	11.036	14.338	18.245	22.307	24.995	27.488	30.577	32.801	15
16	5.1422	5.8122	6.9076	7.9616	9.3122	11.912	15.338	19.368	23.541	26.296	28.845	31.999	34.267	16
17	5.6972	6.4077	7.5641	8.6717	10.085	12.791	16.338	20.488	24.769	27.587	30.191	33.408	35.718	17
18	6.2648	7.0149	8.2307	9.3904	10.864	13.675	17.337	21.604	25.989	28.869	31.526	34.805	37.156	18
19	6.8439	7.6327	8.9065	10.117	11.650	14.562	18.337	22.717	27.203	30.143	32.852	36.190	38.582	19
20	7.4338	8.2604	9.5907	10.850	12.442	15.451	19.337	23.827	28.412	31.410	34.169	37.566	39.996	20
21	8.0336	8.8972	10.282	11.591	13.239	16.344	20.337	24.934	29.615	32.670	35.478	38.932	41.401	21
22	8.6427	9.5424	10.982	12.338	14.041	17.239	21.337	26.039	30.813	33.924	36.780	40.289	42.795	22
23	9.2604	10.195	11.688	13.090	14.848	18.137	22.336	27.141	32.006	35.172	38.075	41.638	44.181	23
24	9.8862	10.856	12.401	13.848	15.658	19.037	23.336	28.241	33.196	36.415	39.364	42.979	45.558	24
25	10.519	11.524	13.119	14.611	16.473	19.939	24.336	29.338	34.381	37.652	40.646	44.314	46.927	25
26	11.160	12.198	13.843	15.379	17.291	20.843	25.336	30.434	35.563	38.885	41.923	45.641	48.289	26
27	11.807	12.878	14.573	16.151	18.113	21.749	26.336	31.528	36.741	40.113	43.194	46.962	49.644	27
28	12.461	13.564	15.307	16.927	18.939	22.657	27.336	32.620	37.915	41.337	44.460	48.278	50.993	28
29	13.121	14.256	16.047	17.708	19.767	23.566	28.336	33.710	39.087	42.557	45.722	49.587	52.335	29
30	13.786	14.953	16.790	18.492	20.599	24.477	29.336	34.799	40.256	43.773	46.979	50.892	53.672	30

9. **Many data sets.** Because the data model is IID, we could also say that the PDF of the members of a large data set would be Gaussian. This is in fact how we will test the assumption, by investigating the distribution of the one data set we have.

10. **Loss of one degree of freedom.** We have given here a standard explanation for the use of $n-1$ in calculating the sample variance when the mean is unknown. We have never found this convincing and place more value on the proof that this leads to an unbiased estimator.

11. **Student's t random variable.** Many students suppose that this random variable is so named to commemorate their suffering in trying to learn this subject, but this is not so. This random variable was first investigated by W. S. Gosset, who published his results in 1908 under the pseudonym "Student" because his employer, the Guiness brewery, did not let its employees publish their work under their own names. The PDF for the Student's t random variable with $\text{dof} = k$ is $\frac{1}{\sqrt{k\pi}}\frac{\Gamma((k+1)/2)}{\Gamma(k/2)}\left(1+\frac{t^2}{k}\right)^{-(k+1)/2}$

12. **Tail probabilities for Student's T distribution.** The table gives t-values for tail probabilities in the top column. For example with $\text{dof} = 1$, $P[T > 3.077] = 0.1$. *Note:* For $\text{dof} > 29$, use the normal distribution, given in the table as $\text{dof} = \infty$.

dof	0.100	0.050	0.025	0.01	0.005	dof
1	3.077	6.313	12.70	31.82	63.65	1
2	1.885	2.919	4.302	6.964	9.924	2
3	1.637	2.353	3.182	4.540	5.840	3
4	1.533	2.131	2.776	3.746	4.603	4
5	1.475	2.015	2.570	3.364	4.032	5
6	1.439	1.943	2.446	3.142	3.707	6
7	1.414	1.894	2.364	2.997	3.499	7
8	1.396	1.859	2.306	2.896	3.355	8
9	1.383	1.833	2.262	2.821	3.249	9
10	1.372	1.812	2.228	2.763	3.169	10
11	1.363	1.795	2.200	2.718	3.105	11
12	1.356	1.782	2.178	2.680	3.054	12
13	1.350	1.770	2.160	2.650	3.012	13
14	1.345	1.761	2.144	2.624	2.976	14
15	1.340	1.753	2.131	2.602	2.946	15
16	1.336	1.745	2.119	2.583	2.920	16
17	1.333	1.739	2.109	2.566	2.898	17
18	1.330	1.734	2.100	2.552	2.878	18
19	1.327	1.729	2.093	2.539	2.860	19
20	1.325	1.724	2.085	2.527	2.845	20
21	1.323	1.720	2.079	2.517	2.831	21
22	1.321	1.717	2.073	2.508	2.818	22
23	1.319	1.713	2.068	2.499	2.807	23
24	1.317	1.710	2.063	2.492	2.796	24
25	1.316	1.708	2.059	2.485	2.787	25
26	1.314	1.705	2.055	2.478	2.778	26
27	1.313	1.703	2.051	2.472	2.770	27
28	1.312	1.701	2.048	2.467	2.763	28
29	1.311	1.699	2.045	2.462	2.756	29
∞	1.282	1.645	1.960	2.326	2.576	∞

13. **Least-mean-square regression line.** The formulas for a and b involve the sample means [Eq. (4.1.2)] and sample variances [Eq. (4.1.55)] for x and y, which are familiar formulas from Sec. 4.1, plus the sample covariance, $\bar{c}_{xy}$, which is given by

$$\bar{c}_{XY} = \frac{1}{n-1} \sum_{i=1}^{n} (x_i - \bar{x})(y_i - \bar{y})$$

In these terms we give

$$a = \frac{\bar{c}_{XY}}{\bar{s}_X^2} \text{ and } b = \bar{y} - a\bar{x}$$

14. **Finding summations in your calculator.** Of course, you can look in the calculator manual to find where summed terms are stored, if you can find it. Another way is to determine what storage registers are used by experiment. Here is a simple experiment to determine this information. Clear the Σ storage registers. Enter $y = 3$ and $x = 2$ and hit Σ. Then look in your Σ storage registers. Somewhere you will find "1", "2", "4", "3", "9", and "6". These values uniquely identify where the various summed values are being stored. For example, in my calculator the registers come out as follows: R11 = 2, R12 = 4, R13 = 3, R14 = 9, R15 = 6, and R16 = 1. This tells me that, for my calculator:

    n, the number of data points, is stored in register 16
    Σx, the sum of the x-values, is stored in register 11
    Σx^2, the sum of the squares of x, is stored in register 12
    Σy, the sum of the y-values, is stored in register 13
    Σy^2, the sum of the squares of y, is stored in register 14
    Σxy, the sum of the product of the x- and y-values, is stored in register 15

15. **In-depth treatment of linear regression.** See *Statistical Analysis for Engineers and Scientists,* by J. Wesley Barnes, McGraw-Hall, Inc., 1994, Chapter 11.

16. **Book pricing.** We once did this experiment with electrical engineering textbooks in the campus bookstore. For the resulting data set, the price proved to be negatively correlated with the prices: the longer the book; the cheaper it was! The explanation was not too difficult to figure out. The long books were the introductory books for circuit theory and electronics, designed for two-semester courses. These books sell in large numbers, so there is some economy of scale. These books are competitively priced, since there are many introductory books in this class. The shorter books were for graduate classes and were very expensive due to the small number sold and the lack of competition. The conclusion is that stated in the text, that there are many factors other than overhead and length that influence the price of a book.

17. **Correlation coefficient.** In Section 3.5, we defined a correlation coefficient between two random variables. Here, we are speaking of the sample correlation coefficient between two data sets. The formula is $\bar{\rho}_{XY} = \frac{1}{n-1} \Sigma (x_i - \bar{x})(y_i - \bar{y}) \times \frac{1}{\bar{s}_X \bar{s}_Y}$. You will note that this is the numerical version of the definition in Eq. (3.5.17), with the mean replaced by the sample mean, and standard deviations replaced by sample standard deviations.

18. In lab courses, it is not unknown for students to fit their data to a theoretical model by creatively editing the data. This is the opposite of what we have in mind here.

19. **The "$n + 1$" factor.** We argue that this factor places the CDF symmetrically between 0 and 1. If we use a more general form $\frac{k-\alpha}{n+\beta}$, we find that symmetry is achieved if $2\alpha + \beta = 1$. We have used $\alpha = 0$ and $\beta = 1$, which is called *mean ranking*. Williams in *Probability, Statistics, and Random Processes for Electrical Engineers,* Brooks/Cole Publisher, in press, uses both mean ranking and median ranking, which uses $\alpha = 0.3$ and $\beta = 0.4$. He does not discuss the virtues of the different experimental CDFs, so we are using the simpler of the two.

20. **Why Rayleigh?** We said there is no serious reason for using Rayleigh, but that does not exclude a frivolous reason. Assume that the people that founded these towns were looking for the best place in Texas to settle down. Because Austin is the best place in Texas, we figure that they wanted to arrive in Austin, but for some reason missed—took a wrong turn, ran out of gas, team of horses ran away, and the like. We recall that random miss distances in a plane tend toward the Rayleigh. The model actually works pretty well.

21. **Natural logarithms.** "Log" is the Mathematica function for the natural logarithm. The common logarithm of x, base 10, is Log[10, x]. In the text we use "ln" because this is standard notation.

22. **Why 8.5?** Because the results of the test are integer values, any number between 8 and 9 would demark the boundary between the acceptance and rejection regions.

23. **Answer to you do it on p. 412.** After much trial and error, I decided that $n = 98$ and $cv = 40$ was the best I could do. You can put those in the cell and confirm that they work.

24. **Times.** We use x to represent time instead of t because we will be using the Student's t random variable later in this section.

25. **Answer to you do it on p. 418.** Not knowing the standard deviation, we must use the Student's t random variable. That requires changing NormalDistribution $\rightarrow$ StudentTDistribution. The rest is trial and error. Here is the code, with the values that we determined. Notice that we were able to satisfy the requirement with $n = 11$.

```
n = 11;
cv = 153.2;
T1 = (cv - 157) / (7 / √n);
α = N[CDF[StudentTDistribution[n - 1], T1]]
T2 = (cv - 149) / (7 / √n);
PowerOfTest = N[CDF[StudentTDistribution[n - 1], T2]]
0.0509884
0.962688
```

26. **Thanks to Dan Magrigal of Mathematica, for designing this code.** The function "boundaries" is defined in the initialization cell at the beginning of this section.

27. **Degrees of freedom in the chi-square measure.** Walpole and Myers, *Probability and Statistics for Engineers and Scientists,* 2d ed., Macmillan Publishing Co, New York, 1987, explain that the dof to be used in the chi-square measure is the number of regions, i, minus the number of parameters from the data set used in the model. Since the number of data points,

n, is always used, this rule reduces to $i - r - 1$, where r is the number of parameters extracted from the data and used in the model, and the "1" represents the use of n.

28. **Degrees of freedom.** This formula comes from Walpole and Myers, *Probability and Statistics for Engineers and Scientists,* 2d ed., Macmillan Publishing Co, New York, 1987, p. 271, where it is given without derivation. Much of the viewpoint of this section on hypothesis testing draws on Chapter 7 of this much-used text. See below for a blank sheet of probability paper.

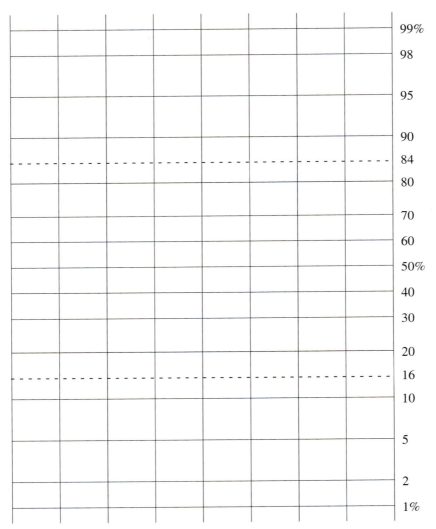

Probability Paper.
The CDF of a Gaussian distribution should be a straight line on this scale.

5

The Poisson Model

5.1 THE POISSON MODEL FOR RANDOM EVENTS IN TIME

5.1.1 The Need for and the Nature of the Poisson Model

Review of models developed thus far

The purpose of this text is to equip you to understand the basic concepts of probability, statistics, and random processes, and to be familiar with the most successful models that are useful in modeling the behavior of real random systems. We have made considerable progress in this project. We now review the main probability models we have developed.

Outcomes occurring "at random." The first model we studied was the equally likely outcomes model. In one sense this model is demanded when we are ignorant of any reason to favor one outcome over another. We use the term *at random* to indicate such ignorance. For the discrete case in which we are dealing with numerical outcomes, this leads to a uniform PMF; similarly, in the continuous case we have a uniform PDF.

The equally likely outcomes model in a discrete space leads to the classical definition of probability and successfully models, among other things, games of chance. Probabilities are calculated by counting the outcomes that favor the event of interest, counting all the outcomes in the space, and dividing the former by the latter.

Repeated trials. The second model we developed involved independent Bernoulli trials in which the probability of "success" (some binary result) is the same on each trial. We used the term *binomial trials* to describe Bernoulli trials of this class, and we found two useful distributions from this basic model:

1. When the number of trials is fixed and we want the probability of a prescribed number of successes, the model leads to the binomial distribution.
2. When the number of successes is fixed and we want the probability of achieving the last success on a given trial, the model is the Pascal distribution.

The model for complexity. Often, many small causes combine to produce a large effect. When that occurs, the resulting distribution is largely independent of the individual distributions of the many small causes. From this model, via the central limit theorem, we get the Gaussian distribution. If two IID Gaussian random variables describe the rectangular coordinates of a point in a plane, then the Rayleigh distribution describes the distance between the X, Y point and the center of the distribution.

Random events in time. In this section we will develop a model to describe random events[1] in *time* or some other dimension such as distance, and even area and volume. The following examples require such a model:

- Supernova events in this galaxy and radioactive decay are two physical processes that occur randomly in time.
- Telephone calls arriving at a telephone exchange and cars arriving at a tollbooth are similar random events.
- The location of birds sitting on a power line or the distribution of red trucks on an interstate highway are examples of events that are random in distance.
- The locations of wildflowers in a forest or flaws on a semiconductor wafer are examples of random events in two-dimensional space.
- The locations of raisins in a cake or supernovas in the galaxy are examples of random events in three-dimensional space.
- From the preceding list we can see that supernovas are randomly located in four-dimensional space, one temporal and three spatial dimensions.

As we develop the Poisson model to model such phenomena, you will come to appreciate its many applications. We will derive the Poisson PMF with time as the independent variable, but the derivation is general enough to include all the possibilities listed.

Random events in time as a random process

The probability macromodel. We must fit this concept of "random events in time" into our probability paradigm. This macromodel requires a repeatable experiment, outcomes of that experiment, events defined on those outcomes, and probabilities associated with those events. In most cases it is convenient to define random variables to map outcomes into numbers, and probabilities to CDFs and PDFs or PMFs. We now show how the "random events in time" phenomenon fits into such a macromodel.

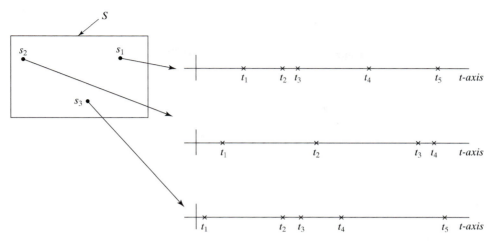

Figure 5.1.1   Each outcome is associated with a series of times, which will be modeled as a random process.

The experiment and its outcomes.   The fundamental experiment is hard to conceive, since its result is a series of random events; however, we can depict, as in Fig. 5.1.1, the macro-model with its outcomes and the associated random events. To be specific, let us consider that we are measuring radioactive decay events, and the data are times recorded by a detector coupled to a counter, with data recorded in a computer. Consider that the sequence of events associated with s_1 are Monday's data; s_2 is associated with Tuesday's data, and so on. Thus the outcome of the random experiment is associated with a pattern of random events, in general an infinite number of events at random times.

Counting the events.   How might we describe such a series of events? One way is to count the events between the origin and an arbitrary time. Let us define $K(t, s)$ as a counting function that counts the number of events in the period from 0 to t. We note that K is a function of t and s because the count will depend on the outcome of the experiment as well as the time. Figure 5.1.2 illustrates the counting function for the first outcome in Fig. 5.1.1. Similarly, we have a $K(t, s)$ for every outcome of the experiment.

Interpretation of the counting function $K(t, s)$.   Figure 5.1.3 gives the various interpretations of the counting function $K(t, s)$.

- If $t = t_j$ and $s = s_i$ are fixed, we have a number, in this case an integer. That integer, $K(t_j, s_i)$, is the number of events between 0 and the fixed time t_j for the events associated with the outcome selected, s_i.
- If $t = t_j$ is fixed, we have an integer assigned to every outcome of the experiment. That number is the number of events in the interval from 0 to t. In this interpretation the counting function $K(t_j, s)$ is a random variable, a number assigned to the outcomes of a random experiment. For fixed t, we can define events and calculate probabilities, such as the probability that $K(t_j, s) = 5$.

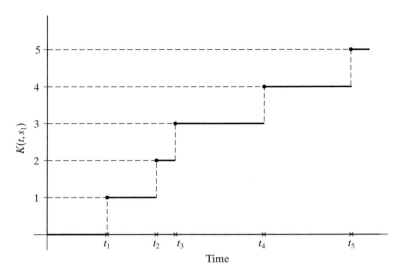

Figure 5.1.2   The counting function $K(t, s_1)$ for the first sequence of random events in Fig. 5.1.1. Random events are a random function of time and are modeled as a random process.

$t \backslash s$	Fixed $s = s_i$	Variable outcome
Fixed $t = t_j$	$K(t_j, s_i) =$ a number	$K(t_j, s) =$ a random variable
Variable time	$K(t, s_i) =$ a time function	$K(t, s) =$ a random process

Figure 5.1.3   The various interpretations for the counting function, depending on what is constant and what is variable. With both time and outcome variable, we have a random process, which is the probability model for a random function of time.

- If $s = s_i$ is fixed and time varies, we have a time function, $K(t, s_i)$, the stair-step time function associated with counting the events for that outcome. This time function is not "random" except in the sense that it is the result of a random experiment. For example, we can print out Tuesday's data after we have completed the experiment.
- If both time and the outcome are variable, then we have a family of functions. Because those functions depend on the outcome of a random experiment, we can define events and calculate probabilities. These events and probabilities will be functions of time. A *random process* is defined as a family of time functions, each of which is associated with the outcome of a random experiment. Thus $K(t, s)$ is a random process.

A random process models a random function.   We spoke previously of counting radioactive decay events. Other examples of random functions would be the fluctuating temperature in a vessel in a chemical plant, the signal from a video camera, and the dynamic load on a column supporting a bridge. Such random functions are vital to the analysis of dynamic systems.

The development of an appropriate mathematical model to describe such systems represents significant progress in modeling random systems.

Summary.   We introduced the concept of a random process because the Poisson process is at heart a random process; however, we leave the full description of random processes to Chapter 6. We derive the important distributions connected with the Poisson process without further elaboration at this time.

5.1.2 The Poisson Process

First-order PMF.   In this section we derive the first-order PMF of the Poisson process. We call this process *first-order* because this PMF refers to the count at one time only. In Fig. 5.1.4 we show the random process and identify two times, t and $t + dt$. We begin by considering the probability that an event occurs or does not occur during the interval dt. Figure 5.1.4 shows three typical sequences of random events, with an event occurring during dt in the third sequence.

Notation.   We use the notation

$$P(k, t) = P[k \text{ events in a time period } t] \qquad (5.1.1)$$

to mean the probability of k events in a period of time of duration t. Eventually, we will derive and solve a differential equation for this function, which is the Poisson distribution. The first consideration is $P(1, dt)$, the probability that one event occurs during the period of time dt.

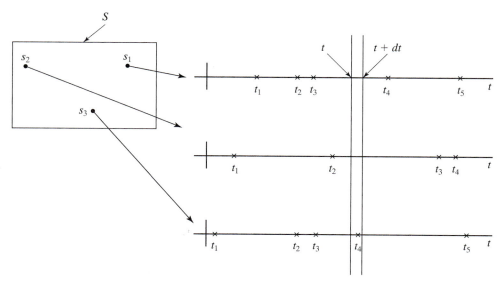

Figure 5.1.4   Here we show three records of random events in time and consider the probability that an event will occur between t and $t + dt$.

Assumptions.   We make three assumptions about the process:

1. **Independent occurrences**. We assume that the numbers of events in nonintersecting time periods are independent. Thus the random variables representing counts of such events are independent random variables. This means that $P(1, dt)$ is independent of however many events have occurred in the past. The process has no memory.

2. **No simultaneous events**. Although it is not impossible in a real system that events will occur simultaneously, such simultaneity would be an event of probability zero, like the event of picking exactly 0.4 in choosing a number at random in the interval 0 to 1. Another way of stating this assumption is that in an infinitesimal time period, dt, either zero or one event can occur, but no more than one. Thus $P(k, dt) = 0$ for $k = 2, 3, \ldots$.

3. **Uniform rate**. We assume that the probability of an event in a small period of time, dt, is $\lambda\, dt$, where λ is a constant. Thus

$$P(1, dt) = \lambda dt \qquad \text{and} \qquad P(0, dt) = 1 - \lambda dt \qquad (5.1.2)$$

At this stage λ is simply a constant. Later we will interpret it as the average rate of occurrence of events. This assumption that $\lambda = $ constant will be relaxed in Sec. 5.2 when we talk about applications in reliability theory.

The differential equation.   We now determine $P(0, t)$ by solving a differential equation. Consider the probability that no events occur during the period 0 to $t + dt$, which is $P(0, t + dt)$, as shown in Fig. 5.1.5. The event $\{0$ events in $t + dt\}$ can be expressed as $\{(0$ events in $t) \cap (0$ events in $dt)\}$. Thus we have

$$P[0 \text{ events in } t + dt] = P[(0 \text{ events in } t) \cap (0 \text{ events in } dt)]$$
$$= P[(0 \text{ events in } t)] \times P[(0 \text{ events in } dt)] \qquad (5.1.3)$$

where we used the first assumption that events in the two periods of time are independent, and thus $\cap \to \times$. Expressing (5.1.3) in the notation of Eq. (5.1.1) and using Eq. (5.1.2), we have

$$P(0, t + dt) = P(0, t) \times P(0, dt)$$
$$= P(0, t) \times (1 - \lambda dt) \qquad (5.1.4)$$

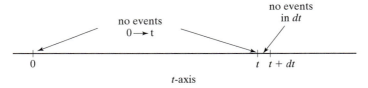

Figure 5.1.5   To find $P(0, t + dt)$, we require the events {no events $0 \to t$} and {no event in dt}.

Equation (5.1.4) can be written as a differential equation:

$$\frac{d}{dt}P(0, t) + \lambda P(0, t) = 0 \tag{5.1.5}$$

which can be directly integrated to the form

$$P(0, t) = A\,e^{-\lambda t} t \ge 0, \text{ zow}^2 \tag{5.1.6}$$

where A is a constant that can be determined from the initial conditions at $t = 0$. Because we are certain to have zero events in no time, we substitute $t = 0$ into Eq. (5.1.6) and set $P(0, 0) = 1$, from which it follows that $A = 1$. We therefore find

$$P(0, t) = e^{-\lambda t}, \ t > 0 \tag{5.1.7}$$

Equation (5.1.7) gives the probability of zero events as a function of the parameter λ, shown in Fig. 5.1.6 for $\lambda = 4$. The probability of zero events decreases with time because the probability of one or more events having occurred increases.

The next of a series of differential equations.   We proceed to derive $P(1, t)$, using similar methods. Consider $P(1, t + dt)$, the probability that exactly one event has occurred in the period $0 \rightarrow t + dt$. The event {1 event in $t + dt$} can be partitioned into {(1 event in t) $\cap$ (0 events in dt)} $\cup$ {(0 events in t) $\cap$ (1 event in dt)}. Recall that a partition breaks the event into

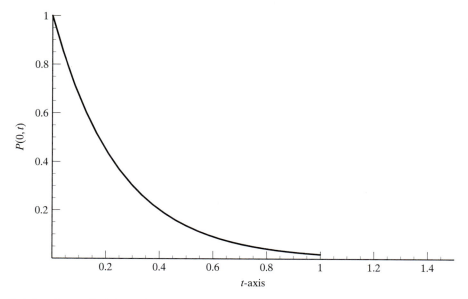

Figure 5.1.6   The probability of zero events as a function of time for $\lambda = 4$. As time increases it becomes increasingly likely that one or more events has occurred, so the probability of zero events decreases.

two or more disjoint events, so that probabilities add [Eq. (1.3.10)]. Adding the probabilities we have

$$P[1 \text{ in } t + dt] = P[(1 \text{ in } t) \cap (0 \text{ in } dt)] + P[(0 \text{ in } t) \cap (1 \text{ in } dt)] \qquad (5.1.8)$$

Because these are nonoverlapping regions in both probabilities and thus describe independent events, we can transform $\cap \rightarrow \times$. Translating Eq. (5.1.8) into the Poisson notation of Eq. (5.1.1) and using Eq. (5.1.2), we have

$$P(1, t + dt) = P(1, t) \times (1 - \lambda dt) + P(0, t) \times \lambda dt \qquad (5.1.9)$$

Routine manipulation of Eq. (5.1.9) produces a differential equation for $P(1, t)$ as follows:

$$\frac{d}{dt} P(1, t) + \lambda P(1, t) = \lambda P(0, t) \qquad (5.1.10)$$

where the term on the right side is known from Eq. (5.1.7). Equation (5.1.10) is of the form known as *exact* with an integrating factor of $e^{+\lambda t}$ and thus can be solved readily. The solution is

$$P(1, t) = \lambda t \, e^{-\lambda t} \qquad (5.1.11)$$

For $\lambda = 4$, this solution looks like Fig. 5.1.7.

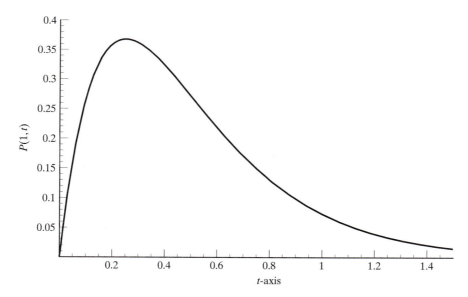

Figure 5.1.7   The probability of {1 event in t} starts at zero, rises to a maximum at $t = \frac{1}{\lambda}$, and then falls asymptotically to zero. Near $t = 0$ it is unlikely that an event has already occurred, and for large time more than one event is likely.

The higher-order Poisson probabilities.   We may derive $P(k, t)$ for $k = 2, 3, \ldots$ using similar methods. The general result is

$$P(k, t) = \frac{(\lambda t)^k}{k!} e^{-\lambda t}, \quad k = 0, 1, 2, \ldots, t \geq 0, \text{ zow} \tag{5.1.12}$$

Notice that Eq. (5.1.12), which is the Poisson distribution, is valid for $k = 0$ if we assume $0! = 1$.

The PMF of the Poisson random variable.   If we use the language of random variables, we define the Poisson random variable, K, as the number of events occurring during the period of time of duration t. This Poisson random variable is discrete, having values of $K = 0, 1, 2, \ldots$. The probabilities of the various values of the random variable are described by the PMF

$$P_K(k) = \frac{(\lambda t)^k}{k!} e^{-\lambda t}, \quad k = 0, 1, 2, \cdots, t \geq 0, \text{ zow} \tag{5.1.13}$$

The Poisson PMF is plotted for $\lambda t = 10.8$ in Fig. 5.1.8.

The most likely value of the Poisson random variable.   This is a good place to look at some of the properties of the Poisson distribution. Let us take the ratio between $P(k - 1, t)$

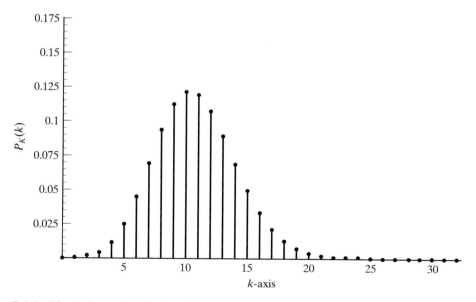

Figure 5.1.8   The Poisson distribution for $\lambda t = 10.8$. For large values of k the distribution approaches the Gaussian. If λt is an integer, there will always be two equally likely values of k, as explained in the text.

and $P(k, t)$. Some simple math yields

$$\frac{P(k, t)}{P(k - 1, t)} = \frac{\lambda t}{k} \qquad (5.1.14)$$

One use of Eq. (5.1.14) is to determine the most likely value of k. Note that if $\lambda t > k$, the ratio in Eq. (5.1.14) is greater than 1, and $P(k, t) > P(k - 1, t)$; hence the probabilities are still increasing. If $\lambda t = k$, then $P(k, t) = P(k - 1, t)$. It follows that the most likely value of k is the integer part of λt, unless λt is an integer, in which case $k = \lambda t$ and $k = \lambda t - 1$ are equally likely.

A recursion formula.　Equation (5.1.14) also gives us a simple way to calculate the Poisson probabilities. Let us assume $\lambda t = 0.5$, and calculate $P(0, t) = e^{-\lambda t} = e^{-0.5} = 0.6065$. The next term will be

$$P(1, t) = \frac{\lambda t}{k} \times P(0, t) = \frac{0.5}{1} \times 0.6065 = 0.3033 \qquad (5.1.15)$$

and the next term will be

$$P(2, t) = \frac{\lambda t}{k} \times P(1, t) = \frac{0.5}{2} \times 0.3033 = 0.0758 \qquad (5.1.16)$$

and so on.

Normalization.　We now show that the Poisson probabilities are normalized to 1. The key to proving normalization as well as to deriving the mean, mean square, and variance is the power series expansion of the exponential function:

$$e^{+x} = 1 + \frac{x}{1!} + \frac{x^2}{2!} + \cdots \qquad (5.1.17)$$

When we add the Poisson probabilities, factoring out the exponential term, we have

$$P(0, t) + P(1, t) + P(2, t) + \cdots = e^{-\lambda t} \left[1 + \frac{\lambda t}{1!} + \frac{(\lambda t)^2}{2!} + \cdots \right] = e^{-\lambda t} \times e^{+\lambda t} = 1 \quad (5.1.18)$$

Thus the Poisson probabilities are normalized.

The mean.　The mean of the Poisson random variable can be determined similarly. By definition

$$\mu_K = E[K] = 0 \times P(0, t) + 1 \times P(1, t) + 2 \times P(2, t) + \cdots$$

$$= e^{-\lambda t} \left[0 \times 1 + 1 \times \frac{\lambda t}{1!} + 2 \times \frac{(\lambda t)^2}{2!} + \cdots \right] \qquad (5.1.19)$$

$$= \lambda t \times e^{-\lambda t} \left[1 + \frac{\lambda t}{1!} + \frac{(\lambda t)^2}{2!} + \cdots \right] = \lambda t$$

where we used Eq. (5.1.18) to make the final simplification. Two important conclusions follow from Eq. (5.1.19). The first follows from

$$\lambda = \frac{E[K]}{t} \tag{5.1.20}$$

which says that λ can be interpreted as the expected number of events in a period of time t divided by t. Thus λ is the average rate of events.

The second interpretation and conclusion is that λ and t always appear together and hence $\mu_K = \lambda t$ is a convenient argument for the Poisson distribution. We will therefore change the notation from "t" to "μ_K" in the Poisson distribution for K. Thus Eq. (5.1.12) can be rewritten in the form

$$P(k, \mu_K) = \frac{\mu_K^k}{k!} e^{-\mu_K} \tag{5.1.21}$$

This shows that the Poisson distribution is a one-parameter distribution: if one knows the expected number of events, then one knows the probability of $0, 1, 2, \ldots$ events. As you will see in the examples to follow, this feature of the Poisson distribution allows us to obtain many results from minimal information.

Equation (5.1.21) also shows the Poisson distribution without reference to λ or t or any underlying assumptions. In this guise, the Poisson random variable may be used as a model for any discrete random variable that takes on all integer values. To cite a far-out example, let us say we are interested in how many keys people carry. The chance experiment is to pick a person at random by some scheme, and the random variable is the number of keys that person is carrying. This random variable could well be approximately Poisson, but there is no obvious connection to the assumptions we made in deriving the Poisson.

The mean square value.   The mean square value of the Poisson distribution can be readily calculated from the following identity that follows from the linearity of expectation:

$$E[K^2] = E[K(K-1)] + E[K] \tag{5.1.22}$$

The second term we determined in Eq. (5.1.19). The first term is similar to Eq. (5.1.19), except the first two terms of the sum vanish and the $k(k-1)$ in the numerator cancels the first two terms in the factorial. The result is

$$E[K^2] = \mu_K^2 + \mu_K \tag{5.1.23}$$

The variance of the Poisson random variable.   The variance can be calculated as

$$Var[K] = E[K^2] - E^2[K] = \mu_K \tag{5.1.24}$$

where Eqs. (5.1.23) and (5.1.19) were used. Thus the mean and variance of the Poisson random variable are the same. This seems dimensionally wrong until one realizes that μ_K is dimensionless.

Summary.   We derived a model for random events in time, such as raindrops hitting in a rain gauge. If we know the average rate, λ, and we have a period of time, t, then we may calculate the probability of k raindrops with Eq. (5.1.12). We may think of the number of raindrops as a random variable, K, described by a PMF, Eq. (5.1.13).

Conditions for using the Poisson distribution.   In addition to the model explored for random events in time, we may think of the Poisson PMF as the distribution of a discrete random variable that satisfies certain criteria. The model is one-dimensional in that μ_K, the mean value, defines the entire distribution. The criteria for modeling with the Poisson distribution follow:

1. The outcomes must be integers in the range beginning with zero and having no upper limit. Thus the Poisson differs from the binomial distribution, for which an upper limit of events (successes) exists. In practice, an upper limit may exist but it should be much larger than the expected number of events; that is, $k_{max} \gg \mu_K$.
2. The random phenomena occur in a continuous medium. We used time as the medium for our derivations, but we might have used area, volume, or some other continuous medium.
3. The physical situation suggests events happening at random and independently in some continuous medium in which the rate or density of events is constant. We will illustrate this criterion in a series of examples that apply the Poisson distribution to situations where events are distributed in time, distance, area, and volume.

If these criteria are met, the Poisson should be a good model. The critical beginning is determining the expected number of events in the region, μ_K. From the mean we may calculate all the probabilities using Eq. (5.1.21). You will see how this approach works in the examples to follow.

5.1.3 Examples Using the Poisson Distribution

Example 5.1.1:   Wrong numbers
As an example of random events in time, consider a family that gets, on average, three wrong-number calls per week. What is the probability they will receive exactly two wrong-number calls during a 4-day period?

Solution   First, let us consider how the assumptions for the Poisson model are satisfied. The first two assumptions are clearly satisfied: a large number of calls could occur in a 2-day period, and time is a continuous medium. The third assumption is a bit shaky, since calls in the evening are more likely than in the early morning. Nevertheless, we will assume the third assumption is warranted and proceed.

We are given the expected number of calls per week, $E[K] = 3 = 7\lambda$, where time is measured in days; $\lambda = \frac{3}{7}$ calls/day. To calculate the probability of two wrong-number calls in a 4-day period, we need the expected number, which is

$$\mu_K = \frac{3 \text{ calls}}{7 \text{ days}} \times 4 \text{ days} = \frac{12}{7} = 1.714 \text{ calls} \tag{5.1.25}$$

Using Eq. (5.1.21), we calculate the probability of exactly two calls in 4 days to be

$$P(2, 1.714) = \frac{(1.714)^2}{2!} e^{-1.714} = 0.2646 \tag{5.1.26}$$

Example 5.1.2:   Cars on a bridge

As an example of random events in distance, consider a highway that has, on average, 20 cars/mile. What is the probability that at any instant of time there will be 3 or more cars on a bridge that is 100 ft long.

Solution   First, we must work out the expected number of cars on the bridge. This we can do by letting the units guide us:

$$\mu_K = \frac{20 \text{ cars}}{1 \text{ mile}} \times \frac{1 \text{ mile}}{5280 \text{ ft}} \times \frac{100 \text{ ft}}{1 \text{ bridge}} = 0.379 \frac{\text{car}}{\text{bridge}} \tag{5.1.27}$$

We assume cars are distributed in distance according to the Poisson model. This means, among other things, that the largest number of cars possible on the bridge would much exceed 0.379 car, which is reasonable. The probability of three or more cars on the bridge is best calculated by the following:

$$P(\geq 3, 0.379) = 1 - P(< 3, 0.379) = 1 - [P(0, 0.379) + P(1, 0.379) + P(2, 0.379)]$$

$$= 1 - e^{-0.379}\left(1 + 0.379 + \frac{(0.379)^2}{2!}\right) = 1 - 0.9932 = 0.006837 \tag{5.1.28}$$

You do it.   At a busy intersection, 22 accidents occur yearly on average. Assuming Poisson conditions are met, what is the probability of having 2 or more accidents in a given week?

```
myanswer = ?          ;
```

```
Evaluate
```

For the answer, see endnote 3.

Example 5.1.3:   IC defects

This example involves random events in an area. In the manufacture of semiconductor integrated circuits (ICs), the process produces an average of 10 defects/wafer, and one wafer contains 20 ICs. Find the probability that an IC selected at random has no defects, and the expected number of good ICs/wafer.

Solution   The expected number of defects is $\frac{10 \text{ defects}}{1 \text{ wafer}} \times \frac{1 \text{ wafer}}{20 \text{ ICs}} = 0.5 \frac{\text{defect}}{\text{IC}}$. From the Poisson distribution [Eq. (5.1.21)], the probability of zero defects on an IC is

$$P(0, 0.5) = e^{-0.5} = 0.607 \tag{5.1.29}$$

Thus an IC picked at random will have a probability of 0.607 of being without defect, or, alternatively, we expect 60.7% of the ICs to be good. That this is more than 50% follows because some of the ICs will have two or more defects if the distribution is truly random.

We now can consider the number of good ICs in the 20 that come from the wafer. For these, the conditions for binomial trials are met: independent results, same probability of success for each, and no concern for order. We may calculate the probability of 0, 1, ..., 20 good ICs with the binomial distribution [Eq. (2.1.9)]:

$$P[k \text{ good ICs}] = B_{20}(k, 0.607) = \binom{20}{k}(0.607)^k(1 - 0.607)^{20-k} \tag{5.1.30}$$

Thus the expected number [Eq. (2.3.10)] of defect-free ICs on a wafer is

$$E[K] = np = 20 \times 0.607, \text{ or approximately 12/wafer} \tag{5.1.31}$$

Example 5.1.4:   Raisins in a cake

This example involves random events in a volume. A cake recipe calls for 1 cup of raisins, which is approximately 360 raisins.[4] The cake is cut into 20 pieces. What is the probability that a piece will have at least 20 raisins?

Solution   The average number of raisins/piece $= 360/20 = 18$ raisins/piece. The conditions for using the Poisson are reasonably met. We may therefore calculate the required probability as

$$P(\geq 20, 18) = \sum_{20}^{+\infty} P(k, 18) = \sum_{20}^{+\infty} \frac{(18)^k}{k!}e^{-18} \tag{5.1.32}$$

which we can use Mathematica to calculate:

```
Sum[PDF[PoissonDistribution[18], k], {k, 20, Infinity}];
N[%]
0.349084
```

If you are stuck on a desert island with only a set of math tables, you can perform the same calculation using the Gaussian as an approximation to the Poisson. We pointed out before that for large μ_K, the Poisson becomes bell-shaped. We can approximate the Poisson with a Gaussian distribution of the same mean and variance:

$$P(k, \mu_K) \approx N(\mu_K, \mu_K) \text{ for large } \mu_K \tag{5.1.33}$$

where we used [Eq. (5.1.24)], which gives $\sigma_K^2 = \mu_K$. The sum in Eq. (5.1.32) can be calculated as

$$\sum_{20}^{+\infty} P(k, 18) \approx \int_{19.5}^{+\infty} N(18, 18)\, dk = 1 - \Phi\left(\frac{19.5 - 18}{\sqrt{18}}\right) = 1 - \Phi(0.3536) = 0.362 \tag{5.1.34}$$

which compares favorably with the exact answer of 0.349, an error of 3.7%. Note that we had to use the continuity correction (see page 249), since half the probability associated with $k = 20$ lies between 19.5 and 20 in the Gaussian PDF.

You do it. A box of Raisin Bran contains 400 raisins. The box claims 10 servings per box. What is the probability of fewer than 36 raisins in a serving?

```
myanswer = ?              ;
```

```
Evaluate
```

For the answer, see endnote 5.

5.1.4 The Exponential PDF

Relationship between Poisson and binomial models. We now consider the exponential and the Erlang random variables, which are intimately related to the Poisson random variable. First, let us compare the relationship between the Poisson and binomial models. With the binomial, we have a discrete number of trials with independent events occurring or not occurring on each trial, with a constant probability of occurrence. If we let the number of trials go to infinity, and let the probability of success go to zero in such a way that the average number of successes remains the same, then we have the Poisson conditions. Thus there is a strong analogy between the Poisson and the binomial distributions, and under certain conditions we may approximate the computationally challenging binomial with the Poisson, which is relatively easy to calculate. This sort of approximation was attractive in precomputer times.[6]

Waiting-time distributions. Recall that the geometric distribution gives the probabilities of having to wait so many trials for the first success (event), and the Pascal distribution gives the probabilities of having to wait so many trials for the kth success (event). In the Poisson model, we have the probability of k events in a certain period of "time". The corresponding waiting-time distributions are the exponential, for the first event, and the *Erlang distribution,* for the kth event, as shown in Fig. 5.1.9.

Derivation of the exponential PDF. We now derive the PDF of the exponential random variable from the Poisson distribution. We begin with the CDF of the exponential random variable, which is defined as

$$F_T(t) = P[T \leq t] = 1 - P[T > t] \tag{5.1.35}$$

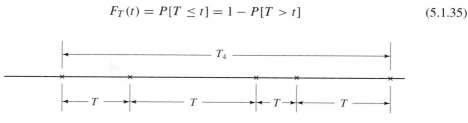

Figure 5.1.9 The random variable T_k is the waiting time for the kth event. Here we show the definitions for $k = 1$ and 4, the first events and the fourth event. We drop the subscript on $T_1 = T$ for notational simplicity. For Poisson conditions, this figure depicts the exponential random variable T and the Erlang random variable of order 4, T_4.

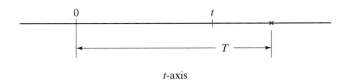

t-axis

Figure 5.1.10   The event $\{T > t\}$ is equivalent to the event {zero events between 0 and t}, which is given by the Poisson distribution.

The second form is readily related to the Poisson distribution. The event $\{T > t\}$ is that pictured in Fig. 5.1.10, and is equal to the event {0 events in $0 \to t$}.

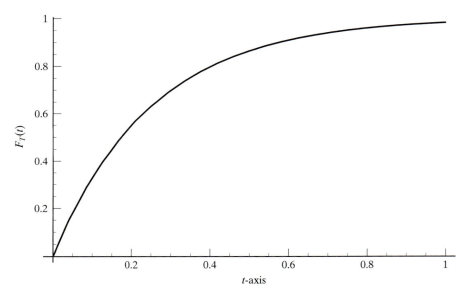

t-axis

Figure 5.1.11   The CDF for T, the time to the first event in a Poisson process. $F_T(t)$ begins at zero because it takes some time for the first event to happen, and $F_T(t)$ approaches 1 asymptotically because the first event must eventually happen.

Thus we can rewrite Eq. (5.1.35) in the form

$$F_T(t) = 1 - P(0, \lambda t) = 1 - e^{-\lambda t}, t \geq 0, \text{ zow} \tag{5.1.36}$$

This CDF is pictured in Fig. 5.1.11 for $\lambda = 4$.

The PDF of T is given by the derivative of the CDF:

$$f_T(t) = \frac{d}{dt} F_T(t) = \lambda e^{-\lambda t}, t \geq 0, \text{ zow} \tag{5.1.37}$$

where λ is the average rate of events. This PDF is shown in Fig. 5.1.12 for $\lambda = 4$.

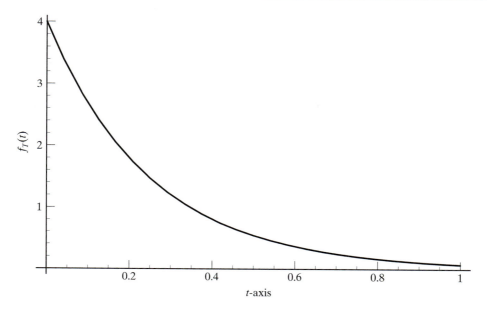

Figure 5.1.12   The PDF for T, the time to the first event in a Poisson process. Note that the most likely time for an event is "now." The time scale is determined by the average rate, λ, and the expectation (average) time to the first event is $\frac{1}{\lambda}$. For this plot, $\lambda = 4$.

Properties of the exponential random variable.   The mean, mean square value, and variance were derived in Sec. 3.1, where we introduced [Eq. (3.1.22)] the exponential PDF as an example, without derivation. We repeat the values here:

$$\mu_T = E[T] = \frac{1}{\lambda}, \qquad E[T^2] = \frac{2}{\lambda^2}, \qquad \text{and} \qquad Var[T] = \frac{1}{\lambda^2} \qquad (5.1.38)$$

Thus the mean and the standard deviation of the exponential random variable are equal.

No memory.   The most striking property of the exponential random variable is that it, like the geometric distribution [Eq. (2.1.21)], has no memory, that it "begins again" at each instant of time. This is implied by the Poisson assumption of independent events, but it still is interesting to see how it works out in the mathematics. We can show this lack of memory by calculating the conditional PDF, with the condition that no event takes place between 0 and some time, call it t_0, as pictured in Fig. 5.1.13.

We begin with the conditional CDF:

$$F_{T \mid T > t_0}(t) = P[T \leq t \mid T > t_0] = \frac{P[(T \leq t) \cap (T > t_0)]}{P[T > t_0]} \qquad (5.1.39)$$

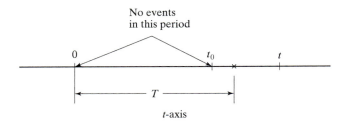

Figure 5.1.13   We are going to calculate the conditional probability of T, the time to the first event, with the condition that no event occurs in the period 0 to t_0, as shown. The result will show that the exponential random variable has no memory.

The numerator is equivalent to the probability of the event $\{t_0 < T \leq t\}$, which we may calculate from the unconditional PDF of T:

$$P[t_0 < T \leq t] = \int_{t_0}^{t} f_T(t)\, dt = \int_{t_0}^{t} \lambda e^{-\lambda t}\, dt = e^{-\lambda t_0} - e^{-\lambda t}, \quad t > t_0 \tag{5.1.40}$$

and the denominator of Eq. (5.1.39) we also can calculate from the unconditioned PDF of T:

$$P[T > t_0] = \int_{t_0}^{\infty} f_T(t)\, dt = \int_{t_0}^{\infty} \lambda e^{-\lambda t}\, dt = e^{-\lambda t_0} \tag{5.1.41}$$

Thus Eq. (5.1.39) reduces to

$$F_{T\,|\,T>t_0}(t) = \frac{e^{-\lambda t_0} - e^{-\lambda t}}{e^{-\lambda t_0}} = 1 - e^{-\lambda(t-t_0)}, \quad t > t_0, \quad \text{zow} \tag{5.1.42}$$

which is shown in Fig. 5.1.14 for $\lambda = 4$.

We see that nothing is changed except the delay. The conditional PDF is the derivative of the conditional CDF, and will show no change except the delay.

$$f_{T\,|\,T>t_0}(t) = \frac{d}{dt}(1 - e^{-\lambda(t-t_0)}) = \lambda e^{-\lambda(t-t_0)}, \quad t > t_0, \quad \text{zow} \tag{5.1.43}$$

which is shown in Fig. 5.1.15 for $\lambda = 4$.

The conditional PDF is merely delayed by t_0; there is no other difference between Figs. 5.1.12 and 5.1.15. This means that the past does not influence the future. This property of the exponential random variable is somewhat counterintuitive because we are accustomed to scheduled events. A city bus, for example, runs on a schedule, so the longer you wait for a bus, the more likely it becomes that the bus will appear. But many events are unscheduled, such as radioactive decay, supernova explosions, and auto accidents. For such unscheduled events, the exponential random variable may well model the times between events.

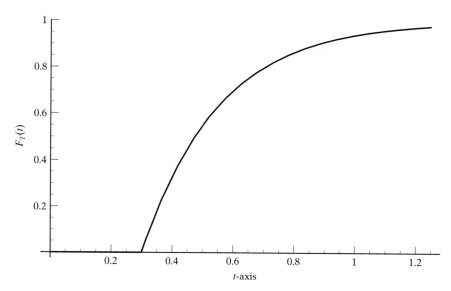

Figure 5.1.14   The conditional CDF of the exponential random variable, the condition being that no event takes place between 0 and $t_0 = 0.3$. This is identical to Fig. 5.1.11, except for the delay, which shows the lack of memory in the exponential random variable.

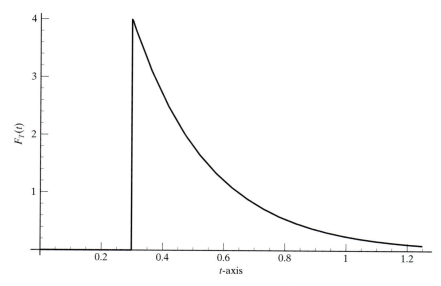

Figure 5.1.15   The conditional PDF of the exponential random variable, the condition being that no event occurs between 0 and $t_0 = 0.3$. Note that this graph is identical with the unconditioned PDF in Fig. 5.1.12, except for the delay. This tells us that the exponential random variable has no memory, that it begins afresh at each instant of time, regardless of when events have occurred in the past.

Example 5.1.5:   Entering a busy street _____

Consider entering from a side street onto a busy thoroughfare. There are 40 cars/minute passing your side street, and it will take you 3 seconds to enter the stream of traffic safely. What is the probability that you will be able to enter without waiting for a break in the traffic?

Solution   The rate of cars is

$$\lambda = 40 \frac{\text{cars}}{\text{minute}} \times \frac{1 \text{ minute}}{60 \text{ seconds}} = \frac{2}{3} \frac{\text{cars}}{\text{second}} \tag{5.1.44}$$

We assume the cars are randomly distributed in time according to the Poisson assumptions, so the time to the first car is exponentially distributed with $\lambda = \frac{2}{3}$. The probability that the first car will reach the intersection 3 or more seconds after you arrive is

$$P[T > 3] = \int_3^\infty f_T(t) \, dt = \int_3^\infty \tfrac{2}{3} e^{-2t/3} \, dt = e^{-2} = 0.135 \tag{5.1.45}$$

___

You do it.   At a busy intersection, 22 accidents occur yearly on the average. Assuming Poisson conditions are met, what is the probability that the next accident will occur in the next 6 days?

```
myanswer = ?            ;
```

```
Evaluate
```

For the answer, see endnote 7.

5.1.5 The Erlang Distribution

As the exponential random variable is the analog in continuous space to the geometric random variable for binomial trials, so the Erlang random variable is analogous to the Pascal. The Erlang random variable, T_k, is the waiting time from $t = 0$ (or any arbitrary time) to the kth event, as is shown for $k = 4$ in Fig. 5.1.16.

Thus the Erlang random variable of order k is the sum of k independent exponential random variables. We may derive the PDF of the Erlang random variable three ways. We will show you two of the three and merely mention the third.

Convolution.   The method we only mention is convolution. Because the Erlang is the sum of independent exponential random variables, we may derive the PDF of the Erlang by multiple convolution of the exponential PDF. Although this method sounds horrible, it works out pretty well. But there is nothing new to be learned from this, so we will not do it here.

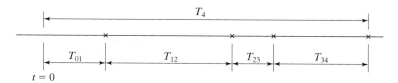

Figure 5.1.16 The time to the fourth event is the sum of the times between the origin and the first event, the first and the second, the second and the third, and the third and the fourth. Whether an event occurs at the origin does not matter, since the Poisson process has no memory.

Direct derivation.   By definition [Eq. (3.1.2)] the PDF of T_k is

$$f_{T_k}(t)\, dt = P[t < T_k \leq t + dt] \tag{5.1.46}$$

The event on the right can be expressed as the intersection of two independent events:

$$P[t < T_k \leq t + dt] = P[(k - 1 \text{ events in } t) \cap (1 \text{ event in } dt)] \tag{5.1.47}$$

We now apply the Poisson assumptions (see page 456). As just stated, the two events on the right are independent because the two regions do not overlap (first assumption). Thus we can change $\cap \to \times$.

$$P[t < T_k \leq t + dt] = \underbrace{P[k - 1 \text{ events in } t]}_{P(k-1,\, \lambda t)} \times \underbrace{P[1 \text{ event in } dt]}_{\lambda dt} \tag{5.1.48}$$

The first term is the Poisson probability of $k - 1$ events in time t, and the second term, by the third Poisson assumption, is λdt. Substituting Eq. (5.1.48) back into Eq. (5.1.46), canceling the dt's, and substituting Eq. (5.1.12), we have the kth-order Erlang PDF:

$$f_{T_k}(t) = \frac{(\lambda t)^{k-1}}{(k - 1)!} e^{-\lambda t} \times \lambda = \frac{\lambda^k t^{k-1}}{(k - 1)!} e^{-\lambda t}, \ t \geq 0, \ \text{zow} \tag{5.1.49}$$

Figure 5.1.17 shows the Erlang PDF for $\lambda = 4$ and $k = 10$.

The Erlang CDF.   The third way to derive the Erlang PDF is to start with the CDF. Usually, we start with the CDF in deriving the PDF, but you will see why we do not favor this approach here, although it does work. The CDF is by definition

$$F_{T_k}(t) = P[T_k \leq t] = 1 - P[T_k > t] \tag{5.1.50}$$

But the event $\{T_k > t\}$ can be partitioned into the events $\{0 \text{ events in } t\} \cup \{1 \text{ event in } t\} \cup \cdots \cup \{k - 1 \text{ events in } t\}$. These events are disjoint, so we may add their probabilities, with the result

$$P[T_k > t] = e^{-\lambda t}\left[1 + \frac{\lambda t}{1!} + \frac{(\lambda t)^2}{2!} + \cdots + \frac{(\lambda t)^{k-1}}{(k - 1)!} \right] \tag{5.1.51}$$

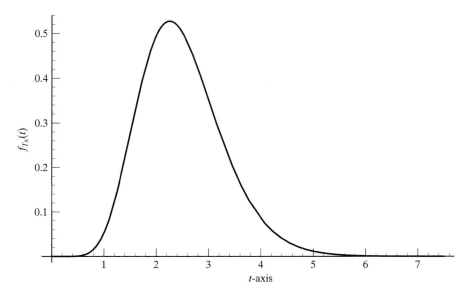

Figure 5.1.17   The PDF of the Erlang random variable of order $k = 10$. The expected value is $\frac{k}{\lambda}$, and the peak value of the PDF occurs at $\frac{k-1}{\lambda}$. The Erlang is the sum of k IID exponential random variables. For this plot, $\lambda = 4$.

and therefore the CDF of the Erlang random variable is

$$F_{T_k}(t) = 1 - P[T_k > t] = 1 - e^{-\lambda t}\left[1 + \frac{\lambda t}{1!} + \frac{(\lambda t)^2}{2!} + \cdots + \frac{(\lambda t)^{k-1}}{(k-1)!}\right], \; t \geq 0, \; \text{zow} \quad (5.1.52)$$

The derivative of the CDF in Eq. (5.1.52) is the PDF in Eq. (5.1.49), since all the terms in the derivative cancel out except the last. Likewise, the integral of Eq. (5.1.49) from 0 to t is Eq. (5.1.52), after you integrate by parts $k - 1$ times. We think you will agree that it is easier to derive the PDF and the CDF from basics rather than from each other.

Properties of the Erlang random variable.   We may derive the mean and variance of the Erlang without doing any calculus. Because the Erlang is the sum of k IID exponential [Eq. (5.1.38)] random variables, it follows from the algebra of expectation that

$$E[T_k] = kE[T] = \frac{k}{\lambda} \quad (5.1.53)$$

Similarly, the variance is

$$Var[T_k] = k \; Var[T] = \frac{k}{\lambda^2} \quad (5.1.54)$$

Because the Erlang is the sum of k exponential random variables, for large k the central limit theorem suggests that the Erlang should approach the Gaussian. Using Eqs. (5.1.53) and (5.1.54), we may express this as

$$f_{T_k}(t) \approx N\left(\frac{k}{\lambda}, \frac{k}{\lambda^2}\right), \quad \text{for large } k \tag{5.1.55}$$

which you may find useful if stranded on a desert isle with some math tables.

Example 5.1.6:   Waiting at the bank

You are waiting in line at the drive-in window at your bank. You are sixth in line, counting the one being served, and it takes, on average, 2 minutes to serve each customer. The service time for each customer is a random variable, which we will assume to be exponential.[8] Thus your time to drive away is the sum of the six exponential random variables, which is the Erlang random variable of order six. What is the probability that you will drive away more than 12 minutes from the present?

Solution   From the expected (average) value of the wait time and Eq. (5.1.38), we derive that $\lambda = \frac{1}{2}$ car/minute. In terms of the Erlang PDF, the required probability is

$$P[T_6 > 12] = \int_{12}^{\infty} \frac{\lambda^k t^{k-1}}{(k-1)!} e^{-\lambda t} \, dt \tag{5.1.56}$$

with $k = 6$ and $\lambda = \frac{1}{2}$. It is better to use the CDF or to simply reason on the basis of the Poisson distribution. We know that the Poisson applies because of the intimate relationship between the Poisson, exponential, and Erlang distributions; that is, they all arise from the same assumptions (see page 456). From the CDF, Eq. (5.1.52), and $\lambda t = \frac{1}{2} \times 12 = 6$, we have

$$P[T_6 > 12] = 1 - F_{T_6}(12) = e^{-\lambda t}\left[1 + \frac{\lambda t}{1!} + \frac{(\lambda t)^2}{2!} + \cdots + \frac{(\lambda t)^5}{5!}\right]$$
$$= e^{-6}\left[1 + \frac{6}{1!} + \frac{(6)^2}{2!} + \cdots + \frac{(6)^5}{5!}\right] = 0.446 \tag{5.1.57}$$

This is readily interpreted as the probability that 0, 1, 2, 3, 4, and 5 events take place in the 12 minutes, but not 6 or more, for then you, the sixth event, would have completed your business and driven away.

   You do it.   The situation is the same, but you are third and it takes 4 minutes per customer. Calculate the probability that you will be gone in 12 minutes, enter your answer to at least three places in the cell box, and click Evaluate for a response.

```
myanswer = ?       ;
```

```
Evaluate
```

For the answer, see endnote 9.

Events and distances in more than one dimension. We have seen that the Poisson process in one dimension, say, time, produces an exponential distribution for the time between events. Let us now consider the corresponding problem in two dimensions.

Example 5.1.7: Wildflowers

To make the situation specific, imagine that you are in the middle of a large field that contains beautiful wildflowers here and there. Specifically, there are on average $\rho = 1$ flower/100 ft^2. From a point picked at random, what is the expected (average) distance to the nearest flower? We assume that Poisson assumptions [following Eq. (5.1.1)] are met, suitably adapted to two dimensions. This means that flowers are independently located, that the average density is uniform throughout the field, and that every location contains either zero or one flower.

Solution   To calculate the expected distance, we need the PDF of R = the distance to the next flower. Because this is a derivation, let us first find the CDF, and then the PDF, then the expectation. The CDF is defined as

$$F_R(r) = P[R \le r] = 1 - P[R > r] \tag{5.1.58}$$

Following the same approach we used in dealing with Eq. (5.1.35), we reason that the event $\{R > r\}$ is equivalent to the event $\{0$ events in a circle of radius $r\}$, which can be calculated from the Poisson distribution. The expected number of flowers in a circle of radius R is $\mu_K = \rho \times \pi r^2$ and

$$P[R > r] = P(0, \mu_K) = e^{-\mu_K} = e^{-\pi \rho r^2}, \ r \ge 0, \ \text{zow} \tag{5.1.59}$$

Thus Eq. (5.1.58) becomes

$$F_R(r) = 1 - P[R > r] = 1 - e^{-\pi \rho r^2}, \ r \ge 0, \ \text{zow} \tag{5.1.60}$$

This is the CDF. The PDF is the derivative with respect to r:

$$f_R(r) = \frac{d}{dr}(1 - e^{-\pi \rho r^2}) = 2\pi \rho r e^{-\pi \rho r^2}, \ r \ge 0, \ \text{zow} \tag{5.1.61}$$

The PDF given in Eq. (5.1.61) is a Rayleigh distribution [Eq. (3.5.6)] with a parameter of

$$\sigma = \frac{1}{\sqrt{2\pi \rho}} \tag{5.1.62}$$

Our goal is to find the mean distance to the nearest flower. This follows from the expectation of a Rayleigh random variable, given in Eq. (3.5.7) as

$$E[R] = \sqrt{\frac{\pi}{2}}\sigma = \frac{1}{\sqrt{4\rho}} \tag{5.1.63}$$

Because our flower density is 1 flower/100 ft^2, the expected distance to the nearest flower given by Eq. (5.1.63) is 5 ft.

You do it.   You are on the *Starship Enterprise* in a star cluster with a star density of $\rho = 0.01$ stars/cubic light-year. You are low on fuel and need to reach the nearest star to extract energy. What is the probability that the closest star is within 4 light-years? Enter your answer in the cell box, and click Evaluate for a response.

```
myanswer = ?              ;
```

```
Evaluate
```

For the answer, see endnote 10.

Summary.   In this section we developed models for random events in time or some other dimension. The Poisson distribution describes the probability of a prescribed number of events in some interval, and the exponential and Erlang PDFs give the distribution of the intervals between events in one dimension. Both are one-parameter distributions defined by the expected number of events in an interval.

In the process of developing the Poisson distribution we introduced the concept of a random process. This important concept is developed further in the remaining sections in this chapter and is the principal subject of Chapter 6.

5.2 APPLICATIONS IN RELIABILITY THEORY

The importance of reliability theory

Reliability theory refers to probability models that are used to describe failure of products. We deal with this situation under the Poisson process because "product failure" is an event in time. As owners of products we know that failure can mean anything from a minor irritation to a total loss: a car can run out of gas or be totaled in an accident, but in the present context we deal with the device or system as being either in service or in standby, or as having failed.

No new mathematical concepts are introduced in this section, but the vocabulary is rather different from that in the previous sections. One reason is that reliability theory has matured independently from the formal mathematical community, in the insurance industry to be specific, and these roots survive in the vocabulary and notations of this application.

Reliability is important to engineers both as producers and consumers of manufactured goods. We seek to build reliability into our designs for the sake of company reputation and profit. Certainly, the people that figure warranty costs need to know about reliability, and the sales-people want to claim that products are reliable.

We are also consumers of manufactured goods in our professional and personal lives. We need to know the basics of reliability theory to make informed decisions about what to buy. In sum, this is an important application of probability and random process theory.

Within reliability theory we have two viewpoints: the user's viewpoint and the manufac-turer's viewpoint. The user generally buys one or a few of the manufactured items, whereas the

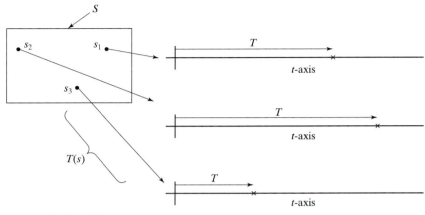

x means the item fails

Figure 5.2.1 The user buys an item and places it in service. It fails at time *T*, the time to failure, which is a random variable. This is the macromodel for a reliability situation from the user's point of view.

manufacturer deals with larger numbers. Because both are talking about the same product the viewpoints are ultimately comparable, but initially, different concerns are being expressed. We begin with the user's viewpoint.

5.2.1 The User's Model for Reliability

The macromodel. Let us say you are going to buy something. You go to the discount store, look at the items on display, make your choice, and place the order with the salesperson. You then go to the pickup area, a box comes down the conveyor system, and you receive your purchase. The "chance experiment" here is your purchase, and the outcomes are the various individual items that may have come down the conveyor system.

You take the item and use it until it fails. The time to failure is a random variable associated with the outcome of the chance experiment, as pictured in Fig. 5.2.1.

Relation to Poisson process. The user model is a random variable model that describes an event, the failure, in a continuous medium, time. The differences from Sec. 5.1 are two: (1) we are interested only in the first occurrence of the event; and (2) the rate parameter, λ, is not generally constant for manufactured items. The more likely times for failures are when the item is initially put into service, owing to defects in manufacture, or long after being put into service, owing to aging and wear effects. Thus the third Poisson assumption [following Eq. (5.1.1)] must be changed to

$$P(1, dt) = \lambda(t)\, dt \qquad (5.2.1)$$

Equation (5.2.1) represents the probability that the failure will occur between t and $t + dt$. In the reliability context, the rate parameter is called the *failure rate* and is traditionally represented by the symbol $h(t)$.[11] Thus we change the notation in Eq. (5.2.1) to

$$P(1, dt) = h(t) \, dt \qquad (5.2.2)$$

We will use Eq. (5.2.2) to derive the reliability function.

The reliability function. The user wants assurance of a long lifetime of service. The reliability function, $R(t)$, gives the probability that the item is still in service at time t. This probability is related to the CDF for T as follows:

$$R(t) = P[T > t] = 1 - P[T \leq t] = 1 - F_T(t) \qquad (5.2.3)$$

Conversely, the CDF for the time to failure can be expressed in terms of the reliability function:

$$F_T(t) = 1 - R(t) \qquad (5.2.4)$$

The reliability function is a probability and thus it must be $0 \leq R(t) \leq 1$. Further, since $F_T(t)$ can never decrease with time, $R(t)$ can never increase with time, only decrease or remain constant. It also must be true that $R(0) = 1$ if we assume that the device operates when first put into service.

We may relate the reliability function to the failure rate by solving a differential equation. In the Poisson notation of Eq. (5.1.1), the reliability function is simply $P(0, t)$, the probability of no failures in time $0 \rightarrow t$. Thus

$$P(0, t) = P[T > t] = R(t) \qquad (5.2.5)$$

where T is the time to failure. We derived a differential equation in Sec. 5.1 for $P(0, t)$, Eq. (5.1.5). Equation (5.2.6) is the same equation using the notation in Eqs. (5.2.2) and (5.2.5):

$$\frac{d}{dt} R(t) + h(t) R(t) = 0 \qquad (5.2.6)$$

The solution to Eq. (5.2.6) is the same as the solution to (5.1.5), with one exception. We put the equation into the form for direct integration,

$$\frac{dR(t)}{R(t)} = -h(t) \, dt \qquad (5.2.7)$$

Here we cannot integrate the right side, as we could when $h(t) = \lambda = $ constant, but rather we can integrate only symbolically. We define the cumulative failure rate, $H(t)$, as

$$H(t) = \int_0^t h(t') \, dt' \qquad (5.2.8)$$

Now, when we integrate Eq. (5.2.7) from 0 to t, we have

$$\ln[R(t')]\big|_0^t = -H(t) \Rightarrow R(t) = e^{-H(t)} = e^{-\int_0^t h(t') \, dt'} \qquad (5.2.9)$$

where $\ln[\ ]$ is the natural log and $\ln[R(0)] = \ln[1] = 0$. The relationship in Eq. (5.2.9) between the reliability function and the failure rate will be investigated in detail later.

The mean time to failure, MTTF.   The mean time to failure is the average lifetime of the product and is the expectation of the time to failure:

$$\text{MTTF} = E[T] = \int_0^\infty t f_T(t)\, dt \tag{5.2.10}$$

where the PDF in Eq. (5.2.10) can be determined from the CDF in Eq. (5.2.4):

$$f_T(t) = -\frac{dR(t)}{dt} \tag{5.2.11}$$

The MTTF can be determined directly from the reliability function by substituting Eq. (5.2.11) into Eq. (5.2.10) and integrating by parts. The result is

$$\text{MTTF} = -t R(t)|_0^\infty + \int_0^\infty R(t)\, dt \tag{5.2.12}$$

The first term vanishes at $t = 0$, since $R(0) = 1$, and also vanishes at $t = \infty$ if we assume that $R(t)$ goes to zero faster than t goes to ∞, which it must.[12] Thus the MTTF is the area under the reliability curve:

$$\text{MTTF} = \int_0^\infty R(t)\, dt \tag{5.2.13}$$

Example 5.2.1:   Constant failure rate
To illustrate the concepts and equations we have developed, we assume that the failure rate is a constant, $h(t) = \lambda = \text{constant} = \frac{1}{4} \frac{\text{failure}}{\text{year}}$. Thus the cumulative failure rate is given by Eq. (5.2.8) as

$$H(t) = \int_0^t h(t')\, dt' = \int_0^t \lambda dt' = \lambda t \tag{5.2.14}$$

and by Eq. (5.2.9), the reliability function is

$$R(t) = e^{-\lambda t} = e^{-\frac{t}{4}}, \quad t \geq 0 \tag{5.2.15}$$

Using Eq. (5.2.13), we find the mean time to failure to be

$$\text{MTTF} = \int_0^\infty R(t)\, dt = \int_0^\infty e^{-\lambda t}\, dt = \frac{1}{\lambda} = 4 \text{ years} \tag{5.2.16}$$

You do it.   Assume the failure rate for a device increases in time according to the function

$$h(t) = 0.0001\, t \tag{5.2.17}$$

where time is in years. Find the mean time to failure for this device. Be warned that this is not a trivial exercise mathematically. You can do the integral using Mathematica, looking it up in a table, or using standard integrals for the Gaussian PDF. In any event, enter your answer in the cell box, and click Evaluate for a response.

```
myanswer =     ;
```

```
Evaluate
```

For the answer, see endnote 13.

5.2.2 The Manufacturer's Model for Reliability

The chance experiment for the manufacturer is different from that of the user. An appropriate chance experiment for the manufacturer would be to design a certain model of product and to manufacture many products with that design. An appropriate outcome of that chance experiment might be one day's production, and with each outcome we would associate the life history of those products, as shown in Fig. 5.2.2.

Because we are dealing with a large number of items, each of which has its own failure time, our model is a random process, $N(t, s_i)$, which is the number of surviving items for that outcome as a function of time. For simplicity, we assume that we begin with the same number of items for each outcome, which we have called $n(0)$. Although we are talking about the failures of individual items, and thus the random process is actually discrete, we assume that sufficient numbers of items are included to allow us to treat $N(t, s_i)$ as a continuous function.

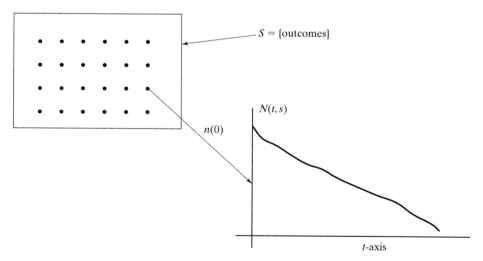

Figure 5.2.2 The manufacturer's model requires a random process, $N(t, s)$, which is the life history of a large number of items for each outcome of the chance experiment. Here we show only the life history of one batch of products.

Relating the manufacturer's model to the user's model.   The user buys one of a large number of identical items. For the user, the outcome is the individual item, and the random variable of interest is the time to failure or the reliability function. For the manufacturer, the outcome is the large number of identical items, and the random variable of interest is the life history of each batch of items. Because this "random variable" is a function of time, it is actually a random process. We now show the connection between the two viewpoints.

The importance of the reliability function.   The reliability function gives the probability of survival for individual items that are manufactured, and the same reliability function applies whether we are speaking of one item (user) or many items (manufacturer). Thus the two models must ultimately be the same, as we now show.

Consider the random process $N(t)$ at a fixed time. Some of the original $n(0)$ items have failed and some have not failed, and the proper model is that of binomial trials because failures are independent and all have the same probability. The number of trials is $n = n(0)$, the probability of success is $p = R(t)$, the probability of failure is $q = 1 - R(t)$, and $K = N(t)$ is a binomial random variable describing the number of successes at any time. From our prior work [Eq. (2.3.59)] on the binomial random variable, we can determine the mean of $N(t)$ to be $n(t)$, which is

$$n(t) = E[N(t)] = np = n(0)R(t) \qquad (5.2.18)$$

The interpretation of $n(t)$ is the average life history of a group of batches of identical manufactured items. We also can determine the variance from binomial theory to be

$$\sigma_N^2 = npq = n(0)R(t)(1 - R(t)) = n(t)(1 - R(t)) \qquad (5.2.19)$$

Because we are dealing by assumption with a fairly large n, we can use the central limit theorem and approximate the binomial distribution by the Gaussian:

$$N(t) \approx N(n(t), n(t)(1 - R(t))) \qquad (5.2.20)$$

where the second "N" stands for the normal random variable, the notation before Eq. (3.4.14). We can use the exact binomial distribution if the situation warrants more accuracy.

Example 5.2.2:   Widget reliability _____

We buy 1000 widgets. Infant mortality takes 1% of them, and the remainder have a constant failure rate of 10%/year. Find the probability that at least 575 are in operation at the end of 5 years.

Solution   Ten widgets die early, and the remaining 990 have a constant failure rate: $H(1) = h \times 1$ and $e^{-H(1)} = 0.9$. Thus $h = -\ln(0.9) = 0.105$. Thus at the end of 5 years we have an expected number of

$$n(5) = 990\,e^{-0.105 \times 5} = 584.6 \qquad (5.2.21)$$

The variance of the survivors is $584.6 \times \left(1 - e^{-0.105 \times 5}\right) = 239.4$. Using the Gaussian distribution, we estimate the probability of 575 or more survivors at 5 years to be

$$P[N(5) \geq 575] = 1 - P[N(5) < 575] = 1 - \Phi\left(\frac{574.5 - 584.6}{\sqrt{238.8}}\right) = \Phi(0.6518) = 0.7427$$

(5.2.22)

You do it. You are the widget czar for your organization and you must have a 90% probability of having at least 300 widgets on hand at all times. Assuming the situation in the preceding example, at what time should you reorder? Calculate your time, enter it in the cell box, and click Evaluate for a response.

```
myanswer = ?      ;
```

```
Evaluate
```

For the answer, see endnote 14.

The failure rate definition. In Eq. (5.2.2), we introduced the term *failure rate,* identifying it as a generalization of the rate parameter, λ, that is familiar from the study of the Poisson process. This section defines $h(t)$, the failure rate, from the manufacturer's viewpoint. We begin with $n(t)$, the expected number of survivors as a function of time. As shown in Fig. 5.2.3, in a period of time dt, the average number of functioning units "increases" by dn, which is numerically negative.

The definition of the failure rate is

$$h(t)\, dt = -\frac{dn}{n}$$

(5.2.23)

In words, the failure rate times a short period of time is the fraction of the units expected to fail in that period of time. The units of the failure rate are failures/unit time, where "time" can be in appropriate units. A special unit is the FIT, *failures in time,* which denotes one failure per 1 million units in 1000 hours. Thus

$$1 \text{ FIT} = \frac{10^{-6} \text{ failures}}{1000 \text{ hours}} = 10^{-9} \frac{\text{failures}}{\text{hour}}$$

If we treat $n(t)$ as a continuous function of time and interpret dn and dt as differentials, Eq. (5.2.23) takes an equivalent form:

$$h(t) = -\frac{1}{n}\frac{dn}{dt} = -\frac{d}{dt}\ln(n(t))$$

(5.2.24)

where "ln" is the natural logarithm. If we integrate both sides of Eq. (5.2.24) from 0 to t, we arrive at the results given in Eqs. (5.2.8) and (5.2.9), scaled by $n(0)$:

$$n(t) = n(0)e^{-H(t)}, \text{ where } H(t) = \int_0^t h(t')\, dt'$$

(5.2.25)

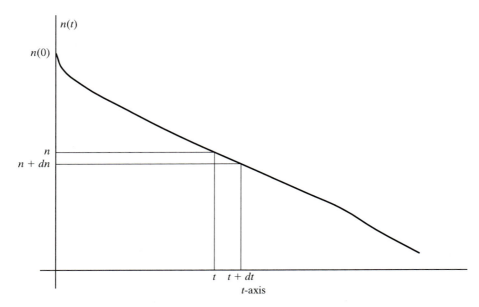

Figure 5.2.3   The average number of survivors as a function of time. This curve has the general shape of the reliability function but is scaled up by $n(0)$, the original number of units. Because the number of working units is always decreasing, dn is negative numerically.

Equation (5.2.25) is identical with Eq. (5.2.18) combined with Eq. (5.2.9). Finally, we might note that the failure rate and the reliability function are related through Eqs. (5.2.24) and (5.2.18) as

$$h(t) = -\frac{1}{R(t)}\frac{dR(t)}{dt} = -\frac{d}{dt}\ln[R(t)] \tag{5.2.26}$$

Summary.   The models appropriate to the user and to the manufacturer use different vocabulary that represent their differing concerns, but the models are basically the same. We presented both models and defined the mean time to failure, the reliability function, the failure rate, and the cumulative failure rate.

5.2.3 Failure Rate Models

Failures occur for a variety of reasons, and different modes of failure lead to differing patterns. In this section we develop several models for failure rates that cover some of the major failure modes.

Early failures.   Early failures, or infant mortalities, indicate manufacturing defects. Such defects lead to failure rates such as pictured in Fig. 5.2.4. An exponential model for early failures, which is chosen for mathematical convenience, leads to a cumulative failure rate for the early failures of

$$H_E(t) = \int_0^t h_E(t')\,dt' = \int_0^t ae^{-bt'}\,dt' = \left(\frac{a}{b}\right)(1 - e^{-bt}) \tag{5.2.27}$$

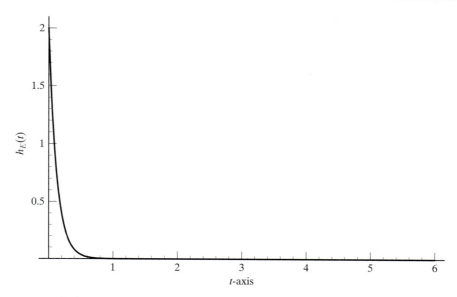

Figure 5.2.4 Early failures are indicated by a failure rate that is large immediately after the units are placed in service but rapidly decreases to zero as units with manufacturing defects are removed from the population.

and the reliability function, considering only early failures, is

$$R_E(t) = e^{-H_E(t)} = \exp\left[-\frac{a}{b}(1 - e^{-bt})\right] \tag{5.2.28}$$

This reliability function is shown in Fig. 5.2.5. The number of survivors of early failure would be this curve times the original number of units, $n(t) = n(0)R_E(t)$.

There are two parameters of interest in the early failure period: (1) the probability of early failure and (2) the period of time during which early failures occur. If we were speaking of a large batch of units, the first would indicate the number of units expected to succumb to early failure. If we were speaking of one unit, this value would indicate the probability of its succumbing to early failure. The probability of early failure depends on the area under the failure rate curve in Fig. 5.2.4. In the present model, the area is $\frac{a}{b} = 0.25$ and the corresponding drop in the reliability function is $1 - e^{-0.25} = 0.221$. Thus 22.1% of the units are expected to have early failures. In general,

$$P[\text{early failure}] = 1 - e^{-\text{area}} \tag{5.2.29}$$

where *area* is the area under the early failure rate curve, Fig. 5.2.4. For a large batch, the expected number of early failures would be

$$\Delta n = n(0)(1 - e^{-\text{area}}) \tag{5.2.30}$$

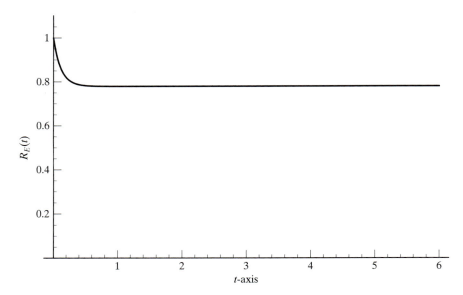

Figure 5.2.5 The reliability curve, or the fraction of survivors, with early failures. For emphasis the curve gives a relatively large number of early failures, about 22%.

The second number of interest in the early failure period is t_E, a time characteristic of the end of the early failure period. No precise definition will be given for t_E. For Figure 5.2.4, $t_E \approx 0.5$. We could also estimate t_E from Fig. 5.2.5 as the time when the curve flattens out.

A constant failure rate.   After the early failure period, a constant failure rate, $h(t) = \lambda$, is often a useful model for failures. A constant failure rate models failures due to accidents and lost items. Failures due to accidents or loss take place without a strong pattern in time, at least to a first approximation. To give a simple example, we bought 36 glasses about 11 years ago. Two glasses remain at this time. The other glasses were broken or lost. Such a failure mode would have a constant failure rate. For a constant failure rate the cumulative failure rate during the midperiod, M, is

$$H_M(t) = \lambda t \tag{5.2.31}$$

and the reliability function is

$$R_M(t) = e^{-\lambda t} \tag{5.2.32}$$

which is characteristic of a pure Poisson process. The reliability curve for a constant failure rate is shown in Fig. 5.2.6 for $\lambda = 0.2$.

Aging and wear.   Aging and wear out lead to increasing failure rates as time increases. We denote this period with a subscript L; hence we have a reliability function $R_L(t)$ due to a failure rate $h_L(t)$ during the late period, whose onset occurs at $\approx t_L$. Figure 5.2.7 shows such a pattern.

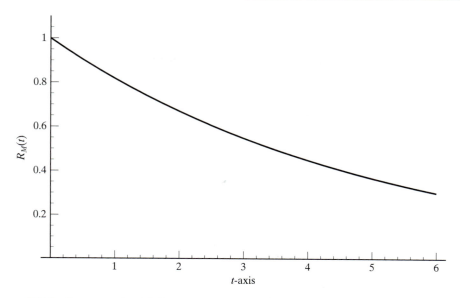

Figure 5.2.6 For a constant failure rate, $\lambda = 0.2$, the reliability function is exponential.

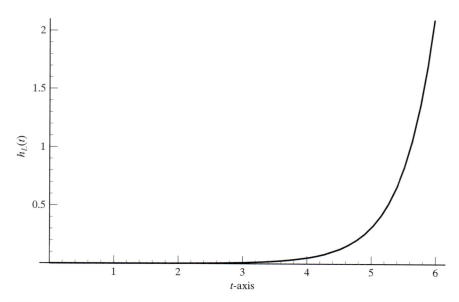

Figure 5.2.7 A failure rate that shows aging and wear out. Here the effects are seen about $t = 4$ and rapidly become severe. Thus we would judge $t_L \approx 4$ for the onset of aging and wear out. The failure rate model was chosen because it looked right; the model has no physical significance.

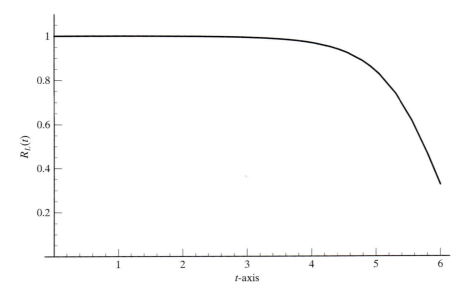

Figure 5.2.8 The effects of aging and wear out is a drop of survivors during "old age." Here we have shown a severe effect for emphasis. The effects of aging and wear out begin to show at $t_L \approx 4$.

The cumulative failure rate for such a model as we have used does not submit to ready calculation, so we resort to numerical calculation to calculate the reliability function. Figure 5.2.8 shows a severe aging and wear-out effect for emphasis. One parameter of the failure pattern is the time of the onset of aging and wear out. The wear-out period begins $t_L \approx 4$ in this model.

The bathtub curve.   In general, systems can have early failures, a midperiod of relatively constant failures, and a period of aging and wear out. The combined failure rate is the sum of the early, mid, and late failure rates. Figure 5.2.9 shows the combined effects in the failure rate. The failure rate pattern in Fig. 5.2.9 is called a *bathtub* failure rate. Figure 5.2.10 shows the resulting reliability function for this bathtub characteristic.

The reliability function shown in Fig. 5.2.10 reveals a drop in reliability in the early period due to manufacturing defects, an exponential decrease in the middle period due to accidents, and a rapid drop in reliability at the onset of the aging and wear-out period. We will soon show how to analyze the critical parameters of the bathtub curve from reliability data.

The Weibull reliability model.   A model that often successfully fits reliability data in either the early or the late period is the Weibull model. The CDF of the Weibull is a generalization of the exponential model:

$$R(t) = \exp\left[-\left(\frac{t}{c}\right)^m\right] \tag{5.2.33}$$

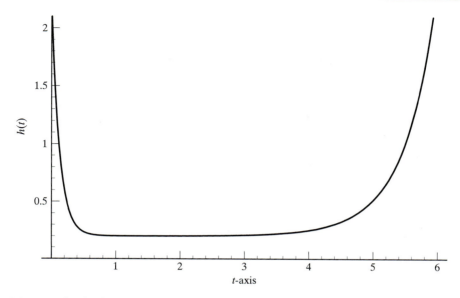

Figure 5.2.9 A "bathtub" curve that shows early and late failures with a period of constant failures in between. Here the effects have been exaggerated for emphasis.

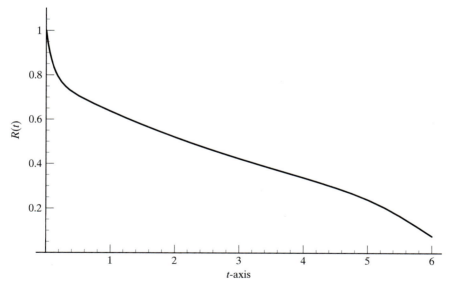

Figure 5.2.10 The reliability function associated with a bathtub failure rate characteristic. We see the effects of manufacturing defects in the early period, a drop in reliability during the late period, and a period of exponential decline during the middle period.

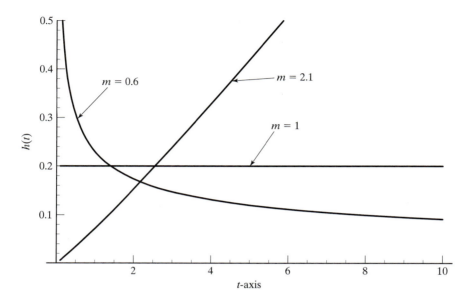

Figure 5.2.11   The failure rate for the Weibull distribution for the same value of $c = 5$ but differing values of the shape factor, m. For $m < 1$, early failures are indicated; for $m = 1$, a constant failure rate results, and for $m > 2$, wear out or aging is indicated.

where c is a characteristic time and m is a shape parameter. The corresponding failure rate is determined from Eq. (5.2.26) as

$$h(t) = -\frac{d}{dt} \ln[R(t)] = -\frac{d}{dt}\left[-\left(\frac{t}{c}\right)^m\right] = m\frac{t^{m-1}}{c_m} \tag{5.2.34}$$

The nature of the failure rate depends on m, as Fig. 5.2.11 shows. As shown in Fig. 5.2.11, the shape factor, m, can be adjusted to fit early failure trends, a constant failure rate, or aging and wear out.

Use of the Weibull distribution.   The Weibull distribution, embracing as it does a wide variety of failure conditions, can be fit to failure data to determine the nature of the failures. After we discuss system reliability theory, we demonstrate how to fit a bathtub failure model and a Weibull model to a set of failure data.

5.2.4 System Reliability

Systems.   So far we have spoken of the reliability of entire systems, such as an automobile, or a single component of a system, such as a tire on an automobile. In this section we deal with systems comprised of many subsystems, each in principle having its individual reliability characteristics. Our purpose is to see how the reliability characteristics of the subsystems contribute to the overall reliability of the system.

Types of systems.   We will deal with four types of systems:

1. **Series or chain systems.** These are systems in which if one subsystem fails the entire system fails. An example is the four tires on an automobile, all of which have to operate for the "tire system" to be functional.
2. **Parallel systems.** Parallel systems fail only if all subsystems fail. An example is the headlight system of an automobile, in which if either of the two headlight fails the headlight system does not fail.
3. **Standby systems.** Standby systems have one or more subsystems in reserve to replace a failed subsystem. An example is the spare tire for an automobile.
4. **Combinations of the preceding.** It is possible to combine series, parallel, and standby subsystems. The entire tire system of an automobile combines the series system of four tires on the ground with one standby tire in the trunk, which would replace any failed tire.

In the following we analyze series, parallel, and standby systems for their MTTFs and reliability functions, given the MTTF and reliability functions of the component subsystems.

Series or chain systems

System model.   In Fig. 5.2.12 we show a series system configuration with the failure times of the three subsystems.

Reliability function for a series system.   We define the failure time for the system as T_S and the failure times for the subsystems as $T_A, T_B,$ and T_C. The reliability function is the

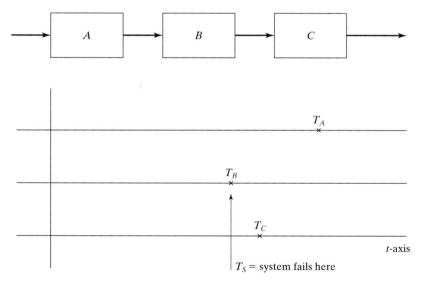

Figure 5.2.12   Subsystems *A*, *B*, and *C* are operated in series. The system fails when the first subsystem fails, in this case *B*.

probability that the system is operating at time t, which requires

$$R_S(t) = P[T_S > t] = P[(T_A > t) \cap (T_B > t) \cap (T_C > t)] \tag{5.2.35}$$

We assume independent failure times, so $\cap \rightarrow \times$ and we have

$$R_S(t) = P[(T_A > t)] \times P[(T_B > t)] \times P[(T_C > t)] = R_A(t) \times R_B(t) \times R_C(t) \tag{5.2.36}$$

Thus the reliability function of the series system is the product of the reliability functions of the component subsystems.

Failure rates. The failure rates for the series subsystems also combine in a simple fashion. We start with the cumulative failure rate of the system. Combining Eqs. (5.2.9) and (5.2.36), we find

$$e^{-H_S(t)} = e^{-H_A(t)} \times e^{-H_B(t)} \times e^{-H_C(t)} = e^{-(H_A(t)+H_B(t)+H_C(t))} \tag{5.2.37}$$

Thus the cumulative failure rates add to give the cumulative failure rate for the system:

$$H_S(t) = H_A(t) + H_B(t) + H_C(t) \tag{5.2.38}$$

Because the cumulative failure rate is the integral [Eq. (5.2.8)] of the failure rate, this additive property applies as well to the failure rates for the subsystems:

$$h_S(t) = h_A(t) + h_B(t) + h_C(t) \tag{5.2.39}$$

MTTF calculation. The mean time to failure (MTTF) for the system is the area under the system reliability function, as shown in Eq. (5.2.13):

$$\text{MTTF} = \int_0^\infty R_S(t)\, dt \tag{5.2.40}$$

This integral cannot be evaluated in general. The following example shows a calculation for a specific model.

Example 5.2.3: The Great Race

An off-road race is through 300 mi of difficult terrain. A tire can be expected to have one failure every 500 mi on average, and so every vehicle is allowed to carry two spares. Find the mean distance to failure, MDTF, for the four tires, and the probability that a vehicle will finish the race with the two spare tires.

Solution Because we are dealing with failure due to accident and not wear out, we assume a constant failure rate, λ failures/mile, for an individual tire. The constant failure rate corresponds to an exponential reliability function, Eq. (5.2.32), and the expected distance to failure is Eq. (5.1.38), the reciprocal of the failure rate

$$E[\text{distance}] = \frac{1}{\lambda} = 500 \Rightarrow \lambda = \frac{1}{500} \tag{5.2.41}$$

Similarly, the system reliability function is constant, given by Eq. (5.2.39) as

$$\lambda_S = 4\lambda = \frac{4}{500} \tag{5.2.42}$$

The system reliability function will be exponential [Eq. (5.2.37)]:

$$R_S(x) = e^{-\lambda_S x} = e^{-4x/500} \tag{5.2.43}$$

where $x =$ distance traveled. The MDTF for the system of four tires is thus

$$\text{MDTF} = \int_0^\infty R_S(x)\, dx = \frac{1}{\lambda_S} = \frac{500}{4} = 125 \text{ mi} \tag{5.2.44}$$

That is why the vehicles carry two spares. We will continue this example when we take up the properties of standby systems.

You do it.   In a new car the failure rate for the motor is $\lambda_M = 0.1$ failure/year, and the failure rate for the drive train is $\lambda_D = 0.08$ failure/year. What is the probability that the first failure occurs within the first 5 years?

```
myanswer = ?         ;
```

```
Evaluate
```

For the answer, see endnote 15.

Parallel systems.   A parallel system with two subsystems is pictured in Fig. 5.2.13. The reliability function of a parallel system can be expressed in terms of the union of the failure times of the subsystems. For two subsystems, this function is

$$
\begin{aligned}
R_S(t) = P[T_S > t] &= P[(T_A > t) \cup (T_B > t)] \\
&= P[T_A > t] + P[T_B > t] - P[(T_A > t) \cap (T_B > t)]
\end{aligned}
\tag{5.2.45}
$$

When independence is assumed, we let $\cap \to \times$ in the last term, and express the results in terms of the reliability functions of A and B. Equation (5.2.45) thus takes the form

$$R_S(t) = R_A(t) + R_B(t) - R_A(t)R_B(t) \tag{5.2.46}$$

The MTTF is the area under the reliability function, Eq. (5.2.13), but no general form is possible. The following example uses a constant failure rate, which is analytically convenient and fairly realistic in this scenario.

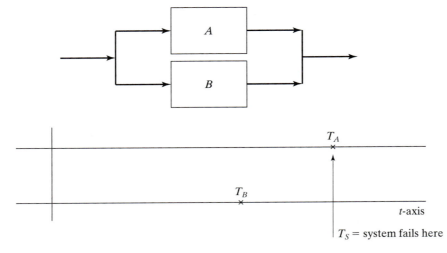

Figure 5.2.13   In a parallel system, the system does not fail until every subsystem fails. In this case subsystem B fails first, but the system does not fail until both B and A have failed.

Example 5.2.4:   Electric power lines

A small town is served by the electric power company through two independent transmission lines. The lifetime of the lines is long, but accidents of various types can cause failures; hence, we assume constant failure rates for the two lines. Failure mechanisms include ice storms, lightning, lines downed by falling trees, transformers shorted out by small animals, and power poles felled by vehicles. We assume independent failures, which in the case of weather-related failures is not very realistic. The MTTFs for the two lines are 6 years and 10 years for lines A and B, respectively. Find the MTTF for the parallel system.

Solution   The failure rates are the reciprocals of the MTTFs of the two lines: $\lambda_A = \frac{1}{6}$ and $\lambda_B = \frac{1}{10}$. The reliability functions for the lines will be exponential [Eq. (5.2.32)], so Eq. (5.2.46) takes the form

$$R_S(t) = e^{-\lambda_A t} + e^{-\lambda_B t} - e^{-\lambda_A t} \times e^{-\lambda_B t} = e^{-\lambda_A t} + e^{-\lambda_B t} - e^{-(\lambda_A + \lambda_B)t} \qquad (5.2.47)$$

The MTTF is the area under this reliability function:

$$\text{MTTF} = \int_0^\infty R_S(t)\, dt = \frac{1}{\lambda_A} + \frac{1}{\lambda_B} - \frac{1}{\lambda_A + \lambda_B} = 6 + 10 - 3.75 = 12.3 \text{ years} \qquad (5.2.48)$$

Note that the MTTF of a parallel system is longer than the MTTF of the subsystems. Parallel systems are used in applications where improved reliability is desired. Standby systems also improve reliability, as shown in the next section.

You do it.   What if the transmission lines are identical in their failure rates? If the town requires a MTTF of 20 years, what is the required failure rate for the lines?

```
myanswer  =    ?   ;
```

```
Evaluate
```

For the answer, see endnote 16.

Standby systems

A standby system has one unit in operation with one or more units in reserve. We represent this plug-in capability with a switch in Fig. 5.2.14.

The failure time for a standby system is the sum of the failure times for the various subsystems. For the system with one standby subsystem, as shown in Fig. 5.2.14, the failure time for the system is

$$T_S = T_A + T_B \tag{5.2.49}$$

from which it follows that the MTTF for the system is the sum of the MTTFs for the subsystems:

$$\text{MTTF}_S = \text{MTTF}_A + \text{MTTF}_B \tag{5.2.50}$$

Finding the reliability function for the standby system is not so easy. A starting point would be to determine the PDF of the system failure time. This would be the convolution of the PDFs of the failure time for the standby subsystems:

$$f_S(t) = f_A(t) * f_B(t) \tag{5.2.51}$$

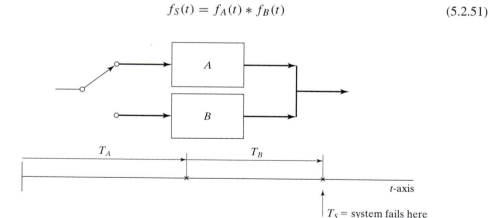

Figure 5.2.14   A standby system with one subsystem in service and one in standby. The failure time for the standby system is the sum of the failure times for the subsystems.

No general form is possible, but for the simplest case, a constant failure rate, the PDFs of the subsystems are exponential, and the PDF of the system is Erlang [Eq. (5.1.49)], if the subsystems have the same MTTFs. The general procedure would be to do the convolution and then calculate the reliability function as

$$R_S(t) = P[T_S > t] = \int_t^\infty f_S(t')\,dt' \tag{5.2.52}$$

Example 5.2.5: The Great Race Revisited
We began Example 5.2.3 involving a 300-m off-road race in the section on series systems. We determined the MDTF to be 125 m for the series system of four tires. We now address the question, What is the probability of finishing the race, considering that two spares are carried. We note that tires are failing owing to accident, not to wear out, and thus a constant failure rate is appropriate.

Solution We note that the MDTF for the series-standby system is three times the MDTF for the series system, or $\text{MDTF}_S = 3 \times 125 = 375$ mi. We might therefore suppose chances to be excellent for finishing the race. We shall see. The failure rate of the series system is $\lambda_S = \frac{4}{500}$. The distance to failure is thus an exponential random variable with this parameter, and the total distance for failure of the series-standby system, X, is

$$X = X_0 + X_1 + X_2 \tag{5.2.53}$$

where 0, 1, and 2 stand for the original tires, the first spare, and the second spare. The PDF of X would be the convolution of three exponential random variables and thus would be Erlang [Eq. (5.1.49)] of order $k = 3$. Thus the probability of finishing the race is

$$P[X > 300] = \int_{300}^\infty \frac{\lambda_S^3}{2!} x^2 e^{-\lambda_S x}\,dx \tag{5.2.54}$$

where $\lambda_S = \frac{4}{500}$. Equation (5.2.54) requires integration by parts three times, so let us let Mathematica do the work.

```
λ=4/500;
Integrate[λ³ x² Exp[-λx] / 2!, {x, 300, Infinity}];
N[%]
```
```
0.569709
```

Thus we are taking a considerable risk by taking only two spare tires, since the chance of not completing the race is over 40%.

You do it. What is the probability of finishing the race if you take three spares?

```
myanswer =       ;
```

```
Evaluate
```

For the answer, see endnote 17.

Summary. We introduced series, parallel, standby, and combination systems. The primary focus was on calculating the MTTF and the reliability functions for these systems. Simple results were obtained only for specific models and limited systems, in view of analytic difficulties.

5.2.5 Fitting Failure Data with Models

The problem. In this section we address the question: Given that we have some reliability data, how can we determine an appropriate model to understand the data and predict reliability performance beyond the range of the measured data? This problem applies the techniques introduced in Sec. 4.2 on fitting probability models to data. Here the data will be survivor data versus time for a group of devices under reliability testing. The devices may be stressed outside their normal operating range to accelerate the failure mechanism, or the data may indicate field data on failures.

The data. The data we will analyze are survivor statistics for California residents in 1998. The table includes men and women and gives, for that year, the number of deaths of individuals in a certain age bracket.[18] We readily admit that these data do not apply to the same group of individuals, as in a batch of computers manufactured the same week, and that lifetime health care will be different for someone 85 years old versus someone 34 years old. Nevertheless, these data will illustrate the analysis of survivor statistics.

The total number of males in the table is 113,554, and we are given how many died that year within the first year of life (1627), between 1 and 4 years (323), etc. The data, with years followed by survivors and a plot appear in Fig. 5.2.15.

```
{{0, 113554}, {1, 111927}, {4, 111604}, {14, 111104},
 {24, 108691}, {34, 105376}, {44, 99189},
 {54, 89484}, {64, 76194}, {74, 52574}, {84, 20102}}
```

We will be fitting an experimental reliability function to these data. The experimental reliability function, like an experimental CDF, would be the survivors divided by the original number in the population $+1$, as

$$R_{\exp}(t) = \frac{n(t)}{n(0) + 1} \tag{5.2.55}$$

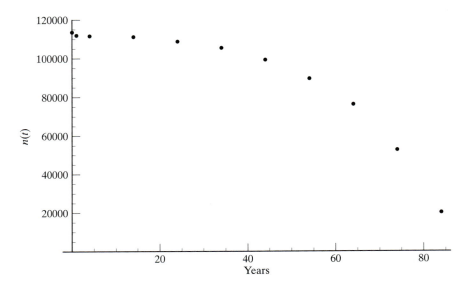

Figure 5.2.15   Population data for reliability analysis. This hypothetical population was constructed from California deaths in 1998. As our analysis will show, the deaths beyond age 25 show the effects of poorer lifetime health care for older members of the population.

The +1 is of no significance here, but generally this is an empirical correction for a finite data set and would matter if the numbers were small.

   Analysis with a bathtub model.   We now analyze the data for a bathtub (Fig. 5.2.9) characteristic. Recall that this model includes early failures, here actual infant mortalities, a period of relatively constant failure rate, and the onset of aging at some time. During the middle period the reliability function takes the form

$$R(t) \approx e^{-(\text{area} + \lambda t)} \tag{5.2.56}$$

where "area" is the area under the failure rate curve for early failures, and λ is the constant failure rate during the middle period, after early failures and before aging and wear out. We may analyze the experimental reliability function as a bathtub curve by taking the natural log of the failure rate. If the result has a linear region, then the bathtub curve is indicated, especially if there is an early drop from early failures and a late drop due to aging and wear out. Thus we plot the natural log of the experimental reliability function versus time and see if we get a linear region. Figure 5.2.16 shows such a plot.

   On this scale it is hard to see if there is a linear region, so we replot with an expanded vertical scale, as in Fig. 5.2.17. Here we see the drop due to infant deaths in the first year, and then something like a straight line through year 24. At that point the reliability begins to drop below the line, suggesting aging. Of course, we know from experience that aging is not a factor at age 34, so there must be some other explanation. One suspects that we are seeing here the improvement of health care during the recent past. Nevertheless, we will continue with the

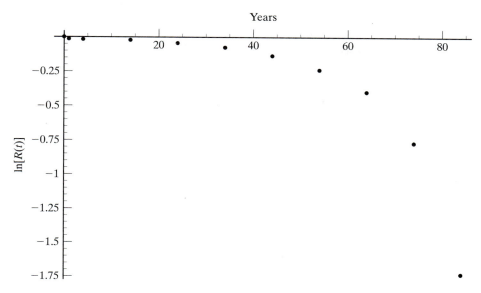

Figure 5.2.16   Plot of the experimental reliability function on a log scale. This plot shows infant deaths, a region of constant death rate, and aging. The next plot expands the scale to show these effects more clearly.

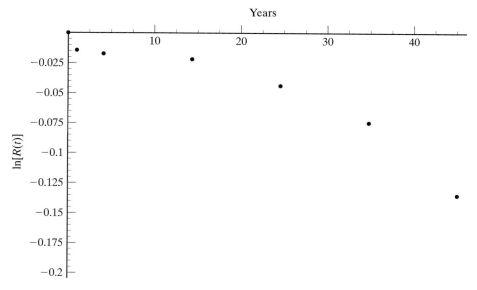

Figure 5.2.17   Here we see the drop due to infant deaths, a short linear region, and the onset of ''aging'' about age 25.

analysis, since these are real data and we have a model we are testing. We now fit a line to the three points to determine the "area" intercept.

```
-0.0114061 - 0.00120338 t
```

We see that the area intercept is -0.0114061. The infant mortality rate is therefore $1 - e^{-0.0114} \approx 1.14\%$. The slope in the constant region is -0.00120338, indicating a death rate of 0.12%/year during the years $1-24$. The early period is 1 year or less, and the onset of "aging" is in the 30s. Of course, we do not believe the latter, but that is what the analysis indicates. As stated before, this artifact is most likely due to the improving health care throughout the lifetime of the individuals in the population.

Analysis with a Weibull model.   The Weibull model is widely used in reliability studies. As stated earlier [Eq. (5.2.33)], it can model either early, mid, or late periods. In this case we will use it to model the late period. The Weibull reliability function, which we will match to the experimental reliability function, is

$$R(t) = \exp\left[-\left(\frac{t}{c}\right)^m\right] \tag{5.2.57}$$

Because our technique is based on linear regression, we mathematically transform Eq. (5.2.57) into the form of a straight line. This requires taking the natural logarithm twice, as shown:

$$\ln[R(t)] = -\left(\frac{t}{c}\right)^m \Rightarrow \ln[-\ln[R(t)]] = m\ln[t] - m\ln[c] \tag{5.2.58}$$

Thus we replace the theoretical reliability function with the experimental reliability function, take the natural log, change the sign, and take the natural log again. This function, plotted against the natural log of time, would be a straight line if the data fit the model perfectly. The slope of the line would be the shape factor, m, and the intercept of the line would lead to a value of the time parameter, c. In this case we take only data after time 24, since that is when the "aging" period begins. Figure 5.2.18 shows the results.

The plot in Fig. 5.2.18, although not a perfect straight line, can be fit with a straight line to make the best Weibull model for these data. The fit is

```
-14.6068 + 3.34726 lnt
```

From the fit, we find that the shape factor is

```
3.34726
```

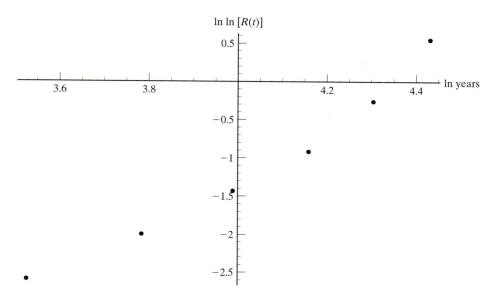

Figure 5.2.18   A log–log plot of the aging portion of the mortality data. If the Weibull model fit perfectly, this would be a straight line.

and the time factor is

```
78.5565
```

Finally, Fig. 5.2.19 shows the experimental reliability function and the fitted Weibull reliability function on the same graph.

Recall that the model was fit to the points 34 years and upward. Whether the model is useful we leave to the reader's judgment. Our purpose was to illustrate the method for fitting the model to the data.

Summary.   We treated reliability theory as a special case of a Poisson process. We defined probability models from the viewpoint of both customer and manufacturer. The concepts of interest to the customer, the reliability function and the MTTF, were related to the concept of interest to the manufacturer, the failure rate. We studied how system reliability is affected by subsystem reliability in chain (series), parallel, and standby systems. We investigated some common models, specifically the bathtub and the Weibull models, and we showed how to fit a model to reliability data.

This chapter introduced the concept of a random process. We treated the Poisson process as a random process and pointed out that the manufacturer's model for the lifetime reliability history of batches of manufactured goods is a random process model. Random processes appear in the next section on queues and are the focus of the next chapter, particularly a special class of random processes called wide-sense stationary random processes.

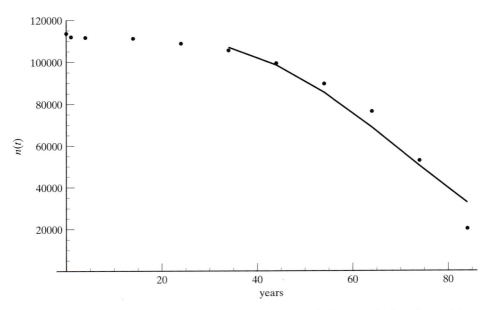

Figure 5.2.19   Plot of the attempt to fit the aging portion of the population data with a Weibull model.

5.3 QUEUING THEORY

5.3.1 Introduction to Queuing Theory

Americans line up to enter a theater; Englishmen "queue" up to enter a theatre.[19] This section on queuing theory investigates models for systems with *servers,* such as cashiers in a grocery store, and *customers,* who are either served immediately or wait in a queue to be served. Of course, these categories are applicable to inanimate servers, such as computers, and inanimate customers, such as communication messages.

Queuing systems can be complicated.   There can be one server, as at a convenience store, or many. There can be one queue, as at many post offices, or many, as at the supermarket. Customers can arrive at random or in batches, as when arriving passengers head for the toilets in the airport. Service times can be more or less constant, as when flu shots are given, or can vary widely, as at a bank.

Queuing disciplines.   Queues involving people are usually first come, first served, but other disciplines are possible. Consider your dinner plates stacked up (in a queue) waiting to be of service. The last one put on the stack is the first one off, a last come, first served queue discipline. In batch computer processing, the queue discipline is influenced by estimated run time and memory requirements of the various jobs.

   In Sec. 5.3 we will deal with queues in which customers arrive at random with a constant average rate, and thus the arrivals are described as a Poisson process. We will analyze a single queue/single server system. Service times are assumed to be exponential, another link with the Poisson process. Even with these simplifications, the operation of a queue is complicated, as the following simulation will show.

Vocabulary.   To reduce confusion in this section, we are careful to call the entire operation, queue plus server, the *queuing system* but to call the customers waiting to be served *the queue.* Thus we may have two customers in the queuing system, one customer being served and one customer in the queue, waiting to be served.

Arrival times.   Arrival times are described as a Poisson process with a constant average rate, λ. Consider a queuing system consisting of one server and one queue. We assume that at $t = 0$ the queuing system is empty, meaning that no one is being served and no one is waiting. The following cell calculates a series of arrival times that are IID exponential random variables:

```
m = 10;
λ = 1; (*the arrival rate*)
betweenarrivals =
  Table[Random[ExponentialDistribution[λ]], {m}];
NumberForm[%, 3]
```
```
{0.854, 0.184, 3.22, 2.65,
 1.59, 0.384, 0.993, 0.07, 2.33, 0.503}
```

These are the times between arrivals. The first number gives the arrival time of the first customer. The arrival times come from the sums of these intervals, as given by the following cell and plotted in Fig. 5.3.1:

```
arrival =
  Table[Sum[betweenarrivals[[k]], {k, 1, i}], {i, 1, m}];
NumberForm[%, 3]
```
```
{0.854, 1.04, 4.26, 6.9,
 8.5, 8.88, 9.87, 9.94, 12.3, 12.8}
```

Service times.   We now generate the service times, for these are needed to calculate departure times. These will also be IID exponential random variables, but we need a higher rate, since the server must be able to service customers faster than they arrive on average; otherwise, the queue will grow in length. Thus the server rate parameter is $\lambda_s > \lambda$. If the server were never idle, he would process customers at a rate of λ_s, but customers do not arrive at this higher rate. The average rate at which customers are processed is λ, the rate at which they arrive in the queuing system, if the system is stable.[20] It follows that the server must be idle some of the time. The next cell calculates the service times for the m customers.

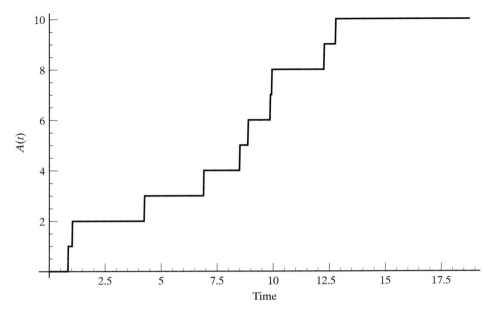

Figure 5.3.1   A plot of the accumulated arrivals of customers in a queuing system. The times between arrivals are IID exponential random variables.

```
Off[General::spell1]
λs = 1.5;
servicetime =
  Table[Random[ExponentialDistribution[λs]], {m}];
NumberForm[%, 3]
```

```
{1.46, 0.442, 0.282, 0.969,
 0.486, 0.57, 0.657, 1.32, 0.0195, 0.71}
```

Departure times.   To calculate the departure times, we must add the arrival time, the time spent in the queue, and the service time. The first customer spends no time in the queue, since it is empty when he arrives; hence the first customer departs at departure[[1]] = arrival[[1]] + servicetime[[1]]. The second customer may or may not have to spend time in the queue. If arrival[[2]] > departure[[1]], then customer 2 is served immediately without waiting in the queue, but if arrival[[2]] < departure[[1]], then customer 2 will wait in the queue and depart at departure[[1]] + servicetime[[2]]. In general, customer i departs at arrival[[i]] + servicetime[[i]] if there is no one in the queue, but at departure[[$i - 1$]] + servicetime[[i]] if forced to spend waiting time in the queue. The queue exists if arrival[[i]] < departure[[$i - 1$]]. In this fashion we can work out the details of arrivals and departures as follows in Fig. 5.3.2:

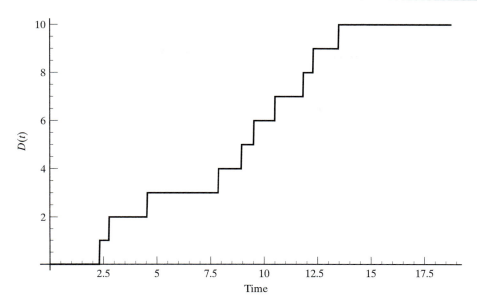

Figure 5.3.2   A plot of the accumulated departure of customers in a queue. The departure times depend on arrival and service times, both of which are random.

```
departure = Table[0, {m}]; (*Creates a table*)
For[i = 1, i ≤ m, i++,
  departure[[i]] =
   If[i == 1, arrival[[i]] + servicetime[[i]],
    If[departure[[i - 1]] < arrival[[i]],
     arrival[[i]] + servicetime[[i]],
     departure[[i - 1]] + servicetime[[i]]]]];
NumberForm[departure, 3]
```

```
{2.31, 2.76, 4.54, 7.87,
 8.98, 9.55, 10.5, 11.9, 12.3, 13.5}
```

The state of the queue is shown by combining arrivals and departures, as in Fig. 5.3.3.

The number of customers in the system is simply the difference between the accumulated arrivals and the accumulated departures, $N(t) = A(t) - D(t)$, as illustrated in Fig. 5.3.4.

We can also work out the time in the system and the time in the queue, as in the following cell:

```
systemtime = departure - arrival;
NumberForm[%, 3]
```

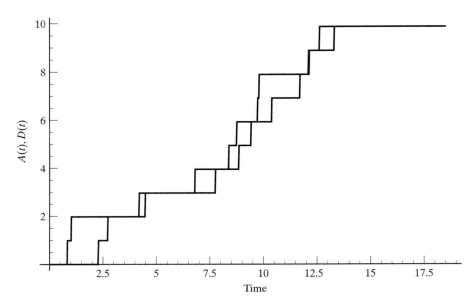

Figure 5.3.3   Cumulative arrivals and cumulative departure times for a queuing system. Note that the vertical distance between the arrival and departure plots at any time is the number of customers in the system at that time. Also note that the horizontal distance between the arrival and departure plots at customer *i* is the time spent in the system by that customer.

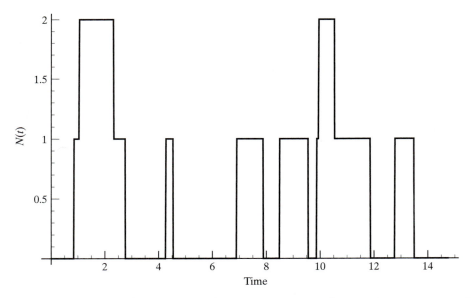

Figure 5.3.4   The number of customers in the queuing system. If $N(t) = 1$, one customer is with the server and there is no one in the queue.

```
queuetime = Chop[systemtime - servicetime];
NumberForm[%, 3]
```

{0.103, 1.79, 1.52, 0.397,
  0.261, 2.08, 1.35, 0.413, 0.733, 0.515}

{0, 0, 1.39, 0, 0, 0, 1.33, 0.374, 0, 0}

Random processes.   A queuing system is modeled by random processes. What we showed in the simulation just completed is one set of member functions of these random processes. The arrivals were generated as IID exponential random variables with a rate parameter λ to model customers arriving at the server at random in a Poisson process. The service times for the customers were also IID exponential random variables with a different rate parameter, λ_s. The arrivals and departures were generated from these two sets of random variables according to the operation of the queue.

To generate another of the member functions of the random processes, one can start at the top (arrival times) and execute all the cells again. Of course, the numbers and plots will come out different, perhaps very different, but they will be part of the same random processes. Indeed, the full random processes would contain the multiple infinities of all such functions that could be generated with this procedure.

Summary.   The simulation just worked through had several purposes. First, we illustrated our statement that operation of even the simplest queuing system is complicated. Second, we introduced many important quantities in queuing systems: arrival and departure times, the number of customers in the system, the times spent in the system and in the queue, and the service times. The next section derives a simple formula that relates the averages of the time spent in the system, the number of customers in the queue, and the average rate of servicing customers.

5.3.2 Little's Formula

Little's formula is one of those back-of-the-envelope derivations that turned out to be extremely general and extremely useful. The derivation depends on observation of some features of Fig. 5.3.3, repeated here as Fig. 5.3.5.

The horizontal distance between the arrival and departure plots for customer i is the time spent in the system by customer i, t_i. Thus the total area between the curves is approximately

$$\text{Area} = \sum_1^m t_i = m \times \bar{t} \tag{5.3.1}$$

where $\bar{t}$ is the average time spent by the m customers in the system. We say "approximately" because the system in steady state is ongoing, and the area between the curves is defined exactly only when the system is empty. Recall that this is a back-of-the-envelope derivation.

The vertical distance between the arrival and departure plots at any time is the number of customers in the system at any time. We show a typical plot in Fig. 5.3.4, and the area under

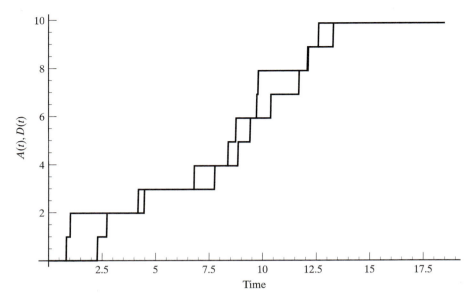

Figure 5.3.5 Cumulative arrivals and cumulative departure times for a queuing system. A repeat of Fig. 5.3.3. Note that the vertical distance between the arrival and departure plots at any time is the number of customers in the system at that time. Also note that the horizontal distance between the arrival and departure plots at customer i is the time spent in the system by that customer.

this curve is the same as the area shown between the plots in Fig. 5.3.5. Thus we can relate the area to the customers in the system as follows:

$$\text{Area} = \int_0^t n(t)\,dt = \overline{n} \times t \tag{5.3.2}$$

where $\overline{n}$ is the average number of customers in the queuing system, and t is a time when the mth customer is departing, a time large enough for meaningful averaging.

A final relationship comes from the average rate of arrival. In our model we have an exact value of λ, but in a real queue the arrival rate would be estimated from the data:

$$\overline{\lambda} = \frac{m}{t} \tag{5.3.3}$$

If we eliminate m, Area, and t from (5.3.1)–(5.3.3), we have Little's formula:

$$\overline{n} = \overline{\lambda} \times \overline{t} \tag{5.3.4}$$

where $\overline{n}$ is the average number of customers in the queue, $\overline{\lambda}$ is the average rate at which they pass through the system, and $\overline{t}$ is the average time they spend in the queuing system.

We can test Little's formula on the preceding simulation. We let departure[[m]] be the end of the experiment. Then we can computed $\overline{n}$ by numerical integration:

```
Off[NIntegrate::"slwcon"]
Off[NIntegrate::"ncvb"]
AveNumber = (1/departure[[m]])
  NIntegrate[Sum[u[t - arrival[[i]]] - u[t - departure[[i]]],
    {i, 1, m}], {t, 0, departure[[m]]}]
```

```
0.662126
```

Although we have specified an average rate of arrival, we can compute the experimental rate from the generated data:

```
AveRate = m/departure[[m]]
```

```
0.712942
```

We can compute the average time in the system as well:

```
AveTime = Mean[systemtime]
```

```
0.915496
```

Little's formula says the first of these three should be equal to the product of the second and third:

```
AveRate * AveTime
AveNumber (*Compare the two numbers below to verify
  that Little's formula is valid for this case.*)
```

```
0.652695
```

```
0.662126
```

Random process. Because Little's formula works for every member of the random process, it must work for the entire random process as well. Making reasonable assumptions,[21] we can replace the time averages in Little's formula with statistical averages over the full random process, as follows:

$$\bar{\lambda} \to \lambda$$

$$\bar{n} \to E[N(t)]$$

$$\bar{t} \to E[T]$$

where λ is the true rate of arrival, $N(t)$ is the random process describing the number of customers in the system, and T is a random variable describing the time spent by a customer in the system. Thus Little's formula becomes

$$E[N(t)] = \lambda E[T] \tag{5.3.5}$$

The generality of Little's formula. The derivation of Little's formula assumes very little about the details of the operation of the queuing system. In the following table, we compare the example calculations with what was assumed in deriving Little's formula.

Table 5.3.1 A comparison between the specific example in the text and the generality of Little's formula

Feature	Example calculations	Requirements of Little's formula
1	Poisson arrivals	Not required; any model of arrivals is valid
2	Exponential service times	Not required; any model of service times is valid
3	Single queue	Not required; any number of queues is valid
4	Single server	Not required; any number of servers is valid
5	System = queue + server	The system can be only the queue or queues
6	System = queue + server	The system can be only the server or servers

Some applications. Let us apply Little's formula to feature 5, such that the "system" is only the queue. The relevant time is a random variable, T_Q, the time spent in the queue; the rate is λ_Q, the rate at which customers are entering the queue; and N_Q is the number of persons in the queue. In these terms, Little's formula becomes

$$E[N_Q] = \lambda_Q E[T_Q] \tag{5.3.6}$$

Consider, for example, the design of a supermarket checkout system, where we need to decide c, the number of checkout stations. We expect the maximum customer stream to be 10 customers per minute. If c is the number of servers, then $\lambda_Q = \frac{10}{c}$, assuming customers divide themselves among the lines. Human factor studies have shown that the longest queue that customers will tolerate is 2.5 in the queue, and that the longest they will wait is 3 minutes. Little's formula gives

$$2.5 = \frac{10}{c} \times 3 \Rightarrow c \approx 12 \text{ stations} \tag{5.3.7}$$

Utilization of the system. A second application follows from feature 6, in which the "system" is a single server. Here one of the relevant variables is N_S, the number of persons being served by the server. Because the server can serve one customer at a time, N_S is a Bernoulli random variable (see page 136), either 0 or 1. If we let $P[N_S = 1] = \rho$, then $E[N_S] = \rho$. The other variables of interest are the average rate of service, λ, and the time of service, T_S. In these terms Little's formula becomes

$$\rho = \lambda E[T_S] \tag{5.3.8}$$

The utilization, ρ, is the fraction of the time that the server is busy, and $1 - \rho$ is the fraction of the time that the server is idle. For exponential service times, $E[T_S] = 1/\lambda_s$, from which it follows that

$$\rho = \frac{\lambda}{\lambda_s} \text{ for exponential service times} \tag{5.3.9}$$

For example, in the preceding example calculations, $\lambda = 1$, $\lambda_s = 1.5$, and hence $\rho = \frac{1}{1.5} = 0.667$. In this system we expect the server to be idle about 33% of the time. From the graph (Fig. 5.3.4), this assumption appears reasonable;[22] however, realize that many more than 10 customers would have to be processed before such averages would be meaningful.

5.3.3 Analysis of a Single-Server Queue

Description of the queuing system. We turn now to the detailed analysis of a single queue system with one server. Arrivals will be Poisson at a rate of λ, and service times will be exponential with a mean service time of $E[T_s] = \frac{1}{\lambda_s}$. The rate λ_s is the average rate at which customers would be discharged from the server if the server was never idle, but of course the average rate at which customers are discharged from the server must be λ, the rate at which they arrive. This last statement assumes that $\lambda < \lambda_s$, which is required for a stable queuing system. From these considerations it follows that the server must be idle part of the time; indeed, the analysis to follow shows an idle server to be the most likely state of the system.

The arrival and departure processes. The operation of the queuing system involves two independent Poisson processes, but this independence is of a special form. The service times are independent of the arrival times, but the discharge times are not independent of arrival times, because the server can service and discharge customers only after they arrive. This coupling can be expressed by the following equations:

$$P[1 \text{ arrival in } dt] = \lambda \, dt \quad \text{and} \quad P[0 \text{ arrivals in } dt] = 1 - \lambda \, dt \tag{5.3.10}$$

and the other Poisson assumptions following [Eq. (5.1.1)] apply as well; however, the departures are conditioned on the state of the queue, as follows:

$$P[1 \text{ departure} \mid N > 0] = \lambda_s \, dt \quad \text{and} \quad P[0 \text{ departures} \mid N > 0] = 1 - \lambda_s \, dt \tag{5.3.11}$$

but

$$P[1 \text{ departure} \mid N = 0] = 0 \quad \text{and} \quad P[0 \text{ departures} \mid N = 0] = 1 \tag{5.3.12}$$

where N = the number of customers in the queuing system, which includes the server.

Requirements for describing the system. We require two related functions: (1) the PMF of N, the number of customers in the system, and (2) the PDF of T, a random variable describing the time that customers spend in the system. We begin with the first, defined in Eq. (5.3.13):

$$P_N(n) = P[N = n] \tag{5.3.13}$$

The PMF of *N*, the number in the queuing system

A stable queue.   In general, N is a random process and thus is a function of time; however, we will not express the time dependence because we are interested in $P[N = n]$, which should be the same at all times if the queue is stable, that is, is neither growing or shrinking in size, on average. This requires that the average rate of arrival, λ, be constant and that the rate at which the server is capable of serving customers, λ_s, is greater than the rate of arrival. If these requirements are met, the length of the queue will vary randomly with time but will not grow or shrink on average.

The system at *t* and *t* + *dt*.   Our analysis considers the state of the queue at two times, t and $t + dt$. During the period dt, at most one customer can arrive and at most one customer can depart. We let ΔN represent the change in the state of the queue during this period. We can express the probabilities of ΔN as follows:

If the system is empty, $N = 0$, then

$$P[\Delta N = +1] = \lambda\, dt$$
$$P[\Delta N = 0] = 1 - \lambda\, dt \tag{5.3.14}$$
$$P[\Delta N = -1] = 0$$

If the system is not empty, $N > 0$, then increasing N by 1 requires one arrival and no departures; keeping N the same requires no arrivals or departures (since simultaneous arrivals and departures are excluded by the Poisson assumptions); and decreasing N by 1 requires a departure but no arrival. These, being independent events, may be expressed by Eq. (5.3.15):

$$P[\Delta N = +1] = \lambda\, dt(1 - \lambda_s\, dt) \approx \lambda\, dt$$
$$P[\Delta N = 0] = (1 - \lambda\, dt)(1 - \lambda_s\, dt) \approx 1 - (\lambda + \lambda_s)\, dt \tag{5.3.15}$$
$$P[\Delta N = -1] = (1 - \lambda\, dt)\lambda_s\, dt \approx \lambda_s\, dt$$

where we have discarded higher-order differentials.

Relating $P_N(0)$ and $P_N(1)$.   We now consider $P_N(0)$, the probability that the system is empty at $t + dt$. A partition of the experiment is that ΔN can be either 0 or -1 during dt, since $\Delta N = +1$ would require that $N = -1$ at t, which is impossible. Thus

$$P_N(0 \text{ at } t + dt) = P[(N = 0 \text{ at } t) \cap (\Delta N = 0)] + P[(N = 1 \text{ at } t) \cap (\Delta N = -1)] \tag{5.3.16}$$

Because the ΔN terms refer to changes during dt, such changes are independent of the state at t, and hence we change $\cap \rightarrow \times$, and obtain the form in Eq. (5.3.17):

$$P_N(0 \text{ at } t + dt) = P_N(0 \text{ at } t) \times P[\Delta N = 0] + P_N(1 \text{ at } t) \times P[\Delta N = -1] \tag{5.3.17}$$

Using the appropriate equations from Eqs. (5.3.14) and (5.3.15), we reduce Eq. (5.3.17) to

$$P_N(0 \text{ at } t + dt) = P_N(0 \text{ at } t) \times (1 - \lambda\, dt) + P_N(1 \text{ at } t) \times \lambda_s\, dt \tag{5.3.18}$$

We now rearrange Eq. (5.3.18) to separate out the terms with dt:

$$P_N(0 \text{ at } t+dt) = P_N(0 \text{ at } t) + [-\lambda P_N(0 \text{ at } t) + \lambda_s P_N(1 \text{ at } t)]\, dt \qquad (5.3.19)$$

If the queue is in equilibrium, then $P_N(0 \text{ at } t+dt) = P_N(0 \text{ at } t)$, and the bracketed term multiplying dt must equal zero; hence we find

$$P_N(1) = \frac{\lambda}{\lambda_s} P_N(0) = \rho P_N(0) \qquad (5.3.20)$$

where $\rho = \lambda/\lambda_s$ is the utilization of the system, discussed earlier in connection with Eq. (5.3.8). Equation (5.3.20) expresses the probability that $N = 1$ in terms of the probability that $N = 0$ and the utilization factor.

Relating $P_N(2)$ to $P_N(0)$ and $P_N(1)$.   We now consider $P_N(1)$ at $t+dt$. A partition of the experiment is that $\Delta N = -1, 0,$ or $+1$ during dt; hence we may express $P_N(1 \text{ at } t+dt)$ as

$$P_N(1 \text{ at } t+dt) = P[(N=1 \text{ at } t) \cap (\Delta N=0)] + P[(N=2 \text{ at } t) \cap (\Delta N=-1)]$$
$$+ P[(N=0 \text{ at } t) \cap (\Delta N=+1)] \qquad (5.3.21)$$

When we substitute terms from Eqs. (5.3.14) and (5.3.15) and collect terms in the manner of Eq. (5.3.19), we obtain the form

$$P_N(1 \text{ at } t+dt) = P_N(1 \text{ at } t) + [-(\lambda+\lambda_s)P_N(1 \text{ at } t) + \lambda_s P_N(2 \text{ at } t) + \lambda P_N(0 \text{ at } t)]\, dt \qquad (5.3.22)$$

For a stable queue, the bracketed term multiplying dt must vanish, from which we obtain

$$\lambda_s P_N(2) = (\lambda+\lambda_s)P_N(1) - \lambda P_N(0) \qquad (5.3.23)$$

Dividing by λ_s and letting $\rho = \lambda/\lambda_s$, we obtain

$$P_N(2) = (1+\rho)P_N(1) - \rho P_N(0) \qquad (5.3.24)$$

Substituting Eq. (5.3.20) and simplifying we obtain finally

$$P_N(2) = (1+\rho)\rho P_N(0) - \rho P_N(0) = \rho^2 P_N(0) \qquad (5.3.25)$$

Repeating the same procedure, we find it generally true that

$$P_N(n) = \rho^n P_N(0) \qquad (5.3.26)$$

Normalizing the distribution.   The PMF $P_N(n)$, must normalize to 1, so we have

$$P_N(0) + P_N(1) + P_N(2) + P_N(3) + \cdots = 1 \qquad (5.3.27)$$

Substituting (5.3.26), we find that (5.3.27) becomes a geometric series [see endnote 4, Chapter 2]

$$P_N(0)(1 + \rho + \rho^2 + \rho^3 + \cdots) = P_N(0)\left(\frac{1}{1-\rho}\right) = 1 \Rightarrow P_N(0) = 1 - \rho \qquad (5.3.28)$$

From Eqs. (5.3.28) and (5.3.26) we find the PMF of N to be

$$P_N(n) = (1 - \rho)\rho^n, \ n = 0, 1, 2, \ldots \tag{5.3.29}$$

where $\rho = \lambda/\lambda_s$.

Discussion. Equation (5.3.28) indicates that $1 - \rho$ is the probability that the server is idle, and

$$P[N > 0] = 1 - P_N(0) = \rho \tag{5.3.30}$$

is the probability that the server is busy. This result is also a consequence of Little's formula [Eq. (5.3.8)]. A consequence of Eq. (5.3.29), which we have already mentioned, is that the most likely state of a stable system is for the server to be idle, since $P_N(0) > P_N(n)$, for all n.

Probabilities of queue length. A useful result that may be derived immediately from Eq. (5.3.29) is the probability that the queuing system will have n or more customers, namely, that

$$P[N \geq n] = \sum_{n}^{\infty} P_N(n') = (1 - \rho)(\rho^n + \rho^{n+1} + \cdots) = (1 - \rho)\rho^n(1 + \rho^1 + \rho^2 \cdots) = \rho^n \tag{5.3.31}$$

The expectation of N. The expected value of N is of considerable importance and is readily calculated from Eq. (5.3.29) and the properties of the geometric series [see endnote 4 in Chapter 2]:

$$E[N] = \sum_{0}^{\infty} n P_N(n) = \sum_{0}^{\infty} n(1 - \rho)\rho^n = (1 - \rho)\sum_{0}^{\infty} n\rho^n$$

$$= (1 - \rho) \times \frac{\rho}{(1 - \rho)^2} = \frac{\rho}{1 - \rho} = \frac{\lambda}{\lambda_s - \lambda} \tag{5.3.32}$$

Thus for the example beginning with the calculation of arrival times, the expected length of the queuing system is $\frac{1}{1.5-1} = 2.$[23]

The variance of N. To calculate the variance, we need the mean-squared value of N, which is

$$E[N^2] = \sum_{0}^{\infty} n^2 P_N(n) = (1 - \rho)\sum_{0}^{\infty} n^2\rho^n = (1 - \rho) \times \frac{\rho(1 + \rho)}{(1 - \rho)^3} = \frac{\rho(1 + \rho)}{(1 - \rho)^2} \tag{5.3.33}$$

where again we used the properties of the geometric series [see endnote 4 in Chapter 2]. The variance of N is therefore

$$Var[N] = E[N^2] - E^2[N] = \frac{\rho(1 + \rho)}{(1 - \rho)^2} - \left(\frac{\rho}{1 - \rho}\right)^2 = \frac{\rho}{(1 - \rho)^2} \tag{5.3.34}$$

For example, in the queue demonstrated earlier in this section, we had $\rho = 1/1.5$, which gives a mean value of 2, a variance of 6, and a standard deviation of $\sqrt{6} = 2.45$. Thus the average size is fairly small, but the length of the queue varies widely, as discussed in endnote 23.

The length of the queue, not counting the person being served.   The number waiting in the queue we will call N_Q, and the number being served we will call N_S. Clearly,

$$N = N_Q + N_S \tag{5.3.35}$$

As stated in connection with Eq. (5.3.8), N_S is a Bernoulli random variable with a mean value of

$$E[N_S] = \rho \tag{5.3.36}$$

From Eqs. (5.3.35), (5.3.36), and (5.3.32), it follows that

$$E[N_Q] = E[N] - E[N_S] = \frac{\rho}{1 - \rho} - \rho = \frac{\rho^2}{1 - p} \tag{5.3.37}$$

Example 5.3.1:   Call-waiting system
A phone company offers call waiting, which tells you that someone is waiting on "the other line" if you get a call while on the phone. We assume that the queuing assumptions made previously are valid. If your average phone conversation takes 3 minutes, and there is a probability of 0.1 that you will receive a call-waiting notice while on the phone, what is your average time between calls?

Solution   Here you are the server, and the people trying to call you are queued up for service. We know $\lambda_s = \frac{1}{3}$ from the average phone conversation. The probability that you get a call-waiting notice is the probability that more than one person is in the queuing system. Thus

$$P[N \geq 2] = \rho^2 = 0.1 \Rightarrow \rho = 0.3162 \tag{5.3.38}$$

This value gives $\lambda = \frac{1}{3} \times 0.3162 = 0.1054$. The average time between incoming calls would be the reciprocal of this value, or 9.487 minutes.

You do it.   For the situation described in Example 5.3.1, what is the probability that you will miss a call with call waiting on?

```
myanswer = ? ;
```

```
Evaluate
```

For the answer, see endnote 24.

The PDF of T

The random variable T describes the time a customer spends in the queuing system. We may work out the PDF of T using a partition of the experiment. When the customer arrives, the state of the system is that $N = 0, 1, 2, \ldots$, so in general, we need the conditional PDFs, $f_{T|N=n}(t)$, and the PMF of N, which we know from the previous section.

Empty system.   Consider that the customer arrives to find an empty system. The customer is served immediately, and the PDF of the time is simply the PDF of the service times:

$$f_{T|N=0}(t) = \lambda_s e^{-\lambda_s t}, \; t \geq 0; \; \text{zow} \tag{5.3.39}$$

Empty queue.   If the customer arrives to find the server occupied but no one waiting, then that customer will have to wait two service times to depart. It does not matter how long the server has been with the customer being served when the new customer arrives because the exponential distribution has no memory, as shown earlier, in Eq. (5.1.43). The PDF of the sum of two independent exponentials is the Erlang distribution of order 2, given in Eq. (5.1.49). For $n = 1$, this distribution takes the form

$$f_{T|N=1}(t) = \frac{\lambda_s^2 t}{1!} e^{-\lambda_s t}, \; t \geq 0, \; \text{zow} \tag{5.3.40}$$

In general,

$$f_{T|N=n}(t) = \frac{\lambda_s^{n+1} t^n}{n!} e^{-\lambda_s t}, \; t \geq 0, \; \text{zow} \tag{5.3.41}$$

Combining the conditional PDFs.   To determine the PDF of T, we now combine the conditional PDFs summarized by Eq. (5.3.41) with the PMF of N in Eq. (5.3.29). The result is

$$f_T(t) = \sum_0^\infty f_{T|N=n}(t) P_N(n) \tag{5.3.42}$$

$$= \lambda_s e^{-\lambda_s t} \times (1-\rho) + \frac{\lambda_s^2 t}{1!} e^{-\lambda_s t} \times (1-\rho)\rho + \frac{\lambda_s^3 t^2}{2!} e^{-\lambda_s t} \times (1-\rho)\rho^2 + \cdots$$

which simplifies to

$$f_T(t) = \lambda_s e^{-\lambda_s t} \times (1-\rho) \left[1 + \frac{\lambda_s t}{1!}\rho + \frac{\lambda_s^2 t^2}{2!}\rho^2 + \cdots \right] \tag{5.3.43}$$

Because $\rho \lambda_s = \lambda$, and the power series is that of $e^x = 1 + \frac{x}{1!} + \frac{x^2}{2!} + \cdots$, with $x = \lambda t$, we obtain the final form for the PDF of T:

$$f_T(t) = \lambda_s(1-\rho) e^{-\lambda_s t} \times e^{+\lambda t} = (\lambda_s - \lambda) e^{-(\lambda_s - \lambda)t}, \; t \geq 0, \; \text{zow} \tag{5.3.44}$$

The remarkably simple form of Eq. (5.3.44) suggests that the queuing system operates as a Poisson process with an equivalent rate of $\lambda_s - \lambda$. An interpretation is that discharges are "positive" events, and arrivals are "negative" events, and the overall rate of the system is the "sum" of the two, counting arrivals as negative departures. Certainly, this would be the case if the queue was long: customers would be discharged at a rate of λ_s, and customers would arrive at a rate of λ, and the queue would diminish with an equivalent rate of $\lambda_s - \lambda$.

Expectations of waiting times. The mean and variance of the exponential random variable were derived in Eqs. (3.1.24) and (3.1.26), respectively:

$$E[T] = \frac{1}{\lambda_s - \lambda} \text{ and } Var[T] = \frac{1}{(\lambda_s - \lambda)^2} \tag{5.3.45}$$

Thus the mean and the standard deviation of T, the time in the queuing system, are the same. Again, this indicates the wide fluctuations in waiting time.

Expectation of waiting time in the queue. Because

$$T = T_Q + T_S \tag{5.3.46}$$

where T_Q is the waiting time in the queue, and T_S is the waiting time while being served, it follows that

$$E[T_Q] = E[T] - E[T_S] = \frac{1}{\lambda_s - \lambda} - \frac{1}{\lambda_s} = \frac{\lambda}{\lambda_s(\lambda_s - \lambda)} = \rho E[T] \tag{5.3.47}$$

Thus for the example with which we began this section, the expected waiting time in the system would be $\frac{1}{1.5-1} = 2$ minutes, and the expected waiting time in the queue would be $\frac{2}{3} \times 2 = 1.33$ minutes.

Example 5.3.2: Waiting for a title transfer _____
You go to the government office to transfer the title on a car you bought from an acquaintance. There are people waiting, and you are sixth in line, not counting the person being helped when you walked in. On the wall it tells you that the average waiting time to be served is 6 minutes and that 40 title transfers are processed per hour. How long before you can expect to leave?

Solution We interpret this problem to require your expected time in the queuing system. We know λ to be 40. Also, we know the average wait time in the queue, which is given in Eq. (5.3.47). Thus

$$\frac{40}{\lambda_s(\lambda_s - 40)} = \frac{6}{60} \Rightarrow \lambda_s = 48.3 \text{ per hour} \tag{5.3.48}$$

Because seven persons must be processed before you can leave, your departure time is Erlang of order 7, and the expectation is given in Eq. (5.1.53) as

$$E[T_7] = \frac{7}{48.3} = 0.145 \text{ hour} = 8.698 \text{ minutes} \tag{5.3.49}$$

You do it.   What is the probability that you will have to wait longer than 10 minutes?

```
myanswer = ? ;
```

```
Evaluate
```

For the answer, see endnote 25.

5.4 PROBLEMS

5.4.1 The Poisson Model for Random Events in Time

Exercises on the Poisson model

P5.1.1   We know that for np not too small or too large, the Gaussian is a good approximation to the binomial. This is also true for the Poisson, so long as the expected number of events, μ_K, is not too small. For np small, the Poisson is a good approximation to the binomial. Several comparisons can be made to get a feel for these approximations:
a. Compare $B_n(k, p)$ and $P(k, np)$ for $k = 3, n = 100$, and $p = 0.05$.
b. Compare $B_n(k, p)$ and $P(k, np)$ for $k = 40, n = 100$, and $p = 0.45$.
c. Compare $B_n(k, p)$ for $k = 40, n = 100$, and $p = 0.45$ with the normal based on the binomial distribution, $N(np, npq)$.
d. Compare $P(k, np)$ for $k = 40, n = 100$, and $p = 0.45$ with the normal based on the Pascal distribution, $N(np, np)$.

> **A5.1.1**   **(a)** $B_{100}(3, 0.05) = 0.1396$, $P(3, 100 \times 0.05) = 0.1404$; they differ by 0.6%; **(b)** $B_{100}(40, 0.45) = 0.04880$, $P(40, 100 \times 0.45) = 0.04716$; they differ by 3.5%; **(c)** $N(100 \times 0.45, 100 \times 0.45 \times 0.55) = 0.04839$; differs by 0.9% from binomial at $x = 40$; **(d)** $N(100 \times 0.45, 100 \times 0.45) = 0.04505$; differs by 1.0% from Pascal at $x = 40$

P5.1.2   The exponential PDF is often successful in modeling the time between random events, such as the times between automobile accidents at a prescribed intersection. Let $f_T(t) = 0.05e^{-0.05t}$, $t > 0$, zow. Describe the PDF of the random variable, $T = $ time between accidents.
a. Find the expected value of T.
b. Find $P[T < t | T < 10]$ for all values of t.
c. Find the expected value of T, given that T is less that 10.
d. Consider the random variable X, where $X = 0$, $T < 0$, $= T$, $0 < T \le 10$, $= 10$, $T > 10$, zow. Find the expected value of X.

> **A5.1.2**   **(a)** 20; **(b)** this is the conditional CDF $F_{T|T<10}(t) = 0$, $t < 0$, $= \frac{1-e^{-0.05t}}{1-e^{-0.5}}$, $0 < t \le 10$, $= 1$, $t > 10$; **(c)** 4.585; **(d)** 7.869

P5.1.3 For the Poisson counting function $P(k, \lambda t) = P[k$ events in the period of time 0 to $\lambda t]$ find the conditional probability, $P[10$ events in $\lambda t_2 = 8|5$ events in $\lambda t_1 = 6]$. Make the usual assumptions for the Poisson process.

A5.1.3 0.03609

P5.1.4 Consider a stream of events described by the Poisson assumptions, with the average time between events 10 milliseconds.

a. Give the marginal PDFs of T_1 and T_2, the times to the next event from an arbitrary time and to the second event, respectively, as shown in the figure. Note that the random variables are defined over separate periods of time and thus are independent.

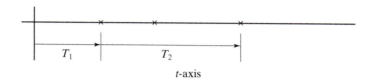

t-axis

b. Give the joint PDF of T_1 and T_2.
c. Find $P[T_1 + T_2 \le 20$ ms$]$.
d. Find $P[T_2 - T_1 \le 10$ ms$]$.

A5.1.4 **(a)** Let $T_1 \to X$ and $T_2 \to Y$. $f_X(x) = 100e^{-100x}, x \ge 0$, zow, $f_Y(y) = (100)^2 e^{-100y}, y \ge 0$, zow; **(b)** $f_{XY}(x, y) = (100)^3 e^{-100(x+y)}$ in first quadrant, zow; **(c)** 0.3233; **(d)** 0.7632

P5.1.5 Let K_1 be a Poisson random variable with an average rate of λ_1, and K_2 be an independent Poisson random variable with an average rate of λ_2. Consider $K = K_1 + K_2$. According to the fundamental assumptions of a Poisson process, K is Poisson with a rate of $\lambda = \lambda_1 + \lambda_2$. Let us now consider the time between events: T_1 and T_2, associated with these different species of Poisson random variables. These should be exponentially distributed with average times $= 1/(\lambda_1 + \lambda_2)$. For the combined process, the time to the first event should be the lesser of T_1 and T_2, that is, $T = \min(T_1, T_2)$. Show that T is exponentially distributed with an average of $1/(\lambda_1 + \lambda_2)$.

A5.1.5 Partition with the events $\{T_1 < T_2\}$ and $\{T_1 > T_2\}$. Then derive conditional CDFs, $F_{T|T_1 < T_2}(t)$ and $F_{T|T_1 > T_2}(t)$. From these get the unconditional CDF of T, which shows its exponential with $\lambda = \lambda_1 + \lambda_2$.

P5.1.6 An exponential random variable is described by the following PDF, $f_T(t) = \lambda e^{-\lambda t}, t > 0$, zow, where λ is a parameter related to the rate of events in a Poisson process. In this problem we will let the rate also be a random variable, specifically an Erlang random variable of second order. Thus we replace λ with Λ, where $f_\Lambda(\lambda) = \alpha^2 \lambda e^{-\alpha \lambda}, \lambda > 0$.
a. Find the joint PDF, $f_{T\Lambda}(t, \lambda)$.
b. Find the expected rate, $E[\Lambda]$.

c. Find the expected time between events, $E[T]$. *Hint:* It is easiest mathematically if you do the double integral first in t, then in λ.

A5.1.6   **(a)** $f_{\Lambda T}(\lambda, t) = (\alpha\lambda)^2 e^{-(\alpha+t)\lambda}$, λ and $t > 0$, zow; **(b)** $\frac{2}{\alpha}$; **(c)** α

P5.1.7   In the exponential distribution $f_T(t) = \lambda e^{-\lambda t}$, $t > 0$, zow, we normally treat λ as a constant. This problem explores letting λ vary with time, specifically, letting $\lambda = 1 + \frac{t}{4}$. Thus the PDF becomes $f_T(t) = ae^{-(1+t/4)t}$, $t > 0$, zow, where a is a constant. With $\lambda = 1$, $E[T] = 1$, with a constant λ. Find $E[T]$ with $\lambda = 1 + \frac{t}{4}$.

A5.1.7   0.6390

P5.1.8   In Example 5.1.7 we derive the PDF of the nearest event in two-dimensional space. In this problem generalize to the nth event in two-dimensional space. Specifically, let $R =$ the distance to the nth event from an arbitrary location and $\rho =$ the density of events in events/square length. Find $f_R(r)$.

A5.1.8 $\frac{(\pi\rho r^2)^{n-1}}{(n-1)!} \times 2\pi\rho r \exp[-\pi\rho r^2]$, $r \geq 0$, zow

P5.1.9   Let $\mu =$ the expected number of events and $K =$ the number of events, a Poisson random variable. Derive formulas for the following:
a. The probability $P[K \neq 0]$.
b. The conditional PMF, $P_{K|K \neq 0}(k)$.
c. The conditional expectation, $E[K|K \neq 0]$.

A5.1.9   **(a)** $1 - e^{-\mu}$; **(b)** $P_{K|K\neq 0}(k) = \frac{\mu^k}{k!}e^{-\mu}/(1 - e^{-\mu})$, $k = 1, 2, 3, \ldots$; **(c)** $\frac{\mu}{1-e^{-\mu}}$

Modeling problems on the Poisson model

P5.1.10   Earthquakes in the range 8–8.6 on the Richter scale occur at an average rate of 0.2 per year. We assume a Poisson process describes the occurrence of such earthquakes.
a. What is the average time between such earthquakes?
b. What is the probability of exactly one such earthquake during the next year starting today?
c. Assume this is 2001.9. What is the probability that the third such event from now will occur in the 2010–2020 decade?

A5.1.10 **(a)** 5 years; **(b)** 0.1637; **(c)** 0.4790

P5.1.11   As an author, I am aware of how hard it is to eliminate all errors from a book. In fact, I just reread the 913-page book I wrote some years ago and flagged 77 pages as containing errors. Some pages had multiple errors. (Assume that I spotted all the errors and the Poisson distribution.)
a. Estimate the number of pages that have multiple errors, based on this count.
b. Estimate the number of errors in the book.
c. Given that a page has at least one error, what is the probability that it has exactly one error?

A5.1.11 **(a)** 3.34; **(b)** 80.4; **(c)** 0.957

P5.1.12   A space vehicle has a detector for micrometeorites. In its mission the expected number of impacts per day is 10. Find the probability that two or more impacts will occur during a 2-hour docking procedure.

A5.1.12 0.2032

P5.1.13   A manufacturer puts prizes at random into packages of cereal by putting 100 prizes into a large batch of cereal, mixing well, and then filling 100 packages with the cereal. How many boxes might we expect to have at least one prize?

A5.1.13 Using a Poisson model, 0.623, so the answer is about 62 or 63.

P5.1.14   According to tradition, a Jewish scribe, in copying the Torah, was allowed to make one mistake on a page, which could be erased, but if two mistakes were made, the page had to be destroyed. If a certain scribe was skilled, in that the probability of exactly one error on a page was 0.05, what is the probability that more than one error would be made? (There are two solutions, but give the one that reflects accuracy.)

A5.1.14 0.00134

P5.1.15   A gardener has a problem with caterpillars on his dill plants. He notes that one plant out of three has no caterpillars. What is the probability that a dill plant selected at random has at least two caterpillars? (Incidentally I allowed some of the caterpillars to complete their life cycle, and they turned into beautiful black butterflies. Amazing!)

A5.1.15 0.3005

P5.1.16   I walk to work every day and frequently find money in the street or on the sidewalks and parking lots, usually coins. In fact, I find money about 40% of the time. What is the probability that I will find two or more coins or bills on any given trip?

A5.1.16 0.0935

P5.1.17   A person is driving the interstate highway system and wants to buy gas. He knows that there is, on average, a gas station every 25 miles. What is the probability that the *second* gas station down the road is between 60 and 75 miles distant? Assume Poisson conditions.

A5.1.17 0.1093

P5.1.18   A shepherdess must get her flock across the highway, which takes 5 minutes. Experience shows that 7 times out of 10 times no cars arrive while the flock is crossing. Estimate the probability that when she finishes there will be two cars waiting.

A5.1.18 0.04453

P5.1.19   A book has 300 pages and contains, on average, one error for every 2 pages. What is the probability that there is no error on a page chosen at random?

A5.1.19 0.606

P5.1.20   I just planted beans in my garden. The package calls for about three seeds per foot in the row, but it is hard to drop them that exactly. In fact, the pattern is somewhat random, except that I try to achieve that density. Furthermore, only about 60% of the seeds germinate and make plants. If a 15-in. section is identified at random, what is the probability that there will be three or fewer plants in that section?

A5.1.20   0.8094

P5.1.21   You are on a side street waiting to enter going right on a busy two-lane street. Traffic moves at 60 mph, and cars pass at a rate of 40 cars per minute. You need 5 seconds to enter the traffic stream safely. What is the probability that you will have to wait to enter the street?

A5.1.21   0.9643

P5.1.22   A large box of Raisin Bran cereal contains 10 cups of cereal and, on average, 400 raisins. A serving is 1 cup, which contains about 16 spoonfuls.
a. Find the probability of having 50 or more raisins in your bowl.
b. Find the probability of getting no raisins in your fourth spoonful.
c. Find the probability of getting more that two raisins in your fourth spoonful.

A5.1.22   **(a)** Using Gaussian, 0.0665; using Poisson, 0.0703; **(b)** 0.08208; **(c)** 0.4562

P5.1.23   On a night the emergency medical service (EMS) has an average of five calls on a 4-hour shift. Assume a call comes in and the EMS vehicle spends 30 minutes out of the station. Find the probability that one or more calls come in during the time when the vehicle is out.

A5.1.23   0.465

P5.1.24   It is customary to examine the beans before you cook them to remove small stones that pass through the harvest/production process. There are 420 beans per cup and on average 1.5 stones per cup of beans. There is a 0.95 probability of observing and removing any given stone. Find the probability that one or more stones end up in the pot, assuming 1 cup of beans/pot.

A5.1.24   0.0723

P5.1.25   A big-game hunting guide guarantees that a customer will get at least two shots at a suitable quarry, or else the money is refunded. Experience has shown that only one refund per 20 customers must be made. Assuming the conditions for the Poisson distribution are met, what is the probability that the customer will get exactly two shots?

A5.1.25   0.09795

P5.1.26   An EMS station deals with random events in two senses: (1) the calls come at random times, and (2) the location of the destination is also random. This problem concerns the randomness in time only. For a given EMS station, the average time between calls is 20 minutes. Assume Poisson assumptions apply in the time of the calls.

a. What is the probability that they get three or more calls during a given hour?

b. If the crew starts watching a 30-minute TV show, what is the probability that they will not be interrupted by a call before it is over?

A5.1.26 **(a)** 0.5768; **(b)** 0.2231

P5.1.27   A gallon of banana nut ice cream has, on average, 100 pieces of nut, distributed at random. Joe's Ice Cream Shoppe gets 20 double-dip ice cream cones out of a gallon.

a. Find the probability that a double-dip cone contains 3 or more pieces of nut.

b. If we know that a cone contains at least 3 pieces of nut, what is the probability that it contains exactly 3 pieces?

c. What is the probability of getting no nut in one bite of a cone, assuming 20 bites per cone?

A5.1.27 **(a)** 0.875; **(b)** 0.160; **(c)** 0.779

P5.1.28   A weary professor grades exams. There are 58 students in the class and it takes him, on average, two and a half hours to grade the stack. (Assume an exponential distribution for the time required to grade one paper.) After what seems like 4 or 5 hours of grading, he notices there are only two papers left. What is the probability that it will take him more than 6 minutes to finish?

A5.1.28 0.3263

P5.1.29   Annually, an average of 27 meteoric events above a certain magnitude occur on the earth. Assume that these are randomly distributed in time.

a. What is the probability that 3 or more such events happen in a month? For simplicity, assume 12 uniform months/year.

b. Making the same assumptions, what is the probability that exactly 5 months in 2005 will have 3 or more such events?

A5.1.29 **(a)** 0.3907; **(b)** 0.2248

P5.1.30   A Geiger counter counts particles emitted by a radioactive material. Consider that the half-life of the sample is sufficiently long that the average rate of emission is constant (λ = constant). The electronics associated with the counter takes 10 μs to respond to the particles, so in effect the instrument has 10 μs of dead time during each count. What is the maximum rate, λ, that the instrument can measure with a 0.1% error due to missed particles?

A5.1.30 100.1 events per second

P5.1.31   A one-shot is triggered by Poisson events that occur at an average rate of $\lambda = 10$ events per second. The one-shot normally stays with its output in a ZERO state, but goes to a ONE for 20 ms after being triggered. While in the ONE state, trigger pulses are ignored. What is the rate of output pulses?

A5.1.31 Output rate $= 8.33/\text{second}$

P5.1.32   A traffic counter has a 0.01 second dead time after every event owing to delays and recovery time inherent to the internal circuits. The accuracy is guaranteed to be 1% up to a certain count rate. What is that count rate?

A5.1.32   1.0101 events per second

P5.1.33   A botany class does field work collecting specimens of a certain plant. The area to be examined is divided into equal areas, A. These are rare plants being studied, so some lots are devoid of specimens. In fact, 10% of the areas have no specimen, on average. What is the expected fraction that have two or more specimens?

A5.1.33   0.6697

P5.1.34   For this problem, we model the foliage of a pecan tree as a sphere of 20-ft radius. The pecan tree has 1000 pecans on it, and the chance experiment is to designate a pecan at random and see where it ends up on the ground. The eventual distribution of pecans on the ground we model as uniform in angle and as a Rayleigh distribution in radius,

$$f_{R\Theta}(r, \theta) = \frac{r}{2\pi\sigma^2} \exp\left[-\frac{1}{2}\left(\frac{r}{\sigma}\right)^2\right]$$

where r is distance from the center of the tree, and θ is the angle around the tree from some arbitrary direction. The distribution goes beyond the edge of the tree owing to the actions of wind, squirrels, and ambitious ants.

a. If there is a 98% chance that a pecan will fall under the tree, in a 20-ft circle, find σ.

b. Determine the probability that three or more pecans fall within a 1 ft^2 area at 10-ft radius from the center of the tree, using a binomial model.

c. Determine the probability that three or more pecans fall within a 1 ft^2 area at 10 ft from the center of the tree, using a Poisson model.

A5.1.34   **(a)** 7.150; **(b)** 0.1141; **(c)** 0.1143

P5.1.35   The Slipshod Computer Corporation (SCC) ships with a minimum amount of testing. The number of flaws that show up during the warranty period is known to be a Poisson random variable.

a. If 96% of the SCC computers have no flaws, what fraction has two or more flaws?

b. You purchase a SCC computer and have a problem during the warranty period. What is the probability that you will have additional problems during the warranty period?

c. Under the conditions of part b, what is the expected number of additional problems you will have during the warranty period?

A5.1.35   **(a)** 8.109×10^{-4}; **(b)** 0.02027; **(c)** 0.021

P5.1.36   In a large forest, black walnut (BW) trees occur at random (Poisson assumptions) at a density of two trees per 10 acres. For your information, 640 acres = 1 square mile.

a. What is the probability of finding more than one tree on a 1-acre plot chosen at random?

b. From a point chosen at random, what is the probability of finding no BW trees within a radius r?

c. From a point chosen at random, what is the PDF of the distance to the nearest BW tree? Let R = the random variable describing the distance to the nearest BW tree.

d. From a point chosen at random, what is the expected distance to the nearest BW tree?

A5.1.36 **(a)** 0.01752; **(b)** $e^{-\pi\rho r^2}$, $r \geq 0$, zow; **(c)** $f_R(r) = 2\pi\rho r e^{-\pi\rho r^2}$, $r \geq 0$, zow, which is Rayleigh; **(d)** 233.3 ft

P5.1.37   During the statistics part of this course I sent a student to the ME building to get some data on the number of passengers leaving elevators on the first floor. I was expecting a Poisson distribution, and was right more or less, but a (not surprising) feature of the data was that no elevators arrived with zero passengers. (We excluded the situation in which someone called the elevator and it arrived empty.) Thus the distribution was Poisson, but conditioned on $K \neq 0$. The average number of passengers per elevator averaged 2.25.

a. Find the value of the expected value of the unconditioned Poisson random variable. This is the μ_K in the usual Poisson formula. This is not 2.25!

b. Find the probability that five persons will step off the elevator, given that the elevator door opens.

A5.1.37 **(a)** 1.92; **(b)** 0.03735

P5.1.38   A forest contains a rare hardwood tree with an average density of one tree per 100 acres (1 square mile = 640 acres). Assume that trees are distributed randomly according to the assumptions for a Poisson distribution.

a. A logging company is seeking to purchase, sight unseen, cutting rights on a 500-acre tract. To be a good deal, the acreage needs to contain more than three hardwood trees. Find the probability that this is a good deal for the company.

b. If a spot is chosen at random in the forest, what is the probability that at least one hardwood tree is within 1000 ft of this spot?

c. Find the PDF of R = the distance from one hardwood tree to its nearest neighbor in feet.

A5.1.38 **(a)** 0.735; **(b)** 0.514; **(c)** $f_R(r) = 1.44 \times 10^{-6} r e^{-7.21 \times 10^{-7} r^2}$, $r \geq 0$, zow

P5.1.39   At the post office, customers stand in one line to be served. There are two clerks, one of whom takes 12 seconds on average to serve a customer, and the other takes 10 seconds on average to serve a customer. (Assume an exponential model for each clerk's service time.) Assume the effective service time is the time to wait for the first free clerk. Let T = the time a customer has to wait for the next clerk, assuming the customer is next to be served and the queue is not empty. Find the PDF of T.

A5.1.39 $f_T(t) = \left(\frac{1}{12} + \frac{1}{10}\right) \exp\left[-\left(\frac{1}{12} + \frac{1}{10}\right)t\right], t > 0$, zow, time in seconds

P5.1.40   I am sitting in the Travis County Tax Office and there are 7 people waiting. I am fifth in line, not including the person being served, according to the sheet I signed when

I entered. They seem to be taking people at a rate of one every 5 minutes. (Assume Poisson assumptions for the process).

a. What is the probability that I will be served in a 30-minute period?

b. Given that they serve exactly four people in 20 minutes, what is the probability that I will get in to be served before 25 minutes elapse?

c. Given that I got in to be served before 25 minutes elapsed, what is the probability that the four people before me were served in 20 minutes or less?

A5.1.40 (a) 0.7149; **(b)** 0.8735; **(c)** 0.8842

P5.1.41   Consider a diode that has a reverse breakdown voltage, V, that is given by the relation $V = 30.0 - 0.1K$, where K is a Poisson random variable representing the number of defects in the junction area. For a given batch of diodes, the average breakdown voltage is determined to be 29.1 V.

a. Find the probability that for a given diode, $V = 30.0$ V.

b. If we regard V as a Gaussian, determine the voltage range within which 90% of the diodes fail.

A5.1.41 (a) 1.234×10^{-4}; **(b)** 90.4% fail between 28.6 and 29.5 V, inclusive

P5.1.42   A new metastable element, Cogdellium, has a variety of isotopes, such that the particle emission rate of a randomly selected sample is uniformly distributed between 120 and 180 particles per minute. Let T represent the time to the first emission, and Λ represent the emission rate in particles per minute.

a. Find $f_{\Lambda T}(t, \lambda)$, the joint PDF.

b. Find the marginal PDF for T.

c. If a sample is selected at random, what is the probability that a particle will be emitted in the next 1 second?

A5.1.42 (a) $f_{\Lambda T}(\lambda, t) = \frac{\lambda}{60} e^{-\lambda t}$, $t > 0$, $120 < \lambda \leq 180$; **(b)** $\frac{1}{60}\left[e^{-120t}\left(\frac{120}{t} + \frac{1}{t^2}\right) - e^{-180t}\left(\frac{180}{t} + \frac{1}{t^2}\right)\right]$, $t \geq 0$, zow; **(c)** 0.9145

P5.1.43   A fire station has two trucks. One or both fire trucks leave the station at random times, day or night (assume constant rate of fires.) In any given 1-hour period, there is a probability of 0.3 that one or both trucks will have to go at least once.

a. Find the average rate of events.

b. Find the probability that more than three events occur in a 6-hour period.

c. When the alarm goes off, 80% of the time one truck leaves, and 20% of the time both trucks leave. What is the probability that in a 6-hour period at least one truck remains in the station at all times?

A5.1.43 (a) 0.3567 per hour; **(b)** 0.1690; **(c)** 0.6518

P5.1.44   I just planted some flowers in my garden. Actually, I planted flower seeds. The seed packet said it contained 1722 seeds with a 78% germination rate. I scattered the seed along a row that is 15 ft long (call that X). Assume the seeds are uniformly distributed along the 15-ft length but distributed laterally according to a Laplace distribution, $f_Y(y) = 0.25e^{-|y|/2}$, where y is in inches.

a. What is the bivariate PDF of the distribution of a single seed?

b. Pick a region in X that is 1 in. long. What is the probability that there are more than 10 germinated seeds in that region?

c. Pick a region that is 1 in. long and in a square $1 < Y < 2$ (one side only). What is the probability that no seed in this square germinates?

A5.1.44 (a) $\frac{0.25}{15 \times 12} e^{-|y|/2}$, $0 < x < 180$, all y, zow; (b) 0.1345; (c) 0.4105

P5.1.45 You are in a long line to get some IRS forms. You begin as twentieth in line, and after 30 minutes you are third in line. Assume that the time required to serve a single customer is exponentially distributed.

a. Approximate the probability that the next customer will take more than 2 minutes.

b. Approximate the probability that you will be served within the next 10 minutes.

A5.1.45 (a) 0.322; (b) 0.9769

P5.1.46 You need to enter traffic on a road. The average distance between cars on your side is 60 ft, and traffic is moving at 30 mph. Assume that all cars are moving at the same speed but that distances are distributed exponentially.

a. Find the PDF of the random variable T, the times between cars passing you as you wait to enter the road.

b. You need a 2.5-second break in traffic to enter and accelerate up to traffic speed. What is the probability that you will be able to enter without waiting for a break in traffic?

c. Traffic on the other side has identical characteristics to traffic on your side. If you are trying to cross the street and you require 2 seconds, what is the probability that you will be able to cross without waiting for a break in traffic?

A5.1.46 (a) $f_T(t) = 0.7333 e^{-0.7333t}$, $t \geq 0$, zow; (b) 0.1599; (c) 0.05322

P5.1.47 An office gets calls at the rate of 10 per hour, on average. Call lengths are exponentially distributed, with an average duration of 3 minutes.

a. After the receptionist hangs up, what is the expected time to the next call?

b. Assume a call comes in and the receptionist answers it. What is the probability that the next caller will get a busy signal?

A5.1.47 (a) 6 minutes; (b) $\frac{1}{3}$

P5.1.48 During the summer in Austin, Texas, it occasionally rains. On average it rains six times during June, July, and August. For simplicity assume each month has 30 days. Assume the rains are distributed according to a Poisson distribution.

a. What is the probability that it does not rain in July?

b. What is the probability that it rains at least once in each month?

A5.1.48 (a) 0.1353; (b) 0.6465

P5.1.49 A switchboard operator at a small business gets 50 calls per hour on average. There are five lines coming in. One day the receptionist is angry about his low pay and poor benefits, so he starts putting all incoming calls on hold. "Let them listen to music for a while," he thinks. Assume calls come in as a Poisson process.

a. From the time he makes this decision, how long on average will it take for all five lines to be filled?

b. What is the probability that the actual time for the lines to be filled falls within ± 1 minute of the answer in part a?

c. Because this problem amounts to the addition of five IID exponential random variables, the central limit theorem suggests that the PDF should approach a normal distribution. Determine the normal distribution with the same mean and variance, and confirm the results of part b using the normal CDF.

A5.1.49 (a) 6 minutes; **(b)** 0.2883; **(c)** 0.2906

P5.1.50 Two children, Abe and Beverly, are looking for Easter eggs in a yard. The eggs are distributed at random at one egg per 10 ft^2. Abe searches out 50 ft^2, and Beverly searches out another 40 ft^2. Assume their searches are effective in finding the eggs in these regions.

a. What is the probability that Abe finds fewer than four eggs?

b. Given that Abe found fewer than four eggs, what is the probability that together they found exactly six eggs?

A5.1.50 (a) 0.2650; **(b)** 0.1881

P5.1.51 John Smith waits in line to be served in a drive-in bank. Specifically, he is fourth in line when he arrives. The clerk takes, on average, 2 minutes to serve a customer. Assume the time to serve a customer is a random variable that is exponentially distributed. Find the probability that John will have to wait more than 8 minutes to be served.

A5.1.51 0.4335

P5.1.52 John then goes home. During the night, his child cries and John goes in to comfort him. There are 100 marbles scattered around the floor of the 8×10 ft^2 room, and John has to walk five steps in the dark. If his footprint is 18 in.^{2}, what is the probability that John does not step on a single marble?

A5.1.52 0.458

P5.1.53 A woman shoots a shotgun against a large target, to study the pattern of the shot. After many tests, she concludes that the pattern is well approximated by a Gaussian distribution. Each shell contains 100 shot. The "experiment" is the firing of one shell. The average density of shot per square foot is

$$d(x, y) = \frac{100}{2\pi(1.5)^2} \exp\left[-\frac{x^2 + y^2}{2(1.5)^2}\right] \frac{\text{shot}}{\text{ft}^2}$$

where the units of x and y are in feet.

a. Find the expected number of shot in a 50 in.^{2} area at the center of the pattern.

b. Find the PMF of the number of shot in a 50 in.^{2} area at the center of the pattern.

    c. How far from the center of the pattern do you have to go before there is a 50% probability of there being no shot in a 50 in.^{2} area?

A5.1.53 (a) 2.456; (b) $\frac{(2.456)^k}{k!} e^{-2.456}$; (c) 2.386 ft

P5.1.54 A lumberman leases 1 mi^2 of forest, which contains 640 acres. He is interested in harvesting black walnut trees. According to his information, there should be an average of three such trees on each acre. Assume Poisson conditions. Consider that the area is mapped into square plots of 1 acre each.
    a. What is the probability that an acre has no black walnut trees?
    b. What is the probability that every acre in the plot has at least one black walnut tree?
    c. What is the probability that the total number of black walnut trees in the plot exceeds 2000?

A5.1.54 (a) 0.0498; (b) 6.4×10^{-15}; (c) 0.0331 (exact is 0.03375)

P5.1.55 a. Certain parts of Missouri recently had a 100-year flood in two consecutive years. What is the probability of this event, using the Poisson model?
    b. Because floods happen generally once a year during the spring, rework the problem using the binomial model.

A5.1.55 (a) 0.000196; (b) 0.0001

P5.1.56 The paper towel dispensers on campus give 4.5 in. of paper each time a lever is pushed. One roll of paper contains 800 ft and will take care of 600 customers, on average. Assume the number of pushes for a customer is a Poisson random variable.
    a. What is the probability that a customer will use more than 10 in. of paper towel on a given visit?
    b. What is the probability that a roll of towels will be used up by the first 580 customers?

A5.1.56 (a) 0.6894; (b) 0.0587

P5.1.57 A photon detector has a 1-microsecond recovery time, during which it will fail to detect a photon event. Thus, if two photons arrive closer together in time than 1 microsecond, the second photon will not be detected. On a given experiment, the detector counts 10,302 photons in 1 second.
    a. Estimate the true rate of photon events, correcting for the missed photons.
    b. Find the probability that the number of actual photon events during this time is 10,402 photons or higher. *Hint:* The 10,302 is not random in any sense. The random variable is the number of missed photon events.

A5.1.57 (a) 10,409; (b) 0.77074 (exact), 0.772313 (Gaussian)

P5.1.58 A series of random pulses having, on average, three pulses per second is generated by a noise source. These pulses are counted by two counters: counter A counts from $0 < t < 2$ seconds, and counter B counter from $1 < t < 3$ seconds. Let N_A and N_B represent the counts of the two counters.

a. Find $E[N_A]$.
b. Find $Var[N_B]$.
c. Find $E[N_A + N_B]$.
d. Find $Var[N_A + N_B]$.
e. Find the correlation coefficient between N_A and N_B.

A5.1.58 (a) 6; **(b)** 6; **(c)** 12; **(d)** 18; **(e)** 0.5

P5.1.59   There are about 70 faculty members on the ECE faculty, but only 16 on average show up at faculty meetings. Assume Poisson statistics as an approximation for the binomial.
a. What is the probability that exactly 16 show up?
b. What is the probability that 16 ± 1 standard deviation show up, exactly?
c. What is the probability that 16 ± 1 standard deviation show up, using the Gaussian approximation?

A5.1.59 (a) 0.0992 (binomial gives 0.113); **(b)** 0.741; **(c)** 0.742

P5.1.60   Consider the random process that results from popping packages of microwave popcorn. Assume the popping rate for the process is that shown in the figure.

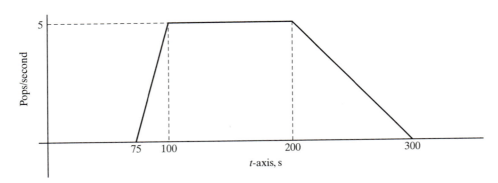

a. Estimate the total number of kernels of corn in the average package.
b. In the period of time between 150 and 151 seconds, find the probability that two or more kernels pop.
c. As a lab project, students designed a system to count the numbers of pops. After many trials it is determined that the average number of pops in the first 150 seconds is 310, but about 25% of the time the number exceeds 330. Estimate the probability that the number is less than 250.

A5.1.60 (a) 813; **(b)** 0.9596; **(c)** 0.0182

P5.1.61   A radioactive atom emits two types of particles: A and B. The average rate of A particles is one every 5 seconds, and the average rate of B is one every 3 seconds. These are independent. Find the probability that, from any arbitrary time, a B particle will come first.

A5.1.61 5/8

P5.1.62 Two species of rabbit inhabit the same area. It is known that species A on average has three rabbits per acre, and species B has two rabbits per acre. A field experiment counts five rabbits of both species in a 1.2-acre region. Assume that the rabbit counts are independent.

    a. What is the *a priori* probability of exactly five rabbits in 1.2 acres?

    b. What is the *a posteriori* probability that exactly two of these five rabbits are from species A?

    A5.1.62 (a) 0.161; (b) 0.230

P5.1.63 A traffic monitoring device is stretched across a major highway's three lanes and records on average 2.7 cars per second during average traffic conditions.

    a. Give the PDF for the time between cars, T.

    b. What is the probability that more than 30 cars go by in a 10-second period?

    A5.1.63 (a) $2.7e^{-2.7t}$, $t \geq 0$, zow; (b) 0.2503 (Gaussian), 0.2447 (exact)

P5.1.64 A highway patrol officer sets up a radar "speed trap" and issues tickets to speeders. Based upon past experience and traffic conditions, she expects to catch an average of seven speeders per hour.

    a. What is the probability that she will write her first ticket between 10 and 15 minutes after setting up?

    b. Given that she writes exactly four tickets in the first half hour, what is the probability that she will write exactly three during the second half hour?

    c. Find the probability that she issues three tickets in the period from 30 to 60 minutes, given that she wrote four in the period 0 to 45 minutes. Note that these periods overlap.

    A5.1.64 (a) 0.138; (b) 0.216; (c) 0.2431

P5.1.65 A cosmic ray detector measures events with momenta up to 15 Bev/c and detects, on average, six events per day. The detector is then upgraded to detect 30 Bev/c particles, which is supposed to increase the number of events detected by 25%. The first day after the upgrade, no events are detected. What is the probability that the new detector is not working at all? Assume that the *a priori* probability that the new system is not working is 0.9.

    A5.1.65 0.99993855

P5.1.66 You are in the middle of a large forest. All you can see in any direction is trees. Indeed, at eye level all you can see are tree trunks. (Assume no underbrush or immature trees.) Assume the average tree density is 10,000 trees per square mile. Let $R =$ the distance one can see in an arbitrary direction.

    a. Use the Poisson to find $F_R(r)$, the CDF of R. Assume all trees are 1 ft in radius.

    b. Find the expected distance you can see.

    c. Let $R =$ the distance to the nearest tree from an arbitrary location. Find $E[R]$.

    A5.1.66 (a) $F_R(r) = 1 - e^{-2\rho r}$, where $\rho = 3.59 \times 10^{-4}$; (b) 1390 ft; (c) 26.4 ft

P5.1.67   The Highway Patrol (police) enforces the laws on Texas highways.
    a. Assume that there is an average of one police car every 50 miles on Texas highways, randomly located. You drive from Austin to Lampasas, 78 miles. What is the probability that you will see two or more police cars?
    b. Assume, instead (different model), that there is one police car between Austin and Lampasas, that drives back and forth between the two cities all the time. The police car drives at 60 mph, but you drive at 80 mph. (1) Find the probability that you will encounter the police car in 5 minutes, given that you and the police car are going the same direction. This is a conditional probability. (2) Find the probability that you will encounter the police car in 5 minutes, given that you and the police car are going in opposite directions. This is also a conditional probability. (3) Find the probability that you will encounter a police car in 5 minutes, generally if the relative direction is totally unknown.

A5.1.67   (a) 0.462; **(b)** 0.0214, 0.150, 0.0855

P5.1.68   A large round of Swiss cheese is cut, and the internal spherical holes are revealed at the cut surface. We assume that the holes are distributed throughout the volume at an average density of 200 holes per cubic foot, and that all holes are 1 in. in diameter. We will ignore the possibility of overlapping holes.
    a. The spherical holes appear as circles on the cut surface, of all sizes up to 1-in. in diameter. What is the density of holes on the cut surface in holes per square foot?
    b. What is the probability that a square foot taken at random contains more than 10 holes? Consider the hole contained if its center falls within the area.
    c. On average, what is the percentage of the cut surface that is cheese and not hole? This value would be 100% with no holes, but is lower because of the holes.

A5.1.68   (a) 16.67; **(b)** 0.94275; **(c)** 93.94%

P5.1.69   Telephone calls come into an office at the rate of 500 per hour and last (to pick a simple model) 5 minutes each. Thus the expected number of calls at any given instant is 41.7 calls. How many lines are needed to have a probability of 90% of getting all calls, that is, 10% or less probability of giving a busy signal? Use the Gaussian PDF to approximate the Poisson PMF.

A5.1.69   50 lines

P5.1.70   Vehicles traveling 60 mph cross a 100-ft-long bridge at a rate of 30 per minute on average. The weight of the vehicles is between 2000 and 5000 lb, uniformly distributed. Find the probability that the total weight on the bridge exceeds 4200 lb at a given instant.

A5.1.70   0.197

P5.1.71   A botany class does field work collecting specimens of a certain plant. The area to be examined is divided into equal areas. These are rare plants being studied, so some areas are devoid of specimens. In that case, students with more than two specimens are to invite students with no specimens to come collect excess plants so that every student has at least one specimen. What is the minimum plant density, μ_K plants per area, for this scheme to work, on average?

A5.1.71 1.57 plants per area

P5.1.72 The number of e-mails a person receives each day is Poisson distributed with an average of three e-mails. The amount of information in an e-mail is exponentially distributed with an average of 1 KB. Find the probability that she receives more than 3 KB on a given day.

A5.1.72 0.58333

P5.1.73 Telephone calls arrive at random at the switch in a small town. There are 400 telephones, and we assume the length of a phone call to be exponentially distributed, with the average length of call being 3 minutes. Let the rate of calls be 12 per hour.
  a. Let T_1 be the time before the present to the most recent call to arrive at the switch. What is the probability that the last call is still in progress at the present time? *Hint:* Let D_1 be the duration of that call. You need $P[T_1 < D_1]$.
  b. Let T_2 be the time before the present to the second most recent call to arrive at the switch. What is the probability that that call is still in progress at the present time?
  c. What is the probability that the switch has no calls at a particular time, assuming the independence of past calls that have ended?

A5.1.73 **(a)** 0.375; **(b)** $(0.375)^2$; **(c)** 0.4928. But the assumption of independence of past calls seems poor, based on intuition. I did a computer simulation and got 0.547 based on 30,000 trials.

P5.1.74 You are at a busy restaurant and you want to eat in a hurry. You order through a computer system that gives the number of orders ahead of you and the predicted wait time until you can expect to get your food. In your case, there are 22 orders ahead of you and a 7-minute wait. But you want more than the expected time to receive your food; you want to be 90% certain of getting your food by a certain time.
  a. Assuming an exponential model for the time to prepare a single order, what is the time for 90% certainly? Then find w such that $P[W < w] = 0.9$, where $W = T_1 + T_2 + \cdots + T_{22}$?
  b. Rework part a assuming that T is uniformly distributed in the range $0 < T < a$, where a is a constant.

A5.1.74 **(a)** 8.921 minutes, using the CLT. The Erlang distribution gives 8.96772; **(b)** 8.109

```
{w → 8.96772}
```

P5.1.75 Consider the following information: In the average college classroom, the probability that a student is carrying keys on his or her person is 0.9. Furthermore, the number of keys on a person chosen at random is known to be a Poisson random variable.

    a. If 10 persons are selected at random, what is the probability that at least 8 of them have keys on them at the time?

    b. If you go down the row asking people if they have keys, what is the average number you will have to ask before you find a person without any keys?

    c. What is the average number of keys that a person carries?

    d. What is the probability that the first person that you find with keys has exactly four keys?

A5.1.75 **(a)** 0.9298; **(b)** 10; **(c)** 2.303; **(d)** 0.1301

P5.1.76 I was at an outdoor restaurant last evening and I noticed that tables with larger groups were having to borrow chairs from tables with smaller groups. Thus throughout the evening a chair would "diffuse" away from its original location. Let's model this diffusion phenomena as follows: the tables are in a random pattern, from 8 to 12 ft apart and at all angles. Assume a chair is moved 10 times during the evening. Under these assumptions estimate the average distance between the original and the final position of a chair. Ignore boundary considerations.

A5.1.76 28.2 ft using the CLT

P5.1.77 A biological experiment is done in the following way. A plot of ground is divided into 1-m^2 areas. The number of species of plants is noted. If the area contains two or more species of plants, then the plot is considered diverse and the total number of species of plants is recorded. If the average number of species for the selected plots is 4.2 (the conditional expectation), what fraction of the plots are not selected, that is, have fewer than two species? Assume Poisson statistics.

A5.1.77 0.103

P5.1.78 Insects are distributed in a plot of native grassland, with an average density of four insects per square foot. A bird alights in the grassland.

    a. Find the probability that the bird lands on one or more insects if the bird's footprint is 0.2 in.^{2} per foot.

    b. Find the PDF of $R_2 =$ the distance to the second bug from the bird.

    c. Assuming that the bird eats 90% of the bugs within a 1-ft radius of the place where it lands, what is probability that it eats more than 10 insects?

A5.1.78 **(a)** 0.01105; **(b)** $f_{R_2}(r) = 315.8r^3 e^{-4\pi r^2}$, $r > 0$, zow with r in feet; **(c)** 0.5766

P5.1.79 The density of stars in the vicinity of the sun is 1 star per 100 cubic light-years.

    a. What is the probability that there is at least one star within 3 light-years of the sun?

    b. What is the PDF of $R =$ the distance to the nearest star from the sun?

    c. Find the expected distance to the nearest star.

A5.1.79 **(a)** 0.6773; **(b)** $f_R(r) = \frac{4\pi r^2}{100} e^{-\frac{4\pi r^3}{300}}$, $r \geq 0$, zow; **(c)** 2.57126 light-years by numerical integration. The nearest star is actually 4.3 light-years away.

P5.1.80   A grocery store has one fast and several slow lines. Let $E[T_f] = 30$ seconds be the average time it takes to check out in the fast line and Let $E[T_s] = 90$ seconds be the average time it takes to check out in the slow line. We assume that T_f and T_s are independent, exponentially distributed random variables.

A couple shops and, being in a hurry, divide their groceries. He takes an armload of the items and gets in the fast line, and she goes in the slow line with the remaining groceries in the cart. By chance they arrive at the checkers simultaneously.
a. Find the probability that she gets finished before he does, $P[T_f > T_s]$.
b. Let $W = T_s - T_f$ be the time that he has to wait. Find the PDF of W. Note that W can be negative.

A5.1.80 (a) $\frac{1}{4}$; (b) $f_W(w) = \frac{e^{+w/30}}{120},\ w < 0,\ = \frac{e^{-w/90}}{120},\ w > 0$

P5.1.81   The number of cars per mile on a busy two-lane highway averages 132 per mile in each direction and follows a Poisson distribution. This implies that the distance between cars follows an exponential distribution.
a. What would be the PDF of the distance between cars if Poisson conditions applied exactly? Let L = the random variable describing the distance between cars in feet.
b. Under the conditions of part a, find the probability that a car follows at less than 10 ft.
c. For safety, cars leave a minimum of a 10-ft distance, so the cars that would be in the 10-ft space follow at exactly 10 ft. The real PDF therefore is zero for $0 < l < 10$ and has an impulse at $l = 10$ ft. What is the area of that impulse? That is, what is $P[L = 10]$? *Hint:* This is not the same as part b.
d. Give the PDF of L, considering the impulse.

A5.1.81 (a) $f_L(l) = \frac{1}{40}e^{-l/40},\ l \geq 0,$ zow; (b) 0.2212; (c) 0.25; (d) $f_L(l) = 0.25\delta(l - 10) + 0.01875e^{-(l-10)/40}u(l - 10),\ l \geq 0,$ zow.

P5.1.82   You are in a restaurant and the waiter takes your order. There are three orders ahead of you in the kitchen. Assume that it takes the cook an average of 2 minutes to prepare an order and that the times are exponentially distributed and independent.
a. What is the expected time until you are served?
b. What is the probability that you will be served in less than 5 minutes?
c. Of the three orders, one takes the longest time to prepare. What is the probability that that order takes less than 3 minutes? In other words, what is the probability that all three take less than 3 minutes each to prepare?

A5.1.82 (a) 8 minutes; (b) 0.2424; (c) 0.4689

P5.1.83   Airplanes arrive at random times at a busy airport at a rate of 1 arrival/minute on average. The planes are not allowed to land within 30 seconds of each other but have to circle the airport until their turn comes. Find the probability that an arriving flight will get to land directly without having to circle the airport.

A5.1.83 (a) 0.5

5.4.2 Reliability Theory

Exercises on reliability theory

P5.2.1   A manufacturer sells 1000 electric drills to an industrial customer and all are put into service immediately. From experience it is known that the failure rate for this tool is $h(t) = 0.005e^{-t/2} + 0.005 + 10^{-5}t^2$ failures/month.
  a. How many units are expected to have early failure?
  b. Estimate the time period during which wear-out becomes a significant factor in the failures.
  c. At what time are half the drills expected to have failed?

A5.2.1   **(a)** about 10 units; **(b)** about 22.4–39 months; **(c)** about 50.5 months

P5.2.2   Consider a device that has a constant failure rate of $h = \lambda = 0.1$/year. One thousand of these devices are put into service at $t = 0$. Let $N =$ the number of devices that survive into the tenth year. We know that N is a binomial random variable but can be well approximated by a normal random variable.
  a. Find the probability that more than 375 survive into the tenth year.
  b. Assuming that exactly 375 do survive into the tenth year, how many devices, Δn, can we expect to fail in the tenth year?

A5.2.2   **(a)** 0.9788 if we take this to mean the beginning of the tenth year; 0.3196 if we take it to mean the end of the tenth year; **(b)** 35.7

P5.2.3   A system has 100 components, each with a failure rate, $h(t) = 0.1e^{-20t} + 0.01$, t in years. All components must function properly for the system to be functioning.
  a. Find the probability that the system will experience early failure owing to manufacturing defects.
  b. Find the probability that the system does not fail during the first year.

A5.2.3   **(a)** 0.3935; **(b)** 0.223

P5.2.4   A system has a reliability function given by the figure.
  a. Find the MTTF of this system.
  b. Find the failure rate, $h(t)$.
  c. Find the probability that the system fails in the first 7.5 years.

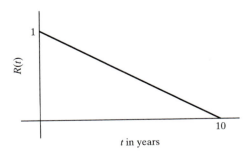

A5.2.4   **(a)** 5 years; **(b)** $h(t) = \frac{1}{10-t}$, $0 < t \le 10$, $= \infty$, $t > 10$; **(c)** 0.75

P5.2.5   A system has a reliability function given by the figure.
    a. Find the MTTF of this system.
    b. Find the failure rate, $h(t)$.
    c. Find the probability that the system fails in the first 7.5 years.

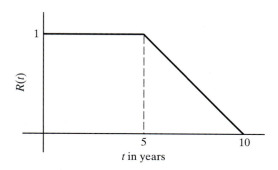

A5.2.5   **(a)** 7.5 years; **(b)** $h(t) = 0$, $t < 5$, $= \frac{1}{10-t}$, $5 < t \le 10$, $= \infty$, $t > 10$;
    (c) 0.5

P5.2.6   A system has the configuration shown in the switches: A and B are operated in series, and together they are in parallel with C. Find the reliability function of the system, R_S, if the reliability functions of A, B, and C, are R_A, R_B, and R_C, respectively. Assume all failures independent.

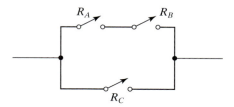

A5.2.6 $R_A R_B + R_C - R_A R_B R_C$

P5.2.7   A system has the reliability function shown.
    a. Find the probability that the system fails in the period of time $90 < T < 100$.
    b. Find the MTTF.
    c. Find the failure rate of this system.
    d. Is the system more likely to fail owing to manufacturing defects or to wear-out?

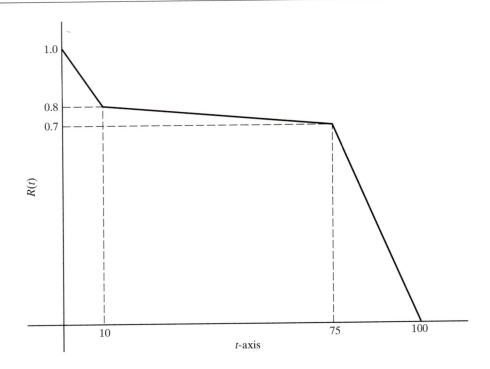

A5.2.7   **(a)** 0.280; **(b)** 66.5; **(c)** $h(t) = \frac{0.02}{1-0.02t}$, $0 < t < 10$; $= \frac{0.001538}{0.8154 - t/650}$, $10 < t < 75$; $= \frac{0.028}{2.80 - t/35.71}$, $75 < t < 100$; undefined for $t \geq 100$; **(d)** wear-out

P5.2.8   A candle will burn between 5 and 6 hours. Assume a uniform distribution in the absence of better information.

            a. Considering the candle a "system," give the reliability function.

            b. If you have two identical candles and you burn them at the same time, what is the PDF of the time until the first one burns out? Consider the candles independent.

            c. If you have two identical candles and light the second when the first goes out, find the PDF of the time until the second candle goes out. Consider the candles independent.

         A5.2.8   **(a)** $R(t) = 1$, $t < 5$, $= 6 - t$, $5 < t < 6$, $= 0$, $t > 6$; **(b)** $f_T(t) = 2(6 - t)$, $5 < t < 6$, zow; **(c)** This is standby. The convolution of the two identical PDFs is an isosceles triangle with height 1 and base between 10 and 12.

P5.2.9   A Gizmo has a failure rate that is described by the equation $h(t) = \frac{10^{-2}}{1+t^2} + 10^{-3} + 10^{-6}t^2$ per year.

            a. Determine the reliability function.

            b. Find the probability of infant mortality.

c. At what time does wear-out become the dominant failure mechanism?

d. Find the probability that a Gizmo will fail during its second year.

A5.2.9 (a) $R(t) = \exp\left[-\left(10^{-2}\tan^{-1}(t) + 10^{-3}t + \frac{1}{3}10^{-6}t^3\right)\right]$; (b) 0.0156; (c) 31.6 years; (d) 4.17×10^{-3}

P5.2.10 The reliability function of a certain device is well approximated by the function $R(t) = \frac{a}{10+t^2}$, t in years.

a. Find a.

b. What is the MTTF?

c. Determine the failure rate at $t = 2$ years.

d. What is the probability that this device will fail in the first 5 years of use?

A5.2.10 (a) 10; (b) 4.967 years; (c) 0.2857; (d) 0.7143

P5.2.11 One hundred systems are put into service at $t = 0$, and the failures are recorded: The first period is 0 to 1 year, and so on.

t	Failures
1	13
2	12
3	4
4	9
6	12
8	10
12	10
20	17

a. Fit to these data a model including infant mortality and a constant failure rate.

b. Determine the number of infant failures and the failure rate on units that survive.

A5.2.11 Plot $-\ln\left[\frac{n(t)}{101}\right]$ as y and t as x to get the form $y = -0.08530 - 0.09818t$, which leads to $R(t) = \exp[-0.08530 - 0.09818t]$; (b) infant mortality $= 8.2$, $h = 0.09818$

P5.2.12 A 6-in. candle will burn between 1 and 3 hours, depending on air currents in the room. (Assume a uniform distribution.)

a. What is the MTTF?

b. Find and plot the reliability function.

c. Find and plot the failure rate.

A5.2.12 (a) 2 hours; (b) $R(t) = 1$, $t < 1$, $= 1 - \frac{1}{2}(t - 1)$, $1 < t \le 3$, $= 0$ for $t > 3$; (c) $h(t) = \frac{f_T}{R(t)} = 0$, $t < 1$, $= \frac{1/2}{1 - \frac{1}{2}(t-1)}$, $1 < t \le 3$, $= \infty$ for $t > 3$. See plots.

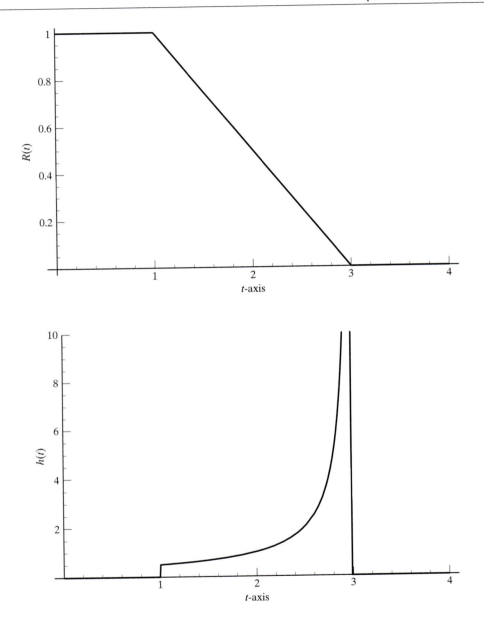

P5.2.13   The bathtub curve for a device is approximated by the function in the figure. Ten thousand of these devices are manufactured and put into service at the same time.

   a. Of this total number, find how many failed due to infant mortality, how many due to accident, and how many due to wear-out. *Hint:* You can estimate how long it takes them all to fail by setting the number of survivors to 0.5.

b. Find the MTTF for this device.

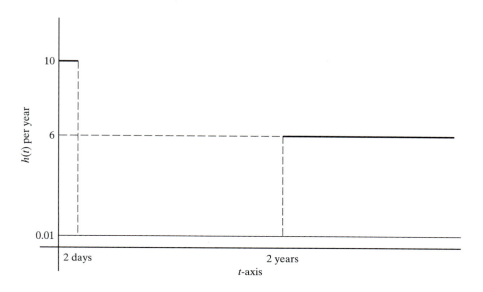

A5.2.13 (a) 533, 338, 9128 over 3.64 years; **(b)** 2.03 years

P5.2.14 The XYZ Corporation purchased 1000 widgets and placed them into service at the same time. Service records revealed the following failures during the period ending with the given year. For example between the ends of the sixth and the tenth year, 137 widgets failed. Making the assumption of constant failure rate plus infant mortality, determine the failure rate using a regression analysis of the empirical reliability function $R(t) = \frac{n(t)}{n(0)+1}$.

Year	Failures
1	53
2	40
3	40
4	45
5	40
6	32
10	137
15	120
20	100

A5.2.14 Fitting a line gives 0.0466 with 10 infant deaths.

P5.2.15   A reliability function for a device is shown.

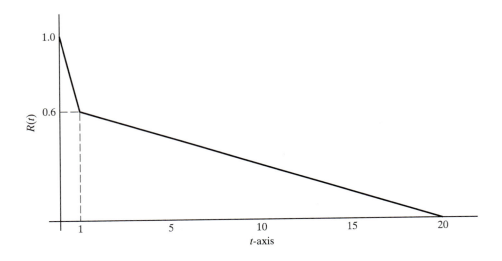

a. Find $P[$fails before 10 years$]$.
b. Find the MTTF.
c. Find the failure rate at 10 years.
d. Two of these devices are used in a series arrangement, find $P[$series arrangement fails before 10 years$]$.
e. Two of these devices are used in a parallel arrangement, find $P[$parallel arrangement fails before 10 years$]$.

A5.2.15 **(a)** 0.684; **(b)** 6.50 yrs; **(c)** 0.100; **(d)** 0.900; **(e)** 0.468

P5.2.16   The failure rate for a device is approximated by the expression $h(t) = 11e^{-92t} + 0.1$ per year.
a. Out of a lot of 1000 units, how many fail during the infant mortality period?
b. How long before half the units are expected to fail?

A5.2.16 **(a)** 113; **(b)** 5.736 years

P5.2.17   The reliability function for a certain device is well approximated by the function $R(t) = \frac{a}{100+t^2}$, where a is a constant and time is in years.
a. Find a.
b. Find the mean time to failure, MTTF.
c. Find the failure rate at $t = 10$ years.
d. If 100 units were purchased in year 0, how many failures would we expect in the tenth year?

A5.2.17 **(a)** $a = 100$; **(b)** 5π; **(c)** 0.1; **(d)** 4.75

P5.2.18   We have two subsystems in parallel. Each has a constant failure rate of $h = \lambda = 0.02$ failures/year if both are working but owing to increased stress the failure rate of the surviving component increases to 0.04 if the other fails.
a. Find the MTTF for the system.
b. What is the probability that the system fails before the MTTF?

A5.2.18 **(a)** 50 years; **(b)** 0.594

P5.2.19   A computer manufacturer has observed a failure rate of $h(t) = 0.002e^{-t/10} + 10^{-5}$ failures/hour (t in hours).
a. What fraction of the computers succumb to early failure?
b. The manufacturer figures the lifetime of the computer is 5 years before the system is totally obsolete. The manufacturer thus offers a warranty on the cost of the system, prorated to zero in 5 years. Thus the warranty costs the manufacturer $C(t) = C(0)\left(1 - \frac{t}{5}\right)$, where here t is in years and $C(0)$ is the original cost to the customer. Find the expected warranty cost per computer.

A5.2.19 **(a)** 0.0198; **(b)** $0.2063C(0)$

P5.2.20   Reliability data are taken on the failure times of $n = 19$ devices, with the results shown in the following table. Two models for the reliability of this device are to be evaluated against these data. These are

$$\text{Model 1: } R(t) = e^{-(a+bt)}, \ t \geq 0, \ \text{zow}$$

$$\text{Model 2: } R(t) = e^{-m \tan(t)}, \ t \geq 0, \ \text{zow}$$

where in both models t is in years and in the second it has radian measure (e.g., $\tan t = 1.56$ for $t = 1$).
a. Test these two models against the data and choose the better model.
b. Evaluate the unknown parameter(s) in the model.
c. From the model, estimate the times at which the eighteenth device is expected to fail.

k	t_k, years
1	0.28
2	0.52
3	0.73
4	0.90
5	1.00
6	1.10
7	1.20
8	1.25
9	1.30
10	1.30
12	1.40
15	1.45

A5.2.20 (a,b) Using the mean ranking technique, model 2 fits well but model 1 does not. From the fit, we find $m = 0.197$; **(c)** 1.49

P5.2.21   A device has a failure rate well approximated by the graph shown.

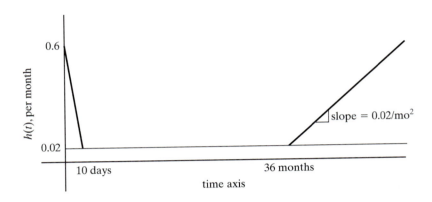

The early failure period is over after $t_E = 10$ days, and the wear-out period starts in $t_L = 36$ months. One thousand of these devices are put into service at $t = 0$.
a. How many units are expected to fail owing to infant mortality?
b. Find the time when the expected number of devices still in service is two.
c. Find the MTTF of the device.

A5.2.21 (a) 92.1; **(b)** 58.25; **(c)** 26.82

P5.2.22   A company does a reliability study on one of its products. The failure history of $n = 1000$ items is given in the following table:

Year	Failures
0.5	27
1	10
2	38
3	40
4	49
5	54
6	53

For example, between 0.5 and 1 year, 10 items failed. In addition to early failures, one late-period model for failure rate that the company wishes to test against these data is of the form $h(t) = a\sqrt{t}$.

    a. Analyze the data and determine the number of infant failures and the constant a in the model.

    b. How good is the fit? Give evidence.

A5.2.22 **(a)** By regression analysis, our model is $\underbrace{-\ln\left[\frac{n(t)}{1001}\right]}_{y} = b + \underbrace{\frac{2a}{3}\,t^{3/2}}_{x}$. Regression gives $b = 0.0199149$, and $a = 0.3030$. Hence infant mortality is about 20 units; **(b)** The correlation coefficient is -0.9999, or show how it looks on a graph, or analyze residuals.

P5.2.23 The failure rate for a system is $h(t) = a(1 - 10t) + b$, $0 < t \leq 0.1$, $= b, t > 0.1$, where t is in years.

    a. Find a if we know that 2.5% of the units fail during the early failure period, and 10% fail by the end of the first year.

    b. If a unit fails during the first year, what is the probability that it failed owing to manufacturing flaws?

A5.2.23 **(a)** 0.3285; **(b)** 0.1629

P5.2.24 One hundred systems are put into service at $t = 0$, and the failures are recorded: The first period is 0 to 1 year, and so on.

t	Failures
1	19
2	2
3	4
4	5
6	13
8	14
12	24

    a. Fit to these data a model including infant mortality and a failure rate that increases with time of the form $h(t) = at$, and determine a.

    b. Determine the number of infant failures.

A5.2.24 **(a)** $a = 0.02032$; **(b)** 18.6 infant deaths

P5.2.25 If the infant mortality period is ignored, the failure rate for a device is well modeled by the expression $\lambda_0 + \lambda_2 t^2$, where the second term describes the wear-out period. Tests show that before the wear-out period the failure rate is approximately 10%/K, but by 1000 hours has risen to 20%/K. ($K = 1000$ hrs.)

    a. Find λ_0 and λ_2.

    b. Find the reliability function for this device.

    c. At what time do we expect half the devices to have failed?

A5.2.25 (a) 10^{-4} and 10^{-10}; (b) $\exp\left[10^{-4}t + 10^{-10}\frac{t^3}{3}\right]$; (c) 2389 hours

P5.2.26   An incandescent lightbulb has a failure rate that is well approximated by a Gaussian curve, $h(t) = 0.05\exp\left[-\frac{1}{2}\left(\frac{t-850}{50}\right)^2\right]$.

     a. Find the reliability function, $R(t)$.

     b. The advertised lifetime of the bulbs is 750 hours. What is the probability that a bulb will last longer than 750 hours.

     c. Estimate the MTTF of a lightbulb.

A5.2.26 (a) $R(t) = \exp\left[-2.5\sqrt{2\pi}\,\Phi\left(\frac{t-850}{50}\right)\right]$; (b) 0.2396; (c) $\approx$790 hours by integrating with Mathematica to 2000 hours.

P5.2.27   One hundred units of Gizmo X are put into service at $t = 0$. The number failing during the first 4 years are shown in the table

Year	Failures
1	17
2	9
3	9
4	5

     a. Investigate a model of constant failure rate plus early failure by regression analysis.

     b. Estimate the number of infant failures.

     c. Estimate the number of failures expected in the fifth year.

A5.2.27 (a) fits an exponential mostly, $R(t) = \exp[-0.0914 - 0.110t]$; (b) 9; (c) 7

P5.2.28   A large company bought 1000 microprocessor-controlled pencil sharpeners. The manufacturer gave the reliability function as $R(t) = \exp\left[-\left(0.01t + 0.001t^2\right)\right]$, t in years.

     a. Find the time when 100 of the units can be expected to have failed.

     b. Find the MTTF of the pencil sharpeners. *Hint:* Complete the square in the exponent and it is of the form of a Gaussian PDF.

A5.2.28 (a) 6.42; (b) 23.7

P5.2.29   A motor has a failure rate that is proportional to time, $h(t) = at$, where a is a constant.

     a. Derive the reliability function.

     b. The MTTF is 5 years. Find a.

     c. Find the probability that the motor will fail in the first 2 years.

     d. Given that the motor has lasted 2 years, find the probability that it will fail in the next month.

     e. Find the PDF of the time to failure, $f_T(t)$.

A5.2.29 (a) $\exp\left[-\frac{at^2}{2}\right]$; (b) $a = 6.28 \times 10^{-2}$; (c) 0.118; (d) 1.05×10^{-2}; (e) $at \times \exp\left[-\frac{at^2}{2}\right]$, where $a = \frac{\pi}{50}$

P5.2.30   The definitions and vocabulary of reliability theory are based on continual usage; however, some systems are used spasmodically and run the risk of failure with each use. Let $p[i]$ = the probability of failure on the ith use, given that the system survives the $i - 1$st use.
a. If $p[i] = $ constant $= p$, derive the reliability function, $R(i)$.
b. If $p(i) = 1 - (0.9)^i$, find the reliability function.

A5.2.30 **(a)** $R(i) = (1 - p)^i$; **(b)** $R(i) = 0.9^{\left(\frac{i(i+1)}{2}\right)}$

Modeling problems on reliability theory

P5.2.31   An all-terrain vehicle sets out on a cross-country trip in territory that is hazardous to tires. Indeed, the average distance a tire lasts before failing is 100 mi. The vehicle carries two spares.
a. What is the probability that the vehicle has no tire trouble in the first 40 mi?
b. Assuming that a spare is installed when a tire fails and no tire repairs are made, what is the expected distance the vehicle can travel before it can go no farther?
c. Find the probability that the vehicle makes it as far as the distance calculated in part b.

A5.2.31 **(a)** 0.202; **(b)** 75 mi; **(c)** 0.423

P5.2.32   You borrow your roommate's car to drive on an extended trip. You do not know how much gas there is in the car, and the gas gauge is broken. In other words, you have a reliability problem. Make the following assumptions: (1) the gas tank holds 20 gal; (2) the mileage is 20 mpg; and (3) all possible states of the tank are equally likely. Let a "failure" of the system be defined as running out of gas.
a. Find the reliability function for this automobile.
b. Find the failure rate.
c. Find the MDTF = mean distance to failure for this system.

A5.2.32 **(a)** $R_M(m) = 1 - \frac{m}{400}$, $0 < m \le 400$, zow; **(b)** $h(m) = \frac{1}{400-m}$, $0 < m \le 400$, zow; **(c)** 200 mi

P5.2.33   In the instructions for my hearing aids, it states that the batteries for both aids should be changed at the same time. In other words, when the first fails, both should be changed. Assume that the failure time of a battery is uniformly distributed between 2.5 and 3.5 weeks.
a. If the instructions are followed, determine the mean lifetime of a battery.
b. If a battery is changed when it fails, what is the mean lifetime of a battery?

A5.2.33 **(a)** 2.833 weeks; **(b)** 3 weeks

P5.2.34   A farmer buys a herd of 100 cattle. The probability that any specified animal will die in the first year is 0.01. Assume constant failure (mortality) rate.
a. Consider the herd as a series system. What is the probability that the herd is intact at 6 months?

b. Find the number of cattle expected to die in the eighth month.

A5.2.34 (a) 0.605; **(b)** 0.0832

P5.2.35   A highly critical aircraft control system has a doubly redundant system consisting of three computers and a decision unit that compares computer outputs and uses a "majority vote" system: if all three agree or if two out of three agree, the system is functional. Assume that the goal is $P[1$ or more failures/month$] = 10^{-6}$. Find the requirement on the individual computers to achieve this reliability, assuming independent failures. Do not consider the reliability of the majority vote system.

A5.2.35 0.9994225

P5.2.36   A computer system has 1 million components. Assuming a stable failure period, and assuming each component has identical probability of failure, calculate the reliability for each component in FITs for a MTTF of 1 month on the computer.

A5.2.36 1.39 FIT

P5.2.37   A machinist buys a socket wrench set with a driver and 40 sockets. Over time, sockets get lost, such that after 10 years only 32 of the sockets remain. Consider losing a socket a "failure" and assume a constant failure rate.
a. Estimate the failure rate for a single socket.
b. Find the MTTF for a single socket.
c. Consider the entire set of sockets a "system" such that the system fails when the first socket is lost. Find the MTTF for the system.

A5.2.37 (a) 0.02478 per year; **(b)** 40.35 years; **(c)** 1.10 years for set

P5.2.38   a. A unicyclist sets out to set the world's record for cross-country unicycling. The only thing that can go wrong is that he might get a flat tire, since he carries no spare. If the failure rate of the tire is 0.001 failure/mile, find his MDTF.
b. A bicyclist sets out on a long trip. The failure rate on each tire on his bicycle is 0.001 failure/mile. Find his MDTF.
c. An automobile sets out on a long trip. The failure rate of any tire on the ground is 0.00001 failure/mile. Consider that if a tire fails, the spare is put on and the trip continued, but the tire is not repaired. Find the MDTF.
d. What is the probability that the auto trip goes farther than the MDTF?

A5.2.38 (a) MDTF $=$ 1000 mi; **(b)** MDTF $=$ 500 mi; **(c)** MDTF $=$ 50,000 mi; **(d)** 0.406

P5.2.39   A seven-segment BCD display must have all seven segments functional to be useful as a display. If all segments have constant failure rates and independent failures, with a MTTF of 20 years:
a. What is the MTTF of the display?
b. What is the probability that the display will last more than 5 years?

A5.2.39 (a) 2.857; **(b)** 0.1738

P5.2.40 A manufactured product involves two major components, A and B, both of which must work for the system to operate properly. Component A tends to have infant mortalities, and its failure rate is $0.001e^{-0.1t}$ failures/Khours, t in Khours. Component B has a constant failure rate of 0.001 failure/Khours.

  a. What is the failure rate for the combined system?
  b. If 1000 units are manufactured, how many might we expect to experience infant mortality?
  c. At what time might we expect all the units to have failed?

  A5.2.40 **(a)** $\lambda_{A \cap B} = \lambda_A + \lambda_B = 10^{-6}(e^{-0.0001t} + 1)$, t in hours; **(b)** about 10; **(c)** 6205 hours

P5.2.41 A janitor uses a certain spray cleaning product that lasts a variable period of time depending on the weather, number of special events in the building, and the like. The time of "failure" is normally distributed with a mean of 3 weeks and a standard deviation of half a week. He gets two cans of this product, and "failure" occurs when both cans are empty.

  a. Considered as a "system" is this a series, parallel, or standby system?
  b. Find the MTTF.
  c. Determine the reliability function, $R(t)$.
  d. Find the failure rate of the system at $t = 7$ weeks.

  A5.2.41 **(a)** standby; **(b)** 6 weeks; **(c)** $1 - \Phi\left(\frac{t-6}{1/\sqrt{2}}\right)$; **(d)** 2.637

P5.2.42 The starting offensive lineup (11 players) for a football team can be considered a "system." Any player may get injured and thus "fail." When one member fails, the system fails. Let the probability of any player's failing during the game be 0.1, so his reliability is 0.9. Because a player tires and is more liable to injury as the game progresses, we assume a failure rate proportional to time, so $h(t) = at$. For the sake of uniformity we let time be $0 < t < 4$, i.e., count quarters of the game.

  a. Find a.
  b. What is the probability that the starting team (system) will be intact at the half ($t = 2.0$)?
  c. Find the MTTF for the starting team.

  A5.2.42 **(a)** 0.0132; **(b)** 0.748; **(c)** 3.29

P5.2.43 An automotive manufacturer writes a warranty for 60,000 miles on the drive train of a new automobile. If the drive train fails during this period, the manufacturer will repair it without charge. The motor has a failure rate of $h_m = 2 \times 10^{-6} + 10^{-20}m^3$ failures/mile, where m is the mileage in miles. The transmission has a failure rate of $h_t = 10^{-6} + 4 \times 10^{-16}m^2$. The marketing guys estimate that the offer of a warranty would allow a price increase of \$300/automobile. If the average repair for a drive train failure is \$600, what is the net gain in profit on a car owing to offering the warranty? Assume that only one repair will be made during the warranty period.

  A5.2.43 \$171.41

P5.2.44   A textbook can be considered a "system" with a reliability function. Let $i =$ the number of times the book is sold; $i = 1$ when the book is sold new. Let us consider the following model: after each sale, there is a probability p_1 that the book will be kept by the student and not sold back to the campus bookstore. From the viewpoint of the bookstore, this represents a "failure," since it makes no more money from that book. There is also a probability p_2 that the book will be so mistreated that the bookstore will not buy back the book for resale, another "failure."
  a. Under these assumptions, derive $R(i)$, the reliability function as a function of the number of times the book is sold.
  b. Find the MTTF of the book.

  A5.2.44 (a) Let $p = p_1 + p_2 - p_1 p_2$; then $R(i) = (1 - p)^i$; (b) $\frac{1}{p_1 + p_2 - p_1 p_2}$

P5.2.45   A student buys a mechanical pencil. It comes with two leads. From experience, she knows that a lead lasts from 4 to 6 days. Assume all times equally likely.
  a. Find the PDF of the time that a lead lasts.
  b. Find the probability that the two leads would last a combined time exceeding 9.2 days.
  c. When the student bought the pencil, she bought and put in a set of 10 additional leads, making 12 in all. Find the mean and variance of the total time expected for all 12 leads before she is out of leads.
  d. Estimate the probability that the 12 leads will be gone before 59 days.

  A5.2.45 (a) $f_T(t) = \frac{1}{2}$, $4 < t \le 6$, zow; (b) 0.820; (c) $\mu = 60$ days and $\sigma^2 = 4$ days^2; (d) 0.3085 using the CLT

P5.2.46   A pencil lead lasts a variable amount of time owing to breakage, differences in paper, pressure, and usage. Let $T = N(3, 1)$ model the time in weeks for a single lead to be used up. Ignore the fact that this model gives a small probability of a negative failure time. A pencil comes with three leads when new. Assume independence of lead lifetimes.
  a. Find the MTTF for the "lead system" consisting of the three leads used in sequence.
  b. Find the reliability function for the "lead system."
  c. Find the probability that the "lead system" is still in service at 12 weeks.

  A5.2.46 (a) 9 weeks; (b) $1 - \Phi\left(\frac{t-9}{\sqrt{3}}\right)$; (c) 0.0416

P5.2.47   A retired professor purchases a recreational vehicle (RV) to travel around the country. He also purchases a small motorcycle (MC), which he places on a rack at the rear of the RV. The idea is to use the motorcycle to go for help should he have an accident, run out of gas, have motor or transmission problems, and the like. If the motorcycle fails, then he has to walk for help, which means that the system has failed totally should that occur. The failure rate for the RV is a constant $\lambda_{RV} = 0.001$/mi, and the failure rate for the motorcycle is $\lambda_{MC} = 0.005$/mi.

a. Find the MDTF for the RV.

b. Find his MDTF of the RV + MC system.

c. Find the probability that the RV + MC system will fail in the first 500 mi.

A5.2.47 (a) 1000 mi; (b) 1200 mi; (c) 0.262

P5.2.48 A hospital must have an electric generator to provide power in case of a power failure. The emergency generator has a reliability function $R(t) = 0.99e^{-0.001t}$, for $0 < t \le$ 120, zow, where t is in minutes, and has 2 hours of fuel. Note that $R(0) = 0.99$ because 1 time out of 100 the generator will not start at all.

a. Why is $R(t) = 0$ for $t > 120$ minutes?

b. Find the probability that the emergency generator fails before it runs out of gas, given that it starts.

c. Find the MTTF for the emergency generator.

A5.2.48 (a) because it runs out of fuel; (b) 0.113; (c) 111.9 minutes

P5.2.49 A candle burns between 1 and 2 hours, depending on how much air is blowing on it. Assume all $1 < T \le 2$ are equally likely, where T represents the time to failure.

a. Find $R(t)$, the reliability function for the candle.

b. Find the MTTF for the candle.

c. If a person has two candles and lights the second when the first is gone (a standby system), find the reliability of the "system" of two candles.

A5.2.49 (a) $R(t) = 1$, $0 < t \le 1$, $= 3 - t$, $1 < t \le 2$, $= 0, t > 2$; (b) 1.5 hours; (c) $R(t) = 1$, $t < 2$, $= 1 - \frac{(t-2)^2}{2}$, $2 < t < 3$, $= \frac{(t-4)^2}{2}$, $3 < t \le 4$, $= 0$, $t > 4$

P5.2.50 Assume that a modern automobile, after the break-in period and before the effects of wear set in, has a constant failure rate per mile due to electrical problems of $h_E = 10^{-5}$, a constant failure rate per mile due to motor problems of $h_M = 10^{-6}$, a constant failure rate per mile due to transmission problems of $h_T = 3 \times 10^{-6}$.

a. Find the overall reliability function for the automobile during this period. This will be a function of the mileage, m.

b. If you see such an automobile stranded at the side of the road, what is the probability that the problem is electrical if the mileage is 5000?

c. What if the mileage is 50,000? What then is the probability that the problem is electrical?

A5.2.50 (a) $R(m) = \exp[-1.4 \times 10^{-5}m]$, m in miles; (b) 0.721; (c) 0.782

P5.2.51 A lighting fixture has four bulbs, any three of which give adequate light. If $R_B(t)$ is the reliability function for each bulb, assumed independent, find $R_S(t)$, the reliability function for the fixture.

A5.2.51 $4R_B^3 - R_B^4$

P5.2.52 A stock car race has 10 cars start the race. On average, 6 cars finish the race. We assume that cars fail owing to mechanical problems with a constant failure rate in failures per unit distance; that is, no collisions occur that take two cars out of the race at the same time.

a. Find the probability that 8 or more cars are still in the race at the halfway point.

b. Let D be the distance the race progresses before the first car fails. Find the expected value of D.

A5.2.52 **(a)** 0.6003; **(b)** 19.6% of the distance of the race

P5.2.53 A piece of electronic equipment has a failure rate model of

$$h(t) = 0.01 \left(1 + \frac{1}{\sqrt{t}} \right) \text{ failures/month}$$

a. Find the cumulative failure rate, $H(t)$.

b. Find the reliability function for this device, $R(t)$.

c. Out of 100 units, how many failures do you expect in the first 6 months?

d. Find the MTTF for this device. This will require some sort of numerical integration.

A5.2.53 **(a)** $0.01(t + 2\sqrt{t})$; **(b)** $\exp[-0.01(t + 2\sqrt{t})]$; **(c)** about 10; **(d)** about 84 months

P5.2.54 A small town in west Texas gets its electric power from two independent transmission lines. Line A uses four transformers, and line B uses two transformers. These transformers are operating in series to supply the power. Assume that the transformers have a MTTF of 30 years, and there is line failure due to lightning or accident (tree limbs, ice storms, etc.) with MTTF of 10 years. Assume constant failure rates (the exponential model) and independent failures.

a. What is the MTTF for the electric power to this city?

b. What is the probability that the city goes longer than the MTTF with no power outages?

A5.2.54 **(a)** 7.79 years; **(b)** 0.391

P5.2.55 A mechanical pencil comes with two leads. Due to breakage, the time a lead lasts is unpredictable, but is somewhere between 1 and 2 weeks, with all times equally likely. Let the pencil be the "system" and its "failure" time be when the second lead is gone.

a. Find and sketch the reliability function, $R(t)$, for this system.

b. Find the MTTF for this system.

A5.2.55 **(a)** $R(t) = 1$ for $0 < t < 2$, $1 - 0.5(t - 2)^2$ for $2 < t < 3$, $0.5(t - 4)^2$ for $3 < t < 4$, and 0 for $t > 4$, see plot following; **(b)** 3 weeks

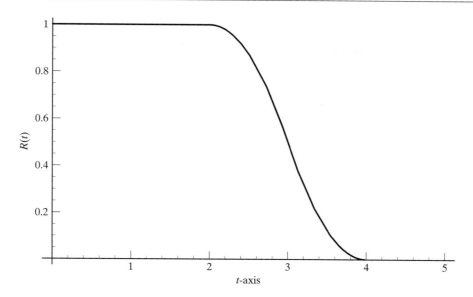

P5.2.56   The normal failure mode for an incandescent lightbulb is evaporation of the filament; hence operating a lightbulb is a bit like burning a candle; apart from accident, the bulb has a predictable lifetime. The failure rate is well approximated by $\lambda(t) = 5 \times 10^{-5} + 0.04 \exp\left[-\frac{1}{2}\left(\frac{t-850}{50}\right)^2\right]$, where t is in hours.
a. Find the probability that a bulb fails by accident.
b. If 1000 bulbs were put into service at the same time, how much later might we expect 500 to have failed?

A5.2.56 (a) 0.0416; **(b)** 769 hours

P5.2.57   A satellite has two nuclear power plants, one with a MTTF of 5 years and a standby unit with a MTTF of 1 year. Assume constant failure rates for both units.
a. What is the MTTF for the system?
b. Determine the reliability function for the system, $R_S(t)$.
c. At what time in years does the satellite have a 50% chance of having power?

A5.2.57 (a) 6 years; **(b)** $R_S(t) = \frac{5}{4}e^{-t/5} - \frac{1}{4}e^{-t}$; **(c)** 4.555 years

P5.2.58   Consider that an automobile has three significant components: the motor, the transmission and the body/suspension system. The failure rate for each system is constant (λ) until the wear-out period commences at 120,000 mi. That is, each system has an equal probability of breaking down at any time during this period. It is known that 75% of the cars manufactured need at least one major repair prior to the wear-out period.
a. Find λ, the failure rate per mile for each of these systems before the wear-out period begins.

b. Considering that a repair for one of these systems costs $500, what are the expected repair costs per automobile before the wear-out period begins?

A5.2.58 **(a)** 3.85×10^{-6}; **(b)** $693.15

P5.2.59 The purpose of a warranty is to make good on an early failure of a device due to improper manufacturing; however, some warranties are "no questions asked," that is, they cover failure for all causes. Let us say the failure rate of a device is $h(t) = 0.02e^{-5t^2} + 0.05$, t in years. The first term represents failures during the early months of life due to manufacturing defects, and the second represents failures due to improper use.
a. If 10,000 units are sold, how many are expected to fail due to infant mortality?
b. If the warranty covers failure for any reason within the first 2 years, and 80% of the units that fail during this period for abuse are actually returned, how many of the units would be returned, including all the early failures?

A5.2.59 **(a)** 762; **(b)** 1465 returned

P5.2.60 Because my front porch lightbulb is hard to change, I buy three long-life lightbulbs at a time to use in that location. The average lifetime for such a bulb is 2000 hours. Because failure is due to a number of factors, we assume that the failure times for a single bulb are Gaussian, $T = N(2000, 100^2)$, where T is the time to failure.
a. For a single bulb, what is the reliability function?
b. Find the failure rate for a single bulb at $t = 2100$ hours.
c. Consider now the three bulbs as a standby system. What is the MTTF of the system?
d. What is the reliability function of the system evaluated at the MTTF?

A5.2.60 **(a)** $1 - \Phi\left(\frac{t-2000}{100}\right)$; **(b)** 0.01525; **(c)** 6000; **(d)** 0.5

P5.2.61 The drive mechanism of a certain naval craft has two driveshafts to increase reliability. Let $\lambda = $ constant represent the failure rate of a single shaft when working in tandem. The shafts can be used singly or in parallel; however, if used singly, the increased strain changes the failure rate to 1.1λ. Consider two strategies: (1) standby operation or (2) parallel operation; however, note that this is not standard parallel operation, since the failure rate changes when the first shaft fails. Calculate MTTF1 and MTTF2, and advise on which system to choose on that basis.

A5.2.61 MTTF1 $= \frac{2}{1.1h}$ and MTTF2 $= \frac{1.41}{h}$. The standby system is superior.

5.4.3 Queuing Theory

Exercises on queuing theory

P5.3.1 Show that the average time between departures is equal to the average time between arrivals.

A5.3.1 Proof, based on the conditional expectation $E[T] = E[T|N = 0] \times P[N = 0] + E[T|N > 0] \times P[N > 0]$

Modeling problems on queuing theory

P5.3.2   A restaurant has one toilet, which accommodates one person at a time. During the rush hour, there is at least one person waiting for 20% of the time. On average it takes each person 2 minutes to use the toilet, exponentially distributed. Assuming Poisson arrivals, what is the rate at which customers need to use the toilet.

A5.3.2   0.2236 per minute

P5.3.3   In a grocery queue, customers arrive at an average rate of one customer every 2 minutes. The checker can check out the average customer in 1 minute. The manager will open a new checkout station if the queue gets more than two customers in the queue, plus one being checked out.
a. At any time, what is the probability that $N > 3$ if a new checkout station is not opened?
b. What is the expected number of customers in the first queue, under this arrangement. That is, what is $E[N|N \le 3]$?

A5.3.3   **(a)** $\frac{1}{16}$; **(b)** 0.7333

P5.3.4   Based on measurements of a given queuing system, it is estimated that customers arrive at a rate of 1.8 per minute. It is also estimated that the average number of customers in the queue is 2.1, and that the average number in the only server is 0.7.
a. What is $\bar{n}$, the average state of the queuing system.
b. What is $\bar{t}$, the average time a customer spends in the queuing system?
c. Make an estimate of the fraction of time that there are more than two customers in the system.

A5.3.4   **(a)** 3.9; **(b)** 1.56 minute; **(c)** about 47.4%

P5.3.5   A mom-and-pop grocery store has an average of 1.5 customers in line waiting to be served during the lunch hour. The average rate of customers coming into the store is 1 per minute during that period. Make the usual assumptions about Poisson arrivals and exponential service times.
a. What is the average time from the time the customer enters the line to when the customer leaves the checkout counter?
b. What is the average time it takes mom or pop to check out a customer?
c. The scanner salesperson claims that the new scanning system will speed up checkout by a factor of 2. If this is true, what fraction of the time will the checkout person be idle?

A5.3.5   **(a)** 2.186 minutes; **(b)** 0.68614 minutes; **(c)** 65.7% of the time

P5.3.6   A queue in a fast-food store has customers arriving at random with an average rate of one customer every 30 seconds. Because the food is already prepared it takes, on average, 21 seconds to bag the food, take the money, and make change.
a. What is the utilization for this queuing system?
b. Find the probability that the queue will have more than two people in it.

c. What is the probability that you will have to wait more than 1 minute for your food?

d. Verify Little's formula for this queuing system.

A5.3.6   **(a)** 0.7; **(b)** 0.343; **(c)** 0.424; **(d)** $2.33 = 2 \times 1.17$

P5.3.7   An air traffic controller at a large airport has planes arriving at random times at an average of one every 2 minutes. The airport has airspace for five planes circling to land, including the plane landing. Assuming exponential times to land, what is the required average landing time such that $P[N > 5] = 10^{-3}$?

A5.3.7   0.9432 minute

P5.3.8   In an auto service shop, the cars arrive at an average of one every 20 minutes. It takes the shop manager 5 minutes on average to hear the owner's story, decide what to do, and write the work order. The manager also does minor repairs when there is no one waiting.

a. What is the probability that, once he clears the queue, he will have more than 15 minutes to work on his repair job?

b. What fraction of his day is spent in managing?

A5.3.8   **(a)** 0.472; **(b)** 0.75

P5.3.9   Driving I-40 between Albuquerque and Amarillo, a traveler notices that there are about 5 cars per mile but twice as many trucks. (Assume that all vehicles move at 70 mph.)

a. What is the probability that there will be fewer than five vehicles in a prescribed mile of highway?

b. At the truck-weighing station near Tucumcari, where all trucks have to pull over to be weighed, the average waiting time for a truck to be weighed is 20 seconds, not counting the time on the scales. Find the average time required to weigh a truck (assume exponential model).

A5.3.9   **(a)** 0.0008566; **(b)** 4.243 s

P5.3.10   An efficient manager wants to hire only one server for a queuing system and wants to have a utilization ratio of 0.8. If people appear at the input to the queue at a rate of three in 10 minutes,

a. What is the average rate at which the server must be able to process the customers?

b. What is the average number of people waiting for the server in the queue?

c. How long is it expected that people will have to wait in the queue before being served?

d. On average, how long does it take for a person to go through the entire system?

A5.3.10 **(a)** 0.375; **(b)** 3.2; **(c)** 10.33 min; **(d)** 13.33 min

P5.3.11   A data repeater accepts messages from a number of sources and, after a possible delay, transmits them to a central station. Messages arrive according to a Poisson process with a rate of one message every 4 milliseconds. The data messages are exponentially distributed in the length of time it take the process them, with an average delay of 3 milliseconds.

a. Find the expected number of messages in the system.

b. Find the expected delay in the system before messages reach the processor.

c. At what arrival rate, with the same service time model, does the expected waiting time in the queue double?

d. For the answer to part c, what is the upper limit for 95% of all the delay in the system. That is, within what delay time do 95% of the delays fall below?

A5.3.11 (a) 3; **(b)** 9 ms; **(c)** 285.7 messages/second; **(d)** about 62.9 ms

P5.3.12 Airplane crashes occur at random times, and all crashes are investigated. In a certain FAA district, crashes occur at an average rate of one every 8 days. Investigations are done by a team that takes an average of 5 days to complete. Assume the time required for an investigation is exponentially distributed.

a. What is the probability that there will be no crashes in a 2-week period?

b. If a monthly rate of crashes is calculated, what is the probability that the rate will exceed four crashes per month, using a 30-day month for the calculation?

c. What is the average time between the time of the crash and the end of the investigation?

A5.3.12 (a) 0.174; **(b)** 0.322; **(c)** 13.3 days

P5.3.13 Trucks along a major highway have a density of five trucks per mile and drive 60 mph. Assume a random distribution of trucks. A weigh station can weigh a truck in 8 seconds on average (assume exponential service time).

a. Consider a time when there is no truck on the scale and no truck waiting. What is the expected time until the next truck drives in, is weighed, and departs?

b. The highway department wants to make sure that there is adequate parking for trucks waiting to be weighed. How many trucks does the department have to have space for, not counting the truck being weighed, such that there is a 99% probability that all waiting trucks have a place to park?

c. What is the probability that a truck will be delayed more than 1 minute by the weighing requirement? Count only waiting and weighing time, not time to stop and time to get back on the road.

A5.3.13 (a) 20 s; **(b)** 11; **(c)** 0.0821

ENDNOTES

1. **Event.** We now have two different meanings for the term *event*. It can mean a set of outcomes from a chance experiment, or it can mean, especially in this chapter, something that happens, such as an earthquake. The context should make it clear which is meant.

2. **Zow.** In the context of this chapter, time is always positive. We do not always define functions for negative time.

3. **Answer to you do it on p. 463.** The weekly average is $\frac{22}{52}$. The probability of two or more is $1 - P[0 \text{ or } 1] = 1 - e^{-\frac{22}{52}}\left(1 + \frac{22}{52}\right) = 0.06784$.

4. **Raisins.** I once offered extra points to anyone who would count the number of raisins in a cup. I had three or four takers, and 360 raisins/cup is close to the average. Another shameless exploitation of students' insatiable greed for points! The details appear in a problem for P4.1.31.

5. **Answer to you do it on p. 465.** We are supposed to use the Gaussian to approximate the Poisson. The expected number is 40, so that will be the mean and variance of the Gaussian. The required probability is $\Phi\left(\frac{35.5-40}{\sqrt{40}}\right) = 0.2384$. We use 35.5 instead of 35 as a continuity correction. The following cell gives the exact value.

```
Needs["Statistics`DiscreteDistributions`"]
Sum[PDF[PoissonDistribution[40], k], {k, 0, 35}];
N[%]
```

```
0.242414
```

6. **Approximating the binomial with the Poisson.** The expected number of successes in a series of binomial trials is np. If p is small, then a good approximation to the binomial distribution is $B_n(k, p) \approx P(k, np)$. For example, let $n = 100$ and $p = 0.03$. Then the exact binomial for 2 successes is $B_{100}(2, 0.03) = \binom{100}{2}(0.03)^2(0.97)^{98} = 0.2254$. The Poisson approximation, since $E[K] = np = 3$, is $P(2, 3) = \frac{3^2}{2!}e^{-3} = 0.2404$—not terribly impressive, but useful in an emergency.

7. **Answer to you do it on p. 470.** This problem calls for $P\left[T < \frac{6}{7}\right] = \int_0^{6/7} \frac{22}{52}e^{-22t/52}\, dt = 0.3042$. This can be done also with the Poisson as the complement of the probability that there are no events in the next 6 days. I find that most problems involving the Erlang can be done with easier math using Poisson.

8. **Exponential service times.** Service times are frequently well modeled by the exponential random variable. A student measured service times at a grocery store for an in-class presentation. We used the process from Chapter 4 to fit an exponential CDF to the data, and the fit was excellent, except there was a shortage of very short times. We figured these represented the effect of the "10 items or less" line.

9. **Answer to you do it on p. 473.** The expected number of customers in 12 minutes would be $\lambda t = \frac{1}{4} \times 12 = 3$. For you to be gone in 12 minutes, they would have to serve three or more in 12 minutes. The complement would be that they serve 0, 1, or 2 in 12 minutes. The probability is thus $1 - e^{-3}\left(1 + 3 + \frac{3^2}{2!}\right) = 0.5768$.

10. **Answer to you do it on p. 475.** Adapting the analysis to three dimensions, the CDF is $F_R(r) = 1 - \exp\left[-\frac{4}{3}\rho\pi r^3\right]$ and the PDF is $f_R(r) = 4\pi\rho r^2 \exp\left[-\frac{4}{3}\rho\pi r^3\right]$. The $P[R \le 4]$ can be derived directly from the CDF as $F_R(4) = 0.9315$. Derived from the PDF, the result is

```
In[8]:= Integrate[4 * 0.01 π r² Exp[-4/3 * 0.01 * π * r³], {r, 0, 4}];
        N[%]
Out[9] = 0.931493
```

11. **Failure rate.** The failure rate is also called the *hazard rate* and the *death rate*. This section does not define the failure rate in the usual way. It merely introduces a name and a symbol for a concept that is familiar from study of the Poisson process. Later in this section we will give the usual derivation and show that it corresponds to the practice followed here.

12. **Convergence of the reliability function.** If $R(t) \to 0$ equal to or slower than $\frac{1}{t}$, then neither part of (5.2.12) converges and no MTTF exists.

13. **Answer to you do it on p. 479.** The cumulative failure rate is clearly $H(t) = \frac{1}{2}0.0001t^2$, so the integral that must be evaluated is $\int_0^\infty \exp\left[-\frac{1}{2}\left(\frac{t}{100}\right)^2\right]dt$. This is basically half the normalization equation for the Gaussian PDF with $\sigma = 100$ and $\mu = 0$, so the result is $\frac{1}{2} \times \sqrt{2\pi}\sigma = 125.331$ years. This is the approach for those who like to do integrals. For those who do not, we can simply paste the expression into an active Mathematica cell and execute, ignoring the warning.

```
∞
∫ Exp[-1/2 (t/100)²] dt
0
N[%]
─────────────────────
50 √2π
─────────────────────
125.331
```

14. **Answer to you do it on p. 481.** This is harder than the example because we do not know the reliability function at the time to reorder. We want $P[N \geq 299.5] = 0.9$, considering the continuity correction. Reverting to the notation of the binomial, we let $p =$ the reliability function at the unknown time and use the Gaussian approximation for the binomial distribution. The result is $\Phi\left(\frac{990p-299.5}{\sqrt{990p(1-p)}}\right) = 0.9$, which leads to a quadratic equation in p. The solution is $p = 0.3216$, which leads to a time of 10.77 years, so you can relax a bit longer before reordering.

15. **Answer to you do it on p. 491.** Because both must work, this is a series arrangement, and the total failure rate is 0.18. The probability that the car has not failed in 5 years is $R(5) = e^{-0.18 \times 5}$. The probability of failing in 5 years is the complement, 0.5934.

16. **Answer to you do it on p. 493.** Using the same formula, we have $\frac{1}{\lambda} + \frac{1}{\lambda} - \frac{1}{\lambda+\lambda} = 20$, which gives 13.33 years.

17. **Answer to you do it on p. 495.** Add another exponential random variable and you have an Erlang of order $k = 4$. Now the integral, followed by its result, is

```
λ=4/500;
Integrate[λ⁴x³Exp[-λx]/31, {x, 300, Infinity}]
N[%]
```

$$\frac{1073}{125\,e^{12/5}}$$

```
0.778723
```

18. **The data** are from www.dhs.ca.gov/hisp/chs/OHIR/cadeathsrates.htm.
19. **Queue.** Derived from the latin for "tail," and coming into English from French.
20. **A stable queue.** A queue in which customers arrive on average faster than they can be processed must grow steadily in length. Even if $\lambda = \lambda_s$, the queue is unstable, as the theory shows. In a store where the queue starts growing long, the server normally calls for another server to come help out. Of course, such a growing queue may be a normal fluctuation, but customers are intolerant of long queues, so stores respond quickly to prevent annoying customers in this way.
21. **Reasonable assumption.** The reasonable assumption of replacing time averages with statistical averages is called the *ergodic assumption*. We deal with ergodic random processes in Chapter 6 because the concept is important in modeling random signals.
22. **Idle times reasonable.** If you rerun the active cells, it may not appear so reasonable the second time. The operations of a queue vary widely, and one would have to average very many longer trials to verify that 33% of the time the server is idle on average.
23. **Average number in the queue.** The time average of N was *calculated* in connection with Little's formula, and the value is considerably lower than the theoretical value. This is an artifact of using a small number of customers. The nature of the queue is such that is remains small most of the time, but occasionally it gets long, and then it takes quite a while to clear out the backlog. You can go back and change m to some much larger number, like 500, and the result should be that the time-average value of N will be much closer to the theoretical value, which is the expectation derived in this section.
24. **Answer to you do it on p. 513.** To miss one or more calls, three or more calls must be in the queue, $P[N \geq 3] = 0.1^{3/2} = 0.03162$.
25. **Answer to you do it on p. 516.** Here is a case in which the Poisson is easier than the Erlang. We require that $0, 1, \ldots, 6$ customers be served, but not 7 or more. Thus we add the Poisson for $0 \to 6$. The expected number to be served in 10 minutes is $48.28 \times \frac{10}{60} = 8.047$. Thus the answer is $e^{-8.047}\left(1 + \frac{8.047}{1!} + \cdots + \frac{8.047^6}{6!}\right) = 0.6924$.

6

Modeling Random Signals

6.1 WIDE-SENSE STATIONARY RANDOM PROCESSES

The need for models of random signals. Engineers deal with a wide variety of random signals. In Chapter 5 we studied the Poisson process, which consists of a series of events at random times. We introduced the concept of a random process to model such phenomena with our probability macromodel. We also used random processes in the section on reliability as a model to describe the life history of a large number of manufactured items. Random processes also were used in describing the behavior of queues.

In this chapter we deal with an important class of random processes called *wide-sense stationary* (WSS) random processes, which are used to model random signals such as

- *Information-bearing signals*. Engineers design, analyze, and use a variety of systems that generate, store, transmit, and process random signals. Models are required to establish design parameters such as the required bandwidth for such signals.
- *Noise*. One enemy of information is noise, which is also random. Although many sources of noise, such as man-made electrical noise on a power line, are not well modeled by WSS random processes, many natural forms of noise are. Examples are resistor noise, antenna noise from the atmosphere and extragalactic sources, and various forms of noise in electronic devices due to the discrete nature of electricity.

The definition of a random process. Although we focus in this chapter on WSS random processes, we begin by reviewing the definition of a random process generally and giving two examples. Definition: a *random process, $X(t)$*, is a family of functions that are associated with the outcomes of a chance experiment. A fuller notation would be $X(t, s_i)$, where t is an independent variable associated with time, and s_i represents the outcomes of a chance experiment.[1] The value of $X(t, s_i)$ can be discrete or continuous, and the time variable likewise can be discrete or continuous.

Example 6.1.1: A random process with two members

Let us assume a chance experiment with two outcomes, s_1 and s_2, where the probability of the elementary event $S_1 = \{s_1\}$ is $P[S_1] = p$, and $P[S_2] = 1 - p = q$. This defines the chance experiment. The random process is defined as $X(t, s_1) = 12\cos(12t)$ and $X(t, s_2) = 12\sin(12t)$. Figure 6.1.1 depicts this random process.

At any time, the random process is a random variable described by a PMF. For example, at $t = 0$, the PMF would be

$$P_{X(0)}(12) = p, \quad P_{X(0)}(0) = q, \quad \text{zow} \tag{6.1.1}$$

This random process is continuous in time but discrete in amplitude, since at any time only two values of $X(t, s_i)$ are possible.

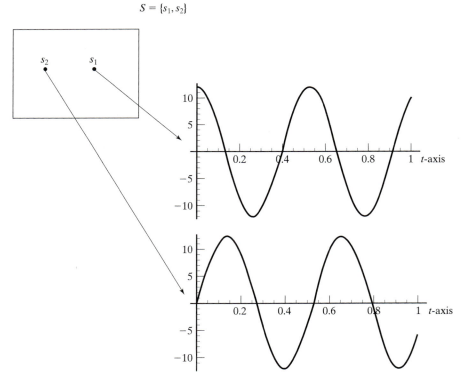

Figure 6.1.1 A random process with two members, a sine and a cosine function. The probability of having the cosine is p, and the probability of having the sine is q.

A random process with an infinite number of members. Consider a chance experiment that produces an exponential random variable, T, where $f_T(t) = 2e^{-2t}$, $t \geq 0$, zow. The random process is defined as

$$X(t) = 1 - \frac{t}{T}, \ 0 < t \leq T, \ \text{zow} \tag{6.1.2}$$

Two of the infinite number of members of this random process are shown in Fig. 6.1.2. The random process in Fig. 6.1.2 is continuous both in time and in amplitude.

Analog and digital signals. In Sec. 6.1 we present WSS models for random analog signals, synchronous and asynchronous digital signals, and the wideband noise inherent to many information systems. We begin with the asynchronous digital signal, which provides a good example of the basic concepts and methods for describing WSS random processes.

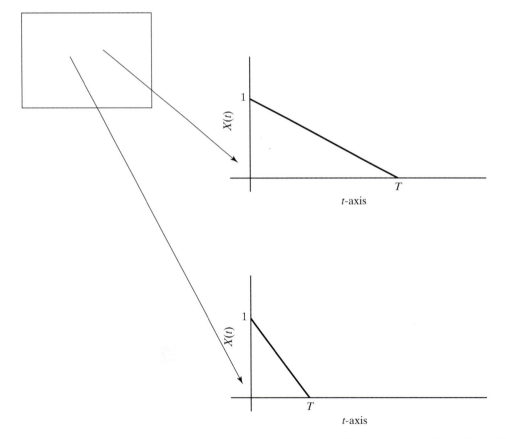

Figure 6.1.2 Two members of a random process that has an infinite number of members. The random variable, T, is exponentially distributed and thus can take any value between 0 and ∞.

6.1.1 Modeling an Asynchronous Digital Signal

Basic model.   We will use a Poisson process as the underlying model for an asynchronous digital signal. The random-process model is based on the Poisson process shown in Fig. 6.1.3.

We model an asynchronous digital signal by using a Poisson point process as the clock input to a toggle flip-flop (FF). The output logic levels are assumed to be 0 and 1 V and the output is preset to 1 at $t = 0$. The circuit is shown in Fig. 6.1.4.

We call this a *semirandom flip-flop* because we have preset the output state to 1. Later, we will eliminate the initial condition to have a fully random FF. The output of the FF for the input sequence in Fig. 6.1.3 is shown in Fig. 6.1.5.

Describing the random processes with PMFs or PDFs.   We now describe the state of the random process with a probability mass function, PMF. The output is discrete, $Q(t) = 0$ or 1, and hence a PMF is required. If the output were an analog signal, we would use a PDF.

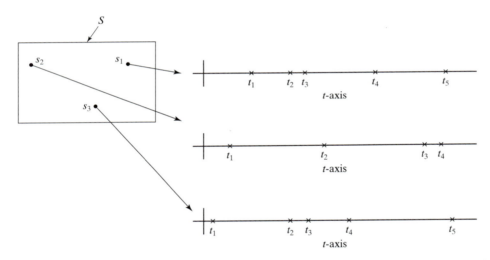

Figure 6.1.3   The Poisson point random process consists of a random sequence of events for each outcome of the chance experiment. We use this process to model an asynchronous digital signal.

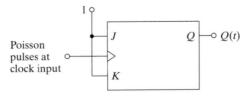

Figure 6.1.4   The output state of the toggle flip-flop will change at every Poisson event at the clock input. Our initial analysis assumes that $Q(0) = 1$ because the output is preset to 1.

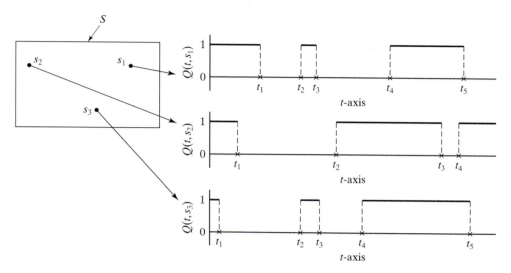

Figure 6.1.5 The output random process is generated by the input random process of Poisson points in Fig. 6.1.3. Note that all output signals begin with $Q(0) = 1$ because we preset the output to 1.

First-order PMF. The first-order PMF gives the output PMF at some time t. By definition,

$$P_{Q(t)}(q) = P[Q(t) = q] \tag{6.1.3}$$

which takes on values at $q = 0$ and $q = 1$ only. Thus $Q(t)$ is a Bernoulli random variable [(Fig. 2.2.6)]. The condition for $Q(t) = 1$ is that there is an even number of clock events between 0 and t. The probability of this event can be calculated from the Poisson process with an average rate of λ as follows:

$$P_{Q(t)}(1) = P[K \text{ even}] = P[K = 0] + P[K = 2] + P[K = 4] + \cdots \tag{6.1.4}$$

We now substitute the Poisson probabilities of Eq. (5.1.12) and obtain the following series:

$$P_{Q(t)}(1) = e^{-\lambda t} + \frac{(\lambda t)^2}{2!}e^{-\lambda t} + \frac{(\lambda t)^4}{4!}e^{-\lambda t} + \cdots = e^{-\lambda t}\left[1 + \frac{(\lambda t)^2}{2!} + \frac{(\lambda t)^4}{4!} + \cdots\right] \tag{6.1.5}$$

The series is unfamiliar, but from the standard power-series expansion of the exponential, given in Eq. (5.1.17), we derive the identity

$$1 + \frac{x^2}{2!} + \frac{x^4}{4!} + \cdots = \frac{e^{+x} + e^{-x}}{2} \tag{6.1.6}$$

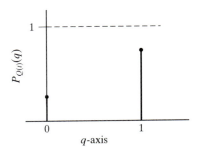

Figure 6.1.6   The PMF of $Q(t)$ at a time when 1 is still favored over 0. As time increases the probabilities become equal.

Using this identity in Eq. (6.1.5) we obtain

$$P_{Q(t)}(1) = e^{-\lambda t}\left[1 + \frac{(\lambda t)^2}{2!} + \frac{(\lambda t)^4}{4!} + \cdots\right] = e^{-\lambda t}\left[\frac{e^{+\lambda t} + e^{-\lambda t}}{2}\right] = \frac{1}{2}[1 + e^{-2\lambda t}] \quad (6.1.7)$$

Equation (6.1.7) gives the result we seek and is easily interpreted in terms of the FF output. Note that for $t = 0$, we have $P_{Q(t)}(1) = 1$, which must be true because we preset the FF to 1. With time increasing, the probability that the output is in the 1 state approaches $P_{Q(t)}(1) \to \frac{1}{2}$, which must be true, since the clock events are random and eventually randomize the output.

The derivation of $P_{Q(t)}(0)$ is similar and leads to a similar result:

$$P_{Q(t)}(0) = \frac{1}{2}[1 - e^{-2\lambda t}] \quad (6.1.8)$$

Note that $P_{Q(t)}(1) + P_{Q(t)}(0) = 1$. As stated earlier, $Q(t)$ is a Bernoulli random variable, so the PMF is that shown in Fig. 6.1.6. Figure 6.1.7 shows the PMF of the output state as a function of time.

Figure 6.1.7 confirms what we would expect from the way $Q(t)$ is generated. Initially, the output is preset to 1 on all members of the random process. As the Poisson pulses arrive at the clock input, either earlier or later in the various realizations of the random function, more and more of the outputs change states, and with time the output states become fully randomized.

Second-order PMF.   We use the results obtained in Eq. (6.1.7) to derive the second-order PMF of $Q(t)$. By definition, this is

$$P_{Q(t_1)Q(t_2)}(q_1, q_2) = P[(Q(t_1) = q_1) \cap (Q(t_2) = q_2)] \quad (6.1.9)$$

Because $Q(t_1)$ and $Q(t_2)$ are not independent, we consider the four possibilities for $q_1 q_2 = 00, 01, 10, 11$. We will work out the last case because we need it later. The other cases are similar. We pick two times, t_1 and t_2, with $t_2 > t_1$, and determine the probability that the output state is 1 at both times, as shown in Fig. 6.1.8.

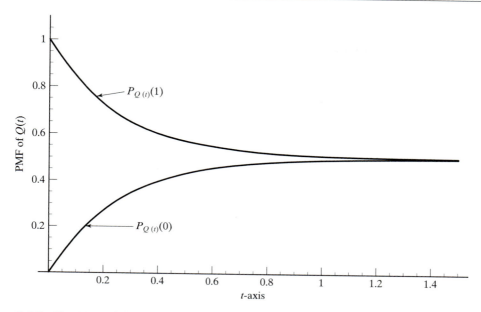

Figure 6.1.7 The PMF of the FF output, $Q(t)$, as a function of time. Initially the output is sure to be 1, but with time the output is randomized by the random input pulses, and eventually 1 and 0 become equally likely. For this part, $\lambda = 2$.

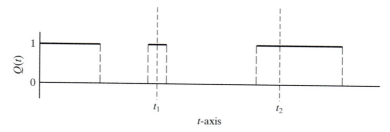

Figure 6.1.8 We pick two times and calculate the probability that $Q(t)$ is 1 at both times, as shown here. The required condition is that there be an even number of transitions between the origin and t_1 and also an even number of transitions between t_1 and t_2.

The probability we will calculate is expressed in Eq. (6.1.10) in terms of a conditional probability:

$$P_{Q(t_1)Q(t_2)}(1, 1) = P[(Q(t_1) = 1) \cap (Q(t_2) = 1)] = P[Q(t_2) = 1 | Q(t_1) = 1] \times P[Q(t_1) = 1] \tag{6.1.10}$$

The conditional probability in Eq. (6.1.10) is the probability of an even number of transitions between t_1 and t_2, which is essentially what we derived in Eqs. (6.1.4)–(6.1.7). Adapting

Eq. (6.1.7), we have

$$P[Q(t_2) = 1|Q(t_1) = 1] = \tfrac{1}{2}[1 + e^{-2\lambda(t_2 - t_1)}] \tag{6.1.11}$$

The second term in the second form of Eq. (6.1.10) is exactly what we derived in Eq. (6.1.7), so we obtain

$$P_{Q(t_1)Q(t_2)}(1, 1) = \tfrac{1}{2}[1 + e^{-2\lambda(t_2 - t_1)}] \times \tfrac{1}{2}[1 + e^{-2\lambda t_1}] \tag{6.1.12}$$

We have thus determined the second-order PMF of the output of the semirandom flip-flop for one of four possible states. If needed, the others can be derived similarly.

PMFs or expectations? The ultimate and complete description of this random process would be the PMFs to any order desired. Such detail is not required for many basic theoretical and practical applications. Expectations, which represent averages, give much less information about a random process, but the information given is often adequate to design systems for processing a signal. We turn, therefore, to the first- and second-order expectations, which are the mean and the autocorrelation function of $Q(t)$.

The mean of $Q(t)$. By mean, we do not mean the time average but the statistical mean. Look back at Fig. 6.1.5, and consider that you have a vertical line at some time t. The intersection of that line and the random process $Q(t)$ is either 1 or 0 for the individual functions in the random process. The average of those 1s and 0s would be the statistical mean at that time. The mean of a Bernoulli random variable is easily calculated from Eqs. (6.1.7) and (6.1.8) as

$$\mu_{Q(t)} = E[Q(t)] = 0 \times P_{Q(t)}(0) + 1 \times P_{Q(t)}(1) = 0 \times \tfrac{1}{2}[1 - e^{-2\lambda t}] + 1 \times \tfrac{1}{2}[1 + e^{-2\lambda t}]$$

$$= \tfrac{1}{2}[1 + e^{-2\lambda t}] \tag{6.1.13}$$

This result looks like the top curve in Fig. 6.1.7, and this makes sense. Because the FF was preset to 1, the mean should start out at 1, but with time the mean should approach $\tfrac{1}{2}$ because the output becomes randomized by the Poisson clock pulses.

The autocorrelation function. The autocorrelation function is defined as

$$R_Q(t_1, t_2) = E[Q(t_1)Q(t_2)] \tag{6.1.14}$$

For discrete bivariate random variables, this function is

$$R_Q(t_1, t_2) = E[Q(t_1)Q(t_2)] = \sum \sum_{\text{all states}} q_1 q_2 P_{Q(t_1)Q(t_2)}(q_1, q_2)$$

$$= 0 \times 0 \times P_{Q(t_1)Q(t_2)}(0, 0)$$
$$+ 0 \times 1 \times P_{Q(t_1)Q(t_2)}(0, 1)$$
$$+ 1 \times 0 \times P_{Q(t_1)Q(t_2)}(1, 0)$$
$$+ 1 \times 1 \times P_{Q(t_1)Q(t_2)}(1, 1) \tag{6.1.15}$$

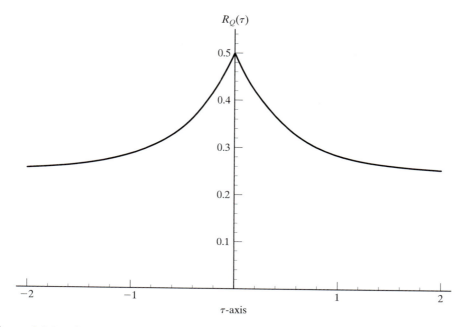

Figure 6.1.9 The autocorrelation function of the output state of the random flip-flop.

Clearly, the only term in the sum that contributes is the last, which requires the probability we calculated in Eq. (6.1.12). The autocorrelation function is

$$R_Q(t_1, t_2) = 1 \times 1 \times \tfrac{1}{2}[1 + e^{-2\lambda(t_2 - t_1)}] \times \tfrac{1}{2}[1 + e^{-2\lambda t_1}] \qquad (6.1.16)$$

The result in Eq. (6.1.16) is hard to interpret because it has an early period before the system randomizes. That is why we call this the "semirandom" FF case. We now remove that preset condition to have a fully random FF. We may do this in two ways: we can randomize the initial output state, or we can examine the results far away from the initial time. The latter is easier, so we make the following changes in Eq. (6.1.16)

- Let $t_1 \to$ large.
- Keep $t_2 - t_1 =$ constant $= \tau$.
- Realize that the expectation is independent of the sign of $t_2 - t_1 = \tau$.

With these changes Eq. (6.1.16) becomes

$$R_Q(\tau) = E[Q(t)Q(t + \tau)] = \tfrac{1}{4}[1 + e^{-2\lambda|\tau|}] \qquad (6.1.17)$$

A plot of Eq. (6.1.17) is shown in Fig. 6.1.9, for $\lambda = 1$.

The autocorrelation is now a function only of time difference, τ. Absolute time does not matter because we have moved far from the time origin, where we preset to 1. Note that under these conditions, the mean is a constant, Eq. (6.1.13).

Example 6.1.2:   Micrometeorite counter ⎯⎯⎯⎯⎯⎯⎯⎯⎯⎯⎯⎯⎯⎯⎯⎯⎯⎯⎯⎯⎯⎯

A satellite is equipped with a micrometeorite counter. The counter records, on average, 3000 events per day. The input stage of the digital counter changes state for each input. Assuming voltage levels of 0 and 2 voltage, what is the value of the autocorrelation function for that output for a time difference of 15 seconds.

Solution   The average rate would be $\lambda = 3000 \times \frac{1}{24} \times \frac{1}{60} = 2.083 \frac{\text{events}}{\text{minute}}$. The autocorrelation function for the output is given in Eq. (6.1.17) for logic levels of 0 and 1 V. For logic levels of 0 and 2 V, the autocorrelation function will increase by a factor of 2^2, since $Q(t)$ is multiplied by itself shifted in time. Thus at $\tau = 0.25$ minute, the autocorrelation function has the value $R_Q(0.25) = 2^2 \times \frac{1}{4}(1 + e^{-2 \times 2.083 \times 0.25}) = 1.353$ V^2.

⎯⎯

Definition of wide-sense stationary (WSS) random processes.   We now are in a position to define WSS random processes. Let $X(t)$ represent a random process. The definition of WSS is that $X(t)$ satisfies two criteria:

1. The mean is constant, $\mu_X = E[X(t)] = $ constant.
2. The autocorrelation is a function of magnitude of time difference only:[2] $R_X(t_1, t_2) = E[X(t_1)X(t_2)] = f(|t_2 - t_1|)$. Another notation for this expression is that $R_X(\tau) = E[X(t)X(t + \tau)] = f(|\tau|)$, where $f(\cdot)$ is an appropriate function.

Interpretation of WSS random processes.   We may interpret WSS random processes as those random processes that look statistically the same at all times, at least as concerns the first- and second-order effects. As we shall see, this means that the total power in the process is constant, and the split between DC and AC power is constant. Thus the DC power and the AC power are constant. This "power" interpretation will be explored later.

The fully random FF random process is WSS. Its mean, Eq. (6.1.13), is constant, $\mu_{Q(t)} \rightarrow \frac{1}{2}$ as $\tau \rightarrow$ large, and its autocorrelation function is a function of $|\tau|$ only, Eq. (6.1.17). Once we get far away from the time of initialization all that matters is differences in time; absolute time does not matter.

Summary and look ahead.   We now have investigated a model for an asynchronous digital signal. Our model is a digital signal that changes states randomly, in accordance with a Poisson process. Some physical realizations of such a signal would be the first stage of a counter monitoring radioactive decay events or monitoring the passage of automobiles on a highway. Our results confirm the WSS nature of the signal. We next develop a model for a synchronous, or clocked, digital signal, then for a random analog signal, and finally for a random noise signal. These remaining sections will be much briefer.

6.1.2 Modeling a Synchronous Digital Signal

The model.   Our probability model for a synchronous (clocked) digital signal is shown in Fig. 6.1.10. The probability model shown in Fig. 6.1.10 is random in two ways. The signal is 1 or 0 V in each clock period, with equal probability. The other random aspect is the delay to the beginning of the first full clock period from the arbitrary time origin. This we represent as D in Fig. 6.1.11.

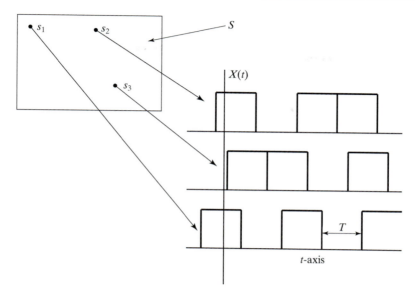

Figure 6.1.10   A probability model for a synchronous digital signal. The clock period is T, and each period contains a 1 or 0 with equal probability. The outcomes of the chance experiment lead to all such sequences. Note that the digital functions are synchronous with themselves but have no synchronism with each other. There is therefore no absolute time origin.

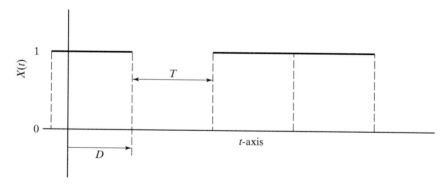

Figure 6.1.11   Definition of the clock period, T, and the delay to the beginning of the first full clock period, D, from the arbitrary time origin. In each clock period, the signal is 1 or 0 with equal probability.

The period, T, in Fig. 6.1.11 is a known constant, but the delay, D, is a random variable that is uniformly distributed between 0 and T:[3]

$$f_D(d) = \frac{1}{T}, \quad 0 < d \le T, \quad \text{zow} \tag{6.1.18}$$

The mean.   Again, the random process is 1 or 0 at any time, and we can easily calculate the mean:

$$\mu_{X(t)} = E[X(t)] = 0 \times P[X(t) = 0] + 1 \times \underbrace{P[X(t) = 1]}_{1/2} = \tfrac{1}{2} \text{ volt} \tag{6.1.19}$$

Thus the mean is $\frac{1}{2}$ V at all times because the signal is equally likely to be 1 or 0.

The autocorrelation function.   The autocorrelation function is defined as

$$R_X(t_1, t_2) = E[X(t_1)X(t_2)] \tag{6.1.20}$$

Because $X(t)$ is binary in nature the expectation is similar to Eq. (6.1.15), and the only term that contributes is

$$R_X(t_1, t_2) = 1 \times 1 \times P[(X(t_1) = 1) \cap (X(t_2) = 1)] \tag{6.1.21}$$

There are two cases to consider.

Case 1: If $t_2 - t_1 > T$, then at least one clock transition between t_1 and t_2 is sure to occur, and the values at $X(t_1)$ and $X(t_2)$ are independent and equally likely to be 1 or 0. In this case Eq. (6.1.21) becomes

$$R_X(t_1, t_2) = 1 \times 1 \times P[(X(t_1) = 1) \cap (X(t_2) = 1)] = 1 \times 1 \times \tfrac{1}{2} \times \tfrac{1}{2} = \tfrac{1}{4} \tag{6.1.22}$$

Case 2: If $t_2 - t_1 < T$, then a clock transition may or may not occur between t_1 and t_2. We denote the event of a clock transition occurring in this period as $CT = \{t_1 < \text{clock transition} < t_2\}$. The probability of this event and its complement are

$$P[CT] = \int_{t_1}^{t_2} f_D(d)d(d) = \frac{t_2 - t_1}{T} \quad \text{and} \quad P[\overline{CT}] = 1 - P[CT] = 1 - \frac{t_2 - t_1}{T}, \ 0 < t_2 - t_1 < T \tag{6.1.23}$$

In the case where $t_2 - t_1 < T$, we may express the autocorrelation function using the law of total probability [Eq. (1.5.7)] as

$$
\begin{aligned}
R_X(t_1, t_2) &= 1 \times 1 \times P[(X(t_1) = 1) \cap (X(t_2) = 1)] \\
&= P[(X(t_1) = 1) \cap (X(t_2) = 1)|CT] \times P[CT] \\
&\quad + P[(X(t_1) = 1) \cap (X(t_2) = 1)|\overline{CT}] \times P[\overline{CT}]
\end{aligned}
\tag{6.1.24}
$$

In the first term, in which a clock transition occurs between t_1 and t_2, $X(t_1)$ and $X(t_2)$ are independent and equally likely to be 1 or 0, and it follows that

$$P[(X(t_1) = 1) \cap (X(t_2) = 1)|CT] \times P[CT] = \frac{1}{2} \times \frac{1}{2} \times \frac{t_2 - t_1}{T} \tag{6.1.25}$$

where Eq. (6.1.23) was used. In the second term in Eq. (6.1.24), in which a clock transition does not occur between t_1 and t_2, $X(t_1)$ and $X(t_2)$ are the same, with 1 and 0 equally probable, and it follows that

$$P[(X(t_1) = 1) \cap (X(t_2) = 1)|\overline{CT}] \times P[\overline{CT}] = \frac{1}{2} \times \left(1 - \frac{t_2 - t_1}{T}\right) \tag{6.1.26}$$

where again Eq. (6.1.23) was used. Substituting the results of Eqs. (6.1.25) and (6.1.26) into Eq. (6.1.24) and combining terms, we have the result in Eq. (6.1.27) for case 2, $t_2 - t_1 < T$:

$$R_X(t_1, t_2) = \frac{1}{4} \times \frac{t_2 - t_1}{T} + \frac{1}{2} \times \left(1 - \frac{t_2 - t_1}{T}\right) = \frac{1}{2} - \frac{1}{4}\left(\frac{t_2 - t_1}{T}\right) \tag{6.1.27}$$

We now combine Eqs. (6.1.27) and (6.1.22) to get the final result, with the following two additional changes. We note that only the difference between t_2 and t_1 matters; thus we substitute $\tau = t_2 - t_1$. Finally, it does not matter which is greater, t_1 or t_2, because the same probabilities will apply, and thus $|\tau|$ is the true variable of the autocorrelation. The final result is

$$R_X(\tau) = \frac{1}{2} - \frac{1}{4}\frac{|\tau|}{T}, \quad 0 < |\tau| < T$$
$$= \frac{1}{4}, \quad |\tau| > T \tag{6.1.28}$$

This autocorrelation function is plotted in Fig. 6.1.12.

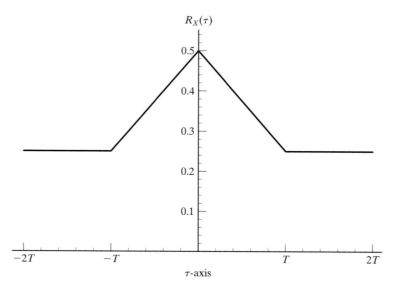

Figure 6.1.12   Autocorrelation function of the model of a synchronous digital signal.

Model is WSS. The model for the synchronous digital signal is WSS, since its mean is constant, Eq. (6.1.19), and its autocorrelation function depends on time differences alone, Eq. (6.1.28). This is a consequence of the stable nature of the statistical properties of the model. The randomization of the synchronous digital signal over the clock period is clearly shown in Fig. 6.1.12.

6.1.3 Modeling a Random Analog Signal

The random sinusoid. In the study of linear systems, we rightly focus much effort in solving problems with sinusoidal waveforms. Sinusoids are used in signal analysis as a basic building block with which more complex waveforms can be analyzed. Sinusoids are also used as carriers for communication signals.

In AC circuit problems, for example, we deal with circuits with known sources, including the amplitude, frequency, and phase of the sinusoidal sources. In contrast, in the real situation that we deal with in a power system we know the frequency quite well, 60 Hz in the United States, and we know the amplitude of the voltage within reasonable bounds, from about $110\sqrt{2}$ to about $125\sqrt{2}$ V, but when we turn on a switch, say to start a dishwasher, we engage the switch at a random time. This is equivalent to turning on the voltage at a random phase. This equivalence is suggested in Fig. 6.1.13.

Semi- and fully random sinusoids. A semirandom sinusoid is a sinusoid turned on at a random time. This model is useful in studying turn-on characteristics of electrical equipment. Here we will study the fully random sinusoid, by which we mean a sinusoid of random phase that exists for all time. Figure 6.1.14 gives the results of a chance experiment that generates six random phases and plots the associated sinusoids.

Properties of the random process. Our main concern is WSS random processes, which require the analysis of the mean and the autocorrelation function. These we can obtain without the PDFs of the random process because we can express this random process as a function of the random variable, Θ, which is the phase of the various sinusoids. Thus we may represent this

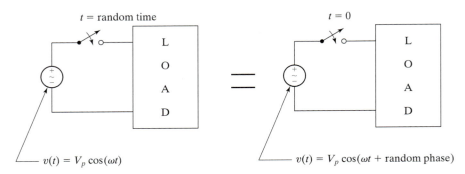

Figure 6.1.13 Turning on a sinusoid at a random time is equivalent to turning on a sinusoid of random phase. The latter would be a semirandom sinusoid. The fully random sinusoid has random phase but no turn-on. This will be our model for a random analog signal.

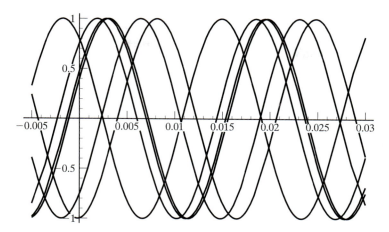

Figure 6.1.14 Six members of the random process modeling a random analog signal. Here we show six sinusoids of random phase. The fully random process treats the phase as a uniformly distributed random variable.

random process simply:

$$V(t, \Theta) = V_p \cos(\omega_1 t + \Theta) \text{ volts} \tag{6.1.29}$$

where V_p is the peak value, ω_1 is the frequency in radians per second (rad/s) and Θ is a uniformly distributed random variable with the PDF

$$f_\Theta(\theta) = \frac{1}{2\pi}, \ 0 < \theta \leq 2\pi, \ \text{zow} \tag{6.1.30}$$

The mean of $V(t)$. We now can calculate the mean and autocorrelation function of the random process by averaging with respect to Θ, as presented in Eq. (3.1.10). The mean is

$$\mu_{V(t)} = E[V(t, \Theta)] = \int_{-\infty}^{+\infty} V(t, \theta) f_\Theta(\theta) \, d\theta = \int_0^{2\pi} V_p \cos(\omega t + \theta) \frac{1}{2\pi} \, d\theta = 0 \tag{6.1.31}$$

Note that the integration in Eq. (6.1.31) is with respect to θ, not time. The results are zero because we are averaging a sinusoid over a full cycle in θ with ωt fixed.

The autocorrelation function. The autocorrelation function can be determined by the same process:

$$R_V(t_1, t_2) = E[V(t_1, \Theta) V(t_2, \Theta)] = \int_0^{2\pi} V_p \cos(\omega_1 t_1 + \theta) V_p \cos(\omega_1 t_2 + \theta) \frac{1}{2\pi} \, d\theta \tag{6.1.32}$$

The integration in Eq. (6.1.32) can be performed with the aid of a trig identity,[4] which gives the form

$$R_V(t_1, t_2) = \frac{V_p^2}{2} \int_0^{2\pi} [\cos(\omega_1(t_2 - t_1)) + \cos(\omega_1(t_2 + t_1) + 2\theta)] \frac{1}{2\pi} \, d\theta \tag{6.1.33}$$

The second term in Eq. (6.1.33) integrates to zero because the average is performed over two cycles of the sinusoid. The first term in Eq. (6.1.33) has no θ dependence; hence the autocorrelation function is

$$R_V(t_1, t_2) = \frac{V_p^2}{2} \cos(\omega_1(t_2 - t_1)) \int_0^{2\pi} \frac{1}{2\pi} \, d\theta = \frac{V_p^2}{2} \cos(\omega_1(t_2 - t_1)) \tag{6.1.34}$$

If again we let $t_2 - t_1 = \tau$, we have

$$R_V(\tau) = \frac{V_p^2}{2} \cos(\omega_1 \tau) \quad \text{volts}^2 \tag{6.1.35}$$

The unit of volts squared relates to power and will be discussed presently.

The fully random sinusoid is WSS.   Note that the mean of the fully random sinusoid is zero, which is a constant, and the autocorrelation function is an even function of $t_2 - t_1 = \tau$. Thus the fully random sinusoid is WSS.

Example 6.1.3:   The power line _____
The power input for domestic appliances is 120 V, rms, and a frequency of 60 hertz (Hz), but phase is arbitrary relative to the clocks in your house. What would be the autocorrelation function of the voltage of an appliance output in your house?

Solution   The peak voltage would be $120\sqrt{2} = 169.7$ V. The frequency would be $\omega_1 = 2\pi \times 60 = 377.0$ rad/s. Using Eq. (6.1.35) we find the autocorrelation function to be $R_V(\tau) = \frac{(120\sqrt{2})^2}{2} \cos(377\tau)$ volts^2.

_____

You do it.   Assume you have an analog clock in your house that has a minute hand 4 in. long. Let $X(t) =$ the horizontal projection of the tip of the minute hand relative to the axis of rotation. Let t be time in minutes from the instant of your birth. Find the autocorrelation of X in feet squared and evaluate at $\tau = 10$ minutes.

```
myanswer = ? ;
```

```
Evaluate
```

For the answer, see endnote 5.

6.1.4 Ergodic Random Processes

Time averages.   The following material relates to WSS random processes and to deterministic as well as to random signals. Figure 6.1.15 shows the definitions of the total signal, $v(t)$, the DC component of the signal, V_{DC}, and the AC component of the signal, $v_{AC}(t)$.

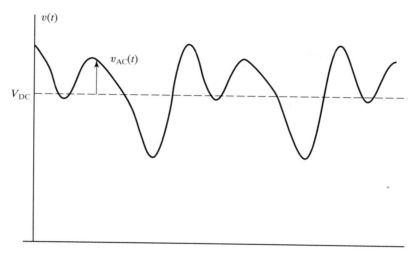

Figure 6.1.15 The definitions of the total signal, $v(t)$, the DC component of the signal, V_{DC}, and the AC component of the signal, $v_{AC}(t)$. Note that in this context "DC" does not mean "direct current" but rather "time-average value," and "AC" does not mean "alternating current" but rather "fluctuating."

For a periodic signal, such as in Fig. 6.1.15, the time average can be determined from one period,

$$\langle v(t) \rangle = \frac{1}{T} \int_0^T v(t)\, dt \tag{6.1.36}$$

but in general one has to average over all time:

$$\langle v(t) \rangle = \lim_{W \to \infty} \frac{1}{W} \int_{-\frac{W}{2}}^{+\frac{W}{2}} v(t)\, dt \tag{6.1.37}$$

where W is the width of a "window" centered on the origin, as shown in Fig. 6.1.16.

"Power" in volts squared. In signal analysis *power* means a measure of the square of the variable. In circuits, the true power would be the voltage squared divided by the impedance level of the circuit in ohms, all multiplied by the power factor if necessary. Here we will deal with power in voltage squared, with the understanding that for real power in watts the impedance level of the circuit must be considered.

The DC value and DC power. The DC value is the time average:

$$V_{DC} = \langle v(t) \rangle \tag{6.1.38}$$

and the DC power is the square of the DC value:

$$P_{DC} = V_{DC}^2 \tag{6.1.39}$$

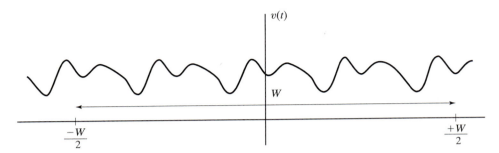

Figure 6.1.16 A "window" over which the function is averaged. The width of the window is allowed to go to infinity, $W \to \infty$, for the time average of the function. This definition of time average works for periodic and random functions.

The AC value and the AC power. The AC value is the total signal minus the DC value:

$$v_{\mathrm{AC}}(t) = v(t) - V_{\mathrm{DC}} \tag{6.1.40}$$

Note that the time average of the AC value is zero:

$$\langle v_{\mathrm{AC}}(t) \rangle = \langle v(t) - V_{\mathrm{DC}} \rangle = \langle v(t) \rangle - \langle V_{\mathrm{DC}} \rangle = V_{\mathrm{DC}} - V_{\mathrm{DC}} = 0 \tag{6.1.41}$$

The time average distributes because averaging is a linear operation. The AC power is the time average of the square of the AC component of the signal:

$$P_{\mathrm{AC}} = \langle v_{\mathrm{AC}}^2(t) \rangle \tag{6.1.42}$$

The total power. The total power in volts squared is the time average of the square of the total voltage, which is also the sum of the DC and AC components, Eq. (6.1.40):

$$P_T = \langle v^2(t) \rangle = \langle (V_{\mathrm{DC}} + v_{\mathrm{AC}}(t))^2 \rangle = \langle V_{\mathrm{DC}}^2 \rangle + \langle 2V_{\mathrm{DC}}v_{\mathrm{AC}}(t) \rangle + \langle v_{\mathrm{AC}}^2(t) \rangle \tag{6.1.43}$$

The middle term in the expansion vanishes:

$$\langle 2V_{\mathrm{DC}}v_{\mathrm{AC}}(t) \rangle = 2V_{\mathrm{DC}}\langle v_{\mathrm{AC}}(t) \rangle = 2V_{\mathrm{DC}} \times 0 = 0 \tag{6.1.44}$$

Thus Eq. (6.1.43) reduces to

$$P_T = P_{\mathrm{DC}} + P_{\mathrm{AC}} \tag{6.1.45}$$

Example 6.1.4:   A square wave ⎯⎯⎯⎯⎯⎯⎯⎯⎯⎯⎯⎯⎯⎯⎯⎯⎯⎯⎯⎯⎯⎯⎯⎯⎯⎯⎯
Consider a periodic square wave having a period T and an amplitude V, as shown in endnote 6. Find the DC and AC power in this signal.

Solution   The DC value is $\frac{V}{2}$, so the DC power is $P_{\mathrm{DC}} = \left(\frac{V}{2}\right)^2 = \frac{V^2}{4}$. The AC signal, $v_{\mathrm{AC}}(t) = v(t) - \frac{V}{2}$, is another square wave going from $+\frac{V}{2}$ to $-\frac{V}{2}$. Since $P_{\mathrm{AC}} = \langle v_{\mathrm{AC}}^2(t) \rangle = \left(\pm\frac{V}{2}\right)^2 = \frac{V^2}{4}$ also. Note that the total power, $P_T = \frac{V^2}{2}$, is the time average of the original square wave squared.

You do it.   If the square wave has the value V twice as long as it has the value 0, what now is the AC power? Let $V = 1$ V.

```
myanswer = ? ;
```

```
Evaluate
```

For the answer, see endnote 7.

The time-average autocorrelation function.   Hitherto we have defined the autocorrelation function as a statistical average, an expectation, as follows:

$$R_V(\tau) = E[V(t)V(t + \tau)] \tag{6.1.46}$$

Thus the (statistical) autocorrelation function involves every member of the family of functions making up the random process. But a time-average autocorrelation function may be defined for a single function. This is true for all periodic deterministic functions, and it is true for each of the "random" functions making up a random process. We replace the expectation operator in Eq. (6.1.46) with the time-average operator for the time-average autocorrelation function:

$$\overline{R}_V(\tau) = \langle v(t)v(t + \tau) \rangle \tag{6.1.47}$$

In words, we average the function times itself shifted τ in the negative t direction. We used the overscore estimator symbol because for a WSS random process the time-average autocorrelation function serves as an estimator for the statistical autocorrelation function.

The time-average autocorrelation function is meaningful for both deterministic and random time functions. In endnote 6 we analyze the time-average autocorrelation function for the square wave used in Example 6.1.4.

Summary.   In this section we gave definitions for the DC and AC components of a signal and of the total, DC, and AC power. These definitions apply to both deterministic and random signals. Power is expressed in volts squared.

The ergodic concept.   We now have in mind two types of averaging: statistical averaging for the mean and autocorrelation function, and time averaging as described in the previous paragraphs and suggested in Fig. 6.1.17. The ergodic concept addresses the relationship between these two types of averages. In general, a WSS ergodic random process, $X(t)$, has the property that statistical averages are equal to time averages. For the mean

$$\mu_{X(t)} = E[X(t)] \quad \text{and} \quad X_{DC} = \langle X(t) \rangle, \text{ but } E[X(t)] = \langle X(t) \rangle \tag{6.1.48}$$

For the autocorrelation functions, we have the corresponding relation:

$$R_X(\tau) = E[X(t)X(t + \tau)] \quad \text{and} \quad \overline{R}_X(\tau) = \langle X(t)X(t + \tau) \rangle, \text{ but } R_X(\tau) = \overline{R}_X(\tau) \tag{6.1.49}$$

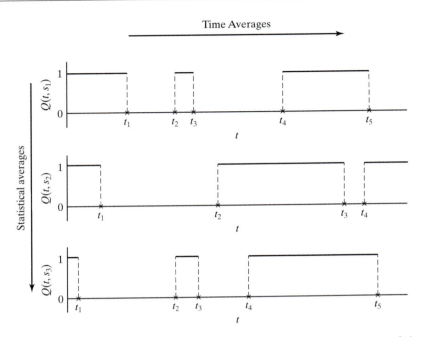

Figure 6.1.17 Time averages must be performed on a single member function of the random process. Statistical averages, the expectation, are performed on the entire random process. The ergodic property requires that the two averages be the same.

Equations (6.1.48) and (6.1.49) are a bit odd in that the statistical averages, $E[X(t)]$ and $E[X(t)X(t+\tau)]$, involve every member function in the random process, whereas the time average, $\langle X(t) \rangle$ and $\langle X(t)X(t+\tau) \rangle$, must of necessity be performed on only one of the member functions of the random process. For Eqs. (6.1.48) and (6.1.49) to be true, the randomness inherent in the entire random process must be present in, and fully represented by, every member function of the random process. The implications of this will be explored after we examine the ergodic property of the fully random sinusoid.

The time-average value and the time-average autocorrelation function of the fully random sinusoid. Because the random sinusoid is a periodic function, we may compute time averages by averaging over one period. Thus the DC value is

$$V_{\text{DC}} = \langle V(t, \theta_i) \rangle = \frac{1}{T} \int_0^T V_p \cos(\omega t + \theta_i) \, dt = 0 \qquad (6.1.50)$$

Note in Eq. (6.1.50) that we have explicitly stated that the random variable, Θ, takes on a specific value, here called θ_i, for the time average. The time average in Eq. (6.1.50) is similar to the statistical average in Eq. (6.1.31), except that we are now averaging in time. Similarly, the result is zero because we are averaging a sinusoid over one full period:

$$V_{DC} = 0 \qquad (6.1.51)$$

The time-average autocorrelation function is

$$\overline{R}_V(\tau) = \langle V(t, \theta_i) V(t + \tau, \theta_i) \rangle = \frac{1}{T} \int_0^T V_p \cos(\omega t + \theta_i) V_p \cos(\omega(t + \tau) + \theta_i) \, dt \qquad (6.1.52)$$

Again we use the trig identity for $\cos A \cos B$ (see endnote 4) with the resulting form

$$\overline{R}_V(\tau) = \frac{V_p^2}{2T} \int_0^T [\cos \omega\tau + \cos(\omega(2t + \tau) + 2\theta_i)] \, dt \qquad (6.1.53)$$

As before, the second term integrates to zero, and the first is constant with respect to the variable of integration. The result is

$$\overline{R}_V(\tau) = \frac{V_p^2}{2T} \cos \omega\tau \int_0^T dt = \frac{V_p^2}{2} \cos \omega\tau \qquad (6.1.54)$$

Comparing time and statistical averages.   The time-average value in Eq. (6.1.51) is the same as the statistical expectation in Eq. (6.1.31), and the time-average autocorrelation function in Eq. (6.1.54) is the same as the statistical expectation in Eq. (6.1.35). We therefore conclude that the fully random sinusoid, which is our model for a random analog signal, is not only WSS but is also ergodic.

Why the ergodic property is important.   The ergodic property is important to the engineering applications of random processes. Consider the following scenario. You are required to design a system to process a certain type of signal. The signal is an ongoing random signal that looks well behaved, so you take a lot of data and study their properties such as the mean and the autocorrelation function. To design your system, you need to generalize that model into a random process. In that generalization you are assuming the ergodic property. Once your system is designed, it needs to work on specific time signals. In effect, you again needed the ergodic property.

Proving that a random process has the ergodic property.   The fully random sinusoid is a random process that is easily shown to be ergodic in mean and autocorrelation function. There are but a few random processes like that. For the rest, the ergodic property is assumed as a matter of convenience, or perhaps necessity. Ultimately, the justification for using the ergodic property is a working system, that is, a good piece of engineering.

Why the autocorrelation function is so important.   When we spoke in Sec. 3.5 about correlation between random variables, we criticized the correlation and the covariance as difficult to interpret, and we focused on the correlation coefficient as the major way that the linear relationship between random variables is described. Yet, in dealing with random processes, we focus on the autocorrelation function, which is the correlation of the random process at one time with itself at another time. In this section we show why the autocorrelation function of a WSS random process contains important information about the random process in a concise form. Our purpose here is to show how to read this information from the autocorrelation function.

The definition of the autocorrelation function of a WSS random process, $X(t)$, is

$$R_X(\tau) = E[X(t)X(t+\tau)] \tag{6.1.55}$$

When the WSS random process is also ergodic, then the time-average autocorrelation function is the same:

$$R_X(\tau) = E[X(t)X(t+\tau)] = \langle x(t)x(t+\tau) \rangle \tag{6.1.56}$$

where $x(t)$ is a member function of the random process.

When $\tau = 0$. Setting $\tau = 0$ gives information about the total power in the random process. From Eq. (6.1.56) at $\tau = 0$, we have

$$R_X(0) = E[X^2(t)] = \langle x^2(t) \rangle = P_T \tag{6.1.57}$$

so the autocorrelation at $\tau = 0$ is the total power in the signal. Because $R_X(0)$ also is the mean-square value of the random process, and since the total power is the sum of the AC and DC powers, it follows that

$$R_X(0) = \sigma_X^2 + \mu_X^2 = P_{AC} + P_{DC} \tag{6.1.58}$$

But for the ergodic random process, the mean is the same as the time average, or DC value, of the member functions, so we assume for all WSS random process that the variance is the AC power and the square of the mean is the DC power:

$$\sigma_X^2 = P_{AC} \text{ and } \mu_X^2 = P_{DC} \tag{6.1.59}$$

When τ gets large. We consider now random processes that lose coherence as τ gets large. This would be true of any random process modeling a physical process without long-term memory. It is true, for example, in our models for synchronous and asynchronous digital signals; however, it is not true for the random sinusoid because this random process never becomes randomized in time. When we let τ get large in Eq. (6.1.55), $X(t)$ and $X(t+\tau)$ become uncorrelated, and the autocorrelation function must approach the square of the mean, as shown by Eq. (3.5.15), when the covariance is zero:[8]

$$R_X(\tau) \underset{\tau \to \infty}{\longrightarrow} E[X(t)] \times E[X(t+\tau)] = \mu_X^2 = P_{DC} \tag{6.1.60}$$

From Eq. (6.1.60) it follows that the difference between the autocorrelation at $\tau = 0$ and at $\tau \to \infty$ is the variance, or the AC power:

$$R_X(0) - R_X(\infty) = \sigma_X^2 = P_{AC} \tag{6.1.61}$$

Thus we can readily derive the total power, the AC power, and the DC power from the autocorrelation function of a WSS ergodic random process.

The coherence function. The correlation coefficient between two random variables, X and Y, is defined in Eq. (3.5.17) as

$$\rho_{XY} = \frac{E[XY] - \mu_X \mu_Y}{\sigma_X \sigma_Y} \tag{6.1.62}$$

Consider now the random process $X(t)$. If we let $X \to X(t)$ and $Y \to X(t+\tau)$, the result is

$$\rho_X(\tau) = \frac{E[X(t)X(t+\tau)] - \mu_X \mu_X}{\sigma_X \sigma_X} = \frac{R_X(\tau) - R_X(\infty)}{R_X(0) - R_X(\infty)} \tag{6.1.63}$$

The function $\rho_X(\tau)$ we will call the *coherence function* because it gives the correlation coefficient between the WSS random process at some time and itself at some increment of time τ later or earlier. Note that $\rho_X(0) = 1$.

The coherence time. A WSS random process that decorrelates as τ increases has a characteristic time during which it maintains a degree of coherence; or one could also say that after a period of time it decorrelates. We define a coherence time as that time in τ beyond which the correlation coefficient remains below 0.1. Thus the coherence time, τ_c, is defined as

$$|\rho_X(\tau)| \le 0.1 \text{ for all } \tau > \tau_c \tag{6.1.64}$$

We could also call the coherence time the *decorrelation time,* since this is the time when the random process loses most of its self-correlation, or even *correlation time,* since this is the time period over which the random process retains a measure of correlation. We give examples later.

A standard form for the autocorrelation function. If we solve Eq. (6.1.63) for $R_X(\tau)$ and use Eqs. (6.1.61) and (6.1.60) we obtain the form

$$R_X(\tau) = \sigma_X^2 \rho_X(\tau) + \mu_X^2 = P_{AC} \rho_X(\tau) + P_{DC} \tag{6.1.65}$$

Thus the autocorrelation function contains information about the total power, the AC power, the DC power, and the coherence properties of the random process. We now apply Eq. (6.1.65) to the three random process models that we have analyzed in this section.

The asynchronous digital signal model. The model for the asynchronous random process, the fully random flip-flop, has an autocorrelation function of Eq. (6.1.66), repeated from Eq. (6.1.17),

$$R_Q(\tau) = \tfrac{1}{4}[1 + e^{-2\lambda|\tau|}] = \underbrace{\tfrac{1}{4}}_{P_{AC}} \underbrace{e^{-2\lambda|\tau|}}_{\rho_Q(\tau)} + \underbrace{\tfrac{1}{4}}_{P_{DC}} \tag{6.1.66}$$

Here the autocorrelation function is readily placed into the form of Eq. (6.1.65), and the various components are evident. Because $Q(t)$ varies randomly between 1 and 0, with equal probability, the DC value is $\tfrac{1}{2}$, and hence the DC power is $\tfrac{1}{4}$. Because 1^2 is also 1, the total power also must be $\tfrac{1}{2}$, and hence the AC power must be $\tfrac{1}{2} - \tfrac{1}{4} = \tfrac{1}{4}$. These values are identified in Eq. (6.1.66). The coherence function shows a steady loss of coherence due to the random clock pulses. The coherence time is found to be

$$e^{-2\lambda|\tau_c|} = 0.1 \Rightarrow \tau_c = \frac{\ln 10}{2\lambda} = \frac{1.15}{\lambda} \tag{6.1.67}$$

The synchronous model.   The model for the synchronous random process yields an autocorrelation function in Eq. (6.1.28) of

$$R_X(\tau) = \frac{1}{2} - \frac{1}{4}\frac{|\tau|}{T}, \quad 0 < |\tau| < T$$
$$= \frac{1}{4}, \quad |\tau| > T \tag{6.1.68}$$

which can be placed in the form

$$R_X(\tau) = \frac{1}{4}\left[1 - \frac{|\tau|}{T}\right] + \frac{1}{4}, \quad 0 < |\tau| < T$$
$$= \frac{1}{4}, \quad |\tau| > T$$

Here again we have a DC power of $\frac{1}{4}$, an AC power of $\frac{1}{4}$, and a coherence function of

$$\rho_X(\tau) = 1 - \frac{|\tau|}{T}, \quad 0 < |\tau| \le T, \text{ zow} \tag{6.1.69}$$

The coherence time for this model is

$$\rho_X(\tau_c) = 1 - \frac{|\tau_c|}{T} = 0.1 \Rightarrow \tau_c = 0.9T \tag{6.1.70}$$

The signal loses all coherence in one clock period, and our definition gives an answer very close to this value.

The analog model.   Although the random sinusoid does not lose coherence, the model in Eq. (6.1.65) still fits very well. The autocorrelation function is given in Eq. (6.1.35) as

$$R_V(\tau) = \frac{V_p^2}{2}\cos\omega\tau \quad \text{V}^2 \tag{6.1.71}$$

which we may place into the form of Eq. (6.1.65) as

$$R_V(\tau) = \underbrace{\frac{V_p^2}{2}}_{P_{AC}}\underbrace{\cos\omega\tau}_{\rho_V(\tau)} + \underbrace{0}_{P_{DC}} \tag{6.1.72}$$

Note the AC and DC power are clearly represented, and the coherence function is

$$\rho_V(\tau) = \cos\omega\tau \tag{6.1.73}$$

This coherence function never goes to zero, which tell us that the random sinusoid never loses coherence. No coherence time exists.

Summary.   We examined three random processes that model digital and analog signals, defined WSS and ergodic random processes, discussed time averages and statistical averages, and showed how to extract from the autocorrelation function important information about power and coherence properties. In Sec. 6.2, Spectral Analysis of Random Signals, we show that additional important information is contained in the autocorrelation function; but first we must give one further model, that for Gaussian noise.

6.1.5 Model for Wideband Noise

Many physical processes generate wideband noise, also called *broadband* noise. Examples are resistor thermal noise, antenna noise from atmospheric and extraterrestrial sources, and a variety of noise mechanisms in electronic devices due to the discrete nature of electricity. Figure 6.1.18 shows something of what such noise looks like.

The random process model.   A random process model for such noise would consist of a large number of outcomes, each with its associated noise signal. We make the following assumptions about this random process.

1. *The noise is Gaussian.* This assumption is appropriate because of the complex mechanisms associated with the generation of such noise. This is logical and is experimentally verifiable in most cases.

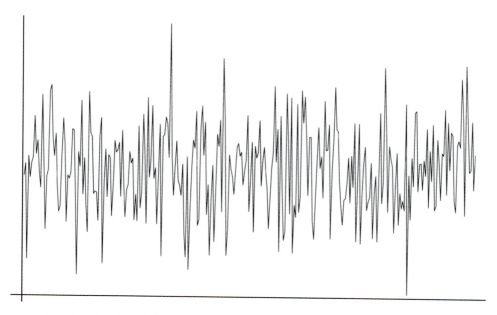

Figure 6.1.18   A noise signal. Such signals are associated with the thermal motion of carriers, discrete carrier phenomena, and other natural sources of noise. Sensitive analog electronic equipment inherently adds such noise to the signal.

2. *The noise is WSS.* This will be true provided the noise source is stable.
3. *The noise is ergodic.* The random properties of the random process are fully contained in any of the member functions.

The autocorrelation model. We assume an autocorrelation model in the form of Eq. (6.1.65)

$$R_X(\tau) = \sigma_X^2 \rho_X(\tau) + \mu_X^2 \tag{6.1.74}$$

In general, we have AC and DC power, represented by σ_X^2 and μ_X^2, respectively, and the coherence function, $\rho_X(\tau)$, is determined by the physical system producing the noise. These three components of the noise could be determined from a time-average autocorrelation function performed on one piece of data. We will give an example in Sec. 6.3.

The PDFs. Because the random process is Gaussian, we can state $X(t) = N(\mu_X, \sigma_X^2)$ at any time. Thus we can establish the probability that the signal exceeds a certain level at any time:

$$f_{X(t)}(x) = \frac{1}{\sigma\sqrt{2\pi}} \exp\left[-\frac{1}{2}\left(\frac{x - \mu_X}{\sigma_X}\right)^2\right] \quad \text{and} \quad P[X(t) > x] = 1 - \Phi\left(\frac{x - \mu_X}{\sigma_X}\right) \tag{6.1.75}$$

From the ergodic property we can also say these properties will be reflected in the time behavior of any member function. For example, the fraction of the time that $X(t)$ spends above x will also be $1 - \Phi\left(\frac{x-\mu_X}{\sigma_X}\right)$. Such analysis is useful in the design of signal-processing devices. Second Eq. (3.5.34), and higher-order PDFs, can also be written, with the coherence function playing the role of the correlation coefficient.

6.1.6 Relationships Between Two WSS Random Processes

In many contexts, two WSS random processes much be considered in the analysis of a random system. In a communication system, we may be dealing with one random process representing the signal and another representing the noise; or in a signal-processing system we may be dealing with one random process representing the input signal and another representing the output signal. In this section we discuss means for relating two such random processes, call them $X(t)$ and $Y(t)$. We assume them to be WSS random processes and jointly WSS, meaning that any relationship between them is also independent of absolute time in first- and second-order matters such as mean and power relationships.

Cross-correlation. The cross-correlations between two jointly WSS random processes, $X(t)$ and $Y(t)$, are defined as

$$R_{XY}(\tau) = E[X(t)Y(t + \tau)] \quad \text{and} \quad R_{YX}(\tau) = E[Y(t)X(t + \tau)] \tag{6.1.76}$$

From the definitions in Eq. (6.1.76) and the time-invariant nature of the WSS random processes, the symmetry property is easily shown to be $R_{XY}(-\tau) = R_{YX}(\tau)$. If $X(t)$ and $Y(t)$ are independent random processes, then the cross-correlations reduce to the product of the means:

$$R_{XY}(\tau) = R_{YX}(\tau) = \mu_X\mu_Y, \text{ if } X(t) \text{ and } Y(t) \text{ are independent.} \tag{6.1.77}$$

A cross-covariance function between $X(t)$ and $Y(t)$ can be defined similar to Eq. (3.5.14). When $X(t)$ and $Y(t)$ are independent, the cross-covariance function is zero for all τ.

An application of cross-correlation as a signal-detection process was presented in the Venus radar experiment described in Chapter 1. There, you may recall, a random sequence of radar pulses was bounced off Venus, and the return signal was compared through cross-correlation with the transmitted sequence. The value of τ that gave the maximum return gave information about the round-trip travel time and hence on the distance to Venus. We will use the cross-correlation function in the analysis of linear systems in Sec. 6.3.

The sum of two jointly WSS random processes.   Let $Z(t) = X(t) + Y(t)$ represent the sum of two random processes. The mean of $Z(t)$ is simply $\mu_Z = \mu_X + \mu_Y$, regardless of any relationship between $X(t)$ and $Y(t)$. The autocorrelation function of $Z(t)$ is

$$R_Z(\tau) = E[(X(t) + Y(t))(X(t + \tau) + Y(t + \tau))]$$

$$= E[X(t)X(t + \tau)] + E[X(t)Y(t + \tau)] + E[Y(t)X(t + \tau)] + E[Y(t)Y(t + \tau)] \quad (6.1.78)$$

$$= R_X(\tau) + R_{XY}(\tau) + R_{YX}(\tau) + R_Y(\tau)$$

Thus the sum of $X(t)$ and $Y(t)$ is WSS and can be expressed in terms of the auto- and cross-correlation functions of $X(t)$ and $Y(t)$. If $X(t)$ and $Y(t)$ are independent, Eq. (6.1.78) reduces to

$$R_Z(\tau) = R_X(\tau) + R_Y(\tau) + 2\mu_X \mu_Y \qquad (6.1.79)$$

which says that if either random process has zero mean, the autocorrelation function of the sum is the sum of the autocorrelation functions.

Example 6.1.5:   Analog signal plus noise _____

Consider the sum of the random analog signal and zero-mean broadband Gaussian noise

$$Z(t) = V_p \cos(\omega_1 t + \Theta) + N(t) \qquad (6.1.80)$$

where Θ is a random phase uniformly distributed between 0 and 2π, and $R_N(\tau) = \sigma_N^2 \rho_N(\tau)$. Find the autocorrelation function of $Z(t)$.

Solution   According to Eq. (6.1.79), the autocorrelation of such a sum is the sum of the autocorrelation functions, plus a constant. The autocorrelation function of the random sinusoid is given in Eq. (6.1.35), and the autocorrelation function of the noise is given in the problem statement. The autocorrelation function of the sum is

$$R_Z(t) = \frac{V_p^2}{2} \cos(\omega_1 \tau) + \sigma_N^2 \rho_N(\tau) \qquad (6.1.81)$$

In this case the constant is zero, since both random processes have zero mean. For $\tau \to$ large, $\rho_N(\tau) \to 0$, and the periodic analog signal will increasingly dominate the sum. Thus periodic signals can be detected in broadband noise by autocorrelation. Indeed, the cross-correlation between the random analog signal and $Z(t)$ would give the first term in Eq. (6.1.81) directly without the noise term.

You do it.   Let the signal-to-noise ratio before autocorrelation be 10 and $\rho_N(\tau) = e^{-10000|\tau|}$. What value of τ improves the signal-to-noise ratio to 100? Give your answer in milliseconds.

```
myanswer =   ?          ;
```

```
Evaluate
```

For the answer, see endnote 9.

The product of two jointly WSS random processes.   Now let $Z(t) = X(t)Y(t)$, where $X(t)$ and $Y(t)$ are independent jointly WSS random processes. As we shall see in Sec. 6.2, this represents some form of modulation. For example, if $X(t)$ were some nonnegative signal, and $Y(t)$ were a sinusoid of random phase, then $Z(t)$ would be an amplitude-modulated signal.

The mean of $Z(t)$ is

$$\mu_Z = E[X(t)Y(t)] = \mu_X \mu_Y \tag{6.1.82}$$

The autocorrelation function of $Z(t)$ is

$$R_Z(\tau) = E[X(t)Y(t)X(t+\tau)Y(t+\tau)] = E[X(t)X(t+\tau)]E[Y(t)Y(t+\tau)] \tag{6.1.83}$$

where we used independence to distribute the expectation operator. The final form in Eq. (6.1.83) is simply the product of the autocorrelation functions of $X(t)$ and $Y(t)$:

$$R_Z(\tau) = R_X(\tau)R_Y(\tau) \tag{6.1.84}$$

Therefore the product of two independent WSS random processes produces a WSS random process whose autocorrelation function is the product of the individual autocorrelation functions of the independent WSS random processes. The significance of Eq. (6.1.84) will be investigated in Sec. 6.2.

6.1.7 Discrete-Time Random Processes

Modern signal-processing methods are increasingly using digital signal processing (DSP) techniques for both linear and nonlinear signal filtering and detection.

In Figure 6.1.19 we show an analog signal with dots representing the information sampled and retained for processing. When the signal is random the random process representing the signal becomes a sequence of random variables representing the random process at the sample times. We might represent this sampling process as

$$X(t) \to X(nT_s) \to X(n) \tag{6.1.85}$$

where T_s is the sampling interval, and n is an index integer associated with each sample. The last form, which omits the sampling interval, would be the form of the data in the information-processing system, since the time interval of the samples is irrelevant to the signal processing

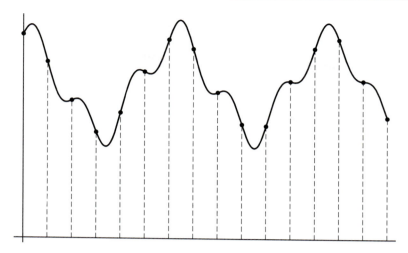

Figure 6.1.19   The continuous line is the signal, and the dots represent the samples that retain the information to be processed. When the signal is random the samples become a sequence of random variables.

system. The end result is that the random process model is reduced to a sequence of random variables, $X(1), X(2), \ldots$. For digital processing the amplitude would be digitized in an A/D converter, but we assume that the number of levels are sufficient to treat the samples as continuous with negligible quantization noise.

The various tools we have developed to represent continuous-time random signals are easily adapted to discrete-time systems. For a WSS sampled process, the autocorrelation function becomes

$$R_X(k) = E[X(n)X(n+k)], \quad k = 0, \pm 1, \pm 2, \ldots \tag{6.1.86}$$

and similarly for cross-correlations and the other matters discussed previously. No new concepts are required in this case, and thus we will not elaborate on discrete-time systems here beyond the following example.

Example 6.1.6:   A sampled random process

A WSS random process with an autocorrelation function $R_X(\tau) = 2 + 5e^{-1000|\tau|}$ is sampled at 1-millisecond intervals. Describe the resulting random variables.

Solution   From the autocorrelation function of the continuous-time process, we know that the DC value of the random process is $\pm\sqrt{2}$, and the variance is $\sigma_X^2 = 5$. The coherence function $\rho_X(\tau) = e^{-1000|\tau|}$ gives us the time scale of the loss of coherence of the random signal. Thus the sequence of random variables representing the sampled system will have a mean of $\mu_X = \pm\sqrt{2}$ (we cannot determine the sign from the information given) and a variance of $\sigma_X^2 = 5$. The autocorrelation function would be

$$R_X(k) = E[X(n \times 1 \text{ ms})X((n + k) \times 1 \text{ ms})] = \underbrace{R_X(10^{-3} k)}_{\text{continuous}-\text{time}} = 2 + 5e^{-|k|}, \; k = 0, \pm 1, \pm 2, \ldots$$

$$(6.1.87)$$

Thus the correlation coefficient of each sample with the adjacent sample before and after is $\rho = e^{-1} = 0.368$.

You do it.   The previous sampling scheme is found to be undersampled, such that information is being lost, so the sample rate is increased to every 200 microseconds. Determine now the correlation coefficient between every other sample.

```
myanswer  =       ?      ;
```

```
Evaluate
```

For the answer, see endnote 10.

Summary.   We offered four models that are useful in the analysis of random signals. We have models for random asynchronous digital signals, synchronous digital signals, analog signals, and noise signals. We explored the concepts of WSS and ergodic random processes and emphasized the autocorrelation function as containing the significant power and time-structure information in the random process. We also defined cross-correlation and discussed the mean and cross-correlation function between two jointly WSS random processes, as well as their sum and product. Discrete time signals were discussed briefly. In Sec. 6.2, we extend the analysis from the time domain to the frequency domain.

6.2 SPECTRAL ANALYSIS OF RANDOM SIGNALS

6.2.1 Review of Spectral Analysis

Sinusoids and spectra.   We may describe a signal in either the time domain or in the frequency domain. A time-domain description gives the signal as a function of time. A frequency-domain description gives the *spectrum* of the signal as a function of frequency. Thus a spectrum represents a signal as the simultaneous existence of many sinusoids of different frequencies.

The frequency domain is introduced in engineering curricula when the response of a linear system to a sinusoidal source is considered. Later, more than one frequency is allowed, as represented by a Fourier series or a Fourier transform. Thus the concept of a spectrum is introduced, and the study of the response of linear time-invariant systems to such spectra is important to many areas of engineering.

Our experience, however, is that these ideas need reviewing at this stage before we apply frequency-domain concepts to the study of random signals. Sections 6.2.1 and 6.2.2 provide such a review of concepts, vocabulary, and notation that will assist us in studying the spectra of random signals.

Four kinds of spectra.   There are four kinds of spectra: voltage spectra and power spectra, and one-sided and two-sided spectra, four combinations in all. We will show the four spectra for a DC plus a simple sinusoid.

The bridge between the time domain and the frequency domain is the formula

$$v(t) = V_0 + V_p \cos(\omega_1 t + \theta) = V_0 + \mathrm{Re}\{\underbrace{V_p e^{j\theta}}_{\underline{V}} e^{j\omega_1 t}\} = V_0 + \frac{\underline{V}}{2} e^{+j\omega_1 t} + \frac{\underline{V}^*}{2} e^{-j\omega_1 t} \quad (6.2.1)$$

where "Re" means real part, $\omega_1 = 2\pi f_1$ is the angular frequency (f_1 is the frequency in hertz), θ is the phase, V_p is the peak value of the sinusoid, and $\underline{V}$ is a phasor representing the amplitude and phase as a complex number and $\underline{V}^*$ its complex conjugate. The DC, with $f = 0$, does not require the complex number or the real part. The phasor representations on the right side suggest two ways to represent the spectrum. The first form, the one beginning with "Re," has one frequency, $f = f_1$. For this form, the spectrum suggested is the one-sided spectrum shown in Fig. 6.2.1.

The rightmost form in Eq. (6.2.1), however, suggests a two-sided spectrum with frequency components at $\pm f_1$, as shown in Fig. 6.2.2. Of course, both show the DC at zero frequency.

We now have two kinds of spectra: one-sided and two-sided voltage spectra. The other two are one- and two-sided power spectra. First, let us review power concepts.

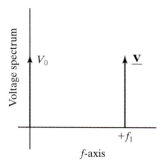

Figure 6.2.1   A one-sided voltage spectrum based on Eq. (6.2.1).

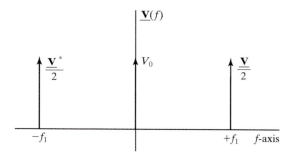

Figure 6.2.2   A two-sided spectrum based on Eq. (6.2.1).

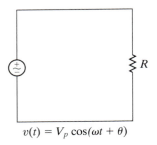

$$v(t) = V_p \cos(\omega t + \theta)$$

Figure 6.2.3   A simple circuit with an AC voltage source and a resistor.

Power in signals.   Consider a simple circuit, as in Fig. 6.2.3, with a sinusoidal source connected to a resistor. The time-average power would be

$$P = \frac{\langle (V_p \cos(\omega t + \theta))^2 \rangle}{R} = \frac{1}{R} \langle \frac{V_p^2}{2} (1 + \cos 2(\omega t + \theta)) \rangle = \frac{V_p^2}{2R} \quad \text{W} \tag{6.2.2}$$

Equation (6.2.2) gives the power in watts. The power in volts squared would simply leave out the resistance in the denominator.[11] We will use the same symbol for power in volts squared and list the units from time to time as a reminder. Thus Eq. (6.2.2) becomes

$$P = \frac{V_p^2}{2} \quad \text{V}^2 \tag{6.2.3}$$

Note that frequency and phase do not matter for power, with one exception. For $f = 0$ (DC), the power is

$$P = V_0^2 \quad \text{V}^2 \tag{6.2.4}$$

where V_0 is the DC voltage. For a DC voltage, the factor 2 in Eq. (6.2.3), which arises in the time-averaging of a sinusoid, is not required.

The power spectrum.   We can associate the power with the frequency of the source as a power spectrum. Again, we can have a one-sided spectrum, as in Fig. 6.2.4, or we can have a two-sided power spectrum, as in Fig. 6.2.5, in which the AC power is split between positive and negative frequency components.

In Figure 6.2.5, we showed the two-sided power spectrum of a sinusoid. We defined a symbol for the power spectrum[12]

$$S(f) = |\underline{\mathbf{V}}(f)|^2 \quad \text{V}^2/\text{Hz (two sides)} \tag{6.2.5}$$

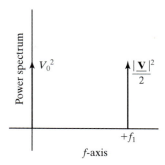

Figure 6.2.4 The one-sided power spectrum. All the power is associated with a positive frequency, $|\underline{V}| = V_p$, plus the DC.

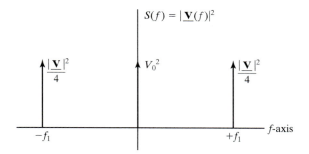

Figure 6.2.5 The power spectrum for a sinusoid plus DC. In the figure we have identified an important advantage of two-sided spectra, namely, that the power spectrum is the square of the voltage spectrum, for both the DC and the AC parts.

and indicated an important feature of two-sided spectra, namely, that the power spectrum is the square of the voltage spectrum. This is true for the DC component also:

$$V(f) = V_0 \quad \text{and} \quad S(f) = V_0^2 \text{ for } f = 0 \tag{6.2.6}$$

The power spectrum is real, involving amplitude only and no phase.

One-sided or two-sided spectra? Both types of spectra express the same information, and both have an important place in our practice. One-sided spectra are appropriate in a laboratory setting or generally when we describe real systems. Two-sided spectra have mathematical advantages for two reasons: the symmetry property for mathematical operations, and the simple relationship between voltage and power spectra. In this chapter we use two-sided spectra to describe signals in the frequency domain. A consequence of using both types of spectra is that one should make it clear, if the context does not, which is being used. For this reason, we will occasionally indicate the type of spectrum we are using (two sides or one side).

Periodic signals. A periodic signal, such as a square wave, can be described in the time domain through a Fourier series:

$$v(t) = V_0 + \sum_{n=1}^{n=+\infty} 2V_n \cos(n\omega_1 t + \theta_n) = \sum_{n=-\infty}^{n=+\infty} \underline{V}_n e^{jn\omega_1 t} \quad \text{V} \tag{6.2.7}$$

where n = harmonic number, ω_1 = the fundamental (also first harmonic), $\underline{V}_n$ = phasor amplitude of the nth harmonic (two sides), V_n = the amplitude of the nth harmonic (two sides), and θ_n = phase of the nth harmonic. The factor 2 in the first form in Eq. (6.2.7) is required because the first sum includes only positive frequencies. The harmonic amplitudes are computed as

$$\underline{V}_n = \frac{1}{T} \int_0^T v(t) e^{-jn\omega t} dt \quad \text{V} \tag{6.2.8}$$

where T = the period of the periodic function = $\frac{2\pi}{\omega_1} = \frac{1}{f_1}$ and $\underline{V}_{-n} = \underline{V}_{+n}^*$. A generic voltage spectrum is shown in Fig. 6.2.6.

The power spectrum is simply the square of the voltage spectrum, as shown in Fig. 6.2.7.

Parseval's theorem. The time domain and the frequency domains are related through Parseval's theorem:

$$\langle v(t)^2 \rangle = \sum_{-\infty}^{+\infty} |\underline{V}_n|^2 \tag{6.2.9}$$

We interpret Eq. (6.2.9) as expressing conservation of power between the two representations of the signal, the left side being power in the time domain and the right being power in the frequency domain.

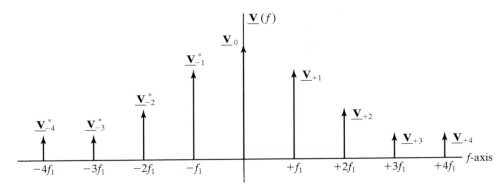

Figure 6.2.6 The two-sided harmonic spectrum of a periodic function. In functions possessing symmetry, some of the harmonics will be missing. The amplitudes of the various harmonics are phasors, with amplitude and phase.

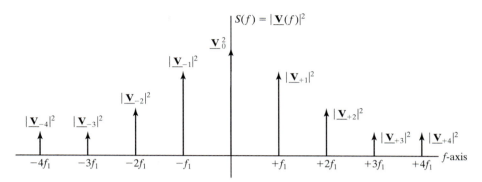

Figure 6.2.7   The power spectrum is the square of the voltage spectrum. For simplicity we left off the complex conjugate signs on the phasor amplitudes of the negative harmonics.

Nonperiodic signals.   The time and frequency domain representations for a signal that occurs only once, such as a single pulse, are represented through the Fourier transform pair

$$\underline{V}(\omega) = \int_{-\infty}^{+\infty} v(t)e^{-j\omega t}\,dt \quad \text{V/Hz} \qquad \text{and} \qquad v(t) = \frac{1}{2\pi} \int_{-\infty}^{+\infty} \underline{V}(\omega)e^{+j\omega t}\,d\omega \quad \text{V} \quad (6.2.10)$$

The first integral is the forward transform, and the second the reverse, or inverse, transform. This review assumes that the reader has familiarity with Fourier transform methods. Endnote 13 gives a short table of useful transforms. Here we hit a critical detail in this subject. The natural mathematical variable in the Fourier transform is ω, the frequency in radians/second. But the natural unit for engineering applications is f, the frequency in hertz. When we do Fourier transforms we will mostly use ω as the variable, but we will always interpret the spectra as V/Hz or V^2/Hz, as we did in Eq. (6.2.10). Attention to this detail is critical to understanding the spectra of random signals.

A single pulse.   A signal often used to illustrate the Fourier transform is the single pulse, Fig. 6.2.8. The Fourier transform of the function in Figure 6.2.8 is

$$\underline{V}(\omega) = \int_{-\tau/2}^{+\tau/2} Ve^{-j\omega t}\,dt = V\tau\frac{\sin \omega\tau/2}{\omega\tau/2} \quad \text{V/Hz} \qquad (6.2.11)$$

The amplitude of this function is shown in Fig. 6.2.9.

Normally the sin x/x function is plotted as going negative, but we have chosen to show the amplitude only. The phase is $0°$ in the center lobe, $180°$ in the adjacent side lobes, and alternates in the outer lobes. The power spectrum is the square of the voltage spectrum:

$$S(\omega) = |V(\omega)|^2 = (V\tau)^2\left(\frac{\sin \omega\tau/2}{\omega\tau/2}\right)^2 \quad \text{V}^2\text{-s/Hz} \qquad (6.2.12)$$

This power spectrum is shown in Fig. 6.2.10.

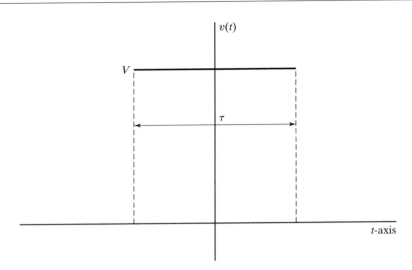

Figure 6.2.8   A single pulse of height *V* and width τ. The Fourier transform is the sin *x/x* function.

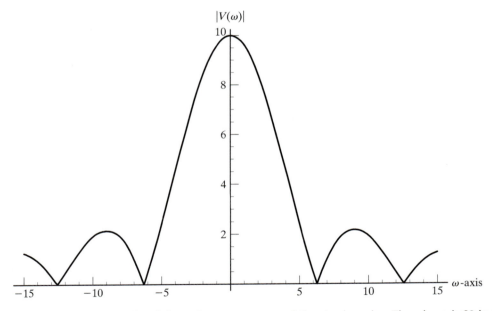

Figure 6.2.9   The amplitude of the voltage spectrum of the single pulse. The phase is 0° in the center lobe, 180° in the adjacent side lobes, and alternates in the outer side lobes. For this plot, $V = 10$ and $\tau = 1$.

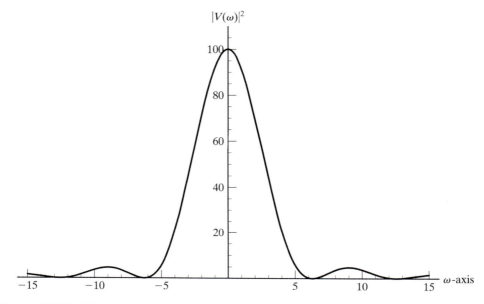

Figure 6.2.10   The power spectrum of a single pulse of height $V = 10$ V and width $\tau = 1$.

The bandwidth of the spectrum.   The required bandwidth is an important characterization of a signal in the frequency domain. For the single pulse, most of the energy in the frequency domain is contained in the main lobe. For convenience, we name the bandwidth, B in hertz, to be the point where the spectrum first goes to zero. Thus the bandwidth for a single pulse is defined by

$$\frac{2\pi B \tau}{2} = \pi \Rightarrow B = \frac{1}{\tau} \text{ Hz} \tag{6.2.13}$$

Thus the required bandwidth is the inverse of the pulse width. It takes a bandwidth of approximately 1 MHz to pass a 1-microsecond pulse, and so forth.

6.2.2 Linear System Theory

Sinusoids and linear time-invariant systems.   One reason we use frequency-domain representations of signals is that linear systems are more easily characterized and understood in the frequency domain than in the time domain. In this section we review spectral concepts as applied to linear systems. We will use a low-pass filter as an example.

Time-domain analysis.   The time-domain representation of an RC low-pass filter is shown in Fig. 6.2.11.

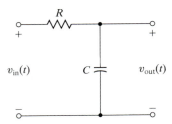

Figure 6.2.11   A low-pass filter in the time domain. The circuit is characterized by a differential equation.

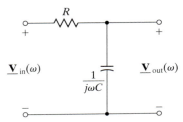

Figure 6.2.12   The low-pass filter in the frequency domain. The signals are represented by spectra, and the circuit is represented by impedances.

The input and output of the low-pass filter are related through the following differential equation:

$$RC\frac{dv_{\text{out}}}{dt} + v_{\text{out}} = v_{\text{in}} \tag{6.2.14}$$

The differential equation (DE) is readily solved for certain cases, such as a single pulse or a square wave, but in general, the DE does not lend much insight to the properties of the filter. (We will deal later with the convolution relationship between input and output.)

Frequency-domain analysis.   We may transform the circuit to the frequency domain by replacing R and C values with their impedances and replacing input and output signals with their spectra. The circuit now takes the form in Fig. 6.2.12.

In the frequency domain the input and output are related by a multiplication with the system function:

$$\underline{\mathbf{V}}_{\text{out}}(\omega) = \underline{\mathbf{V}}_{\text{in}}(\omega) \times \frac{1}{1 + j\omega RC} = \underline{\mathbf{V}}_{\text{in}}(\omega) \times \underline{\mathbf{H}}(j\omega) \tag{6.2.15}$$

where the system function is

$$\underline{\mathbf{H}}(j\omega) = \frac{1}{1 + j\omega RC} \tag{6.2.16}$$

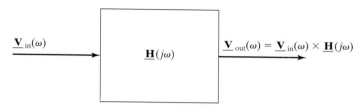

Figure 6.2.13   The input spectrum is multiplied by the system function to produce the output spectrum.

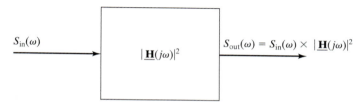

Figure 6.2.14   The output power spectrum is the input power spectrum multiplied by the system function for power. The power system function affects the amplitude of the power spectrum, but phase is irrelevant for power spectra.

The effect of the low-pass filter in the frequency domain is to reduce the high frequencies, indicated by the ω in the denominator, and to produce a phase shift at high frequencies, indicated by the j in the denominator. We can generalize the system as in Fig. 6.2.13.

Power spectra.   Equation (6.2.15) can be multiplied by its complex conjugate to give a relationship between input and output power spectra:

$$|\underline{V}_{\text{out}}(\omega)|^2 = |\underline{V}_{\text{in}}(\omega)|^2 \times \left|\frac{1}{1 + j\omega RC}\right|^2 = |\underline{V}_{\text{in}}(\omega)|^2 \times |\underline{H}(j\omega)|^2 \tag{6.2.17}$$

Because the squares of the input and output voltage spectra are the input and output power spectra, we may rewrite Eq. (6.2.17) as

$$S_{\text{out}}(\omega) = S_{\text{in}}(\omega) \times |\underline{H}(j\omega)|^2 \tag{6.2.18}$$

where the system function for power is

$$|\underline{H}(j\omega)|^2 = \left|\frac{1}{1 + j\omega RC}\right|^2 = \frac{1}{1 + (\omega RC)^2} \tag{6.2.19}$$

The system function for power affects only the amplitude of the spectrum, since phase is not included in the power spectrum. The system diagram of Eq. (6.2.18) is given in Fig. 6.2.14.

Back to the time domain: convolution and the impulse response.   Although we dismissed a time-domain approach for analyzing the effect of the system on the signal, we may

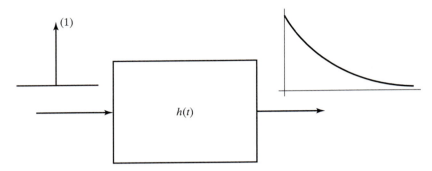

Figure 6.2.15 The impulse response is the response of the system to an impulse of unit area at the input. Mathematically the impulse response is the inverse Fourier transform of the system function.

revisit the time domain by considering the convolution relationship among input, system function, and output. Specifically, if we take the inverse Fourier transform, Eq. (6.2.10), of (6.2.15), we obtain the convolution relationship

$$v_{out}(t) = \int_{-\infty}^{+\infty} v_{in}(\alpha)h(t-\alpha)\,d\alpha = \int_{-\infty}^{+\infty} v_{in}(t-\beta)h(\beta)\,d\beta \qquad (6.2.20)$$

where $h(t)$ is the impulse response of the system, the inverse Fourier transform of the system response.

$$h(t) = \frac{1}{2\pi}\int_{-\infty}^{+\infty} \mathbf{H}(j\omega)e^{+j\omega t}\,d\omega \qquad (6.2.21)$$

For the low-pass filter, the impulse response is known to be

$$h(t) = \frac{1}{RC}e^{-t/RC}, t \geq 0, \text{ zow} \qquad (6.2.22)$$

The interpretation of the impulse response is conveyed by the name: if the input is an impulse of unit area, the output is the impulse response

$$v_{in}(t) = \delta(t) \Rightarrow v_{out}(t) = h(t) \qquad (6.2.23)$$

This relationship is suggested in Fig. 6.2.15.

Convolution and Fourier transform theory. Although we used Fourier transform theory to define the impulse response and to derive the convolution, which uses the impulse response, you need to be aware that the meaning of the impulse response and its use in the convolution do not depend on Fourier transform theory. Rather, the impulse response is an intuitive and experimental concept, and the convolution relationship among input, output, and impulse response is a simple consequence of the linear time-invariant character of the system. Consider

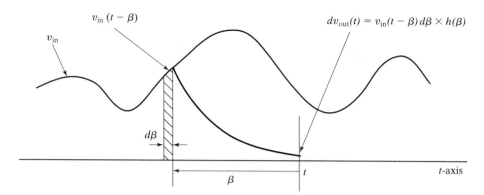

Figure 6.2.16   The convolution integral may be interpreted as a consequence of superposition. Thus the convolution principle depends on the linear time-invariant nature of the system, not on Fourier transform relationships.

the interpretation of the rightmost form of Eq. (6.2.20), repeated in Eq. (6.2.24) with the lower limit of the integral changed to zero because the impulse response is zero for negative arguments.

$$v_{out}(t) = \int_0^{+\infty} v_{in}(t - \beta)h(\beta)\,d\beta \tag{6.2.24}$$

This integral is readily interpreted in terms of superposition from Fig. 6.2.16.

In Fig. 6.2.16 we show an input voltage, v_{in} (the three humps), a time t, and an increment $d\beta$ at a time β earlier than t. The crosshatched area amounts to an impulse of area

$$\text{impulse area} = v_{in}(t - \beta)\,d\beta \tag{6.2.25}$$

This input impulse is affected by the impulse response to make an incremental contribution to the output at t of

$$\text{contribution of impulse to output} = v_{in}(t - \beta)d\beta \times h(\beta) \tag{6.2.26}$$

When all the contributions of past inputs are summed up with an integral, the result is Eq. (6.2.24). Thus the convolution relationship results from linear time invariance and does not depend on Fourier transform theory. This point is crucial to the analysis of random signals in linear systems, as we will soon address. We have one more important matter to cover in this review of spectral analysis of nonrandom signals.

Two ways to get to the power spectrum.   Every function has a time-domain autocorrelation function, as we stated in Sec. 6.1. The autocorrelation function is defined as

$$\overline{R}_V(\tau) = \langle v(t)v(t + \tau) \rangle \tag{6.2.27}$$

Here we investigate the relationship between the autocorrelation function and the power spectrum. The line of argument we will follow is summarized in Fig. 6.2.17.

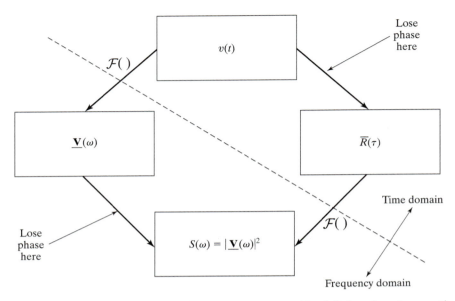

Figure 6.2.17   The two ways to get to the power spectrum. The left-hand route uses the voltage spectrum, which is the Fourier transform of the signal. The right-hand route uses the Fourier transform of the autocorrelation function. Fourier transforms are designated by $\mathcal{F}()$. Note that phase is lost in the second operation on the left-hand path but in the first operation on the right-hand path. Time-domain representations are separated from frequency-domain representations by the dashed line.

The left-hand path is familiar: first perform the Fourier transform of the signal to obtain the voltage spectrum, and then square the voltage spectrum to obtain the power spectrum. The right-hand path is unfamiliar, and we will show here that it works just as well: first, perform the autocorrelation, and then Fourier transform the autocorrelation to obtain the power spectrum. We will now demonstrate that this right-hand path works for a simple sinusoid. Before proceeding, you might visit endnote 14 for some ideas about impulse functions involving frequency.

For a sinusoid: left-hand path.   First, we review the left-hand path for a sinusoid. The Fourier transform of a sinusoid is[13]

$$\underline{\mathbf{V}}(f) = \int_{-\infty}^{+\infty} V_p \cos(\omega_1 t + \theta) e^{-j\omega t} \, dt = \frac{V_p}{2} e^{-j\theta} \delta(f + f_1) + \frac{V_p}{2} e^{+j\theta} \delta(f - f_1) \text{ volts/Hz}$$

(6.2.28)

where $f_1 = \frac{\omega_1}{2\pi}$. This is the spectrum we plotted in Fig. 6.2.2 with DC added.

The power spectrum of a simple sinusoid is the square of the voltage spectrum in Eq. (6.2.28):

$$S(f) = |\underline{\mathbf{V}}(f)|^2 = \left(\frac{V_p}{2}\right)^2 \delta(f + f_1) + \left(\frac{V_p}{2}\right)^2 \delta(f - f_1) \text{ volts}^2/\text{Hz}$$

(6.2.29)

This is the spectrum plotted in Fig. 6.2.5 with DC added.

For a sinusoid: right-hand path.   The time-average autocorrelation function of a sinusoid is performed with the aid of the familiar trig identity (see endnote 4).

$$\overline{R}_V(\tau) = \langle V_p \cos(\omega_1 t + \theta) V_p \cos(\omega_1(t + \tau) + \theta) \rangle$$
$$= \frac{V_p^2}{2} \langle \cos(\omega_1 \tau) + \cos(\omega_1(2\,t + \tau) + 2\,\theta) \rangle \qquad (6.2.30)$$

The first term is constant with respect to time and thus averages to itself. The second time is a pure sinusoid and averages to zero. The result is

$$\overline{R}_V(\tau) = \frac{V_p^2}{2} \cos(\omega_1 \tau) \qquad (6.2.31)$$

This is the first box on the right in Fig. 6.2.17. We now take the Fourier transform of the autocorrelation function[13]:

$$S_V(f) = \int_{-\infty}^{+\infty} \frac{V_p^2}{2} \cos(\omega_1 \tau) e^{-j\omega\tau}\,d\tau = \frac{V_p^2}{4}\delta(f + f_1) + \frac{V_p^2}{4}\delta(f - f_1) \text{ volts}^2/\text{Hz} \qquad (6.2.32)$$

Because we see that Eq. (6.2.32) agrees with (6.2.29), we conclude that *for a simple sinusoid* both paths lead to the power spectrum.

Generalizing.   Because we are dealing with deterministic signals, we recall that we can express all deterministic signals as the sum or the integral of sinusoids. We reason, therefore, that if both paths work for a sinusoid, they must work for all deterministic signals. We work out the details for the square wave in endnote 15.

Back to the main plot.   We began this section with a review of spectral analysis to fix concepts, refresh memories, and standardize vocabulary and notation. We return now to the announced subject of this section, the spectral analysis of random signals.

6.2.3 The Spectral Analysis of WSS Random Processes

No voltage spectra.   Random processes do not have voltage spectra. Consider the following thought experiment. You have a source of a random signal. On Monday, you take a lot of data and analyze the spectrum in a high-performance computer. After considerable number crunching, the computer outputs a spectrum, both amplitude and phase. On Tuesday you do the same. When you compare the two spectra, you see that the amplitude spectrum is very similar, but the phase of the spectrum bears no resemblance to the previous one. Perhaps the computer had problems, so you repeat the procedure on Wednesday. Again, the amplitude spectrum is the same, but the phase of the spectrum is different from the first two.

What the computer is telling you is that the random signal has an amplitude spectrum but no stable phase spectrum. In effect, it is telling you to forget about voltage spectra and focus on power spectra. Thus the left-hand path from the signal to the power spectrum does not work for a random process, as pictured in Fig. 6.2.18.

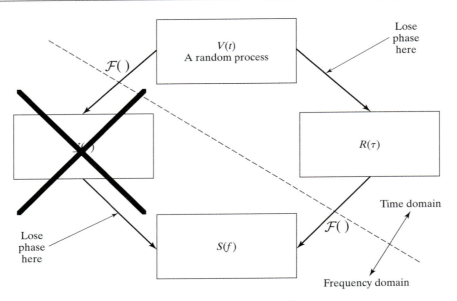

Figure 6.2.18 A random process has no voltage spectrum but does have a power spectrum. The only way to get the power spectrum is through the autocorrelation function.

The definition of power spectral density, PSD. Following the right-hand path, we define the PSD of a WSS random process as

$$S_V(\omega) = \int_{-\infty}^{+\infty} R_V(\tau)e^{-j\omega\tau}\,d\tau \text{ volts}^2/\text{Hz} \qquad (6.2.33)$$

where $R_V(\tau) = E[V(t)V(t+\tau)]$, $V(t)$ a WSS random process. The remainder of this section addresses the question, Does the definition of PSD in Eq. (6.2.33) make sense? We have led you to this definition by showing it to be plausible. We will continue to investigate its plausibility through a number of means, to increase your understanding of and intuition about the spectral analysis of random signals.

The inverse transform. Because Fourier transforms come in pairs, we get the inverse transform of Eq. (6.2.33) for free:

$$R_V(\tau) = \frac{1}{2\pi} \int_{-\infty}^{+\infty} S_V(\omega)e^{+j\omega\tau}\,d\omega \text{ volts}^2 \qquad (6.2.34)$$

Thus if we know the PSD of a random process, we can derive the autocorrelation function by Eq. (6.2.34).

Ergodic random processes. Recall that an ergodic random process is one in which statistical averages are equal to time averages. Because the right-hand path in Fig. 6.2.18 works for all time functions, it must therefore work for every member of an ergodic random process.

Therefore it works for the random process itself, and we conclude that the definition of PSD for an ergodic random process is valid; however, since the ergodic property is difficult to prove, but is usually assumed for convenience, we continue to investigate Eq. (6.2.33) for all WSS random processes.

Properties of the PSD

1. *Total power.* If we set $\tau = 0$ in Eq. (6.2.34), we have

$$R_V(0) = \frac{1}{2\pi} \int_{-\infty}^{+\infty} S_V(\omega)\, d\omega = \int_{-\infty}^{+\infty} S(f)\, df \text{ volts}^2 \qquad (6.2.35)$$

But $R_V(0) = E[V^2(t)] = \sigma_V^2 + \mu_V^2$, which is associated with the total power in the random process. For an ergodic random process, this *is* the total time-average power in every member function in the random process and, according to Eq. (6.2.35), is equal to the integral of the two-sided power spectral density over all frequencies. This result is equivalent to Parseval's theorem, which expresses that power is conserved between the time and frequency domains.

2. *Even symmetry.* Using the Euler identity, $e^{-j\omega\tau} = \cos\omega\tau - j\sin\omega\tau$, we can express Eq. (6.2.33) as

$$S_V(\omega) = \int_{-\infty}^{+\infty} R_V(\tau)(\cos\omega\tau - j\sin\omega\tau)d\tau = 2\int_0^{+\infty} R_V(\tau)\cos\omega\tau\, d\tau \text{ volts}^2/\text{Hz}$$

$$(6.2.36)$$

Recalling that the autocorrelation function, $R_V(\tau)$, is an even function of τ, we see that the $R_V(\tau)\cos\omega\tau$ term in Eq. (6.2.36) is even, and the $R_V(\tau)\sin\omega\tau$ term is odd. The odd term drops out when integrated from $-\infty$ to $+\infty$. Also, we integrate the even term in the second form of Eq. (6.2.36) from 0 to $+\infty$ and double the result. From the second form of Eq. (6.2.36) we see that the PSD is an even function of ω: $S_V(-\omega) = S_V(+\omega)$.

3. *Nonnegative.* It can be shown that $S_V(\omega) \geq 0$ for all ω. This mathematical property accords with our physical interpretation of $S_V(\omega)$ as a power spectrum. We conclude that not all mathematical functions can be autocorrelation functions; only even functions that have Fourier transforms that are nonnegative everywhere can be autocorrelation functions.

Cross-power spectra.   We defined the cross-correlation function between two jointly WSS random processes, $X(t)$ and $Y(t)$, as $R_{XY}(\tau) = E[X(t)Y(t+\tau)]$ and $R_{YX}(\tau) = E[Y(t)X(t+\tau)]$. The cross-power spectra are defined as

$$S_{XY}(\omega) = \int_{-\infty}^{+\infty} R_{XY}(\tau)e^{-j\omega\tau}\, d\tau \quad \text{and} \quad S_{YX}(\omega) = \int_{-\infty}^{+\infty} R_{YX}(\tau)e^{-j\omega\tau}\, d\tau \qquad (6.2.37)$$

The symmetry properties of the cross-power spectra are readily shown to be

$$S_{XY}(-\omega) = S_{XY}^*(+\omega) = S_{YX}(+\omega) \qquad (6.2.38)$$

Cross-power spectra can provide a means for measuring the frequency response of a system that does not admit of direct measurement. For example, the frequency response of the ionosphere/atmosphere system can be measured using naturally occurring radiation as a signal.

In Sec. 6.1 we presented and investigated four WSS random processes that model four important random signals. We now extend that presentation to include the frequency domain. Our purpose is to demonstrate the plausibility of the PSD concept and to give insight into the properties of these models.

Model of a random asynchronous digital signal

The model.   We modeled a random asynchronous digital signal (Sec. 6.1.1) by triggering a toggle flip-flop with a Poisson process of average rate λ. The results were that the model was WSS and that the autocorrelation function was of the form Eq. (6.1.17),

$$R_Q(\tau) = \tfrac{1}{4}e^{-2\lambda|\tau|} + \tfrac{1}{4} \tag{6.2.39}$$

Although we did not show that this random process is ergodic, we pointed out that the total power, AC power, and DC power were reasonable for a digital signal that spends half its time in the 1 state and half in the 0 state.

The PSD.   Using a common Fourier transform pair,[13] we find the PSD of the model to be

$$S(f) = \frac{1}{4}\delta(f) + \frac{\lambda}{(2\lambda)^2 + (2\pi f)^2} \text{ volts}^2/\text{Hz} \tag{6.2.40}$$

This spectrum is plotted in Fig. 6.2.19.

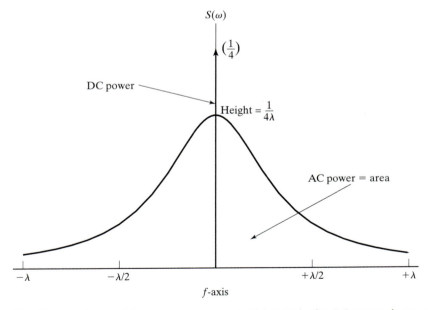

Figure 6.2.19   The spectrum of the asynchronous digital signal. The DC power is represented by an impulse at $f = 0$. The AC power is spread over a continuous spectrum.

The spectrum shows the DC power as an impulse at $f = 0$ and the AC power as a continuum of frequencies.

The bandwidth.   The bandwidth is related to the width of the AC spectrum. Somewhat arbitrarily we define the bandwidth as the range of frequencies in hertz (one-sided) that contains 90% of the AC power. The integral of the AC portion of the spectrum in Eq. (6.2.40) is

$$\text{power in } B \text{ Hz} = 2 \int_0^B \frac{\lambda}{(2\lambda)^2 + (2\pi f)^2} \, df = \frac{1}{2\pi} \int_0^{\pi B/\lambda} \frac{1}{1 + x^2} \, dx = \frac{1}{2\pi} \tan^{-1} \left(\frac{\pi B}{\lambda} \right)$$

(6.2.41)

We were able to integrate from 0 to B and double the results owing to the even symmetry of the integrand. We also changed variables from $f \to x = \frac{\pi f}{\lambda}$ to get the familiar form for $\tan^{-1}$. Note that as $B \to \infty$, the total AC power in the frequency domain approaches $\frac{1}{4}$, which is the total AC power in the time domain. To find the required bandwidth for 90% of the AC power we solve

$$\frac{1}{2\pi} \tan^{-1} \left(\frac{\pi B}{\lambda} \right) = \frac{0.9}{4} \Rightarrow B = 2.01\lambda$$

(6.2.42)

Let us put in some numbers and get a feel for this result. Let $\lambda = 1000$ pulses/second. This is the input to a toggle flip-flop, which divides by 2 and produces output bits with an average pulse width of 2 milliseconds and an average frequency of 500 Hz. Equation (6.2.42) tells us that we need 2000 Hz to pass 90% of the AC power in this signal. The average pulse width and average frequency are therefore not good indicators of the required bandwidth. The problem is that there are some very short pulses in the mix, and these require more bandwidth.

Bandwidth and coherence time.   Combining Eqs. (6.2.42) and (6.1.67), we find the relationship between the bandwidth and the coherence time to be

$$B = \frac{2.312}{\tau_c}$$

(6.2.43)

As expected, the usual inverse relationship exists, although the constant, 2.312, is larger than usual. This occurs because the pulses vary widely in length: the short pulses require a wide bandwidth, and the long pulses give a long coherence time.

Example 6.2.1:   Photodetector

A system is designed to count the output of a photocell that produces a 0.1-μs pulse for each photon and has an average count of $\lambda = 50$ kHz in the application of interest. What bandwidth is required at the input and output of the first stage of the counter?

Solution   For the input bandwidth Eq. (6.2.13) shows the required bandwidth to be $B = \frac{1}{0.1 \times 10^{-6}} = 10$ MHz. For the output Eq. (6.2.42) gives the required bandwidth to be $2.01\lambda = 100$ kHz.

You do it.   For such a counter some input pulses will be missed because of the 0.1-μs response time of the photodetector. What would be the correction factor in percent to be added to the recorded count? Enter a number as **myanswer,** but do not include the % sign.

```
myanswer =        ?    ;
```

```
Evaluate
```

For the answer, see endnote 16.

Summary. The random process model for an asynchronous digital signal leads to a spectrum with the correct AC and DC power and a reasonable bandwidth. The bandwidth we derived is based on 90% of the AC power.

Model of synchronous digital signal

The model.   In Sec. 6.1 we investigated a random process model for a synchronous digital signal. We assumed a clock period of T, equally likely 1s and 0s during each clock cycle, and an arbitrary time origin. The random process proved to be WSS and the autocorrelation function was Eq. (6.1.28)

$$
\begin{aligned}
R_X(\tau) &= \frac{1}{2} - \frac{1}{4}\frac{|\tau|}{T}, 0 < |\tau| < T \\
&= \frac{1}{4}, \ |\tau| > T
\end{aligned}
\tag{6.2.44}
$$

Using the table of Fourier transform pairs (see endnote 13), we find the PSD to be

$$
S_X(f) = \frac{1}{4}\delta(f) + \frac{T}{4}\left(\frac{\sin \pi Tf}{\pi Tf}\right)^2 \text{ volts}^2/\text{Hz}
\tag{6.2.45}
$$

The spectrum in Fig. 6.2.20 shows the DC power as an impulse at $f = 0$, and shows the AC power spread into a continuum of frequencies.

The bandwidth.   The bandwidth in hertz can be set equal to the frequency of the first null.

$$
B = \frac{1}{T}
\tag{6.2.46}
$$

We consider that this is a reasonable bandwidth. The digital signal alternates between 1 and 0 with each clock cycle. The fastest-moving signal it can create is when it alternates between 1 and 0 regularly, making a square wave. To get 90% of the power the bandwidth of a square wave goes to the third harmonic, which would be a bandwidth of $\frac{3}{2T}$ in the notation of this problem. This is the worst case and it requires more bandwidth than is given by Eq. (6.2.46). But the alternating structure of the square wave is highly improbable, for at each clock transition the state changes with probability 0.5. We conclude that Eq. (6.2.46) gives a reasonable bandwidth for the random synchronous digital signal. We show in endnote 17 that the power to the first null in the spectrum is 90.4% of the total AC power.

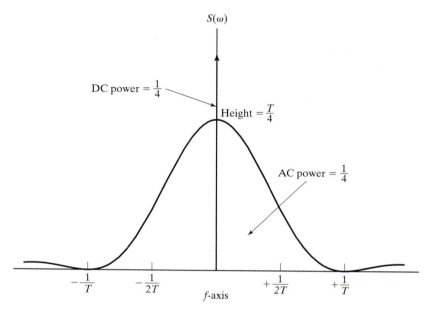

Figure 6.2.20   The spectrum of the model of the synchronous digital signal. As before, the AC and the DC power are the same, as is appropriate for a signal that spends half its time in the 1 state and half in the 0 state. The bandwidth to the first null is $\frac{1}{T}$.

Example 6.2.2:   Computer CPU speed

A computer runs with a CPU speed of 560 MHz. What bandwidth is required for the busses bringing the instructions from memory?

Solution   The clock period is $T = \frac{1}{560 \times 10^{+6}}$. The required bandwidth for 90% of the signal power is $B = \frac{1}{T} = 560$ MHz.

Summary.   Again, we find that the PSD of the model of the synchronous digital signal gives the right AC and DC powers and a reasonable bandwidth.

Model of a random analog signal

The model.   Our model for a random analog signal is a sinusoid of fixed amplitude and frequency but random phase. We showed that this random process is WSS and is also ergodic.

The PSD of the model.   The autocorrelation function for the random sinusoid was Eq. (6.1.35):

$$R_V(\tau) = \frac{V_p^2}{2} \cos \omega_1 \tau \text{ volts}^2 \qquad (6.2.47)$$

This function is identical with the example we used to present the two ways to get to the power spectrum, Eq. (6.2.31). The PSD is worked out there and given in Eq. (6.2.32), which we repeat:

$$S_V(f) = \int_{-\infty}^{+\infty} \frac{V_p^2}{2} \cos(\omega_1 \tau) e^{-j\omega\tau} \, d\tau = \frac{V_p^2}{4} \delta(f + f_1) + \frac{V_p^2}{4} \delta(f - f_1) \text{ volts}^2/\text{Hz} \quad (6.2.48)$$

Equation (6.2.48) gives the spectrum we expect for a sinusoid of frequency f_1: half the power appears at $-f_1$, and half appears at $+f_1$. There is no DC component.

Model for wideband noise

Our model for wideband (broadband) noise was a Gaussian random process with a first-order PDF of $X = N(\mu_X, \sigma_X^2)$. The form of the autocorrelation function (which is, in fact, valid for all WSS random processes) was given in Eq. (6.1.74) as

$$R_X(\tau) = \sigma_X^2 \rho_X(\tau) + \mu_X^2 \quad (6.2.49)$$

The PSD would be the Fourier transform,

$$S(f) = \mu_X^2 \delta(f) + \sigma_X^2 \int_{-\infty}^{+\infty} \rho_X(\tau) e^{-j2\pi f\tau} \, d\tau \quad (6.2.50)$$

We cannot do the integral without an explicit form for the coherence function, $\rho_X(\tau)$. Equation (6.2.50) shows the DC component and the AC component. We will work an example in Section 6.3; however, we may make a guess for the bandwidth. We defined a coherence time, τ_c, as the delay beyond which the coherence function remains below 0.1. The coherence time characterizes the time structure of the random process. We would expect the bandwidth to be approximately

$$B \approx \frac{1}{\tau_c} \quad (6.2.51)$$

Next, we discuss the physics, circuit theory, and random-process model for a common form of broadband noise, thermal noise in resistors.

6.2.4 Modeling of Broadband Noise

This is the third time we have taken up the subject of broadband noise. We treated broadband noise in Sec. 6.1 as an important signal to model with a WSS random process. We just discussed the spectrum of broadband noise without giving specifics. We now have the tools for a fuller treatment of this important subject.

Sources of broadband noise.   There are a number of physical processes that produce broadband noise in electrical circuits. Thermal motion of carriers in lossy structures such as resistors is a major source. The discrete nature of electrical carriers leads to broadband noise due to partition and recombination processes in semiconductors, and shot noise in vacuum tubes. For several reasons we focus on resistor noise in this section.

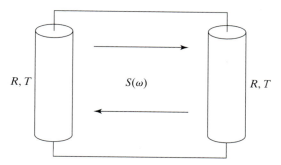

Figure 6.2.21   Two resistors in equilibrium. We may think of the resistors as noise sources, the wires as a transmission line, and the source and load impedances as equal. Therefore there is no reflection, and the radiation of one resistor is absorbed by the other, and vice versa. Thus this is *blackbody* radiation.

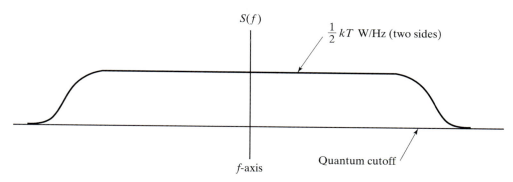

Figure 6.2.22   The emitted spectrum of a resistor is flat throughout the normal electronic frequency range provided the resistor is not cooled to cryogenic temperatures. The magnitude of the emitted spectrum into a matched load is $\frac{1}{2}kT$ W/Hz, where k is Boltzmann's constant, and T is the temperature in kelvin.

Blackbody radiation.   Classical physics had some problems understanding the radiation of hot bodies until quantum mechanics yielded adequate models. Resistor noise, also called *Johnson noise,* is blackbody radiation confined to an electrical circuit. Because the noise is produced by the energetic thermal motion of carriers and because collision distances are on the atomic scale, the collision times are extremely short. This leads to a short coherence time and a broad bandwidth. The context and results of the physics of this subject are summarized by the circuit in Fig. 6.2.21. Two resistors of value R and temperature T kelvin (K) are in equilibrium through an equal exchange of energy.

The spectrum of the exchanged radiation is shown in Fig. 6.2.22. The emitted power spectrum into a matched load is

$$S(f) = \tfrac{1}{2}kT \ \text{W/Hz (two sides)} \tag{6.2.52}$$

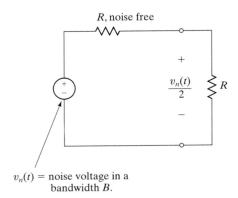

$v_n(t)$ = noise voltage in a
bandwidth B.

Figure 6.2.23   The Thevenin equivalent circuit for a hot resistor coupled to a matched load. Because any circuit has a limited bandwidth, we have indicated the noise voltage in the bandwidth appropriate to the circuit. Later, we will extend the model to include more details about this bandwidth.

where k = Boltzmann's constant = 1.38×10^{-23} J/K, and T is the resistor temperature in kelvin. Note that the units of spectra are watts per hertz. The quantum mechanical drop-off is at a frequency of approximately $2.5 \times 10^{10}\ T$ Hz. For room temperature, this cutoff falls in the far infrared. For liquid helium temperature of 3 K, the cutoff frequency is approximately 60 GHz, in the millimeter region. Therefore, for normal electronic and microwave work, the noise spectrum can be considered flat.

The circuit theory of resistor noise.   Consider the two resistors in Fig. 6.2.21. We will consider only the noise going from left to right, so we will model the left resistor as a source and the right resistor as a load. The Thevenin equivalent circuit allows us to separate the internal noise source from the output impedance, with the model shown in Fig. 6.2.23.

By combining the results of thermal physics with circuit theory we can determine the rms value of the noise voltage. Because the frequency cutoff of thermal noise is far beyond the bandwidth of the circuit, the power in the load from physics is

$$P = \frac{1}{2} kT \times 2\,B = kTB \quad \text{W} \tag{6.2.53}$$

where B is the bandwidth (one side) of the coupling. From circuit theory we calculate the power in the load as

$$P = \frac{\langle (v_n(t)/2)^2 \rangle}{R} = \frac{V_{\text{rms}}^2}{4\,R} \tag{6.2.54}$$

Equating the two powers, we have

$$V_{\text{rms}} = \sqrt{4\,kTRB} \quad \text{volts} \tag{6.2.55}$$

In Eq. (6.2.55), V_{rms} is the rms noise voltage, open circuit, out of a resistor R, at a temperature T with an effective bandwidth B (one-sided). This result, which is quoted in many handbooks on electronics, is useful for studying the noise properties in sensitive electronic circuits.

Random-process model.   We have already discussed modeling wideband noise as an ergodic, Gaussian random process. We now are in a position to give values for the mean and variance of thermal resistor noise. The mean is zero, and the variance, from Eq. (6.2.55), is

$$V_{rms}^2 = R_V(0) = \sigma_V^2 = 4\,kTRB \tag{6.2.56}$$

The power spectrum of the open-circuit voltage comes from assuming a constant-noise spectrum, S_N, over a bandwidth (two sides) of $2B$.[18] From Eqs. (6.2.56) and (6.2.35) we have

$$R_V(0) = \int_{-B}^{+B} S_N\,df = 2\,S_N B = 4\,kTRB \Rightarrow S_N = 2\,kTR \text{ volts}^2/\text{Hz (two sides)} \tag{6.2.57}$$

This model of a constant PSD over a bandwidth also allows the determination of the coherence function in Eq. (6.2.49). We can determine the autocorrelation function as the inverse Fourier transform of the PSD:

$$R_V(\tau) = \int_{-B}^{+B} S_N e^{+j2\pi\tau f}\,df = S_N \left.\frac{e^{+j2\pi\tau f}}{j2\pi\tau}\right|_{-B}^{+B} = 2\,BS_N\left(\frac{\sin 2\pi B\tau}{2\pi B\tau}\right) \text{ volts}^2/\text{Hz} \tag{6.2.58}$$

The coherence function, $\rho(\tau)$, is the $\sin x/x$ term in Eq. (6.2.58). We can determine the coherence time for the wideband noise signal by plotting the coherence function and seeing when it remains below 0.1. Figure 6.2.24 shows such a plot.

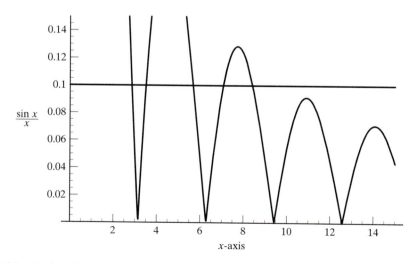

Figure 6.2.24   A plot of the coherence function of Eq. 6.2.58. Setting $\rho(\tau) = 0.1$ produces five solutions, the largest of which is $x = 2\pi B\tau_c \approx 8.5$.

The coherence time corresponds to $x \approx 8.5$, which gives a coherence time of

$$2\pi B \tau_c \approx 8.5 \Rightarrow \tau_c \approx \frac{8.5}{2\pi B} \approx \frac{1}{B} \qquad (6.2.59)$$

The relationship derived in Eq. (6.2.59) was anticipated in Eq. (6.2.51) based on intuition. Although the bandwidth model is crude, with its sharp cutoffs, the general results are useful. We will revisit this problem in Sec. 6.3 under more realistic assumptions.

White noise.   Because most sources of wideband noise have a bandwidth much wider than that of electronic and microwave systems, mathematical modeling of such noise is simplified by assuming that the noise has infinite bandwidth. Such a model is called *white noise* in analogy with white light, which contains all frequencies. The assumed spectrum for white noise is

$$S(f) = S_N, \ -\infty < f < +\infty \ \text{volts}^2/\text{Hz (two sides)} \qquad (6.2.60)$$

The corresponding autocorrelation function is the inverse Fourier transform,

$$R_N(\tau) = S_N \delta(\tau) \ \text{volts}^2 \qquad (6.2.61)$$

We note that $R_N(0) = \infty$, which indicates infinite power. This is no surprise, since the frequency-domain model has a finite spectrum magnitude over an infinite bandwidth. We also note that the coherence time for white noise is zero.

The white noise model, a useful fiction, will help us in analyzing the effect of linear systems on broadband noise.

6.2.5 Modulation of Random Processes

What is modulation?   By *modulation* we mean the multiplication of one signal by a carrier signal that shifts it to a different frequency band. These processes are descriptive of amplitude modulation. We will analyze the process pictured in Fig. 6.2.25. We assume that the signal is band limited and in the baseband.[18] The analysis also applies to mixing, but in this case the signal is originally in a high-frequency band and is shifted to another frequency band by the nonlinear properties of the mixer. These processes of modulation and mixing are vital to the hardware of communication systems.

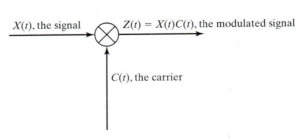

Figure 6.2.25   The modulator creates the product of the signal and the carrier.

Our goal is to derive the autocorrelation function and spectrum of the modulated signal. Normally, the carrier is a sinusoid, but we will carry out the analysis generally and then specialize to a sinusoidal carrier.

The autocorrelation function of Z(t).   We model the signal, $X(t)$, and the carrier, $C(t)$, with independent WSS random processes. The autocorrelation function of $Z(t)$ is shown in Eq. (6.1.84) to be

$$R_Z(\tau) = R_C(\tau)R_X(\tau) \tag{6.2.62}$$

The spectrum of Z(t).   To derive the spectrum of the modulated signal, we begin with the Fourier transform of the autocorrelation function, which is by definition the spectrum of $Z(t)$:

$$S_Z(\omega) = \int_{-\infty}^{+\infty} R_C(\tau)R_X(\tau)e^{-j\omega\tau}\,d\tau \tag{6.2.63}$$

Our approach is to express $S_Z(\omega)$ in terms of the spectra of the carrier and the signal. We may express the autocorrelations in Eq. (6.2.63) as inverse Fourier transforms of these spectra:

$$R_X(\tau) = \frac{1}{2\pi}\int_{-\infty}^{+\infty} S_X(\alpha)e^{+j\alpha\tau}\,d\alpha \quad \text{and} \quad R_C(\tau) = \frac{1}{2\pi}\int_{-\infty}^{+\infty} S_C(\beta)e^{+j\beta\tau}\,d\beta \tag{6.2.64}$$

We use α and β as "dummy" variables of integration for frequency because we will next substitute Eq. (6.2.64) into Eq. (6.2.63) and we do not want to confuse the various variables of integration. The results of the substitution are

$$S_Z(\omega) = \left(\frac{1}{2\pi}\right)^2 \iiint_{-\infty}^{+\infty} S_X(\alpha)e^{+j\alpha\tau}S_C(\beta)e^{+j\beta\tau}e^{-j\omega\tau}\,d\tau\,d\alpha\,d\beta \tag{6.2.65}$$

We integrate first in τ. The term to integrate is simply the exponential term that combines the three terms involving τ. Focusing only on that integration, we have

$$\int_{-\infty}^{+\infty} e^{-j(\omega-\alpha-\beta)\tau}\,d\tau = 2\pi\delta(\omega-\alpha-\beta) \tag{6.2.66}$$

which is a standard Fourier transform (see endnote 13). Thus after the integration in τ, Eq. (6.2.65) reduces to

$$S_Z(\omega) = \frac{1}{2\pi}\iint_{-\infty}^{+\infty} S_X(\alpha)S_C(\beta)\delta(\omega-\alpha-\beta)\,d\alpha\,d\beta \tag{6.2.67}$$

Next we integrate in β. The impulse will "happen" when its argument is zero, that is, when $\omega - \alpha - \beta = 0$, or when $\beta = \omega - \alpha$. Thus the integration in β yields

$$S_Z(\omega) = \frac{1}{2\pi}\int_{-\infty}^{+\infty} S_X(\alpha)S_C(\omega-\alpha)\,d\alpha, \quad \omega \text{ and } \alpha \text{ in rad/s} \tag{6.2.68}$$

which is, except for the scaling factor in front, the convolution of the two spectra. The $\frac{1}{2\pi}$ in front results from integrating in radians per second. If we integrate in frequency in hertz, Eq. (6.2.68) takes the form

$$S_Z(f) = \int_{-\infty}^{+\infty} S_X(\gamma) S_C(f - \gamma)\, d\gamma, \quad f \text{ and } \gamma \text{ in hertz} \tag{6.2.69}$$

which is a true convolution. The convolution in the frequency domain is, of course, to be expected, since we are multiplying autocorrelation functions in the time domain.

A sinusoid carrier.   Normally, the carrier is a sinusoid, which we model with the random process

$$C(t) = V_p \cos(\omega_1 t + \Theta) \tag{6.2.70}$$

where Θ is a random variable with $f_\Theta(\theta) = \frac{1}{2\pi}$, $0 < \theta \leq 2\pi$, and ω_1 is the modulation frequency in rad/s. The autocorrelation function for this WSS random process is worked out in Sec. 6.1; see Eq. (6.1.35)

$$R_V(\tau) = \frac{V_p^2}{2} \cos \omega_1 \tau \quad \text{volts}^2 \tag{6.2.71}$$

and the spectrum is worked out in Sec. 6.2, with the results in Eq. (6.2.48):

$$S_C(\omega) = \int_{-\infty}^{+\infty} \frac{V_p^2}{2} \cos(\omega_1 \tau) e^{-j\omega\tau}\, d\tau = \frac{V_p^2}{2} \pi \delta(\omega + \omega_1) + \frac{V_p^2}{2} \pi \delta(\omega - \omega_1) \text{ volts}^2/\text{Hz} \tag{6.2.72}$$

When we substitute Eq. (6.2.72) into Eq. (6.2.68) we obtain two terms. We work next with the first of these. The integral to be performed is

$$S_Z(\omega)(\text{due to the first term}) = \frac{1}{2\pi} \int_{-\infty}^{+\infty} S_X(\alpha) \frac{V_p^2}{2} \pi \delta(\omega - \alpha + \omega_1)\, d\alpha \tag{6.2.73}$$

Again, the impulse will "happen" when its argument is zero, which is when $\alpha = \omega + \omega_1$. Thus we substitute $\omega + \omega_1$ for α in the spectrum of $X(t)$, with the result

$$S_Z(\omega)(\text{due to the first term}) = \frac{V_p^2}{4} S_X(\omega + \omega_1) \tag{6.2.74}$$

Clearly, the second term is similar, and we obtain the full spectrum:

$$S_Z(\omega) = \frac{V_p^2}{4} S_X(\omega + \omega_1) + \frac{V_p^2}{4} S_X(\omega - \omega_1) \tag{6.2.75}$$

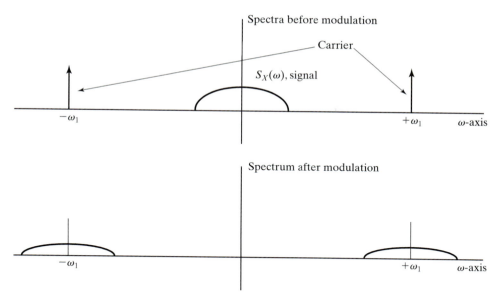

Figure 6.2.26   The two-sided power spectra before and after modulation. The signal in the baseband is shifted to a band at the frequency of the modulation frequency.

Speaking in terms of two-sided spectra, we say that the modulation process has shifted the signal spectrum in the baseband to bands at $\pm \omega_1$. The spectra before and after modulation are pictured in Fig. 6.2.26.

Speaking in terms of one-sided spectra, which is appropriate for a physical process like modulation, we say that modulation shifts the signal spectrum in the baseband to the frequency band of the carrier, creating upper and lower sidebands in the process. The one-sided spectra are pictured in Fig. 6.2.27.

Summary.   In the time domain, amplitude modulation is a multiplication process. In the frequency domain, amplitude modulation is a frequency-shifting process. Other modulation processes, such as frequency modulation, have similar effects in the frequency domain.

The units of spectra

One of the confusing matters in the discussion of spectra is the units of the various spectra. We have been dealing generally with power in volts squared (see endnote 11), but matters are not quite so simple, as the following shows. Throughout this section we have associated units with various definitions and spectra. This section pulls together this information in an ordered discussion.

Units are a great aid in solving problems and in clarifying understanding. You are encouraged to develop the habit of including units, or at least discussing units in connection with derivations and problems.

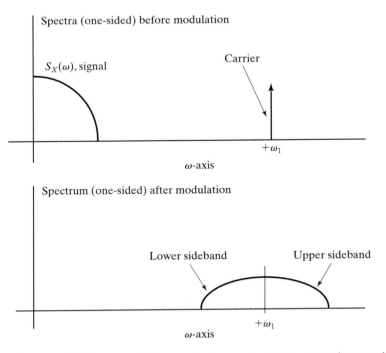

Figure 6.2.27   The one-sided spectra before and after modulation. Note that modulation not only shifts the spectrum from the baseband but also creates a lower sideband image of the signal spectrum below the carrier frequency.

Fourier series.   A periodic signal has finite power and thus infinite energy. Consider the two-sided Fourier series

$$v(t) = V_0 + \sum_{1}^{\infty} 2V_n \cos(n\omega_1 t + \theta_n) = \sum_{-\infty}^{\infty} \underline{\mathbf{V}}_n e^{jn\omega_1 t} \quad \text{volts} \tag{6.2.76}$$

As indicated, the unit of the various harmonic amplitudes is volts. The voltage spectrum would be

$$\underline{\mathbf{V}}(f) = \sum_{-\infty}^{\infty} \underline{\mathbf{V}}_n \delta(f - nf_1) \quad \text{volts/Hz} \tag{6.2.77}$$

The units of Eq. (6.2.77) require some explanation. The first point, which we have mentioned before, is that a unit impulse has units reciprocal to its argument.[14] Thus $\delta(f)$ has units of frequency^{-1} or seconds. The formal units of Eq. (6.2.77) are volts-second; however, in the spirit of a spectrum that spreads the voltage over a region in frequency space, we have our choice of volts/(radians per second) or volts per hertz. We choose the latter because the Fourier integral is an integration in frequency in hertz, as shown by the inverse transform

$$v(t) = \int_{-\infty}^{+\infty} \mathbf{V}(2\pi f) e^{+j2\pi ft} \, df \text{ volts} \tag{6.2.78}$$

What matters in Eq. (6.2.78) is not the argument of the voltage spectrum, which could just has easily have been written as $\mathbf{V}(f)$, but the "df" for the increment of the space over which the integration is taking place.

The power spectrum is the square of the voltage spectrum with appropriate units

$$S(f) = \sum_{-\infty}^{\infty} |\mathbf{V}_n|^2 \delta(f - nf_1) \text{ volts}^2/\text{Hz} \tag{6.2.79}$$

Fourier transforms. An aperiodic (one-time) signal, such as a pulse, has finite energy but zero power. The Fourier transform

$$\mathbf{V}(\omega) = \int_{-\infty}^{+\infty} v(t) e^{-j\omega t} \, dt \text{ volts/Hz} \tag{6.2.80}$$

has formal units of volts-seconds, but we choose volts per hertz for the reasons given previously. The power spectrum

$$S(f) = |\mathbf{V}(\omega)|^2 \tag{6.2.81}$$

has units of volts squared-second per hertz. This unit bespeaks an energy spectrum. If we put in the circuit impedance level by dividing by R in ohms, then volts squared per ohm = watts, and the units would be watts-seconds per hertz or joules per hertz.

Random signals. Wide-sense stationary random processes model signals that extend over all time and thus have infinite power. The autocorrelation function is defined as

$$R(\tau) = E[V(t)V(t + \tau)] \text{ volts}^2 \tag{6.2.82}$$

The expectation operator has no units, since $f_V(v) \, dv$ has the units of probability, a pure number. The power spectrum is the Fourier transform of the autocorrelation function:

$$S_V(\omega) = \int_{-\infty}^{+\infty} R_V(\tau) e^{-j\omega\tau} \, d\tau \text{ volts}^2/\text{Hz} \tag{6.2.83}$$

Again, we choose volts squared per hertz because the integral of the PSD with respect to frequency in hertz is the total power in the signal

$$\text{Total power} = R_V(0) = \frac{1}{2\pi} \int_{-\infty}^{+\infty} S_V(\omega) \, d\omega = \int_{-\infty}^{+\infty} S(f) \, df \text{ volts}^2 \tag{6.2.84}$$

Summary. In this section we discussed the units of the various functions involved in spectral analysis. Such information is useful in problem solving and in thinking carefully about the spectral concepts. In Sec. 6.2 we made the units explicit in many equations.

6.3 WSS RANDOM PROCESSES IN LINEAR SYSTEMS

6.3.1 Time- and Frequency-Domain Analysis

We began Sec. 6.2 with a review of spectral analysis. We dealt there with the analysis of signals in linear systems. Generally, we introduced the voltage spectrum, $\underline{V}(\omega)$, and the system function, $\underline{H}(j\omega)$, and from these we derived the power spectrum, $S(\omega)$, and the system function for power, $|\underline{H}(j\omega)|^2$. We also introduced the convolution relationship between the time-domain input signal and the impulse response of the system. We showed that convolution depends on the concept of the impulse response and the linear time-invariant nature of the system. Fourier transform relationships need not be involved.

When we discussed the spectra of random signals, as modeled by WSS random processes, we stressed that no voltage spectrum exists but that a power spectrum does exist. This means that we cannot use the relationship between input and output power spectra based on the reasoning that led to Eq. (6.2.18), at least not until we prove its validity by other means. Such proof we now give based on time-domain analysis. This proof completes the explication of the definition of the PSD as the Fourier transform of the autocorrelation function.

A double convolution.   Because the frequency-domain path is not available to us, we take the time-domain approach. We consider a linear system with a random process input, as shown in Fig. 6.3.1.

Because each member function of the input random process is related to a corresponding member function of the output random process by convolution, we attribute the convolution relationship to the entire random process:

$$V_{\text{out}}(t) = \int_{-\infty}^{+\infty} V_{\text{in}}(t-\alpha)h(\alpha)\,d\alpha \qquad (6.3.1)$$

We calculate the output autocorrelation function by taking $E[V_{\text{out}}(t)V_{\text{out}}(t+\tau)]$, which involves two convolution integrals and an expectation on the right-hand side. Because integration and expectation are linear operations we take the expectation inside the convolution integrals. We also let the variable of integration in the second convolution integral be $\alpha \to \beta$. The result is

$$E[V_{\text{out}}(t)V_{\text{out}}(t+\tau)] = \int_{-\infty}^{+\infty}\int_{-\infty}^{+\infty} E[V_{\text{in}}(t-\alpha)V_{\text{in}}(t-\beta+\tau)]h(\alpha)h(\beta)\,d\alpha\,d\beta \qquad (6.3.2)$$

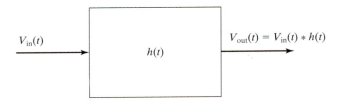

Figure 6.3.1   The input random process and the output random process are related by a convolution relationship.

The two expectations give the input and output autocorrelation functions, except the argument for the input autocorrelation function is the difference between the two arguments, $t - \beta + \tau - (t - \alpha) = \tau + \alpha - \beta$. Thus Eq. (6.3.2) becomes

$$R_{\text{out}}(\tau) = \int_{-\infty}^{+\infty} \int_{-\infty}^{+\infty} R_{\text{in}}(\tau + \alpha - \beta) h(\alpha) h(\beta) \, d\alpha \, d\beta \qquad (6.3.3)$$

Equation (6.3.3) is a double convolution. It gives us a means for calculating the output autocorrelation function, given the input autocorrelation function and the impulse response of the system. In certain simple cases this would be a reasonable way to solve a problem; however, our goal is to take the analysis into the frequency domain, where matters are usually simpler. We therefore perform the Fourier transform of Eq. (6.3.3) to obtain the output power spectrum:

$$S_{\text{out}}(\omega) = \int_{-\infty}^{+\infty} R_{\text{out}}(\tau) e^{-j\omega\tau} \, d\tau = \int_{-\infty}^{+\infty} \int_{-\infty}^{+\infty} \int_{-\infty}^{+\infty} R_{\text{in}}(\tau + \alpha - \beta) e^{-j\omega\tau} h(\alpha) h(\beta) \, d\alpha \, d\beta \, d\tau$$
$$(6.3.4)$$

The triple integral divides nicely into three integrals when we make the substitution $x = \tau + \alpha - \beta$. The key factor in this separation is what happens to the exponential term:

$$e^{-j\omega\tau} \rightarrow e^{-j\omega(x - \alpha + \beta)} = e^{-j\omega x} \times e^{+j\omega\alpha} \times e^{-j\omega\beta} \qquad (6.3.5)$$

Substitution of Eq. (6.3.5) into Eq. (6.3.4) and separation of the result into three single integrals give the following:

$$S_{\text{out}}(\omega) = \underbrace{\int_{-\infty}^{+\infty} R_{\text{in}}(x) e^{-j\omega x} \, dx}_{S_{\text{in}}(\omega)} \times \underbrace{\int_{-\infty}^{+\infty} h(\alpha) e^{+j\omega\alpha} \, d\alpha}_{\underline{\mathbf{H}}(j\omega)^*} \times \underbrace{\int_{-\infty}^{+\infty} h(\beta) e^{-j\omega\beta} \, d\beta}_{\underline{\mathbf{H}}(j\omega)} \qquad (6.3.6)$$

In Eq. (6.3.6) we have identified the first term as the input PSD. The last term is the Fourier transform of the impulse response and thus is the system function, and the middle term is the complex conjugate of the last term. Thus Eq. (6.3.6) reduces to

$$S_{\text{out}}(\omega) = S_{\text{in}}(\omega) \times |\underline{\mathbf{H}}(j\omega)|^2 \qquad (6.3.7)$$

which is the same relation, Eq. (6.2.18), we derived for deterministic signals by squaring the voltage spectrum relationship between input and output. Equation (6.3.7) allows us to use frequency-domain techniques for PSDs of WSS random processes and hence is the final vindication of the definition of the PSD as the Fourier transform of the autocorrelation function and its interpretation as a power spectrum.

Input and output DC.   Other relationships between input and output can be investigated. For notational simplicity, let the input be $V_{\text{in}}(t) \rightarrow X(t)$ and the output be $V_{\text{out}} \rightarrow Y(t)$. The relationship between input and output given in Eq. (6.3.1) in this notation is

$$Y(t) = \int_{-\infty}^{+\infty} X(t - \alpha) h(\alpha) \, d\alpha \qquad (6.3.8)$$

If we take the expectation of Eq. (6.3.8) and take the resulting constant outside the integral, we have

$$\mu_Y = \mu_X \int_{-\infty}^{+\infty} h(\alpha)\, d\alpha \tag{6.3.9}$$

The impulse response, $h(\alpha)$, is related to the system function by the inverse Fourier transform in Eq. (6.2.21). The associated forward transform is

$$H(j\omega) = \int_{-\infty}^{+\infty} h(\tau)e^{-j\omega\tau}\, d\tau \tag{6.3.10}$$

If we set $\omega = 0$ in Eq. (6.3.10), we have

$$H(0) = \int_{-\infty}^{+\infty} h(\tau)\, d\tau \tag{6.3.11}$$

Thus Eq. (6.3.9) merely tells us that the output DC is the input DC times the system response at DC.

Cross-correlation between input and output.   We may cross-correlate the input and output as

$$R_{XY}(\tau) = E[X(t)Y(t+\tau)] = \int_{-\infty}^{+\infty} E[X(t)X(t-\alpha+\tau)]h(\alpha)\, d\alpha \tag{6.3.12}$$

where we used Eq. (6.3.8) and took the expectation inside the convolution integral. The result is

$$R_{XY}(\tau) = \int_{-\infty}^{+\infty} R_X(\tau - \alpha)h(\alpha)\, d\alpha \tag{6.3.13}$$

Thus the cross-correlation between input and output can be expressed as a convolution between the input autocorrelation function and the impulse response of the system.

Cross-power spectra between input and output.   If we take the Fourier transform of Eq. (6.3.13), we have

$$S_{XY}(\omega) = S_X(\omega)H(j\omega) \tag{6.3.14}$$

Note in Eq. (6.3.14) that $S_X(\omega)$ is a real function, but the system response, $H(j\omega)$, has both amplitude and phase, so the cross-power spectrum has both amplitude and phase associated with it.

We will now illustrate some of these general relationships by passing our four models through a low-pass filter.

6.3.2 Modeling a Random Analog Signal Through a Low-Pass Filter

To keep the mathematics manageable, we will consider a low-pass filter for our linear system and treat in turn the four models for random signals that we have been exploring in this chapter.

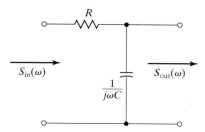

Figure 6.3.2   The *RC* low-pass filter in the frequency domain. The input is a WSS random process, described in the frequency domain by its PSD function.

System properties.   The low-pass filter in the frequency domain is shown in Fig. 6.3.2. The power system function for the *RC* low-pass filter is given in Eq. (6.2.19) as

$$|\underline{\mathbf{H}}(j\omega)|^2 = \left|\frac{1}{1 + j\omega RC}\right|^2 = \frac{1}{1 + (\omega RC)^2} = \frac{1}{1 + (f/f_c)^2} \tag{6.3.15}$$

where $f_c = \frac{1}{2\pi RC}$ is the half-power frequency of the filter, also called the *cutoff frequency*. The relationship we will use to determine the output spectrum is given in Eq. (6.3.7) as

$$S_{\text{out}}(\omega) = S_{\text{in}}(\omega) \times |\underline{\mathbf{H}}(j\omega)|^2 \tag{6.3.16}$$

Generally, our method of analysis follows the pattern $R_{\text{in}}(\tau) \rightarrow S_{\text{in}}(\omega) \rightarrow S_{\text{out}}(\omega) \rightarrow R_{\text{out}}(t)$. Matters of concern are the DC and AC power in the output, the coherence function, and the bandwidth and coherence time. In Sec. 6.1 we determined the input autocorrelation function for our four models. The $R_{\text{in}}(\tau) \rightarrow S_{\text{in}}(\omega)$ part of the analysis was accomplished in Sec. 6.2 for the four models. We here complete the remainder of the analysis.

Model for a random analog signal

Input characteristics.   We begin with the model for a random analog signal because the math is simplest. Our model is a sinusoid with fixed amplitude and frequency but random phase. We showed that this model is WSS and ergodic. The autocorrelation function was given in Eq. (6.1.35) as

$$R_{\text{in}}(\tau) = \frac{V_p^2}{2} \cos \omega_1 \tau \text{ volts}^2 \tag{6.3.17}$$

The input PSD function is given in Eq. (6.2.48) as

$$S_{\text{in}}(f) = \frac{V_p^2}{4}\delta(f + f_1) + \frac{V_p^2}{4}\delta(f - f_1) \text{ volts}^2/\text{Hz} \tag{6.3.18}$$

The output PSD function is given by Eq. (6.3.18) multiplied by the power system response, Eq. (6.3.15), with the result

$$S_{\text{out}}(f) = \left[\frac{V_p^2}{4}\delta(f + f_1) + \frac{V_p^2}{4}\delta(f - f_1) \right] \times \frac{1}{1 + (f/f_c)^2} \text{ volts}^2/\text{Hz} \qquad (6.3.19)$$

The filter function gives its response at $\pm f_1$ and diminishes the amplitude by the factor $\frac{1}{1+(\pm f_1/f_c)^2}$, with the final result

$$S_{\text{out}}(f) = \frac{V_p^2}{4(1 + (f_1/f_c)^2)}\delta(f + f_1) + \frac{V_p^2}{4(1 + (f_1/f_c)^2)}\delta(f - f_1) \text{ volts}^2/\text{Hz} \qquad (6.3.20)$$

Finally, the inverse transform of Eq. (6.3.20) is identical with Eq. (6.3.17), except the amplitude is diminished by the power system response.

$$R_{\text{out}}(\tau) = \frac{V_p^2}{2(1 + (f_1/f_c)^2)} \cos 2\pi f_1 \tau \text{ volts}^2 \qquad (6.3.21)$$

Summary. The low-pass filter has the expected effect of reducing the amplitude of the random sinusoid. The magnitude of the effect depends on the relationship between the frequency of the random sinusoid and the cutoff frequency of the filter. For $f_1 \ll f_c$, the filter has little effect; for $f_1 \gg f_c$, the effect will be strong; and for $f_1 = f_c$, the signal power will be reduced by a factor of 2.

6.3.3 Model for Broadband Noise in a Low-Pass Filter

Resistor noise output. The effect of a low-pass filter on broadband noise is best considered as a problem in circuit theory. The question we will address is, How much noise voltage comes out of a real resistor? The problem is stated, and translated into circuit theory, in Fig. 6.3.3.

The source resistance and stray capacitance amount to a low-pass filter. We model the input PSD as white noise of magnitude $S_N = 2kTR$ (two sides) [Eq. (6.2.57)]. The output PSD is therefore

$$S_{\text{out}}(\omega) = S_N \times \frac{1}{1 + (\omega RC)^2} \text{ volt}^2/\text{Hz} \qquad (6.3.22)$$

and the output autocorrelation function is the inverse Fourier transform. The form of Eq. (6.3.22) requires in the table,[13] $\alpha = \frac{1}{RC}$ and some juggling of the constants, with the result

$$R_{\text{out}}(\tau) = \frac{S_N}{2RC}e^{-|\tau|/RC} \text{ volts}^2 \qquad (6.3.23)$$

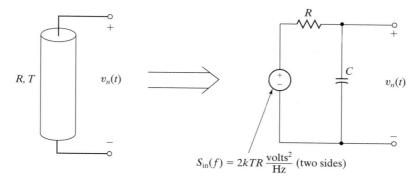

$$S_{\text{in}}(f) = 2kTR \,\frac{\text{volts}^2}{\text{Hz}} \text{ (two sides)}$$

Figure 6.3.3   A resistor has output noise owing to thermal movement of carriers. The equivalent circuit shows the internal noise source, with its PSD, the output impedance of the resistor source, and a capacitance to account for stray, or parasitic, capacitance inherent to the physical structure.

If we insert the value for $S_N = 2kTR$, we find that the output autocorrelation function has the form

$$R_{\text{out}}(\tau) = \frac{kT}{C}e^{-|\tau|/RC} \text{ volts}^2 \qquad (6.3.24)$$

Character of the output.   We consider now the broad features of the output. The output voltage will still be Gaussian and ergodic. There is no mean, but the variance has the value

$$R_{\text{out}}(0) = E[V_{\text{out}}^2(t)] = \sigma_V^2 = \frac{S_N}{2RC} = \frac{kT}{C} \qquad (6.3.25)$$

The rms value of the output noise is therefore

$$V_{\text{out}} = \sqrt{\frac{kT}{C}} \text{ rms volts} \qquad (6.3.26)$$

For example, at room temperature with 1 pF stray capacitance, we have an rms voltage of 64 μV, independent of R.

A noise bandwidth, B_n, is found by equating the total noise power given in Eq. (6.3.23) to

$$S_N \times 2B_n = \frac{S_N}{2RC} \qquad (6.3.27)$$

It follows that

$$B_n = \frac{1}{4RC} \text{ Hz} \qquad (6.3.28)$$

The half-power point of the low-pass filter is $f_c = \frac{1}{2\pi RC}$, and therefore the noise bandwidth is about 1.6 times the half-power frequency.

The coherence function for the output noise is

$$\rho_V(\tau) = e^{-|\tau|/RC} \tag{6.3.29}$$

The coherence time, defined as the value of τ after which the coherence function remains below 0.1, is therefore

$$\tau_c = -RC \ln(0.1) = 2.303 \; RC \tag{6.3.30}$$

The noise bandwidth and the coherence time are related as

$$B_n = \frac{0.576}{\tau_c} \tag{6.3.31}$$

An application of this theory.   Let us say we have a sample of wideband noise and we wish to estimate the variance. Of course, with a true rms voltmeter that has adequate bandwidth one can measure the noise directly, but we will use an oscilloscope. Our method will be to display the noise on the scope and estimate its peak-to-peak (PP) value. The scope trace looks like that plotted in Fig. 6.3.4.

Let us say the known bandwidth of the signal, either from the source or from the scope, is B, and that the trace speed is S cm/s. Because the coherence time is roughly $\frac{1}{B}$, the 10-cm trace contains approximately $n = 10B/S$ independent samples of the voltage. For example, if the scope bandwidth is 30 MHz, and the trace speed is 1 cm/μs, the number of independent samples

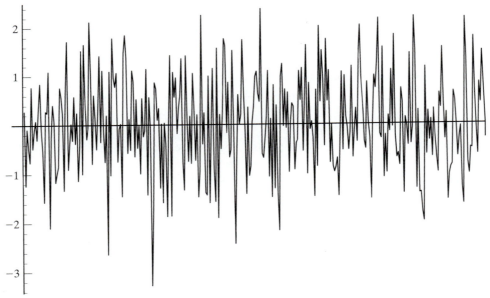

Figure 6.3.4   Simulated noise as it would appear on the screen of an oscilloscope. There are $n = 300$ independent samples in this scan.

is approximately $10 \times 30 \times 10^6 \times 1 \times 10^{-6} = 300$, which corresponds to the number of samples pictured in Fig. 6.3.4. We measure the peak-to-peak voltage and find this to be PP volts (about 5.5 in the plot). We reason as follows: The samples spaced $\frac{1}{B} = 33$ ns apart are IID random Gaussian random variables. A probability statement about these random variables is

$$P\left[\left(|V_1| < \frac{PP}{2}\right) \cap \left(|V_2| < \frac{PP}{2}\right) \cap \left(|V_3| < \frac{PP}{2}\right) \cap \cdots \cap \left(|V_n| < \frac{PP}{2}\right)\right] = 0.5 \quad (6.3.32)$$

Why 0.5? Well, if you did it again, would you expect the PP value to be larger or smaller? Not knowing, you can comfortably say the probability that you would get just what you got is 0.5. Because these are IID variables, we may turn the $\cap \rightarrow \times$, and we have the result

$$P\left[|V| < \frac{PP}{2}\right]^n = 0.5 \text{ or } 2\Phi\left(\frac{PP}{2\sigma_V}\right) - 1 = \sqrt[n]{0.5} \quad (6.3.33)$$

Here we took the nth root of the equation and used the standard formula [Eq. (3.4.9)] for the central probability of a Gaussian random variable. We may solve Eq. (6.3.33) for σ_V, which is the standard deviation, or the rms value, of the noise. The formula is a bit awkward and is best illustrated by an example. We have 300 samples and a PP value of approximately 5.5. For $n = 300$, we have

$$\frac{PP}{2\sigma_V} = \Phi^{-1}\left(\frac{1 + \sqrt[300]{0.5}}{2}\right) = \Phi^{-1}(0.9988) \approx 3.09 \quad (6.3.34)$$

where we used the inverse CDF table [see endnote 34 in Chapter 3]. We solve Eq. (6.3.34) for σ_V with the result that $\sigma_V \approx \frac{5.5}{6.18} = 0.89$. (We generated Fig. 6.3.4 with a standard deviation of 1, so this is acceptable agreement.)

Summary.   We showed how to estimate the standard deviation, or the rms value, of wideband noise based on the peak-to-peak value and the number of independent samples. The results amount to dividing the PP noise by a factor in the range of 6 to 7. Use 6 if you have hundreds of samples, 7 if you have thousands.

6.3.4 Model for an Asynchronous Digital Signal in a Low-Pass Filter

Model.   Our model for an asynchronous digital signal was a flip-flop triggered by a Poisson process with an average rate of λ. The random process was WSS with an autocorrelation function, Eq. (6.1.17), of

$$R_{\text{in}}(\tau) = \frac{1}{4}[1 + e^{-2\lambda|\tau|}] \text{ volts}^2 \quad (6.3.35)$$

The PSD is given in Eq. (6.2.40):

$$S_{\text{in}}(f) = \frac{1}{4}\delta(f) + \frac{\lambda}{(2\lambda)^2 + (2\pi f)^2} \text{ volts}^2/\text{Hz} \quad (6.3.36)$$

We pass this signal through the low-pass filter to produce the output spectrum

$$S_{out}(f) = \frac{1}{4}\delta(f) + \frac{\lambda}{(2\lambda)^2 + (2\pi f)^2} \times \frac{1}{1 + (f/f_c)^2} \text{ volts}^2/\text{Hz} \qquad (6.3.37)$$

We leave the first term alone because this is a DC term, which passes unaffected through the filter. The second term gives the effect of the filter on the AC spectrum of the digital signal. We now determine the autocorrelation function by performing the inverse Fourier transform on Eq. (6.3.37). For this purpose we make a partial-fraction expansion of the second term, which is of the form

$$\frac{1}{x^2 + a^2} \times \frac{1}{x^2 + b^2} = \frac{1}{b^2 - a^2}\left[\frac{1}{x^2 + a^2} - \frac{1}{x^2 + b^2}\right],$$
$$\text{where } x = 2\pi f, \ a = 2\lambda, \text{ and } b = 2\pi f_c \qquad (6.3.38)$$

Using this partial fraction expansion, we obtain the form

$$S_{out}(f) = \frac{1}{4}\delta(f) + \frac{4\pi^2\lambda f_c^2}{(2\pi f_c)^2 - (2\lambda)^2}\left[\frac{1}{(2\pi f)^2 + (2\lambda)^2} - \frac{1}{(2\pi f)^2 + (2\pi f_c)^2}\right] \text{ volts}^2/\text{Hz}$$
$$(6.3.39)$$

From the table of Fourier transform pairs, we find the inverse transform to be[13]

$$R_{out}(\tau) = \frac{1}{4} + \frac{4\pi^2\lambda f_c^2}{(2\pi f_c)^2 - (2\lambda)^2}\left[\frac{1}{4\lambda}e^{-2\lambda|\tau|} - \frac{1}{4\pi f_c}e^{-2\pi f_c|\tau|}\right] \qquad (6.3.40)$$

Equation (6.3.40) is not easily interpreted. We consider two extremes.

Signal bandwidth ≪ filter bandwidth.   If $2\lambda \ll 2\pi f_c$, then the first term in the bracket dominates the second term in the bracket, and the second term in the denominator out front is negligible. In that case, the output autocorrelation function approaches the input,

$$R_{out}(\tau) \underset{2\lambda \ll 2\pi f_c}{\longrightarrow} \frac{1}{4} + \frac{1}{4}e^{-2\lambda|\tau|} = R_{in}(\tau) \qquad (6.3.41)$$

This is what we would expect to happen. Essentially, the bandwidth of the low-pass filter is much wider than the spectrum in the input and thus the signal goes through the filter with little change. The frequency-domain picture of this situation is shown in Fig. 6.3.5, where $2\lambda = \frac{1}{20}2\pi f_c$.

The time-domain picture shows the input pulses slightly rounded due to the loss of high frequencies. Figure 6.3.6 shows the output when the filter bandwidth is much larger than the signal bandwidth, $\lambda = \frac{\pi}{20}f_c$. The main effect is that the pulse corners are rounded.

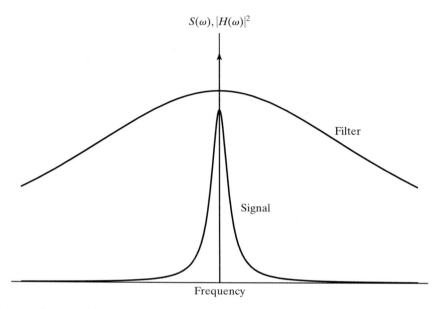

Figure 6.3.5   The signal bandwidth is 5% of the filter half-power bandwidth. The filter has little effect on the signal in this case. The vertical scale is arbitrary.

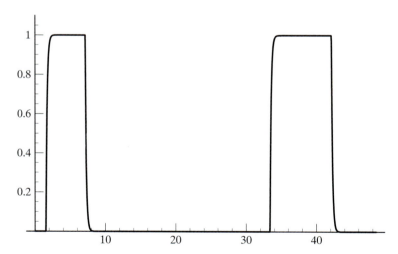

Figure 6.3.6   The output of the low-pass filter with an asynchronous digital signal input. The filter bandwidth is much broader than the signal bandwidth, so the effect of the filter is to round the corners slightly.

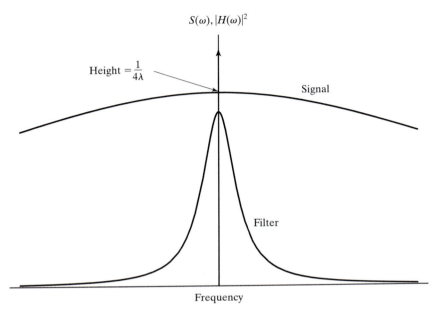

Figure 6.3.7   The input spectrum is much wider than the filter bandwidth, so the input spectrum is like white noise of height $\frac{1}{4\lambda}$.

Signal bandwidth $\gg$ filter bandwidth.   If $2\lambda \gg 2\pi f_c$ then the output autocorrelation function approaches the form

$$R_{\text{out}}(\tau) \rightarrow \frac{1}{4} + \frac{\pi f_c}{4\lambda}e^{-2\pi f_c|\tau|} = \frac{1}{4} + \frac{1}{4\lambda} \times \frac{1}{2RC}e^{-|\tau|/RC} \tag{6.3.42}$$

In the second form of Eq. (6.3.42) we inserted the circuit theory variables so that we can compare these results with the case in which we studied a white-noise input to the low-pass filter. Compare Eq. (6.3.42) with Eq. (6.3.23) and you will observe that the form is the same, with the $\frac{1}{4\lambda}$ playing the role of the white-noise input, S_N. Figure 6.3.7 gives the picture in the frequency domain.

To confirm that the input spectrum has the value $\frac{1}{4\lambda}$ in its low-frequency region, we take the limit of $S_{\text{in}}(f)$ as $f \rightarrow 0$. The spectrum is given in Eq. (6.2.40) as

$$S(f) = \frac{1}{4}\delta(f) + \frac{\lambda}{(2\lambda)^2 + (2\pi f)^2} \text{ volts}^2/\text{Hz} \tag{6.3.43}$$

Considering only the AC portion of the spectrum, we note that

$$S(f) \underset{f\rightarrow 0}{\rightarrow} \frac{1}{4\lambda} \tag{6.3.44}$$

Summary.   When the spectrum of the digital signal is much greater than the bandwidth of the low-pass filter, the input acts as white noise and the output of the filter is the DC component of $\frac{1}{2}$ with a very small fluctuation riding on top of the DC. The time-domain picture would be uninteresting, essentially a constant. All information is lost.

6.3.5 Model for a Synchronous Digital Signal in a Low-Pass Filter

The model.   The model for a synchronous digital signal has 1s and 0s equally likely in each clock period, T, and no absolute time origin. The model was found to be WSS, with the autocorrelation function given in Eq. (6.1.28) as

$$
\begin{aligned}
R_X(\tau) &= \frac{1}{2} - \frac{1}{4}\frac{|\tau|}{T}, \quad 0 < |\tau| < T \\
&= \frac{1}{4}, \quad |\tau| > T
\end{aligned}
\tag{6.3.45}
$$

The spectrum for this model was derived in Eq. (6.2.45) as

$$
S_{\text{in}}(f) = \frac{1}{4}\delta(f) + \frac{T}{4}\left(\frac{\sin \pi Tf}{\pi Tf}\right)^2 \text{ volts}^2/\text{Hz}
\tag{6.3.46}
$$

The output spectrum.   The output spectrum is Eq. (6.3.46) multiplied by the power system function, with the result

$$
S_{\text{out}}(f) = \frac{1}{4}\delta(f) + \frac{T}{4}\left(\frac{\sin \pi Tf}{\pi Tf}\right)^2 \times \frac{1}{1 + (f/f_c)^2} \text{ volts}^2/\text{Hz}
\tag{6.3.47}
$$

As before, we left the DC term alone because it is not affected by the filter. The inverse transform of Eq. (6.3.47) is not apparent, so we must be content with the frequency-domain treatment. This situation is similar to that for the asynchronous digital signal. With adequate bandwidth, the bits pass through the filter with slight rounding of the edges. Without adequate bandwidth, the filter will destroy information. The bandwidth of the digital signal was derived to be $B = 1/T$, where T is the clock period, and the bandwidth of the filter was approximately $\frac{1}{RC}$. Therefore the requirement for little information loss is $T \gg RC$. The information is more robust for the clocked system because the minimum time between transitions is T.

Summary.   In this section we studied the passage of random signals through linear systems. We began by showing that the familiar analysis techniques of the frequency domain are still valid, provided the random signal is WSS and only power spectra are used. We illustrated the method of analysis for the four models we used throughout this chapter. We spent extra time with the model for wideband spectra because of the practical importance of wideband noise in system analysis.

6.4 PROBLEMS

6.4.1 WSS Random Processes

Exercises on WSS Random Processes, Including Many Random Processes That Are Not WSS

P6.1.1   A random process is defined as $X(t) = t$, $0 < t \leq T$, zow, where T is an exponential random variable with a mean of 1.
           a. Find the PMF of X, $P_{X(t)}(x, t)$.
           b. Find $E[X]$.
           c. Find the autocorrelation function, $R(t_1, t_2)$, with $t_1 < t_2$.

           A6.1.1 **(a)** $P_{X(t)} = 1 - e^{-t}$, $x = 0$, $= e^{-t}$, $x = t$, zow; **(b)** te^{-t}, $t \geq 0$, zow; **(c)** $t_1 t_2 e^{-t_2}$, $0 < t_1 < t_2$, zow

P6.1.2   A chance experiment has three equally likely outcomes, $S = \{s_1, s_2, s_3\}$. A random process, $X(t)$, is defined on these outcomes as follows:

$$X(t, s_1) = 5$$
$$X(t, s_2) = \sin t$$
$$X(t, s_3) = -\sin t$$

           a. Find the mean of the random process.
           b. Find the autocorrelation function of the random process.
           c. Is the random process WSS? Explain.

           A6.1.2 **(a)** $\frac{5}{3}$; **(b)** $R_X(\tau) = E[X(t)X(t + \tau)] = \frac{25}{3} + \frac{\cos(\tau)}{3} - \frac{\cos(2t+\tau)}{3}$; **(c)** no, since autocorrelation is not an even function of τ

P6.1.3   A chance experiment has two outcomes, $S = \{s_1, s_2\}$, equally likely. A random process is defined on these outcomes as follows: $X(t, s_1) = e^{+0.01t}$ and $X(t, s_2) = e^{-0.01t}$.
           a. Find the mean of the random process, $\mu_X = E[X(t)]$.
           b. Find the autocorrelation function of the random process, $R(t_1, t_2) = E[X(t_1)X(t_2)]$.
           c. Is the random process WSS? Explain.
           d. Is the random process ergodic? Explain.

           A6.1.3 **(a)** $\cosh(0.01t)$; **(b)** $R(t_1, t_2) = \cosh[0.01(t_1 + t_2)]$; **(c)** no, the mean is not constant; **(d)** no, not WSS

P6.1.4   A random process is defined in terms of a random variable, Z, that is exponentially distributed, $f_Z(z) = e^{-z}$, $z \geq 0$, zow. The random process is $X(t) = Zt$, for all time.
           a. Sketch a typical member of this random process.
           b. Find the mean of the random process, $\mu_X = E[X(t)]$.
           c. Find the autocorrelation function of the random process, $R(t_1, t_2) = E[X(t_1)X(t_2)]$.
           d. Is the random process WSS? Explain.
           e. Is the random process ergodic? Explain.

           A6.1.4 **(a)** see plot; **(b)** t; **(c)** $R(t_1, t_2) = 2t_1 t_2$; **(d)** no, mean is not constant; **(e)** no, not WSS

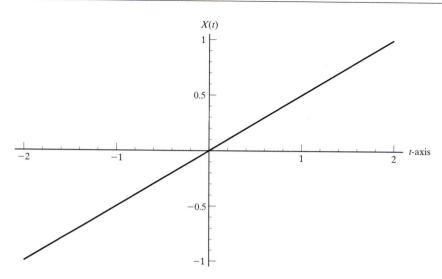

P6.1.5 A random process is defined in terms of a random variable, Z, that is exponentially distributed, $f_Z(z) = e^{-z}$, $z \geq 0$, zow. The random process is $X(t) = Z - t$, for all time.

a. Sketch a typical member of this random process.
b. Find the mean of the random process, $\mu_X = E[X(t)]$.
c. Find the autocorrelation function of the random process, $R(t_1, t_2) = E[X(t_1)X(t_2)]$.
d. Is the random process WSS? Explain.
e. Is the random process ergodic? Explain.

A6.1.5 (a) see the figure; **(b)** $1 - t$; **(c)** $R(t_1, t_2) = 2 - t_1 + t_2 + t_1 t_2$; **(d)** no, mean is not constant; **(e)** no, not WSS

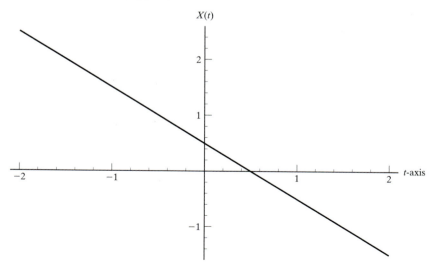

P6.1.6   The simplest random process imaginable is simply a constant, $X(t) = Z$. Assume the random variable, Z, is uniformly distributed between 10 and 20.
a. Find the mean, $E[X(t)]$.
b. Find the autocorrelation function, $R(t_1, t_2)$.
c. Is the random process WSS? Ergodic? Explain.
Note: Normally, we think of a function as *depending* on the independent variable, like $f(x) = x^2$. But $f(x) = 5$ is also a legitimate function, even though x does not appear on the right-hand side of the equation.

A6.1.6 (a) 15; **(b)** 233.3; **(c)** The random process is WSS but not ergodic, since the time average $= Z$, a random variable, but the mean $= 15$.

P6.1.7   A random process is created in the following way: $X(t) = At$, where t is time, $0 < t$, zow, and A is a uniformly distributed random variable in the range $-1 < A < +1$.
a. Find the mean, $\mu_{X(t)}$.
b. Find the autocorrelation function, $R_X(t_1, t_2)$.
c. Is $X(t)$ WSS? Ergodic? Explain your answers.

A6.1.7 (a) zero; **(b)** $t_1 t_2 / 3$; **(c)** not WSS, not ergodic, autocorrelation not an even function of $\tau = t_2 - t_1$, so not WSS

P6.1.8   A WSS Gaussian random process has an autocorrelation function of the form $R(\tau) = 16\left(1 - \frac{|\tau|}{50}\right)^2 + 100$, $0 < |\tau| < 50$, $R(\tau) = 100$ otherwise. Assume a positive mean.
a. What is the mean value of the random process?
b. What is the variance of the random process?
c. Write the first-order PDF, $f_{X(t)}(x)$, for the value of the process.

A6.1.8 (a) 10; **(b)** 16; **(c)** $N(-10, 16)$

P6.1.9   A WSS Gaussian random process has an autocorrelation function of the form $R(\tau) = 16e^{-|\tau|/50} + 100$. Assume the mean is negative.
a. What is the mean value of the random process?
b. What is the variance of the random process?
c. Write the first-order PDF for the value of the process at a given time.

A6.1.9 (a) -10; **(b)** 16; **(c)** $N(-10, 16)$

P6.1.10   A random experiment has three outcomes, $S = \{1, 2, 3\}$, with $P[1] = \frac{1}{2}$, $P[2] = \frac{1}{3}$, and $P[3] = \frac{1}{6}$. A function is assigned to each outcome as shown. This constitutes a random process, since functions are assigned to the outcomes of a chance experiment.
a. Find the mean of this random process at $t = 1$ second; $\mu_{X(1)} = ?$
b. Find the autocorrelation function of this random process at $t_1 = 1$ and $t_2 = 1.5$; $R_X(1, 1.5) = ?$

A6.1.10 (a) ≈ 0.229; **(b)** ≈ 0.0490

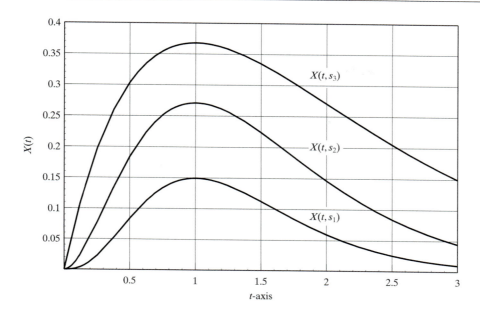

P6.1.11   A chance experiment has three equally likely outcomes, $S = \{s_1, s_2, s_3\}$. A random
process is defined: $X(t, s_1) = 2\cos 10t$; $X(t, s_2) = 2\sin 10t$; $X(t, s_1) = 2$.
a. Find the first-order PMF of this random process at $t = 0.1$.
b. Find $E[X(0.1)]$.
c. Find $R_X(0.1, 0.2) = E[X(0.1)X(0.2)]$.

A6.1.11 **(a)** $\frac{1}{3}$ at $x = 2\cos 1$, $2\sin 1$, 2, zow; **(b)** 1.59; **(c)** 2.05

P6.1.12   A random process consists of four equally likely outcomes, $S = \{s_1, s_2, s_3, s_4\}$, which
map into the following functions,

$$X(t, s_1) = \cos \omega_c t$$
$$X(t, s_2) = -\cos \omega_c t$$
$$X(t, s_3) = \sin \omega_c t$$
$$X(t, s_4) = -\sin \omega_c t$$

a. Find the mean of the random process.
b. Find the autocorrelation function of the random process.
c. Is this random process WSS? Explain.
d. Is this random process ergodic? Explain.

A6.1.12 **(a)** 0; **(b)** $\frac{1}{2}\cos \omega_c \tau$; **(c)** yes, since the mean is constant, and the autocorrelation function is an even function of τ; **(d)** yes, since all four members have the mean and autocorrelation function of the random process

P6.1.13   A WSS Gaussian random process, $X(t)$, has an autocorrelation function of $R(\tau) = \frac{10^{-6}}{1+10^{6}\tau^2} + 10^{-6}$ volts^2, with τ in seconds.

a. Find $E[X^2]$.

b. Find the decorrelation time.

c. Find the probability that $X(t)$ exceeds 0.002, assuming a positive mean.

A6.1.13 (a) 2×10^{-6} volts^2; **(b)** 3×10^{-3} s; **(c)** 0.1587

P6.1.14   A random process is defined as $X(t) = At$, $0 < t \leq T$, zow, where A is a uniformly distributed random variable between 0 and 1, and T is an exponential random variable with an expected value of 1, and the two random variables are independent. A typical member function is shown in the figure.

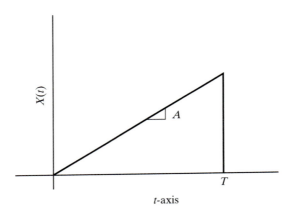

t-axis

a. Find the mean $E[X(t)]$.

b. Find the autocorrelation function, assuming $t_1 < t_2$.

A6.1.14 (a) $\frac{t}{2}e^{-t}$, $t \geq 0$, zow; **(b)** $\frac{t_1 t_2}{3}e^{-t_2}$, $0 < t_1 < t_2$, zow

P6.1.15   Consider a random process in which there are four equally likely outcomes, $S = \{s_i\}$ for $i = 1, 2, 3, 4$. We define a random process based on this experiment as $X(t, s_i) = 10\cos\left(5t + \frac{i\pi}{2}\right)$.

a. Find the mean of this random process.

b. Find the autocorrelation of this random process.

c. Is this random process WSS? Explain.

A6.1.15 (a) 0; **(b)** $R_X(\tau) = 50\cos 5\tau$; **(c)** yes, since the mean is constant, and the autocorrelation function is an even function of τ

P6.1.16   Consider a random process that consists of one pulse. The start of the pulse is exponentially distributed, and the length of the pulse is also exponentially distributed and is independent of the start time. Let T represent the start time and D represent the duration of the pulse, with $E[T] = E[D] = 1$. See the figure for a picture of one member of this random process.

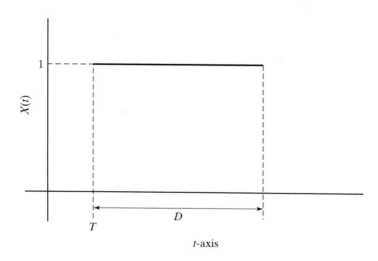

t-axis

a. Find the mean of this random process.
b. Find the autocorrelation of this random process, $R_X(t_1, t_2)$. *Hint:* Conditional probability helps, and let $t_1 < t_2$.

A6.1.16 (a) te^{-t}, $t \geq 0$, zow; (b) $t_1 e^{-t_2}$, $0 < t_1 < t_2$, zow

P6.1.17 A random process depends on the random variable T, where T is exponential with a PDF of $f_T(t) = 2e^{-2t}$, $t \geq 0$, zow. The random process is

$$X(t) = 0, t < T$$
$$= 1, t \geq T$$

a. Find the CDF of the random process for all time.
b. Find the expected value of the random process for positive time.
c. Find the autocorrelation function for the process, $R(t_1, t_2), t_2 > t_1 > 0$.

A6.1.17 (a) $u(x)e^{-2t} + u(x - 1)(1 - e^{-2t})$, $t > 0$, zow; (b) $1 - e^{-2t}$, $t > 0$, zow;
(c) $1 - e^{-2t_1}$

P6.1.18 Consider a random process $X(t) = u(t - T) - u(t - T - a)$. The random variable, T, is exponentially distributed with an average value of b. Find and plot the expected values of $X(t)$. A typical member of the random process is shown in the figure.

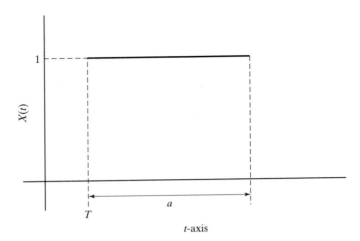

A6.1.18 The function is $E[X] = 1 - e^{-t/b}$, $t < a$; $= e^{-(t-a)/b} - e^{-t/b}$, $t > a$. See the plot for $a = 1$ and $b = 2$.

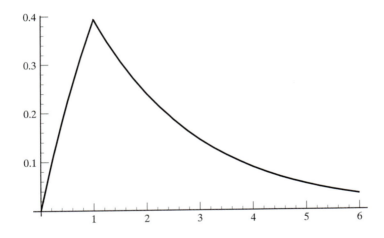

P6.1.19 Consider a random process consisting of functions $V(t) = V_p \cos(\omega t + \Theta) + V_A$, where Θ is a random variable uniformly distributed between 0 and 2π, and V_A is a random variable uniformly distributed between 0 and V_p and independent of Θ. V_p is a fixed constant.

a. Find the expected value of the random process.

b. Find the autocorrelation function of the random process.

c. Is the random process WSS? Explain.

d. Is the random process ergodic? Explain.

A6.1.19 (a) $\frac{V_p}{2}$; (b) $\frac{V_p^2}{2}\cos\omega\tau + \frac{V_p^2}{3}$; (c) yes, since the mean is constant and the autocorrelation is a function of the magnitude of the time difference; (d) no, since the time average is not the statistical mean because of the DC term

P6.1.20 Let $V(t) = A\cos\Omega t$, where Ω is a random variable uniformly distributed between 0 and $2\pi B$. The amplitude, A, is constant.
  a. Find the mean of $V(t)$.
  b. Find $R_V(t_1, t_2)$, the autocorrelation function of $V(t)$.
  c. Is $V(t)$ WSS?
  d. Is $V(t)$ ergodic?

A6.1.20 (a) $\frac{A}{2\pi B}\sin(2\pi Bt)$; (b) $R_V(t_1, t_2) = \frac{A^2}{4\pi B}\left[\frac{\sin 2\pi(t_2-t_1)}{t_2-t_1} + \frac{\sin 2\pi(t_2+t_1)}{t_2+t_1}\right]$; (c) no, the mean is not constant, and the second term in the autocorrelation function is not a function of $t_2 - t_1$; (d) no, not WSS

P6.1.21 The following random process is based on Bernoulli trials. Trials are made on integer values of $t = 1, 2, 3, \ldots$, and the probability of success is p. The random process starts at $X(0) = 0$ and increases 1 for each success. For example, the realized function for the sequence S, F, F, S, F, S, F, F, S looks as shown in the figure.
  a. Find the PMF, $P_{X(t)}(x)$.
  b. Find the expected value, $E[X(t)]$, where t is an integer.
  c. Find the autocorrelation function, $R_X(1, 3)$.

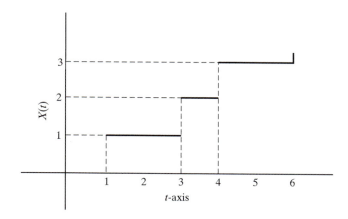

A6.1.21 (a) $B_n(x, p)$, $0 < x \le t$; (b) $t \times p$; (c) $pq^2 + 4\,p^2q + 3\,p^3$.

P6.1.22 A random process is constructed by first choosing a random variable, T, that is uniformly distributed between 0 and 10 seconds and then defining the random process in terms of T: $X(t) = 1$, $0 < t \le T$; $X(t) = -1$, $T < t \le 10$, zow. A typical member of this random process is shown in the figure.

a. Find the PMF of this process, $P_{X(t)}(x)$.
b. Find the mean of the process, $E[X(t)]$.
c. Find the autocorrelation function, $R_X(t_1, t_2) = E[X(t_1)X(t_2)]$. For simplicity, let $0 < t_1 < t_2 < 10$.

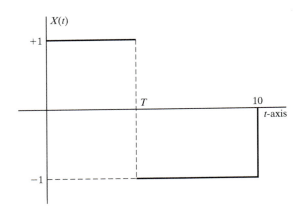

A6.1.22 (a) $P_{X(t)}(1) = 1 - \frac{t}{10}$, $0 < t < 10$, zow, $P_{X(t)}(-1) = \frac{t}{10}$, $0 < t < 10$, 0 otherwise; (b) $1 - \frac{t}{5}$, $0 < t < 10$, zow; (c) $1 - \frac{t_2 - t_1}{5}$, $0 < t_1 < t_2 < 10$, zow

P6.1.23   A discrete random process starts at $X(0) = 0$ and increases by increments of 1 with a probability of $p = 0.4$ at $n = 1, 2, 3, \ldots$. A typical member of this process is shown in the figure. *Hint:* This random process can be formed through a series of Bernoulli trials.
a. Find $E[X]$, for $n = 1, 2, 3, \ldots$.
b. Find $R_X(2, 4)$, the autocorrelation function evaluated at $n = 2$ for the first sample and $n = 4$ for the second.

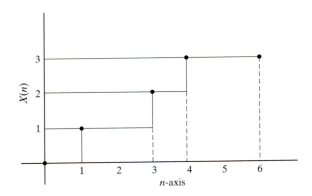

A6.1.23 (a) $0.4\, n$, where $n = 1, 2, 3, \ldots$; (b) 1.76

P6.1.24   A random process consists of $X(t) = 0$ or 1, with transitions described by a Poisson process with an average transition rate of λ. The value $X(0)$ is 0 or 1 with 50% probability. Find
a. $E[X(t)]$.
b. $E[X(t)X(t + \tau)]$.
c. Is $X(t)$ wide-sense stationary? Explain.

A6.1.24 (a) $\frac{1}{2}$; (b) $\frac{1}{4}(1 + e^{-2\lambda|\tau|})$; (c) yes, if you stay away from the origin. If τ is larger than t, then you get into trouble, because the output is undefined for negative time

P6.1.25   A coding scheme uses the phase of a sinusoid to convey a bit of information.

$$V(t) = A\cos(\omega t + \theta_i), \text{ where } \theta_i = 0 \text{ for } \{0\}, \text{ and } \theta_i = 180° \text{ for a } \{1\}.$$

The amplitude, A, is a constant. Assume the random experiment is the selection of the state $\{0,1\}$, with both outcomes equally likely. The result of this scheme is a random process with two member functions.
a. Is this random process WSS? Explain.
b. Is this random process ergodic? Explain.

A6.1.25 (a) no, mean is OK, but $R(t_1, t_2) = \frac{A^2}{2}[\cos\omega(t_2 - t_1) + \cos\omega(t_2 + t_1)]$, which has the wrong form; (b) only WSS random processes can be ergodic

P6.1.26   A toggle flip-flop is triggered by Poisson events, with $\lambda = 1000$ pulses per second, on average. The flip-flop output signal has values of 0 and $+1$. The output autocorrelation function is given by Eq. (6.1.17),

$$R_Q(\tau) = E[Q(t)Q(t + \tau)] = \frac{1}{4}\left[1 + e^{-2000|\tau|}\right]$$

Give the autocorrelation function as affected by the following changes. The changes are made one at a time and are not cumulative.
a. The output logic levels are 0 and V.
b. The output logic levels are 0 and -1.
c. The output logic levels are $+V$ and $-V$.
d. The rate of trigger pulses doubles.

A6.1.26 (a) $R_Q(\tau) \rightarrow \frac{V^2}{4}\left[1 + e^{-2000|\tau|}\right]$; (b) no change; (c) $R_Q(\tau) \rightarrow V^2 e^{-2000|\tau|}$; (d) $R_Q(\tau) \rightarrow \frac{1}{4}\left[1 + e^{-4000|\tau|}\right]$

P6.1.27   A random process is defined as $X(t) = t$, $0 < t \le T$, zow, where T is a random variable with the PDF $f_T(t) = e^{-t}$, $t > 0$, zow. A typical member of this random process is shown in the figure.

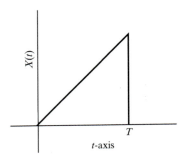

a. Find $E[X]$.
b. Find the PDF of X, $f_{X(t)}(x)$.
c. Find the autocorrelation function, $R_X(t_1, t_2)$.

A6.1.27 **(a)** te^{-t}, $t > 0$, zow; **(b)** $f_{X(t)}(x) = \delta(x - t) \times e^{-t} + \delta(x) \times (1 - e^{-t})$;
(c) $t_1 t_2 e^{-t_2}$, $0 < t_1 < t_2$, zow

P6.1.28   A sinusoidal function has known frequency and phase but uncertain amplitude: $V(t) = A \cos 100t$, where A is a random variable uniformly distributed between $+8$ and $+10$ V.
a. Find the first-order PDF of $V(t)$ at $t = 0.005$ s.
b. Find $E[V(t)]$.
c. Find $R_V(t_1, t_2)$.
d. Is this random process wide-sense stationary? Explain.

A6.1.28 **(a)** $f_V(t) = 0.570$, $7.02 < v < 8.77$, zow; **(b)** $9\cos(100t)$; **(c)** $81.3\cos 100t_1$
$\cos 100t_2$; **(d)** no, the mean is not constant, and the autocorrelation function
is not an even function of the time difference

P6.1.29   A random process is defined as $X(t) = 0$ for $t > T$ and $X(t) = 1$ for $t \leq T$, where T is uniformly distributed between 0 and 10. A member of this random process is shown in the figure.

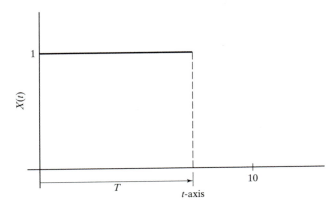

a. Find $E[X(t)]$.

b. Find $R_X(t_1, t_2)$ Assume $0 \le t_1 < t_2 \le 10$.

A6.1.29 (a) $1 - t/10$, $0 < t < 10$, zow; (b) $1 - t_2/10$, $0 < t_2 < 10$, zow

P6.1.30   A random process is defined as $X(t) = A\cos(100t + \Theta)$, where A and Θ are random variables. The random variable A takes on values $+10$ or -10, equally likely, and the random variable Θ is uniformly distributed between $-\pi/2$ and $+\pi/2$. Assume A and Θ are independent.

a. Find $E[X(t)]$.

b. Find $R_X(t_1, t_2)$.

c. Is this a WSS random process? Explain.

d. Is this an ergodic random process? Explain.

A6.1.30 (a) 0; (b) $50\cos 100(t_2 - t_1)$; (c) yes, since the expectation is constant and the autocorrelation function is an even function of $t_2 - t_1$; (d) yes, the time-average mean is zero, and the time-average autocorrelation function is equal to the statistical autocorrelation function.

P6.1.31   Consider a toggle flip-flop, triggered by Poisson pulses with an average rate of λ. The flip-flop starts with a cleared state, $Q(0) = 0$.

a. Find the first-order PMF.

b. Find the second-order PMF for $t_2 = 1$ and $t_1 = 0$.

c. Find $E[Q(t)]$.

d. Find $R_Q(t_1, t_2)$ for $t_2 = 1$ and $t_1 = 0$.

A6.1.31 (a) $P_Q(1) = P[k \text{ odd}] = (1 - e^{-2\lambda t})/2$, $P_Q(0) = P[k \text{ even}] = (1 + e^{-2\lambda t})/2$, zow; (b) $P_Q(0, 1) = \frac{1}{2}(1 - e^{-2\lambda})$, $P_Q(0, 0) = \frac{1}{2}(1 + e^{-2\lambda})$, $P_Q(1, \text{ either state}) = 0$, since it begins in the cleared state; (c) $\frac{1}{2}(1 - e^{-2\lambda t})$; (d) $R_Q(0, 1) = 0$, since it starts in the cleared state

P6.1.32   Consider that the flip-flop in the previous problem begins in an uncertain state, with 1 and 0 equally likely.

a. Find the first-order PMF.

b. Find the second-order PMF for the 1, 1 state.

c. Find $E[X(t)]$.

d. Find $R_Q(1, 1)$.

Hint: Use conditional PMFs with the state at $t = 0$ as the conditioning event.

A6.1.32 (a) $P_Q(0 \text{ or } 1) = \frac{1}{2}$; (b) $P_Q(1, 1) = \frac{1}{4}(1 + e^{-2\lambda(t_2 - t_1)})$; (c) and (d) same as (a) and (b)

P6.1.33   Consider two WSS Gaussian, ergodic random processes, $X(t)$ and $Y(t)$, and a third random process that is formed from them, $Z(t) = X(t) - Y(t)$. Furthermore, the autocorrelation functions of X and Y are $R_X(\tau) = 2e^{-|\tau|} + 2$ and $R_Y(\tau) = 3e^{-2|\tau|} + 1$, and $X(t)$ and $Y(t)$ are independent random processes.

a. Find the autocorrelation function of Z. There are two possible answers; please give both.

    b. Find the AC power in Z.
    c. Find the coherence function for Z.
    d. Find the decorrelation time for Z, τ_c.

A6.1.33 **(a)** $R_Z(\tau) = 2e^{-|\tau|} + 3e^{-2|\tau|} + 3 \pm 2\sqrt{2}$; **(b)** 5; **(c)** $0.4e^{-|\tau|} + 0.6e^{-2|\tau|}$;
       (d) 1.641 s

P6.1.34 A random process is defined on the basis of a series of binomial trials at $i = 1, 2, 3, \ldots$. The initial value is zero, $X(0) = 0$, but with success, 0.5^{i-1} is added. Thus

$$P[X(0) = 0] = 1$$

$$P[X(1) = 1] = p$$

$$P[X(1) = 0] = q$$

$$P[X(i + 1) = X(i) + 0.5^i] = p$$

$$P[X(i + 1) = X(i)] = q$$

    a. At $i = 2$, what are the possible values for $X(2)$ and the probability of each?
    b. At $i = 3$, what are the possible values for $X(3)$ and the probability of each?
    c. Find $E[X(i)]$.
    d. Find $Var[X(i)]$.
    Hint: For parts c and d, let X_1 be a Bernoulli random variable representing success on the first trial, X_2 on the second, and so on.

A6.1.34 **(a)** $P[0] = q^2$, $P[0.5] = pq$, $P[1] = pq$, $P[1.5] = p^2$; **(b)** $P[0] = q^3$, $P[0.25] = pq^2$, $P[0.5] = p^2q$, $P[0.75] = p^2q$, $P[1] = pq^2$, $P[1.25] = p^2q$, $P[1.5] = p^2q$, $P[1.75] = p^3$; **(c)** $2\,p(1 - 0.5^n)$; **(d)** $\frac{4}{3}p\,q(1 - 0.25^n)$

P6.1.35 According to mathematicians, the digits that appear in an irrational number such as π are purely random, with no patterns whatever. This problem investigates this hypothesis by making comparisons between the first 30 digits of $\pi = 31415\ 92653$ $58979\ 32384\ 62643\ 38327$ and the theoretical properties of random, independent digits.
    a. Define a probability model for a random digit, and determine the mean and variance. This model should be calculated and not merely stated.
    b. Determine the sample mean and sample variance of the first 30 digits of π.
    c. Does comparison of the results of parts a and b favor the null hypothesis that the digits are random? Because there are 30 data points, consider that the mean is Gaussian and test at a significance level of $\alpha = 0.05$.
    d. Let us now examine independence. Calculate the sample autocorrelation function, $\overline{R}(\tau)$, where $\tau = 0, 1, 2, \ldots$ refers to the same digit (3, for example), adjacent digits (3 and 1), digits separated by two places (3 and 4), and so on. Calculate $\overline{R}(0)$ and $\overline{R}(1)$ and discuss whether these favor the hypothesis. A subjective discussion is welcome, but numerical comparisons are more impressive.

A6.1.35 (a) Equally likely integers have a mean of 4.5 and a variance of 8.25; (b) for these data $\bar{x} = 4.7$ and $\bar{s}_X^2 = 6.29$; (c) with 30 samples, we can use the CLT to claim that the sample mean will be Gaussian. For 5% significance, the sample mean should fall between 3.6 and 5.4, so our sample passes this test; (d) $\bar{R}(0) = 28.167$, and $\bar{R}(1) = 22.241$; we use $\bar{R}(0) = \sigma_X^2 + \mu_X^2$, and $\bar{R}(1) = \bar{R}(\infty) = \mu_X^2$. These lead to a mean of 4.716 and a variance of 5.926, which compare favorably with the theoretical values. So the hypothesis passes by these rather informal tests.

P6.1.36 A discrete random process $X(n)$ is defined in the following manner: $X(n) = 1$ or 0; $X(0) = 1$. At $n = 1$, the probability that $X(n)$ will change to 0 is p and the probability that $X(n)$ will remain at 1 is $1 - p$. Likewise, at $n = 2, 3, \ldots$, the probability that $X(n)$ will change states is p and the probability that $X(n)$ will not change states is $1 - p$. Note that this process is fundamentally binomial, with independent state changes.
a. Find $E[X(1)]$.
b. Find $E[X(1)X(2)]$.
c. What is the probability that $X(4) = 1$?
d. Find $E[X(n)X(n + 1)]$ if t is a very large integer.

A6.1.36 (a) $1 - p$; (b) $(1 - p)^2$; (c) $(1 - p)^4 + 6p^2(1 - p)^2 + p^4$; (d) $(1 - p)/2$
Part (d) assumes $p \neq 0$. If $p = 0$, then the answer is 1.

P6.1.37 A semi-random flip flop with output logic levels of 0 V and 3.0 V for 0 and 1, respectively, is cleared at $t = 0$. That is, $Q(0) = 0$. The triggers are Poisson events at a rate of 1000 events/second on the average.
a. Give the PMF of $Q(t)$, the output voltage for positive time.
b. Give the autocorrelation function of $Q(t)$ for positive time.
c. For $t = 1$ ms, what is the mean and variance of $Q(t)$?
d. For large time, what is the correlation coefficient of the output at two times separated by 1 ms?

A6.1.37 (a) $P_Q(0) = P[\text{even}] = \frac{1}{2}(1 + e^{-2000t})$ and $P_Q(3) = P[\text{odd}] = \frac{1}{2}(1 - e^{-2000t})$, zow; (b) $R_Q(t_1, t_2) = 3 \times 3 \times \frac{1}{2}(1 + e^{-2000(t_2 - t_1)}) \times \frac{1}{2}(1 - e^{-2000t_1})$; (c) 1.297 volts and 2.209 volts^2; (d) 0.1353

Modeling Problems on WSS Random Processes

P6.1.38 A student taking a test in circuit theory gets an answer to an AC problem of $10/\underline{0^\circ}$ V, but the student cannot remember if the time-domain answer ought to be $10 \cos \omega t$ or $10 \sin \omega t$. So the student flips a coin and uses "cos" for heads and "sin" for tails. The answer is therefore a random process since it is a time function that depends on the outcome of a chance experiment. Let us call this random process $A(t)$.
a. Find and sketch the probability mass function of the random process at $t = 0$, $f_{A(0)}(a)$.
b. Find the expectation, $E[A(t)]$.

c. Is the random process WSS? Explain.

d. Is the random process ergodic? Explain.

A6.1.38 (a)

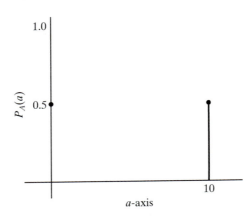

(b) $E[A(t)] = \frac{10}{2}[\cos \omega t + \sin \omega t]$; **(c)** no, the mean varies; **(d)** no, not WSS

P6.1.39   A toggle flip-flop is triggered by Poisson events, with 100 pulses per second being the rate of clock pulses, on average. The flip-flop output signal has values of 0 and +1 V, equally probable at any time. The output autocorrelation function of the output, $Q(t)$, is given by the formula

$$R(\tau) = \frac{1}{4} + \frac{1}{4} \, e^{-200|\tau|} \text{volts}^2$$

Give the autocorrelation function after the following changes, made one at a time. In all cases, these are changes from the original and are not cumulative.

a. We subtract 0.5 from the output, such that the signal goes from +0.5 to −0.5.

b. We double the average rate of the clock pulses.

c. We multiply the signal by 2 such that the output states are 0 and 2.

d. We reverse the signal: $Q(t') = Q(-t)$.

A6.1.39 (a) $R(\tau) = \frac{1}{4} \, e^{-200|\tau|}$ volts²; **(b)** $R(\tau) = \frac{1}{4} + \frac{1}{4} \, e^{-400|\tau|}$ volts²; **(c)** $R(\tau) = 1 + e^{-200|\tau|}$ volts²; **(d)** no change

P6.1.40   A synchronous digital system has logic levels of 0.6 V for a zero and 3.2 V for a one. This is a clocked system with a clock period of 0.05 μs. Ones and zeros are equally likely, and you may assume an arbitrary time origin. Let the WSS random process $X(t)$ model the signal.

a. Find the mean of the random process.

b. Find the total power and the AC power.

    c. Find the autocorrelation function of this signal.

    d. Find the coherence time for this random process.

A6.1.40 (a) 1.9 volts; (b) 5.3 and 1.69 volts^2; (c) $R_X(\tau) = 1.69\left(1 - \frac{|\tau|}{T}\right) + 3.61$ V^2, $|\tau| \leq T$; $= 3.61$volts^2 otherwise; (d) 0.045 μs

P6.1.41 An ergodic, Gaussian random process, $V(t)$, has an autocorrelation function of $R(\tau) = 100e^{-1000\tau^2} + 91$ volts^2.

    a. What is the DC value of the signal, assumed negative?

    b. What is the total power in volts squared?

    c. Find the decorrelation time.

    d. Find the probability that the signal is negative at a time chosen at random.

A6.1.41 (a) -9.54 volts; (b) 191 volts^2; (c) 0.04799 s; (d) 0.8305

P6.1.42 A random process model for a synchronous digital signal has logic levels of 0 and 1 and a clock period of T. The "pulses" or bits in all clock periods are independent, but 0 and 1 are not equally likely. Let $P[1] = p$ at any time and $P[0] = 1 - p$.

    a. Find the mean of this random process.

    b. Find the autocorrelation function of this random process.

    c. Is this random process WSS? Explain.

A6.1.42 (a) p; (b) $R_X(\tau) = p\left(1 - \frac{|\tau|}{T}\right) + p^2 \times \frac{|\tau|}{T}$, $0 < |\tau| \leq T$, $= p^2$, $\tau > T$; (c) yes, because $\mu = $ constant and $R_X = f(|\tau|)$

P6.1.43 A random process is defined on the basis of a series of binomial trials at $n = 1, 2, 3, \ldots$. The initial value $X(0) = 0$. After a trial, with success we add 1 and with failure we subtract 1, where $P[\text{success}] = p$.

    a. Find the mean, $E[X(n)]$, where $n = 1, 2, 3, \ldots$ is the time.

    b. Find the variance, $Var[X(n)]$.

    c. Is the random process WSS?

A6.1.43 (a) $n(2\ p - 1)$; (b) $4pqn$; (c) no, the mean is not constant if $p \neq 0.5$

P6.1.44 A 12-V battery is connected in series with a switch, a resistor, and a 1-H inductor, and the output voltage is taken across the inductor. The resistor is randomly chosen, all values between 2 and 4 Ω being equally likely. The switch is closed at $t = 0$, thus creating a random process, $V(t) = 12e^{-Rt}$, $t \geq 0$, zow.

    a. Derive the PDF of the random process, $f_{V(t)}(t, v)$. *Hint:* Do the CDF first. Drawing pictures helps.

    b. Determine the expectation of the random process, $E[(V(t)]$.

A6.1.44 (a) $f_V(v) = \frac{1}{2tv}$, $12e^{-4t} < v \leq 12e^{-2t}$, zow; (b) $6\left(\frac{e^{-2t} - e^{-4t}}{t}\right)$, $t > 0$, zow.

P6.1.45 A model for a clock signal of unknown phase is shown in the figure, with D, the time to the leading edge nearest the origin, a random variable uniformly distributed between $-\frac{1}{2f}$ and $\frac{1}{2f}$, where f is the clock frequency. Note that all members of the random process are periodic with period $1/f$; hence the only times that need to be considered are during the first period of the function.

a. Find the PMF: $P_{X(t)}(x)$.

b. Determine the autocorrelation function, $R_X(t_1, t_2)$. *Hint:* Because all phases are equally likely, set t_1 to zero.

c. Is this random process WSS?

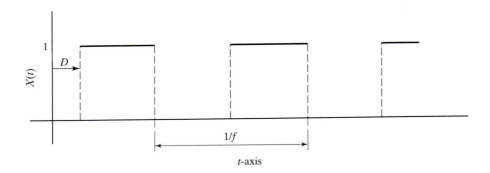

t-axis

A6.1.45 **(a)** $P_{X(t)}(0) = P_{X(t)}(1) = \frac{1}{2}$, zow; **(b)** $R_X(\tau) = \frac{1}{2}(1 - 2|\tau|f)$, $0 < |\tau| < \frac{T}{2}$ and is a sawtooth pattern generally; **(c)** yes

P6.1.46   The circuit shown in the figure has a known battery and inductor but a resistance that is chosen at random between 10 and 20 Ω.

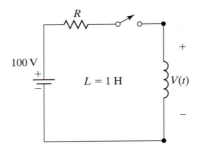

When the switch closes, the resulting voltage depends on the outcome of a chance experiment and is thus a random process, $V(t)$.

a. Find the mean of the process, $\mu_{V(t)}(t)$.

b. Find the PDF of the process, $f_{V(t)}(v)$.

c. Find the autocorrelation function of the process, $R_V(t_1, t_2)$.

A6.1.46 **(a)** $\frac{5}{t}(e^{-20t} - e^{-40t})$; **(b)** $\frac{1}{20vt}$, $100e^{-40t} < v \leq 100e^{-20t}$;
   (c) $\frac{10^4}{t_1+t_2} \left[\frac{e^{-20(t_1+t_2)} - e^{-40(t_1+t_2)}}{20} \right]$

P6.1.47 Consider a WSS random process, $Y(t) = X(t-2) + 5$, where $X(t)$ is a random process with autocorrelation function

$$R_X(\tau) = \frac{4}{1+\tau^2} + 4 \text{ volts}^2$$

Clearly, $Y(t)$ is $X(t)$, delayed 2 seconds and increased by 5 V. Assume that the mean of $X(t)$ is negative.
a. Find $R_Y(\tau)$.
b. Find $R_{XY}(\tau)$.

A6.1.47 (a) $R_Y(\tau) = \frac{4}{1+\tau^2} + 9 \text{ volts}^2$; **(b)** $R_{XY}(\tau) = \frac{4}{1+(\tau-2)^2} - 6 \text{ volts}^2$

P6.1.48 A binary counter counts random events that are Poisson distributed. The autocorrelation function of the output of the first stage of the counter is

$$R_1(\tau) = 2.25e^{-10^6|\tau|} + 4.24 \text{ volts}^2$$

a. What are the logic levels being used in the system for binary 0 and binary 1 assumed positive?
b. What is the average rate of the events being counted?
c. What is the autocorrelation function, $R_2(t)$, of the second stage of the counter if it uses the same logic levels? Assume the first stage is a binary divide-by-2 circuit.

A6.1.48 (a) $V_0 = 0.56$, and $V_1 = 3.56$ volts; **(b)** 500 kHz; **(c)** $R_2(\tau) = 2.25e^{-5\times10^5|\tau|} + 4.24 \text{ volts}^2$

6.4.2 Spectral Analysis of WSS Random Processes

Exercises on Spectral Analysis of WSS Random Processes

P6.2.1 The autocorrelation function of a WSS Gaussian random process is shown in the figure.

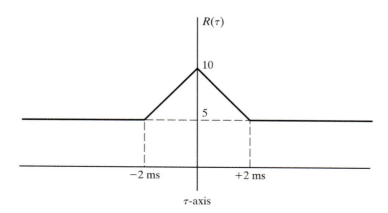

a. What is the AC power in the signal?
b. Give the approximate bandwidth of the signal.
c. If the signal is positive most of the time, what is the probability that at a random time it will be negative?

A6.2.1 (a) 5 volts^2; **(b)** $\approx$500 Hz; **(c)** 0.1587

P6.2.2   Consider a random model for a synchronous digital signal similar to that analyzed in Sec. 6.1, except that we no longer assume ones and zeros equally likely. Let $P[1] = p$, and $P[0] = 1 - p = q$. The clock period is T.
a. Find the autocorrelation function, $R(\tau)$.
b. Find the DC power, the AC power, and the total power.
c. Give the spectrum of this random process.

A6.2.2 (a) $R_X(\tau) = p - pq\frac{|\tau|}{T}$, $0 < |\tau| \le T$; $= p^2$, $|\tau| > T$; **(b)** $P_{DC} = p^2$, $P_{AC} = pq$, $P_T = p$; **(c)** $S_X(\omega) = p^2 2\pi\delta(\omega) + pqT\left(\frac{\sin(\omega T/2)}{\omega T/2}\right)^2$

P6.2.3   For the previous problem, let $p = \frac{1}{2}$, such that it reduces to the problem analyzed in the text. Assume a clock speed of 100 MHz, such that $T = 10$ ns. Thus the spectrum is

$$S_X(\omega) = \frac{1}{4}2\pi\delta(\omega) + \frac{1}{4} \times 10^{-8}\left(\frac{\sin(5 \times 10^{-9}\omega)}{5 \times 10^{-9}\omega}\right)^2$$

Consider the effect of the following changes, made one at a time. These are not cumulative but rather always are changes from the original. Give numerical values where possible.
a. Give the spectrum if the clock speed is lowered to 80 MHz.
b. Give the spectrum if the signal is inverted such that a one is -1 V.
c. Give the spectrum of the random process if the value of a one is 5 V and the value of a zero is 1 V.

A6.2.3 (a) $S_X(\omega) = \frac{1}{4}2\pi\delta(\omega) + \frac{1.25}{4} \times 10^{-8}\left(\frac{\sin(6.25\times 10^{-9}\omega)}{6.25\times 10^{-9}\omega}\right)^2$ volts^2/Hz; **(b)** no change; **(c)** $S_X(\omega) = 18\pi\delta(\omega) + 4 \times 10^{-8}\left(\frac{\sin(5\times 10^{-9}\omega)}{5\times 10^{-9}\omega}\right)^2$ volts^2/Hz

P6.2.4   A WSS random process, $X(t)$, models a synchronous digital signal similar to that modeled in Sec. 6.1, except the logic levels are $+10$ V and -10 V, and the clock period is 10 μs. The figure shows a sample function for this waveform.

a. Give the total power, the AC power, the DC power, and the coherence function for this random process.
b. Give the autocorrelation function of this random process.
c. What is the coherence time for this random process?
d. Give the PSD for this random process.

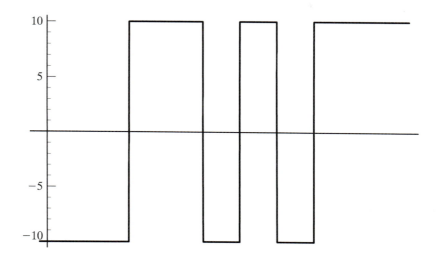

A6.2.4 **(a)** $P_{AC} = P_T = 100$ volts^2, $P_{DC} = 0$; **(b)** $R_X(\tau) = 100\left(1 - \frac{|\tau|}{T}\right)$, $|\tau| < T$, zow, where $T = 10$ μs; **(c)** 9 μs; **(d)** $S_X(f) = 10^{-3} \times \left(\frac{\sin \pi \times 10 \, \mu s \times f}{\pi \times 10 \, \mu s \times f}\right)^2$ volts^2/Hz

P6.2.5   A WSS ergodic Gaussian random process, $V(t)$, has a DC value of 10 mV, an AC value of 20 mV, rms, and a coherence function of $\rho(\tau) = e^{-10^{+5}|\tau|}$.
a. Find the first-order PDF, $f_{V(t)}(v, t)$.
b. Find the second-order PDF, $f_{V(t_1)V(t_2)}(v_1, v_2, t_1, t_2)$.
c. Find the autocorrelation function, $R_V(t_1, t_2)$.
d. Find the power spectrum, $S_V(f)$.

A6.2.5 **(a)** $N(10, 20^2)$, units of mV; **(b)** bivariate with each $N(10, 20^2)$ and $\rho = e^{-10^{+5}|\tau|}$, the formula is Eq. (3.5.34); **(c)** $R_V(\tau) = 400e^{-10^{+5}|\tau|} + 100(\text{mV})^2$; **(d)** $S(f) = 10^{-4}\delta(f) + \frac{80}{10^{+10}+(2\pi f)^2}$ volts^2/Hz

P6.2.6   An ergodic Gaussian random process has an autocorrelation function of $R(\tau) = 10^{-6}$ $e^{-10000\tau^2} + 4 \times 10^{-6}$ volts^2
   a. Find the DC value of the random process.
   b. Find the variance of the random process.
   c. What is the average power in a typical member of the random process?
   d. What is the two-sided power density spectrum of the random process? Check the table of Fourier transform pairs in endnote 13.

   A6.2.6   (a) $\pm 2 \times 10^{-3}$ volts; **(b)** 10^{-6} volts^2; **(c)** 5×10^{-6} volts^2; **(d)** $S(f) = 4 \times 10^{-6}\delta(f) + \sqrt{\pi} \times 10^{-8} \exp\left[-\left(\frac{2\pi f}{200}\right)^2\right]$ volts^2/Hz

P6.2.7   Consider a WSS random process, $X(t)$, with an autocorrelation function of $R_X(\tau) = \frac{4}{1+\tau^2} + 4$ volts^2.
   a. Find the coherence time.
   b. What fraction of the total power lies in the DC power?
   c. Give the PSD for X, $S_X(\omega)$.

   A6.2.7   (a) 3; **(b)** 50%; **(c)** $4\pi e^{-|\omega|} + 8\pi \delta(\omega)$ volts^2/Hz

Modeling Problems on Spectral Analysis of WSS Random Processes

P6.2.8   Your new-hire comes to you and claims that he has measured the autocorrelation function of the output of his new system as $\overline{R}(\tau) = 5$ volts^2, $-1 < \tau \leq +1$, zow.
   a. If you asked him for the power spectrum of the output, what should he give you?
   b. As the boss, should you congratulate him on his design or tell him to go back and try again? Explain.

   A6.2.8   (a) PSD $= \frac{10}{\omega} \sin \omega$; **(b)** impossible spectrum

P6.2.9   A counter for counting particles due to cosmic rays must count random particles up to bursts of 10^6 particles per second. Assume logic levels of 0 and 1 V.
   a. Find and plot the autocorrelation function of the output of the first stage of the counter for the maximum count rate.
   b. Find and plot the spectrum of the output of the first stage of the counter for the maximum count rate.
   c. What approximate bandwidth is required for the output of the first stage of the counter?

   A6.2.9   (a) $\frac{1}{4}(1 + e^{-2\lambda|\tau|})$, with $\lambda = 10^6$; see figure **(b)** $\frac{1}{4}\delta(f) + \frac{\lambda}{(2\lambda)^2 + (2\pi f)^2}$, with $\lambda = 10^6$; see figure; **(c)** 2 MHz

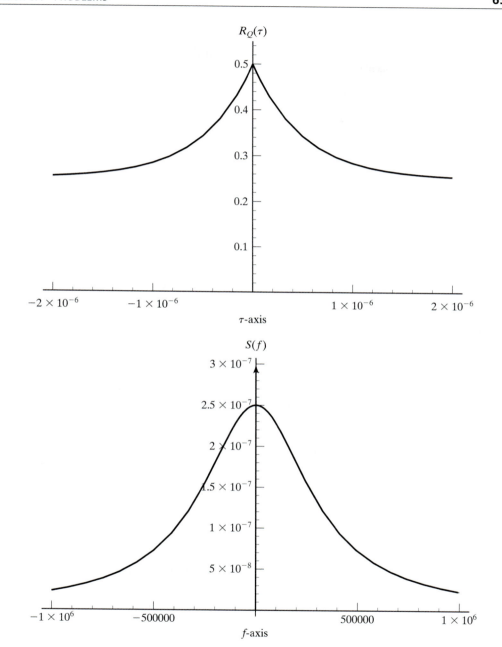

P6.2.10 Write a one-sentence definition of each of the following. No equations or mathematical symbols are allowed.
a. Random process
b. The mean of a random process
c. Wide-sense stationary random process
d. Ergodic random process
e. Time-average autocorrelation function
f. Power spectrum of a random process

> **A6.2.10** (a) A random process is a set of functions, each of which is associated with the outcome of a chance experiment. (b) The mean of a random process is the summation of the values of the member functions at a prescribed time, weighted according to the probability that function will occur. (c) A WSS random process is a random process with a constant mean and an autocorrelation function that is an even function of the difference between two times. (d) An ergodic random process is a random process in which time averages of member functions are equal to statistical averages taken over the entire process. (e) The time-average autocorrelation function is the average over infinite time of a function times itself displaced in time. (f) The power spectrum of a WSS random process is the Fourier transform of the autocorrelation function.

P6.2.11 A random process, $X(t)$ is WSS.
a. Give the definition of the autocorrelation function.
b. Give the definition of the time-average autocorrelation function.
c. Give the definition of the power spectrum.
d. Which of the above is a random variable?
e. Which of the above cannot go negative?

> **A6.2.11** (a) $R_X(\tau) = E[X(t)X(t+\tau)]$; (b) $\overline{R}_X(\tau) = \langle x(t)x(t+\tau)\rangle$, averaged over all time, where $x(t)$ is one member function of the random process; (c) $S(f) = \int_{-\infty}^{+\infty} R_X(\tau)e^{-j2\pi f\tau}d\tau$; (d) b, the time-average autocorrelation function for a fixed value of τ; (e) c, the power spectrum

P6.2.12 A toggle flip-flop is triggered by Poisson events, with 100 pulses per second being the rate of trigger pulses, on average. The flip-flop output signal has values of 0 and $+1$ V, equally probable at any time. As shown in Sec. 6.2, the spectrum of the output is given by the formula

$$S(\omega) = \frac{\pi}{2}\delta(\omega) + \frac{100}{\omega^2 + (200)^2} \text{ V}^2/\text{Hz (two-sides)}$$

Give the power spectrum after the following changes, made one at a time. In all cases, the changes are from the original and are not cumulative.
a. We subtract 0.5 from the output, such that the signal goes from $+0.5$ to -0.5.
b. We double the average rate of the clock pulses.

c. We multiply the signal by 2, such that the output states are 0 and 2.

d. We express the spectrum as a one-sided spectrum.

A6.2.12 (a) $S(\omega) = \frac{100}{\omega^2+(200)^2}$ volts^2/Hz; (b) $S(\omega) = \frac{\pi}{2}\delta(\omega) + \frac{200}{\omega^2+(400)^2}$ volts^2/Hz;
(c) $S(\omega) = 2\pi\delta(\omega) + \frac{400}{\omega^2+(200)^2}$ volts^2/Hz; (d) $S(\omega) = \frac{\pi}{2}\delta(\omega) + \frac{200}{\omega^2+(200)^2}$
volts^2/Hz (one side)

P6.2.13   A random process, $X(t)$, has the spectrum

$$S_X(\omega) = 10\pi\delta(\omega) + 10 \text{ volts}^2/\text{Hz}, \; -2\pi < \omega < +2\pi, \text{ zow}$$

a. Find the autocorrelation function, $R_X(\tau)$.

b. Find the AC and DC power in the signal.

c. Find the coherence function, $\rho(\tau)$.

d. If we define the effective bandwidth of the signal as that band, B, in hertz (one side) in which 90% of the total power lies, including the DC power, what is B?

A6.2.13 (a) $5 + 20 \times \frac{\sin 2\pi\tau}{2\pi\tau}$ volts^2; (b) $P_{DC} = 5$ volts^2, and $P_{AC} = 20$ volts^2;
(c) $\frac{\sin 2\pi\tau}{2\pi\tau}$; (d) 0.875 Hz

P6.2.14   A WSS Gaussian random process consists of a signal plus noise, $X(t) = S(t) + N(t)$. Both signal and noise are Gaussian but uncorrelated. The autocorrelation function of the signal is $R_S(\tau) = 10^{-6}e^{-10^7|\tau|} + 10^{-5}$ volts^2, and the autocorrelation function of the noise is $R_N(\tau) = 10^{-12}\delta(\tau)$.

a. What is the total power in the signal?

b. Find the probability that the total signal has the same sign as the DC component of the signal.

c. What is the PSD of X, $S_X(\omega)$?

A6.2.14 (a) 1.1×10^{-5}; (b) $\Phi(3.16) = 0.9992$; (c) $S_X(\omega) = \frac{20}{\omega^2+10^{14}} + 2\pi \times 10^{-5}\delta(\omega) + 10^{-12}$ volts^2/Hz (two sides)

P6.2.15   A toggle flip-flop is triggered by Poisson events, with $\lambda = 1000$ pulses per second, on average. The flip-flop output signal has values of 0 and $+1$. The output power spectrum is given by the formula [Eq. (6.2.40)], $S(f) = \frac{1}{4}\delta(f) + \frac{1000}{(2000)^2+(2\pi f)^2}$ volts^2/Hz (two sides).

Give the power spectrum as affected by the following changes. The changes are made one at a time and are not cumulative.

a. The output logic levels are 0 and V.

b. The output logic levels are 0 and -1.

c. The output logic levels are $+V$ and $-V$.

d. The rate of trigger pulses doubles.

A6.2.15 (a) $S(f) \to \frac{V^2}{4}\delta(f) + \frac{1000V^2}{(2000)^2+(2\pi f)^2}$ volts^2/Hz; (b) no change; (c) $S(f) \to \frac{4000V^2}{(2000)^2+(2\pi f)^2}$ volts^2/Hz; (d) $S(f) \to \frac{1}{4}\delta(f) + \frac{2000}{(4000)^2+(2\pi f)^2}$ volts^2/Hz

P6.2.16   Assume that the power line frequency is 60 Hz on average but varies over time with an rms deviation of ± 0.03 Hz, such that the overall shape of the spectrum is Gaussian. Find the autocorrelation function of the time-domain voltage function, assuming 120 V rms. *Note:* The Fourier transform of a Gaussian is itself a Gaussian. See the table in endnote 13 for the Fourier transform. Do not forget to model this as a two-sided spectrum.

A6.2.16 $R(\tau) = 120^2 \exp\left[-\frac{1}{2}(2\pi \times 0.03)^2\tau^2\right]\cos(120\pi\tau)$ volts^2/Hz

P6.2.17   A WSS random process, $X(t)$, has an autocorrelation function given by $R_X(\tau) = 10e^{-10^6|\tau|} + 5$ volts^2.

a. Find the spectrum of the random process.

b. The spectrum is modulated by a sinusoid of unknown phase, which we model as the independent random process $C(t) = 2\cos(10^7 t + \Theta)$ V, where Θ is a random variable uniformly distributed between 0 and 2π. Hence $Y(t) = X(t)C(t)$. Find the autocorrelation function of $Y(t)$.

c. Find the spectrum of $Y(t)$, $S_Y(\omega)$.

d. Is power conserved in the modulation process? Explain.

A6.2.17   **(a)** $10\pi\delta(\omega) + 10 \times \frac{2 \times 10^6}{\omega^2 + 10^{12}}$ volts^2/Hz; **(b)** $(10e^{-10^6|\tau|} + 5) \times 2\cos 10^7 \tau$;

(c) $10\pi\delta(\omega + 10^7) \times \frac{20 \times 10^6}{(\omega + 10^7)^2 + 10^{12}} + 10\pi\delta(\omega - 10^7) \times \frac{20 \times 10^6}{(\omega - 10^7)^2 + 10^{12}}$;

(d) $R_Y(0) \neq R_X(0) + R_C(0)$, so power is not conserved

P6.2.18   A random sinusoid is modeled by $V(t) = 12\cos(100t + \Theta)$, where Θ is a random variable uniformly distributed between 0 and 2π. In a modulator this sinusoid multiplies the random process $X(t)$ in Problem 6.2.13 to produce a third random process, $Z(t) = V(t)X(t)$, where $V(t)$ and $X(t)$ are independent.

a. Find the autocorrelation function of Z, $R_Z(\tau)$.

b. Find and sketch the spectrum, $S_Z(\omega)$.

c. Is energy conserved in the modulation process?

A6.2.18   **(a)** $\frac{12^2}{2}\cos(100\tau) \times \left(5 + 20 \times \frac{\sin 2\pi\tau}{2\pi\tau}\right)$; **(b)** $S_Z(\omega) = 360\pi\delta(\omega + 100) + 360\pi\delta(\omega - 100) + 360$, $|\omega \pm 100| < 2\pi$, zow; the sketch is shown in the figure; **(c)** $R_X(0) + R_V(0) = 97$; $R_Z(0) = 1800$; no, power is not conserved

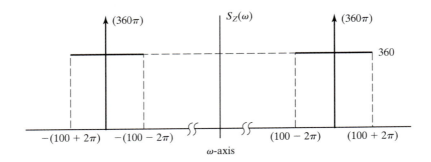

6.4.3 WSS Random Processes in Linear Systems

Modeling problems on WSS random processes in linear systems

P6.3.1 A 1-MΩ resistor with a temperature of 290 K has 2-pF stray capacitance associated with it.

a. Give the power spectrum of the terminal voltage (one-side).
b. Find the rms value of the output voltage.
c. Give the autocorrelation function.
d. Find the decorrelation time, τ_c.

A6.3.1 **(a)** $1.601 \times 10^{-14} \times \dfrac{1}{1+(\omega/5\times10^5)^2}$ volts^2/Hz (one side); **(b)** 44.7 μV; **(c)** $2.001 \times 10^{-9} e^{-|\tau|/2\times10^{-6}}$ volts^2; **(d)** 4.605 μs

P6.3.2 Wide-sense stationary broadband noise with $S_N = 10^{-8}$ volts^2/Hz (two sides) is put through an ideal low-pass filter with $|H(j\omega)| = 1$, $|\omega| < 10^6$, zow.

a. Find the output power spectral density.
b. Find the output autocorrelation function.
c. Find the output rms voltage.

A6.3.2 **(a)** $S_o(\omega) = 10^{-8}$, $|\omega| < 10^6$, zow; **(b)** $\dfrac{2\times10^{-8}}{2\pi} \times \dfrac{\sin 10^6 \tau}{\tau}$ volts^2/Hz; **(c)** 0.0564 V

P6.3.3 White noise with a PSD of $S_N = 10^{-15}$ volts^2/Hz (two-sided) is passed through a single-pole low-pass RC filter with a cutoff frequency of 500 kHz. Find the autocorrelation function of the output of the filter.

A6.3.3 $\pi \times 10^{-9} e^{-\pi \times 10^6 |\tau|}$ volts^2

P6.3.4 Consider a random process, $V(t) = V_p \cos(\omega_1 t + \Theta)$. The random variable representing the phase, Θ, is uniformly distributed between 0 and 2π. This random process is put into a high-pass filter with the filter function $\mathbf{H}(j\omega) = \dfrac{j\left(\frac{\omega}{\omega_1}\right)}{1+j\left(\frac{\omega}{\omega_1}\right)}$.

a. What is the autocorrelation function of the input function?
b. What is the power spectral density of the input random process, $S_{in}(f)$?
c. What is the power spectral density of the output random process, $S_{out}(f)$?
d. What is the autocorrelation function of the output random process?

A6.3.4 **(a)** $R(\tau) = \dfrac{V_p^2}{2} \cos \omega_1 \tau$ volts^2; **(b)** $\dfrac{V_p^2}{4}\delta(f + f_1) + \dfrac{V_p^2}{4}\delta(f - f_1)$volts^2/Hz; **(c)** $\dfrac{V_p^2}{8}\delta(f + f_1) + \dfrac{V_p^2}{8}\delta(f - f_1)$volts^2/Hz; **(d)** $R(\tau) = \dfrac{V_p^2}{4}\cos \omega_1 \tau$ volts^2

P6.3.5 White noise that has a flat spectrum of magnitude $S_N = 10^{-17}$ volts^2/Hz (two sides) is put through an RC low-pass filter with an RC product of 10^{-7} second.

a. What is the output spectrum?
b. What is the output autocorrelation function?

A6.3.5   **(a)** $S_{\text{out}}(\omega) = \dfrac{10^{-17}}{1+(10^{-7}\omega)^2}$ volts²/Hz; **(b)** $R_{\text{out}}(\tau) = \dfrac{10^{-17}}{2\times10^{-7}}e^{-10^7|\tau|}$ volts²

P6.3.6   A power spectrum is given in the figure in volts squared.

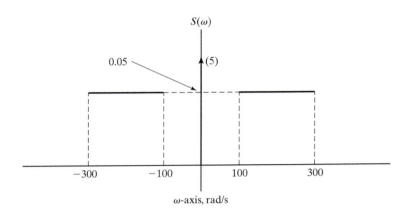

a. Find $R_X(0)$, the autocorrelation function at $\tau = 0$.
b. Find $R_X(\infty)$, the autocorrelation function at $\tau = \infty$.
c. Estimate τ_c, the coherence time.

A6.3.6   **(a)** 3.979; **(b)** 0.7958; **(c)** The inverse of the bandwidth gives about 21 ms, but a plot of the inverse Fourier transform shows more like 80 ms. This is one of those autocorrelation functions that has lots of structure, owing to the corners in the spectrum.

P6.3.7   White noise with a noise spectrum of $S_N = 10^{-14}$ volts²/Hz (two sides) is input to a filter with the characteristic shown in the figure.

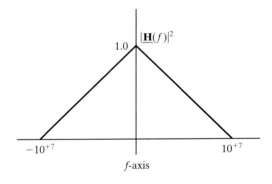

a. Find $R_{\text{in}}(\tau)$.
b. Find the output spectrum.

c. Find the rms voltage out of the filter.

d. Find the coherence time of the output noise.

A6.3.7 (a) $10^{-14}\delta(\tau)$ volts^2; (b) $10^{-14}\left(1 - \frac{|f|}{10^7}\right)$, $0 < |f| < 10^7$, zow; (c) 3.164×10^{-4} V; (d) The reciprocal of the bandwidth is 0.1 μs. A plot of the inverse Fourier transform gives more like 0.08 μs.

P6.3.8   Ergodic, Gaussian white noise has a spectrum of $S(f) = 10^{-10}$ volts^2/Hz (two sides) and is input to a filter described by the filter function in the figure.

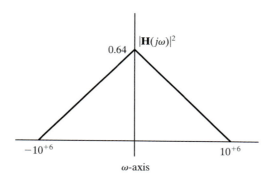

a. What is the mean of the output?

b. What is the variance of the output?

c. *Estimate* the peak-to-peak voltage for 1000 independent samples of the output.

d. *Estimate* the decorrelation time for the output.

A6.3.8   (a) 0; (b) 1.02×10^{-5} volts^2; (c) about 0.0173 V; (d) about $4-6$ μs

P6.3.9   A 1-MΩ resistor at a temperature of 77 K will exhibit broadband thermal noise.

a. Consider that the thermal noise is not limited by quantum effects or any system bandwidth. This means that we have ideal white noise over infinite bandwidth. Give the PDS and the autocorrelation function of this noise, including units.

b. We now consider the effect of 3-pF stray capacitance. Find the rms value of the noise voltage at the resistor terminals.

c. What is the autocorrelation function of the noise voltage, considering the capacitance?

d. What band of frequency, B in hertz, (one side), contains 95% of the noise power, considering the effect of the capacitance?

A6.3.9   (a) 2.125×10^{-15} volts^2/Hz, $R(\tau) = 2.125 \times 10^{-15}\delta(\tau)$ volts^2; (b) 3.542×10^{-10} volts^2; (c) $3.542 \times 10^{-10}e^{-|\tau|/3\mu s}$ volts^2; (d) 674.1 kHz

P6.3.10   A communication system has a coherent signal modeled by $V(t) = V_p \cos(\omega_1 t + \Theta)$, where Θ is a random variable uniformly distributed between 0 and 2π. This signal has additive white noise, $N(t)$, where $S_N(\omega) = S_N$ volts^2/Hz (two sides), a constant for all ω. Thus the sum of signal and noise is $X(t) = S(t) + N(t)$.

a. Find $R_X(\tau)$.

b. The sum, $X(t)$, is put through a low-pass filter with a 3-dB frequency of $2\omega_1$. Find the spectrum of the output signal, plus noise.

c. Find the autocorrelation function of the output signal plus noise.

d. What is the output signal-to-noise ratio, S/N, defined as the output signal power divided by the output noise power?

A6.3.10 **(a)** $\frac{V_p^2}{2}\cos(\omega_1\tau) + S_N\delta(\tau)$ volts^2; **(b)** $\frac{V_p^2}{2}[\pi\delta(\omega+\omega_1) + \pi\delta(\omega-\omega_1)] \times \frac{1}{1.25} + S_N\frac{1}{1+(\omega/2\omega_1)^2}$; **(c)** $\frac{V_p^2}{2.5}\cos(\omega_1\tau) + S_N\omega_1 e^{-2\omega_1|\tau|}$; **(d)** $\frac{V_p^2}{2.5S_N\omega_1}$

P6.3.11   White noise with $S_N = 10^{-18}$ volts^2/Hz (two-sided) is put through an ideal bandpass filter with a one-octave bandwidth, as shown in the figure. $\omega_1 = 2\pi \times 1000$ MHz.

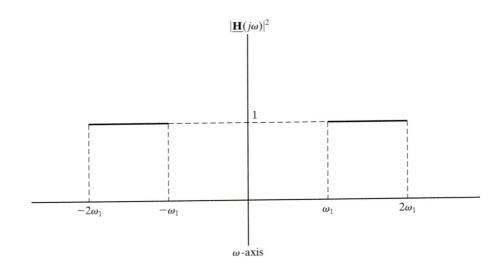

a. Find the total power out of the filter.

b. Give the autocorrelation function of the output signal. *Hint:* Because of the symmetry of the integral, you can perform the cosine transform rather than the full Fourier transform. Both work fine.

c. Find the decorrelation time, τ_c, defined as the time at which the coherence function drops to and remains below 0.1.

A6.3.11 **(a)** 2×10^{-9} volts^2; **(b)** $2 \times 10^{-9}\left[\frac{\sin 2\omega_1\tau - \sin \omega_1\tau}{\omega_1\tau}\right]$ volts^2; **(c)** The reciprocal of the bandwidth in hertz is 0.5 ns. Plotting the coherence function and finding the value beyond which it remains below 0.1 gives $\tau_c \approx 0.789 \times 10^{-9}$ s.

P6.3.12 White Gaussian noise plus DC has the autocorrelation function $R_X(\tau) = 100\delta(\tau) + 1$ volt^2.

a. Find the power spectral density function, $S_X(\omega)$.

b. If this signal is put through a low-pass filter with a 3-dB bandwidth of 0.05 Hz, find the output spectrum, $S_Y(\omega)$.

c. Give the autocorrelation function of the output.

d. Assuming a positive DC value, find the probability that the output of the filter is positive at a random time.

A6.3.12 **(a)** $100 + \delta(f)$ volts^2/Hz; **(b)** $\dfrac{100}{1+(10\omega/\pi)^2} + \delta(f)$ volts^2; **(c)** $5\pi e^{-\pi|\tau|/10} + 1$ volts^2; **(d)** 0.5996

P6.3.13 Consider two jointly WSS random processes, $X(t) = V_X \cos(\omega_1 t + \Theta)$ and $Y(t) = V_Y \sin(\omega_1 t + \Theta)$, where Θ is a random variable uniformly distributed between 0 and 2π, and the amplitudes, V_X and V_Y, are constants. Let the random process $Z(t) = X(t) + Y(t)$.

a. Find the autocorrelation function of $Z(t)$.

b. Find the spectrum of $Z(t)$.

c. If $Z(t)$ was put through an RC low-pass filter with a cutoff frequency of $\omega_c = \omega_1$, what would be the output AC power?

A6.3.13 **(a)** $R_Z(\tau) = \dfrac{V_X^2 + V_Y^2}{2} \cos \omega_1 \tau$; **(b)** $\dfrac{V_X^2 + V_Y^2}{4} \times 2\pi[\delta(\omega + \omega_1) + \delta(\omega - \omega_1)]$; **(c)** $\dfrac{V_X^2 + V_Y^2}{2} \times \dfrac{1}{2}$

P6.3.14 A random process is given by $V(t) = V_c \cos \omega_1 t + V_s \sin \omega_1 t$, where V_c and V_s, the amplitudes of the cosine and sine terms, respectively, are independent random variables uniformly distributed between -10 and $+10$ V.

a. Find $E[V(t)]$, the mean of the random process.

b. Find the autocorrelation, $E[V(t_1)V(t_2)]$, of the random process.

c. Is the random process WSS? Explain.

d. Is the random process ergodic? Explain.

e. The random process is put through a low-pass filter with a cutoff frequency $\omega_c = \omega_1$. Find the autocorrelation function of the output of the filter.

A6.3.14 **(a)** 0; **(b)** $\dfrac{400}{12} \cos \omega_1(t_1 - t_2)$; **(c)** yes, since the mean is constant and the autocorrelation function is an even function of $t_1 - t_2$; **(d)** clearly not, since each member function has a different time-average autocorrelation function; **(e)** $\dfrac{400}{24} \cos \omega_1(t_1 - t_2)$

P6.3.15 A Gaussian random process is generated by running white noise through an RC low-pass filter. The output random process has a variance of 0.01 volt^2 and a 20-dB bandwidth of 120 Hz, one-sided.

a. Find the intensity of the input white noise (two-sided) in volts^2/Hz.

b. Find the value of τ in the autocorrelation function that gives a correlation of 0.1 in the random process.

A6.3.15 (a) 2.64×10^{-4} volts^2/Hz; (b) 30.4 ms

P6.3.16 A sinusoid with a frequency of 100 Hz but uncertain phase has additive white noise: $V(t) = 10^{-3} \cos(200\pi t + \Theta) + N(t)$ V, where Θ is uniformly distributed between 0 and 2π, and $N(t)$ is the noise with a power spectrum of $S_N = 10^{-12}$ volts^2/Hz.
a. What is the power spectrum of this random process?
b. The signal is low-pass filtered with a cutoff frequency of 200 Hz. What is the autocorrelation function of the output of the filter?

A6.3.16 (a) $\frac{10^{-6}}{4}[\delta(f + 100) + \delta(f - 100)] + 10^{-12}$ volts^2/Hz; (b) $10^{-12} \times \frac{400\pi}{2}$ $e^{-400\pi|\tau|} + \frac{10^{-6}}{2} \times \frac{4}{5} \cos(200\pi|\tau|)$ volts^2

P6.3.17 Let $X(t)$ be a WSS Gaussian ergodic random process with the following autocorrelation function: $R(\tau) = \frac{100}{1+\tau^2}$ volts^2, τ in seconds.
a. Find $P[|X(2)| > 12]$.
b. Find the rms value for the signal.
c. If 100 independent samples of $X(t)$ were required, how much time would that require?
d. This signal is filtered through an ideal low-pass filter, $|\mathbf{H}(j\omega)| = 1$, $-1 < \omega \leq +1$, zow. Find the rms value of the signal out of the filter.

A6.3.17 (a) 0.2302; (b) 10 V; (c) $\approx$300 seconds; (d) 7.951 V

P6.3.18 A WSS random process has a coherence function of $\rho(\tau) = e^{-1000|\tau|}$, a DC value of -1 V, and a total power of 100 volts^2.
a. Give the autocorrelation function.
b. The random process is put through an ideal low-pass filter with a bandwidth of 1 Hz. Give the DC power of the output.
c. Estimate the probability that the output of the filter is positive.

A6.3.18 (a) $99e^{-1000|\tau|} + 1$; (b) $+1$ V^2; (c) 0.0559

P6.3.19 An ergodic Gaussian random process with a positive mean value has an autocorrelation function of $R(\tau) = 10^{-8}e^{-10^5\tau^2} + 10^{-9}$ volts^2.
a. Find the DC value of the voltage.
b. Find the rms value of the voltage, including both DC and AC components.
c. Estimate the bandwidth in hertz of the power spectrum of this signal.
d. Find the probability that the voltage exceeds 120 μV at an arbitrary time.

A6.3.19 (a) 31.6 μV; (b) 104.9 μV; (c) 210 Hz; (d) 0.188

P6.3.20 A low-pass filter (*not* a standard RC low-pass filter) has a noise input with an autocorrelation function of $R_{in}(\tau) = 10^{-8}e^{-10^6|\tau|} + 10^{-8}$ volts^2. The output autocorrelation function is $R_{out}(\tau) = 10^{-9}e^{-10^5|\tau|} + 10^{-9}$ volts^2.
a. Find the DC gain of the filter.
b. Find the approximate bandwidth of the filter.
c. Find the approximate coherence time of the input noise.

A6.3.20 (a) 0.1 in power; **(b)** $\approx$45 kHz; **(c)** about 2 μs

P6.3.21 A WSS ergodic random process has an autocorrelation function given by the formula
$R(\tau) = \sqrt{20 + \frac{20}{\tau^4+1}}$ volts^2.
a. Does the signal have a DC value? If so, what is it?
b. What would be the time-average power in watts given to a 5-Ω resistor by this voltage?
c. This random process is passed through a low-pass RC filter with $R = 100$ Ω and $C = 100$ μF. Is the autocorrelation function of the output greatly different from that of the input or about the same? Explain your answer.

A6.3.21 (a) yes, DC $= \pm2.115$ V; **(b)** 1.265 W; **(c)** 15.9 Hz is the bandwidth of the filter. The coherence time is about 1.8 s, so the bandwidth is very small, about 0.55 Hz. Thus no change will be effected by the filter.

P6.3.22 Pure white noise has no DC component. This problem is about a signal that is white noise plus a DC signal: $S(\omega) = 10^{-14}\delta(\omega) + 10^{-20}$ volts^2/Hz.
a. What is the autocorrelation function of this signal?
b. This signal is the input to an RC low-pass filter, with $RC = 10^{-6}$. What is the spectrum of the output?
c. What is the total power in the output signal?

A6.3.22 (a) $\frac{10^{-14}}{2\pi} + 10^{-20}\delta(\tau)$ volts^2; **(b)** $S(\omega) = 10^{-14}\delta(\omega) + \frac{10^{-20}}{1+(10^{-6}\omega)^2}$ volts^2/Hz;
(c) 6.59×10^{-15} volts^2

P6.3.23 Ergodic Gaussian white noise has a spectrum of $S_N = 10^{-10}$ volts^2/Hz (two sides). This spectrum is input to an RC low-pass filter with $RC = 0.001$ s.
a. What is the mean of the output?
b. What is the variance of the output?
c. Estimate the peak-to-peak value for 1000 independent samples of the output.
d. Estimate the coherence time for the output.

A6.3.23 (a) 0; **(b)** 5×10^{-8} volts^2; **(c)** 1.52×10^{-3} volts; **(d)** 2.3×10^{-3} s

P6.3.24 Gaussian white noise with $S_{in}(f) = 10^{-13}$ volts^2/Hz (two-sided) is put into a low-pass filter with a cutoff frequency of 10^6 rad/s.
a. Find the filter power response, $|\underline{H}(j\omega)|^2$.
b. Find the output spectrum of the filter.
c. Find the autocorrelation function of the output signal.
d. Find the variance of the filter output.
e. Estimate the coherence time of the filter output.
f. Estimate the peak-to-peak variation of the filter output in 1 ms of output.

A6.3.24 (a) $\frac{1}{1+(10^{-6}\omega)^2}$; **(b)** $S_{out}(\omega) = \frac{10^{-13}}{1+(10^{-6}\omega)^2}$ volts^2/Hz; **(c)** $R(\tau) = 5 \times 10^{-8}$
$\exp[-10^6|\tau|]$ volts^2; **(d)** 5×10^{-8} volts^2; **(e)** about 2.3 μs; **(f)** 1.41×10^{-3} V

P6.3.25 A 1000-Ω resistor at room temperature (300 K) has 10-pF stray capacitance.

  a. What is the magnitude of the two-sided power spectrum across the resistor in the region where the spectrum is relatively flat?

  b. Write the equation for the two-sided power spectrum of the voltage across the resistor. This is a function of frequency.

  c. Determine the autocorrelation function.

  d. What is the time increment during which the output voltage becomes 90% uncorrelated?

  e. Write the PDF for the output noise voltage.

  A6.3.25 **(a)** 8.28×10^{-18} volts^2/Hz; **(b)** $\frac{8.28 \times 10^{-18}}{1 + 10^{-16}(2\pi f)^2}$; **(c)** $4.14 \times 10^{-10} \exp[-10^8 |\tau|]$;

  (d) 23 ns; **(e)** $V = N(0, (20.3 \ \mu V)^2)$

P6.3.26 A signal that is a pure sinusoid, $A \cos(\omega_1 t)$, has additive white noise with a one-sided spectrum of S_N volts^2/Hz. The signal is processed through a single-pole low-pass filter with a cutoff of $\omega_c = \omega_1$.

  a. What is the autocorrelation function of the output of the filter?

  b. What is the signal-to-noise ratio of the output?

  A6.3.26 **(a)** $R(\tau) = \frac{A^2}{4} \cos \omega_1 \tau + \frac{S_N \omega_1}{4} e^{-\omega_1 |\tau|}$; **(b)** $\frac{A^2}{S_N \omega_1}$

P6.3.27 A 50-Ω resistor at room temperature ($T = 290$ K) is connected to a 100-Ω resistor in liquid nitrogen (77 K). Consider that the connection between the resistors, made with ordinary unshielded wire, provides coupling between the resistors up to a frequency of 10^{10} Hz. Find the net power leaving the hot resistor, that is, its power out minus power in.

  A6.3.27 2.613×10^{-11} W

P6.3.28 Broadband Gaussian white noise has a spectrum of $S_N = 2.5 \times 10^{-16}$ volts^2/Hz (two sides). The spectrum is amplified by $G_{dB} = 100$ dB by a broadband amplifier and then passed through a low-pass filter with R and C for components, with $RC = 5 \times 10^{-6}$ second. The output of the RC filter is input to a square-law detector with a characteristic $v_{out} = \frac{v_{in}^2}{1000}$ for $v_{in} > 0$ and $v_{out} = 0$ for $v_{in} < 0$.

  a. Find the rms value of the input signal to the square-law detector.

  b. Find the PDF for V_{in}, the random process modeling the input voltage to the square-law detector.

  c. Find the PDF for V_{out}, the random process modeling the output voltage from the square-law detector.

  d. Show that the DC component of the output voltage, modeled by $E[V_{out}]$, is proportional to the power in the input voltage. *Hint:* You do not have to evaluate any integrals.

  A6.3.28 **(a)** 0.5 V; **(b)** $N(0, 0.25)$; **(c)** $0.5\delta(v_{out}) + \frac{12.6}{\sqrt{v_{out}}} \exp[-2000 v_{out}]$, $v_{out} \geq 0$,

  zow; **(d)** $E[V_{out}] = E[V_{in}^2]/2000$, which is proportional to input power

P6.3.29   A resistor is connected in parallel to an inductor and capacitor, as shown in the left
circuit. The equivalent circuit, showing the thermal noise source in the resistor is
shown in the right circuit. We will model the resistor noise as white noise filtered by
the power passband of the *RLC* circuit. This passband is graphed below the circuit
diagrams. The component values are $R = 10\ k\Omega$, $T = 300\ K$, $L = 2\ \mu H$, $C = 10\ pF$.

a. Estimate the rms voltage across the *RLC* combination. *Hint:* You can estimate the
bandwidth from the graph. You can calculate the exact bandwidth by integrating
the filter function. Do not forget to consider one-sided and two-sided spectra.

b. Does the presence of the inductor increase or decrease the noise voltage? Support
your answer with numerical comparisons.

c. If the output noise is sampled at 10-ms intervals, will the resulting random variables
be uncorrelated, independent, or both uncorrelated and independent?

d. Estimate the fraction of the time that the magnitude of the noise voltage exceeds
20 μV.

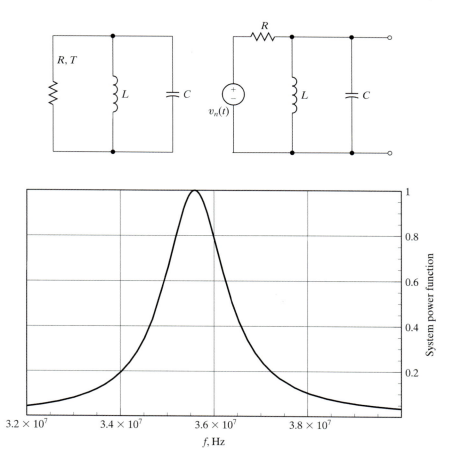

A6.3.29 **(a)** 18.2 μV based on the half-power point on the graph (20.3 μV based on integrating the curve exactly); **(b)** 20.3 μV, so it does not increase the noise, just shifts it to a higher frequency; **(c)** 10 ms $\gg \frac{1}{B} \approx \tau_c$, so uncorrelated; since Gaussian, also independent; **(d)** 32%

P6.3.30 The autocorrelation function of an ergodic WSS Gaussian random process is given as $R(\tau) = 12e^{-40\tau^2}$ volts^2.

a. What is the magnitude of the time-average value of a member function of the random process chosen at random?

b. What is the mean square value of the random process.

c. Estimate the bandwidth of the random process in hertz.

d. The random process is put through a half-wave rectifier that eliminates the negative part of the signal but does not affect the positive part. What is the magnitude of the time-average value of a member function of the output random process chosen at random?

A6.3.30 **(a)** 0; **(b)** 12 V^2; **(c)** about 4.17 Hz; **(d)** 1.38 V

P6.3.31 A Poisson process provides triggers at an average rate of 1000 events per second to the clock input of a toggle flip-flop. Let $Q(t)$ be the output of the flip-flop. The logic levels are +5 V for a one and 0 V for a zero. The output of the flip-flop is put through an RC low-pass filter.

a. Give the autocorrelation function of the output of the flip-flop.

b. Give the power spectral density of the output of the flip-flop.

c. If the RC time constant of the filter is 1 μs, give the approximate output autocorrelation function of the output of the low-pass filter.

d. If the RC time constant of the filter is 1 s, give the approximate output autocorrelation function of the output of the low-pass filter.

A6.3.31 **(a)** $6.25(1+e^{-2000|\tau|})$ volts^2; **(b)** $6.25\delta(f)+\frac{25\times1000}{(2000)^2+(2\pi f)^2}$ volts^2/Hz; **(c)** The time for the transitions on the order of milliseconds, and the time constant is 1 μs. The filter will have insignificant effect on the signal. **(d)** For a 1-s time constant, the flip-flop output is like white noise; the output is mostly DC. The answer is given in Eq. (6.3.42) as $R_{\text{out}}(\tau) = \frac{1}{4} + \frac{1}{4\lambda} \times \frac{1}{2RC}e^{-|\tau|/RC} = \frac{1}{4} + \frac{1}{8000}e^{-|\tau|}$ volts^2

P6.3.32 A WSS ergodic, Gaussian random process, $X(t)$, has an autocorrelation function of $R_X(\tau) = 5e^{-|\tau|}$ volts^2, where τ is measured in milliseconds.

a. $P[X(t) > 2] = ?$

b. $X(t)$ is run through a comparator. The output, $Y(t)$, is +10 if $X(t) > 2$, and is -10 if $X(t) < 2$. Find $\langle Y(t) \rangle$, the time average of the output of the comparator.

c. $X(t)$ is run through an ideal low-pass filter as shown in the figure with $Z(t)$ being the output. Find the filter bandwidth, B, in hertz, such that $R_Z(0) = 0.9R_X(0)$.

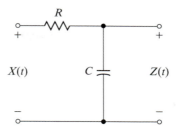

A6.3.32 (a) 0.1855; **(b)** 6.290; **(c)** 1005 Hz

P6.3.33 White noise is passed through an RC low-pass filter. The output spectrum is $S(f) = \frac{10^{-18}}{1+10^{-12}(2\pi f)^2}$, volts^2/Hz (two sides). The autocorrelation function of the output is $R(\tau) = 5 \times 10^{-13} e^{10^6|\tau|}$ volts^2.

Explain the effect(s) of the following changes make one at a time (not cumulative).
a. How does $R(\tau)$ change if 1 μV of DC is added to the input?
b. How does $R(\tau)$ change if the value of the capacitor is doubled?
c. The white noise is run through in inverter, changing the sign of the instantaneous voltage. How is $R(\tau)$ affected?
d. What is the spectrum if expressed as a one-sided spectrum?

A6.3.33 (a) $R(\tau) \to 5 \times 10^{-13} e^{10^6|\tau|} + 10^{-12}$; **(b)** $R(\tau) = 2.5 \times 10^{-13} e^{10^6|\tau|/2}$; **(c)** no change; **(d)** $S(f) \to \frac{2\times 10^{-18}}{1+10^{-12}(2\pi f)^2}$

P6.3.34 A WSS Gaussian ergodic random process has a white noise spectrum of $S_N = 10^{-15}$ volts^2/Hz (two sides). The process is input to an amplifier with a gain of $+60$ dB (power gain $= 10^6$) and a low-pass filter passband with a half-point frequency of 1 MHz. The output of the amplifier is input to an ideal half-wave rectifier that has $v_{out} = v_{in}$, $v_{in} > 0$; $= 0$, $v_{in} \geq 0$. Let $X(t)$ be the input to the amplifier, $Y(t)$ be the output of the amplifier and input of the rectifier, and $Z(t)$ be the output of the rectifier.
a. Find the output spectrum of the amplifier.
b. Find the total power out of the amplifier, $R_Y(0)$.
c. Find the PDF of $Z(t)$.
d. Find the time-average value of $Z(t)$.

A6.3.34 (a) $S_Y(f) = 10^{-15} \times \frac{10^6}{1+(f/10^6)^2}$ volts^2/Hz; **(b)** $\pi \times 10^{-3}$ volts^2; **(c)** $f_Z(z) = \frac{1}{2}\delta(z) + N(0, \pi \times 10^{-3})u(z)$; **(d)** 22.4 mV

P6.3.35 Wideband noise with a broadband noise spectrum of S_N volts^2/Hz (two sides) is passed through a low-pass filter with a cutoff frequency of ω_c. Ignore loading considerations.

The filter is followed by an amplifier with power gain A and a square-law detector with the characteristic $v_2(t) = \alpha v_1^2(t)$, $v \geq 0$, zow.

a. Find the spectrum of the output of the filter.

b. What is the total power in volts squared out of the filter?

c. At what delay time does the correlation reach 0.05?

d. What is the rms voltage at the output of the filter?

e. Find the DC component out of the square-law detector.

A6.3.35 **(a)** $\dfrac{S_N}{1+(\omega/\omega_c)^2}$; **(b)** $\dfrac{S_N \omega_c}{2}$; **(c)** $\dfrac{3.0}{\omega_c}$; **(d)** $\sqrt{\dfrac{S_N \omega_c}{2}}$; **(e)** $\dfrac{\alpha A}{2} \dfrac{S_N \omega_c}{2}$

P6.3.36   A spectrum of $1/f$ noise is put through a high-pass filter to reduce its effects. The noise spectrum is $S_N(f) = \dfrac{10^{-6}}{|f|}$ volts^2/Hz, $0.1 \leq |f| \leq 1000$ Hz (two sides), zow. The characteristic of the high-pass filter is $\mathbf{H}(jf) = \dfrac{j2\pi f RC}{1+j2\pi f RC}$, with $RC = 100$ μs.

a. Find the output spectrum from the high-pass filter.

b. Calculate the total noise out of the filter.

c. Find the factor in decibels by which the filter reduces the noise power. The formula for decibels is dB $= 10\log_{10}\left(\dfrac{P_{\text{out}}}{P_{\text{in}}}\right)$.

d. Estimate the coherence time of the output noise.

A6.3.36 **(a)** $S_{\text{out}}(f) = \dfrac{4\pi^2 |f| \times 10^{-6}}{10^8 + 4\pi^2 |f|^2}$ volts^2/Hz (two sides); **(b)** 3.33×10^{-7} volts^2; **(c)** -17.4 dB; **(d)** ≈ 1 ms

P6.3.37   The autocorrelation function of a random process model for an asynchronous digital signal is $R(\tau) = 4(1 + e^{-500|\tau|})$ volts^2.

a. What are the logic levels for this signal? Assume a positive value for the DC component. What is the average frequency of the trigger events?

b. If the value of the signal is a digital 0 at $t = 0$, what is the probability that it will be a digital 1 at $t = 1$ ms?

c. The mean and standard deviation of this random process have the same numerical value. If the random process is low-pass filtered, the standard deviation will be reduced, and the mean will be unchanged. Find the 3-dB bandwidth of a filter that reduces the standard deviation by a factor of 2.

A6.3.37 **(a)** 0 and 4 V, $\lambda = 250$; **(b)** 0.1967; **(c)** 26.5 Hz

P6.3.38   A wideband Gaussian random process with $S_N = 10^{-12}$ volts^2/Hz (two sides) is passed through an ideal amplifier with a gain of 90 dB and a bandwidth of 100 Hz. More specifically, $|H(f)|^2 = 10^9$, $-100 < f < +100$.

a. Find the PDF of the output voltage.

b. The output voltage is rectified with an ideal half-wave rectifier, which is $V_r(t) = V_o(t)$, $V_o(t) > 0$, zow, where $V_o(t)$ is the output voltage of the amplifier. Find the PDF of the output of this rectifier.

c. Find the DC component in the output of the rectifier.

A6.3.38 **(a)** $N(0, 0.2)$; **(b)** $f_{V_r}(v) = \frac{1}{2}\delta(v) + \dfrac{1}{\sqrt{2\pi \times 0.2}} \exp\left[-\dfrac{v^2}{0.4}\right]$; **(c)** 0.178 V

P6.3.39   Two resistors, 100 Ω and 50 Ω, both 300 K in temperature, are connected by ideal leads (no C, no L), as shown in the figure.

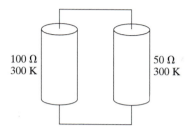

     a. Calculate the noise spectrum $S_N(50)$ in volts²/Hz (two sides) entering the 50-Ω resistor from the source representing the 100-Ω resistor. *Hint:* Now that the resistors are not matched, this requires some circuit theory, like a voltage divider, for example.

     b. Calculate the noise spectrum $S_N(100)$ in volts squared per hertz (two sides) entering the 100-Ω resistor from the source representing the 50-Ω resistor.

     c. Which way is energy flowing in this situation? Explain.

A6.3.39   (a) $2kT \times \frac{50 \times 100}{(50+100)^2}$; (b) the same; (c) They are at the same temperature and thus are in thermodynamic equilibrium. This merely shows that our theory conforms to this part of thermodynamics.

P6.3.40   A WSS ergodic random process has an autocorrelation function given by the formula $R(\tau) = \left(\frac{3}{10^6\tau^2+1} + 10\right)^{1.5}$ volts², time in seconds.

     a. Does the signal have a DC value? If so, what is it, assumed positive?

     b. Find the AC power in a typical member of this random process, which is the variance of the random process.

     c. Find the coherence function, $\rho(\tau)$, for this random process.

     d. Find the decorrelation time for this random process.

     e. This random process is passed through a low-pass RC filter with $R = 100\ \Omega$ and $C = 10\ \mu$F. Is the autocorrelation function of the output greatly different from that of the input or about the same? Explain your answer.

A6.3.40   (a) 5.26 V; (b) 15.2 volts²; (c) $\left[\left(\frac{3}{10^6\tau^2+1} + 10\right)^{1.5} - 31.6\right]/15.2$; (d) 2.90 ms; (e) The decorrelation time for the input signal is 2.9 ms. The time constant for the filter is 1 ms. Because these are comparable, the filter will have an effect on the signal.

ENDNOTES

1.   **Continuous random processes.** Here we have defined a random process as having to be continuous in the independent variable. This is not required, as will be shown, and certainly we can model discrete-time processes by random processes as well.

2. **Even symmetry of WSS autocorrelation functions.** From the definition $R(-\tau) = E[X(t)X(t - \tau)]$, but if we change variables to $t - \tau = t'$, this definition takes the form $E[X(t' + \tau)X(t')]$, which is $R(\tau)$. Thus the autocorrelation of WSS random processes has even symmetry: $R(-\tau) = R(+\tau)$.

3. We normally reserve uppercase letters for random variables, but in this case the period is described by the usual symbol, T, a constant.

4. **Trig identity.** We will often use the identity $\cos A \cos B = \frac{1}{2}[\cos(B - A) + \cos(B + A)]$.

5. **Answer to you do it on p. 574.** The amplitude is $\frac{1}{3}$ ft, and the frequency is $\frac{2\pi}{60}$. The phase is random, so the autocorrelation function is $\frac{1}{2} \times \left(\frac{1}{3}\right)^2 \cos \frac{2\pi}{60}\tau$. At $\tau = 10$, the value is 0.02778.

6. **Time-average autocorrelation function for a square wave.** The definition is $\overline{R}(\tau) = \langle v(t)v(t + \tau)\rangle$, where $v(t)$ is a square wave. In the figure we show such a square wave, the same square wave translated τ in the negative time direction, and the product, which is crosshatched. (For drawing convenience, we assumed $V = 1$.) The area of the overlap is $V^2\left(\frac{T}{2} - \tau\right)$, and hence the average is $\overline{R}(\tau) = \frac{V^2}{2}\left(1 - \frac{|\tau|}{T}\right)$. We indicated the absolute value of τ because the average clearly has even symmetry with respect to τ. The time-average autocorrelation function is also shown. It has the same period as the square wave.

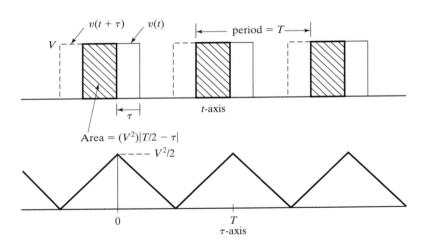

7. **Answer to you do it on p. 577.** The DC value is $\frac{2}{3}V$. Thus the AC value is $\frac{1}{3}V$ for $\frac{2}{3}$ of the time and $-\frac{2}{3}V$ for $\frac{1}{3}$ of the time. The average of the square is $\frac{6}{27}V^2$.

8. **Uncorrelated or independent?** Here we are not asserting that $X(t)$ and $X(t + \tau)$ are independent. We are saying that the correlation coefficient is zero, meaning they are uncorrelated, and thus the covariance is zero. It follows that the correlation is equal to the product of the means.

9. **Answer to you do it on p. 586.** For the factor-of-10 improvement, the coherence function would have to be 0.1, which leads to a time of 0.2303 ms. Of course, it would depend a bit on the frequency of the signal.

10. **Answer to you do it on p. 588.** Sampling at 200 μs would make the coherence function $e^{-0.2}$ between samples, but for every other sample would be $e^{-0.4} = 0.6703$.

11. **On the units of power.** We are using the units "volts squared" for power to make the application of this theory concrete. We realize that the variable could be amperes, centimeter, pounds per square inch, or any other physical variable. Thus we might have for the units of power amperes squared, centimeter squared, and so forth.

12. **Spectra.** At this stage of the development, we are being a bit casual about the mathematical dimensions of the spectra. After we introduce the Fourier transform, we will be more precise and put in the impulse functions such as $\delta(f - f_1)$ that make for a true function.

13. **Fourier transform pairs.** The following table gives Fourier transform pairs that are used in the text and in problems in this chapter. In the table, α is positive, and $2\pi f = \omega$. Also, you may substitute $\delta(f) = 2\pi\delta(\omega)$.

Basic transforms

$$v(t) = \frac{1}{2\pi} \int_{-\infty}^{+\infty} \underline{V}(\omega) e^{+j\omega t}\, d\omega$$

$$v(t) = \int_{-\infty}^{+\infty} \underline{V}(f) e^{+j2\pi ft}\, df$$

$$\underline{V}(\omega) = \int_{-\infty}^{+\infty} v(t) e^{-j\omega t}\, dt$$

$$\underline{V}(f) = \int_{-\infty}^{+\infty} v(t) e^{-j2\pi ft}\, dt$$

Time or τ function $\Longleftrightarrow$ Frequency function (ω or f)

$$\delta(\tau) \Longleftrightarrow 1$$

$$1 \Longleftrightarrow \delta(f) = 2\pi\delta(\omega)$$

$$e^{j\omega_1 t} \Longleftrightarrow \delta(f - f_1)$$

$$\cos 2\pi f_1 \tau \Longleftrightarrow \frac{1}{2}\delta(f + f_1) + \frac{1}{2}\delta(f - f_1)$$

$$\sin 2\pi f_1 \tau \Longleftrightarrow -\frac{1}{2j}\delta(f + f_1) + \frac{1}{2j}\delta(f - f_1)$$

$$\text{pulse of area } VW \Longleftrightarrow VW \frac{\sin \pi f W}{\pi f W}$$

$$2\, SB \frac{\sin 2\pi B\tau}{2\pi B\tau} \Longleftrightarrow \text{Spectrum of height } S \text{ from } -B \text{ to } +B \text{ Hz}$$

$$\text{Symmetric triangle of height } V \text{ and width } 2W \iff (VW)\left(\frac{\sin \pi f W}{\pi f W}\right)^2$$

$$\alpha e^{-\alpha \tau} u(\tau) \iff \frac{\alpha}{\alpha + j2\pi f}$$

$$e^{-\alpha |\tau|} \iff \frac{2\alpha}{\alpha^2 + (2\pi f)^2}$$

$$\frac{\beta}{\pi(\beta^2 + \tau^2)} \iff e^{-\beta |\omega|}$$

$$\alpha e^{-\pi(\alpha \tau)^2} \iff e^{-\pi(f/\alpha)^2}$$

14. **Impulses in radians/second and in hertz.** Dealing with spectra can be tricky because we like to do the math in ω, but the natural units for a spectrum are volts per hertz or volts squared per hertz. These can be converted through the identity $2\pi \delta(\omega) = \delta(f)$. At first glance we think this is wrong because we are used to seeing $2\pi f = \omega$. But the impulse function has meaning only when integrated with respect to its argument. To show that the equation relating the delta function is correct, integrate it with respect to frequency:

$$\int_{-\infty}^{+\infty} 2\pi \delta(\omega)\, df = \int_{-\infty}^{+\infty} \delta(f)\, df$$

The right-hand side integrates to 1 immediately. To integrate the left-hand side, we change units from f to ω by moving the 2π inside the $d(f)$ to have $d(2\pi f) = d\omega$. In this form the left-hand side clearly integrates to 1. In general, the impulse function has units that are the inverse of its argument, since it integrates to a pure number, 1. Thus $\delta(x)$ has units of cm^{-1} if x is in cm.

15. **The power spectrum of a square wave.** The Fourier series for a square wave has a DC value of $\frac{V}{2}$, and odd AC harmonics with amplitudes of $\frac{2V}{\pi n}$. These lead to powers of $\frac{2V^2}{(\pi n)^2}$. The Fourier series expansion of the sawtooth function given in endnote 6 has a DC value of $\frac{V^2}{4}$ and odd harmonics of magnitude $\frac{V^2}{(\pi n)^2}$. These agree except for a factor of 2 because the spectrum from the Fourier series is a one-sided spectrum and that from the autocorrelation function is a two-sided spectrum.

16. **Photometer correction.** Consider a 1-second period. We will count approximately 50,000 photons, so the dead time is about 5 milliseconds, which means that 250 photons will be missed, on average. Thus the correction factor is $+0.5\%$.

17. **AC power to first null for the spectrum of the synchronous digital signal.** We use Mathematica to integrate the $(\sin x/x)^2$ function to a large value and to the first null. We also give the ratio of the two integrals.

```
T = 1;
NIntegrate[
 2 (T/4) (Sin[πTf]/(πTf))², {f, 0.000001, 100}]
NIntegrate[2 (T/4) (Sin[πTf]/(πTf))², {f, 0.000001, 1/T}]
N[%]/N[%%]
```

0.249746

0.225705

0.903739

18. **Noise temperature.** Because a thermal source gives a flat spectrum that is proportional to temperature, any spectrum can be assigned a noise temperature, even if the source of the noise is nonthermal. If the one-sided spectrum intensity is S_N W/Hz, then the noise temperature of the spectrum is $T_N = \frac{S_N}{k}$.

19. **Baseband.** Also written *base band*, this term refers to the low-frequency source of the information, such as a voice or a bit stream, occurring naturally in the system. For voice, the baseband is considered something like 20–5000 Hz. After modulation, the information is transferred to another, higher-frequency band.

Appendix A

Tutorial on Mathematica

Introduction

I chose Mathematica as a platform for this book for a number of reasons. Mathematica gives me powerful authoring tools for formatting text and headings, for numbering equations, figures, and problems, for text processing, and for using hyperlinks to navigate around the book, not to mention the World Wide Web. Mathematica also gives me calculation and plotting capabilities, as I will illustrate in this appendix.

Mathematica gives you as a reader some interactive capabilities as well. I have formulated examples and review information such that you input your answers and get a response from the system. The calculations and plots are coded in a notation and form that should make it easy for you to make simple changes and play around with the results.

Mathematica is a very powerful system for doing mathematics. I know and use perhaps 1% of its capabilities, and this tutorial explains about 20% of what I know; but that will get you into the book, where you will learn some more by observing the code. This is not a book about Mathematica but a book about the applications of probability in engineering. What you learn about Mathematica is the icing on the cake, not the cake itself. This appendix is written primarily for those who are reading the book on screen under control of Mathematica. This material should interest readers of the hard-copy book as well, except they will be unable to explore the described features.

The electronic book appears in 14-point font on the screen and 12-point font when printed. Some of the formatting, like fractions in questions, is pretty small. If you wish to see the screen material in a larger format, go to the Format menu and choose a Magnification greater than 100%, whatever is comfortable for you.

Cells.   First, you need to know about *cells*. From the beginning of this tutorial to here, there are two cells. The first contains the title, and the present cell contains some text. You can identify the cells by the leftmost brackets at the right side of this window. (You do not need to worry about the nesting rules for cell brackets.) Most of the cells are open, meaning that you can read them, but some are closed, meaning the opposite. Many of the cells that create the graphics are closed to save paper in printing the book. You are welcome to open those cells and experiment with the commands to investigate the behavior of the functions being plotted or displayed. In fact, I hope you do that a lot.

The next cell is closed. Open it by clicking on the tiny bracket, then going to the Cell menu → Cell Properties → Cell Open.

Initialization and evaluation of cells.   The book is arranged in sections (= files = "notebooks," Mathematica's name for a file). Most of these require initialization at the beginning. For example, a typical initialization cell looks like

```
(*This is an initialization cell.*)
Needs["Statistics`ContinuousDistributions`"]
```

The (*Comment*) is just that. To perform the initialization, you must *evaluate* the cell. To evaluate, you click anywhere in the cell and hit the Enter key if your keyboard has this key or Shift-Return if it does not. When you initialize the cell, it will ask you if you want to automatically initialize all the initialization cells in the notebook. Your answer is Yes. Go ahead and initialize this notebook by executing the preceding cell. If you forget to initialize, the system will ask you about initializing when you first execute an active cell. In that case your answer will again be Yes.

Input cells.   This and the previous cell are *text* cells and do not involve calculation from our point of view. The initialization cell was an *input* cell, and Mathematica assumes that it contains code that calls for some action or calculations. To perform the action or calculation, you click anywhere in the cell and hit the Enter key on a Macintosh (or PC if it has an Enter key) or Shift-Return on a PC. For another example, to plot the following parabola, click in the cell and tell the computer to execute the cell by hitting the Enter key on a Macintosh or Shift-Return on a PC.

```
Plot[x^2, {x, -1, +1.5}];
```

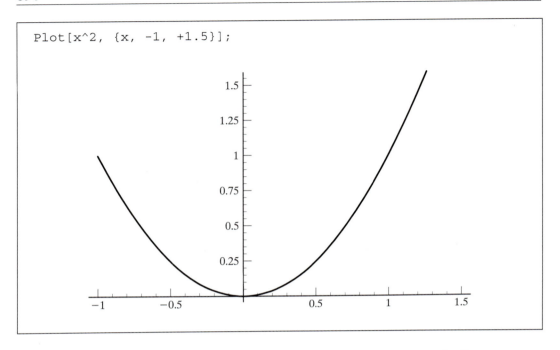

"Plot" is a command in Mathematica that produces a graph of the function in the first parameter, over the range given in the second parameter. A range is expressed as three symbols within braces: an independent variable, a lower bound, and an upper bound. For your first example of using Mathematica, change the exponent $(2 \rightarrow 3)$ and the range of the calculation range $\{x, -1, +1.5\} \rightarrow \{x, -2, +1\}$, and execute the cell again to see a cubic curve.

Lists.   Mathematica handles arrays of numbers or text with nested lists. In the next cell we use the Table command to generate a one-dimensional list and a two-dimensional list, to illustrate that format.

```
OneDList = Table[i, {i, 2, 6}]
TwoDList = Table[{i, i^2}, {i, 2, 6}]

{2, 3, 4, 5, 6}

{{2, 4}, {3, 9}, {4, 16}, {5, 25}, {6, 36}}
```

Note that Mathematica returns both lists. Sometimes we ask the system to format a two-dimensional list like a matrix. This is done with the TableForm command as follows:

```
TwoDList = Table[{i, i^2}, {i, 2, 6}]
TableForm[%]
```

```
{{2, 4}, {3, 9}, {4, 16}, {5, 25}, {6, 36}}
```

```
2       4
3       9
4       16
5       25
6       36
```

The percent symbol, %, refers to the output of the previous command. In this case it takes the output of the Table command, which is shown in the customary list form, and converts it to the array shown. Mathematica is fussy about case and syntax. For example, if you change "TableForm" to "Tableform" or "Table Form" you will get an unhappy response from the system. Try it and see. Then change back to "TableForm" for the next time or person to visit this tutorial. In this case the diagnostic message is easy to understand; usually it is not. Unhelpful diagnostics is one of the weaknesses of Mathematica, in my view.

Interactive responses.   Finally, you need to know how to input answers and get responses. Let us say that you are asked the question, What is the square of $\frac{3}{2}$? You enter your answer in the input cell after "myanswer =" and execute the cell to get a response. You may use a decimal or fraction for the answer.

```
myanswer = ;
```

```
Evaluate
```

Some interactions call for text to be entered and evaluated. For example, you are asked to perform the following algebra: "Multiply out the following, "$(a + b)(x + y)$," and enter your answer between the quotes in "myanswer = " ". Of course, the correct answer is "$ax + bx + ay + by$"; but there are many ways to write the answer, especially if you make blanks optional. You can enter your answer in the cell between the quotes and execute the cell for a response. Blanks do not bother the system; you can use as many or as few as you wish, but the order in which you write the terms does matter. Of the 24 ways to write the answer, two are considered to be logical and the system is coded to approve them. The remaining variations are illogical, not wrong. See if you can identify by trial and error the logical way to write the answer. Because this is text we are testing, you must enter your answer between quotation marks that are supplied.

```
myanswer = "  "
```

```
Evaluate
```

Note that on the first interactive test, when you gave the square of $\frac{3}{2}$, the system did not print out what you put in "myanswer = ", whereas on this test it did print out your input. The difference is the semicolon in the first instance and the lack of a semicolon here. Ending a line with ";" suppresses output. In the text, output in many intermediate steps is suppressed, just to keep the output to the essentials. If you want to see the output from the intermediate stages, just remove the semicolons.

Hyperlinks.   Hyperlinks work on a cell basis. When you click a link it goes to a destination cell, and the bracket at the right of the cell is darkened. For example, go to the target cell next.

Target cell.   Notice that the bracket at the right is darkened. When you Return to the cell you came from, that cell bracket is also darkened.

Things you should never do.   Never go to the Kernel menu and Delete All Output. For some reason, this deletes the Evaluate cells in the interactive exercises. In that case you will have to reload the system from the CD to recover the interactive features.

Another thing you should never do is to call a function that is in a "package" before you load that package. Let me explain. Mathematica has many add-on features, which are called *packages,* that are loaded only upon request. The initialization cell above loads the package Statistics'ContinuousDistributions', which contains statistical functions we will be using. If you forget to load the package and use the function, Mathematica simply outputs your command, in effect telling you that it does not know what you are asking it to do. Then you realize your error and load the package. This does not fix the problem but makes it worse, because the system now thinks the function has two definitions.

The fix is either to reboot your computer or else to remove the confusing definitions. For example, let us say you need to use the Poisson distribution. This is part of the package Statistics'DiscreteDistributions', which is not yet loaded into the system. Then, when you call the function with the following code

```
PDF[PoissonDistribution[1], 0.5]
PDF[PoissonDistribution[1], 0.5]
```

you will not get any output except a diagnostic message saying in effect that PoissonDistribution is undefined. Mathematica does not know what to do, so it returns your command to you. To fix the problem, you can execute the following cell:

```
Remove[PoissonDistribution]
Needs["Statistics`DiscreteDistributions`"]
```

Then it should work when you try again.

```
PDF[PoissonDistribution[1], 2]
```
$$\frac{1}{2e}$$

If you want a numerical value, you use the command

```
N[%]
```
0.18394

Thanks for visiting this tutorial. You have my best wishes as you return to Chapter 1.

Appendix B

Tutorial on Convolution

This tutorial is designed to be read through and to have all the cells executed. That makes it more interesting; but you can read through with the MathReader or hard-copy book also, and see the full results.

The convolution integral is

$$f_Z(z) = \int_{-\infty}^{+\infty} f_X(x) f_Y(z - x) \, dx \tag{B.1}$$

We present convolution as a four-step process and illustrate with moderately difficult functions. The key to doing a convolution is to **DRAW LOTS OF PICTURES**. Usually I do not shout at you, but here I must. I've dealt with many students who thought they could perform convolutions without drawing lots of pictures. They were wrong. You will need to draw pictures if you are serious about doing a convolution and getting the correct answer.

We will convolve the following two functions:

$$f_X(x) = 0.5, \ 0 < x \le 2, \ \text{zow}, \quad \text{and} \tag{B.2}$$

$$f_Y(y) = 4 - 2y, \ 1 < y \le 2, \ \text{zow} \tag{B.3}$$

These are plotted here.

```
fX[x_] := If[x < 0, 0, If[x > 2, 0, 0.5]]
Plot[fX[x], {x, -1, +3}, AxesLabel → {"x-axis", "fX(x)"}];
```

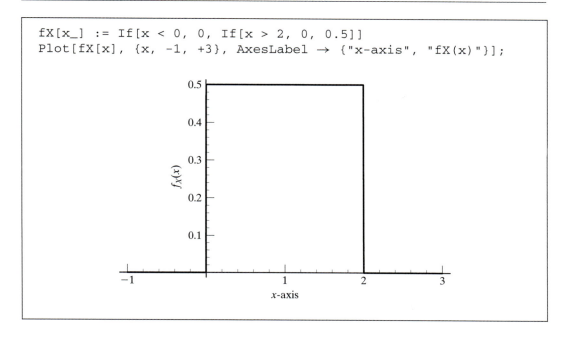

```
fY[y_] := If[y < 1, 0, If[y > 2, 0, 4 - 2y]]
Plot[fY[y], {y, -1, +3}, AxesLabel → {"y-axis", "fY(y)"}];
```

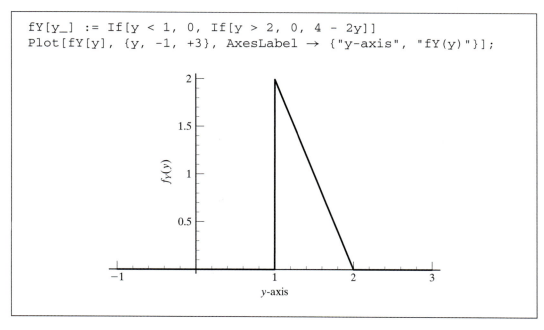

Step 1.   Step one is a notational change only. Change y to x in f_Y. Thus we have

$$f_Y(y) \rightarrow f_Y(x) = 4 - 2x, \ 1 < x \le 2, \ \text{zow} \tag{B.4}$$

This change allows us to plot f_X and f_Y on the same axis. Here are the plots:

```
p1 = Plot[fX[x], {x, -1, +3},
    AxesLabel → {"x-axis", "fX(x),fY(x)"},
    DisplayFunction → Identity, PlotRange → {0, 2.2}];
p2 = Plot[fY[x], {x, -1, +3},
    AxesLabel → {"x-axis", "fX(x),fY(x)"},
    DisplayFunction → Identity, PlotRange → {0, 2.2}];
Show[p1, p2, DisplayFunction → $DisplayFunction];
```

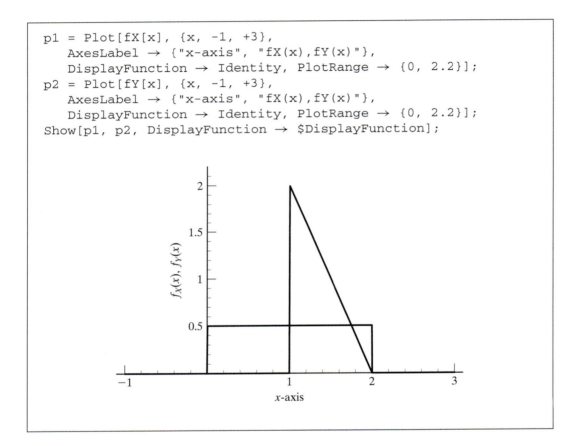

Step 2.   Step 2 is to shift f_Y by z in the $+x$ direction. This means we replace x with $x - z$. Thus

$$f_Y(x) \rightarrow f_Y(x - z) = 4 - 2(x - z), \ 1 < x - z \le 2, \ \text{zow} \tag{B.5}$$

This looks as follows. We set $z = 1.6$, but you can use other values if you wish.

```
z = 1.6    ;
p1 = Plot[fX[x], {x, -1, +3},
    AxesLabel → {"x-axis", "fX(x),fY(x-z)"},
    DisplayFunction → Identity, PlotRange → {0, 2.2}];
p2 = Plot[fY[x - z], {x, -1, +3},
    AxesLabel → {"x-axis", "fX(x),fY(x-z)"},
    DisplayFunction → Identity, PlotRange → {0, 2.2}];
Show[p1, p2, Graphics[{Text["z = 1.6", {1.6, 1.2}],
    Arrow[{1.6, 1.0}, {1.6, 0}]}],
  DisplayFunction → $DisplayFunction];
```

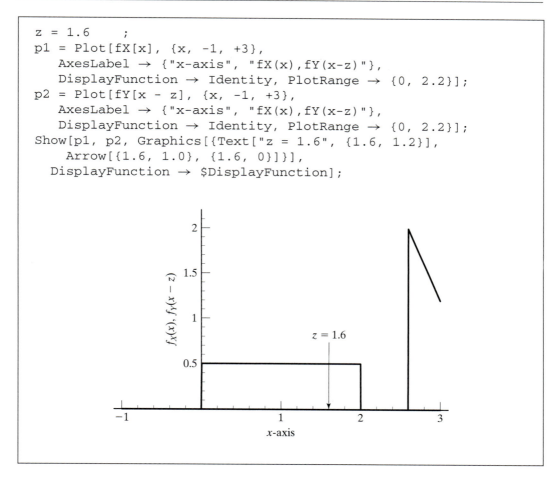

An important part of this step, and subsequent steps, is to keep up with the limits of f_Y. The PDF of Y now goes from $x = z + 1$ to $x = z + 2$. Because we used $z = 1.6$, that means that $f_Y(x)$ is nonzero in the range $2.6 < x \le 3.6$, as shown.

Step 3.   Reflect f_Y about its own axis. This requires replacing $x - z$ with $z - x$. Mathematically this requires the change

$$f_Y(x - z) \to f_Y(z - x) = 4 - 2(z - x), \ 1 < z - x \le 2, \ \text{zow} \tag{B.6}$$

Note that the region of nonzero PDF in terms of x is $z - 2 \le x < z - 1$. Now the picture looks like

```
z = 1.6;
p1 = Plot[fX[x], {x, -1, +3},
    AxesLabel → {"x-axis", "fX(x),fY(z-x)"},
    DisplayFunction → Identity, PlotRange → {0, 2.2}];
p2 = Plot[fY[z - x], {x, -1, +3},
    AxesLabel → {"x-axis", "fX(x),fY(z-x)"},
    DisplayFunction → Identity, PlotRange → {0, 2.2}];
Show[p1, p2, Graphics[{Text["z = 1.6", {1.6, 1.2}],
    Arrow[{1.6, 1.0}, {1.6, 0}]}],
  DisplayFunction → $DisplayFunction];
```

Again, we need to keep up with the region where f_Y is nonzero. Because the origin for f_Y has moved from $x = 0$ to $x = z$ ($= 1.6$ in our case), the PDF of Y is nonzero from $z - 2(-0.4)$ to $z - 1(+0.6)$. These values are evident in the graph, but when you do the sketching on your own problems, you will have to keep up with this information on the sketch.

Step 4. Step 4 is the big step because it involves four parts, namely, (a) letting z start from a "large" negative value and increase to "large" positive values; (b) identifying critical regions in z; (c) writing appropriate limits to the convolution integral for those regions; and (d) doing the math. Most people remember the moving of one function through another (step 4a) but forget why this is done: to note the critical regions in z (step 4b) and to write the convolution integral with appropriate limits for those regions (step 4c). First let us move f_Y through f_X by letting z start with $z = +0.6$.

```
z = 0.6;
p1 = Plot[fX[x], {x, -1, +3},
    AxesLabel → {"x-axis", "fX(x),fY(z-x)"},
    DisplayFunction → Identity, PlotRange → {0, 2, 2}];
p2 = Plot[fY[z - x], {x, -1, +3},
    AxesLabel → {"x-axis", "fX(x),fY(z-x)"},
    DisplayFunction → Identity, PlotRange → {0, 2.2}];
Show[p1, p2, Graphics[{Text["z = 0.6", {0.6, 1.2}],
    Arrow[{0.6, 1.0}, {0.6, 0}]}],
  DisplayFunction → $DisplayFunction];
```

With $z = 0.6$, f_Y is fully to the left of f_X, and there is no overlap. This makes $z = 0.6$ a suitable "large negative value." This is the first critical region, and it runs from $-\infty < z \le 1$. In this region the integrand of the convolution integral is zero, so the limits are irrelevant. Thus

$$f_Z(z) = \int_{-\infty}^{+\infty} f_X(x) f_Y(z - x)\,dx = \int 0\,dx = 0, \quad -\infty < z \le 1 \tag{B.7}$$

The next critical region is where f_Y partially overlaps f_X. For example, we let $z = 1.6$, as before. Here the picture is

```
z = 1.6;
p1 = Plot[fX[x], {x, -1, +3},
    AxesLabel → {"x-axis", "fX(x),fY(z-x)"},
    DisplayFunction → Identity, PlotRange → {0, 2.2}];
p2 = Plot[fY[z - x], {x, -1, +3},
    AxesLabel → {"x-axis", "fX(x),fY(z-x)"},
    DisplayFunction → Identity, PlotRange → {0, 2.2}];
Show[p1, p2, Graphics[{Text["z = 1.6", {1.6, 1.2}],
    Arrow[{1.6, 1.0}, {1.6, 0}]}],
  DisplayFunction → $DisplayFunction];
```

This critical region is $1 < z \le 2$, and here the appropriate limits for the convolution integral are between $x = 0$ and $x = z - 1$. Thus the convolution integral is

$$f_Z(z) = \int_{-\infty}^{+\infty} f_X(x) f_Y(z - x)\, dx = \int_0^{z-1} \frac{1}{2}[4 - 2(z - x)]\, dx, \quad 1 < z \le 2 \qquad \text{(B.8)}$$

The integral is routine but tedious. Let us let Mathematica do it:

```
Clear[z]
Integrate[(4 - 2 (z - x)) / 2, {x, 0, z - 1}]
```

$$\frac{1}{2} (-3 + 4z - z^2)$$

Let us save that for future plotting with the command

```
f1[z_] := 1/2 (-3 + 4z - z²);
```

Now we get to the region where f_Y and f_X fully overlap. This region runs from $2 < z \le 3$, and looks typically as we show next for $z = 2.5$.

```
z = 2.5;
p1 = Plot[fX[x], {x, -1, +3},
    AxesLabel → {"x-axis", "fX(x),fY(z-x)"},
    DisplayFunction → Identity, PlotRange → {0, 2.2}];
p2 = Plot[fY[z - x], {x, -1, +3},
    AxesLabel → {"x-axis", "fX(x),fY(z-x)"},
    DisplayFunction → Identity, PlotRange → {0, 2.2}];
Show[p1, p2, Graphics[{Text["z = 2.5", {2.5, 1.2}],
    Arrow[{2.5, 1.0}, {2.5, 0}]}],
    DisplayFunction → $DisplayFunction];
```

In this case the appropriate limits of overlap are from $z - 2 < x \le z - 1$, and the convolution integral becomes

$$f_Z(z) = \int_{-\infty}^{+\infty} f_X(x) f_Y(z - x)\, dx = \int_{z-2}^{z-1} \frac{1}{2}[4 - 2(z - x)]\, dx, \ 2 < z \le 3 \qquad \text{(B.9)}$$

This integral is trivial, since it contains the full PDF of Y, multiplied by a constant. Because the PDF integrates to 1, the full result is the constant, $\frac{1}{2}$. Thus we have

$$f_Z(z) = \frac{1}{2}, \ 2 < z \le 3 \tag{B.10}$$

Now we move into the region where the end of f_Y overlaps f_X, which requires that $3 < z \le 4$. We can look at that by setting $z = 3.3$, as shown next.

```
z = 3.3;
p1 = Plot[fX[x], {x, -1, +3.5},
    AxesLabel → {"x-axis", "fX(x),fY(z-x)"},
    DisplayFunction → Identity, PlotRange → {0, 2.2}];
p2 = Plot[fY[z - x], {x, -1, +3.5},
    AxesLabel → {"x-axis", "fX(x),fY(z-x)"},
    DisplayFunction → Identity, PlotRange → {0, 2.2}];
Show[p1, p2, Graphics[{Text["z = 3.3", {3.3, 1.2}],
    Arrow[{3.3, 1.0}, {3.3, 0}]}],
  DisplayFunction → $DisplayFunction];
```

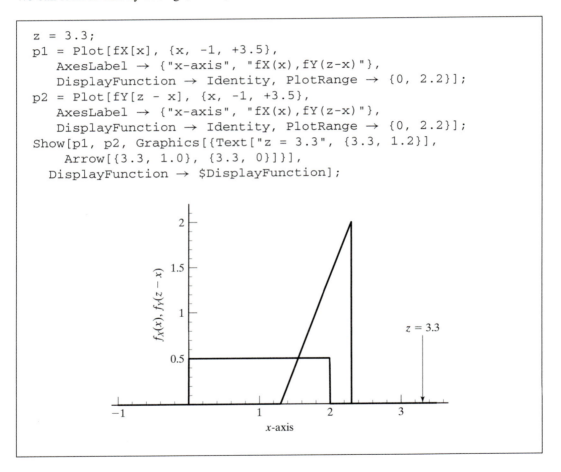

Here the appropriate limits for the convolution integral are from $x = z - 2$ to $x = 2$. Thus

$$f_Z(z) = \int_{-\infty}^{+\infty} f_X(x) f_Y(z - x) \, dx = \int_{z-2}^{2} \frac{1}{2}[4 - 2(z - x)] \, dx, \ 3 < z \le 4 \tag{B.11}$$

Again this is a simple integral, but we let Mathematica do it:

```
Clear[z]
Integrate[(4 - 2 (z - x)) / 2, {x, z - 2, 2}]
```

$$\frac{1}{2} \ (16 \ - \ 8z \ + \ z^2)$$

We can save this as

```
f2[z_] :=    1/2  (16 - 8z + z²)
```

$$\texttt{f2[z\_]} \ := \ \frac{1}{2} \ (16 \ - \ 8z \ + \ z^2)$$

Finally, we reach the region where f_Y again does not overlap with f_X, which requires $z > 4$. We can plot with $z = 4.1$ as shown.

```
z = 4.1;
p1 = Plot[fX[x], {x, -1, +4},
    AxesLabel → {"x-axis", "fX(x),fY(z-x)"},
    DisplayFunction → Identity, PlotRange → {0, 2.2}];
p2 = Plot[fY[z - x], {x, -1, +4},
    AxesLabel → {"x-axis", "fX(x),fY(z-x)"},
    DisplayFunction → Identity, PlotRange → {0, 2.2}];
Show[p1, p2, DisplayFunction → $DisplayFunction];
```

Here, of course, the convolution integral will be zero:

$$f_Z(z) = \int_{-\infty}^{+\infty} f_X(x) f_Y(z - x) \, dx = \int 0 \, dx = 0, \ 4 < z \leq +\infty \qquad (B.12)$$

We now can plot our results by combining the various piecewise functions. This is done in the following plot:

```
fZ[z_] := If[z < +1, 0,
            If[z < +2, f1[z],
              If[z < 3, 0.5,
                If[z < 4, f2[z], 0]]]]
Plot[fZ[z], {z, 0, 5}];
```

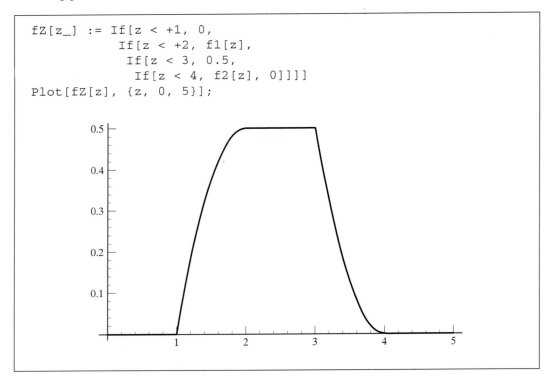

Note that the convolution process generally smooths and broadens the functions being convolved.

Appendix C

Summary of Common Probability Models

This appendix summarizes the basic information about the random variables that are discussed in this book. The reader should refer to the text for fuller discussion.

DISCRETE RANDOM VARIABLE MODELS

Uniform distribution

The PMF. By uniform distribution, we mean that probability is distributed uniformly between the integers $a, a + 1, a + 2, \ldots, b - 1, b$. The PMF is

$$P_X(x) = \frac{1}{b - a + 1}, x = a, a + 1, a + 2, \ldots, b - 1, b, \text{ zow} \tag{C.1}$$

Mean and variance. The mean and variance of this random variable are

$$\mu_X = \frac{a + b}{2} \text{ and } \sigma_X^2 = \frac{(b - a)(b - a + 2)}{12} \tag{C.2}$$

Assumptions and applications. The assumption is that all integers between a and b, inclusive, are equally likely. This random variable models a situation in which an integer occurs in a range and there is no reason to prefer one integer over another.

Bernoulli random variable

The PMF.   The Bernoulli random variable describes the results of one trial or action with probability p for success and probability $q = 1 - p$ for failure. We assign $X = 1$ for success and $X = 0$ for failure. Thus the PMF is

$$P_X(x) = q \text{ for } x = 0 \text{ and } P_X(x) = p \text{ for } x = 1, \text{ zow} \tag{C.3}$$

Mean and variance.   The mean and variance of the Bernoulli random variable are

$$\mu_X = p \text{ and } \sigma_X^2 = pq \tag{C.4}$$

Assumptions and applications.   The Bernoulli random variable finds application in the analysis of a sequence of Bernoulli trials as an indicator of success or failure.

Binomial random variable

The PMF.   The binomial random variable gives the probability of $K = k$ successes in n binomial trials. In the notation of a PMF, we have

$$P_K(k) = \binom{n}{k} p^k q^{n-k} = \frac{n!}{(n-k)!k!} p^k (1-p)^{n-k}, \quad 0 \le k \le n, \text{ zow} \tag{C.5}$$

where p is the probability of success on a trial and $q = 1 - p$ is the probability of failure.

Mean and variance.   The mean and variance are

$$\mu_K = np \text{ and } \sigma_K^2 = npq = np\,(1-p) \tag{C.6}$$

Assumptions and applications.   The assumptions of binomial trials are:

1. Binary result, "success" or "failure."
2. Independence of the results of trials.
3. Constant probability of success $= p$.

For the binomial distribution we also assume

4. Order of successes does not matter; rather, the total number of successes in n trials is of interest.

Applications are found in sequential trials such as repeated attempts to complete some task and also in parallel trials, for example, having K of n channels active in an instrumentation system.

Geometric random variable

The PMF.   The geometric random variable describes the probability of the first success occurring on the nth trial in a sequence of binomial trials. The PMF is

$$P_N(n) = P[\text{first success on } n^{\text{th}} \text{ trial}] = q^{n-1} p, \quad n = 1, 2, \ldots, \text{ zow} \tag{C.7}$$

where p is the probability of success on a trial and $q = 1 - p$ is the probability of failure. The probability of success occurring on *or before* the nth trial is

$$P[\text{first success on or before } n^{\text{th}} \text{ trial}] = 1 - q^n, \quad n = 1, 2, \ldots, \text{zow} \qquad (C.8)$$

Mean and variance.   The mean and variance of the geometric random variable are

$$\mu_N = \frac{1}{p} \text{ and } \sigma_N^2 = \frac{q}{p^2} \qquad (C.9)$$

Assumptions and applications.   The assumptions of binomial trials are

1. Binary result, "success" or "failure."
2. Independence of the results of trials.
3. Constant probability of success $= p$.

Applications are found in sequential trials such as repeated attempts to complete some task, for example, sending a message. The geometric distribution has the property that it is memoryless in the sense that the past does not affect probabilities in the future, which is consistent with the assumptions of binomial trials.

Pascal random variable

The PMF.   The Pascal random variable of order k describes the probability of the kth success occurring on the nth trial in a sequence of binomial trials. The PMF is

$$P_N(n) = P[k^{\text{th}} \text{ success on } n^{\text{th}} \text{ trial}] = \binom{n-1}{k-1} p^k q^{n-k}, \quad k \le n < \infty, \text{ zow} \qquad (C.10)$$

where p is the probability of success on a trial and $q = 1 - p$ is the probability of failure.

Mean and variance.   The mean and variance of the Pascal random variable of order k are

$$\mu_N = \frac{k}{p} \text{ and } \sigma_N^2 = \frac{kq}{p^2} \qquad (C.11)$$

Assumptions and applications.   The assumptions of binomial trials are

1. Binary result, "success" or "failure."
2. Independence of the results of trials.
3. Constant probability of success $= p$.

Applications are found in sequential trials such as repeated attempts to complete some task, for example, sending k messages. The Pascal distribution is a generalization of the geometric distribution.

Negative binomial distribution

The PMF. The negative binomial distribution is closely related to the Pascal. The only difference is that with the negative binomial distribution the independent variable is the number of failures before the kth success. The formula is

$$P[j \text{ failures before } k \text{ successes}] = \binom{k+j-1}{k-1} p^k q^j, \quad 0 \le j \le \infty \qquad \text{(C.12)}$$

where j is the number of failures before the kth success. As before, p is the probability of success on a trial and $q = 1 - p$ is the probability of failure.

Mean and variance. The mean and variance of the negative binomial random variable are

$$\mu_J = \frac{kq}{p} \text{ and } \sigma_J^2 = \frac{kq}{p^2} \qquad \text{(C.13)}$$

Watch out. Be warned that many authors consider that the "negative binomial distribution" is the same as the Pascal distribution; this is incorrect. When someone refers to this distribution, ask a few questions to make sure that you know what they are asking for.

Poisson random variable

PMF. The Poisson random variable has the PMF

$$P_K(k) = \frac{(\lambda t)^k}{k!} e^{-\lambda t}, k = 0, 1, 2, \ldots, \text{zow} \qquad \text{(C.14)}$$

Where K is the number of discrete events in a span "λt." Usually λ is an average rate and t is time. In general, λ is a density of events and t is the region in one or more dimensions to which this density applies.

Mean and variance. The mean and variance of the Poisson random variable are

$$\mu_K = \lambda t \text{ and } \sigma_K^2 = \lambda t \qquad \text{(C.15)}$$

Assumptions and applications. The assumptions used to derive the Poisson distribution, expressed in terms of time, are

1. *Independent occurrences.* We assume that the numbers of events in non-intersecting time periods are independent. The process has no memory.
2. *No simultaneous events.* Thus in an infinitesimal time period, dt, either zero or one event can occur but no more than one.
3. *Uniform rate or density.*

The applications where the Poisson might be a good model are as follows:

1. The values of the random variable must be integers in the range beginning with zero and having no upper limit. In practice, an upper limit may exist but it should be much larger than the expected number of events, that is, $k_{max} \gg \mu_K$.
2. The random phenomena occur in a continuous medium. We may have length, area, volume, or some other continuum.
3. The physical situation suggests events happening at random and independently in some continuous medium in which the rate or density of events is constant.

When these conditions apply, all one needs to know is the expected number of events, μ_K. In terms of the mean, the Poisson distribution is

$$P_K(k) = \frac{\mu_K^k}{k!} e^{-\mu_K}, \quad k = 0, 1, 2, \ldots, \text{zow} \tag{C.16}$$

CONTINUOUS RANDOM VARIABLE MODELS

Uniform distribution

PDF. The uniformly distributed random variable has a PDF of

$$f_X(x) = \frac{1}{b - a}, \quad a < x \le b, \text{ zow} \tag{C.17}$$

where a and b are the lower and upper limits of the distribution, respectively.

The CDF. The CDF of the uniform distribution is

$$F_X(x) = 0, x \le a, = \frac{x - a}{b - a}, a < x \le b, = 1, x > b \tag{C.18}$$

Mean and variance. The mean and variance of the uniform distribution are

$$\mu_X = \frac{b + a}{2} \text{ and } \sigma_X^2 = \frac{(b - a)^2}{12} \tag{C.19}$$

Assumptions and applications. The assumption is that all values between a and b are equally likely. This distribution models ignorance in that there is no known reason to prefer one value over another. Some system that seeks to simulate randomness, such as a random number generator, presumably would fit this distribution. Of course, any real system would output a discrete value, but a continuous model might be useful.

Gaussian, or normal, random variable

PDF. The Gaussian random variable has a PDF of

$$f_X(x) = \frac{1}{\sqrt{2\pi\sigma_X^2}} e^{-\frac{1}{2}\left(\frac{x - \mu_X}{\sigma_X}\right)^2} \text{ for all } x \tag{C.20}$$

where μ_X and σ_X^2 are the mean and variance, respectively.

The CDF. The CDF of the Gaussian random variable is a tabulated function. The CDF of the normalized Gaussian random variable, $Z = N(0, 1)$, we denote as $F_Z(z) = \Phi(z)$, although a few authors use $\Upsilon(z)$. The CDF of the general Gaussian random variable may be derived from the CDF of the normalized Gaussian as $F_X(x) = \Phi\left(\frac{x - \mu_X}{\sigma_X}\right)$.

Assumptions and applications. The assumption is that we have a continuous random variable arising from complex causes. The Central Limit Theorem lends mathematical support to this interpretation, as does experience. The Gaussian can also give approximate values for other distributions under appropriate conditions. In practice the mean and variance of the target distribution are used to fit the Gaussian, and a continuity correction must be applied in some instances. See the text for examples.

Applications are legion. The Gaussian is the model of choice for most physically random quantities such as thermal noise, for error analysis, and for sociological data. Any complex process could produce a Gaussian result.

The Rayleigh random variable

The PDF. The Rayleigh random variable is described by the PDF

$$f_R(r) = \frac{r}{\sigma^2} e^{-\frac{1}{2}\left(\frac{r}{\sigma}\right)^2}, r \geq 0, \text{ zow} \tag{C.21}$$

where σ^2 is a parameter. When the Rayleigh is derived from the Pythagorean sum of two IID Gaussian random variables, σ^2 is the variance of the component Gaussians.

The CDF. The CDF is

$$F_R(r) = 1 - e^{-\frac{1}{2}\left(\frac{r}{\sigma}\right)^2}, r \geq 0, \text{ zow}. \tag{C.22}$$

Mean and variance

$$\mu_R = \sqrt{\frac{\pi}{2}}\sigma \text{ and } \sigma_R^2 = (4 - \pi)\frac{\sigma^2}{2} \tag{C.23}$$

Assumptions and applications. The Rayleigh describes radial miss distance from a target when errors in two orthogonal directions are IID Gaussian random variables. The Rayleigh also describes distance to the nearest event in a two-dimensional Poisson field.

Chi square random variable

The PDF. The PDF of the chi square random variable, V, with k degrees of freedom is

$$f_V(v) = \frac{v^{(k-2)/2} e^{-v/2}}{2^{k/2} \Gamma(k/2)}, v > 0, \text{ zow}, k = 1, 2, 3, 4, \ldots \tag{C.24}$$

where $\Gamma(\cdot)$ is the gamma function.

Mean and variance. The mean and variance of the chi square random variable with k degrees of freedom are

$$\mu_V = k \text{ and } \sigma_V^2 = 2k \tag{C.25}$$

Assumptions and applications. The chi square random variable is derived as the sum of the squares of k IID normalized Gaussian random variables. It describes the distribution of sample variances calculated from Gaussian data sets.

Student's t random variable

The PDF. The PDF of the Student's t random variable, T, with k degrees of freedom is

$$f_T(t) = \frac{1}{\sqrt{k\pi}} \frac{\Gamma((k+1)/2)}{\Gamma(k/2)} \left(1 + \frac{t^2}{k}\right)^{(k+1)/2}, k = 1, 3, 4, \ldots, \text{zow} \tag{C.26}$$

where $\Gamma(\cdot)$ is the gamma function.

Mean and variance. The mean and variance of the chi square random variable with k degrees of freedom are

$$\mu_T = 0 \text{ and } \sigma_T^2 = \frac{k}{k-2}, k \geq 3 \tag{C.27}$$

Assumptions and applications. The Student's t random variable relates to the Gaussian and the Chi Square random variables and is used in range estimation of the mean of Gaussian data sets.

Exponential random variable

The PDF. The exponential random variable has the PDF

$$f_T(t) = \lambda e^{-\lambda t}, t \geq 0, \text{ zow} \tag{C.28}$$

where λ is a parameter related to average rate or interval between discrete events.

The CDF. The CDF of the exponential random variable is

$$F_T(t) = 1 - e^{-\lambda t}, t \geq 0, \text{ zow} \tag{C.29}$$

Mean and variance. The mean and variance of the exponential random variable are

$$\mu_T = \frac{1}{\lambda} \text{ and } \sigma_T^2 = \frac{1}{\lambda^2} \tag{C.30}$$

Assumptions and applications.   The exponential random variable arises from the same assumptions as the Poisson random variable, which are, expressed in terms of time:

1. *Independent occurrences.* We assume that the numbers of events in non-intersecting time periods are independent. The process has no memory.
2. *No simultaneous events.* Thus is an infinitesimal time period, dt, either zero or one event can occur but no more than one.
3. *Uniform rate or density.*

The exponential random variable expresses the time between events that are random according to the Poisson assumptions. The exponential random variable has no memory in the sense that the probabilities of future events are unaffected by the past. In reliability theory, an exponential distribution of failure times bespeaks failure by accident or loss.

The Erlang random variable

The PDF.   The Erlang random variable of order k, T_k, is the sum of k IID exponential random variables and has the PDF

$$f_{T_k}(t) = \frac{\lambda^k t^{k-1}}{(k-1)!} e^{-\lambda t}, t \geq 0, \text{ zow}, k = 1, 2, \ldots \tag{C.31}$$

The CDF.   The Erlang CDF is closely related to the Poisson distribution:

$$F_{T_k}(t) = 1 - e^{-\lambda t} \left[1 + \frac{\lambda t}{1!} + \frac{(\lambda t)^2}{2!} + \cdots + \frac{(\lambda t)^{k-1}}{(k-1)!} \right], t \geq 0, \text{ zow} \tag{C.32}$$

Mean and variance.   The mean and variance of the Erlang random variable are

$$\mu_{T_k} = \frac{k}{\lambda} \text{ and } \sigma_{T_k}^2 = \frac{k}{\lambda^2} \tag{C.33}$$

Assumptions and applications.   The Erlang random variable arises out of the cluster of assumptions that leads to the the Poisson and exponential random variables, given above. In a sequence of random events in time, T_k is the time from an arbitrary time to the kth event to follow. It also finds application in queuing theory when service times are assumed to be exponential.

The Weibull distribution

The CDF and PDF.   The Weibull random variable generalizes the exponential random variable. The CDF is

$$F_T(t) = 1 - \exp\left[-\left(\frac{t}{c} \right)^m \right], t \geq 0, \text{ zow} \tag{C.34}$$

and the PDF is

$$f_T(t) = \frac{mt^{m-1}}{c^m} \exp\left[-\left(\frac{t}{c}\right)^m\right], t \geq 0, \text{ zow} \tag{C.35}$$

where m is a shape parameter and c is a characteristic time. For $m = 1$, the Weibull becomes the exponential distribution with $c = \frac{1}{\lambda}$. The mean and variance of the Weibull random variable will not be given here.

Assumptions and applications.   Your author has, with admittedly limited effort, been unable to discover the underlying assumptions leading to the the Weibull distribution. In this book we have dealt with applications in reliability studies.

Index